UNDIPLOMATIC DIARIES

UNDIPLOMATIC
DIARIES

1937–1971

CHARLES RITCHIE

EMBLEM
McClelland & Stewart

Library and Archives Canada Cataloguing in Publication

Ritchie, Charles, 1906–1995.
    Undiplomatic diaries, 1937–1971 / Charles Ritchie.

Originally published in 3 separate volumes titled: The siren years, Diplomatic passport and Storm signals.

ISBN 978-0-7710-7538-4

    1. Ritchie, Charles 1906–1995 – Diaries.   2. Diplomats – Canada – Diaries.   I. Title.

FC616.R58A3   2008   327.71'0092   C2008-901955-5

We acknowledge the financial support of the Government of Canada through the Book Publishing Industry Development Program and that of the Government of Ontario through the Ontario Media Development Corporation's Ontario Book Initiative. We further acknowledge the support of the Canada Council for the Arts and the Ontario Arts Council for our publishing program.

Typeset in Minion by M&S, Toronto
Printed and bound in Canada

McClelland & Stewart Ltd.
75 Sherbourne Street
Toronto, Ontario
M5A 2P9
www.mcclelland.com

1 2 3 4 5   12 11 10 09 08

CONTENTS

III. STORM SIGNALS:
MORE UNDIPLOMATIC DIARIES, 1962–1971

INTRODUCTION

by Allan Gotlieb

Few Canadian diplomats have had as illustrious a career as the beak-nosed, angular, nasal-sounding scion of an old Nova Scotian Conservative family, Charles Stewart Almon Ritchie. Canadian High Commissioner to London, Canadian ambassador to the United States, the United Nations, NATO, and Germany – he graced all of these posts during his approximately four decades as a member of Canada's foreign service. No other Canadian before or since has occupied so many top diplomatic positions. Although there were many gifted intellectuals, scholars, and writers who, as career foreign-service officers during the middle of the last century, impressed the international community with their ability and creativity ("the best foreign service in the world," the Oxford philosopher Stuart Hampshire once told me), Ritchie alone published a diary that recorded his experience throughout his entire career. The only other Canadian diplomat who published a diary was me but, except for a few short intervals, it was limited to my term in Washington. Had Charles Ritchie not put the idea of a diary in my head at my farewell party in Ottawa – he told me it was absolutely necessary to keep one – I doubt that I would have written a single line.

It is difficult to explain the circumstances that brought such an extraordinary collection of young, high-minded Canadians into the Department of External Affairs during that era. Among this mid-century group were a number of outstanding men (there were no women) who made their mark on Canada and sometimes the world – Lester Pearson, Norman Robertson, Escott Reid, Hume Wrong, Herbert Norman, Arnold Smith, Chester Ronning, Jules Léger, Marcel

Cadieux, John Wendell Holmes, Robert Ford, and of course Charles Ritchie. While sometimes giving the impression – deliberately, no doubt – that he was somewhat frivolous (disappearing from meetings to watch movies in mid-afternoon) or an eccentric, as a professional Charles Ritchie was a match for the most brilliant of the dedicated band. But, once again, he was different from all his colleagues. He had panache. And he flaunted it on the international stage.

Arriving in London before the Second World War, still in his early thirties, Ritchie served under Vincent Massey, perhaps the foremost Canadian snob of the era. But in no time Charles penetrated the precincts of high culture that probably would not have been familiar even to Massey. Regular weekend visits to the country estate of the arch-eccentric and -connoisseur Sacheverell Sitwell, lunches with Loelia, the Duchess of Westminster, more lunches with Nancy Mitford, constant intimate encounters with Elizabeth Bowen – accounts of all these and a host of other social relationships abound in his memorable portrayal of London among the falling bombs of the German blitz.

How did these extraordinary relationships actually come about? Being a third secretary from the colonies would hardly have made him an attraction to people in the most cultivated circles in London. Although Ritchie's diary entries in *The Siren Years* (covering his early assignment in London) illuminate the world around him, they are extremely reticent about how he came to inhabit, so rapidly and effortlessly, the upper regions of London society.

When Ritchie is posted to Paris after the Second World War, the mystery only deepens. In no time at all the diarist, still only a mid-level diplomat, finds himself at the centre of one of Europe's most sophisticated scenes. Lady Diana Cooper, the extraordinarily beautiful, aristocratic wife of the British ambassador to Paris, Duff Cooper, adopts Ritchie into her brilliant circle.

Again, the diary entries in *Diplomatic Passport* – Ritchie's account of those years – are reticent about how his social conquests came about. One of the most remarkable incidents in Canadian diplomatic life abroad occurred when Lady Diana Cooper, in response to some querulous remarks by Ritchie about feeling out of things, declared a "Ritchie Week" in Paris. It was, Ritchie writes, "a week of non-stop parties, dinners, even a ball in Ritchie honour. She roped in half Paris." How does one explain this phenomenon? Readers can only surmise. The answer has to be found in Ritchie's extraordinary sense of style, his gaiety, his delight as a companion, his joie de vivre, and in the impression he gave of being a grand Whig aristocrat from the eighteenth century transplanted into the twentieth.

My exposure to Charles Ritchie began shortly after my years spent as a don at Oxford, where I encountered some of the great eccentrics of mid-century England. Ritchie was definitely in their league. In 1957, I was sent to the UN General Assembly, with the status of third secretary, to be an adviser to the Canadian delegation. There, I found myself working for Ritchie, who was then Canadian ambassador to the United Nations.

My first encounter was sharing an elevator with him and a few others in the tall office building of the Canadian Permanent Mission. With his high-pitched voice, he said loudly and plaintively, "Will someone press a button in this damn thing, I have no mechanical ability." A short time later, the ambassador asked my wife and me to lunch along with a middle-ranking woman who had just been recruited into the department. When the bill was presented at the end of our leisurely lunch at his favourite spot, Gatsby's, he reached into his wallet, pulled out a wad of bills, raised them high, and scattered them over the table, saying "Please, sort this out, I'm not good at these things."

This mischievous, even devilish, side of his personality could appear at the most unexpected moments, such as during the regular morning meeting of the Canadian delegation to the assembly, when the entire group would gather solemnly around a long table to discuss the issues of the day. On one occasion, the chairman of the delegation, a rather obtuse gentleman from Newfoundland entirely without credentials, slowly read out loud an editorial from the New York *Daily News* stating that the problem in the Middle East was that the Arabs wanted to push the Jews out of Israel and into the sea. "Is that right? Do you agree with that, Mr. Ambassador?" Ritchie, who appeared to be barely listening to the chairman's long reading, sat bolt upright, hesitated a moment, and responded to the challenge, "Ah, an excellent question, Mr. Chairman, but on all matters relating to the

Middle East, I defer to the much greater knowledge of my colleague John Holmes." Holmes, known for his earnestness, flushed to a scarlet purple as he was handed the poisoned chalice, managing only to mutter a few incoherent remarks while Ritchie looked on with a mischievous, triumphant little smile on his face. Now that's style.

In spite of his pranks and performances and his habit of enjoying an afternoon movie when Ottawa was frantically trying to reach him on the telephone, the final volume of his diaries, *Storm Signals*, bears witness to the fact that Ritchie understood the difficult and distrustful Diefenbaker government far better than most of his colleagues did.

I was not the only young man in the diplomatic service to be bewitched by Charles Ritchie. To most of us in the ranks, tales of his irreverence brightened our days. On his death some twelve years ago, a colleague, Colin Robertson, wrote of his reaction upon reading *The Siren Years*: "It was like living on the set of a Nick and Nora Charles 'Thin Man' film. In what other profession could you read *Henry V*, cultivate rococo Romanian princesses and baroque dilettantes, bed ballerinas, and then be paid to write 'impressionistic' dispatches on what you learned at dinner! There was no better advertisement for a career in the foreign service than Ritchie's diaries."

If there is anything missing in the Ritchie diaries, it is discussion of the grand foreign-policy issues of the day. They are, of course, always there, enveloping the diurnal activities of the diarist – the conduct of the Second World War, the emergence of the Soviet threat, the establishment of NATO, the Cuban missile crisis, Canada-U.S. relations at their most strained and fractious. But Ritchie explains over and over again in his entries that he is not recording foreign-policy conflicts. At times he seems almost to apologize to his reader for this. Or is it a mock apology? One knows from the moment one begins to read Ritchie's diaries that he was wise in leaving the substantive battles to the historians, the political scientists, the archivists.

In my experience as a diarist, when one records something one thinks important, it is rarely seen that way many years hence. What attracts, entices, and endures is the trivia, the personalities, the ambience of the cafés, the conversations, the conduct of crowds, the pretensions, the vanity, the unique odours of the place and the moment.

This is what Ritchie's diaries provide, so authentically and with such verve. In this manner, Ritchie created something that will endure far longer than accounts of the great policy and bureaucratic battles he declined to record.

THE SIREN YEARS

A Canadian Diplomat Abroad
1937–1945

FOREWORD

It was with adolescence that the diary addiction fixed its yoke on me – a yoke which in the succeeding fifty years I have never been able entirely to shake off, although there have been merciful intervals of abstinence. The habit had begun even earlier – had sprouted furtively when I was a schoolboy. Its seed was perhaps already sown when I would write on the front of school books, Charles Stewart Almon Ritchie, King's Collegiate School, Windsor, Nova Scotia, Canada, North America, The World, The Universe, September 23rd, 1918, 3:17 p.m. – an early compulsion to fix myself in space and in time. Once given over to this mania there was no cure for it. With obstinate obsessiveness I continued to scribble away. Now the toppling piles of my old diaries are mountains of evidence against me, but I still postpone the moment to destroy them. Their writing and subsequent concealment were intentionally secretive – to have them discovered and read would have meant to be caught in the practice of "solitary vice."

The diaries included in this book begin in Washington in 1937 and end in Ottawa in 1945 but are in the main my record of the years I spent in London during the Second World War. They show the scenes and people described as viewed by an outsider–insider – one immersed from boyhood in English life but not an Englishman.

The writer was during these years an officer of the Canadian Foreign Service but these are not diplomatic diaries in any sense of that word. The deliberate exclusion of official business from the record leaves the odd impression that I was floating about London in idleness. One might well ask not only, "What was his war effort?" but "What did the Canadian Government pay him for?" The answer is that I was an obscure and industrious junior diplomatic official who was thrown by chance and temperament into the company of a varied cast of characters who lived those years together in London in the stepped-up atmosphere of war, with its cracking crises, its snatched pleasures, and its doldrums. The diaries are personal – too personal to see the light of day? I once would have thought so. Now thirty years later the personal seems to me to merge into "we" of wartime London days. I resist any temptation to patronize or justify the writer. His faults, follies, and errors of judgement show plainly enough. To paper them over would seem a smug betrayal of my younger self. The diaries are as I wrote them at the time, save for occasional phrases which have been altered for the sake of clarity.

While I spare the reader a leisurely tour of my origins, childhood, and early manhood, a brief backward glance may be helpful in making the narrative and the narrator more comprehensible.

I was born at our family home, The Bower (which crops up from time to time in these diaries), then on the outskirts of Halifax, Nova Scotia, in 1906. The Halifax of those days – at any rate the Halifax of my mother and her friends – looked back to its past as a garrison town and a base for the Royal Navy. I was brought up in an atmosphere – which must be incomprehensibly remote to modern Canadians – in which everything British was Best and "Upper Canada" was a remote and unloved abstraction. Yet my family had been in Nova Scotia for four or five generations. Their devotion to Crown and Empire was a romantic fidelity, quite different from the satisfied acceptance of the English by themselves as English. They might look to England but it was hard for the individual Englishman to pass through the eye of their needle. They were Nova Scotians first, Canadians second. They were North Americans with a difference and they clung tenaciously to the difference. They belonged to Nova Scotia, the land where memories are long, legends, loyalties, and grudges unforgotten, a land where a stranger should tread warily.

My mother was widowed when I was ten. My father, twenty-five years older than she, was a barrister and a brilliantly effective one, to whom the law, which he had in his bones from generations of lawyers and judges, was a devotion. My mother was left with two boys to bring up, my brother Roland and myself. She tackled the job with love and a touch of genius. Never possessive, she held us by the magnetism of her personality.

Our home always seemed full of people coming and going, relations and near-relations, friends young and old, and those whom my mother was sorry for or thought to be lonely. Then there was our own coming and going as a family to and fro from England in the slow boats from Halifax to Liverpool, until England began to seem the other half of one's life.

Our education never stood still in one place – in and out of schools – on and off with tutors – now at a preparatory school in England, then back to Nova Scotia, then to an Anglican concentration camp of a boarding school in Ontario.

It was in 1921 while at the squalid age of fifteen I was incarcerated in this establishment that an envelope emblazoned with the Arms of Canada reached me as unexpectedly as the invitation to Cinderella to attend the court ball. The letter within was from Sir Robert Borden, then Prime Minister. He and my father had been law partners and lifelong friends. His kindly letter now informed me that he hoped in due course to see established a Canadian Foreign Service and that hearing (from my mother) of my interest in international affairs he suggested that one day I might be interested in such a career. Thus was planted the germ of an ambition.

As for my later education it seemed destined to extend to infinity, from King's University in Halifax to Oxford – to Harvard – to the École Libre des Sciences Politiques in Paris and back to Harvard. In no hurry to earn my own living, I was in danger of becoming a perpetual student. There were intermissions, a short-lived spell of journalism in London, an amateurish but exhilarating bout of teaching French irregular verbs in an "experimental" school in Canada, but no settled profession until the Victorian Gothic portals of the Department of External Affairs opened in August 1934 to receive me as an acolyte third secretary.

The Department of External Affairs at that time was small, as was Canada's place on the map of international politics. Its future was being shaped by a handful of unusually gifted men who shared the belief that Canada had its own role to play in the world and a conception of what that role should be. They worked together without feeling for respective rank, without pomposity, with humour, despising pretence, intolerant of silliness, and scathing in their contempt for self-advertisement. They were my mentors and later to become my friends.

My first posting abroad in 1936 was to the Canadian Legation (now Embassy) in Washington. At first this was a sunny and enjoyable interlude. Not overemployed, the diplomatic bachelor had a full and easy hand to play in that sociable city. It was by fits and starts that the approaching war made its presence felt. Ominous newspaper head-lines came and went and then business continued as usual, but by 1938 reality was coming inescapably closer. The Americans whom I knew in Washington and the American papers which I read were vehemently opposed to the appeasement of Germany. Their anti-Nazi feeling was more intense than what I was to meet on arrival in England. They felt that compromise with this evil was immoral and unforgivable. Perhaps they understood the implacable nature of the enemy better than the rest of us did. But there was this difference: emotionally committed as they were, it was not their war that was at stake.

In January 1939 I was transferred from Washington to the Office of the High Commissioner for Canada in London. The London to which I came turned out to be less concerned with the likelihood of war than the Washington I had quitted. We were permitted, indeed encouraged, to hope that the danger had passed. Whether anyone fully believed this is another matter. People behaved as if they did.

Nowhere was this state of mind more firmly ensconced than at Canada House and in this the High Commissioner Vincent Massey accurately reflected the views of his Government and in particular of his Prime Minister, William Lyon Mackenzie King – himself a fervent supporter of the Munich settlement.

On my arrival at Canada House I found that in addition to my diplomatic work I was to act as a private secretary to Mr. Massey. Despite occasional explosions of irritation to be found in the diaries, I was devoted to him. I was attracted by his personality, his sense of drama (he was a born actor), his susceptibility, the alternations of closeness and coolness in his dealings with people, and the delight of his company. It was not an uncritical devotion, but no man is a hero to his private secretary, especially a private secretary who was not himself cast in the heroic mould.

It was impossible to think of Vincent Massey without his wife, Alice. The contrast between them was as striking as their deep mutual attachment – his fastidiousness, her impulsiveness, his discretion, her outspokenness. There was a physical contrast too between his meticulous almost finicky gestures and her exuberant smiles and greetings. She was a handsome woman: prominent eyes of piercing blue, abundant reddish hair piled high. He had the austere visage of an Indian chief belied by his small, frail-appearing form. She was, or seemed to be, the stronger nature emotionally and physically. She wore herself down in the war by hard work for Canadian servicemen in England. I see her plodding along Cockspur Street laden with provisions for the Beaver Club, which the Masseys founded for Canadian soldiers, sailors, and airmen, or at her desk writing hundreds of letters to the relatives of Canadians serving abroad.

The Masseys made their successive homes my second homes. When I was bombed out in the blitz they put me up as their guest in the snug safety of the Dorchester Hotel where they lived at the time. Their sons, Lionel and Hart, were my friends.

The second in command at Canada House was Mike Pearson, the most stimulating of companions in and out of the office. He was at the beginning of a career which was to see him become Prime Minister of Canada. In all the changing scenes of that career he remained the same Mike I knew in those days, incapable of self-importance, ready in wit, and undaunted in the pursuit of his objectives and ideals.

The position of the High Commissioner and his staff in wartime London was not made any easier by the ambivalent attitude of our own Prime Minister Mackenzie King. *Canada at Britain's Side* was the title he chose for his own book on Canada's war effort. The title was certainly justified by the contribution made by Canada to the defence of Britain and to the conduct of the war. Yet Mr. King was obsessed through these years by the suspicion that Whitehall was plotting designs against Canada's independent nationhood and trying to draw us back into the old imperial framework. Unfortunately for us at Canada House the Prime Minister came to believe that his representative, Vincent Massey, had succumbed to these sinister British influences. Even Mr. Massey's successes in London were held against him. He had during his time there consolidated his personal and official position in the inner bastions of pre-war London. Cabinet ministers, editors of newspapers, directors of art galleries, the higher ranges of the peerage, not to mention Royalty itself, enjoyed his company and respected his views. This did him no good in the eyes of his own Prime Minister, who reacted with intense irritation to the Masseys' familiarity with the Great.

To mutual resentment was added a difference of political views. Vincent Massey was a stout defender of Canada's interests, but he believed in Canada as an actively participating member of the British Commonwealth. Mr. King emphatically did not. Whatever the rights and wrongs of their respective opinions, the resulting estrangement between them put the staff of Canada House in a difficult position. The disembodied presence of the Prime Minister brooded over us. It was not a benevolent influence. In the flesh he was thousands of miles away, but he needed no modern bugging devices to detect the slightest quaver of disloyalty to his person or his policies. Perhaps through his favoured spiritualist mediums he was in touch with sources of information beyond Time and Space.

As will be seen, these discords did not unduly affect the diarist. London scenes and people and the conduct and misconduct of his own life were too absorbing.

In these diaries people appear and disappear. For a time one character occupies the centre of the stage only to vanish as if down a bolt-hole. Intimacies develop quickly and sometimes dissolve as quickly. Wartime London was a forcing ground for love and friendship, for experiments and amusements snatched under pressure. One's friends came and went, some to war zones, others evacuated to the country. There was an incessant turnover of occupations from civilian to military and sometimes back to civilian. People drifted apart and together again as the war pattern dictated. This sometimes leaves the diary record disconnected. Situations are left up in the air; questions are not answered. All one can say is that this is what that life was like.

A diary is not an artistic creation. It has – or should have – a breath of immediacy but at the expense of form and style. Life is not transmuted into art. Anyone who wishes to see how that miracle can be achieved should read the work of genius set in the London of those years, *The Heat of the Day* by Elizabeth Bowen.

1937–1938

1 July 1937. Washington.

The Canadian Legation is housed in the former home of a millionaire, one of the palaces in such varied architectural styles which line Massachusetts Avenue. The Legation is both office and also the residence of the Minister, Sir Herbert Marler, and his wife. Sir Herbert is an impressively preserved specimen of old mercantile Anglo-Saxon Montreal. He looks like a painstakingly pompous portrait of himself painted to hang in a boardroom. He is not a quick-minded man – indeed one of my fellow secretaries at the Legation says that he is "ivory from the neck up." Nevertheless he has acquired a handsome fortune and his successful career has been crowned with the diplomatic posts of Tokyo and Washington and with a knighthood.

I am acting as a sort of a private secretary to him for the time being. He is extremely nice to me although each has habits which irritate the other. He has large square hands of immaculate cleanliness with the largest, broadest fingernails I have ever seen on a hand. When reflective or puzzled he has a habit of snapping the end of his index fingernail with his thumb making a distinctly audible clicking sound while gazing meditatively into space. This little repetitive clicking echoes through the large panelled office ornamented with elaborate carved foliage in the manner of Grinling Gibbons. I stand attentively before him awaiting his command and choke back the words, "For Christ's sake stop doing that."

If he is unconscious of my irritation I have been equally unconscious of a trick of my own which must madden him. One day last week Lady Marler drew me aside and said that the Minister had wanted to speak to me about something personal but had asked her to do so instead. Her manner made me wonder whether it was halitosis or a moral misdemeanour of mine which had offended him, but she said, "His Excellency would much appreciate it if you would stop whistling in the hall outside his office."

The Marlers are quite strong on the use of the word Excellency. Once when they were leaving the Legation with their small son I heard Sir Herbert say to the chauffeur, "His little Excellency will sit in the front with you."

There are two other junior secretaries at the Legation with me. We share offices on the top floor. When I arrived they told me that it was a tradition in the Legation that the most newly arrived officer must walk along an extremely narrow parapet running under the office windows. I obediently climbed out of the window and took a few precarious steps looking down at a drop which would have brained me if I had faltered. Then I climbed back in again to be told that I was the first person to be such a bloody fool as to believe this story.

16 July 1937.

Staying in the house in Georgetown which Dudley Brown has lent me. Woke in a state of stupid irritation with Dudley's Negro manservant who had neglected to call me. He is a handsome creature with a peculiarly rich voice and a glib talker. His name is Vernon.

19 July 1937.

There was no hot water. Vernon's face was thunderous. I ate breakfast nervously conscious of his mood and feeling unable to cope with it. "There's a heap of small things in the house that just have to be attended to," he said. "Mr. Brown forgot to have the boiler filled. I spoke to him about it before he went away too." He spoke with the grim, tight-lipped disillusionment of the stern father of an incurably feather-brained offspring. I felt that I could hardly admit this tone in speaking of a fellow "white master." "Oh, he forgot," I said, with a nervous attempt at nonchalance. "Yes *indeed*," said Vernon, allowing his magnificent, sultry, dark eyes to dwell on me for a moment in contemptuous disapproval. Then he withdrew to the pantry. I turned again to *Anna Karenina*. In a minute or two I would have to shave, but what with? There was no hot water. Then unfortunately for my peace of mind it occurred to me that Vernon could quite easily heat up some water – not that it really mattered – I have often shaved in cold water. Why go and face him? Am I afraid of him? I thought, putting down *Anna* to look this disagreeable thought in the face. No, of course not, but I do not like meeting those sullen, disgusted eyes. This is getting too much, I thought, and went into the pantry. "Vernon," I called in quite a loud, confident voice. He was in the kitchen sitting beside the table with a black silk stocking twisted around his head – I suppose to keep the kink out of his hair. "Vernon." He did not get up, but rolled his eyes at me. "I wonder if you could heat up a little water to shave in." I spoke rapidly. "Well, I will have to get some kind of a pot or pan, and it will take some little time to do." This brought me to myself. I said sharply, "Of course, only get it heated up." I felt better after that. Later I was able to go down to him and in quite a calm voice ask him the road I should follow to get to the town in Virginia where I was lunching. Feeling my change of mood he became more amiable himself and gave me the directions I asked for. "What is there to do when I get there?" "Well, there are some places of considerable inter-est," he said gravely, "there is the home of Nathan Freeman, the great Negro Emancipator, now turned into some kind of *mu*seum, and then also there is St. Elizabeth's Hospital for the *In*sane." "Indeed," I said politely. I was so pleased with this information that on impulse I nearly asked him to make me a small picnic luncheon, but although I felt better about Vernon I did not feel equal to this.

3 November 1937.

Michal Vyvyan[1] said on the telephone that he would come around in twenty minutes to show me the draft of the telegram of greetings to Canadian War Veterans. With him came a new man just out from the Foreign Office, a smooth-faced Etonian with an air of sophistication. What happens to them at Eton? However innocent, stupid, or honest they may be they always look as though they had passed the preceding

---

[1] Secretary at the British Embassy in Washington, later Tutor at Trinity College, Cambridge.

night in bed with a high-class prostitute and had spent the earlier part of the morning smoothing away the ravages with the aid of creams, oils, and curling tongs. This graceful young man handed me an elegantly worded little draft message typed out on a piece of paper. I said it was very pretty – "Good morning" – and when they had left went down to tell the Minister about it. "What," said he, "was the significance of this move on the part of the British Embassy?" "A gesture of politeness – of co-operation," I hazarded. But no, it was not as simple as all that. He had to be very careful in his dealings with the Embassy. "They are a queer lot, Ritchie." I was to call Vyvyan and ask him the significance of the whole thing. On second thoughts he would do it himself. Then Vyvyan must needs come down and explain it in person and the Minister explained that we would have to consult our Government. And this was all because they had shown us a message of welcome to Canadian Veterans. The Minister is obsessed with the dangers of any dealings with the British Embassy.

Miss C. the accountant is reading a book on *How to Make Friends and Influence People*. She says that she goes down to see the Minister and after five minutes, despite all the lessons she has learned from the book, she is longing to say, "Oh, to hell with you, you damned old fool." He wears down one's tolerance and amiability like a dentist's drill.

17 November 1937.

The secret telegrams sent by the Dominion Governments to the Government of the United Kingdom during the Rhineland occupation crisis in 1936 have been an eye-opener to me. I have just been reading them. Not much "rallying around the Mother Country in time of danger," and if a similar crisis blew up tomorrow would it be the same song? If the United Kingdom Government could publish these telegrams it might give their Collective Security critics something to think about. The Dominions are not going to fight on account of the rape of Spain nor an indecent assault on Czechoslovakia. The United Kingdom must choose her ground very carefully. I am not sure that a German invasion of France would do the trick. Perhaps not until the first air raid on London.

I was sitting at the bar in the Club tonight beside a man on a visit from New York. "So I took this woman out to dinner," he said, leaning his two elbows on the bar and looking into his brandy and soda. "Marvellous-looking woman and from what my brother had told me I thought it was, well, a foregone conclusion." "An open and shut proposition," I suggested. "Exactly as you say – an open and shut proposition. First of all she ordered three chops straight off like that. That was not all." He twisted his ragged moustache in an agony of remembrance. "I picked up the menus – one was table d'hôte. I really shoved the other at her more as a gesture. It was à la carte – everything three times as expensive in it, of course. She chose a dollar apéritif – there were several at forty cents – then right the way through, a three-dollar entrée, lobster mornay, always the most expensive thing in sight, and after dinner seven double whiskies in the course of the evening, and I never came near to first base." He said, "There must have been something wrong with the woman – physically I mean."

17 February 1938.

At the Soviet Embassy hordes of fat, bespectacled women, young and old, "Radical" newspaper columnists with jowls and paunches shouting their phrases the second time lest they should not be heard or appreciated the first time, a few senators and political big-shots whose faces give one a feeling of familiar boredom like picking up an old twice-read newspaper.

The Soviet Embassy was first the house of Pullman, the inventor of the Pullman car, and then the Imperial Russian Embassy. It is full of tasteless carving, red silk panelling, heavy chandeliers, and marble. Now everything is slightly soiled and shoddy, the silk is frayed, the carved floral designs are encrusted with dust. Paunchy Russian Jews wander about through the marble halls in their shirt sleeves with cigars dripping ashes on their ties, or muttering together in the corners of the big saloon.

18 February 1938.

Reading Shakespeare's *Henry IV*, the scene between Hotspur and his wife. From that glimpse we know what Hotspur is in bed and at table, how he would make love, how he would flick impatiently through his morning paper, how he would drive a car, how he would bring up his children. Hotspur the falcon-eyed aviator, reckless skier is easy to imagine. The jesting, unsentimental tone when talking with his wife and his quick come-backs are startlingly "modern."

7 March 1938.

I went for a walk in the country with the Australian Minister at the British Embassy. His blue, candid eyes, his silver hair, his ruddy cheek, his kindly, wholesome air all announce the fair-minded man of good digestion. He takes snapshots of old forts and churches, he observes the lie of the land, the names of the plants – he walks a steady pace, stout stick swinging at his side, pausing to appreciate a pretty stretch of country or to smile with good humour at a child playing in the village street. He is so nice – why then does one feel stealing over one a faint disgust at the man? Is it because for the best of all possible reasons his bread is always buttered on the right side? His house is in excellent taste, his dinners are not fussy but well cooked, suitable for a manly bachelor, his guests are sensibly chosen, the conversation is cheery and pleasant. On his shelves are Foreign Office reports, official war histories, biographies, and the novels of Galsworthy. In his garden are crocuses planted by an ambassadress. In the mirror in his neat, manly dressing-room are stuck dozens of invitation cards from those who appreciate his jolly niceness. He is too shrewd and too dignified to let the cat out of the bag, but it is for these invitations he lives. They are wife and children to him. The man of the world with his silver-clasped evening cloak, his signed picture of the Duke of Gloucester on the drawing-room mantelpiece, his brandy in old glasses. The Australian without an Australian accent.

8 March 1938.

I went to the district jail to see a Canadian who had been kept thirty-five days awaiting trial for illegally entering the United States. I sat on a bench in the stone-flagged rotunda where visitors may talk to prisoners. The rotunda is in the centre of the prison and is lined with iron grating, beyond which one floor on top of another of the prison is visible, rising right up to the glass roof of the rotunda five floors above your head. The floors are connected by iron staircases. It is like being in the central hall of a zoo, an impression which was heightened by the figures sprawling on the staircases in attitudes of recumbent boredom. They were some of the prisoners and seemed mostly to be Negroes. Why they were sitting about on the stairs instead of being in cells I do not know. It is one of those illogical details which usually occurs in dreams. My prisoner came towards me across the floor. He was a pale boy with romantic, brown eyes and a shadow of a moustache. His features were delicately chiselled and rather trivial. He had on a very clean shirt open at the neck. He must have put it on a minute or two before coming to meet me. He seemed from his name to be of Greek origin and was in show business. "My brother," he said, "had sworn out a warrant for my arrest." "What did he do that for?" I asked. "I do not know what he would do a thing like that for," the boy replied in a gentle, speculative tone as though pondering the vagaries of human nature. I felt my question had been impertinent. His reply was so gracefully said that it could hardly be called a snub, but I did not pursue the subject. I left him a tin of cigarettes. "It has made me feel good to have you come here," he said with cordiality as I got up to go.

9 June 1938.

How many nights have I sat alone in my room listening to the laughter in the streets, looking furtively at my watch to see if I could get up and go to bed. All those nights in my stuffy little room in Paris, in my room at Oxford with the clock of Tom Tower striking nostalgia on the night air, at school with the movements and muffled voices of the boys in the corridors, and at home at the table which faced the window looking out on the lawn with the single oak tree. And always this piece of staring, white paper in front of me with the few and feeble words strung across it. These wasted nights are most remarkable. Nothing could be more stubborn than my devotion, nothing more stupid than my persistence. After all, I have written nothing – I will write nothing. Twenty years have not been enough to convince me of my lack of talent.

23 June 1938.

After dinner at Dumbarton Oaks[1] our hostess Mrs. Robert Woods Bliss led us by circuitous paths to the little lake in the "wilderness" beyond the formal gardens. The night was cool, the sky clear, and there was no shiver of breeze among the box hedges that line the path. When we reached the lake she went ahead of us alone with a flashlight to spot the path under her feet. We remained standing in a little group on a high bank that overlooked the water. We watched her treading lightly and gracefully in the spots of torchlight as she went around the edge of the lake to the other side. There she vanished beyond a tree and touched a switch so that an electric light cleverly placed high in the trees above shone down with a clear, bright, but not too bright, light on the surface of the water. She pressed another switch and a second light shone. The lake and the trees around it were illuminated so that every shadow was given its precise value. When our hostess was within earshot again we murmured our admiration of the ingenuity of the lighting and the beauty of the scene. Quietly she accepted our praise. There was a pause while we stood there gazing at the discreetly illuminated lake conscious of a scene which must be photographed on our memories. In the silence created by our dumb appreciation our hostess's voice sounded in a tinkling falsetto, "It has I think a quality of stillness about it which is most appealing." We nodded agreement. It was a sentiment which could not be enlarged upon. Meanwhile with surprising stealth the moon had slid up over the trees and was regarding us with an expression of indifference.

3 July 1938.

We walked beside the lake arm in arm and stopped every now and then to kiss. The lake and its surrounding circle of trees was still as the empty sky. We saw a white house on an incline among the trees with a big plate glass in the front like the window in a shop. The glass was a blinding gold from the setting sun. "What a view they must have from there over the lake." We wished the house was ours, but then we had said that about so many houses and we nearly always found some

---

[1] This house and its estate were presented for public use by former Ambassador Robert Woods Bliss; the conference which made the plans for the United Nations was held there in August 1944.

objections. This time it was the mosquitoes. "There must be clouds of them rising off the lake in the summer." Instead of the houses we would have we talked for a little about trips to Bermuda, to Provence, or to rocky coasts with inlets of pale sand somewhere in Donegal or Nova Scotia. One place would be too far, another too expensive, another perhaps dull. It was not that we disagreed, but we both knew that none of these things would happen to us – that we would not have a house together nor visit the coasts of Donegal or Nova Scotia.

5 July 1938.

With no rules that I put faith in, no instinct to guide me except the instinct of self-preservation, a soft heart, a calculating head, and a divided mind, is it any wonder that I cause confusion when what I want is so simple – a woman who will love me and who will sleep with me sometimes, who will amuse me and listen to me and not flood me with love.

9 July 1938.

Until I touch her she seems not to be made of flesh – her clothes are of one material, her skin is of another. It seems madness to kiss her cheek, which is made of some soft stuff not silk or velvet. As one might put a piece of velvet to one's face to feel its texture I put my lips close to her skin. I feel a casual pleasure in the softness of her cheek. A moment later a miracle has been achieved – her body is no longer a stubborn material thing of painted wood covered in velvet. It is now fluid and sparkling and electric with life. I can bathe in this moving stream and drown in this strong current.

12 July 1938. Dance at the Leiters'.

The house built in the nineties is rightly famous for its appalling ugliness. The ballroom of inlaid marble was a monument of frigid vulgarity. Other interesting features included the enormous green malachite mantelpiece in the dining-room and the portrait of old man Leiter in the hall which justifies the worst that could be said of the Leiter family.[1] I suffered less than usual during this party as a

---

[1] Levi Ziegler Leiter was a self-made man who amassed a fortune. His daughter married Lord Curzon and his granddaughter Sir Oswald Mosley.

result of consuming one glass of champagne after another in quick succession. I realized that this was necessary when somebody came up to me and said, "You look like Banquo's ghost." After that I felt I must go home immediately or get tight. I am glad I chose the latter course. I danced with Mrs. Legare who was the local beauty. Platitudes dropped from her lovely lips, each platitude as smooth and flawless as a perfect pearl. "Paris is so beautiful in spring when the chestnuts are out." "Women should wear what becomes them, not what happens to be the fashion." Her beauty too is that of a pearl – smooth and flawless. She wore a full-skirted dress of some stiff, shiny material which seemed to radiate a sort of moonlight brightness. Her gestures with her arms and hands, her way of dancing, were of a liquid grace.

15 July 1938.

I am longing to get to Nova Scotia. I want to breathe air from the Atlantic, to lie in bed at night and listen to the fog bell's warning and to live in a family again – tea and gossip in the middle of the morning – my mother sinking exhausted into a chair, lighting a cigarette, beginning an impassioned attack on the stupidity or the ingratitude of the worldly-wise or telling one of those spontaneous masterpieces of mimicry, humour, and pathos, which give such depth of variety and colouring to a small incident.

23 July 1938.

Walked home last night through the dark jungle of the Negro quarter. The groups of Negroes – women sitting on the steps of their houses, young braves under a street lamp at the corner – are waiting for an artist who can render the grace of their movements, their natural nobility of posture or repose.

31 July – 1 August 1938. Newport (Staying at The Breakers, the Vanderbilts' house).

When I stepped out of the station there was the car gleaming like patent leather and a small chauffeur in a greying livery, a pink and crumpled face and an accent which I presumed to be Hungarian.[1]

---

[1] The house now belonged to Gladys Vanderbilt who was married to Count Laszlo Szechenyi, Hungarian Minister in Washington.

"Two things in the United States not good – dogs and children – both too fresh," wheezed the chauffeur in a piping, choking voice as he swerved the car to avoid a dog and again to miss hitting a child. "How much must I tip you?" I thought. "There is the home of Mrs. Vanderbilt," he said. Our Mecca was in sight. In another minute we passed through high iron gates, past great trees – even the grass was a rich man's grass. No house was grander than ours I thought, as we curled in through the iron gates under the massive trees. After glancing at the immense marble hall, I was in the lift and then along a red carpeted corridor and then in my room. It appeared to have been designed for an Edwardian lady of fashion. It was panelled in faded chintz. There was her upright piano, her chaise-longue with its frilled and faded pink cushions. On the walls hung the pretty pictures which one sees nowadays only in the darkest corner of a second-hand dealer's shop where they are piled on dusty shelves asking a shilling a lot for them and glad to get rid of them. I went out into the upper stone terrace and looked over the perfection of green lawns, the fountains and two little groves of trees which framed the seascape beyond. There was the sea – a magnificent blue carpet spread in front of the house, the breakers broke obediently at the foot of the cliff as if performing for the special benefit of the Vanderbilts and their guests. It was all very gratifying.

On my breakfast tray was a gardenia in a glass of water. Anxious to miss nothing I was sniffing at it when the footman appeared. I felt that I looked slightly silly sniffing at the gardenia and I hastened to engage him in conversation about the day's boat race.

On the doorstep that morning we all stood waiting for the car to arrive. My host in white flannels had a cotton cap with a small, transparent, green window in its peak, my hostess in a pink dress and her little girl who was like an old-fashioned doll with circular pink cheeks, china-blue eyes, and golden ringlets. A Hungarian nurse went with the child as though they were two pieces of the same set of chinaware, as she too had the pinkest of cheeks and the bluest of eyes. The nurse and child both shone with cleanliness. I am not particularly fond of sailing, and I know less than nothing about boats, but the day was agreeable. I was sustained by the sensation that people would envy me seeing the *America's* Cup Races on such a fine, fast boat and with such knowledgeable and truly sporting men. I was sustained too by the caviare and champagne and by the slightly heady feeling of association with people whose incomes outdistanced my own by astronomical proportions. The harbour was full of ships, and people kept on saying, "This is the sight of a lifetime." I believed them readily enough. There was in fact nothing remarkable to see. The two yachts were somewhere on the horizon, the English one well in the rear.

That night there was a dance. It took all my energies to wear an easy, pleasant expression. I was frightened of catching a glimpse in one of the mirrors of a pallid, ghost-like face and recognizing with horror that it was my own. As I knew hardly anyone there it was necessary to hide the anxious and slightly embarrassed air of one "who does not belong," particularly in this case because, in the eyes of the guests, those "who did not belong" at this party could belong nowhere mentionable. All were talking the same unmistakable cosmopolitan language of the dollar, but it was not their money that filled me with exhaustion – it was their vitality.

In the garden I was led up to old Mrs. Vanderbilt, who received me with the cordial simplicity of royalty. Her husband with his seedy beard does in fact look like an eccentric member of the German ruling family. One suspected him of epileptic attacks and a passion for collecting birds' eggs. I was paired off with a woman who had recently with unflagging zest embarked on her fourth marriage. She was one of those invulnerable American women set in motion by some secret spring of energy who go dashing through life at such high speed that it is impossible to think of them except in terms of motion – from hotel to hotel – from party to party – from cocktail to cocktail – from bed to bed – and doubtless too from book to book, for American women have of course read *everything*. Her present husband is a pink-cheeked and amiable guardsman who, with a reckless courage which does more credit to a stout heart than to any appreciation of the laws of possibility, seeks to satisfy her.

The young girls at the dance had skins the colour of warm sand which the sun has burnished and the grace of movement and easy buoyancy of those who swim through life on golden tides.

9 August 1938. Halifax, Nova Scotia.

The clammy air comes in through the windows. There is fog in that air, and at intervals there is the melancholy mooing of the foghorn. A tram goes by in the quiet street. As it recedes, its sad monotonous chant grows thin upon the air. When it stops at the corner it puffs like a stout woman with too many parcels. All sounds here are in a minor key, all colours dimmed by a slight disparaging mist.

10 August 1938.

The miasma of the small town – the terror that comes as you are shaving the next morning and remember the things you said the night before. Will it be repeated and distorted? Will your employer hear of it? Will it cause people to think you odd or affected or depraved? Will people say you are a communist or an advocate of free love? Have you *hurt somebody's feelings?*

The last of the three old Miss Odells is dead – foolish, ugly, innocent ladies coming down the aisle after Holy Communion, their silks creaking, their gold bangles tinkling. Now their big solemn town house is for sale and its contents will be offered at an auction next Wednesday, the proceeds to go to the cathedral diocesan fund. Already the china, the glass, and the silver are laid out on tables in the dining-room in preparation for the sale. The little silver vinaigrettes and snuff-boxes on the occasional tables – each has attached to it a numbered cardboard label as big as itself. Even the old mourning ring enclosing a twist of chestnut hair belonging to some dim great-aunt is labelled for the sale. A group of ladies of the diocesan guild of the cathedral are supervising the arrangements. Some are enthusiastic and stand in ecstasy before the Crown Derby dinner service. "Oh, what lovely old things," they say. Others are disparaging, "I must say I thought the silver would have been finer than this – it is mostly plate and the dining-room chairs are falling to pieces." One lady in particular richer than the others insists that the Waterford glass decanters are modern imitations. Her attitude is felt to be too superior and is resented accordingly.

The Miss Odells during their lifetime had no desire to make new acquaintances. Most of the women who wander briefly through the bedrooms would not have been invited to tea in that house because they were "new people" and one did not know them. Now they open private little drawers in the old desks and stare at the religious prints over Miss Ella's bed. An auctioneer pulls books out of the shelves in the library. The maids, still kept on until the house is sold, laugh and call out to each other in the upper rooms. I do not think the old ladies looking down from their Anglican heaven can escape being pained at the intrusion and the noise but perhaps as it is for "the dear cathedral" they do not mind. Most of the things in the house are not beautiful, but in the drawing-room placed on the closed top of the piano is a dessert service of ivory white Wedgwood with urn-shaped sauce-boats painted in Pompeian red with classical motifs of helmets, laurels and harps. It gleams immaculate among the heavy furniture and carved oriental screens. And high on the walls of the tall library are hung plates of Old Blue patterned in willows and waterfalls. From the bedrooms where every table is petticoated in white muslin one can see the wet lawns, the dripping trees, and (for the gardener cannot yet have been dismissed) yellow chrysanthemums tied neatly to small stakes. Then the fog rolls in from the harbour and all vanishes in a white mist.

It is hard to open the heavy front door – there are so many polished brass bolts and bars – enough perhaps they thought to keep out time and change. As one walks away down the street the grave, pillared portico and the elms beside the stables disappear in mist. When the fog dissolves the house may have gone and in its place will be an ugly shadow that haunts all private homes. There will be a boarding-house, leering and shabby with an ingratiating grin and frowsty smell.

12 September 1938. Washington.

I had my first taste of Hitler's style today. I heard the broadcast of his eagerly awaited speech at Nuremberg dealing with Czechoslovakia. He is certainly remarkable entertainment value. I listened for nearly an hour to him speaking in German with brief interpretative interpolations. At the end of that time my nerves were jumping so that I could hardly sit still. This was not because of the subject with its implied danger of war – it was that voice, those whiplash snarls, those iron-hammer blows of speech. What a technique! The Germans get their money's worth all right – the long-drawn sentences with the piled up climax upon climax until the nerves are quivering – shudders of hate and fear and exaltation going through the audience. This cock-teasing oratory drives its victims frantic. If they do not have their grand orgasm of war soon they will burst.

But every good story must have a point and the point of Hitler's story is the outbreak of war. Instinctively every listener longs to get to that point. I heard an American woman say today, "I could not sleep a wink last night after reading the papers and listening to the broadcasts. I was so worried about this war scare." How much anticipation do you suppose was mixed up with this genuine dread?

As I believe that England will not fight for the Czechs if it is possible not to do so, I think it probable that there will be no war at present. The above reflections can be kept in cold storage until *der Tag* comes. What is striking is the lack of a moral cause for and also the absence of any objective to be gained by, a war. If war comes it will be an exasperated reaction to continuous blackmail.

14 September 1938.

This may be one of those historical dates and may be fated to figure in future schoolbooks as the beginning of the Second Great War. The various steps leading up to this climax have had the dramatic excitement of a grand historical drama. One is prepared for the blood-and-thunder finale and it has become almost unbearable to have it so often postponed. We have been going about for months pulling grave faces about the horrid possibility of war, talking about the destruction of civilization, etc., etc., but deep down in our jungle depths have we not been longing for what we fear? Have we been willing this war? This is the same impulse which makes Emerson's saying true, "A person seldom falls sick but the bystanders are animated with a faint hope that he will die." It is human love of disaster to others, and living on this continent it has been possible to feel that one is watching a distant drama. This emotional desire for a climax has been heightened by the newspapers. The familiar vocabulary of exaggeration and dramatization, the horrific illusion are all employed to build up a story – the story of the European crisis, the outbreak of war – the greatest *news story* in the world.

28 September 1938.

We are now on the very edge of war. Already my feelings have changed since I last wrote. Perhaps I am already beginning to suffer from war blindness. I feel more and more part of my generation and my country and less an individual.

The war offers us no ideal worth dying for – we make no sacrifice for a noble cause. We fight with no faith in the future. It is too late to pretend (though we shall pretend) that we are defending the sanctity of international obligations or the freedom of individuals. We are fighting because we cannot go on any longer paying blackmail to a gangster. Whoever wins, we who belong to what we call "twentieth century civilization" are beaten before we start. We have had our chance since 1918 to make a more reasonable and safer world. Now we have to go and take our punishment for having missed that chance. We have willed the ends but we have not willed the means to attain those ends. That must be our epitaph.

Here in America it is "business as usual." Tonight I have been listening to the radio for hours. It reflects the stream of normal American existence, the advertising, the baseball games, the swing music, but every few moments this stream is interrupted by a press bulletin from Europe. More mobilizations. Hitler may march before morning. These warnings from another world give Americans shivers down their spine, make them draw the curtains closer and huddle around their own fireside thanking God that they are safe from the storm outside.

29 September 1938.

Today it seems as though we are not going to have our war after all. I feel tired and slightly hysterical now that the strain is released. The crisis that we have been through shocked some of us temporarily at least out of a lot of our nonsense. Perhaps all this gab about the uplifting effects of war has something in it.

15 December 1938.

I am to be posted to London to the High Commissioner's Office, leaving next month. This means the end of this holiday in Washington, for no one could take too seriously my marginal responsibilities in the Legation. If I have learned anything here it is thanks to Hume Wrong, the Counsellor of the Legation. Each of my draft dispatches has been returned to me with detailed emendations in his elegant script. He has applied acid to what he terms my "impressionistic" manner of expressing myself. He will not allow the word "feel" as in "there is a feeling that the United States Administration's attitude is hardening." "Members of the Canadian Foreign Service," he says, "do not feel – they think." The most gratifying moment of my time here has been seeing his report on my work which states that I have "an instinct for political realities."

I have loved Washington – the beautiful city itself. I have made friends here, friends made in this happy interlude who may last a lifetime. I shall miss Nora very much.[1]

I feel a strong tug of attraction to this country and these people, yet I know that it is time for me to go. The prospect of London means taking up the real pattern of my life and responsibilities again. It has its dreary side – the oyster-coloured skies, the waiting for buses in the rain, the staleness and *main morte* of the class system everywhere. All the same I cannot wait to get back.

---

[1] The beautiful Magee sisters, Willa and Nora, decorated and enlivened the Legation as successive social secretaries to Lady Marler.

1939

17 February 1939. London.

Being a Private Secretary is a busy unreal sort of life – unreal because it makes one's day such a programme of events. One does things in a certain order not because one feels like doing them at the time or even because this is the order of their importance, but because they appear in that order on the day's programme. This programme is dictated by the engagements of the Chief, who is in turn a victim of his engagements and spends most of his day in doing unnecessary things which he does not want to do. Yet neither of us is unhappy. We feel that the ritual of our lives is obligatory – we grumble but we submit with satisfaction to the necessity. A day of telephone conversations, luncheon parties, notes acknowledged, visitors received, memoranda drawn up. Exhaustion is merely staleness – we return with zest to the game. What an extraordinary amount of time is spent in saving our own face and coddling other people's vanities! One would really think that the people we deal with were a collection of hypersensitive megalomaniacs.

28 February 1939.

Levée at Buckingham Palace. I fancied myself in my diplomatic uniform hired for five guineas from Morris Angel, theatrical outfitters, Shaftesbury Avenue. With me was my French-Canadian colleague. We waited for upwards of an hour standing about in a succession of dull rooms in the Palace – the ceilings were ornamented with plaster nymphs of pallid respectability – the walls with portraits of the Royal

Family through the ages by artists who were very consciously on their best behaviour. The crowd of well-brushed men in the Army, Navy, and Civil Service did not make a striking colour scheme. It was only saved from drabness by the strong note of scarlet supplied by liveried footmen, beefeaters, and officers of the Guards. These latter were magnificent – the old ones who were court officials seemed as inhuman as heraldic birds with their tall white plumes, their wasp-waisted uniforms with monstrous epaulettes. Their aristocratic beak noses were so appropriate that they might have been ordered for the occasion with the rest of their costumes. The young guardsmen glistened with superhuman elegance – their crimson faces matched their uniforms – their hair and moustaches had been worked over by scrupulous hands. They did what Englishmen wished to do – they looked their part. The rest were middle-class and muddled by comparison. Groups of officers in khaki were as out of place as stage-hands who had strayed into the midst of a gala performance. Judges pushed back their wigs and looked irritable – their stooping backs and loose bellies in contrast with the military rectitude of the rest. One thin little man with horn-rimmed spectacles wore white duck and carried a topee under his arm. A doctor from Borneo? Civil Servants in knee-breeches had to be careful not to be mistaken for the Palace waiters. It was boring waiting like that and exchanging stares of assumed hauteur with other nonentities. My French-Canadian colleague paused before each mirror to examine his legs – he was worried about the prominence of his calves in their tight casing. "And this is costing me five guineas," I said to him. "Cinq femmes," he answered. At last we trooped into the picture gallery – Rembrandts, Vermeers – but we were too close to the Royal presence for aesthetic appreciation. Before I had time to take in how the man in front of me was executing his bow, I was walking across the floor, standing a second, and bowing, I fear from the waist, instead of from the neck only, as I had been taught. As I raised my head I had a glimpse of a surprisingly unreal and kingly figure in a scarlet tunic with a pink face. There was a flash of Royal azure eyes, a half-smile, and I was walking out like a patient emerging from ether.

George VI looked his part. I am told that his ruddy air of health was due to make-up. This gives that touch of unreality which to my mind is a principal charm of royalty.

The distinction of the occasion lies in incongruities – the superb pictures in the gallery and the Victorian clocks and vases on the tables, the splendour of the Guards, the shabbiness of the judges, the Tudor beefeaters, the Regency Hussars, and the Great War khaki, the mixture of style and colour which would be unthinkable if it had been planned, but which has grown up with the monarchy. Beside all this how made to order is the best of dictatorial display!

5 March 1939.

In the Park on a windy, spring day shadows come sliding along and vanish again, the breeze shifts, and the faces of people change with the light and shade. Everywhere is movement – nothing to seize. A painter was sitting with his canvas facing the bridge and the distant towers, ignoring the life around him. Ducks on ruffled cold-blue water, men rowing with certain strength as though we were in leisured summer. Three sailors sitting on a bench – two reading papers – one his legs apart and his elbows on his knees gazing at the ground, safe from the sound of command. A fair goddess of a woman – how unjust to be so sure that she was stupid. Little laughing cockneys with mis-shapen teeth – city-bred runts enjoying jokes. Two well-bred friends or flirts or lovers exchanging smiles of radiant supremacy as they watched the bouncing or slack-bellied nobodies riding in The Row. A young man with a neck of strength and a head of arrogance riding a fine horse. The shuttered pride in a few ruling faces – the quiet joy in moving within their well-cut clothes. The gazing, haunted, jeering, half-impressed, half-sardonic German Jews who move in and out of the English cavalcade. In the middle distance the black trunks and branches of trees backed by a mist of poetic blue. Damp fresh grass. From beyond the Serpentine came the pulse of a distant band and one's feet fell obediently into step.

15 March 1939.

Posters in the streets announce German troops enter Prague. My neighbour said at lunch, "It may seem cynical but I really cannot get excited over this. I do dislike all this sentimentality about the Czechs – as long as the Germans are going towards the east . . ." This seems to be the general view among the "people one meets at dinner."

Went to the House of Commons. Chamberlain spoke of the disappearance of Czechoslovakia like a Birmingham solicitor winding up an estate. Eden was moved – even eloquent. I wish I could get rid of the haunting impression that he is still an undergraduate. Looking down from my place in the gallery in the House of Commons on the pomaded ringlets of a brace of young Conservative M.P.s who were lounging below I reflected on the excessive attraction which style exercises over my imagination. I would not like to be on the opposite side of the fence from beings so elegant, however clumsy and vulgar the ideas inside those sleek heads.

The moral weakness of the government's foreign policy lies in the fact that they talk the language of trust while arming to the teeth. If Chamberlain believed in Hitler's good faith we would not need our big guns. He does not believe in it, but wouldn't it be better to give up a pretence which takes in nobody? Where are politeness and consideration for German susceptibilities getting us? The Germans evidently consider this façade meaningless.

Yet I cannot forget the remark of a middle-aged woman I met one day at a cocktail party. "If we had gone to the help of the Czechs my twenty-five-year-old son might be dead fighting in Central Europe by now, and what good would that do the Czechs?"

Chamberlain, if he used phrases, might have said, "Czechoslovakia is not worth the bones of a British Tommy." That is what he means, and most Englishmen agree with him. They do not think of the corollary, "England is not worth the bones of an American or Canadian soldier." They know that while the second proposition may seem as sensible as the first it is not true politically.

19 March 1939.

This latest crisis was at first exciting. One had the illusion of participating in "an historical event." As I hurried from Trafalgar Square to the Foreign Office[1] my brain was buzzing with clichés – "The

---

[1] I was acting as liaison officer between Canada House and the Foreign Office.

Chancelleries of Europe are humming" – "The hour of destiny is at hand," etc. The wireless transmitters over at the Admiralty would soon be tingling with commands to the fleet. This was the "pulse of the Empire." It was in these buildings, the Admiralty, 10 Downing Street, and the Foreign Office, that fateful decisions would be taken. I hastened to the Foreign Office, my mind moving among images consecrated by historians, journalists, and radio broadcasters. This feeling of excitement and importance underlay my pessimistic language and my grave actor's face. It was only today that I got bored with my role and bored with the crisis. I wanted to close the book, leave the theatre, turn off the radio. But I am no longer in America, so I cannot do any of these things. Boredom, worry, bewilderment, fear – these unpleasant sensations will be with us for months.

6 April 1939.

This is to say what it was like to be sitting in my office this afternoon after lunch, looking out of the window and wishing that I could settle down to work. There were memoranda of telephone calls which must be made immediately and notes for a speech to be ready by tomorrow morning. I would not touch this welter of paper but stared gloomily, nervously, out at Trafalgar Square. The sky was a stale grey of three days' standing. St. Martin-in-the-Fields and the National Gallery were grey too, so was the water in the fountains – so were the pigeons. People passed in their dreary mackintoshes; the traffic filtered around the Square. There were sudden flights of pigeons – false alarms started by some panicky bird and obeyed in a perfunctory fashion by the others. As they flew they showed the paler grey of the underside of their wings. A wet wind blew the water in the fountains in fine showers over the passers-by. A man and a woman with their arms around each other stood near one of the fountains. He bent his head to her with some lover's joke which made them laugh a little. Her arm tightened around him. Scarlet buses supplied the invariable London colour combination and the note was carried out by the red letters of the posters telling Londoners that Civil Defence is the business of every citizen. The day was too sterile to breed even a good war scare. Who could be frightened when there seems so little to lose? A good bomb I thought is just what this Square wants.

16 April 1939.

My mother is here[1] and I refuse to wear an overcoat because I will not have my health fussed over. I refuse to turn out lights because of resentment at bourgeois economies. I also resent being waked up and being told I am late for breakfast. With this goes a revival of adolescent escapism. I wish for a new mistress or to risk my life in an airplane stunt. At the same time I insist on lecturing her on modern painting, reading aloud to her passages from Auden when she likes Shelley.

17 April 1939.

Quite another story. My mother and I went to a movie, came home, sat by the fire and talked – and this time it was like my youth again, but like the happy part of it. My mother seemed, as she does every now and then, to come back to herself. The ailing old woman disappears. She starts on one of her anecdotes full of mimicry, with a cruel eye for the comic effect – and sentimentality like a chapter of Dickens. She seems then for the moment as strong in vitality as ever she was.

20 April 1939.

Went to the Foreign Office to get telegrams.[2] Hadow, who is in charge of the Foreign Office relations with the Dominions, looked grey with fatigue and says that the Chief of the Southern Division, who is the man most responsible in this crisis, has been working until two or three in the mornings for days.

10 May 1939.

Lunched at the Ritz in the Edwardian Louis Quinze dining-room. The women in feathered and flowered straw hats seem pre-last-war. It was like the opening chapter of an old-fashioned society novel. The London season seems unrealistic in the face of anti-gas precautions and evacuation orders. Snobbery must indeed be a lusty plant that grows even on the edge of the precipice.

---

[1] My mother was in England on one of her annual visits from Canada. While in London she took a flat in the same house in Tregunter Road in which I had a room.

[2] The Canadian Government was supplied with a selection of telegrams exchanged between the Foreign Office and British diplomatic posts abroad.

14 *May 1939.*

Family life makes me long for the brothel or the anchorite's cell.

16 *May 1939.*

I said to Mike Pearson today, "Well, we are out of danger of war for the time being." "Do not be so sure," he said, "if the Germans attack the Corridor, Poland will fight, and so will France, and then we shall be in." One of the few independent acts in recent French foreign policy has been the guarantee to Poland to fight if the Germans seize Danzig and their definite promise to send army divisions. These assurances were given only four days ago. They may not keep their word if the British refuse to promise their support. Plainly the British attitude towards the threat to Poland is the most important question of the moment. I cannot believe that this country will go to war for the Polish Corridor. Therefore, I think the French will probably desert their Polish allies.

29 *May 1939.*

To be always patient, to win all the skirmishes with one's own irritability and selfishness is to drain family life of its vitality. One has no right to pose for one's obituary fan-mail to those one loves.

9 *July 1939.*

A picnic lunch party in the gardens of Eccleston Square – pickled herrings, meat pies, lemonade, and laughter. I shall remember this sunny week in the London season of 1939. It seems to belong to the past almost before it has had time to happen – sometime before the war – the next war I mean. The London season survived the last war and may survive the next. Will there always be cultivated rich girls who have read all this year's books and been to Algiers and will not admit to themselves that marriage is now as tiresomely inevitable for them as it was for their grandmothers? And clever young men in the Foreign Office? And little luncheons of eight in Bryanston Square with an actress, an M.P., a girl three years "out" and getting on with her conversation, an American married woman, and a vigorous Edwardian hostess?

Bernard Shaw passed me today bowling down Jermyn Street in a grey tussore silk suit like a man of twenty-four with false eyebrows and a cotton beard.

And Margot Asquith[1] sat next to me in the cinema treating the performance as a background for her showing-off. No one shushed her – I suppose they recognized her and knew that it was useless, as no one in the last half century from King Edward VII on has succeeded in shutting her up.

Edwardian London,

Between interruptions – the first one 1914–1918 – the next 1939–.

The pink and white telegrams in the worn Foreign Office leather boxes – "Urgent and Secret," "According to your Lordship's instructions I sought an interview with Signor Mussolini," "The situation has deteriorated," "His Holiness said," "Monsieur Molotov with his habitual mixture of peasant naïveté and cunning." For a mixture of naïveté and cunning give me any British Ambassador – and their prose – the casual style, the careful avoidance of purple patches and fine phrases, and every now and then the rather wry, tired, little joke.

I went down to Southampton to see my mother off – the usual discouraging lot of passengers – yellow discoloured American women of no particular age. On the way home the tube was full of soldiers and young men in suits carrying rifles and kitbags. Someone said, "They have called up the militia."

9 July 1939. Sunday.

Took a solitary walk by the river at World's End – swans making scanty meals in the mud flats craning their necks after filthy crusts and paddling about on their clumsy snow-shoes. In Chelsea Old Church elderly women with wispy hair were squatting on their haunches to read the inscriptions at the base of the monuments.

The dreariness of these slum streets on a Sunday afternoon is something almost supernatural. The pubs are still closed, but here and there a small magazine and sweet shop is open, the overcrowded little interiors give some colour for the eye – bright, shiny, flesh colours of nudes on the backs of magazines – the yellows and reds of candies in glass jars.

---

[1] The widow of Lord Oxford and Asquith, who had been Prime Minister 1908–16. She was a formidable personality in London political and social life.

At World's End a Salvation Army band was practising in a drizzle of rain – trumpet notes and the tumpity-tumpity tune – the women of the Army in their bonnets seemed a piece of Victorian London.

10 July 1939.

To the House of Commons where Chamberlain made his statement of support for Poland over Danzig. It was in so tepid a tone, delivered in such a mechanical manner and received in such silence that one felt chilled. The German Ambassador must have felt relieved – the Pole disappointed.

29 July 1939.

From my porthole window at the top of Stansted[1] I could admire the grand park in the manner of Le Nôtre with its noble avenues sweeping through the Sussex woods into the mist.

The Bessboroughs have made me feel at home at Stansted – Lord Bessborough has been kindness itself and is relaxed away from the fetters of Governor Generalship.

Moyra was there. I am getting more and more devoted to her. She has a charm compounded of candour and courage.

Lord Bessborough is a mixture of Whig magnifico and a modern businessman – the ruby ring on his hand – the occasional resonance of a phrase and amplitude of a gesture reveal his origins under the surface of a director of city companies. Someone said they had seen Lord Portarlington at Goodwood wearing a straw hat with a ribbon around it – "Such a paltry hat!" said Lord Bessborough. He puffed at his cigar and repeated with satisfaction "a very paltry hat." When I asked him what he thought of Sam Hoare[2] he said he shared a study with Hoare at Harrow. "He was always the same – twitter, twitter, twitter."

Lady Bessborough glides through the flower-filled rooms of Stansted in an ever-changing succession of costumes. Her effects are

---

[1] The country house in Sussex of the Earl of Bessborough. He had been Governor General of Canada from 1931 to 1935. Moyra was his daughter.

[2] Sir Samuel Hoare, who had been forced to resign as Foreign Secretary over the Hoare-Laval Pact in December 1935, had been brought back into the government the following June, and was now Home Secretary.

calculated with French flair – the right jewels with each dress, the right flowers for each room, the right sauce for the fish.

9 August 1939.

Dined with Tony Balásy, Counsellor of the Hungarian Legation. He feels, coming from Washington where he was posted, the oppression of the preparation for war. He talked about the Hungarian minority in Romania. "Dear old Charles," laying his long hand on my arm, "I should not perhaps pretend to be impartial but there are two million Hungarians in Romania – that dates to the Peace Treaty. Well, you know these countries in Central Europe, how many hatreds there are among them. What do I mean? Since the day that England gave her guarantee to Romania the Romanians have begun ill-treating the Hungarian minority. They say now, 'What does it matter about those damn Hungarians? We have the British guarantee.'

"Then you must not judge Hungary by what you read in the newspapers. What do I mean? Hungary has no freedom of choice. We export sixty per cent of our products to Germany. Before these exports were divided among Czechoslovakia, Germany, and Austria. Now they are all Germany. What I mean is, take a look at the map. As for the Hungarian Nazis they have forty seats out of a parliament of two hundred and sixty. If Hungary was Nazi, why don't the Hungarians vote Nazi?"

I did not tell him that the statistics of votes cast for the Nazis and Fascists did not strike me as conclusive. Poor Tony! He will soon be in a concentration camp if the Nazis get in. There is not much place for gentle liberals in Central Europe, and unless he is harder-boiled and more unscrupulous than he seems he will never stand the pace.

14 August 1939.

Lunched with Robert Byron[1] who is going on a visit to the Kaiser. He hopes to be at Doorn when the next war breaks out (this September). He went last year to the Nuremberg Conference "disguised

---

[1] Travel-writer and aesthete, author of several books including *The Road to Oxiana*, killed at sea during the war.

as a Mitford" with Lord Redesdale.[1] The latter, he says, treated the Nazi Party Conference as though it were a house party to which five hundred thousand rather odd and unexpected guests had turned up.

Looked at Poussins in the National Gallery. My heart swelled at their beauty and was subdued by their finality. This is art in the grand manner – no restlessness.

15 August 1939.

We are to sell out the Poles apparently although I still find it hard to credit, but the advice going out to them from the Foreign Office over Danzig is just what we told the Czechs this time last year over the Sudeten crisis. Hitler says that if absolute calm prevails and his prestige is not attacked the problem can wait, but at the slightest incident he will attack Poland. Hadow at the Foreign Office says we led the Poles down the garden path and now we must lead them back again. He was always against the Polish guarantee. He said then, "We shall promise them too much and go back on our word. Better make a realistic settlement now." He may be proved right. It is sickening. But how can one blame the Government with the sneaking desire inside one that they behave dishonourably as long as they avoid war. "Let them do the dirty work and then we will curse them later for it." Such must be the subconscious feelings of many critics of the Government.

21 August 1939.

An ominous, thunderous, heavy day – close grey weather – a weight on one's chest – not panic but a dull certainty that it is coming. This is a most peculiar crisis. It has not broken yet – it is like one of these heavy, leaden clouds which have been hanging over London all day and which must break in loud thunder and lightning. People are mystified and bewildered by the news. It is menacing but imprecise. No one has defined the immediate danger. Hitler has not said a word in public about Danzig or about Poland. There is nothing ostensible

---

[1] The 5th Baron Redesdale, father of the six Mitford sisters, Nancy, Pamela, Diana (married Sir Oswald Mosley), Unity Valkyrie, Jessica, Deborah (Duchess of Devonshire).

to make this immediately necessary – simply "his patience is exhausted." "We cannot go on like this" – that is what everyone is saying. With fatalism we drift into the alternative; we almost embrace the alternative. This tragedy which, when I was in America, seemed too stupid to be true now seems inevitable. I could no more go back to America than I could leave this planet. There will be a war.

22 August 1939.

Coming down Hollywood Road on my way to the bus I saw the placards "Russo-German Pact." During the morning several journalists came to my office – they were as stunned by the news as I was. It is probably no exaggeration to say that a war to defend Poland with Russia benevolent to Germany would be suicide for this country. The present Government will in the end do anything to stay out of such a war. They should never have given the guarantee to Poland without a prior arrangement with Russia. However we get out of it, it will be so discreditable that the Government will not be able to go on unless they could participate in some kind of European Conference which would save their faces – "undoing the wrongs of Versailles." The results would be a further and far-reaching surrender to Germany who would promise for the time being to leave us alone. This seems the most likely upshot unless Beck, the Polish Prime Minister, either cannot or will not give in to the Germans.

Mr. Massey went to a High Commissioners' Meeting. The British Government pointed out that if Germany had access to Russian raw materials it would be impossible to blockade her. They said, however, that they were going to issue a press communiqué stating that they would stand by their obligations to Poland. Bruce, the Australian High Commissioner, protested against this and said it would lead Poland to resist and she would then be destroyed. Halifax was impressed and took him to put his arguments to the Prime Minister. He should find a ready listener. Of course there is the possibility that Parliament will revolt against the Government and then we shall have a war. If we can still get Russian support we should not discourage the Poles, but unless we can get Russia or the United States to come into this I suppose we must tell the Poles to give in. It all depends how far the Russians are committed. If they are really deep in with the

Germans we might as well climb down. If they are likely to switch to us if it comes to a war, then we should fight. My God, how often have I heard the Foreign Office say that a Russo-German pact was an impossibility. They do not seem to have believed what any journalist in London or New York could have told them was likely to happen. Poor Mr. Massey – he has a cold and no role to play and no idea what he would do if he had such a role. He is as undecided as I am as to what is the proper line for the Canadian Government to take. He put the pros and cons to me without any idea of interpreting them and said pathetically, "Of course Bruce" – the Australian High Commissioner – "has a fine mind." He left relieved at my view that in the end the Poles would have to give in.

23 August 1939.

Weekend in the country – When Sally Gordon-Ives met me at the bus stop at Chippenham she had a stranger with her, a man with the oval face of a Gainsborough portrait, an impression partly derived from his white, wavy hair. As he drove the car he kept waving his long fine hands. "Where are we to turn now, Sally?" "This is where I always get confused." "Oh, this is *worse* than death." We arrived at the house before dinner in time for passion fruit and gin cocktails. The small white drawing-room was sweet with the smells of lilies and carnations. Sally's son, Victor, came downstairs in a dinner jacket with a carnation in his button-hole – long legs, lounging Eton manners, and abundant dark locks. He seemed dripping with softness like a young Orsino. He is a caricaturist, a lover of music and a photographer of talent. "Let's play Beethoven's Eighth on the gramophone just once, Mummy, before dinner. I do so love the part that goes ..." and he hummed it in a pure, rounded, full voice. No doubt when war breaks out he will be among the first killed leading the lower classes into action.[1]

At dinner we had a discussion of literature. It crackled up quite suddenly and spread like a forest fire, started by John Davies (who is also staying here) saying that Dostoevsky was superior to Tolstoy. After drinking some sparkling hock I demolished him entirely.

---

[1] He was, in fact, killed in the war.

John had just come back from exercises as a trooper – "For three days I only slept three hours a night carrying a weight of fifty pounds all the time. Nothing saved my bottom but wearing silk pyjama trousers under my cavalry breeches. One morning I was so weak with exhaustion that I wept into my gas-mask. Have you heard about the cavalry officer who was so stupid that the other cavalry officers noticed it?" The white-haired man's name was David. He kept on saying, "*Worse* than death" and "Too tiresome for words to tell" all the weekend. John says he really is a typical New College highbrow. There was a girl there whom they called "Society" because she was a débutante. "Society will not play tennis with a man in braces." After dinner we played bridge and danced to gramophone records in the drawing-room. Young Victor and Society danced with grave seriousness – he a sensitive dark youth, she the perfect answer to his question. She had been to forty-five débutante dances and never leaves until they are over. She dances with a somnambulistic certainty of timing. I went out and stood in the garden, searchlights guarded our revels. I could hear the music of the "*Kleine Offizier*" coming through the window and could see the lighted, flower-filled room with the figures dancing and David's lounging figure. I went back to my pub through the empty streets of the village. They were still dancing and I could hear the drawing-room floor vibrating as they practised new tap-dancing steps. When I got into bed the sheets were damp as they always are in village pubs, and I soaked up my French three-volume saga by the light of a candle.

26 August 1939.

Yesterday Hadow of the Foreign Office suggested that the High Commissioners should ask Mr. Chamberlain to represent to Poland the full danger of the Russian position. It was a way of asking them to climb down. As I walked back across the Horse Guards I thought, "Should I suppress this suggestion?" but I passed it on to Mr. Massey. If I believed that nothing must be done to discourage the Poles I would not have passed it on. I knew that I had to make up my mind in a hurry. I suppose my feeling was that as a Canadian I should be right in doing anything, however small, in the direction of postponing war. Mr. Massey took up the suggestion with Bruce, the Australian High

Commissioner. Bruce took it up with the Prime Minister. Mr. Massey himself had the idea at second hand and understood it very imperfectly. Bruce must have understood it even less. They just got the essential part of it – to warn off the Poles. Mrs. Massey said, "I saw the film of Mr. Bruce going to Downing Street – the irony of it that he should have the credit of making this suggestion to Mr. Chamberlain which really originates with Vincent." As a matter of fact it is a double irony – the idea originated with Hadow, was brought from him by me to Mr. Massey, and Bruce made the effect. That is a historical fact for you – like a stone dropped in a pool.

Still not a word of enquiry or guidance from the Canadian Government. They refuse to take any responsibility in this crisis which endangers the future of Canada. Mackenzie King is condemned in my eyes as unworthy to hold office as Prime Minister.

Mrs. Massey and I sat up until 11 p.m. drinking whisky and water in the High Commissioner's big Mussoliniesque office awaiting his return from his meeting with Halifax.[1] London seems very calm – everyone appears resigned to war if it comes. They have lost any positive will to peace. The last year of peace has been too insufferable. If Russia was on our side I think people would not be sorry that war had come at last.

29 August 1939.

This is like one of those dreams in which images appear in incongruous juxtaposition. One sees one's maiden aunt riding through the park naked on a polar bear.

At the end of the quiet stuccoed streets hang the great silver elephants of the balloon barrage floating airily high in the evening sky. These captive monsters may be seen between their ascents pinned to the ground in the parks or public places – lying exhausted, breathing faintly with the passing puffs of wind. While the general London scene is the same, there are oddities of detail – brown paper pasted over fan-lights and walled-in windows on the ground floors of the buildings, the sandbags around hospitals and museums, the

---

[1] Viscount Halifax had been British Foreign Secretary since Eden resigned in 1938. He became Ambassador to the United States in 1941 until 1946.

coffin-like enclosures around the statues in the central court of the Foreign Office. And there are odd tableaux too – glimpses of people in shirt-sleeves digging air-raid shelters in their back gardens, or offices debouching typewriters and desks for removal to country premises. Then there is the outcropping of uniforms, raw-looking young soldiers in very new uniforms unload themselves from Army trucks and stand about awkwardly in front of public buildings. Women in uniform looking dowdy as old photographs of the last war, full-bosomed, big-bottomed matrons who carry their uniforms with a swagger, and young girls copying their brothers – a spectacle to make their lovers quail.

1 September 1939.

A day which may have lasted a week or a year. It began when that severely black-clad spinster in my office handed me the *Evening Standard* with the text of Hitler's proclamation to the German army. Until then I suppose I had not really taken in that there would be a war. There followed an interminable period of sitting about. It was like waiting for a train that would not turn up. People made their appearances in my office, stayed and disappeared. Voices from what seemed to be every part of my life spoke to me on the telephone. It was like the anteroom to Hades in which one expects to run into an ill-assorted variety of company.

This drawn-out waiting in the close, grey day was interspersed by my visits to the Foreign Office where Hadow was sitting, stunned, among his telegrams. "These bloody pigs," he said of his Foreign Office colleagues, "want to set up a Jewish-cum-Leftist régime in Germany." Like a man possessed he repeated his old anti-communist ravings but weakly like a gramophone running down.

At seven in the evening Mr. Massey came back from the House of Commons. By then there was a black-out. Three or four of us gathered in his huge office, its walls marked where the oil paintings had been removed to safety, its windows curtained. Mr. Massey stood under the vast chandelier. He was excited – unnatural or too natural "We shall be at war some time tonight."

I dined in the candlelit gloom of Boodle's Club dining-room. All but two waiters had been called up. It was the first time in history that members were permitted to dine in the dining-room in day clothes. After dinner I emerged into the coal-black St. James's Street of Pepys or Dr. Johnson. Through the driving rain I walked along the Mall. I half expected to see a crowd outside the Palace, but its grey mass did not show a light. I hailed passing cars, unable in the blackout to see whether they were taxis or private cars. As I squelched through the mud by the park railings I thought that this compact city civilization, inter-related like a switchboard, is overturned. One's friends join up or go to the country, sail to America, or evacuate school children. If you see a friend you cling to him. For when he is gone he is swept away, and God knows when you will see him again. Telegrams are not delivered, telephones not answered, taxis do not run. I suppose once the war gets under way we shall get back to more normal conditions.

3 September 1939.

The war feeling is swelling. I believe it would sweep aside any compromise with Germany if the Government at the twelfth hour could secure one. I think we may have cheering, weeping crowds in the streets yet. This thing is a drug which alternately depresses and elates its victims and which gives them release from the slow death of their daily lives. No one who has not felt this war-feeling inside him can know how it shakes the foundations and lets loose hate, generosity, lust, fear, courage, love – all the bag of human tricks. Some thought they had been analyzed away, but it was just that the right button had not been pressed.

At the doors of the houses in my neighbourhood stand cars laden with luggage. Little groups of Kensingtonians are evacuating their aunts, their canaries, and their small dogs.

8 September 1939.

Is that humming an aircraft? That faint fluting sound – is it a siren? Our ears have been sharpened. Who would have thought of using "our" of Londoners before?

Was there a time when we did not all carry gas-masks? Only a few days ago.

The liner *Athenia* has been sunk by the Germans. The absurd wicked folly of these utterly unwarlike people being drowned. This war has a quality which no other had. We do not approach it with our former innocence. We are in cold blood repeating a folly which belongs to the youth of mankind. We are driven to it by the force of sheer human stupidity, laziness, and error which we have been unable in the last twenty years to overcome.

We awake at three in the morning to sirens. I go for my overcoat, my gas-mask, my shoes and stumble through the french window into the garden where the other inhabitants of this boarding-house are already in the shelter. They are making jokes and meeting with sleepy or nervous responses from their neighbours. The cook says, "We shall be used to this in ten years." Then she goes off to the kitchen and comes back with a tray of tea. I get bored with the shelter and come up for air in the quiet garden. The old man we call "Uncle" is looking at the stars. He has appointed himself an outside watcher. He often thinks he can hear sounds of enemy planes coming over. So far he has been mistaken. His wife "Auntie" talks all the time in the shelter. She gave us quite a clear little description of different kinds of poisonous gases. I think she has a relish for horrors. "Chris" appears in the shelter with her hair tied up in a pink gauze scarf. She looks better like that than she does in the daytime with her blondined curls – a little better but not enough to matter. I came in and had a bath before the all-clear signal went. People will get less careful each time – especially if we have so many false alarms.

15 September 1939.

Living in London is like being an inmate of a reformatory school. Everywhere you turn you run into some regulation designed for your own protection. The Government is like the School Matron with her keys jangling at her waist. She orders you about, good-humouredly enough, but all the same, in no uncertain terms. You need look no further to know what British fascism would be like. Nothing but acute physical danger can make such a regime bearable. So far we have had the restriction without the danger, and there is healthy discontent as a result. After the first air raid we may feel differently. Meanwhile London is a waste of dull desolation. Never has there been such a colourless war – not a drum, not a flag, not a cheer – just sandbags and khaki and air-raid shelters and gas-masks and the cultivated, careful voice of the BBC putting the best complexion on the news. London is waiting for the first raid like an anxious hostess who has made all the preparations to receive formidable guests – but the guests do not seem to be going to turn up. Every time the door-bell rings she thinks, "At last there they are," but it turns out to be the grocer's boy delivering a parcel. So the days pass. We look at our watches, turn on the wireless, pick up a novel, and wait. There are reports in from Denmark that five hundred German bombers are collected in the Sylt and that we may expect a raid in a few days. Meanwhile the Poles have begged the British Ambassador to press the Government to raid German military objectives as the one action which we could take which would really be helpful to the Poles. I do not see how we can avoid doing so any longer unless – Is this a token war fought to save our faces to be followed in a few weeks by a peace conference? The suspicion exists in England and is strong on the continent.

What a relief to be spending an evening alone in my room without thinking, "the so-and-sos are giving a dinner-party – I should rather like to have gone." There are no dinner-parties.

I have been reading *"New Writing"* which is full of bloody death and the symbolism of decay and destruction. The editors have collected the omens of our impending disaster from China and Spain. This monster which was grazing in exotic fields is now approaching England's garden cities.

16 September 1939.

I went to a typical American comedy film with Ginger Rogers in it. There is a country thirty-eight hours away by Clipper where it is still important that women should be smart and attractive, where the most irreverent wisecracks are permitted, where people are still trying to get rich, where individual happiness is still an aim. The selfish, free world of America seems electric with vitality and with hope compared to this scene of grey submission. All this comes from going to an American film. The truth is that I would not leave this country now if I was presented with a ticket to America and a cheque for one hundred thousand pounds.

17 September 1939.

Weekend with the Masseys. Mike Pearson was there. He went to a night-club last night and says there was a crowd of RAF chaps all having a good time pretending to be tight, pretending to fight over the girls, etc. This was fine and as it should be. But he was disgusted by a group of middle-aged men, survivors of the last war, back in uniform again, singing the old songs of the last war, trying to fancy themselves heroes to the night-club hostesses, trying to get back the glamour of their own youth. Certainly one war generation should be allowed to die off before another war is started.

18 September 1939.

Dined with Robert Byron.

He was very amusing in his richly baroque style with his love of exotic places and extravagant episodes. He is an English eccentric – there is nothing quite like them – with their fear of losing face, their wit, their courage, their thin skins and their thick hides, the rudeness they dole out to others and their own palpitating sensitiveness to the snub.

19 September 1939.

I saw Hadow at the Foreign Office today. He says that the Germans and the Russians will merge into one barbarian horde. They will sweep into the Balkans on a tide of pan-Slavism. Turkey will never fight Russia – her western frontiers are too vulnerable to Russian attack. Therefore, the Turks will not come to the help of Romania when it is attacked by Germany and Russia. We may be able to hold the old line of the Roman Empire along the Rhine against the barbarians. Michal Vyvyan on the other hand says that the Russians and Germans will never be able to agree, and that the Russians must know that they have everything to gain from an eventual German defeat. I dined with Michal last night. He wants to join the Army as a private but at the moment he is employed by the Ministry of Economic Warfare. He says there is no use clinging to comfort. It is all so bloody anyway that one might as well enlist. He says he will not mind seeing people in uniforms killed half as much as it makes one lose one's sense of their individuality, whereas if a bomb landed in this restaurant it would be awful watching all the people in their different clothes and with their various manners of suffering making different kinds of faces over it.

There is no war spirit as there was at the beginning. We are just jogging along in a state of some mystification about this peculiar contest. There seem to be such a lot of cultivated intelligent, youngish men about who have nothing to do in this war. They cannot *all* get into the Ministry of Information.

27 September 1939.

Jock Colville[1] told me of a communication from the Shah of Persia to a Victorian Foreign Secretary which he had seen in the Foreign Office Archives. The Shah wrote as follows:

"Last night I dreamed a dream. I was walking in my garden and I saw a great tree growing whose branches overshadowed the lily pond and the rose garden. Lo, as I approached nearer I saw that it was no tree but Queen Victoria of England. Then I gave orders that it be cut down and cast into a pit."

19 October 1939.

I shall be sorry to leave this quarter for my chic new flat.[2] I have got attached to the dowdy, genteel streets off the Fulham Road. It is part of the ritual of life here to have a stack of pennies for the telephone and a stack of shillings for the gas fire. The boarding-house breakfasts are all right too. I do not mind the young men existing on three pounds a week, keeping their umbrellas rolled and their shoes shone and living for the weekends of golf in the country. And the daughters of small-town doctors and country clergymen who have taken jobs at Harrods. They may be dull but at least they want things – to have enough money for smart cars and smart restaurants, to chat easily with earls or live in sin in Mayfair flatlets. They get a kick out

---

[1] J. R. Colville had been Assistant Private Secretary to Neville Chamberlain since the outbreak of war, and was to hold the same post under Winston Churchill and Clement Attlee when they were Prime Ministers.

[2] I was leaving my room in Tregunter Road and had taken a furnished flat in Arlington Street.

of thinking of things like that. Far be it from me to look down on them on that account. Earls and Mayfair flats floated before my youthful eyes.

14 November 1939.

When she appeared at the door of my flat I was taken aback to see how smart, how almost beautiful, she looked. In two minutes she had the valet and myself moving sofas and chairs and changing the look of the flat. Tonight the Irish maid said to me, "It is better this way – before it looked too much like a bachelor's flat – a real bachelor's flat I mean, sir."

29 December 1939.

She and I went into the sitting-room and drew back the curtains and saw Arlington Street covered with snow and the beautiful sun in the sky. I ate toast and spoonfuls of honey and blissfully drank the unpleasant, cold coffee. Then we went out. She wore a fur cap that covered her ears and that checked blue coat I am not sure of and fur-lined boots that made her stumble. She clung to my arm. I was seized with irritation at this woman stumbling along beside me, clinging to me. Then when I looked into her bright, gay face, with her dark, witty eyes and her pink cheeks I felt proud, amused, happy, and loving. We went into St. James's Park. The canal was frozen over – the sea-gulls were sitting perfectly immovable on the ice like birds made of white china. We walked all the way to the end of the canal and back. We passed a lot of Canadian soldiers who stared at her. "People are looking at me," she said, "it must be my fur cap."

1940

13 February 1940.

The man in the room next to Miriam at Claridge's sleeps with his mother in the same bed. The maids do not like it.

Dined with Victor Cazalet. His overbearing flouncings nonplus me. The party was for Lord and Lady Baldwin.[1] He seems less gaga than I had expected and said in tones of evident sincerity, "The loneliness of living in the country is past belief." There were a lot of Members of Parliament there. The more I talk to M.P.s the more the House of Commons sounds like a private school in which everyone has his rating. "So-and-so is a swat," another "a good sort," another "a teacher's pet."

13 March 1940.

Mr. Massey wanted me to include in my dispatch something to contradict the illusion that England is a class-ridden society. Why illusion? He says that the majority of Civil Servants did not go to the public schools. This may be true of the obscurer clerks, and is obviously not true of the men at the top. Lunched with John Tweedsmuir.[2] He does not agree that England will be much changed after the war.

---

[1] Stanley Baldwin had been raised to the peerage when he ceased to be Prime Minister in 1937. He was popularly blamed for Britain's unpreparedness for war, and rather ostracized at this time.

[2] He had just succeeded to the title on 11 February, when his father, John Buchan, first Lord Tweedsmuir, had died while Governor General of Canada. He served with distinction in the Canadian army during the war. His younger brothers, William and Alastair, were also friends of mine.

"People who hunt six days a week will only hunt four days and when things pick up again they will hunt six days a week again."

Everyone is stunned by the Finnish surrender. The Foreign Office only a week ago had no idea of Finland suing for peace with German connivance. The Foreign Office has had more disagreeable surprises in the last twelve months than ever before in its history. The dictatorship countries move suddenly, boldly, and secretly. We carry on our fumblings in an irritating half-light of partial censorship.

17 March 1940.

She has gone. There is nothing to show that she has been here except the toothbrush glass of faded violets and some talcum powder on top of the dressing-table – that and my own feeling that other people do not exist, have no solidity or meaning, that they are figures cut out of illustrated papers, photographs of people. I am alone in the flat. I wonder whether I could sit through a dinner at the club. No – I do not think so. The sight of those pink-faced, silver-haired, old boys and those well-kept young men drinking their claret and eating their jugged hare would be too much. The whole settled order of daylight comfort and daytime wisdom has become insufferable. I am beyond any consolation to be derived from the cosiest and most sympathetic friend. My heart hurts – I should like to have it removed and taken away on a silver salver.

3 April 1940.

The housekeeper in these flats is like the enchanted woman in the fairy tale. Every time she opens her mouth toads drop out. As she does not seem to dislike me particularly I think this must be simply "her way." Today she came in to arrange my chestnut branches in a vase. "Very pretty they are, but it *was* naughty of you to pick them. Why it is a whole branch taken off." "Well Mrs. Haines," I said, "I need them to brighten up my life." "*You* need brightening up," she cried with a raucous laugh. Whether she meant that I was a particularly dull dog or whether this was a sarcastic reference to my life of immorality I cannot quite make out. To any complaint she always has an answer ready. A lifetime of dealing with complaining lodgers has taught her the technique of always keeping on the offensive. For instance, one day I said that my room was rather stuffy. "It is because you keep the electric fire on. It is not 'ealthy." The price of the fire is included in the rent so that every time I burn it they lose money. I gained this arrangement after long-drawn-out fencing with Mrs. Haines. The other flat dwellers pay for electricity by the hour.

4 April 1940.

Dined with Jock Colville who is in the Prime Minister's Office. He sees everything that is going on in home and international affairs, but tells one nothing, and the questions that one is too much of a gentleman to ask hang heavily over the conversation.

8 April 1940.

Went to the House of Commons to the last day of the great debate on the conduct of the war. There they sat on the front bench – the three of them – Chamberlain, Simon,[1] and Hoare, the old-fashioned, solid, upper-middle-class Englishmen, methodical, respectable, immovable men who cannot be hurried or bullied, shrewd in short-term bargaining or political manipulation, but with no understanding of this age – of its despair, its violence, and its gropings, blinkered in solid comfort, shut off from poverty and risk. Their confidence comes from their certainties. They are the old England. When Chamberlain goes, that goes and it will not return.

Lloyd George attacked the Prime Minister – that old poseur, that mischievous mixture of statesman and minor prophet and tricky Welsh politician. But what an orator! His speech made me think of King Lear's ranting – shot through with gleams of vision. He and Churchill are the only orators in the House. As for Chamberlain, he has authority when he speaks and a sense of the weight of words and an admirable precision. He has at least a standard of speaking.

13 May 1940.

The war has begun all over again in these last few days with the invasion of Holland and Belgium. Events have the same air of

---

[1] Sir John Simon had been an M.P. since 1906 and was then Chancellor of the Exchequer.

unreality that we experienced in the first week in September after the declaration of war. One has the dazed feeling of being dragged in the wake of a runaway destiny. On we go bumping along at a terrific rate with the dust of passing events in our eyes. We are trying to clutch at some meaning in the landscape that rushes past us but it is no good. We are too close to what is happening. This closeness to history puts everything out of focus.

War itself is not unnatural, only the modern weapons of war are unnatural. The weapons dominate us. The pilot is the tool of his plane, the gunner of his gun. That is what makes modern war a new predicament. We are caught in the same trap as the Germans, and we are closer to them than to any neutrals and having got into this mess we long to drag in everyone else. The Germans know the same joys and sorrows that we do. They are the mad dogs who have bitten us and infected us with their madness.

15 May 1940.

They tell us that the greatest battle in history is beginning. London is sultry with the rumour of it. The possibility of defeat appears in whispers and averted glances.

18 May 1940.

I cannot believe that the French are as demoralized as I hear they are. If they have gone to pieces, we have not been beaten yet, and we will have to go on fighting. We know the history of conquered races, the eternal resentment and the eventual revolt. Better to let this generation go through hell and beat the buggers.

22 May 1940.

Last night I wrote a speech for Mr. Massey to deliver to Canada on the general theme of "the darkest hour before the dawn," "British spirit is unbreakable," "the nightmare of horror and destruction that hangs heavy in the air in these lovely days of English spring." Mr. Massey delivered it. It was a great success, I believe. Writing these speeches gives me an outlet for my feelings. Hume Wrong says I shall develop into a jelly-bellied flag flapper. Before the war I used to say that I could not understand how any man of conscience could write propaganda, and in my mind I was always critical of my father for the recruiting speeches he made in the first war and *he*, unlike me, was trying to go to the war himself.

Bad reports on French morale, which is said to be undermined by subterranean communism and fifth column activities. Poor old Franckenstein, the Austrian Ambassador, came to see me today. He wants now to get out to Canada. He is usually so suave and mannered but today he looked shattered. He is partly Jewish and he knows that if the Germans come he will be shot at once. N. says, "Well, he has had a pretty good time all his life. Now he is old – why shouldn't he be knocked on the head? Look at all the chaps who are being killed in France."

A Canadian RAF pilot came back on leave. He seemed a dull young man, but he and the rest of them are our only hope. All I could do was try to talk to him normally, as he must find it awkward to be treated with the reverence he deserves.

19 May 1940.

When Haines, the valet who works in all these service flats, came to see me this morning he was in a state of high excitement. "The news this morning is awful. We have got the men and the spirit, but we have not got the planes. *Somebody* is responsible for this."

Michal Vyvyan said today at lunch, "How absurd to blame a liberal social democracy for not being organized to deal with war. It is like blaming a fine flower garden for not moving at sixty miles per hour."

Meanwhile two French journalists who attended a lunch in Lord Athlone's[1] honour the other day returned in a state bordering on nervous hysteria. They found all the Blimps at the luncheon discussing sports for the British troops behind the lines. "Men must have some rugger and cricket. Keep them fit," etc.

Refugees are beginning to arrive from the Continent – tough-looking Norwegian seamen with shocks of coarse blond hair, dressed in blue serge suits, lunching at Garland's Hotel – Dutch peasant girls in native costume like coloured photographs in the *Geographical Magazine* – walking down Cockspur Street carrying their worldly

---

[1] The Earl of Athlone was about to take up his post as Governor General of Canada.

possessions tied up in bundles. A group of Dutch soldiers in the street in German-looking uniforms gives one a turn. (Shall we see German soldiers in London streets?)

My brother Roley[1] has cabled asking me to do my best to get him a commission in the British Army to get him over here quicker than he could with the Canadians. Why should he be hurled into that hell in France? Why can't he wait until his turn comes to come over with the Canadians? It is not *his* England. It would be more appropriate if I went, as I have always been so bloody English.

I cannot get out of my mind my cousin Jack Grant's face when I saw him the other day. He came over from Canada to join the RAF and has been with them in France since October and now in the Battle of Britain. Earlier he was beginning to have a good-natured, gross look. Now he is pale with fatigue and thin. His eyes look blazing blue and he has two clearly-defined and quite new lines at the corners of his mouth.

This office is being invaded by women of the aristocracy wanting to send their children overseas. Lady S. who came in today is typical of the old-fashioned kind. She was most anxious not to do anything which might divert English currency from this country. But they are all looking to Canada now. We are to provide them with men and ammunition, take their children, intern their fifth column, etc.

29 May 1940.

I could hear the guns plainly tonight as I sat writing in the club library – I suppose at the mouth of the Thames. Natalie Hogg says that last weekend she sat in the garden at her place in Kent and could hear the gunfire from France all afternoon long.

The Canadians here are becoming disillusioned about the English. Mike Pearson says, "Never have I been so glad to be a Canadian as in these last days – at least we are not responsible for this mess." Patterson of the CPR says, "If I ever have to go through another war let it not be with the English – their slowness drives me mad." Even the loyal Mr. Massey (more in sorrow than in anger) admits the flaws.

---

[1] He came to England with the Canadian army and was wounded in Normandy in 1944; he later became a judge of the Supreme Court of Canada.

But so do the English themselves. Lord Davies[1] said today, "Things must go better now – after all we have made every bloody mistake that can be made so that we shall be reduced to doing something right in the end." What makes one fear for the result of this war is not merely Nazi military success but the fact that they have faith in their rulers and we have not – or should not have. Yet we may win in the end because inertia rolling at last into action will be heavy with reserves of strength and wealth, whereas the German will keyed to this tremendous tempo must crack unless it has respite. Perhaps it is nearer cracking than we dream of. To me it is a sheer impossibility that Nazi power, if it triumphed in this war, could live for more than fifteen years. Because it cannot rest. It has no principle of growth in it and so must always be moving on until it meets an immovable object against which it is dashed to pieces. May the British Empire be that immovable object.

2 June 1940.

Went with Mike Pearson to Dover. There we really had the feeling of being in an extension of the actual war zone. Destroyers were coming in and out of the harbour, going to Dunkirk to embark the remains of the British Expeditionary Force and the French Army of the North.[2] As we walked along the pier we saw one of the destroyers returning, its stern had been blown clean off by a bomb. It was limping home with flags still flying. We went alongside two more destroyers, one English and one French. They began landing French soldiers who were herded into a troop train by a thin young officer in riding breeches. Looking down on the decks of the British destroyer we could see a bearded sailor lying asleep beside his gun. On the French destroyer the sailors were clustered in a chattering group – one was showing the others a postcard of a nude woman and they were gossiping and laughing. Soon a tug drew up alongside and began to debouch German prisoners. They were pallid and grimy

---

[1] Formerly a Liberal M.P. and Parliamentary Secretary to Lloyd George, he was a keen supporter of the League of Nations.

[2] The Dunkirk evacuation from 27 May to 3 June brought over 300,000 men, French as well as British, to England.

and looked as if they had been kept underground for a year, the result I suppose of being packed together under the hatches while they were being bombed by their own people from the air. They came shambling out on to the deck in the sunshine and began running up the companion-way as if they had the devil behind them. There they formed into a file waiting to be taken away in buses. I remember the German prisoners-of-war at Calais, when I was a boy after the last war, carrying slop-pails around the British camps. They had shaven heads. These men had long hair which fell over their eyes as they stumbled along the gangplank. Some were aviators, and these had an air of arrogance. The privates ran and huddled like sheep. Prisoners without their guns and helmets have the look of having suffered an amputation, as if they were deprived of a vital limb or had been castrated. Then came the German wounded. They were swung from the decks of the ship by a crane. None of them moved or cried out but lay in waxen immobility as if they were already dead. While the procession of prisoners and wounded moved by, the Tommies who were guarding the pier remained silent. Anyone who spoke spoke in lowered tones. Out in the harbour a mist hung over the smooth sea and dozens of craft lay there at anchor after coming and going to Dunkirk time after time. About the cliffs the eternal gulls circled. Two little girls were shrilly calling to each other from their bicycles as they rode in and out of the small gardens in front of a row of houses at the foot of the great bluff of cliff behind the docks. These docks, and in fact the whole of Dover, are now within range of German shell-fire from Boulogne. But the life of the town is going on just the same. We could see the groups of old ladies coming out of church after eleven o'clock service and standing for a minute to chat in the sun. In the field of buttercups outside the town some little boys were rolling about wrestling – they each wore their little cardboard gas-mask case.

From Dover they can see Boulogne at night burning across the Channel and hear the bombs as they fall. Why the Germans do not bomb the small inner harbour at Dover, so crowded with shipping, one cannot guess. The naval officer who took us around, a lean individual with a sardonic, leathery face, indicated the cliffs of Dover with a wave of the hand, "They may come over here," he said, "but if they do, not one will get out alive."

6 June 1940.

Having half an hour to spare this afternoon I strolled down to the Foreign Office. No one would have thought that a German invasion is just around the corner. There were three or four pleasantly satirical and studiedly casual young secretaries draped about the room drinking their tea and eating strawberry shortcake. It might have been a scene from a skit on His Majesty's Diplomatic Service. In fact I am sure they are all conscientious, hard-working civil servants more aware than most people of what is at stake. After all their cup of tea and their ironic little jokes are pleasures shared by this whole nation and are no doubt part of *What We Are Fighting For.*

Our standards are being overturned. What is brought home to me is my existence as a member of a community in a way that I never dreamed of before. I rather fancied myself as a cosmopolitan who laughed at blimpish patriotism. Now I subscribe to all the old cries – "My country right or wrong," I could have my room plastered with these cracker mottoes which have now become for me eternal truths. Meanwhile we are all waiting, almost longing for these bombs. Hart Massey said to me today, "I wish they would start bombing us." And Michal said with relish, "Soon the bombs will be landing on our heads." This must be the mentality of the civilians behind the lines. The soldiers do not swell the chorus, nor have I heard any women express a pious hope for a bombing raid. The soldiers and the women must be right.

15 June 1940.

Lunched with Mrs. Andreae. She wanted to ask me about taking her grandchildren to America to escape the war. She is a shrewd, worldly, old woman but she is waiting to make her decision until she has consulted a fortune-teller. I should not laugh at her as for the last few days I have had a sort of obsession that the continuation of Hitler's successes was bound up with this unnaturally fine weather that goes on and on. "Hitler weather" they call it. It is not only the effect of the weather in speeding up the movement of his mechanized forces but a purely silly and superstitious association in my mind.

17 June 1940.

The French have declared that organized resistance is at an end and the French Government have asked the British Government if with their approval they may sue for an armistice. The British Government have replied, "Yes, provided the French fleet is handed over to us intact." Apparently the French do not intend to resist in North Africa. It is difficult to see how they can hand over their fleet to us if they are going to make peace with Germany. A full-dress German attack on England is expected this week or the next. We have about five divisions trained and equipped. The Germans have one hundred divisions. They have a pronounced superiority in the air and in equipment. It is estimated that by bombing they could reduce the produce of our factories to twenty-five per cent of the present output. It would take the Americans at least six months to begin supplying this country on a scale equal to the needs.

Whatever the odds this country is not prepared to surrender and would not stand for it, although there are elements at the top and bottom of the social scale who secretly lean towards it. If after three months of total war this country cannot take it (any more than the Finns or the French could take it, and they are both brave races), then I suppose we shall make peace as France is doing now after thousands of men, women, and children have been killed. Mike Pearson says, "If this country makes peace I hope Canada will become a republic and that would be the end of this business of our duty to the Empire."

I got my promotion today as Second Secretary – an odd time to get it.

22 June 1940.

Several exhausting days during which the office has been flooded with people trying to arrange for their children to get out to Canada. I have been impressed by three things:

1. The unnatural coolness of English parents – no broken voices or tear-filled eyes.

2. The incredible confusion caused when civil servants are taken

by surprise and by a sudden onrush of events. I see how "government" breaks down. The picture of such a breakdown is a queue of people with urgent problems and a distracted civil servant, his desk covered with forms and regulations, cornered by "reality."

3. I am impressed by the sacrosanct importance of the British Nanny. People here would rather let their children run the risk of being bombed than send them out on a sea voyage without their Nanny.

Refugees are arriving from our Legation staff in Paris. They have left most of their possessions behind them. Madame Vanier, the wife of our Minister to Paris, stood at the front door watching the boxes of documents from the Paris Legation arrive. Suddenly she gave a cry of emotion, threw herself upon one package – "My hatbox – my hatbox. I never thought I would see it again."

Saw Roger Makins of the Foreign Office at the club today. He says the French Government are completely demoralized and will accept anything the Germans dish out to them. He says it is a question of the collapse of the whole fabric of the Third Republic.

If these politicians of ours ever read any serious modern literature they might not be so surprised at what is happening in France. For years now there has been bad news from France. Their best writers have given a shaking picture of the dry rot which has overtaken the French bourgeoisie. The fascist and communist undercurrent in French literature has been quite audible. Books like Céline's *Voyage to the End of the Night* are social documents as important as white papers or ambassadors' dispatches.

Mr. R. B. Bennett[1] has just made a speech at some school prize-giving saying that there can never be a fifth column in England because it is such a land of liberty, etc. Let him go and take a look at the slums in this country.

I dined with Tony Balásy of the Hungarian Legation. He talked about the overthrow of the small states in Europe by Hitler, and said that to understand the mentality of the people of those states one would have to have lived there through the post-war years. He said, "You have the Big Power point of view. If the British Empire were

---

[1] Bennett, who had been Canadian Prime Minister from 1930 to 1935, was now living in retirement. He was created Viscount Bennett in the Birthday Honours in June 1941.

destroyed you would have all lost something real, but it is not the same for us – we have known all along that our independence, the independence of a country like Hungary, depended on a precarious balance of Big Power rivalries. Such independence was always something of a fiction, although we might come ahead of Germany or England in the alphabetical lists for committees of the League of Nations. Our politicians had to repeat that we would die rather than give up a lot of this precious independence – still at heart we knew we had it on sufferance."

I can see that despite his hatred of Nazis Tony is half fascinated by the idea of a united European bloc by whatever means achieved. Some Europeans may be tempted to think that if the small sovereign state entities can be broken down and Europe united it is worth the price of temporary Hitler domination, because Hitler will not last forever, and after he is gone it will be as impossible to reconstruct the Europe of small states as it was to reconstruct feudal Europe after the fall of Napoleon.

26 June 1940.

Walked today along the Broad Walk through Kensington Gardens. It was thronged with soldiers, the remains of the shattered continental armies, Dutch, French and Norwegian. Then the Canadians who have become almost part of the London streetscape, and the newly arrived New Zealanders including many Maoris, and then, the altogether more solid, as if carved out of some other material, Guardsmen. Moving in this procession of soldiers of the nations I had the sense of swimming in the full tide of history.

My office is the door of escape from hell. Day after day the stream of people press in. Today, for example, some of the Austrian Rothschilds (escaped from a concentration camp) are trying to pass their medical examination to go to Canada. Would I arrange a financial guarantee for them? The wife of one of the wealthiest men in England is trying to get out of the country. Her husband is a Jew and a leading anti-Nazi. Will I get her a letter to prove (on very flimsy grounds) that she is a Canadian? Lady B, looking radiant, comes to ask if I would arrange for her son's prep-school to be affiliated with a boys' boarding school in Canada and to migrate there *en masse*. The

Marchioness of C, in the uniform of the Women's Naval Auxiliary Unit, wants to get three children out to Canada at once. Two Canadian journalists want to get their wives out but there is a mysterious delay in getting their exit permits. The Spanish Ambassador wants us to get accommodation for his daughter, his mother, and a troop of maids and governesses on board the next ship. They are going to Canada for a little rest from the nervous tension of the war. He knows he is slipping with his own Government and may be in exile himself any day. The Polish Ambassador wants us to take the wives and daughters of one hundred high Polish political and diplomatic dignitaries. Count X, the anti-fascist with a price on his head, must leave for Canada at once on a mission of great importance. I have only touched the edge of one day's work. I do not mention my own friends and relatives who want to get out. Here we have a whole social system on the run, wave after wave after wave of refugees, and these are only the people at the top, people who can by titles, letters of introduction, or the ruling manner force their way into Government offices and oblige one to give them an interview. What of the massed misery that cannot escape?

The sense of the dissolution of civilized society is overpowering.

7 July 1940.

Mr. Massey says there will be no revolution in England – if socialism comes it will be a gradual kindly English socialism. There will still be country houses but only the smaller ones. Chatsworth[1] will go. He foresees an early German attempt at invasion and the early establishment of martial law in England.

16 July 1940.

Lord Cromer, the former Lord Chamberlain, came in to see me today to explain some complicated business about the Suez Canal Company which boiled down, as usual, to our taking another refugee into Canada, this time a French Jewish financier. Lord Cromer was very deliberate, very formal, very detailed, and conducted the whole

---

[1] The great house of the Dukes of Devonshire; it has in fact survived, and the present Duke lives there.

negotiation with the leisurely flourishes proper to the transaction of business between gentlemen in the reign of Queen Victoria. It always amuses me to see how much these old boys enjoy getting what they set out to get and how much charm, manner, and wiliness they are willing to expend; sometimes on objectives which only remotely concern them. But such negotiations are the breath of life to them.

I have a hankering to get the Hutterite Brotherhood out to Canada. They are a sect of pacifist community-livers – many of them Germans at present residing in the Cotswolds where their life is being made impossible by the suspicions of the country folk. My weakness for obscure and unpopular religious sects of a pacifist or quietist complexion makes me susceptible to them. Their leader, a man called Arnold, looks an Oberammergau Christ with beard, smock, and knee-breeches. He seems somewhat sly and smooth. The Canadian Government do not want them.

Lunched with Mrs. Andreae and the wife of the British Minister to Sofia. Mrs. Andreae says she has it on good authority that a French refugee approaching the cliffs of Dover on his way to escape from France saw a cloud of angels armed with spears hanging in the heavens over England. She firmly believes we are protected by God or . the stars or something – I cannot quite make out what – as she alternates so much between Christianity and astrology. There is even a suggestion there was more than meets the eye in the British escape from Dunkirk – meaning that it was arranged for our special benefit by God. The latter idea is quite widely spread, with the corollary that it was the response to our National Day of Prayer. It is not only old women who believe this but at least one contemporary of my own – a naval officer now in charge of a destroyer. However, naval officers do have strange beliefs.

I now hear that the ferocious internees whom the British Government begged us on bended knees to take to Canada to save this country from their nefarious activities are mostly entirely inoffensive anti-Nazi refugees who have been shovelled out to Canada at a moment's notice where they may have a disagreeable time, as our authorities have no files about them and will not know whom or what to believe. Part of the trouble is due to the fact that the Home Office and the War Office seem barely to be on speaking terms.

5 August 1940.

The intermingling of various ingredients of English social life is proceeding apace. War is stirring up the mixture. English men and women of different classes, localities, sets, and tastes are for the first time talking to each other. This appeared to be an impossibility in England. The weather was previously the one subject upon which everyone had fixed for conversations with strangers.

15 August 1940.

Garnons, Hereford, the country house taken by the Masseys as a convalescent hospital for Canadian officers – big rambling house – early Gothic revival about 1820 – battlements and a great tower. Looks its best by moonlight (like all imitations of the Gothic). A nice house – big rooms full of chintz-covered sofas and bad Italian paintings collected by an eighteenth-century ancestor on the Grand Tour. Some beautiful mirrors – Lelys, Romneys, and Laszlos in the dining-room. The view from my room was like the background of an eighteenth-century hunting print. The house was on a hill with a prospect over a valley and the Black Mountains as a back-drop – a lovely stretch of skyscape across which the airplanes pass and return on their way to intercept German bombers over Bristol. We live a country-house life – croquet, conversation, billiards, and flirtation, while a few miles away the air battles go on which are to decide our fate. When one of these noisy monsters zooms across our neat, snug valley it is as though it had flown straight back into the old England of port and leisure in which we are incongruously living.

A terrifying night. There are old and evil spirits in this part of the world. A friend who spent his childhood in just such an old house as this set in a lush and misty park, told me that all this Welsh border country is haunted. Here one believes in the fears of peasants and one prays their ancient prayers.

I was led in a dream of circles through my private hell and all the images which congeal my blood and scarify my soul. My daytime self was abolished, I looked out from my window at the quiet moonlit valley and hoped for an air raid to break the silence and deliver me back in the world where courage and intelligence could still avail me.

As the days went by, one after another of those staying here let slip that they had been unable to sleep and nervously laughing asked, "Is this house haunted?" All day the sun glows steadily through the mist. The heat haze lingers like smoke over the clumps of oak trees in the park and the airplanes pass and return across the slumbrous valley.

In the game book which goes back to 1860 I see that this week in August has always been oppressively hot here with the birds lying close. I like to turn the pages of this record with its thumbnail sketches of days' shooting kept by the successive squires of Garnons – of days when it was "wild and wet" and "I never remember to have seen the birds behave so badly" and the days when all went well and the score of the day's bag tells its own story.

Our nerves have been too long taut and this sudden relaxation, this enchanted castle, these long idle days – it is all somehow too much. Today's was only a small incident but for an hour it filled the sky. We were motoring to the Black Mountains and Mrs. Massey decided just as we were climbing the mountain road to Llantony through the close green lanes, to turn back. The rest of us had wanted to go on – impossible to describe the spell of dumb rage that seized us – the heavy clash of her will against our silent resistance. We motored back down from the cool mist-soaked mountain air into the summer languor of the valley. No one in the car spoke all the way back. When we reached the front door we separated to our rooms as if frightened to face each other and to reveal how strongly we had been shaken for no reason.

17 August 1940.

Complete change of atmosphere. The rest of the party have arrived from London. Most successful expedition to Llantony Abbey where the monks kept a Christian oasis during the Dark Ages of the Norse raids. The ruins are deep in a valley buried in the recesses of the Black Mountains, almost inaccessible most of the year, as the roads are a morass. Now part of the Abbey is farm buildings, washing hangs in the ruined nave, chickens step delicately among the cowpats in the roofless lady chapel. I am glad the attempt to restore it in the 1900s by a Roman Catholic monastic order was a failure. Modern

Roman Catholic priests would have ruined it with their atrocious taste in buildings and they would have given it a horrid, preserved, or worse still, "revived" air.

Came back and read David Cecil's[1] description of eighteenth-century country-house life in an eighteenth-century country-house library – cream and gilt with classical busts and blue and white china urns over the bookcases. Mr. Massey and I are both bitten with this place. We cannot escape the charms of the past. Their institutions were made for men and women human in scale. Now everything is over life-size. We are no good for the future. It is not our picnic. I tell myself it will be exciting to be alive in an age of change after the war, but it would only be exciting if we could rebuild the human scale.

26 August 1940. London.

There go the sirens again! I do not know what will be left of our nerves after a winter of this. First the wail announcing impending doom. Then the city holds its breath as the last dying sound of the siren fades and we wait. Of course everyone is calm enough on the surface, but one gets jumpy at sudden noises. At first raids were exciting and frightening. Now they are getting unpleasant, risky and tiring.

3 September 1940.

Weekend with the Bessboroughs who are living on in the middle of the glorious Le Nôtre-style park which is now in the direct line of the German bombers attacking Portsmouth. During the night six bombs landed in the park. On Sunday morning we set out in a little procession to examine the damage. Lord Bessborough, wearing a panama hat, led the way. He prodded the bomb craters with his walking-stick and chatted with magnificent and old-fashioned condescension to the local farmers. Once this insidious process is under way, affability on the one side and an answering feeling of proud gratification are established, the silken cord binds all parties in their respective places in the social order.

---

[1] Younger son of the 4th Marquess of Salisbury, Fellow of New College, Oxford, and later Professor of English Literature at Oxford. The description is in his book, *The Young Melbourne.*

5 September 1940.

Visit to the Canadian Headquarters installed in an ugly country house surrounded by repulsive yew-hedges. General McNaughton[1] holds forth surrounded by a Greek chorus of red-faced generals and brigadiers whose inertia (dating from the close of the last war) is troubled by his incessant darting vitality. They dare not meet that eye. He may or may not be a great man. He is a prima donna. The star of the party was R. B. Bennett, in a ponderously playful vein. Conversation was not brilliant – food none too good – atmosphere creaking with military courtesies enough to make the hackles rise on the back of any good civilian like myself.

6 September 1940.

Lunched with Sir J. M., Scotland Yard, to talk about internees.[2] He is "liberal-minded," slightly malicious, a rather donnish sort of elderly civil servant with a passion for the science of finger printing. Very nice to me – rather stern with the Club's temporary waitresses.

Met that ballet dancer in the street. I wonder? She has magnificent pools of greenish eyes in a naïve, shrewd, American face – slight golden down on her cheek bones and the strong neck of her craft. She adopts a sort of little-girl trustful posture towards me and wears a small white bow in her hair.

7 September 1940.

Dinner with R. B. McCallum, my former tutor at Oxford, at the National Liberal Club, a portentous place, vast and gloomy with walls of dark green and brown tiles. The dining-room is like the main hall of a railway station with an enormous marble statue of Gladstone at one end of it. The whole place is the morgue where the remains of the Liberal Party might be laid out. Our conversation was appropriate. He began by saying that he had that day been motoring through the

---

[1] General A. G. L. McNaughton was officer commanding the First Canadian Division, and later the First Canadian Army. He resigned in 1944 to become Minister of Defence.

[2] Part of my work at Canada House was concerned with the arrangements for transferring suspected enemy aliens from British internment camps to Canada.

industrial suburbs off the Great West Road. "A cheering sight," he said. I suppose I may have winced at this description of that nondescript waste of dreary, characterless little houses. "You," he went on, "and other lovers of the picturesque may lament the green fields and pretty villages which once stretched about London, but remember that those villages housed a desperately poor population of agricultural labourers. You may say that the factory workers' houses which now stand there are ugly and depressing, but remember that the fathers and grandfathers of these workers lived four or five in a room in some filthy slum where misery, dirt, gin, and incest flourished. Now these people have attained respectability, the dearest craving of the working classes. That is a great achievement. You with your apocalyptic talk of the spiritual deadness of the babbitry ignore all this, but it is the triumph of our civilization, and we are too slow to praise it. You talk to me of our failure to turn the Industrial Revolution to good account in human terms, but when war broke out we were busily engaged in doing just that, although I admit that the pace was slow and that there was still a great deal of slack to be taken up."

13 September 1940.

A week of air raids. Our ears have grown sharp for the sounds of danger – the humming menace that sweeps from the sky, the long whistle like an indrawn breath as the bomb falls. We are as continually alive to danger as animals in the jungle.

During a raid the silent empty streets wait for the shock like "a patient etherized upon a table." The taxis race along carrying their fares to the shelters. A few pedestrians caught out in the streets make their way with as much restraint as possible to the nearest shelter, keeping an eye open for protection – for friendly archways. They try to saunter but long to run.

In the parks the fallen leaves lie thick upon the paths. No one has time to collect them into bonfires and burn them. The paint is beginning to peel off the great cream-coloured houses in Carlton House Terrace and the grand London squares. The owners will do nothing about it until "after the war." London is beginning to look down-at-heel and a bit battered. Every now and then one comes upon a gap in a row of houses or a façade of shops. In the gap is a pile of rubble where the bomb has hit. I suppose gradually there will be more and more such gaps until the face of London is pitted and furrowed with them.

The other night I was caught on my way home from Chelsea in a heavy barrage with falling shrapnel and turned into a public shelter to wait until things were quieter. There were half a dozen old women of the Belcher charwoman variety, two conversational old men in battered bowlers, and a drunken Irish maid-servant who kept mocking the English for their credulity and stupidity, "You English, sure you're the dumbest nation on earth. Now do you believe all this you read in the papers about how many German planes were shot down. Don't you see it is all propaganda now." Her harangues were greeted with sardonic amusement. These people were all cold and all sleepless. They had spent three nights in this shelter and outside was the recurrent roar of the barrage. Their homes in Chelsea have been badly pasted. The shelter itself was a feeble affair giving no protection from bombs. But their stolidity was unshaken. Their retort was the Englishman's immemorial reply to danger – irony. The kind of joke which hinges on the thought, "Well it ain't the Ritz exactly." They were not afraid but they did want one thing – "a cup of tea."

14 September 1940.

The attacks on London have only been going on for ten days. So far people are steady, there has been no panic. But they are depressed. Everyone is suffering from lack of sleep and nervous tension. There is some feeling that the poor are taking it the hardest and many complaints about lack of shelters. The ideal thing from Hitler's point of view would be to continue this all winter and then to attack in the spring. Is he strong enough to wait? That is the question hanging over us. His raids certainly have not been a spectacular success, but they are making a dent all right.

My new girl is a ballet dancer. She is an American girl who studied ballet in Paris and is now dancing with a Polish company in London. She seems very dumb. We were walking along Jermyn Street the other day and by way of conversation I said, "This is a great street for tarts." "What are tarts?" I nearly fell flat on my face in the street and then I explained it was an English term for prostitutes. She clucked her tongue disapprovingly. She has been in England six months and she does not know what a tart is. Sometimes she seems almost half-witted. She looks exactly like all ballet dancers. She has ivory, pale skin and a hard body like an athletic boy. The extraordinary thing about her are her eyes which are enormous – the eyes of a tragedy queen. She herself says she feels her eyes "do not seem to belong to her." She seems very truthful and quite without artifices.

15 September 1940.

The luxury restaurants of the West End are dying on their feet. I went into the Apéritif the other night for dinner. It was completely empty. Groups of tired-looking waiters muttering together in corners, the bartender brooding over his deserted bar. Miss Lily who does the accounts was listlessly turning over the pages of *The Tatler.* "My gawd – what freaks!" she observed studying the wedding groups. She too looked tired and strained, and there was an edge of excitement and irritability beneath her carefully casual Mayfair manner.

16 September 1940.

It has come to a state where none of us can be sure that we shall meet each other the next day and we begin to look for a gap in the party. Bombs have been raining around here, Berkeley Square, Park Lane, and Regent Street. So far none in St. James's Street or Pall Mall,[1] but this must be pure luck, and there is more than a chance that we shall get it in the next week. Life is "nasty, brutish and short."

I went to the lunch-time ballet. It was wonderful to see *Les Sylphides* and the meticulous attention that went to each movement and step. The permanent importance of an art compared with the noisy, accidental crashing of tons of high explosives. Aesthetic standards are the only ones that stand up in these times. They are not mixed up with the current political-moral mess – not mouthed by Hitler nor by the Archbishop of Canterbury – not understood by either, although the first knows enough of them to hate them. In this world there is still an escape – not away from reality – but back to reality.

Drove home through the endless mean streets around the Battersea Power Station – glass out of all the shop windows – gaps

---

[1] I had moved again to a furnished flat off Pall Mall.

and piles of rubble in every street – signs saying "Police Warning – Unexploded Bomb" at almost every street corner, but still women coming out of pubs with mugs of beer. Children still playing in the streets and a patriarchal old man with a beard sitting serenely on a porch looking at the sunset. Yet this thing is beginning to get people down. There are desperate faces of fatigue, not so much the danger as the sleeplessness and the dreary discomfort, the long Russian-style queues waiting for the buses, waiting to get into the shelters.

In the Dorchester the sweepings of the Riviera have been washed up – pot-bellied, sallow, sleek-haired nervous gentlemen with loose mouths and wobbly chins, wearing suede shoes and checked suits, and thin painted women with fox capes and long silk legs and small artificial curls clustering around their bony, sheep-like heads.

This is one of those stimulating nights on which I feel a complete immunity from fear. I put it down to brandy – a blessed drink which the war has made me discover. I walked home down St. James's Street under a brilliant moon to the usual orchestra of guns. There were autumn leaves thick on the street, leaves on the pavements on St. James's Street! It is like the Fall of Rome! These minor symptoms of dissolution make one sad. No tarts anywhere. If I had met one I should have been compelled to go home with her. The barrage seems lighter tonight and the bombs more frequent.

22 September 1940.

The moment I stepped out of the station I smelt the familiar smell of Oxford. What nonsense the woman was talking the other day when she said that it did not matter if a city were destroyed physically, if its soul lived. Cities are nothing without their bodies. When you have destroyed Paris and Oxford what happens to their souls? Oxford rebuilt in this age! It would be easy to see what it would be like by looking at the new Bodleian Extension – that blankly commonplace hulk which they have dared to plant in the face of the Sheldonian. *That* is the most distressing thing about Oxford – for the rest the changes are temporary. The streets surge with people – air force pilots and mechanics, soldiers, civil servants, evacuees from the East End and from the West End too, refugees from Europe – French, Austrian, Polish.

In the George Restaurant where aesthetes willowed and whinneyed, where hearties roared and roistered, the tables are taken by heavy-bottomed foreign women or local tradesmen turned majors (Oxford restaurant proprietors must be in seventh heaven). Occasionally one sees a few undergraduates up here on some kind of course edging their way with a self-consciously aloof air among this rabble. Absurdly enough one's own face instinctively takes on this same expression of superiority.

I walked back today part of the way from Marston under a rainy grey sky appropriate to an Oxford Sunday (indeed in my experience rain and Sunday are inseparable in Oxford). In the village street a group of little girls were collected under an umbrella held by the tallest of them. Two ancient dames dressed alike in black with touches of mauve at the throat and clutching prayer books and ebony walking-sticks trundled timidly to church, glancing up and down for fear of cyclists. Earlier I had met the vicar bicycling along a country lane with his black straw hat pushed on the back of his head. All this made me remember that life in England has not been touched – that the raids are only superficial wounds. I stood waiting for my bus in Marston churchyard. I could hear the organ grinding out the music for the evening service and could see lights in the church windows. Outside in the churchyard was a modest war memorial "Lest We Forget" and lower down "Their names are recorded within the Church." The bus lolled slowly up the hill.

That night after dinner I went for a short walk, passing the gate of Christ Church – went in – Tom Quad was deserted and I walked through to Peckwater. Mist hung thickly over the buildings, and the damp smell of the Thames valley filled my nostrils. There were chinks of light at a few windows where the blackout curtains were not tightly drawn and the rickety music of a gramophone came from one corner of the Quad where a family of evacuees were living. Inevitably I thought of that night at Oxford when I penetrated the Quad for the first time. I felt at once sad and quite unsentimental – sad and impersonal.

These two days in Oxford have passed in a trance-like state of convalescence. The absence of noise makes me feel as though I were in a dream. The misty atmosphere, the grey sky, the slight persistent rain and the ghost-like familiar notes of the clock in Tom Tower have induced a state of mild hypnosis. I have been passively suspended without will or desire. The hope of happiness and the wish for gratification seem memories, as if I were already in some dim Lethe.

25 September 1940.

Two Poles and a Hungarian journalist for whom I got visas to go to Canada have been drowned in the *City of Benares* by enemy action on their way to Canada. One of the Poles, the Manager of the Gdynia Shipping Line, was a pleasant, pale man with spectacles who looked like a young professor. His wife and family had gone to Canada and he was going out to pay them a visit. The Hungarian was a very unattractive individual with whom I had had "words" before he left. Tony Balásy says, "There was a man moving heaven and earth to get out of the country because he was in such a panic of fear and then he meets with this dreadful end. That is fate." Tony has no use for cowards or, as he calls them, "people who do not control their nerves." He is a very nervous person but totally disciplined. He is rather proud that he has never been in an air-raid shelter and always sleeps in his own bed. He does this from conviction and on principle. I do the same from laziness. If we were both caught in our beds by a bomb no one would know how much more praiseworthy Tony's motives were than mine.

28 September 1940.

This new American girl of mine is a starry-eyed little number from Portland, Oregon. She tells me that she comes from a fine family in Portland and that they have a lovely home there and she has a brother called Bugs because he is interested in the study of insects. She has taken a course on flower arrangement and says that in her opinion "simplicity is more elegant than anything else." She says she could not bear to marry a man she could not look up to and respect and he must be in a good position. She despises everything to do with ballet (she is a ballet dancer by occupation) because it is not respectable and the men she meets there she treats with scorn because they have not a good position by Portland standards.

Weekend with Ted Achilles of the United States Embassy. In the party was Colonel Lee, U.S. Military Attaché, with old-fashioned bristling moustache, the sort who I am sure likes a woman with a figure – "none of your new-fangled ideas." Very optimistic about English victory – thinks the war is going along very satisfactorily; a Secretary of the United States Embassy, a bullet-headed obstinate type with the habit of lowering platitudes into the conversation which really make one pause and look in embarrassment at one's boots. The Air Attaché described the new flying Fortresses – four-engined planes – ten times the size of the Hurricane and Spitfire. They think the Germans are making a poor showing in the air war.

6 October 1940.

Weekend with H.L. at his house on the slope of Hog's Back. You could not have a more perfect example of the eccentric, comfortable, self-absorbed bachelor. Everything in the house has its own story. Nothing can be moved from its place without upsetting the owner. His taste is his own. It includes baroque, wooden, gilt candelabra, varnished copies of Italian primitives, small plaster figures of St. Francis of Assisi and the Christ Child and (the *clou* of the collection and of the collector) a painting in oils of a very handsome young American man. H. by occupation fills a prosaic job, but once at home he lives a life of play-acting and dressing-up. He came down to breakfast this morning in a pair of impossibly tight riding-breeches, a tweed coat and a kind of silk stock arrangement. He was not going to ride – it was just his idea of a "costume." With pride he showed me a silk and velvet dressing-gown which he had made for him at the cost of two hundred dollars; it was given to him as he says "by a man with more money than sense." Portly and priestly in appearance, ecclesiastical in taste, exuberant in dress, he is a slave of food and comfort. These are provided for him by a Scottish housekeeper who rules him by her concentrated attention on his stomach. A man of a dozen fads, he is a medievalist, an authority on local history, a believer in herbal pills, an ardent Anglo-Catholic, and a student of yoga. If you open a drawer anywhere in the house you are likely to find a crucifix or a string of beads. In the bathroom every kind of unguent cream and bath salts flourishes exuberantly. There are even glass pots of powders and creams. A bath becomes a minor sensuality. His beds (by a special bed-maker) are so vast and deep that, as he says, "You have to be rescued from them in the morning." In the end this concentration upon his manias, this obsession with comfort, this minute regulation of time and food and sleep are oppressive and even frightening. One smells the sexual repression through all the smokescreen of his whims. One scents the possessive tyrant in the genial host. He swells in one's eye by the very force of his obsessions into a sort of magician in whom kindliness and malice are mingled, but who has long since lost all real connection with the world of men in which he moves with such false affability.

9–11 October 1940.

How much does this continual danger to our lives make us forget our smaller fears? Do we still suffer from shyness, or feel that a cold in the throat may turn into pneumonia? If we do, I think it is more by habit than by conviction. We are accustomed to our familiar fears; in the same way even in the midst of a bombardment with planes droning overhead and the noise of the barrage I can sleep quite comfortably, but if through this monstrous uproar I hear the still, small voice of a dripping tap, I get out of bed unable to sleep until the sound is stopped.

Places I hope will not be destroyed – the unregenerate streets of Soho, the chilly splendours of Carlton House Terrace. But I would rather see them bombed than torn down to make way for blocks of flats. My fury against the German bomber is not nearly so great as the rage I feel against the speculative builder and his supine accomplices – the local authorities and the bovine public. We are at least doing everything possible to prevent the destruction of historic London from the air. I wrote just now of fury against the German bomber, but I feel none. The random bombing of central London is like an act of nature, like a volcano erupting nightly. The bombers are like the agents of some blindly destructive force. Their bombs fall, like rain, on the just and the unjust. They do not hate me nor I hate them. We are caught in a fated mechanistic duel of forces which maims and kills bombers and bombed. This is a war fought in cold blood. That is my feeling about it, but I often hear people say, "Why don't we give them hell in Berlin?" I sense a lack of conviction, a sort of nervous irritability in this question as though those who asked it knew the futility of the query. But I may be reflecting in others my own feelings.

Sometimes I feel brave for no good reason and then I wish for danger. Why should one always be brave twenty-four hours a day any more than one is always amorous. The rest of the time one has to act courage or love because it is not admitted to say "Today I am feeling cowardly" or "Tonight I do not want you."

12 October 1940.

Hart (Massey) and I went to an American movie – a saga of a small town in America. We sat there lapped in a feeling of false security while the cinema shook from the explosion of bombs outside. As we came out it seemed as though all Piccadilly were on fire. Tongues of flames were licking the colonnade at the top of the London Pavilion. We drove to the Dorchester Hotel through bombs and shrapnel – there seemed to be fire everywhere. For once London had a catastrophic appearance worthy of American newspaper accounts. At the Dorchester we found the Masseys pacing the floor nervously. In our elation Hart and I seemed childishly excited in telling them what was going on. Mr. Massey lost his temper, and, his voice rising to a peak of exasperation, he said, "You seem to be pleased at what is happening. I do not understand you. These places that are being destroyed are irreplaceable – to me it is like a personal loss." We looked somewhat shamefaced. Then he led the way on to the Dorchester roof. We could see fires in all directions. A bomb came whistling down and we all ran for shelter except Hart, who remained standing where he was – an obstinate figure. I was annoyed with myself for taking shelter not because I was afraid but because the others had run for shelter and I had instinctively imitated them instead of waiting as Hart did to see if it was necessary. I noticed that when Mr. Massey came down from the roof he was in the same exalted state that we had been in when we arrived. There is an exhilaration in this orgy of destruction and in the danger, but next day was the morning after the debauch. I was awakened by the sound of shovelling glass.

16 October 1940.

Dined at the Dorchester Hotel, which is like a luxury liner on which the remnants of London society have embarked in the midst of this storm. Through the thick walls and above the music of the band one could hear the noise of the barrage and at intervals the building shook like a vibrating ship with the shock of an exploding bomb falling nearby. Meanwhile there was N. coming swaying into the dining-room, his hands resting affectionately – reminiscently – on his buttocks, with the pale, grey face of a tired but impudent and dishonest waiter. He stopped at several tables on his way to join a bird of gleaming and immaculate plumage whose habitat might be Cannes, Newport, Le Touquet, or Mayfair. She wore in her hair a little velvet bow which by its irrelevancy pointed up the polished chic of her person. At another table was Lady Diana Cooper – the postcard beauty of the First Great War whom every officer in those days carried in his eye. I remember as a boy having her pointed out to me walking in Bond Street. "There," said my aunt, "is Lady Diana, the Great Beauty." In my anxiety to see what was meant by a Great Beauty I left my aunt's side and hurried to the other end of the street and walked down it again so that I could pass her once more. I caught a confused glimpse of a marble white arm and a glance from those azure eyes so often described and still so magical.

18 October 1940.

I went with Mary[1] to Bath to visit her mother, Mrs. Adlington. I have hardly seen Mary since she joined the ATS at the beginning of the war. We have been swept apart – she out of London. Yet at once it was as if we had never been separated. Will it always be like this, this deep underlying feeling between us? Dear Mrs. Adlington, now very old and very small, sits up erect with her knitting, her jokes, her prejudices, and her cast-iron loyalties. I love her. She has kept a kind of innocence through eighty years and like Mary she is true-hearted.

26 October 1940.

The Pheasantry is a new underground eating club for the new, classless, Americanized English who before the war had grapefruit for breakfast and preferred the *New Yorker* to *Punch*. So far as I know they are limited to London, Maidenhead, and weekend cottages in

---

[1] My cousin Mary Adlington.

the home counties. The men are apt to be subject to ulcers. The women wear "simple" black dresses with diamond clips and have an arrogant manner which follows the third gin. In politics they are against the "Old Gang," whom they think slow-witted and blimpish, but an instinct of self-preservation makes them distrust "parlour-pinks." Connected with no tradition and with no part of the country they are a floating population financed on the money made during and after the last war.

Margery, Frank,[1] and I went after dinner at this club off the King's Road to their house in Blantyre Street; they are still living in this dangerous outpost near Lot's Road Power Station. It is the only street in World's End which has not yet been bombed. Their house, like the others, is a little square box of bricks of the type that falls down when a bomb comes anywhere near it. On this occasion the bomb fell in the next street. We all rushed out and I found myself helping to remove the people from the remains of three bombed houses. There was a large crater where one house had been, and in the centre of the crater were Margery and a doctor, trying by the aid of a torch to see who was injured and how badly. People were being pulled and pushed up the sides of the crater, to be taken off to the nearest pub to wait for the ambulance to come. These were the "shock" cases – an old man who let them make an injection in his tattooed arm without question or even tension of the muscles – an old distraught mother gasping for breath and trying to collect what had happened to her – a tall, scraggy daughter, her cheeks blackened with smoke powder and her hair wisping wildly about her head. Margery called in imperious tones from her crater, "Hot water." I rushed panting through the dark and empty streets to the nearest police station then to the nearest public house in search of water. By now the sky was an ugly "fire pink" glow from a row of houses burning noisily in a street nearby. Bombs were steadily falling and the members of the Air Raid Precautions and Rescue Squad whom I encountered in the streets cowered in carefully restrained attitudes against walls as the bombs came down. In the end when I came back with the hot water it was only to find that full supplies had been brought up already. It was the same with everything I

---

[1] Frank and Margery Ziegler; he was an old Oxford friend of mine.

tried to do. I helped shock cases to walk to the First Aid station when it was plain that they needed no help. Frank and some men in tin helmets emerged from the crater carrying a wounded woman stretched out on one of the doors of her house. We carried the stretcher, Frank calling, "Go easy there," "Gently now." When we put the woman down on the pavement a man came out of the mobile ambulance, felt her pulse and heart, and said, "She is dead." Frank contradicted in a pettish tone, "The other doctor found a pulse." "No she is dead." "Do not cover her face up," said Frank as we walked away. We all went to a pub where a fat landlady, her hair in papers, was offering cups of strong sweet tea, while her husband with a conspiratorial air offered to break the law and give us beer or "take-away ports" although it was 2 a.m.

We all went back to Blantyre Street and slept on the floor in the basement passage.

29 October 1940.

I was thinking today of the last time I was in Halifax, Nova Scotia, and went for a walk to my old home, The Bower.

That day I was trying to look outward from an introspective bout of indigestion by reconstructing the road as it used to be. Only it was more a question of destruction than construction. First of all that row of white clapboard bungalows would have to be swept away and replaced by scrub and pine trees. Then over the stone wall of Gorsebrook – green fields must stretch to woods beyond where now hulked St. Mary's newly-built Catholic College in a monumental freestone, priests pacing its cement-filled paths. Where that stone wall ran my eye could detect the gap built in of new stones where had been a gate on which Peter and I had leaned on a summer afternoon, undirected sex driving us clumsy and breathless. In the Gorsebrook fields I had walked in my new beige Oxford bags reciting Rupert Brooke and trying to keep my pace steady when the small boys from the village catching sight of me through the gap called names after me.

The wall ended at the turn into The Bower drive. Here I was thrown back on memory with no stick or stone to help me – gone the gateposts, gone the lodge, gone the woods on either side of the drive and the tall trees that cast a green gloom until you came out on the slope which curved between rough lawns towards the house. I turned into the cul-de-sac of new houses which with their gardens had obliterated the former drive and woods. My walk was becoming an archaeological expedition but instead of being buried under this new layer of living the old had vanished without a trace, swept off into space and time existing only in my memory.

There seemed to be an excessive number of dogs about. From each porch or garden gate of the new houses a barking dog bounded out sniffing my ankles. Children on bicycles circled the end of the cul-de-sac where The Bower house stood – for it still stood, though crowded into a corner by the new houses so that it hardly had room to breathe. Shorn of its approaches it was at an awkward angle to the street. Altogether the house looked sheepish and out of place among its brisk new neighbours – too large – but without giving any impression of grandeur. They had painted it a musty pale yellow and torn down the vine from the front wall. All that was left of the lawns was a wedge of grass on which still stood the big oak tree. The house would, as they say, have been "better dead." Its physical presence there stopped the power of my imagination like a leaden block. I could not go into the house in my memory while that solid door stood facing me. Yet in that room above the porch on the left I was born. In that room I had shivered and sweated out my adolescence. From that window I had watched for Katherine coming up the curve of the drive from under the summer green of the trees into the sunlight in her pink cotton dress, swinging her straw hat in her hand. But it was no use – these memories were manufactured.

6 November 1940.

Things one will forget when this is over – fumbling in the dark of the blackout for one's front door key while bits of shrapnel fall on the pavement beside one – the way the shrapnel seems to drift – almost like snow-flakes through the air in an aimless, leisurely way, and the clink of it landing on the pavement.

9 November 1940.

Dined alone at Brooks's off silver plate among the prints of eighteenth-century Whig lords to the sound of German bombers overhead.

At the next table the Duke of St. Albans, an old boy in battledress who had spent the day on guard at the Admiralty Arch was saying, "I hate all the Europeans, except Scandinavians. I have always been for the Scandinavians – of course I loathe all dagoes."

16 November 1940.

I came back from spending the night at Aldershot to find my flat a heap of rubble from a direct hit, and I have lost everything I own. That is no tragedy but a bore – and doubtless a cash loss, as the Department of External Affairs will never approve replacing suits from Sackville Street at twenty pounds per suit. I am most annoyed at losing my new "woodsy" tweed suit, the picture of the Rose that Anne gave me, volume two of the book I am reading, my edition of Rimbaud, and the little green book of my own chosen quotations. I do not much regret all the pigskin which used to jar on her so much.

I am enjoying the publicity attendant on this disaster, particularly the idea which I have put abroad that if it had not been for a chance decision to go to Aldershot for the night I should have been killed. I should probably only have been cut about or bruised. The rest of the people living in the flats were in the cellar and escaped unhurt. Hart and I went to see the ruins, and the youth next door was full of the fact that Lord A and Lady A too had had to be pulled out of the débris – so had fourteen other people, but what struck him was that even a lord had not been spared by the bomb. A further fascinating detail was that Lord A's naval uniform was still hanging on the hook on the open surviving wall for all the world to see. Now I know that the *Evening Standard* is right when it prints those items "Baronet's kinswoman in a bus smash" etc.

I feel like a tramp having only one suit and shirt and in particular only *one pair of shoes.*

Last week when I wrote this diary I was sitting on my sofa in front of my electric fire in my perfectly real and solid flat with my books at arm's length – the furniture had that false air of permanence which chairs and tables take on so readily – the drawn curtains shut out the weather. Now all that is a pile of dirty rubble, with bits of my suits, wet and blackened, visible among the bricks.

On top of the pile my sofa is perched (quite the most uncomfortable and useless article in the flat but it has survived) – this violent, meaningless gesture like a slap from a drunken giant has smashed my shell of living into a heap.

17 November 1940. Dorchester Hotel.

It certainly feels safe in this enormous hotel. I simply cannot believe that bombs would dare to penetrate this privileged enclosure or that they could touch all these rich people. Cabinet Ministers and Jewish lords are not killed in air-raids – that is the inevitable illusion that this place creates. It is a fortress propped up with money-bags. It will be an effort to go back to an ordinary house which can be blotted out by one bomb.

I went for a walk in the park with my ballerina. I am trying to talk her into coming to live with me, but am getting nowhere. She says her brothers back in Portland always told her it cheapened a girl in a man's eyes – he never would want to marry a girl who had done that. We walked round and round the equestrian statue of William of Orange in St. James's Square arguing the point until an elderly gentleman called out to us, "I do not want to interrupt you but I feel I should tell you, just in case you did not notice, that there is a police warning on the railings saying that there is an unexploded bomb in the garden!"

17 November 1940.

The ballerina is ridiculous, but I must not begin to think that she is pathetic because she is really very well able to look after herself, and what is more she has succeeded in making me a little bit in love with her.

18 November 1940.

I could have strangled her today while she was eating her chocolate cake, but I was so disagreeable that I do not think she enjoyed it much. Poor little devil – I am sorry for her. She looked so gay and pretty today with her little coloured umbrella in the rainy after-luncheon Jermyn Street. It is rather touching the way she sticks to her

American small-town gods in the midst of this London. When I first knew her only a few weeks ago she was excited at being taken to a smart restaurant. Now she thinks it fashionable to complain – "The smoked-salmon here is not as good as at the Ritz" – "I like the way they pull the table out for you here" (if the waiter has not pulled the table aside for her to pass).

27 November 1940.

I am living at Brooks's Club, a combination of discomfort and old-fashioned comfort. Magnificent coal fires in the living-rooms, icy bedrooms, the kind of confidential valeting that you get in a good country house, the superb bath towels, yards of them, impossible to manoeuvre – the only thing to do is to wrap yourself up in one and sit down until you dry.

As I write I hear the ever-menacing throb of a bomber coming out of the fog. Tonight there is an old-fashioned London fog. Fumbling my way along Piccadilly I could hardly – as they say – "see my hand before me." I hear the hall porter saying in a grieved tone, "There is no air-raid warning gone." This is one of the nights when I feel interested in life, when I should much resent a bomb removing me from the scene. There are other nights when I feel it could not matter less.

Came back last night in the tube from Earl's Court. I hear that the drunks quite often fight it out by throwing each other on to the live wire, which contrary to superstition does not always kill you. If the toughs in the shelter tube do not like a chap they wait for him and throw him on to the wire. I must say that I saw nothing of this – just people sleeping, and not the poorest of the poor. They were all fully dressed and looked clean and quite prosperous, some pretty girls who might be serving in a big store, quite a lot of men and children. I have never seen so many different ages and types of people asleep before. Their sprawled attitudes, arms flung out, etc. made me think of photographs of the dead in battlefields – their stark and simplified faces. What one misses in the sleeping and the dead are the facial posturings prompted by perpetual vanity.

I am off the ballerina – she is rude to waiters who cannot answer back.

3 December 1940.

If that bloody ballerina does not come across tomorrow I am through with her. She gave me a model of Our Lady of Lourdes today, but she seems positively to be getting colder the fonder she gets of me.

6 December 1940.

Weekend with the Sacheverell Sitwells. He is charming with a sort of gentleness, which is most attractive, and manners that show his delicacy and sensibility. He would disappear after tea with, "I am going to my room to scribble for a little while" or "I will withdraw to my apartment." It was exciting to feel that up there he was distilling another of those magic potions of his. He thinks it is all up with Europe, its culture and vitality exhausted. There I think he is mistaken, although certainly his European tradition – that of the civilized aristocrat – is hard hit. His wife Georgia is a Canadian – a beauty – tall with pale skin and dark eyes. She is amused and amusing and impulsively warm-hearted. I came down on the train with Princess Callimachi (Anne-Marie), a lively little Romanian with the look of a lizard, who lives with the Sitwells at present.

21 December 1940.

Evening with the ballerina – some progress to report. We dined, thank God without music and away from the frowsy hotel atmosphere at a small but expensive restaurant in Shepherd Market. She felt, I think, that we were rather slumming. As usual she talked an immense amount about "Mommy and Daddy," and at one stage of dinner I was sunk in such a stupor of boredom that even she noticed it and I had to pull myself together and begin talking rapidly, desperately, and at random. The night was cold and starry outside, with quite a heavy blitz. We walked back to the flat. She has more sense and feeling than one would give her credit for at first. What is shocking about her is the contrast between her romantic looks and her flat commonplace mind. Her mainspring in life appears to be an intense desire to show that she comes from the right side of the railroad tracks. Like many completely uninhibited bores she wins in the end by sheer persistence. She has talked to me so much about people I do not know or care about, her family, the members of the ballet company, etc., that I am beginning to feel I do know them and find myself taking an interest in their doings. Later in the evening we went out to Lyons' Corner House, where we were joined by two RAF pilots, both DFCs, one drunk, Irish and very funny. The RAF have a line laid down for them – the gay, brave, young pilot with a joke on his lips, irresponsible, living to the full because they may die any day.

22 December 1940.

Dined with Alastair Buchan at Pratt's Club – the best sole in London, that is to say in the world. I always enjoy Pratt's, the atmosphere of open fires and easy unbuttoned chat, the equality where cabinet ministers sit around the table and argue with subalterns – the décor of red curtains and the stuffed salmon caught by His Royal Highness the Duke of Edinburgh in 1886. The other night a rather tight, junior lieutenant back from the Middle East was dining there. Anthony Eden began holding forth at length on the Mediterranean situation. This youth, after listening for some time, turned to a friend and said, "I do not know who that man is but he is talking awful balls." Immense satisfaction of all members.

25 December 1940.

Spent Christmas Eve in the country, came back on the morning train to London on Christmas Day – waited of course for nearly an hour at Horsley Station for the train. How well I know those English country stations in the morning after a weekend when you have tipped the chauffeur and told him not to wait and you walk up and down the station platform in the raw air that smells of babies' diapers, with a little view of the railway line and fields and a couple of cows, fields rough-surfaced and untidy seen at close range, although a billiard board of green if you flashed over them in a plane; or a flooded meadow, mist hanging about the trees. Two porters whistling and stamping, a lady in a fur coat taking leave of her rosy-cheeked niece, who wears tweeds and no hat – "My dear, remember when you come to London there is always a roof." Then the soldiers – bold-eyed Canadians with a slouch and a swagger, New Zealanders with overcoats hanging untidily, Australians often with girls, and English soldiers going back to London saying goodbye to plain, sensible, loyal wives wearing spectacles and sometimes carrying babies. The soldiers from the Dominions are invading armies of irresponsible younger brothers. The English soldiers look at them not unkindly but with a sober ironic air – puppies and old hound dogs. London was deserted.

29 December 1940.

Walked home tonight by the pink light of an enormous fire somewhere in the City. Heavy blitz. I dined alone at Brooks's. Read R. G. Collingwood's book on Roman Britain – sandy but with oases. I also tried unsuccessfully to put into dispatch form some intuitions of how things may develop in this country after the war, provided, of course, that we win it. Funny, though reason may tell me that that is open to doubt, I never really contemplate our not winning. It is eerie tonight, the streets are so light from the fires and so completely deserted and silent now that the planes seem to have passed. Was that a distant barrage or somebody moving furniture upstairs? No, the only sound is the tinkle of ambulance bells in the empty street. This is not very pleasant. I think I will have a whisky and soda. Supposing that some day one of these days I just was not there to meet Billy for lunch at the RAC The others were there – Billy and Margery and Hart but not me. *Now* – that was the barrage, and I can hear a plane right overhead. The man at the Club said that a lot of our fighters were up tonight. That was a bomb that time. When the building shakes from the floor upwards it is a bomb.

Spent last night at Stansted. We went to church this morning. Lord Bessborough reading the lessons – "The flesh is as grass and like grass shall wither away." He read it well – the rustic choir boys piped up "Come All Ye Faithful" – clear voices like a running stream. The clergyman ranged from arrangements for the local paper chase to God's purpose. An iconoclast – he announced that God had other preoccupations in addition to the defence of the British Empire. We should will victory – call on the power of thought – pause for a minute every day before the BBC announced the news. It bothers me this talk about calling on the power of thought and willing things to happen to our advantage, as if we were trying to force a lock when, had we the key, it would open itself.

1941

10 January 1941.

The ballerina was rather sweet really. We had breakfast in the Mayfair Hotel – rashers of bacon and great cups of American coffee. She did look beautiful this morning. People turned around in the street to look at her.

12 January 1941.

Reading Gide – the best antidote possible to the triumphant commonplace of an English Sunday. Not even the Blitzkrieg has been able to break the spell which the Sabbath casts over the land. One could not fail by just putting one's head out of the window and smelling and looking and listening for two minutes to recognize that this is Sunday. In my mind's eye I can see the weary wastes of the Cromwell Road beneath a sullen sky where a few depressed pedestrians straggle as though lost in an endless desert. One's soul shrinks from the spectacle.

Symptoms of Sexual Happiness

1. I look at people, men and women, from the physical point of view, not by class or taste but in terms of the senses. Which ones are out of the stream of sex? (How easy it is to see these!) And why? 2. I am temporarily cured of my mania for seeing things in a straight line. I admit and enjoy confusion. The relief is enormous. 3. Time no longer seems to be slipping away from me. I am happy to spend it carelessly. 4. Other people do not seem worth the usual effort. I

cannot help treating them casually, often interrupting them and not listening to what they say. 5. I definitely am very much less amusing. The ballerina leaves today with the ballet company on tour. I am looking forward to early and varied infidelities during her absence.

12 January 1941.

Walked across Grosvenor Square to dine with Lady Malcolm at Claridge's. A London evening – damp air and mist. The guns in Hyde Park reverberated above the square and further away the guns in St. James's Park replied. Clouds slid past a full silver moon.

Lady Malcolm is really only interested in the work she is doing at the canteen at the Beaver Club and in her struggle for power with the other women workers. "We are gettin' along very nicely." (She is Edwardian about her g's.)

Her son-in-law, Basil Bartlett, was there, the playwright now in Military Intelligence, clever and amusing, and Thesiger, the actor – looking at him Lady Malcolm murmured to me, "Cooks perfect *petits pois à la française* and always wears a pearl necklace under its shirt – rather sweet – don't you think?" He was too, with his cosy humour. You felt – there is a talented old creature who does not give a damn one way or the other but will not be bullied. (That was when Basil was trying to force us all to drink white wine because he was eating salmon, although the rest of us obviously wanted red with our fillet of beef.) "I am for red," said Thesiger, with a light flick in his tone, and red it was. He told us about the time in London about 1900 when it used to be the fashion to go down after dinner and sing patriotic songs outside Buckingham Palace to cheer Queen Victoria up. (It must have been during the South African War.) People would give dinner parties to go on to Buckingham Palace. One night he was there among the crowd singing with some friends – a foggy, misty London night with the front of the Palace (not the present façade – that was added later) lit up by gas jets. Suddenly there was a light in one of the windows, then the window opened and onto the balcony stepped two huge footmen bearing each in his hands vast lighted candelabra – "and between them," said Thesiger with feeling, "and between them a little black figure of a woman."

Then Lady Malcolm told us how when she was a little girl King Edward VII came one afternoon to see her mother (Lily Langtry). When she was brought into the drawing-room by her nurse he said to her, "Would you like to go for a drive, my dear, in the Park?" He did not ask her nurse if she could go – he asked *her* and she was sent out in his carriage with his monogram on the door. People in the streets took off their hats as she drove by alone in his carriage. She had to make up her mind whether to acknowledge their bows – as though she were a little princess – or whether to stare at the horizon. She decided on the latter. Thus began a career of doing the right thing.

14 January 1941.

Lunched with Tony Balásy, who told me that he resigned from the Hungarian Diplomatic Service when Hungary joined the Axis in November. It must have taken more guts than I gave him credit for to break the chain of twenty years' habit, especially for such a cautious creature of habits. Now he is going back to his beloved United States without a job and with the somewhat dreary prospect of perhaps doing some writing on political subjects to earn himself a living. He quoted to me a sentence from Roosevelt's speech, "Those who prefer security to liberty deserve to lose both." He says he could not go on any longer without his heart in it. What makes it harder is that he was to have been appointed Hungarian Minister to Washington. I asked him if some people in his Foreign Office would sympathize with him. "The consensus of opinion in Budapest will be the fellow is a damn fool, but maybe in 1943 they will say that Balásy is a shrewd fellow." I admire him for what he has done and doubt if I would have had the nerve to do the same.

Last night was the Russian New Year. I took D. out to dinner and we walked home in brilliant moonlight – no blitz. Passing through Grosvenor Square we found the door to the square garden open and went in. There is a tennis court in the middle concealed by trees, very convenient for the square dwellers, but very disappointing to me. I had hoped for a little lake with even a few birds living on a miniature island. It would be impossible to explore a secret garden by moonlight with a woman like D. without a stirring of excitement. I kissed her. From the sensational point of view it was a sensation.

15 January 1941.

A routine day, worthy but not inspiring. This is the way my "Better Self" would like me to behave all the time. Went to a War Office meeting in the afternoon. Waste of time. We all repeated what we had said a month ago about prisoners-of-war. It is so hard to resist the temptation to score at a meeting of this sort. One is giving a sort of performance, one has an audience, as one talks one becomes possessed by the wisdom of what one is saying and the folly or wickedness of those who oppose one. I find myself getting angry and aggrieved about something which does not matter a damn, when the only thing that does matter is to find the essential and stick to it. The general in the chair, the "tactful" type of soldier who thinks he is conciliating the touchy susceptibilities of the "colonials," and wears a soothing smile while he is determined to get his own way. The only technique with such a man is to flatter him in his own coin and never give an inch.

29 January 1941.

I am ashamed of the dispatches we send to Ottawa. They give an officialese picture of England at war without conveying any sense of the cross-currents. Above all they leave out any pictures of the social changes stirring just under the surface. Mr. Massey does not want the Government at home to glimpse these abysses lest they should be disturbed in their belief that they are fighting for the survival of political democracy, liberal ideas, and human individualism side by side with the traditional England. He thinks that anything that disturbs this set-piece might weaken the war effort and distract our will. (He says that my dispatches read like socialist speeches!)

I dined the other night with Anne-Marie, one of the largest landowners in Romania, now on the German blacklist and unable to get any money out of the country. She is clever, full of wit and disloyalty. In her spare time she has dabbled in the arts, gambled on the Black Bourse, and conducted a good many highly personal political intrigues and vendettas. I met her at the Ritz Bar where she holds court every day, surrounded by half a dozen cosmopolitan perverts, smooth young French success boys, professional photographers, English and White Russian interior decorators. Throughout the evening she was always tipping and ordering and changing tables and bullying the waiters. At intervals soft-spoken young men appeared at her table, kissed her hand, murmured a sentence of greeting in French, and slid away again. Meanwhile she sat smoking cigarettes and darting her lizard head from side to side as she observed the company – "*Cherchée et pas trouvée*," she remarked as a young woman came in wearing a dress more remarkable for elaborate effort than for effectiveness.

30 January 1941.

If we cannot be strong enough to make peace with Germany within two years, Europe will go communist when the Germans do break. Our only chance is to be so strong in planes and navy that with the assistance of the blockade German power will collapse. We cannot alone defeat Germany militarily on the continent of Europe.

The papers are full of butchery in Romania. Rivers of hate, flowing blood all over Europe. How difficult it is for us comfortable creatures to understand all this hate, all this will to cruelty – that people who have lived next door to each other in a street in some small town for years should – the minute the policeman's back is turned – fall on each other like hyenas and butcher each other. What years of bitter, suppressed loathing and fear must lie behind that.

1 February 1941.

It is a relief to plunge into the warmly-coloured, variegated women's world of Colette, whose novels I am reading, to turn one's back on this man-made time when duty and team spirit are the dreary necessities for survival. Never have I so thanked God for women as in these months. While they still care more about their clothes, their children, and their lovers than about the war it is still possible to breathe even in this constricted atmosphere.

Anne-Marie received me in her bedroom at the Ritz – marble mantelpiece, red satin panelling, rose-shaded lamps, and a big double bed standing high off the ground – a period piece cosmopolitan Ritz style 1912. It exactly suits her. We were joined by a young lieutenant who, talking of a friend of his, said, "He has such an adorable sense of humour." "Now, there I do not agree," she said. "Funny, yes, but no sense of humour, you cannot bully him." Her equation – sense of humour equals niceness equals susceptibility to being bullied.

It is getting very hard to obtain matches. It becomes a game to see how long one can make a spill of paper last. I go to buy some shaving-cream and the man at the hairdressers says, "It is the pots for the cream that are our difficulty. The shop in the City that supplied them was burnt out in the last blitz." It is the same with our office stationery – shops that kept it have been blitzed. At the Indian restaurant they give you curry without onions that tastes like hot mud. There is a shortage of French novels and French wines, of glass for spectacles, of rouge. I do not speak of necessities like butter and eggs. In fact there is a shortage of everything except potatoes, bread, and fish, and I believe the last is too expensive for the poor.

7 February 1941.

This morning I had to leave her house early before the maid-of-all-work arrived. It meant staggering up, getting dressed, and out into the dark rainy street, but I was happy. I could see and smell again after days of planning, of talk, of papers. I felt like a living creature not a sort of filing cabinet of resolutions and schemes.

It was impossible to do any serious work today. I went for a walk in St. James's Park. It was a day like early spring – one expected to see crocuses but there were ridges of dirty left-over snow. I was walking along purposefully in my black hat swinging my umbrella thinking damn the war, oh damn the bloody war. I only curse the war when I am happy. When I am miserable it suits me that the world should be sliding down into disaster. Then, realizing that I was happy, I thought that this must not be wasted, let me sit on this bench in the sun, and say to myself as I watch the ducks, "At this moment happiness is right here at my elbow."

I am every day hearing of some new and horrific gas which is to be used against us – soporific, made at Bayer's works in Germany which puts you to sleep all right but from which you awake paralyzed, gas that makes you sick in your mask – you remove the mask and they send over the mustard gas. Certainly people are far more frightened of gas than of anything else, yet it is obvious to me that it can be effective only over a small area and will cause relatively few casualties.

I think the worst would be physical, personal, direct bullying, the sort of intimate cruelties that go on in the concentration camps.

I have been reading Colette's *Chéri* – her style light as thistledown, without a pretentious phrase, full of wit, so effortlessly and brilliantly constructed that you never feel a bump of transition. Is it too facile? No, because when you come to think it over you find you have not been cheated anywhere along the line.

10 February 1941.

Weekend at Oxford – motored down with Alastair and went over to Elsfield to the christening of Billy Buchan's child. Lady Tweedsmuir, gentle, intelligent, loyal-hearted, a few friends and relatives, champagne, little pink marzipan sweets in a white Sèvres bonbonnière – little jokes in the library afterwards. Met Elizabeth Bowen, well-dressed, intelligent handsome face, watchful eyes. I had expected someone more Irish, more silent and brooding and at the same time more irresponsible. I was slightly surprised by her being so much "on the spot."

Oxford.

I walked with M. around Magdalen Park. The newer buildings looked decayed like obsolescent Palladian mansions. There are no deer left in the Park. Dined at Anderson's, the new restaurant next to the George. The Bullingdon Club members came pouring in – children they looked – pink cheeked with long hair and the look of being hot from their baths – innocent and insolent past belief. Then the aesthetes with dangling hands and signet rings, brushing back the locks from their foreheads and swaying on their feet.

M. was very defeatist. He is now serving in the Military Intelligence and doing a course at Oxford. He thinks the Germans will invade simultaneously at four or five different points at the same time. They will concentrate on small areas and cut off communications, and none of our officers will have any initiative to act on their own without orders from the centre. (Quite unconvincing to me, but he knows more about military possibilities than I do.) He foresees a Pétain government in England with Gauleiters for Wales and Scotland. He believes that the Germans would encourage separatist national movements in these countries and that they would find plenty of material to work on. He views the prospect with malicious satisfaction. Failing invasion he thinks a patched-up peace is the only hope of saving us all from another thirty years of war. He is convinced that only the Germans are capable of organizing Europe, that Britain would never be able to do the job and we should turn our backs on Europe. Despite all this he is very anxious to get a chance of fighting and blames the Catholics who he says run the Military Intelligence and are preparing to sell out for a compromise peace. Consistency was never his long suit.

Dinner with my former tutor, Ronald McCallum. Long argument about his beloved "succession states," Czechoslovakia, Romania, the Baltic Republics, and Scandinavia, that promised land of modern liberalism, the country of sound architecture, cleanliness, sexual freedom, and painless socialism. I asked him why, in all these model states, there has been no resistance to the Germans to compare to unpopular Poland.

12 February 1941.

On Tuesday I motored down with the Masseys to see the Canadian Neurological Hospital at Hackwood. The doctors who make up the Neurological Unit are the best Canadian surgeons from Montreal and Toronto. They specialize in brain surgery – Cohen and Penfield of Montreal are probably two of the best brain surgeons in the world. The hospital is full of both military and civilian cases. The doctors and nurses are of the highest standard technically and still seem to be human. They make most of their English opposite numbers seem old-fashioned amateurs. Also they are a great relief after the military – no fuss and flummery here, no prima donnas of generals, no bone-headed brigadiers swaggering in kilts. Quiet, sensible men with a scrupulous tradition. Their uniforms may not fit, but they understand their jobs and do not show off. What a change from politicians.

They are housed in Hackwood Park, Lord Camrose's house, and formerly the scene of Curzon's grandeur.

After our visit to this hospital we went on to the Canadian Army workshop. There again we saw technical men who knew their job. They are skilled workers from Canadian factories. Some of them earned ten dollars a day at home. Now they get seven shillings and sixpence a day. They were repairing tanks, making tunnelling equipment, medical instruments, and doing general repairing. Some were working with acetylene blowtorches or melting iron in forges. Others were mending engines. They are proud of their high standard of skill. The men are said to be tough customers and heavy drinkers. They had the absorbed look of mechanics who are captured by their work. The younger men without much training who are drafted into the unit learn quickly. They have the North American flair for machinery. I asked their officer how they compared with English mechanics. "The English," he said, "are not too bad if they are not hurried. They cannot get a move on."

23 February 1941.

It is being dinned into my mind with persistence that after all we may be going to lose this war. No one admits the possibility publicly, but you could hardly expect us to do that.

It looks as if the Germans might defeat us within the next six months, but if we survive, we shall be embarked on a long struggle against Germany, Japan, Italy, backed by the U.S.S.R., and our success in carrying on would depend on the U.S.A. If we repel the German invasion, as I believe we shall, then we shall enter a new phase of the war – a deadlock, and after a year or so of this it is possible that both sides may come to a compromise peace. It is even just conceivable that an Anglo German combine might result, but that would imply the disappearance of Hitler. On the other hand, if this country is invaded successfully there is the possibility of a Pétain government here whose names one can already guess plus, perhaps, an Anglo-German alliance. This is an ugly picture, but the other, the picture of Germany crushed, of England and America restoring democratic governments in Europe seems to me incredibly remote. All this gloomy speculation goes on in the back of people's minds. They do not talk like this, they hardly allow themselves to think such things. Most are content to repeat that Britons never will be slaves and that Britain can take it. They do not think ahead of the next move, and this is doubtless very sensible. Also they are pretty well blanketed by propaganda.

25 February 1941.

Stayed with Mike Pearson. He has a general and a colonel living with him. The general thinks the solution after the war in Germany would be to shoot one in every four Germans. Why one in four? On that theory it would be logical to shoot the lot.

Read Sir Robert Vansittart's *The Black Record*, a compilation of his broadcasts and a violent attack on the Germans. It is the kind of propaganda that used to flow freely in the last war – full of inaccurate generalizations and written in a "hot gospeller" style which one would hardly expect from a man of his education. Its thesis is that the Germans are an accursed race differentiated from the rest of Europe by their savagery. This in itself is dubious. We know how unpleasant they are, how cruel, and how treacherous, but are they more cruel than the Russians or the Turks, or the Spanish, more treacherous than the Japanese? It is a mistake for a member of a Foreign Office to take this line in propaganda (even if it were true in fact). This makes nonsense of our official line, i.e. the Germans are being misled by the Nazi Party. That is the line to stick to in propaganda. It is a long-term investment which may pay off in the end. When the Germans have received some knocks in battle, when – or if – their morale is softened by setbacks, then propaganda of this kind could be very useful. It is obvious that if they think we intend to make mincemeat of them and that we lump them all together as a criminal nation they will fight with desperate obstinacy.

27 February 1941.

Obviously the biggest influence on all our lives at present is Hitler – as he is in a position to change or terminate our lives. Also his phrases have got under our skins, affected our language, made it impossible to think without his shadow falling across our thoughts. Never has so much hung upon the life of one man, never has one man so dominated the imagination of the world. Even if the Nazis went on, his death would be release from an evil spell. He is the incarnation of our own sense of guilt. When he attacks our civilization we find him saying things that we have thought or said. In the "burrows of the nightmare" such a figure is born, for as in a nightmare the thing that pursues us seems to have an uncanny and terrifying knowledge of our weakness. We spawned this horror; he is the byproduct of our civilization; he is all the hatred, the envy, the guile which is in us – a surrealist figure sprung out of the depths of our own subconscious.

2 March 1941.

Lunched with the Dashwoods at West Wycombe Park – Helen Dashwood looking pretty and being amusing. The house is in a state of slight disrepair, peeling statues with their noses knocked off, holes on the drive. In the big saloon the furniture is under dust-covers, the tapestry room is full of bundles for the troops – there are packing cases in unexpected places. It is the home of the Dashwoods, and down the road at Medmenham Abbey the Hell-Fire Club celebrated their boring black masses. Staying there was one of these aesthetic intellectuals or intellectual aesthetes who leave their London flats, their left-wing politics, and their rather common "boyfriends" at the weekends for the more decorative and well-heated English country houses. When one asks what becomes of the Oxford aesthetes in later life, this is the answer. They are peering at old family letters in pillared libraries or adjudicating the origin of rugs or china – or else they are simply sitting on the sofa before the fire with their legs curled up having a good gossip with the wife of their host.

Field-Marshal Sir Philip Chetwode was there too, and his wife, a solid hull of an old woman of intelligence who likes old houses and to know of skeletons in aristocratic cupboards. After lunch the men talked about the war. Those who might be susceptible to defeatist influences were mentioned. "I do not trust the press," said Johnnie Dashwood. Sir Philip says Archie Wavell[1] came to see him the other day. "When I saw him come in I said to him, 'What are you doing here – have you been given a bowler hat?' (I thought they must have sacked him), but he said he was home to report. The Prime Minister has no use for him – says, 'There is one of your dumb generals.' But it is

---

[1] General Sir Archibald Wavell was then Commander-in-Chief of British forces in the Middle East and under the greatest pressure from Churchill to stretch his forces to the utmost. Field-Marshal Chetwode had been Commander-in-Chief, India, from 1930 to 1935, but was now retired.

because he does not know how to talk to politicians. Soldiers are not stupider than other men. They say what they mean and politicians think they must be damn fools for doing that."

6 March 1941.

I walked to the office a new way across Berkeley Square. The rain was dripping from the trees. They have taken away the railings and laid bare the mystery of the garden. It is so sensible that people should be allowed to walk and sit in these gardens. The railings will never be put back again. It is impossible to argue that they should be, but I loved those shut-in secret gardens. These oases of privilege and mystery seem disappointingly commonplace now that they are exposed to view – just a little grass and a few trees. West-End London had been a place of railed gardens and non-committal Georgian façades – behind these defences in clubs and drawing-rooms shut away from the vulgar, the ladies and gentlemen of England have disposed of their affairs – and the affairs of the nation. Now bomber and builder have conspired to attack these well-bred squares. What looked so solid and seemed so eternal has vanished.

I was talking to the Masseys' chauffeur today about the bombings. "What astonishes me," he said, "is the way those old houses fall down so easy. You take that big house on the corner of Berkeley Square – used to belong to Lord T. My mother used to work there when I was a lad. It always seemed such a fine well-built old house and now it's just a pile of rubble. I would have thought that they would have stood up better – some of these big houses." Although his tone was practical I thought I could catch an undernote of dismay queerly mixed with relief. That great gloomy house may have hung on his memory since childhood. It must have seemed as permanent as a natural feature of the landscape and clothed in dim prestige. Now brutally it vanishes. This sudden destruction of the accustomed must shake people out of the grooves of their lives. This overnight disappearance of the brick and mortar framework of existence must send a shock deep into the imagination. These high explosions and incendiaries are like the falling stars and blazing comets – noted of old as foretelling great changes in the affairs of man.

10 March 1941.

I have just been losing my temper with Laurie Audrain, our Press Officer, in an argument over what the Americans are or are not doing to help us in the war. He was saying that if he were an American he would turn his back on the whole thing and say, "to hell with England and her war!" I suddenly found myself shouting that, "My God, I hoped we would lose this war first to see the spot it would put the American isolationists in." I felt ashamed of myself afterwards because I remembered a resolution I had made to myself when I was in the United States that whatever happened I would never be one of those who cursed the Americans for staying out of the war just because I was in England and it was getting too hot for me.

All the same I feel that I never shall forgive the Americans for not being in this war. It is a purely emotional state but we are all rather emotional at the moment. That bloody blitz on Saturday night partly accounts for it. They hit the Café de Paris and killed forty-seven people including most of the band. I was opposite at the 400 Club. Just afterwards I turned around when I heard a young girl say to her guardsman escort, "Darling, it was *rather* awful when they brought out all those *black* men." This couple had come on from the Café de Paris where they had been in the lounge waiting for a table when the bomb fell and had seen them bringing out the bodies of "Snake-Hips" Johnson and his coloured band, who were all killed but two. Many young officers on leave and their girls were killed. It was a bad blitz because they got so much that I had been hoping would escape. Worst of all Garland's Hotel, which was the great meeting place for myself and all my friends. Miss Clayton, the barmaid whom we all loved, was buried under the débris for six hours and was rescued because she managed to make herself heard and give directions to the men who were digging her out. Laurie and I were walking along Suffolk Street on Sunday afternoon; when we saw what had happened to Garland's we stopped on the street and said to each other, "Bugger them, *bugger* them." But that is about all there is to do – just curse and go home and wait to wake up the next morning to see what else is gone. There goes the siren. It is just like September all over again, and this will go on all spring and all summer and, as far as we can see, forever and ever.

Amen. Having this interval of normality has spoiled us for raids. This diary tonight is whimpering – and war does make one callous too. We were making jokes yesterday about "Snake-Hips" Johnson, the band leader, and his death. Jokes that none of us would have thought anything but pointless and disgusting a year ago, but then I never used to think that soldiers' jokes in the last war ("Ha! Ha! George got his blooming 'ead knocked off!") were very funny.

Meanwhile the Americans are getting their toes dug in in Newfoundland and Bermuda preparatory to inheriting what is left of the British Empire in the Western Hemisphere.

13 March 1941.

An American newspaper correspondent called Lake appeared. He was suffering from what he solemnly called acidosis and he spent the evening railing at the inefficiency of the British censorship and the superiority and maddening "slowness" of British officialdom. Slowness! Why don't the Americans hurry up and convoy over to us the war materials we need to defend them and us, or at least get their industry keyed up to producing them in sufficient quantities. The truth is that we are living on a different planet from the Americans. Their observations from the world of commonsense seem irrelevant and irritating. For the neutral to talk to the belligerent is like a sober man talking to a drunk. The sober man's fear is that the drunk will knock over his best furniture, break his glasses, assault his wife – "Go easy, be reasonable" is his cry. "Don't seize Brazilian shipping for fear of the effect on South American shipping in general. Don't hold up wheat for France in case the children perish," say the Americans. But this is mixed up with a contradictory cry which is, "Why don't you *do* more – be more ruthless. We will scream while you are doing it but admire you for it afterwards." Let us never forget our friends among the Americans – Roosevelt, Bullitt, Dorothy Thompson, Lippmann, or our enemies – La Follette, Lindbergh, Nye, Wheeler.

Dupuy[1] back from France – still optimistic. He says Pétain is as pro-British as ever, full of vigour and master of the situation. Pétain does not entirely trust Admiral Darlan, and he is making use of him

---

[1] Pierre Dupuy was Canadian Minister to the French Government at Vichy.

for just as long as he may wish to. Then he will put someone else in his place and send out a new younger man to North Africa. Pétain is pleased with himself, "N'est-ce-pas que je me suis bien débarrassé de Laval?" Dupuy says that what Pétain aims for now is an agreement – wheat for France under United States control against a promise for Vichy to guarantee no German infiltration into North Africa.

18 March 1941. Garnons.

There are about twenty Canadian officers here mostly recuperating from pneumonia or bronchitis. The place is presided over by a big-boned, big-bosomed old woman – a sort of a Hindenburg of a woman. Apparently she is proving somewhat stiff-necked and cantankerous. In perpetual attendance on her is a Canadian girl brought up here and on the continent. There does not seem to be much point about her. She is sulky and introspective but not enough to be *farouche*.

The masseur employed here was talking to me about the Canadian officers today. "They are all the same, same opinions, same swearwords. They are not interesting men in themselves, but I have only met two since I have been here who I would not be quite happy to serve under in the front line. What I foresee in Canada is an aristocracy beginning to grow up there. You will have aristocrats – the grandsons of the Eatons, Masseys, Flavelles, and the other millionaires." Of course he is dead wrong. There is no aristocratic principle alive in Canada and you will not make it by a few rich men mimicking English lords.

In 1815 Russia was in some ways in relation to Europe what Canada is now, a new country with a deep feeling that the future belonged to her. The Russian officers quartered in France during the occupation soaked up so much of the "spirit of the age" that when they went home to Russia they kept the Secret Police busy for a generation with their dangerous new ideas. Now England is in the midst of a social revolution and the continent is in travail with new forms of political and economic organization. How much of this penetrates to our Canadian officers? So far as I can see, nothing whatsoever; they still think in terms of the last war. To them this is just another war against Germany – Hitler instead of the Kaiser.

As for the Englishman, he looks upon the Canadians as an army of friendly barbarians who for some incomprehensible reason have come to protect him from his enemies.

The Royal Tour in Canada was the occasion for an overpowering manifestation on the part of at any rate some Canadians of a deep yearning towards the *mother* country. (England never thinks of herself as a mother country nor is the phrase ever heard here.) Above all the whole Tour was an example of the English genius for making use of people – a genius so highly developed in both their political and private lives.

28 March 1941.

1. Plutodemocracy is finished as a form of government.
2. The small national sovereign state is finished.
3. American culture based on optimism and the perfectibility of man through technical progress and education has had the bottom of it knocked out.
4. It follows from all this that we are groping for a new organization and a new expression for our faith in the dignity of our destiny. After this war there will be no let-down into materialism. There will be another Age of Faith.

29 March 1941.

I am sick of my present hectic life – the work, the miscellaneous loveless affairs, and the mixed drinks. I wish I lived in a small provincial town and spent the evenings reading aloud the Victorian novelists to my wife and my adoring daughters.

1 April 1941.

The Queen came to tea with the Masseys the other day. Acute suspense among those invited (only seven or eight). Each was to be presented, each wished to show that this was not at all weighing on his spirits, each was hagridden by the thought that through some mischance he or she would not be presented. Mrs. Massey would forget them or the Queen would get tired and want to go home before it came to their turn. I was led in with the other Secretaries – we sat down in front of a blazing fire in a circle around her. She sat very upright and talked to us in her sweetly modulated gentle voice. Yes, the charm is there all right, fabulous charm! You wonder, "Is it done with mirrors?" To see that familiar postage stamp face, those gestures of the hands known to millions, that smile that moves strong men to tears, and what is behind it all? Intelligence, enormous control. She was tired by the time she got to us, but the timing of her departure, the unhurried certainty of her going, the faint regret that tiresome things made it necessary not to go on talking forever to three Secretaries at Canada House. No, it was a perfect performance.

16 April 1941.

Tonight is, I think from the war point of view, a new low. There is another of these infernal, eternal blitzes going on. The sky is crimson again from another great fire, this time in the direction of Victoria – planes are overhead all the time. The Irish porter has just come in to tell me that there is light showing from my window and I have been up on the roof with him watching the flares – great clumps of them – "They're beautiful," he says, "though for such a bad purpose, you have to admit they are beautiful. Why, the sky is lit up like a ballroom." He is right – they are like chandeliers suspended from heaven. All the same this raid has got me scared for the first time in months. I feel like going downstairs to the shelter, but that is a thing I have not done yet. There are guns firing next door in Grosvenor Square and bits of shrapnel crackling down into the wall of the courtyard outside my window.

I saw in the paper the other day a letter recovered from a bombed house from a girl to her sweetheart describing a raid play-by-play and ending, "I am writing this under the table, the planes seem to be getting nearer and nearer. They seem almost in the room with us now . . ." There the letter stopped. It was found a few yards from the girl's body.

There were two explosions then which shook this building considerably – it swayed each time and the blast has made my eardrums feel as they do when one is going up fast in a lift. I do not suppose there is much point in my going downstairs – if the building collapsed it would collapse on top of us. Besides, shelter conversation is insufferable – everyone standing about nervously making jokes. It seems at moments as though the Battle of Britain were being fought just above my bedroom. Someone is whistling tranquilly in the street outside as though it were an ordinary spring evening and he was strolling back with his girl on his arm from an evening in the park or at the cinema. Will there ever be such evenings again? But when other people say that we cannot win the war I immediately begin to preach optimism and victory. Bathos – but the universal bathos of people in all countries at war.

Virginia Woolf's house – Bloomsbury – has been bombed.

Someone was describing it the other day – the frescoes by her sister Vanessa Bell, the book-lined sitting-room where Lytton Strachey and Virginia conducted conversation in the twenties. Now the house is gone, and she has committed suicide because she thought that a mental derangement she had suffered from before was coming back on her again. A fear far worse than the fear of any bombs. For she found it so insufferable that she drowned herself in the peaceful countryside while we in London cling hard to life among the bombs.

What is meant by the collapse of civilization? It means that we are glad when we hear that Berlin is getting the same bombing we are. It means that when I said I was sorry that our bombers had hit Frederick the Great's palace at Potsdam, someone replied, "I cannot say I share that sentiment. I should like all their beautiful and historic places to be destroyed." It means the Italians being prepared (if that story is true) to bomb the Vatican themselves and then put the blame on us.

The unending tale of death and destruction goes on piling up all over the world. And it is too much. General Franco (the Christian Catholic knight) makes a speech saying there is no such thing as peace – all peace is simply the period of preparation for the next war. I should say that war-weariness will soon show itself among all the peoples of the world. That is a thing which has not yet happened. Perhaps it has not yet begun to happen in Germany. I do not know. It is a feeling that takes a long time to assert itself in practical or political form.

Perhaps we are entering a new phase in which war no longer seems a titanic struggle between rival systems and nations, no longer seems even tragic nor glorious, but just an intolerable burden, a bloody pointless waste.

The grass is green at last in St. James's Park, but the gates are locked and one is not allowed in because it is full of time-bombs. I look through the railings at the deserted paths and lawns. Even the ducks seem to have been moved away.

I think of those Australians in that hell in Greece being bombed by planes that outnumber them three to one and by tanks that outnumber them three to one and by armies that outnumber them God knows how many times. It is like the feeling we had last year over Dunkirk and again Norway – the feeling of waste and impotent rage, the feeling that one has no right and very little desire to be alive when better men are lying dead by the hundreds.

The above gloomy entries in my diary have done me some good. It is better that I should pour all this stuff out in a private diary – than after a drink or two begin to talk like this to my friends or write it in letters. There is much self-pity here, mixed with the higher forms of gloom. My own vitality seems to have given out.

21 April 1941.

An Edwardian period piece is Maggie Greville whose luncheons in Charles Street have been famous for at least thirty years. She was the daughter of a Scottish millionaire and possessed by that energetic worldliness which pushes the lowland Scot so far up the English social ladder. Just as whenever in England you meet with a genuine interest in the arts you may suspect Jewish blood, so whenever you meet with respect for the human intelligence you may guess that there is a lowland Scot about. Mrs. Greville is very old, lame, half-blind, and has as she says, "everything wrong with her except leprosy," but she still puts on a great act, and cabinet ministers still ring her up and ask if they may drop in and spend an evening with her in her room at the Mayfair Hotel. "My husband," she told us, "was in the Grenadier Guards. We had been married two years and were very happy together, but I could not bear army society, so I said 'If you must stay in the regiment I'll have to go away with somebody else and begin over again. These people are intolerable.'" He left the army and thus began her social career in London. She talked of her interviews with Hitler, who evidently had charmed her by taking the trouble to talk to her quietly and intelligibly. Someone asked, "Didn't you find him appallingly – well – common?" "Not at all – one doesn't notice that with a great man – now Mussolini, yes, the only great man I have ever known who was truly pompous." I liked her story of Mrs. Cornelius Vanderbilt saying to her at the time when New York was talking about the dangers of communism, "If the revolution comes in America, Neely (her husband) and I will go first – like Louis XVI and Mary Antoinette."

How the English hate being rescued by the Americans. They know they must swallow it, but God how it sticks in their throats. The Americans are thoroughly justified in their suspicions of the English, and the English I think are justified in their belief that they are superior to the Americans. They have still the steadiness, stoicism, and self-discipline that make for a ruling race, but what will these qualities avail them if the tide of history and economics has turned against them? How will the volatile, generous, imaginative, spoiled, and impatient Americans manage city populations in the after-war world?

24 April 1941.

Mr. Massey has said to me that he would not like to think that the National Archives contained no account from this post of affairs in this country during the greatest war in history. I quite agree, but how is one to report anything which does not appear in the propaganda press when he exercises a censorship over everything which could be considered critical of England? He fears that anything critical might weaken the purpose of our people at home. But we are in too deep to get out, and surely our people have the right to know what is going on and read things which, if they were over here, they would hear from half the Englishmen they met in the clubs. He has an unrivalled opportunity to compile a secret history of the conduct of the war – to illustrate it with social anecdotes and personal impressions of men. But he is too patriotic ever to publish anything that could be considered critical, and what is worse he is too blinded by wishful thinking ever to face the conclusions even when he is alone with his confessional diary before him. Some day he will publish his memoirs. In fact he is looking forward to doing so – but they will be composed in the prose he loves best – that of a *Times* leading article. It is a pity, because he has in conversation the vivacity of phrase to produce a vivid, if superficial, account of the London scene. Alas, his reverence is too much for him.

28 April 1941.

I am thinking not in military terms but in social and historical terms. The ruling class in this country has nothing to gain from victory. The loyalty of the ruling class is not open to doubt. They will die for England and will let themselves be bled white for England. They are Englishmen before they are capitalists or landlords (unlike the same class in France). But the fact remains that if the war continues for some years, as it must if we are to obtain the victory, they will be ruined financially and in the event of a British victory they face – not the return of the *status quo* – but the completion of a bloodless, social revolution which will deprive them of all their privileges and bring about the destruction of all the things they hold dear. The reverse is true in Germany where the leaders know that victory means not only the triumph of the Reich but their own continuance in power and ever-increasing spoils of victory. England's ruling class are committing suicide to save England from defeat – it shows the stuff of which they are made, but all the same no one commits suicide with élan, and élan is a valuable quality in time of war.

2 May 1941.

We are in danger of losing the war. This is the way things might go if Hitler has his way as he has had it up to now. The "pincer movement" in Egypt may succeed. If it does, and the Germans reach the Suez Canal, Japan will move south, Spain will attack Gibraltar and French Morocco. The Germans will then be able – for who is to stop them? – once the British army in Egypt is eliminated, to drive through Africa to the Cape. South Africa has neither arms nor men to defend itself. A quisling government will be set up there, Germany can then cut our communications not only with India but with Australia and New Zealand which will be threatened by Japan.

As for England she will be outflanked on a world scale and left like the Maginot Line, a graveyard of equipment and static armies with nothing to defend except herself. These possibilities were outlined by General Smuts in a memorandum addressed to the United Kingdom

Government in July 1940. They now seem to me to represent the most likely objectives of German strategy. It is possible that when the Germans have reached Suez they will make another peace offer on the basis that we can keep our Empire (except of course that they will control it by establishing themselves on the main routes of communication) and let them run Europe. They might join this with the announcement that they propose to turn their attention to the U.S.S.R., thus appealing both to our wish to save the Empire and to our hope that they may get embroiled in a grapple with Russia. Needless to say they will not have finished with us nor with the U.S.A. but they may prefer to transfer the war temporarily back to the sphere of pressure politics and to avoid their biggest risk, a frontal invasion of the U.K.

3 May 1941.

Went to a concert with Anne-Marie. Bach, to which I am deaf – though Anne-Marie says, "He is a god." As she had said a few minutes before that what she liked in music was "sex – the frisson," I cannot think that she enjoys Bach much. Then Beethoven's piano concerto with Moiseiwitsch at the piano. The Beethoven was what I had come for, but Anne-Marie somewhat spoiled it for me by leaning her shoulder against mine and "vibrating" during the more exciting passages, at the same time glancing at me with a "faint smile of pleasure" to make sure that I was sharing her ecstasies in the appropriate manner. This technique disturbed me, as what I like to do is to shut my eyes and concentrate like hell.

I always enjoy it when Anne-Marie talks of her fabulous youth. "When I was a girl," she says, "I was a very precious person. My father of a very old family in Romania going back to 1200 – pedigree perfect. My mother came from nothing, but she was very rich. She died when I was eighteen months old, and half her fortune went to my father and half to me – forty thousand pounds a year each – so you see I was an heiress – for those days in Romania before the war it was a lot of money." She adds this last deprecatingly out of worldly *convenance* – knowing perfectly well that forty thousand pounds a year is a lot of money anywhere at any time. "My father was a charming person, but good for nothing. He went through his share of the fortune in a year – every penny of it – and nothing was left but bills. Under the Romanian inheritance laws if I died before coming of age my money went to my father – so now you see why I was so precious. I was brought up by my grandfather and grandmother – my father's parents. They were always terrified in case anything should happen to me. I might be kidnapped by some of my father's creditors who, if I was out of the way, could collect their money, or I might die. So if I flew into a rage they did not dare to refuse me what I wanted in case it should turn to a fever, and upset my health. My grandfather I disliked, but he was a very intelligent man – to him I owe any taste or knowledge I may have. But I got on badly with him, first because he made my grandmother, who was a saint, miserable – but that is another story – then because he was after my money all the time. But they were all after my money, like sharks – he, my father, my uncle – all of them.

"I never went to school, but I had all kinds of governesses – Swiss, English, German, Italian, French. It was that way that I learned languages. I have never studied a language in my life. I was allowed to read almost anything I liked. I was allowed to travel where I liked – Venice, Paris, Munich – anywhere so long as it was by land. My grandparents were frightened of sea travel in case anything should happen to me. I was too precious. My grandfather used to take me to the Salon Carré at the Louvre when I was twelve years old. In those days the pictures had not been divided into the schools. In the Salon Carré was the best of Rubens, Rembrandt, Titian – everything – 'Go and look for yourself,' he would say, 'and come back and tell me what you liked and try to explain to me why you liked it.'

"I was brought up to sit on top of the pyramid of my fortune. I was taught nothing practical, but after the war when it became necessary I turned into an excellent business woman. I must have had that from my mother's side – where the money came from. So you see I am a mixture of everything, only I have no Jewish blood."

5 May 1941.

I have just got back from a day in the country lunching with Loelia, Duchess of Westminster. She is witty, worldly, and sensible. She lives in a house full of rococo white china and pretty little eighteenth-century chandeliers and lovely abundant flowers, and is herself opulently handsome, with dark eyes and an independent swing of the hips. If there was a revolution she would open an interior decorating establishment on Fifth Avenue and do handsomely out of it. People like her just cannot lose.

I spent last evening at Margery Ziegler's. I shall remember that funny little converted box of a house and her window-boxes of dust-laden pink carnations and blue front door and the little drawing-room full of flowers and the slum neighbours going to and from the pub with caps pulled down over their eyes, and the river at the end of the street. She loves the house and has stayed in it all through the blitz, although it is only a box of bricks, and it is just luck that it has not already collapsed about her ears with all the land-mines that have fallen around it – for it is almost under the shadow of Lot's Road Power Station, one of the principal German objectives. If there is an air raid I always think first of her sleeping on a mattress down in the passage below the level of the area railings, quite sure that she is not going to leave her own house to live anywhere else.

We are all publicly agreed that it would be better to be dead than to be defeated. On this principle any one of us would risk his life tomorrow. Yet do we really feel this to be true? I do not. Yet if necessary I would act on it.

21 May 1941.

I do not know how to account for the extraordinary feeling of happiness and of completeness which I have felt in this past year in London. I have a premonition that it must mean that I have gone as far as I can go – that I am being shown happiness like a stretch of fair landscape that I have been in search of for a long time but that once having seen the promised land I must lose it. Tonight sitting in the park in a deck-chair, smoking a cigarette, watching the searchlights, smelling the lilacs, I felt – this is too much – retribution must follow.

I dined with the Masseys – if only their enemies could see them like that they could not help being touched. Their love for each other is the most attractive thing about both of them.

25 May 1941.

Dined with Lady Malcolm after the ballet – *Orpheus and Eurydice*, music by Gluck – so unbelievably badly done that the only thing to do was to treat it as a joke, and even as a joke it was too long, choreography infantile, costumes ludicrous, dancers ugly, graceless, and amateurish – they do not even know how to get across the stage, much less any technique – practically no dancing in it and I must say it is music which makes no impression on me at all. The only interesting thing was Constant Lambert's face – he was at the piano – a remarkable face – sensitive, highly intelligent, and, I think, repulsive.

Well, I got Jack Grant out to Canada today with his wife and child. I have paid that debt in a way certainly never expected. I remember this time last year when he came reeling into my office. He was in the Bomber Command and had been going up in France six and seven times a day and making night flights over Germany. In a few months he had aged years from a boy into a tired man – so dizzy with fatigue that he did not know if he was coming or going. I wrote him off as one of the war's losses – never thought somehow that he would come out of it alive. Here he is a year later with a wife, a superbly healthy son, and a good job, on his way to Canada out of the war – and what is more the desperate look which he has always had – the look of a man who is gambling against himself – has gone. He is a responsible husband and father. I thought of him as a tragic figure, a man who cannot compromise successfully with the world or his fate and so butts his head against stone walls. He is going as a Training Instructor with the Air Force. Now he is safe unless, of course, his ship is torpedoed on his way to Canada or he is killed in an accident.[1]

30 May 1941.

I took the ballerina to lunch at the Ritz. She was a little nervous of the place and kept her checked mackintosh on in the bar because it was new and under it she was wearing an old tweed suit. I told her

---

[1] He was in fact killed in a plane crash while a training instructor with the RCAF.

today that I was falling a little bit in love with her and so I am a little bit. She is my perennial type. When I die they will find some woman's name written on my heart – I do not know myself whose it will be!

1 *June 1941.*

I like to remember the mornings after I have spent a night out when I have got up very early to be away before the daily charwoman arrives and standing in the damp grey morning air waiting to get one of the first buses with the people starting out for their day's work coughing and gossiping and grousing and waiting stolidly – patiently – for the bus – working men with coat collars turned up and stout women going scrubbing who spent last night at the local. I am unshaven and drifting and happy and with all the pores open to physical sensation and the tight core of will melted. Then to get into my smart pseudo-New York flatlet that always smells of whatever they clean the carpets with, and I have a hot bath and sausages for breakfast to celebrate the fact that I feel fine.

Love affairs. In my youth (that is until this year, for my youth was one of the protracted kind) I used to be bewildered by my own lack of feeling in affairs of the heart. I felt that my love affairs were not up to scratch. I did not yearn or suffer enough – not nearly enough. I still feel that – I believe it to be a much more common state than people suppose. For to hear me talking of my loves you would think me to be a creature of burning passions and palpitating feelings, particularly if I am telling a woman of my ecstasies and sufferings in love's lists. This is just advertising one's own temperament by exaggerating what one is capable of feeling in love. Most other people knowingly or not must employ the same trick. It is true that promiscuous love-making knocks a lot of the nonsense out of one, and at the same time it "hardens a' within and petrifies the feelings!"

2 *June 1941.*

The common people of England deserve a few breaks and if it is socialism they want they should have it. I would trust them to make any form of government into something tolerant and tolerable.

5 June 1941.

It has begun to thunder – *that* is what I have been expecting all evening without knowing what it was. I walked alone in the park. It was hot for the first time this year and everything was in bloom at once – lilacs (white lilacs leaning over the garden wall at Apsley House), hawthorn everywhere, and chestnut. The grass is long and shaggy – people have trodden paths across what used to be smooth preserved lawns. There are cigarette boxes and papers everywhere, but the trees are in full magnificence and there are lovers on the grass and solitary ladies reading lending library books in their deck-chairs, and old dirty human bundles of tramps, and everywhere soldiers. I think of last year walking in the parks after Dunkirk when they were full of the remnants of half the armies of Europe with foreign voices and tired strained faces. Again we are on the edge of something momentous. And next spring?

7 June 1941.

The mournfulness – more than that – the terror of being alone is upon me. I am really frightened of these walls. I do not like the way my self seems to expand and fill the whole room when I am alone like this. I am more frightened than I dare to write.

We have had a little Scottish factory manager here who has escaped from Lille telling us about conditions in the north of France, the extent of the sabotage and the decline in morale of the Germans stationed in France. This is all to the good and gives one the much-needed refreshment of realizing that the Germans have their own difficulties and the hope that if pressed they might crack under them, if only we had the power to press them. From what one can piece together from unoccupied France it is rather different there. The richer people are adapting themselves to the new life. They no doubt vastly prefer the socially safe Pétain regime to the Blum government – they have not, apparently, been ruined financially by the defeat of France. It is the same kind of situation in Romania and probably all through central and south-east Europe. The richer classes are not doing too badly – business is good. They are picking up the strings of their lives again and cushioned by cash are accepting the inevitable. There is greater freedom to travel in Europe and conditions are coming around to a new kind of normalcy. "You cannot," says Basil, "get the rich down." People who are adapting themselves like that must wish for German victory – a British success means continuation of the war indefinitely, more destruction and danger, more interruption of business, and finally the probability of a social upheaval. The lower classes and the city intelligentsia are pro-British. But this class line of sympathy is blurred in thousands of cases by other elements, patriotism, race (e.g. the Jews), and individual temperament and experience.

I was talking to an officer of the United States Embassy who has lately been transferred from Berlin. I detect in him what I find in most people who have lived on the Continent since the war began, an unexpressed but apparent acceptance of the invincibility of Germany. He has been in Berlin during our raids there and says they are nothing – nothing at all – compared with German raids on London – that of course one knew already. Some believe that the German crack up will come in the end through the lack of inner toughness of the German people – their nervosity. They picture the fat men sitting around the bar at the Adlon Hotel in Berlin wiping their brows with their handkerchiefs and saying, "*Ich bin nervös*." I tried that picture of the German temperament on my American friend who said it applied to the older generation but not to the young men. He obviously feels that the Germans understand the nature of war much better than we do and says they throw themselves into it one hundred per cent because they want to get it over with and see that is the only way to do it.

With the Americans more than with most people nothing succeeds like success. If we are defeated in the Middle East this summer, if Germany then proposes peace and we have to turn to the United States and say, "It is up to you – do we continue the struggle or come to terms?" that will be America's hour of testing. We went through the same test and after failing twice came through with the goods in the end.

12 June 1941.

Went with Vincent Massey to the Conference of Allied Representatives[1] held at St. James's Palace in a long saloon panelled in

[1] The representatives of the Allied Governments in exile in London.

rather worn green silk and hung with copies of royal portraits. Winston Churchill delivered a melodramatic and moving oration and made a historic occasion of what could so easily have been just a formal gathering of politicians and diplomats sitting around a green baize table ("quite like a meeting of the Council of the League of Nations" as Belinski, the Pole, said). The Prime Minister made one see it as the assembly of all the duly constituted governments of Europe who had sought refuge in the embattled fortress of England and who would in due course issue forth to deliver their oppressed lands from the heel of Hitler. He indulged in one of his usual diatribes against the Nazis with all his usual relish. These terrific castigations always make me feel a little uneasy. He so obviously enjoys piling into Hitler and the Nazis – and you feel it is just too easy for him. Also you wonder if he won't one of these days overdo it and reduce the whole thing to a music-hall level. He is very near the music-hall sometimes, but he always manages to get away with it. One of the secrets of the hold of his oratory over the English people is that he makes them feel that they are living their history, that they are taking part in a great pageant. He gives them his own feeling of the continuity of English history. All the same there are murmurs. Crete was a blow to his prestige, already one hears again that phrase which used to be ever on the lips of Tory back-benchers, "Churchill, oh yes – but he lacks judgement." The Tory wives are beginning to say that again now, and that shows that their husbands have begun to say it to them again, although they dare not say it in public – yet.

Mr. Massey was made a Privy Councillor today – it was Churchill's own idea and Mr. King concurred. The Masseys are so excited and happy about it. It is really touching the way Mr. Massey reacts to praise and recognition. He is so open about it like a schoolboy who just cannot resist ice-cream. Brendan Bracken wrote and told him that few men living had done more for the Empire.[1] Certainly the Empire has no more loyal servant. Bennett's peerage provides me

[1] Massey's appointment and Bennett's peerage were announced in the Birthday Honours. Bracken, who was to become Minister of Information on 20 July, was then Churchill's Parliamentary Private Secretary, and so may have been writing on Churchill's behalf. Bennett's actual title was Viscount Bennett of Mickleham and of Calgary and Hopewell.

with the headache of writing to him. Lord Stampede of Calgary is the best title suggested.

Crossing the park I took a minute or two off and sat in a deckchair beneath two May trees of varying hues of pink – under a parasol of blossom. I thought that I would like to spend the day drifting through the parks without object and without personality, watching the lovers, looking at ducks and flowers, listening to the bands – neither imposing myself on other people nor receiving their imprint and above all not having to observe with precision, not making mental notes – just drifting – as if into a sunny impressionist picture where everything swims vaguely in light and colour.

16 June 1941.

It really is most interesting about Billy Coster[1] brought up in the smart Paris-American world of Ritz bars, promiscuity, and snobbishness. He now finds the only real fun he gets out of life is serving behind the bar in a small pub in a poor street in Chelsea. The people he enjoys being with are Bill Epps, the local plumber, and Millie Lighthouse, the barmaid at "The Surprise." Those social charms which he would not dream of displaying at Newport are lavished upon the working people who come in for a half-pint. They obviously love him, and I suppose it satisfies his need of affection. I think he would do well to marry his barmaid, but then I am all for experimental marriages – where other people are concerned. In my advice to others I notice that I scorn worldly considerations and always counsel them to take a chance – a chance that nothing would induce me to take myself. I was thinking tonight at dinner with Billy how much more difficult it is to talk freely to one's friends than it used to be when one was young. There was a time when I would have told Billy quite freely anything about my private life – and now – no. The things that one cannot talk about accumulate each year – each month there are more things that one suppresses. One grows more polite, more guarded – why? How I cling to the few people to whom I still speak freely, yet no doubt they despise me for it.

---

[1] An old friend from Oxford and Harvard days.

Mackenzie King has been putting on the most remarkable display of panic – was invited to come to the get-together of Commonwealth Prime Ministers. He has cabled the longest apologies to Churchill. 1. He cannot leave the country because of the problem of unity. 2. Labour difficulties. 3. Conscription. 4. External Affairs. 5. Possibility of the United States coming into the war. 6. Needed to campaign the country. 7. Knows nothing about strategy. I do not know why he does not add that he cannot leave because he is having his front parlour repapered and is needed to choose the design. When he says that anyway he does not think the meeting would serve much purpose he is on surer ground – in fact he may be quite right on the whole position. But what maddens one is that it is such a demonstration of cowardice, personal and political. If the cables were published surely he would be dished politically.

As someone has said (General McNaughton) he must be a very brave man to refuse to take the risk of coming. He cuts such a figure. It has put Mr. Massey in a spot – although he thinks that King should come, he does not want to put himself on record as opposing or supporting or confirming King's line – lest he should be made the public scapegoat – and at the same time the ball has been thrown to him, and he is in trouble if he will not play. Personally I would feel very tempted to try to put King on the spot, but that would be shortsighted. 1. The issue is not important enough – it does not involve anything really essential to winning the war. 2. Much as one would enjoy putting a spoke in the old hypocrite's wheel, the fact remains that there is no one who could take his place with anything like the same chance of keeping the country together. He is easy to rail at but not easy to replace.

We had an interesting Canadian lunch the other day – Graham Spry and I, and three Conservative army officers, all imbued with contempt for Mr. King and all agreed that the Canadian war effort is nil compared with what it might and should be. Graham, an ex-socialist, agrees with them on the last point and in fact considers that Canada has relaxed its efforts since September of last year. Certainly, unless King's telegrams are entirely bluff, the situation at home must be very tricky. Now we need a few victories or else some bombing blitzes on North America to make us know what we are up against.

X. was talking about Churchill yesterday and said that when he first met him he was not impressed. It was in Canada – he was recovering from his accident in New York and was drinking too much brandy. Then he met him again a few years ago at lunch. He dominated the table with his compelling monologue which fascinated everybody, although he did not agree with his argument which was a scathing attack on the lower classes – the plebs – for whom he had no use. In summing him up he said, "He has plenty of spirit but no soul." In fact he is an old pirate and if things go wrong people will find out and will turn on him and he will end in disgrace and they will forget that he is the only thing that kept England – so far – from a Vichy Government.

I had sandwiches with D. in the Park. It was not a great success. She had dressed for the Ritz and was not too pleased at my enthusiasm for the simple life. If women only knew how endearing it would be if they occasionally expressed a desire for a cheap, simple meal instead of always exacting their full pound of flesh. But they all act on the assumption that the price you pay for their dinner is the measure of your regard for them. Just to prove to D. that I loved her I took her afterwards to the Apéritif where we had peaches and white wine for the price that would keep a working woman for a week, and I must say that she was right in wanting a smart restaurant as a background. It suited her and made one feel that this was Page 1 Chapter 1 of a new and exciting story. Also it restored my lust for the things that money can buy – smart women, fashionable glitter, all the frivolities that charm the eye. What I really dread from the sober reasonable socialism of the future is the eclipse of style, the disappearance of distinction – for mixed and intermingled with the vulgarity of our age is the survival of pleasant, ornamental, amusing people and things – and one's soul shrinks from the austere prospect of cotton stockings. The intellectuals do not mind, because they despise the glitter and speciousness of rich life. But the aesthetes – like myself – have their misgivings.

23 June 1941.

Went down to the House of Commons. Eden spoke on Russia.[1] He is not impressive – he never sounds as if he really means what he

---

[1] Germany had invaded Soviet Russia the day before.

says. It is not that he seems insincere, but there is a lack of conviction or temperamental failure in power to convey his convictions to others. And one feels his lack of intellectual power. A nonentity, although not obstructionist nor actively harmful in any way. I walked through Westminster Hall – the sunlight coming through the gaps caused by the bombing above the rafters in the magnificent roof. The House met in the Lords[1] – sitting on very new red leather benches. Churchill spoke about the postponement of the Prime Ministers' Meeting – a most instructive episode the secret history of which will never – presumably – be revealed to the Canadian people.

Lunched with the Poles – Marlewski, rather boring and vulgar, and Belinski in cool grey flannels with his quiet, sympathetic manner and his cynicism. Poor buggers – the Russians are laying waste their homes as they retreat.

The modern Englishman does not seem to have any desire to impose his will on anyone or even to impose his view of life. I cannot imagine that, even if the war is won, these people are destined to reorganize the Continent of Europe. They have nothing to say to Europe. They do not even believe any longer in their own mission as empire builders. Yet it is nonsense to say that they are decadent any more than the Dutch are, or the Swedes. It is just that what they are principally interested in is improving living conditions and spreading the "advantages" in this island. They are aiming straight for a moderate socialist state run on rational lines – "a little England" of the type which English socialists and radicals have always preferred. People of that sort who may be expected (if we win) to rule England have no use for the Empire which they consider an embarrassment and a bore. They will never apply force to continental politics but will expect continental states to be reasonable – like the English.

The younger writers, painters, and poets who congregate in London and dine in the Charlotte Street restaurants form very much of a club. Most of them are middle-class young men, sons of schoolmasters, civil servants, doctors, colonels, and clergymen – that is to say they were brought up in the religion of snobbery. They are trying desperately hard but usually with incomplete success to escape from the

---

[1] The House of Commons had been bombed on the night of 10 May 1941.

strait-jacket of the English social hierarchy. But who buys their books, pictures, and magazines? Is it the working man? Whom do they like to dine with and spend the weekends with? Is it with the workers? If they prefer the manual workers to their own class, why have they not flocked to join the army? Instead they are, many of them, filling white-collar jobs in America.

4 July 1941.

This war between Germany and Russia has made things seem different all over again. We have entered into yet another phase of the war. This war is like a complicated piece of music – a great symphony in which motifs are started then disappear and reappear in many combinations. Now in a way it is like not being in the war any longer and yet it is not in the least like being at peace. We are back again in the "phoney war" feeling of that first year before Dunkirk. Of course the situation is completely different but the feeling of it is rather the same. The German pressure has momentarily been removed. We are not in physical danger. Apart from this unreal and unnatural war in Syria between Australians, Arabs, and the Foreign Legion our people are not engaged in fighting.

I still believe that this German attack on Russia was an act of madness on Hitler's part. All the experts here said that Germany would easily overwhelm the Russians, but then these same experts said that there would never be a Russo-German Pact and believed up to a week before the attack took place that Germany would not fight Russia. One thing seems at least likely and that is that even the German military machine will be in no condition to attack England for several months after the Russian campaign even if they do succeed in conquering Russia. This means that the attack on England is off for the time being.

Meanwhile we go from one cloudless, high-summer day to another in a kind of daze. The parks are full of soldiers and girls in summer dresses. It is difficult to get a table in a restaurant. My friends indulge their love affairs and their vendettas. Cabinet ministers gossip in clubs and the press print daily jeremiads warning us to prepare lest a worse thing befall us. From the endless plains of Russia comes news of vast combats between alien hordes, between armies of tanks, and our lives may be being settled somewhere between the Dvina and the Dnieper. We know this but we cannot realize it. We seem to be moving in a trance towards the day when Hitler's tanks are lumbering past the Kremlin and he is ready to settle his score with us. We feel that day must come and may come soon but we cling to the hope – the wonderful, white hope – that the Russians may hold him – may even, though this would be too miraculous to be mentioned – defeat him.

18 July 1941.

I went to the Air Ministry meeting this morning. On one side of the table sat "Chubby" Power, the Canadian Air Minister, and his staff. On the other side were the high officers of the Air Ministry. They are an attractive lot – low-voiced, sensible men without the stiffness or the affectations – and above all without the bloody breeziness – of the army. Our people, especially Power, were moderate, plain-spoken, and willing to waive their own proposals if it was made clear to them that they would impair the efficiency of the war effort.

There was an interesting question over the Canadian request that we should be allowed to publish in the Canadian press the names of individuals in the Air Force who had performed outstanding exploits. This violates the sacred RAF tradition of anonymity for individuals. Power pointed out that it was necessary for recruiting in Canada. He said that the British might think it "Hollywood ballyhoo," but in our country "you must make things human and above all personal." It was plain that the Air Ministry did think it "Hollywood ballyhoo," and that no Englishman in the room knew what Power meant, yet all the Canadians, whatever their inner reservations on other points, agreed with Power on this one. The English could not bear the idea of individuals thinking themselves heroes. We could not understand the blank refusal to admit the human and popular approach – "The home-town boy makes good" myth.

10 August 1941.

Weekend at Miriam Rothschild's. Waddesdon is another of these monstrous Rothschild houses scattered through the Chilterns, and is a copy of Chambord. The state apartments are closed and the pictures (some I believe are magnificent) sent to Canada. The family are living in a wing and somewhere in the house tucked away are one hundred and fifty orphans and their attendants. It gives an idea of the scale of the house that never during my visit was I aware of their existence. The inhabited part of the house is furnished exactly as it was in the 1880s. It is decorated entirely in deep crimson – the carpets, curtains, even the leather sofas and chairs are crimson.

There are certain peculiarities about staying in a country house in wartime, one is the problem of the blackout. When you retire to your room for the night you find that it has been most thoroughly blacked out in several layers. First the extremely tall heavy windows have been securely closed and fastened (these can only be opened by pulling on two long cords with white bobbles attached to the ends of them). Then the shutters have been closed and fastened with mighty crossbars fitting into grooves. The black-out curtain hangs the whole length of the window and then come the long heavy curtains which also can only be made to come apart by pulling the correct pulleys, so that one gazes in dismay at the number of possible cords all twined around knobs. If you pull the wrong combination of pulleys (i.e. one of the curtain cords and *one* of the cords that open the window) you are involved in a breathless struggle which yields no results save frustration. It must be remembered that the business of opening the windows has to be done in the pitch dark as the light must be turned out before you begin playing about with curtains. One night staying at Stansted I was completely defeated by the combination of obstacles and panting with exhaustion after wrenching at shutters and pulling at cords I took to my bed and tossed all night, in breathless confinement. But at Waddesdon I triumphed, and what a relief to hear the wind sighing in the trees and to feel the soft night air! Then, of course, fumbling your way by the light of a small hand-torch along black corridors filled with unfamiliar furniture, to the W.C. (which one had failed to mark by daylight) or alternatively to the bedroom of your girl-friend is another country-house hazard. At Waddesdon the valet asked me what I would like for breakfast. "Coffee," he suggested, "toast or anything cooked, sir?" What a question in any English country house! But I stood out for an egg – felt the Rothschilds should be able to manage it – somehow!

2 September 1941.

The first time I saw Elizabeth Bowen I thought she looked more like a bridge-player than a poet. Yet without having read a word of her writing would not one have felt that something mysterious, passionate, and poetic was behind that worldly exterior?

17 September 1941.

The night porter said to me, "I don't want my daughter to be in domestic service – to be a servant. When she is three years old I am going to buy her a typewriter so that it will be second nature to her. I waited until I was fifty to have her, not like some young people who have children right away like animals.

"I look upon you as a friend, not like some of them who look down on me. I have an encyclopaedia – the latest one – *Pears Cyclopaedia*. What I like about it is it always settles an argument. There is one man on the staff who says to me 'I don't care what the book says.' Now that can only be ignorance or else he envies me and my knowledge."

I lunched today with de Selliers of the Belgian Embassy and another Belgian, a civil servant, and Berkeley Gage of the Foreign Office. We discussed the settlement after the war in a muddled way. What was chiefly shown up was the great divide which separates the Englishman from everyone else on earth. Gage said that it would be fatal to have another peace of bitterness. He would like the peace conference to take place in Peking. In that atmosphere the delegates would take their time and get to know each other. It would take them months to reach the final solution but so much the better – a peace that was made amid the passions of war would never be any good. Peking was the place – and then he typically added, "I am afraid I am not being absolutely serious about this." The two Belgians protested – so did I. De Selliers said, "We Belgians – like all Continentals – would want to have things reduced to writing." "Oh," said Gage, "if only you Continentals could get tight with an Englishman we would understand one another and trust one another and it would not be necessary to put everything in writing. The English have never been in favour of writing everything down." De Selliers said, "When you say you do not want a peace made until the passions of war have cooled you mean let us give the Germans another chance – that you will begin your old policy of equilibrium in Europe, playing off one power against another. We want peace made while you are still angry. The work of Bismarck must be undone. Germany must be split up – Bavaria, the Rhineland, Saxony, etc., must be revived as separate states. We in Europe will take the Anglo-Saxon lead – but you must use your power."

18 September 1941.

There is only one question of any real importance at this moment. Everyone is asking "Why can't we make a landing in France or Italy or Greece, anywhere provided it is in time to divert some German troops and planes from the Eastern Front before it is too late?" The Russians are on the verge of being pushed right out of the war, and still we do not move. And to think that there are still people in the Foreign Office and elsewhere who want to be sure that Russian strength is annihilated and that G. of the Foreign Office said at lunch the other day before two foreign diplomats, "After this is over I suppose we shall have to fight the Russians." "Whom the gods would destroy they first make mad."

24 September 1941.

Dinner with Elizabeth Bowen and her husband Alan Cameron and a few writers and critics. So far in my excursions into High Bloomsbury I have not encountered, except for Elizabeth, any striking originality of thought, phrase, or personality but rather a group of cultivated, agreeable people who think and feel very much alike.

Inter-Allied Conference all morning and most of the afternoon – pious speeches in English and French from case-hardened exiled continental politicians who abjure all aggression, talk of the rights of man and the territorial integrity and self-determination of nations. At least Hitler uses a new vocabulary and not this Genevese jargon.

25 September 1941.

Dinner at a dining club got up by Berkeley Gage of the Foreign Office. I sat between Archduke Robert of Austria and de Selliers of the Belgian Embassy, the former rather like someone seen in a distorted mirror. His head seems preternaturally shallow, his neck elongated.

He has the romantic Austrian charm which springs from an inveterate superficiality. He never asserts himself, but he is a Hapsburg and one cannot help knowing it. His mother, Empress Zita, and younger children are living near Quebec.

29 September 1941.

"Take it from one of the best living novelists that people's personalities are not interesting," Elizabeth said in a dry voice. "Except," she added, "when you are in love with them." Her books show much that you would expect if you knew her only as an acquaintance, her intelligence, her penetrating eye, her love of houses and flowers. These things you would have gathered from talking to her in her drawing-room. But there are certain passages in which her peculiar intensity, her genius, come out, which would be hard to reconcile with this cultivated hostess. That purity of perception and compassion seem to come from another part of her nature of which she is perhaps not completely aware.

This afternoon, Elizabeth and I went to see the roses in Regent's Park. For days we had been talking of those roses, but I could never get away from the office before nightfall, and it seemed as if we should never go together to see them. Then one perfect September afternoon she telephoned to say that if we did not go today it would be too late – they were almost over. So I put away the Foreign Office boxes in the safe, locked up the files, and took a taxi to Regent's Park. As we walked together I seemed to see the flowers through the lens of her sensibility. The whole scene, the misty river, the Regency villas with their walled gardens and damp lawns, and the late September afternoon weather blended into a dream – a dream in which these were all symbols soaked with a mysterious associative power – Regent's Park – a landscape of love. A black swan floating downstream in the evening light – the dark purplish-red roses whose petals already lay scattered – the deserted Nash house with its flaking stucco colonnade and overgrown gardens – all were symbols speaking a language which by some miracle we could understand together.

Weekend staying with Miriam Rothschild. She is a remarkably handsome woman, heavy dark eyebrows, dark eyes which nothing escapes, a slow deliberately cockney voice, and a free-ranging bold experimental intelligence which is beautiful to watch, an antiseptic wit which can puncture a pretension or exorcise a neurosis, a glorious capacity for gossip and fantastic invention. Add to these endearing qualities that she is a respected research scientist, is keenly interested in problems of airplane construction, is an authority on plant and animal life, buys and looks at modern pictures, runs her own business affairs, sits on Jewish welfare committees, and manages a large agricultural estate, and one has some idea what her energies must be. With all of this she has the most generous good heart for people in trouble, and is the most loyal friend and the most ruthless critic. People are frightened of her because her intelligence is free and she does not bother with English circumlocutions.

1 October 1941.

Old men in clubs are puzzled by the Russians' successful resistance. "My nephew who was in the Navy was out there after the last war, time that Denikin was fighting in the Crimea, he used to tell me, 'You can never organize the Russians to do anything. They are feckless, absolutely feckless.' Everyone said the same thing – now how are they managing all the organization of a modern war?" "Well," says another old boy, "scratch a Russian and you find a Tartar – you know they are slow to rouse but once roused – why at Tannenberg five divisions of them marched unarmed straight at the Germans." "What beats me," says a third club member, "is that the Orthodox Church is praying for the success of the Soviet Union." The attitude of officialdom about the U.S.S.R. is "Necessity makes strange bedfellows." When at one moment optimists were proclaiming the possibility of a Russian counter-offensive which would drive the Germans back across the borders, people in London were already getting very exercised about the possibility of the Russians being the ones to liberate the Poles, Czechs, etc., instead of the English. The idea of a smashing Russian victory and communism in Central and south-eastern Europe appalled them. What would suit them best would be a stalemate in the East with the Russians holding the Germans, and if by any – as it now seems – remote chance the Russians did seem to have the Germans on the run – they no doubt would do their (probably successful) best to stop any more aid to Russia. As it seems unlikely that we shall ever have a land army big enough to finish off the Germans ourselves that seems a somewhat dog-in-the-mangerish attitude. It is worth noticing that the argument which you hear quite freely expressed now that maintenance of the Russian army in the field is the only way of defeating Germany on the European continent implies that if Germany had not attacked Russia we ourselves would never have been able to defeat Germany, which is true enough but used to be hushed up.

Meanwhile the Russians do not trust us any further than they can see us. The present accusation that certain members of the British Merchant Marine have been expressing anti-Soviet views is not surprising. Sailors have a habit of saying what they think.

Anne-Marie says that the Germans are physically frightened by the Russians and are terrified of the country itself with its immense empty spaces. This may well be so – if it is, it is another proof of the courage of the German soldier as well as of the vaulting boldness of conception which has inspired them – probably the most ambitious offensive in the history of war.

18 October 1941.

The gloom of these times is inescapable. It is a grey Sunday with a warm, restless, futile wind blowing London leaves about streets and squares. There are even dead leaves on the red carpet of the Ritz vestibule, blown in through the swinging door.

19 October 1941.

I cannot get away from the dilemma that Sachie Sitwell put to me last weekend. If we cannot land an army on the Continent now while the Russian army is still in existence and holding the mass of German power in the East, how are we ever to defeat the German army? Why not give up the Continent to its fate and withdraw into isolation just defending our own if it is attacked? Of course we all know that such a programme is an impossibility, that we must go on until the Germans' will or our own is broken.

22 October 1941.

I was thinking this morning about that time in Boston when we went there as boys with Mother and Aunt M. We had a furnished apartment at the wrong end of Commonwealth Avenue. They thought it would be a relief to have a winter away from The Bower – not to have a house to bother about, and of course it would save money too. But it was not a success – the flat was too small – we were always falling over each other, and there was a horrid little gate-legged table in the sitting-room on which we had our meals. It was so low that we always had to stoop down, to eat. There was always a wind in Commonwealth Avenue and dust blowing and glare on the pavements. One day I went out to the bus in my patent-leather shoes and without a hat. Two girls in the street turned around and made some sort of crack. I felt ridiculous and humiliated. When I think of my youth it makes me angry even now. I feel that I ought to have my own back at someone for all that that vain, timid, harmless dreamer had to put up with. Now I have the weapons – then I was unarmed.

Elizabeth was saying the other day that a sense of guilt seems to be specifically a middle-class complaint – not enough humility and sense of limitations.

23 October 1941.

They were beginning to hold a meeting in Trafalgar Square for more aid to Russia. I thought of staying to see what it was like, but it was so cold. There were a lot of scrubby men in dirty mackintoshes with packages of red leaflets. They looked like the sweepings of the Communist Party hoping to stir something up. Charlie Hébert (a Canadian officer friend of mine) was with me – solid, military, well-fed. They seemed to look at him with envious, hating sidelong looks, as if they longed to be strong enough to pull him down.

I should like to have seen the Masseys standing next to Maisky (the Soviet Ambassador) and singing the Internationale at the private viewing of the Soviet films. It is quite a long step from "dear Alba" (the Spanish Ambassador) "the last great gentleman in Europe" and Lord Halifax and "all of us." When I came here two and a half years ago there was no more devoted adherent of Chamberlain than Mr. Massey. Churchill, of course, in those days had "no judgement." I could never get Mr. Massey to accept an invitation to Maisky's ("I feel uncomfortable with that little man") but the Masseys have followed the English ruling class in the most spectacular somersault in all recorded history and never have they felt consciously insincere except perhaps now they do feel their conversion to the U.S.S.R. a little – shall we say – sudden. The more candid just go on hating communism as much as ever – "Anything to save our bacon." But they will not feel comfortable for long in this open cynicism. Already the Archbishop of Canterbury has found that communism contains the seeds of Christianity – even if the Russians wear their religion with a difference. A few really consistent Tories are in danger of being locked up in Brixton jail. They are guilty of the unpardonable sin of putting ideas before the interests of England. The English always said they were not interested in an ideological war. Mind you, I think they are quite right, but what does a little appal me is that when the storm is past they will bring back the old prejudices and what is much worse – the "old principles."

27 October 1941.

The sights – the long tree-lined avenue in Hyde Park at dusk echoing with the noise of soldiers' boots as they come strolling, swinging, whistling, singing, or alone looking for a girl, and the girls plain – most of them – little working girls in short skirts and sweaters with fancy handkerchiefs around their necks. They know they are wanted – they twist and turn as they walk and break into sudden gusts of giggles and cling to each other's arms. The whole length of the avenue is alive with desires. There are satyrs behind every tree. Silhouetted against the hall-light soldiers with their girls sit on the deck-chairs on the grassy stretches that border the avenue. The flicker of a cigarette lighter reveals for a long second – the pose of a head – the movements of hands. Near the park gates the Military Police in their rose-topped caps stand in groups of twos and threes hoping for trouble, longing to exercise summary justice.

In the expensive restaurants at this hour pink, well-scrubbed schoolboys masquerading in guards uniforms are drinking bad martinis with girl-friends in short fur capes and Fortnum and Mason shoes, who have spent the day driving generals to the War Office or handing cups of tea and back-chat to soldiers in canteens. Grass widows in black with diamond clips or pearls are finding the conversation of Polish officers refreshingly different from that of English husbands. Ugly vivacious ATS are ordering *vin rosé* at the Coquille. A film actress (making the best of a patriotic part at present) is just going through the swinging door of the Apéritif with David Niven at her elbow. Ageing Edwardian hostesses whose big houses are now shuttered and silent are taking little naps in their hideouts on the third floor ("so much the safest floor, darling") at Claridge's or the Dorchester. Cedric (in a yachtsman's jacket) and Nigel are hipping their way through the crowd of pansies in the Ritz bar (they all have the most madly peculiar jobs in the Ministry of Information or the BBC). At the Travellers' Club Harold Nicolson in his fruity voice is embellishing a story as he settles on the leather sofa. Anne-Marie is sitting on the side of her bed at the Ritz making eyes at herself in the mirror and trumpeting down the telephone in Romanian French. It is a world of hotels and bars and little pubs that have become the fashion overnight – of small drinking clubs run by gangsters who make a nice profit out of prostitutes and the dope racket – packed with RAF pilots, Canadian officers, blondes, and slot-machines, and perhaps a baccarat table in the upstairs rooms.

And along Piccadilly from the Circus to Hyde Park Corner is an incessant parade of prostitutes, and out of the black-out an acquisitive hand on your arm and "Feeling lonely, dearie?" "Hello, my sweet," (in a Noël Coward voice) or "*Chéri*." In Berkeley Square the railings are down. An old man is making a bonfire of dead leaves beside the little pavilion in the centre of the garden.

28 October 1941.

Until this war began I never felt that I was a member of a community and that I had an obligation to others. The idea of "doing my bit" had always seemed to me a piece of schoolboy morality, not applicable to me. I was still the bullied schoolboy who gets his own back in the end. Now this attitude seems to me not so much wicked as childish and dangerous too. It was because so many of us thought that "the world" was something alien to ourselves which owed us the plunder of a living and as many privileges as we could lay our hands on that we are in our present spot. That lonely but pleasurable anarchism we shall never enjoy again in my lifetime. We shall never be safe enough to afford it. We are bound together now either in brotherhood or in fraternal hate. After this we either have a state based on human relationships or we have civil war.

2 November 1941.

I suppose I ought to cultivate the society of solid civil servants instead of rococo Romanian princesses and baroque dilettantes.

8 November 1941.

I have been reading with singularly little pleasure some modern poetry in *Horizon* magazine. What can you expect of poets who keep on thinking about "the happiness of the common people," as if happiness could be an "ideal." They remind me of those thick-headed Babbitts who drew up the American Declaration of Independence and who announced "the pursuit of happiness" as a political aim. The poets' contemporary left-wing opinions have no real political significance; they have not faced up to the fact that the new world for which they are rooting will be just as immoral and selfish as the old. They still believe in Santa Claus. To me that makes all that they have to hint about the future childish and silly. The only hope for the future is that more political intelligence will be applied to our problems so that the machine will not break down again. It is first of all a *technical* problem. But that it will be a better world for poetry to flourish in is poisonous nonsense.

10 November 1941.

I used sometimes during last autumn's air raids to say to myself in a stupid bewildered way, "I wonder if those people in Berlin ever think of the hell we are going through." Now I feel quite sure that they never did. We never stop to think that they are now having just the same terrifying experience. We shut our eyes to that fact and only think how many bombers we have lost. The capacity for sympathizing with other people's troubles seems to have completely dried up. Do we ever think of the thousands of starving people in Europe? Do we sympathize with the sufferings of the Russians? I doubt it. Think of our sympathy for the persecution of the Jews in the early days of Hitler. It seems that now the response to suffering is dead. Peter Quennell was saying the other day that he was surprised at the apathy of the people over the Russian war news on which, after all, our skins depend and that the fall of Moscow would hardly make people buy an "extra." We have long ceased to find the war thrilling – any excitement in the movement of historic events is gone. There is a vague but persistent worry in people's minds about the coming air raids this winter, but like everything else this is accepted as inevitable. The truth is that the war has become as much a part of our lives as the weather, the endless winter, and when the ice does break there will be no cheering in the streets.

So far as I know we have only one fascist poet in England – Roy Campbell – and his poetry is worth reading not only as poetry but as fascism. It is full of vitality, blazing with heat and colour. He is a Catholic and a romantic. He rides a high horse and takes you for some splendid gallops although he comes some bad croppers. The croppers in taste and feeling are mostly the result of showing off – for the poet rams his legend down the reader's throat. He is the gay and spirited cowboy herding on the plains of Castile with a rose between his teeth and a song in his heart and cocking snooks the while at the suburban "Charlies" as they trot obediently to their city offices. Such uninhibited posturing takes us back to the early days of the Romantic movement when every man was his own Byron. All the same it is rather refreshing to find someone with the spirit to cut such capers, and if Campbell has a touch of Byronic silliness he has a touch of Byronic fire too. For the man is a poet and his poetry strikes sparks. It is easy to see his faults, his damn "picturesqueness," his blatancies, and his lack of discrimination. The first poems in the series called *Mithraic Emblems* are his most careful works and some of them are magnificent. In the second poem "The Solar Enemy" he sweeps into his stride.

> Enemy of my inward night
> And victor of its bestial signs
> Whose arm against the Bull designs
> The red veronicas of light:
> Your cape a roaring gale of gold
> The scarlet of its outward fold
> Is of a dawn beyond the world.

24 November 1941.

Visited by my familiar devils which I fondly thought I had exorcised. I do not know what brings on these attacks when I am reduced almost to idiocy by ridiculous nervous compulsions, tics, obsessions, and all manner of foolishness. I used to think they were brought on by living "too chaste" but that can hardly be the case at the moment. Or it may be discovered when they have my brain in a bucket that there has been some recurrent form of pressure on it.

My finances are in a bad way which means dining alone in clubs and missing good chances. Now is the time for culture to come to the rescue and fill up the void. She seems to come on lame feet.

Went with Miriam to a party given by Lady Victor Paget for Bea Lillie.[1] Noël Coward sang "London Pride" in a manner which I found all the more revolting for being sincere. There was a gathering of pansies and theatrical blondes interspersed with Lord S. and latest girl-friend and Hore-Belisha[2] – an obscene spectacle. Old Lady Crewe[3] having a "diplomatic" conversation with the Counsellor of the Washington Embassy. David Herbert[4] looking more *racé* than he knew. General atmosphere: a réchauffé of a gay twenties party with everyone looking that much older and trying to get back something which is not there any more.

29 November 1941.

Weekend at Miriam Rothschild's at Ashton. Miriam is becoming a friend – she certainly has no time for me in any other capacity.

She was talking about her cousin Baron Louis's imprisonment by the Nazis in Vienna. He was kept in solitary confinement in a space four feet by six feet. His glasses were taken away from him and he was not given anything to read. He was not ill-treated physically. Almost

---

[1] Beatrice Lillie was in London after touring with E.N.S.A. entertaining the forces.

[2] Leslie Hore-Belisha had been Minister for War from May 1937 until January 1940. He held no office in the Coalition Government.

[3] Daughter of Lord Rosebery, wife of the former British Ambassador in Paris.

[4] Second son of the 15th Earl of Pembroke. He served in the Navy during the war.

every day some neighbouring prisoner was taken away and shot, and he was continually expecting to be the next. One thing that worried him was that he was never able to make out how the Germans' minds worked. For instance, they legalized every step they took to deprive him of his fortune in the most tortuous manner instead of just grabbing it. One day a whole string of lawyers came into his cell laden with account books. He thought, "Now it has come – they want me to sign something which will show that I have been swindling the shareholders." The lawyers said, "We regret to inform you that there has been a swindle in your affairs." "Yes," he replied, "I know. Who have I swindled?" "No, Baron, it is you who have been robbed." Then they explained to him in detail how one of his agents in Germany had been cheating him. The lawyers then went away leaving him baffled that when they were robbing him they should take the trouble to show him that someone else had been cheating him.

One day Himmler was announced in the cell. He came in, sat down and after a few platitudes said, looking around at the absolutely bare cell with nothing in it but a palliasse and a chair, "Now is there anything you want?" "No," said Baron Louis, "but what I should like to know is why I am here." Himmler's face clouded – looking at him coldly he left the room without a word of reply. Three or four days later a parcel arrived for Baron Louis from Himmler. It contained a pink satin eiderdown for his bed. (This is pure surrealism.)

There was a Belgian Jewish banker staying at Ashton. He and Miriam talked about their connections and friends on the Continent. They have cousins in every capital in Europe. I got an impression as they talked of the international *haute juiverie* of the days before the Nazis – energetic, experimental, cultivated, sensual people, fond of sport and pleasure and by far the best educated aristocracy the world has ever seen. He struck me as an almost sentimental idealist who would change once he got into his bank into a steely intelligence. He is now serving in the Belgian army. There was also a young Hungarian who was in the Pioneer Corps. He said bitterly, "I am not allowed to have the honour to fight the Nazis although I hate them worse than any Englishman." I do not like what I hear about the Pioneer Corps. It seems to be officered by a poor type of English officer who has been a flop in his own regiment. Half the NCOs are English – half are foreign. He says the English NCOs are the bad lot who have been got rid of out of their own regiments.

4 December 1941.

Elizabeth has been telling me how she goes about writing a novel. She talked about *The Death of the Heart*. I see the two women in *The Death of the Heart* as the two halves of Elizabeth. – Portia has the naïveté of childhood – or genius. She is the hidden Elizabeth. The other woman is Elizabeth as an outside hostile person might see her. But all this is my own surmise and not what she told me. She said that besides this Eddie–Portia theme there was a second situation – that of the poor unworldly girl who comes lonely with her pathetic trunk containing all the things she owns to live in the house of grand relations. Portia is in the position of the governess in *Jane Eyre*.

Baudelaire quotes Edgar Allan Poe who said that no one would dare write a book called *My Heart Laid Bare* which was true to its title because "the paper would shrivel and blaze at every touch of the fiery pen." That is not quite what I am afraid of. My pen is not, alas, fiery. I am afraid to face my own smallness.

Elizabeth says that T. S. Eliot told her that without alcohol he could never have got in the mood for his poems. That is good news!

George Ignatieff[1] was talking today about the "German smell." He remembers that smell in the changing room at Amsterdam when he was playing hockey against a German team. He says it comes from their gross eating of coarse heavy meats.

4 December 1941.

Thinking over what I have written. What a pack of lies intimate journals are, particularly if one tries too hard to be truthful.

This autumn has been curiously characterless. After being the centre of the world's stage London has become unexciting. As soon as

---

[1] Then a member of staff at Canada House, subsequently Canadian Ambassador to the U.N. and the N.A.T.O. His elder brother Nicholas was in the Russian and Scandinavian section of British Military Intelligence, and was chief of M.I.3C, 1943 to 1945.

Russia was invaded and the direct threat diverted, the temperature of the town went down. We are not as heroic, desperate, and gay as we were last winter. London seems drab. The tension is removed – the anxiety remains.

7 December 1941.

The attack on Pearl Harbor has caused very human sardonic satisfaction to everyone I have happened to see today. This will take the Americans by the scruff of the neck and bounce them into the war. The picture is that of an over-cautious boy balancing on the edge of a diving-board running forward two steps and back three and then a tough bully comes along and gives him a kick in the backside right into the water! And only yesterday they were still hovering, saying they felt almost sure they might back us up if the Japanese attacked the Kra Peninsula, but they would feel happier if we could give a guarantee of the territorial integrity of Thailand before we invaded its territories. The President had a hot tip that the Japanese objective was Rangoon – but, lo and behold! it was Pearl Harbor. For years I have seen movies of United States reconnaissance planes ("the eyes and ears of the U.S. Navy," as the announcers portentously described them) circling away from the U.S. base at Pearl Harbor to spy out the Pacific for just such an attempt as this. What were they doing when those five aircraft carriers sneaked up close enough to disgorge those planes? Mr. Massey says, "They have been living in a Hollywood world of unreality." We listened to Roosevelt's address to Congress on the wireless in Mr. Massey's big office at Canada House under the great glass chandelier – the room where he told us of the declaration of war on Germany. Roosevelt was moving and had dropped his mannerisms. He sounded profoundly shocked and bitterly angry. His speech was exactly right.

At the Admiralty they suggest, "Why not a British naval adviser on every American battleship." At first the news of American unpreparedness and its results was an immense *soulagement* of a long-stored, carefully restrained grudge in this country, but when the number of U.S. battleships sunk began to come in an Admiralty official said, "This is getting past a joke." I have not heard one word of sympathy for the United States here. The note of outraged American indignation at the treachery of which the U.S.A. has been a victim meets with no real echo here. It is like a hardened old tart who hears a girl crying because a man has deceived her for the first time. We have become very much accustomed to treachery – now let the Americans learn the facts of life and see how they like them.

We Canadians feel all the same that once the Americans have got over the initial shock they will get on the band-wagon and will get into the war one hundred per cent and be producing tanks, planes, etc., by the million when the Japs are finished. The English have no real faith in the United States. Now it is our business to begin boosting the Americans here.

17 December 1941.

Reading Peter Quennell's *Byron in Italy*. This is the irresistible Byron of the letters and of the early cantos of *Don Juan*. I can hardly imagine any man, certainly any young man, reading Byron's letters from Italy to Hobhouse and Kinnaird without loving the writer. I do not know if a woman would be so delighted with them. I doubt it. One could hardly blame them, for no man can read about Byron without having his own egoism reinforced and without experiencing a frantic desire to show off and to find a woman to show off before. This deleterious influence at one time swept the entire European continent. But alas, what puny creatures we all are beside the Great Originals. Hamlet and Byron – the modern world is unthinkable without them.

I enjoy my walks to the office in the mornings – the elegance of Grosvenor Street, the Maisons de Haute Couture, behind their ageing façades, Jacqmar's interior seen through the long plate-glass windows with the soignées salesgirls drifting about among the lengths of patterned silk. It looks as a temple of fashion should look – dimly lit and solemn, but luxurious – a proper place to stir the imagination of the passing woman. Oh God, leave us our luxuries even if we must do without our necessities. Let Cartiers and the Ritz be restored to their former glories. Let houseparties burgeon once more in the stately homes in England. Restore the vintage port to the clubs and the old brown sherry to the colleges. Let us have pomp and luxury, painted jezebels and scarlet guardsmen, – rags and riches rubbing shoulders. Give us back our bad, old world.

21 December 1941.

Stayed in bed in my new flannel pyjamas reading Byron's letters with a Christmas fog outside. I had not the will-power even to change the water in which Elizabeth's flowers were dying. I liked the picture of Byron's life at Ravenna playing with his animals writing to his friends, or sitting before the fire remembering the past which weighed heavily on him with Proustian power. I like the sketch of him yawning in the fog in Bennet Street on just such a day as this. I walked down Bennet Street today past where his lodgings used to be before they were destroyed in the last reprisal blitz.

Elizabeth came to tea in her smart black coat with a pink flower in her buttonhole. She lay on the sofa as she likes to do in an oddly elegant and relaxed pose. She never sprawls – mentally or physically. Her long, high-bred, handsome face was pink from the outside damp. She had on her gold chains and bangles.

On the way home tonight Raymond Mortimer said to me, "Oh Elizabeth, she has such charm and is so kind and makes most of one's friends seem irremediably vulgar."

28 December 1941.

Just back from Christmas – the Sitwells' at Weston – my favourite house – fire in the bedroom with a view of a piece of lawn with conifer-shaped shrubs. White frost on Christmas day. We sang carols in the family pew in the stone, stone cold of the little church. It was only the family – Sachie, Georgia, and their son, Reresby, at home from Eton. At the moment I am happier with them than anybody. My sadness and staleness went away. Sachie is sensitive, lovable, and very funny – an ageless creature. He does not seem any older than his four-teen-year-old son. He has altogether escaped pomposity and has no desire to impress. The boy looks seventeen but he seems, too, no particular age and can talk about anything that comes along, but yet is a spontaneous, excitable child. Georgia sparks all talk with her wit and warmth and looks a young beauty. There is a magic about the place that must be distilled in some mysterious manner by Sachie.

1942

11 January 1942.

Elizabeth came to see me in the morning and brought me a cyclamen.

She talked about women's friendships, apropos of Virginia Woolf and her niece and Jane Austen and her niece, Fanny Knight. She says that every young woman has such friendships and that the older woman puts into them all the lyrical, poetic side of her nature and that she lives her youth again. The girl finds so much pleasure in being seen through the eyes of love and admiration that she may have a flirtation with a man simply for the pleasure of telling the other woman about it. This is all quite apart from Lesbianism.

The river in the park was frozen today, and the gulls slid on the ice, looking as if they were doing it for fun, although it probably annoyed them. There was a wintry sun, what, for the lack of a nearer word for the colour, is called an orange sun.

I had an embarrassing dinner with the Masseys. She was irritable and he was making Balliol answers to her haphazard remarks and beginning his sentences with, "But, my dear." I did not know what to say or where to look, as my unfortunate face always gives me away. She said, "You have a very guilty look this evening." I should have answered, "I always look guilty when anything unpleasant is said, even if I am in no way responsible for it." It is an idiotic characteristic, but I cannot help it.

13 January 1942.

Miriam and I were talking about love. I said that the words "Do you love me?" said earnestly had a putting-off effect. Miriam said that on the contrary – this repetitious earnestness is a very good line for women. I said, "But it is such a bore." She said, "Look how often it works with a man."

The sheets are cold and I have just drunk two glasses of ice-cold barley water – emblem of chastity.

20 January 1942.

I am reading *Tristan et Iseult*, the story reconstructed by Joseph Bédier from twelfth-century sources. It is giving me as much pleasure as it used to give the inhabitants of draughty, medieval castles when it was recited or sung to them by passing troubadours. It has the same variety of incident and lack of proportion as the scenes in old tapestries in which some detail in the foreground – a dog or a group of flowers – has interested the artist so much that it crowds out the knights and the castle. It is certainly one of the most enjoyable books I have come across.

They have taken my chairs and sofa away to have them covered in "off-white" (as the manageress calls it). Meanwhile I have a temporary sofa which looks as if it belonged in an undergraduate's room at Oxford.

Elizabeth and I dined at Claridge's. She was in an easy and cheerful mood. She said, "I would like to put you in a novel," looking at me through half-closed eyes in a suddenly detached way like a painter looking at a model. "You probably would not recognize yourself." "I am sure I wouldn't," I lied.

A red-haired young man came up to me in Claridge's and said, "I have met you somewhere before." Neither of us could think where or how. He kept on coming back to our table while we were dining and suggesting clues which led nowhere. "Was it playing tennis in Surrey or dining with mutual friends in Cambridge?" In the end I remembered it was on a Sunday afternoon when I was staying with the Fullertons. He played Chopin in the drawing-room while we all sat around on chairs draped in dust-covers. There was a thick mist outside – we sat listening to him until dinner-time and after dinner he did ingenious and boring parlour tricks. Since then he has been shot down in an airplane, lost a lung, and gets six pounds and six shillings a week disability allowance. I think he must have landed on his head. He has a wild look in his eye.

22 January 1942.

Dined with Elizabeth at her house. She always manages to have unheard-of quantities of smoked salmon. The house was so cold that we put the electric heater on a chair so as to have it on a level with our bodies. Elizabeth was wearing a necklace and bracelet of gold and red of the kind of glass that Christmas tree ornaments are made of. Some woman friend had given them to her – she considered Elizabeth to be "a Byzantine type." She had on a white silk jacket over a black dress. We sat on the sofa and talked.

23 January 1942.

I feel that this country cannot – in the end – escape the European civil war. My friends seem to me to be waiting offstage to take up their parts. James Peel is going to be the out-of-work ex-officer trained in methods of violence (and yet the most kindly creature), an adventurer and a patriot. There are other friends of mine of the same stamp mostly now employed in Military Intelligence who might qualify for a post-war secret police. My role is indicated – the diplomat who hangs on until the last moment, feeling it his duty to defend his country's actions right or wrong, reluctant to give up his career.

26 January 1942.

Fascinated by the Tristan and Iseult legend. I have been reading Swinburne's "Tristan in Lyonesse." It is much too heavily upholstered, the passion is stifled in ninetyish verbiage. Occasionally a line strikes – Laurence Binyon is better with the same subject. But his last dialogue between Tristan and Iseult is flat. Nothing so far touches the twelfth-century French legend.

27 January 1942.

Heard the Prime Minister defend the Government's conduct of the war in the House. It was the greatest speech I have ever heard. For an hour and a half he developed the central theme of the grand strategy of the war and at recurrent intervals sounded the note of his own desire for a vote of confidence from the House. It was an orchestral performance, lesser motifs interspersed were all handled with the same easy strength. To read it would be to lose half of it – the implications in his slightest side-glance were significant.

One small thing that struck me before the Prime Minister got up to speak was the reception given to a question asked by a Labour M.P. as to why certain people were still allowed to have three or four domestic servants in their employ. The question was greeted with ironical laughter from Conservative M.P.s, the implication of the laughter being that there were no such persons. The Cabinet Minister who answered the question pooh-poohed it and said that he could not accept that such a situation existed. "Of course not," laughed the Conservative M.P.s scornfully. Yet they must have known as well as I do (better, since most of them no doubt have still got three or four domestic servants of their own) that in any country house you choose to go into there are still domestic servants in threes and fours. A small thing but typical.

George Ignatieff is shocked that behind closed doors in the War Office the MI boys express the hope that the Russians will be defeated and that *three days* later the German army itself will collapse. It is and has been all along the ideal British solution. The Russians know this as well as we do. It is the obvious reason for the so-called "mysterious peasant suspicions" of our Soviet allies. But it is not a state of opinion peculiar to this country. You would get just the same reaction in Ankara, Vichy, Rome, Madrid, Stockholm, in the State Department and in Wall Street.

29 January 1942.

Dined last night in the Guardroom at St. James's Palace, a pleasant eighteenth-century white-panelled small dining-room. The lights were turned out during the whole of dinner. Candlelight from heavy Victorian candelabra and firelight. A perfect example of a Guards colonel passing the port says, "Will you try some of this Grocer's Blood?" It was port of a kind you never taste these days. Politics consisted of railing at Hore-Belisha (of course, they say his real name is Horeb-Elisha). "If they put him back at the War Office I personally would lead a meeting at the head of the regiment and go and kick the little bugger out." Around the table the young subalterns, a nice crowd most of them lately from Oxford, more interested and intelligent than the peacetime Guards officer. One of them when the subject of genealogy was being discussed (his name was Cayzer) said something about his family's claim to be descended from Julius Caesar, and in quite an inoffensive boyish way he said, "I believe the descent was quite well established." "Nonsense," said the colonel, "Your uncle paid the College of Heralds five hundred pounds to say so." A very English evening.

5 February 1942.

Mr. Massey signed the Agreement for Exchange of Consuls between Canada and the U.S.S.R. at the Soviet Embassy. I had forgotten to provide for a seal so we had nothing to seal with on behalf of Canada. Otherwise everything went well. I feel I have played some part in getting this Agreement safely signed. Did my best to get into the press photographs. Actual signing was in the drawing-room full of yellow silk-covered chairs, with daffodils in a vase in the embrasure of the window and snow outside. Talked with S. of the Tass Agency and he said the war could be over this year if

(a) We and the United States gave the Russians enough tanks and planes so that they could finish the job themselves, or

(b) We would start an offensive in Europe.

What was happening in the Far East was tragic but it did not matter in the long run if Germany could be knocked out. We must go for the weakest link in the chain. Afterwards we and "perhaps my country" (i.e. the U.S.S.R.) could go for Japan and finish her off.

Elizabeth has gone to Ireland. Miss her even more than last time. I am getting dependent on her.

10 February 1942.

Lunch at the Royal Empire Society for a leading lady of the ATS. She made a speech afterwards about ATS work. I thought her a detestable woman, a hard-bitten clever careerist. Reminds me of the manageress of these flats. She has a soft voice and a piquant manner calculated to go over big with cabinet ministers and generals.

Dined at the Conservative Club. Gossip about Stalin – they say he wishes Cripps would not come and bore him by talking communism to him.[1] Stalin hates bores but takes a great interest in the Windsor–Simpson story. He cannot understand why Mrs. Simpson was not liquidated.

16 February 1942.

Maisky, the Soviet Ambassador, to lunch – very amiable with an amusing attractive face. Madame Maisky won the Masseys' heart by taking an interest in the claret and talking about the days of her courtship in Omsk. When they left the Masseys subscribed to the opinion that they were "a dear little couple."

17 February 1942.

A cold wind blowing all the dust in the streets. I went down to the House of Commons to hear the Prime Minister make his speech on the escape of the *Gneisenau* and *Scharnhorst*.[2] The House in an agitated and restive mood, a series of short speeches and questions. A fumbling about for a voice in which to express the wish for a new deal. A fag-endish, nervous, inconclusive semi-debate, the rattling together of dry twigs that only wanted a flaming voice to stir them into a blaze of public indignation. The Prime Minister, strained and tired, keeping his voice low and being very patient and restrained in a perfectly obvious manner like a parent dealing with naughty children and determined not to lose his temper. The control snapped when he spoke of the House being in a mood of "anger and panic." At the word panic an angry wave of protests spread through the House.

27 February 1942.

Dinner with George Ignatieff and a friend of his, an instructor from Harvard. If the Russians win and Europe is Sovietized, at least

---

[1] Sir Stafford Cripps, left-wing Labour former Solicitor-General, had been British Ambassador to Russia since 1940. A few days after this entry was written he was recalled from Moscow to become Lord Privy Seal.

[2] These two German battle-cruisers had been stuck in Brest from March 1941 until they escaped through the English Channel on 12 February, despite the RAF and the Royal Navy.

to the Rhine, the English socialists will want a socialist England to join up in some sort of federal union with the countries of the "New Europe." On the other hand, the governing class here pin their hopes more and more on the United States. Which way will England go? If history and geography can be relied on, I should say with Europe, and what about Canada? Probably under the United States' umbrella, where some of our professors of economics have been telling us for years we ought to be. I cannot imagine going back to the old small-town Canada with its narrow, intense, local interests and sitting down under it again.

My brother Roley's mess is a depressing place.[1] They live in slum conditions – they have taken over an ugly, characterless country house in Sussex. The mess is beaver-boarded – I suppose to protect the panelling – not a picture on the walls, just dirty beaver-board. Three uncovered dirty old sofas, each adorned with the person of a pot-bellied, bored, senior Canadian officer in a recumbent position, with a glass of brassy whisky in hand. A few hard wooden chairs with younger and equally bored officers seated on them.

Politics have caught up with me at last. Here I am reading G. D. H. Cole in preference to Rimbaud. (Rimbaud's phrases are time-fuse bombs – I read them without understanding and their meaning explodes later in my mind.)

3 March 1942.

Elizabeth was discussing her method of writing the other night. She says that when she is writing a scene for the first time she always throws in all the descriptive words that come to her mind. She over-does the situation, puts in everything which will heighten the effect she wants to get, like, as she says, someone doing clay modelling, who smacks on handfuls of clay before beginning to cut away and doing fine modelling. Then afterwards she cuts down and discards and whittles away. The neurotic part of writing, she says, is the temptation to stop for the exact word or the most deliberate analysis of the situation when one should hurry, get the general effect and then come back and write over, but sometimes one gets stuck like a needle in the

---

[1] He was now stationed with the Canadian army in Sussex.

groove of a gramophone record and cannot stop going over and over one point.

She says that characters must not be made to say things which fit into situations intellectually conceived beforehand. The best writers of dialogue in English, she thinks, are Jane Austen and E. M. Forster in *Howards End*.

Sat with Miriam in her room at Claridge's while her maid curled and brushed her hair – felt like a French abbé in an eighteenth-century boudoir print.

I wish I could get a job for Mrs. Elliott Smith – poor old girl. I think one should do one's best to provide for one's friends if one is in office. I cannot bear the assumption of impersonality by civil servants. I am all for nepotism and jobs arranged over the luncheon table by feminine influence, etc., etc. – provided it is not at my expense. Still I would take a chance on that.

7 March 1942.

For some time now I seem to be getting more and more greedy about food. It may be partly due to having considerably less to eat, but the way I wolfed my food at the Masseys' tonight was rather too much. What a curious and fascinating character Mr. Massey has – that blend of acuteness and superficiality. He has enormous susceptibility to more phoney forms of charm. What he loves in life is delicatezza – the pleasant surface style. He is a puzzling person because behind his London *Times* leading article official views and his carefully polished manner there lurks an ironic appreciation of things as they are and of himself as he is. When he has a decision to make – disappointingly – he always decides in favour of the conventional. His charm is remarkable. It springs, as charm so often does, from his own insecurity. He is painfully easy to hurt or ruffle and full of *prévenances* for the feelings of others if he happens to like them. If not, he is ruthless. Sometimes I have been stifled by the too strong atmosphere of the Masseys' love of power, but I am very fond of them and diverted by them. Their relationship to each other is the most admirable thing about them. I never expect to have another chief who is so personally sympathetic – after all, I share so many of his weaknesses. His critics may have a great deal on their side, but he is so much more interesting as a personality than they are.

6 April 1942.

Weekend in the country. Nancy Mitford staying there – witty in a high-pitched, restless way, clever, and giving off that impression of courage which some people convey even when making small talk around a tea-table. She belongs to the world of Evelyn Waugh's novels and to the set of which Evelyn Waugh is a member. They have a definite tone of their own. They are all now in their thirties or early forties and were the bright young things of the 1920s. Except for one or two who have become Roman Catholic or Communist they are as bored by religion as they ever were. In the arts they admire Baroque and Regency (in architecture cathedrals and Tudor beams are their aversion), Mozart in music, in literature anything that shows style and exuberance – nothing that is soulful, formless, or introspective. In love as in conversation a flavour of insolence is appreciated. With both sexes the thing admired is to do what you want just as long as you want to and not a moment longer. Hence the speed with which people change partners in this game, which requires a good eye, a cool nerve, and a capacity to take punishment as in any other kind of sport. Toughness is the favourite virtue. Any form of cry-babyishness (wistful yearnings, hopeless passions, plain self-pity) is taboo except among pansies, in whom it is recognized as an innate characteristic which does not affect their essential toughness. In this little world almost none are stupid. Some have "dumb" husbands or wives whose excuse for existence is that they are rich, good-looking, or superlatively bed-worthy. There are also a few "holy idiots" tolerated who are "rather sweet" and who are often rich and sometimes American and who pay the bill. Their gossip is so frank, so abundant, and so detailed it is a wonder that their lives are not even more complicated than they are. Discretion is looked upon as a paltry virtue like thrift. Their closest friends' reputations are ripped to pieces at the tops of their voices usually in a restaurant. Among themselves they practise a mixture of delicate sympathy and charming attention, alternating with dive-bombing attacks of brutal frankness. Rows are frequent but seldom lasting. They stick by each other in misfortune with the loyalty the English usually show to their friends.

13 April 1942.

I am reading *Barometer Rising*, Hugh MacLennan's book about the Halifax Explosion.[1] It is the first time that anyone has succeeded in giving the feeling of the town and the poetry peculiar to the place, the dreariness and yet the fascination of those fogbound days when the town is smothered and shut in, half asleep, half in a slow trance, snow running in the gutters, horses on the cobblestones of Water Street, the sound of trains whining over the uneven rails, the recurrent melancholy of the foghorn, the feeling of the sea – February in Halifax, Nova Scotia.

In the afternoon I went with Elizabeth to Hampstead. On the way back, walking through Keats Grove and the quiet French provincial streets full of flowering shrubs, Elizabeth talked about Virginia Woolf, saying how tall and graceful she looked wearing some flowing dress of mauve or grey. Elizabeth said she had a sort of "fairy cruelty" but she did not know how much she could hurt. There were many forms of being hurt about which she knew nothing. She had never been humiliated herself although she used half jokingly to say how shy she was and that she could never go into a room full of strange people without feeling that they thought her odd. In fact, she had always lived in a sort of Chinese world of intelligent, complicated people who had made a cult of her. From that world she never issued – she led a guarded life.

Elizabeth met a female admirer last night at dinner who said to her, "To meet you is like meeting Christ."

14 April 1942.

Dined with the Masseys – Margot Asquith was the big attraction. I was amazed – I had expected her to be pretty gaga and to have the depressing job of trying to reconstruct the original from among

---

[1] A French ship, carrying 3,000 tons of explosives, collided with a Norwegian vessel in Halifax harbour on 6 December 1917 and devastated about one-tenth of the city.

the ruins, instead of which I am inclined to agree with Mr. Massey that she is still the best woman or perhaps man conversationalist in England. What put her on her form was the presence of Sir Andrew Duncan, the Minister of Supply, who was there. She arrived in full war-paint, crossed swords with him at the close of the fish course, and carried on a duel all evening. Her enjoyment of her own skill is still infectious. Her vanity is stridently insistent, but she has a streak of humility – a sort of refreshing honesty running through all her boasting. I believe she is considered an old nuisance, but I think she is a phenomenon. She brought with her a protégé, a boring German Jew editor. She said she brought him because he was such a remarkable man that she wanted the Masseys to meet him, but he hardly got a word in and looked, I thought, slightly bitter about it. He has probably had a good dose of Margot, who is obviously like all these entertaining Edwardian relics an impossible woman at close quarters.

I must add that we each had a filet mignon for dinner – one week's meat ration for three people! How?

16 April 1942.

David Cecil had dinner at Elizabeth's. I was charmed by him, his quick responsive flicks of attention, his irony and his wit, his contempt for the middle-brow, the snob, and the inflated personality. At one point in talk he said, "One does not often have to put one's foot down, but I feel it is useful to have a Foot to Put Down." I like him and Cyril Connolly best of Elizabeth's literary friends.

Later in the evening Stephen Tennant came in. He and David had a lovely little conversation – effusive, sprightly, and prickly.

Lunched with Anne-Marie at Claridge's. She looked pure Paris. When I asked her how she did it she replied that first, she always dressed her age (forty-nine), never a year younger and that gave her an extra five years' margin, second, she always wore black, and thirdly, she attended to detail. She said that every Englishwoman should be presented with three more clothes-brushes than she has at present and told how to use them. Her territory at the country house where she is living with rich friends has been invaded by a parasitic bugger called Mr. Midge. Anne-Marie says that he has "cried his way out of the army."

30 April 1942.

Dined with the Masseys off salmon-trout and asparagus. Mrs. Ronnie Greville was there – sitting up in a bath chair with her feet dangling on to a footstool. Her small hands covered with diamonds, and with her painted face – she looked like a monstrous baby – something in *grand guignol*. This was also the impression given by her having only one eye – the other is dead and blind – and that one eye raked the table round – illuminated by intelligent malice. The conversation was on a royal plane during a great deal of dinner, highly aristocratic titbits of scandal. (Lady Y who has run away with the groom. Lord X who has eloped with his stepmother.) Resigned prophecy that Cripps will be the next Prime Minister. The old girl is kept alive by her sleepless snobbery, her still unquenchable zest for the great world. She is a lowland Scot, and the lowland Scot from Boswell on is the most insatiable animal on earth when it comes to worldly glitter and bustle. I should know – I am one.

10 May 1942.

Yesterday was a day of flowers. The tulips are out in St. James's Park – they are at their time of perfection – not one has fallen out of the ranks. Three unattractive little girls were picking the faded bluebells that grew on the bank above me and stuffing them into a shabby leather handbag that must have belonged to one of their mothers. It irritates me that since the railings have gone people pick the flowers and trample the grass in the parks until it becomes hard dry earth. The lilac is out. It gives me a feeling of urgency – its time is so short – only about a fortnight.

Something of the panic of middle age is coming over me. It is the bald spot beginning on the back of my head. This morning I combed the longer hair from the sides back over the place where it is thin. I felt as if I were adjusting a wig which the wind might blow out of place. I seem surrounded by nice but ugly girls.

19 May 1942.

Went to the House to hear Attlee on the war situation. He treated the House to an insulting meagre string of platitudes. The Members were impatient and rather badly behaved like schoolboys when the headmaster is away and a weak under-master is temporarily in charge. L., who is in the Dominions Office says, "I now serve under Attlee who would be ideally suited as an assistant manager of a bank in a small town in the south of England."

Margot Asquith waylaid me in the passage outside the gallery wearing a green tulle dress and a brown fur hat, her make-up dashed on with a careless hand, rather gaga – but only when the wind blows nor-nor-west.

24 May 1942.

A perfect May day. Elizabeth and I went to Kew. It is hardly worth my while to describe the scene or dwell upon the dreamlike state in which we drifted among ravines of rhododendrons and azaleas. It was a day like a page from one of her books, the involved relationship between the two people who are wandering among the flower beds. They sit together on a bench to look across the narrow muddy Thames at the set-piece of Syon House and discuss projects of happiness, voyages they may never take, childhood, but never Love. There is sun and then a shower – they take shelter under the green tent of a weeping willow and go together through the modest, white-panelled rooms of Kew Palace where hang the framed embroideries of dead princesses. Then tea among the devitalized inhabitants of Kew in a room full of small tables each with its white tablecloth and its groups of whispering, mumbling people who are bound by some spell not to raise their voices, not to laugh, and not to gesticulate. At moments I could see Elizabeth peering about her – her head a little back, her eyes half closed (how affected it sounds – how utterly unaffected the gesture was) focusing on the memories of the place.

Elizabeth has been going to an Austrian psychoanalyst to be cured of her stammer (which is so much part of her). So far it seems to me that she has told him nothing while he has told her the story of his life. This hardly surprises me.

25 May 1942.

My feelings are mixed when I read speeches like that of Wallace in the United States – "this is the century of the common man." Apparently we are to devote ourselves after the war to bringing the blessings of mass production, hygienic American civilization, and American uniformity and materialism to the world.

26 May 1942.

I had lunch with Nancy Mitford. She fluted away in her light, modish voice, being amusing and looking so distinguished with her beautiful head and thin arms. She says there is no use speculating on what will come out of Europe after the war because no one dreamt of fascism twenty years ago and something equally unexpected is brewing now. Yet one ought to have anticipated fascism – all the signposts were there and had been for the previous one hundred years. I had drinks with Billy Coster – his politics are wonderful. He blames everything on "Mr. Morrison, the Duke of Bedford, and the Archbishop of Canterbury"[1] and thinks it would be possible with the scientific use of gas and the RAF to exterminate at least fifty per cent of the German people.

2 June 1942.

I went to see Elizabeth this afternoon and found her standing on the balcony of her sitting-room that looks over Regent's Park. The tall, cool room is full of mirrors and flowers and books. She wants to dedicate her next novel to me. I hope she will, and that it will be her best.

Later we walked out into Regent's Park. It was a blazing June day – we sat on the bank by the canal watching the swans "in slow indignation," as she says, go by.

Of what is her magic made? What is the spell that she has cast on me? At first I was wary of her – "*méfiant*" – I feared that I should expose my small shifts and stratagems to her eye which misses nothing. Her uncanny intuitions, her flashes of insight like summer lightning at once fascinated and disturbed me. Now day by day I have been discovering more and more of her generous nature, her wit and funniness, the stammering flow of her enthralling talk, the idiosyncrasies, vagaries of her temperament. I now know that this attachment is nothing transient but will bind me as long as I live.

---

[1] Herbert Morrison, Labour Home Secretary in the Coalition Government, had been a pacifist in 1914–18; 12th Duke of Bedford, pacifist with sympathies for fascism; William Temple, Archbishop of Canterbury.

5 June 1942.

Some slightly drunk and defiantly cheerful American soldiers were piling into a taxi tonight in Berkeley Square shouting and in general throwing their weight about. Surprised looks on the faces of two elderly English gentlemen of military bearing who were waiting to cross the square – an "old-fashioned look" – contempt concealed by policy.

11 June 1942.

Dined at Nesta's – J. was there. I drew him out to see what his line is at the moment and he gave me my money's worth. He says that Russia will be defeated this summer which he thinks is highly desirable. After that we and America will defeat an exhausted Germany. He thinks that is the secret plan of the War Cabinet. There would be two stages in Germany's defeat, the first will be that the German General Staff will get rid of Hitler and offer peace and to liberate the occupied countries. He says that the masses in the occupied countries do not hate the Germans – it is only the intellectuals. Hatred of the Germans would disappear if their troops were actually withdrawn, etc. His immediate concern is that the British people should be warned of the approaching collapse of Russia. He asked me what my reaction to the fall of Moscow would be. I said, "Blank dismay and discouragement but not despair." "Ah," he said, "that is what I am afraid people's reaction would be." I might have asked him if he expected me to hang out flags in the street. I do not say the man is a German agent but his line of talk, though a farrago of nonsense, is about the best a German agent in England could produce at the present time. I do not think it would be at all a bad thing to lock him up. I think it is monstrous that he should still be printing his bloody pamphlet. He gave me a lift home in his ostentatious Rolls-Royce, which must be the only one of its kind left in London and which is usually parked outside Claridge's or the Ritz.

13 June 1942.

Worked all afternoon on my dispatch about the future organization of Europe, application of the Atlantic Charter, the treatment of Germany after the war, etc. I have almost decided not to send this dispatch at all. I think it would be too vague to be useful or interesting.

Dined with Elizabeth. Drank a lot of red wine. Who could help becoming attached to her?

23 June 1942.

This morning was interesting because the work was about something that really may matter – the control of trans-Atlantic airways now and after the war and the part that Canada should play. Had lunch with the new Dominions Office appointee to Canada. He must be as sick of meeting me at lunch as I am certainly sick of meeting him. Mentally and socially he is a permanent pre-last-war subaltern in a not too good line regiment. What a man to send to Ottawa to cope with that little group of bristling professional Canadian nationalists who would welcome him as a heaven-sent confirmation of all they have ever said about the Old School Tie! The anti-British members of the Canadian intelligentsia will never be happy until they have pulled down the Old England of Tradition and can dance on its grave. He is the sort of Englishman who makes one understand why.

28 June 1942.

Pierre Dupuy came to pay me a visit. What an enjoyable war that little man is having! He exudes high politics and dark diplomacy. He is intelligent – yes – but nine-tenths of it is his capacity to put himself across. From being a dim little diplomat he has become an international figure – the only Canadian except for the Prime Minister whose name is known in Paris and Berlin political circles and in the inner circle in London.

Dined with the Masseys. Mrs. Greville rang up in the middle of dinner to say, "Winston must go – some of our friends are here with me and we all agree – go he must. I have known him for fifty years and he has never been right yet." Just the sort of party I should have thought would be sitting there in Claridge's spinning trivial but not harmless gossip.

10 August 1942.

Although there are no indications that we are winning the war, I feel that the Germans are committing suicide, that even if they won they would be incapable of profiting by their victory. They have not got what it takes to organize Europe and rule it as the British ruled India. They are not healthy in themselves. Perhaps they have too much imagination. The rebound from their tensed up national effort must be towards materialism, individualism, and a wish for the cosy and pleasurable. Once beaten they may not prove so hard to handle for the time being. People talk of the Dark Ages, of a reversion to semi-barbarism, but is that really possible? The dream of the masses everywhere is comfort – the American standard of living. It will be the same for the Germans. Once out of the iron circle of fear, hate, slaughter, and revenge they will turn passionately to materialism.

Dined at the St. James's Club among the remnants of the Diplomatic Corps. It was pleasant for a change to be back among the *chers collègues* – not an atmosphere in which ideas are encouraged certainly, but of anecdote, amiability, and polite enquiries about "so and so who was at Teheran or Washington at the same time I was." A feeling of complicity in belonging to a class or craft which has its own mysteries – although the initiates know these to be trivial. Outside the narrow windows a November-like gale tossed the trees in Green Park. From the walls the blank frames stared eyeless forth. The Club sent its pictures into retirement in the days of the Blitz. They have moved their funniest marble nymph from the foot of the stairs to the lavatory where she shares pride of place with a steel engraving of Paolo and Francesca whirling through space in their endless loves.

Talking of endless loves makes me think of Saturday night which was a grand catharsis – getting drunk, making love, spending more money than one can afford – things one should never regret. How innocent in comparison with the poisoned pleasures of boasting, showing off, giving false impressions or phoney confidences, or the wicked glooms of sterile introspection.

10 August 1942.

The waiter in these flats is trying to get me to give him one of my suits. He talks to me as though the revolution had already come. If it ever does, God defend me from the city hotel servants and all hangers-on of the rich, spoiled and eaten up with envy, full of dirty tricks and cruelty to each other. Gorky in one of his books suggests that the revolution should protect itself by bumping off such people.

Reading Rebecca West's book about Yugoslavia.[1] What the Croats felt about the Serbs is (I hope in a minor degree) what the French-Canadians feel about us. What the top-dogs cannot imagine or understand is the degree of resentment which the under-dogs feel. Because we know ourselves as Anglo-Canadians to be fairly mild and good-natured we feel injured that we can be so hardly thought of, but it is not only cruelty that people resent, it is unconsciousness, lack of insight, the bland shrug of incomprehension. The British are paying for this attitude now all over the world and we British-Canadians will pay for it with the French-Canadians in Canada before we are through.

19 August 1942.

Dined at the Allies' Club – afterwards a Polish exile played Chopin and jazz in the former Rothschild drawing-room. I sat next to a Polish Countess, a county family type (Polish version) – her country house has been burned down by the Germans, and her brother and his wife have been murdered by the Bolsheviks. As the pianist played a Polish peasant dance she said, "It is funny, but the last time I heard that tune was when I was dancing it over and over again with that Polish officer over there at home in Poland – and now we are both here."

Lunched with Anne-Marie by the open window at the Étoile in Charlotte Street. She arrived in a new summer dress, saying, "Imagine a Canadian soldier twenty-four years old but intelligent and a poet – he fell in love with me at first sight. Such a nice present on my fiftieth birthday. It has given me so much confidence."

Street fighting in Stalingrad – I heard the news at the St. James's Club where I dined with Archduke Robert, who seems to have loosened up and become less careful in manner. He has a love of fun underneath the Hapsburg reserve and *calcul.*

29 August 1942.

There is summer lightning tonight. At first I thought it was guns. I dined alone at the St. James's Club among diplomats and old prints – rather dreary.

---

[1] *Black Lamb and Grey Falcon*, which had just been published.

3 September 1942.

Anne-Marie's young soldier came to see me today about getting transferred from the army to something in which he could "use his power to create." He has written a poem about Canada "in six movements." I do not know what the hell I am supposed to do about it. Although he is an American with a Scottish name he looks like a half-breed Filipino with large and lustrous dark eyes and a pale pink tongue. He came in trailing clouds of Anne-Marie's extremely cloying perfume after him. He gave me an oration in deep and thrilling tones about his own genius. I could see he had made up his mind to make the biggest possible impression on me. He is such a bounder and so humourless that the poem may be some good. I could see how an older woman might find him touching. When he left he said he would "always be my slave" if I could get him transferred from the army.

Last night Margery and I started drinking at a pub with a drunk with whom I got into an argument because he said that no woman could be called beautiful if she had "bad legs" and went on to say that he would never sleep with anyone who was not physically perfect – "not if I fault them." This infuriated me for some reason. Margery and I went back to her house and had rice and pickled walnuts and drank red wine and gin while the cat and Pekinese joined actively in our dinner-table conversation.

4 September 1942.

Staying with a Canadian friend, Anson McKim – a cold day like November. I have escaped to my room. The others are playing tennis. Even the park here is ugly – detestable fir trees and a tree with leaves the colour of a bloodstone. The wind is making a loud melancholy sound which suits my state of heavy sensual melancholy. The millionaire who built this dreary expensive barracks of a house came to tea today. A brisk air battle is going on overhead, rumbling anti-aircraft fire far off.

Four Montrealers, including Anson, staying here – all about thirty-three years old – one stockbroker, one businessman, one lawyer – all now in the army – all with that Montreal voice that echoes from the locker-rooms of good clubs, all coming from the solid homes of the Montreal merchant aristocracy. Good chaps and good company with a pleasant debunking humour, no side, and a canny tendency to under-play their hand. Anything excessive, strange, or alarming can be brushed aside in a tolerant bantering tone. They are far from stupid, though – without mannerisms yet they manage to establish a type.

A young Belgian named Moreau came to see me who had just escaped from a Nazi concentration camp, arriving with nothing but the suit he wore – having got across to France – then in a Spanish concentration camp and here via Gibraltar. These people who are working in illegal organizations on the continent come from another world. They stare at our food and our normal lives and still have something of the trapped animal about them.

14 September 1942.

Spent the day with dearest Elizabeth to whom I owe everything.

19 September 1942.

What is going to happen to Canada after the war? Then what is a Canadian? We are a new type among the nations of the world. As the British Empire becomes less able to protect us our future will need more statesmanship and more knowledge of the world. Our greatest enemy is the parish pump. How are we Anglo-Canadians and the French-Canadians to get on together in the future? We have never succeeded and indeed never seriously attempted to become a bilingual nation, and there is the feeling of the French-Canadians that they are being exploited, although that we also feel in the Maritime Provinces.

This war is digging deeper the gulf between Anglo-Canadians and French-Canadians – the fatal word "conscription" may haunt us after the war. If the casualties are big and still there is no conscription, things will be worse. But supposing a Conservative government came in and introduced conscription, it would undo so much and gain so little. The uneasy but tolerable relationship between French and English Canadians has only been possible because we have used our strength sparingly. We owe much to Mackenzie King for not being panicked into throwing all that overboard. Where we have been the weakest is in making any effort to understand each other, and this is a two-way accusation – the French have been just as bad. But it is a disgrace that these Anglo-Montrealers do not speak French.

The Canadian war effort may be weak in spots, but if we ever get together to the same extent to achieve anything in peacetime Canada it would be a different country. Our social services are backward, our protection of the really poor from exploitation is nearly non-existent. We have done nothing to encourage the growth of civilized standards of taste, and we are harnessed with an absurdly old-fashioned and cumbrous Dominion–Provincial relationship which just must be over-hauled. The Mackenzie King Government has not had the guts to tackle any of these questions. The Tories represent the business community plus some honest imperialists. The Liberals have no programme, they represent everybody and nothing. They stand for equilibrium which has to be preserved to keep the country from splitting seriously on any issue. It is a matter of papering over the cracks. The C.C.F. are old-fashioned socialists, but they do propose certain economic and social adjustments. Canada cannot go in for revolutionary constitutional and social changes in the middle of a war but she can and does tend in the direction of change. For example, the innumerable state controls introduced and efficiently worked during the war by youngish men with no strong party affiliations.

Canada will not go in for pure socialism but we do not want to develop into an unco-ordinated group of "interests." The war will make people impatient and ready for a change. The post-war period is our great opportunity.

I have a new feeling about my fellow Canadians – a feeling that there is good material among the young – idealism, energy, practical ability which somehow never gets a chance to express itself in the public life of the country. I feel that if we can break the crust on top we could make Canada a much better country to live in. What is stifling us is the system – social, economic, and political.

20 October 1942.

I went to see Ernest – found him in his dressing-gown with a muffler around his neck in his large dark sitting-room furnished in Curzon Street Baroque. "Bored," he said. "That is what I am. When I was eighteen years old I swore I would commit suicide on my thirty-first birthday. Now I am thirty-one and I have not committed suicide. I cannot get hold of a girl who attracts me, the old women cling like ivy." He looked the spoilt fractious not-so-young Frenchman with a sensual mouth and bad teeth. We had a cold dinner, and I left immediately afterwards with the feeling that there was a wounded snake.

These days with their falling leaves and bland autumn weather make the shabby parks seem like Tuileries of memory. The waiter here has been wearing my suits, which I suppose is flattering of him. The confident voices of American girls at Claridge's make me feel that the past is still the present and that there is still a comfortable world safe for American humour.

26 October 1942.

I have been reading George Moore's *Memoirs of My Dead Life*. The mixture of sensuality, sentiment, and cloying knowing caddishness is more than one's stomach can take, but the impressions of places in London and of a journey to Paris via Dieppe are nostalgic and remind one of the civilized silver age before the barbarians had broken through. I like the part about my favourite Soho. "The smell of these dry faded streets is peculiar to London. There is something of the odour of the original marsh in the smell of these streets. It rises through the pavements and mingles with the smoke." That smell is still there, and I have often caught it on my way to the office on autumn mornings.

I lunched with Mary Bartlett at the Étoile. She showed me the tongue motion that women make when they are cleaning lipstick off their front teeth and I feel that I have gained a valuable piece of information.

27 October 1942.

Tonight we had our first fog with a full moon. I walked home with a bunch of violets in one hand and *Mademoiselle de Maupin* in the other, thanking my stars that any attempt to move me from London has been frustrated and acknowledging to myself that what holds me is not duty or patriotism but London and the spectacle of its decay and the continuance of its fascination.

I was talking to a man who was telling me of his escape from a concentration camp in France – sawing his way through iron bars with a saw smuggled into the prison in a loaf of bread – "Scarlet Pimpernel stuff" he calls it. He was in a camp composed of Englishmen caught on the continent – these ones were the most sordid type of pseudo-pimps and book-store agents-cum-pimps. When he had first proposed to escape the camp leaders put a guard of fellow prisoners on him to stop him in case his escape should bring reprisals on his fellow prisoners. He says that from the moment he arrived at the camp and witnessed the beating to death of a French prisoner his nervous reactions and sensitivity seemed dead – he was "like an ox being led to the slaughter" and felt only dull fatalism. He has that same peculiar look as others who have escaped from a concentration camp – shifty, nervous, and on the defensive – slightly mad by our standards, or is it just the contrast between the wild and the tame?

30 October 1942.

I thought I would have a look again at the New Testament and began reading St. John's Gospel. I wanted to see how much of a Christian I still might be. I was looking for some sort of copy-book tags to help one along. Instead I met a blazing fire so hot and dazzling that I shield my eyes from it. I read on for ten chapters without ever coming on a moral precept. All is a challenge to believe in the divinity of Christ – not even a challenge – an affirmation. This Christ is a comet miraculously lighting up the skies and He does not want our partial approval or our attempt to find that something can be salvaged from Christian doctrine.

23 November 1942.

Went to the 400 Club with Margery and stayed drinking there until 4 a.m. That place has become part of my life. It is the only place of pleasure left in London with any character that is not infested with middle-aged stout gentlemen and their blondes. At the 400 Club there is always the same background – nostalgic music, half-lighting, eternal youthfulness, guards officers and girls, and myself – not so eternally youthful – always well in the foreground.

What will happen in Canada after the war? Both the state and our own nationalism are growing stronger. I suppose we shall attempt some kind of an egalitarian planned state, where the power is hidden. There will be a monstrous increase in the hypocrisies of government and a monstrous growth of peddling politicians of the lowest and most dangerous sort. The country will be run behind the scenes by powerful quiet men whether financiers or Treasury officials. It will in that way be different from our old-fashioned Canada but in no circumstances can the people have an effective voice in administering the modern state – it is far too big a machine.

27 November 1942.

Went to a party at Nancy Mitford's – I had a long conversation with Unity Mitford. She started the conversation by saying, "I have just hit my left breast against a lamp-post as I was bicycling here." She said, "I tried to commit suicide when I was in Germany but now I am a Christian Scientist – not that I believe a word of it, but they saved my life so I feel I owe it to them to be one." "I hate the Czechs," she said suddenly in a loud, emphatic voice, "but that is natural – they tried to arrest me and I had not done anything. I did not even have the Führer's picture in my suitcase as they said I had." She has just recently returned to England where her role as Hitler's English friend does not make her popular. I must say I liked her better than anyone else at the party. She has something hoydenish and rustic about her.

Great discussion with George Ignatieff about the future of Europe. He sees the great age of the Slav people dawning. I see our being drawn gradually into supporting every and any regime in Europe that offers a bulwark against communism, i.e., in terms of power politics against a triumphant Russia with overwhelming influence at least as far as the Rhine. Of course we shall try to get rid of the more stinking quislings and put in progressive governments, but above all, we must hold the *cordon sanitaire* against Bolshevism. Could there be two worlds after the war – the Atlantic and the Middle European plus the Balkans – the former dominated by Anglo-Germany – the one democratic and semi-capitalist, the other communist?

What will our relations with Russia be after the war if they win against Germany? As long as they remain behind the Curzon Line and busy themselves with reconstruction we might get along all right, but Russia will inevitably be on the side of every revolutionary government in Europe. We shall become suspicious of her and will tend, for the sake of balance, to back anti-revolutionary forces. Thus a new war will be prepared. Indeed we can see the forces that are already preparing it.

23 December 1942.

Went down to spend last weekend – Elizabeth and I – with Stephen Tennant. It was a dreamlike and unrepeatable occasion. From the moment of coming out of the rainy December country-side into his apartment all was under a magician's spell. It was partly the sense of being picked up on a magic carpet out of the prosaic into the midst of everything that is extravagant and strange. In one wing of what was formerly his country-house and is now a Red Cross Hospital he has furnished a set of rooms to suit his own fantastic taste. Such huge white velvet sofas, piles of cushions, and artificial flowers, chandeliers, such a disorder of perfumes, rouge pots, and pomades, such orchid satin sheets and pink fur rugs, toy dogs, and flounced silk curtains, mirrors at angles, shaded lights and scented fires. But the unreality of it attained to an intensity which was pure artistic illusion – too fantastic to be vulgar or funny and with a strange honesty as a natural mask for Stephen's high-strung, high-coloured, but never vulgar nature.

On the train down we found ourselves sitting opposite Augustus John wearing a tweed cap which he removed to reveal that noble head of a moth-eaten lion. Fixing us with his unfocussed gaze he made an effort to assemble meaning and made charming light conversation, full of malice and fun. At intervals he dozed off – his beautiful hands in his lap.

At Salisbury Stephen met us coiffed in a blue knitted helmet – his too-golden hair arranged in a becoming crest. Through the driving rain under a gun-metal sky with sodden leaves piled high in the ditches we drove to Wilsford and were wafted up into the pink rococo of his apartment. "Rich stains of former orgies," he said giggling at the spots on the silver-satin cushion covers; but he is not a comic. His drawings are brilliant evocations of the Marseilles underworld. His notebooks are full of them and all the same characters reappear – *matelots* and tarts, procurers and pimps – faces which have obsessed him. Perhaps he is too undisciplined to express his obsessions in terms of writing.

Elizabeth talked to Stephen of dialogue in the novel – of how every sentence must bear directly or indirectly on the theme – must be a clue or the counter-point to a clue. In that sense how "every novel is a detective novel." It does no harm to linger in places where one has pleasure in writing provided one makes it up by skimming quickly elsewhere so that the tempo of the whole is not slowed up. How a phrase should be written down when it occurs because it may be fruitful of unexpected developments; may contain seeds which would only come to life when it is on paper.

Then they talked about the sticky passages that haunt writers. Whether it was best to make a frontal attack on such difficulties and never rest until they were overcome or, as Elizabeth said, to sidestep the dragon in the path and to go on to what one wanted to write and return to the difficulty later, perhaps from a different angle or aspect. She told us how Virginia Woolf when writing her last book *Between the Acts* was heard to say, "For six weeks I have been trying to get the characters from the dining-room into the drawing-room and they are still in the dining-room."

Virginia Woolf haunts the lives of all who knew her. Almost every day something is added to my knowledge of her – that she was a snob – that she could be cruel, as when one lovely May evening a young, shy girl came into her drawing-room in Bloomsbury to be greeted with the overwhelming question from Virginia, "What does it feel like to be young in May?" The girl stood shambling in silent consternation in the doorway. But how they revolved around Virginia Woolf, how much she must have done to liberate them all, to give them weapons of coolness and wit, and how often they say, "Virginia would have enjoyed it" or "she would have enhanced it." But to me her reflected atmosphere is rather alarming – the exquisite politeness –

but an eye that misses nothing and a power to puncture gracefully, opportunely, and mercilessly if occasion arises or the mood changes.

28 December 1942.

To have heard (as I did the other night) T. S. Eliot on the subject of Charles Morgan[1] was to be entertained at a most delicate feast of malice – the sidelong, half-pitying, good-natured, kindly approach – ("Poor old Morgan, etc.") the closing in on the prey, the kill, so neat and so final, and then the picking of the bones, the faint sound of licking of lips and the feast is over.

---

[1] Novelist, playwright and essayist, author of *The Fountain*, *The Flashing Stream*, etc., sometimes subject to similar disparagement in England, much respected in France.

1943

1 January 1943.

Last night the end of the year with a wind howling down the steep gully of flats outside my window. I feel both sad and excited as though I were seventeen and in my bedroom at The Bower on some winter night in my youth. Christ! Why has it all happened?

3 January 1943.

Elizabeth has borne with all my attempts to play-act my life, although she has so little patience with histrionic characters, without ever making me feel a fool. She has shown me up to myself – good money to some extent has driven out bad.

People in Russian novels stand for hours – sometimes all night – gazing out of a window dreaming over a landscape or lost in a mood. I have never been able to stand at a window for more than a few minutes at any time in my life.

4 January 1943.

Now arises the question of whether or not I should join the army. Elizabeth thinks that I might make a "useful soldier." She says if I join the army she will join the ATS I doubt if either of us will do either. I can see that this idea of joining the army is closing in on me unless I can prove to myself that it would be unfair to the service I am now in and just a piece of heroics. Unfortunately the work here has been so slack recently that I find it impossible to believe that I am pulling my weight in the war.

Walked alone in Regent's Park beside the grey waters of the canal, under a grey winter sky. I tried to get Elizabeth but she was out and the house was shuttered and looked as if it had been unoccupied for years. I felt as though I had come back years later to find her gone and the whole thing in the past.

What a joke it is – a cosy bachelor pried out of his shell and being drawn principally for reasons of face-saving into the horrid prospect of army life. What a short story for someone. By suggesting that I should become a soldier I have put myself in for stakes which I know I cannot afford to play, and depend on other people to get me out of the situation. Perhaps no one will be bothered to do so, and that in itself has a sort of attraction for me. I have now a card to play against myself.

30 January 1943.

I saw a Duncan Grant painting today that made me want to go in and ask the price. I suppose it would have been about two hundred pounds. It was a picture of a small closed café with blue shutters by the sea-front somewhere not far from Wimereux – I should think painted in the early morning before opening time – before the patron had come down to give a perfunctory polish to the linoleum bar – on a morning of damp and shifting weather. The paint had the wetness of the weather and the indecisive cloud shiftings. This morning was just such a morning. I got up early with the idea of going to Holy Communion but decided while shaving that I was not fit to receive Communion – too selfish and sin-satisfied. So I went to the little Anglo-Catholic church and knelt facing the altar while the Service went on – "It is meet, right, and our bounden duty" etc. I was cut off and felt it.

I asked Elizabeth last night whether it was possible to regard oneself – not with violent disgust but with a steady cold distaste as one might feel towards an unattractive acquaintance whose character one knew all too well. She thought, "Yes, if one had been over-praised for the wrong reasons."

31 January 1943.

A day like a day at the seaside. You expected to hear the waves lapping and pictured rain-swept piers. In fact I was nowhere near the sea. I went to visit Roley in the hospital with jaundice at Horsham in the heart of the Canadian-occupied district. Everywhere Canadian soldiers, often with local girls. I suppose somewhere under the surface a Sussex rustic life goes on. An occupying army irons out the character of a neighbourhood – everything looking down-at-the-heel as in London. The rich settled bloom has gone, the stripped naked country-houses are all barracks or hospitals, the avenues morasses of mud from military vehicles, the fences down, the gardens neglected – the little towns submerged in khaki.

6 February 1943.

A sunny, almost spring morning spent in solitary bachelor fashion like so many similar solitary mornings of self soliloquizing – in Oxford to the sound of bells – at Harvard a breakfast of waffles and maple syrup, the good and abundant coffee, Sunday papers, the North American sunlight – in Paris, in Ottawa, in Washington, and in Tregunter Road with the Salvation Army band in the street outside and even the cats and dogs oppressed by a London Sunday. All those Sunday mornings and now another with the wireless in the distance and the servants banging and whistling in the courtyard. Mornings when I have repaired the holes in my ego.

Shaftesbury Avenue was lined with American soldiers just standing there, very quiet and well-behaved, watching the crowds or waiting to pick up a girl. The American troops are everywhere in the West End. They make a curious impression, very different from the legend of the swashbuckling, boasting Yankees abroad. I wonder what they really think about it all. They are so negative that they arouse one's curiosity. They themselves seem completely incurious. They look as though they were among strange animals. The Canadian soldiers up against the British try at once to establish human contact – they make jokes, pick quarrels, make passes, get drunk, and finally find friends.

13 August 1943.[1]

Conclusion of the Civil Aviation Talks. This is a test case for our post-war relations with the Empire. Unless Ottawa reacts strongly we

---

[1] My diary lapsed during much of 1943.

shall have accepted in these talks the idea of a Commonwealth body presiding over an "all-red route." What functions and powers such a body would have is as yet by no means clear, but the precedent is interesting. It is the first post-war Empire body to be set up. The initiative came from Australia. The Australian concept of the future of the Commonwealth is in contradiction to the Canadian and South African. It obviously suits the British book to have projects for greater centralization come from a Dominion. Australia has served notice that she will continue to be a member of the Club at her own price. I should be much surprised if there is not a fight from Ottawa.

6 November 1943.

Talked to Elizabeth about the way women seem, however they purport to be employed, to have the leisure to spin a cocoon of imaginings and questionings around their personal relationships so that when a man blunders into this area he so often finds it thoroughly mined beforehand.

16 November 1943.

Saw Archduke Robert of Austria at the St. James's Club. He surprised me by suddenly saying, "I am the cat's whiskers." He had just been weekending with de Courcy who, he said, would embarrass him in the train coming up to London by addressing him in consciously loud tones as, "Your Imperial Highness" before a carriageful of suburbanites.

4 December 1943.

Dined with Simon, the gold-haired pretty-faced son of a doting and strong-minded mother with a damp old country-house in the Shires and not enough money to keep the old name going. He went from Oxford into the Guards and has now married a Viscount's daughter. He reminds me of the young officers whom Litvinow happens on at their picnic near Baden in Turgenev's *Smoke*. He has a smattering of liberalism, a survival of Oxford days and a core of gentlemanly *arrivisme*. He was talking about the discussion groups that have now been instituted in the army. At the last group meeting he had put up for discussion the inevitable release of Mosley.[1] He found the soldiers solidly but incoherently against the release. Then they talked about the Hereford Birching case,[2] and there again the men were, as he put it "silly and soft" and all against beating children – said it did no good. He explained to them about the merits of corporal punishment but refrained from quoting from his own experiences at public school because public schools are a "tricky subject" with the men.

The night after the release of Mosley, Barrington-Ward, the editor of *The Times*, came to dinner at the Masseys'. He was cagey. He said it was a bad blunder, but he did not intend to publish any letters of protest yet until he had heard Mosley defend himself. In fact he never has published one. I think most Englishmen were disgusted at the release, but within the next day or two it was clear that the Extreme Left were making political capital out of it. "All of us" closed their ranks. *The Times* published a guarded leader in support of Mosley. On the division the Tory Party went solidly into the lobbies to vote in defence of his release. The Liberal individualists rushed to the support of the Habeas Corpus.

20 December 1943.

Spent the entire day at the International Labour Organization Conference and ended by being rather fascinated by the play of interests and personalities and absorbed by the family party atmosphere of an international conference. It has been interesting to watch the skilful old hands at this sort of game.

About the usefulness of our proceedings I am in some doubt. There is a good deal of mass self-hypnosis engendered at such gatherings and confirmed in this instance by visits from Mr. Eden, blessings from Ernest Bevin and a laudatory article in *The Times*. But the doubts persist. A code of labour legislation and social security for the liberated

---

[1] Sir Oswald Mosley, founder of the British Union of Fascists, had been detained under regulation 18B in May 1940. He was released in November 1943.

[2] In October 1943 the Lord Chief Justice quashed the sentence and severely rebuked a magistrate who had ordered an eleven-year-old boy to be birched.

European countries? Splendid, but who is to apply it and in what conditions? In the chaos of a half-starved Europe ridden by class conflict? Are the Balkans ripe for such an utopia? Is Spain? Will Russian commissars order the rhythm of reconstruction by this measure? Will they agree to it in the parts of Germany they may occupy?

21 December 1943.

Lunched with Derek Patmore – he and Peter Quennell are editing Anne-Marie's memoirs and are bringing it out in a very *Almanach de Gotha* manner – I think quite wrongly. It ought to be given a full Romanian flavour – a sort of rococo Ritz 1912 affair. I am afraid they will make her a bore by treating her too seriously.

22 December 1943.

Dined with Elizabeth, Maurice Bowra, and Raymond Mortimer[1] – a most unusually entertaining evening. Every now and then in London you have such an evening and feel at the end of it that this is what is described in memoirs as "brilliant" conversation. Bowra fascinated me by his vitality, malice, and wit. Although a very Oxford product he looks like a Midland businessman – stocky, bullet-headed, with very small hands and feet. He has donnish tricks like "that is a good point," if he is pleased with what you say. Raymond Mortimer seemed young and vulnerable beside him and was on the defensive throughout. At dinner Bowra made a dive bombing attack on him, "Catholic! Conshie! Cagoulard!" Raymond seemed to love it.

25 December 1943.

In the morning Elizabeth and I went to the Christmas service at the Abbey. It was crowded. The procession had to make a path between the people as it wound its way through the nave and into the choir. One saw the banners moving unsteadily over the heads of the people – an immemorial lurching movement. Candles were

---

[1] C. M. Bowra, classical scholar, was Warden of Wadham College, Oxford; Mortimer, a literary critic, was then working for the French service of the BBC; he had long ago given up Roman Catholicism (see Bowra's remarks below).

blazing against the iron-black pillars. We came back to lunch with Alan, off cold duck and white Corton 1924.

I sat next to Margot Asquith at dinner. We talked about the place of the bed in marriage. She is too old and there is nothing left but senile vanity and play-acting. Once with a trace of her old verve she said, "The man who never falls in love is filleted." She horrified me by saying, "I should like to live forever." I was thinking at the very moment how tragic it must be for her not to have been able to die before now. She wore a black tricorne hat with a long black crêpe veil, a shrilly bright green silk jacket and a flaring skirt of black and white tartan silk. She looked like a witch – a surrealist witch – in a modern fairy tale.

1944

17 January 1944.

Just back from a weekend with Roley at Bournemouth where his regiment is stationed. He is a local legend in the regiment and he lives up to it. Dark, restless, warm-hearted, caustic, and above all natural. He has captured the imagination of the men in his regiment by being more alive than any of them.

In the morning I went for a solitary walk down the steep Bournemouth streets full of soldiers and airmen. I think I was the only male civilian in Bournemouth under eighty. The whole atmosphere of the mess was like a school just before the holidays – high spirits, jokes, and friendliness. They made the discomforts, most of which are avoidable, seem fun. With dozens of soldier servants they live in unimaginable squalor. Nowhere a picture or a curtain or even an armchair, but plenty to drink – cars right and left – the slipshod cheerful untidiness of bachelor life lived in common. An atmosphere in which even the most pompous, touchy or old-maidish get into the habit of taking jokes against themselves and resigning their privacies. Also like school – the photographs of wives and mothers and children beside every other bed. I think what has cheered them up so much is the consciousness that they will be joining in the coming invasion of Europe.

18 January 1944.

The news of Jock Colley's death – killed in the RAF– a lamb to the slaughter.

19 January 1944.

Talked to George Ignatieff about this ghastly raid on Sofia where we have wiped out the whole centre of a town, which has no shelters, is built of wood, and is inhabited by people most of whom seem to be pro-Ally. The horror of these destructive attacks on the cities of Europe! It is such a revolting way of waging warfare and no one seems to try to realize what we are doing. It may be necessary, but at least we should accept the guilt and not send out brave, callow youths as our scapegoats to bomb in our names while we treat the news like a cricket score. If the clergymen were worthy of their salt they would make themselves unpopular by voicing our inner doubts about this methodical slaughter.

19 January 1944.

Dined with dearest Elizabeth and Cyril Connolly. He was suffering from a sore throat, but he said when he began to say critical things about his friends his voice came back to him.

27 January 1944.

Our minds much occupied with the incident of Lord Halifax's speech in Toronto.[1] It was not a speech calculated in terms which could appeal in Canada. It was ineptly put and showed no understanding of our psychology. It ought to have been argued in terms of Canadian self-interest. Mr. Massey says that the Prime Minister told him, "In peace-time I would have gone to the country on it." Yet Halifax's general argument is hard to answer.

Might it not be more satisfactory if we gave up being in the Empire at all and concluded a self-respecting alliance with England? Of course that would not be practical politics – it would divide Canada. But it is important that the loyalty theme, making sacrifices for the Home Country, should not be stressed – they are preaching to the converted and enraging the unconverted. Also the combination of Lord Halifax, Tory Toronto, and an Empire Club is so unfortunate as a starting point for a debate over the future of Canada.

---

[1] Halifax argued that for Great Britain to be an effective power in the post-war world, she would need a closely unified Commonwealth.

2 February 1944.

Mr. King says that Empire conferences should be for consultation and co-operation but not for the formulation or preparation of policies.[1] Presumably he means that you have a talk but commit yourselves to nothing. While one can agree with him about the dangers of formal machinery, surely that does not mean a totally negative attitude, and how in hell can you co-operate unless you have something to co-operate about, and what can you co-operate in except in plans and policies? The question really is the spirit in which you approach Commonwealth problems. The proper approach it seems to me would be to try to arrive at common objectives towards which we can all work in our separate ways. Where some or all of us can co-operate closely and in detail over plans let us do so without trying to enforce policies on members to whom they do not appeal. Let us have in mind how best these Empire plans can be merged in the wider objectives which the U.N. will have set before them, but Mr. King does not want to work through the Empire towards broader affiliations. He mistrusts the whole thing.

9 February 1944.

I did not think I was still capable of the friendship I feel for George Ignatieff and I am touched by his demonstrativeness. He has a noble and generous nature.

18 February 1944.

Elizabeth says that she works around to getting what she wants like a cat trying to get out of a room, and like a cat forgets in the middle what it was she wanted and remains standing vaguely gazing into space.

Victor Gordon-Ives[2] killed in Italy – he was looking forward to enjoying life if there was anything left for an Eton and Oxford young man to enjoy after this war. He used to say how much he envied us having lived in the gay twenties. He did not have a chance – only twenty-two – straight from school into the army. Oh hell!

---

[1] Mackenzie King repudiated Halifax's argument in a speech in the Canadian House of Commons. He rejected any notion of a shared Commonwealth foreign policy.

[2] See above, page 35.

2 April 1944.

Dined with Nancy Mitford. She is a queer mixture of county and sophistication – you never know which reaction you are going to strike. She talked about Chatsworth where she has just been staying – says that the wind in the corridors blows your hat off like in an underground and that the portraits are being ruined by the breaths of the evacuee orphans who are occupying the house – that they have fat legs in black stockings and are always charging about playing hockey in the state rooms.

20 April 1944.

On Sunday morning at six o'clock Mary Rose Thesiger and I were walking through Hyde Park. It was only four o'clock by the sun and had the desolating stillness of four a.m. We walked down to the bridge with the ground mist still rising. The Park guns looked forlorn and powerless like the débris of some long-forgotten war – débris resting in a deserted field, yet still sinister like prehistoric remains.

When we got to the bridge we lit cigarettes and looked out over the Serpentine stretching to dreamlike mist-enshrouded distances grey and silent. The dawn wind came up – a woman passed with a small boy in a school cap. Why were they there in the Park before dawn on Easter morning, 1944?

22 April 1944.

Went down to the House of Lords and heard a pretty thin debate on the Empire. They just do not know much about the subject. There was one old bugger who made me feel like personally establishing a secession group in Canada – Lord W. who had had "three hundred lads from the Dominions" stay with him since the war began. "My imperial conferences, my friends call them." Patronizing old Pecksniff!

No one in the House showed any real understanding that Canada is a nation with a soul of its own. They all say it but none of them really understand it.

7 May 1944.

Lunched with Elizabeth in the downstairs grill in the Ritz. There were pink tulips on the table with pinkish lights. It was odd coming into it from the sunlight and wind. We talked as we did when we first got to know each other. It was one of those times which we shall both remember afterwards and say to each other, "That fine, windy Sunday in spring when we lunched underground in the Ritz."

12 May 1944.

Perhaps it is the invasion. We live for D-Day, and after D-Day I suppose we will settle down to some way of living – the same way but with everything shifted a bit. After each of these crises – September 1939, June 1940, September 1940, there has been an adjustment – like a building that has been just missed by a bomb. It "settles" a little – one or two cracks appear. It is still standing the next day, and you are so surprised to see it there that you only notice later that a bit is gone off the cornice and the drawing-room ceiling is sagging badly.

I met my brother, Roley, last night. He appeared in his beret – the first time he has worn it. He said it was to impress me that he was a Commando now. We walked up the towpath from Richmond to Kew. It was a beautiful evening – the enormous chestnut trees in full bloom – the May-trees dusty with white. Before he came when I was saun-tering among the people waiting for him I felt a premonition, "That last time I saw him at Richmond." When I met him in the hall of the Elephant and Castle Hotel it was like meeting him in a dream – just that touch of irrelevance, "Why Richmond? What were we doing there? Why was he wearing a beret and looking so brown?" – the sort of questions one asks oneself when one wakes up.

28 May 1944.

Reading Lady Ottoline Morrell's[1] memoirs which should cer-tainly be published. They have the same mixture of vitality and silli-ness as George Moore's memoirs of a young man, and for all her wild fumbling she has an artist's gift for describing people and places. At one point she brings in Henry James who said of Clive Bell, "that little soiled piece of humanity," and on being invited to meet an ageing actress, said to his hostess, "A tightrope, a banister,

---

[1] Lady Ottoline Morrell, patron of Bloomsbury writers and of D. H. Lawrence, died in 1938. A selection of her memoirs was eventually published in 1963.

backstairs – anything to save me from meeting that battered mountebank, dear Lady."

6 June 1944.

D-Day has come. It had become a hallucination – something like the Second Coming or the End of the World. Roley has not yet gone. He rang me on the telephone yesterday. I hope Peter[1] will be all right.

The soldiers who have been left behind in London look forlorn and subdued. The town seems empty. The gaiety and sense of pressure and excitement have gone. There is a morning-after feeling abroad. The taxis have become plentiful again and the drivers are beginning to be quite polite now that the American debauch is over.

7 June 1944.

The relief of having got home from that party. Not Daniel escaping from the lions' den, not Marie Antoinette escaping from the Paris mob can have felt a more profound sense of deliverance than I do. The scene – a converted mews, a vast underground saloon – like the vestibule of a cinema or like the anteroom of Hades – light percolating only from the ceiling. In this "luxurious interior" the most deadly effort at social gaiety ever perpetrated. In a space which could have held four hundred people was collected a handful of American officers mixed with a smattering of peculiarly snobbish women – endless dry martinis, interminable whisky. The final touch for me was added by a lame American with silver hair and dignified appearance who was a "specialist on Russia" and who was in the last stages of gin-intoxication. He got it firmly into his head that I was a spy, and when I said that I could not understand Russian he said angrily, "Don't you try to pretend with me."

Mary Rose has a collection of Victorian Valentines thrust in the drawers of an old cabinet and a scrap book of her life. I understood more about her when I saw the photographs of her and her two sisters acting in the play that J. M. Barrie had written for them when they were children. Then I saw the connection with her "little girl" dresses – the schoolgirl dresses that she wears to the 400 Club. She poses as a

---

[1] My cousin, and later brother-in-law, Peter Smellie.

lost girl and she is one. She and Stephen Tennant are companion pieces
– those exquisite children growing up in a world of taste and imagination, of green lawns, strawberries and cream, footmen and
whimsicality – those last blooms from the hot-house. The photographs
of the pre-war débutante with a half-boiled guardee-peer – the
fashionable marriage and now this strange lost child – this cheerful
little waif – and anyone – a waiter, a policeman, a man or woman –
would come to her help if she needed them.

9 to 14 June 1944.

At this point I became unendurably restless and determined by
hook or crook to get to the Normandy beachhead. This was strictly
forbidden to all civilians, as the landing had only taken place on 6
June and troops were still landing. However, I had the inspiration to
sell Mr. Massey the idea that a message of good wishes should be sent
to the Canadian troops in Normandy from Mr. Mackenzie King. I
then drafted the message in Mr. King's name and induced Mr. Massey
to get the Prime Minister's approval. Admiral Nelles of the Royal
Canadian Navy arranged a passage for me on a troopship, but said
that I would have to arrange my own landing in Normandy as it was
impossible to obtain permission for a civilian to land.

I left London on Wednesday, 14 June, in the company of Lieut.-
Commander B., Royal Canadian Navy, who had been told off by the
Admiral to look after me. He was a tiresome little man, in appearance and also temperament not unlike Mr. Mackenzie King, a
neurasthenic bachelor whose job was to look after the Canadian
personnel on the large troop landing craft which are about two
hundred and fifty tons and have eight diesel engines. There are
about twenty of these manned by the Royal Canadian Navy and the
Royal Canadian Naval Volunteer Reserve, who had been serving in
combined operations with the Royal Navy. B. described these men
as "his children" and spoke feelingly of how they were neglected by
the Canadian authorities and bullied by the Royal Navy, of how they
had been given ships in bad repair and expected to keep them in
order. The officers and crews were of an average age of nineteen. I
was to get to know a good deal more about these landing craft and
their crews.

B. and I took a train to Portsmouth that night and we repaired to a hotel on the front at Southsea which had been taken over by the Royal Navy – its lounge serving as an unofficial meeting place where officers newly arrived from "the other side" sat in wicker chairs drinking beer and talking shop. B., who had a violent anti-English complex, on being asked for his identity number by the woman at the reception desk said, "Canadians do not have identity numbers – you people know nothing about us do you? Except that our boys fight for you and we feed you." The woman flushed and looked embarrassed. I did the same. My natural dislike for B. was tempered by my feeling that as he was my naval guide and I was completely off my own ground I must bear with him.

15 to 17 June, 1944.

Thursday, 15 June, was fine – we started off to join our troop-ship *Prince William*, going first by ferry to Ryde and thence by Jeep to Cowes, which consisted of a narrow winding street packed with the Royal Navy. It was at this point that I first became conscious of my civilian clothes. (I was later to be the only male out of uniform to be seen anywhere in the course of my time in France, except for the Norman shopkeepers and peasants.) I was eyed with curiosity and – not quite – hostility. It was apparent to all that I must be some sort of a bloody nuisance, most probably a journalist. Not for the last time on the trip I longed for the protective colouring of khaki. We took off for the troopship in a small troop-carrying craft guided by a remarkably pert young RCN officer who treated me in the slightly insolent manner common among junior officers to civilians until they have gauged by the behaviour of their seniors what their attitude should be. This cue was readily and warmly given by the Commanding Officer of the *Prince William*, Captain Godfrey, and in addition my old friend, Rastus Reid, now an Admiral, was on board.

The first day we went over to lunch with the Captain of the sister cruiser, the *Prince Henry*, and I had my first insight into naval rivalries. The Captain of the *Prince Henry* was a six-foot Irish-cop type called Kelly. He was Royal Canadian Naval Volunteer Reserve, not Royal Canadian Navy, not in fact a Straight Striper. I soon discovered that the RCNVR hate the Royal Navy as being stuck-up, stuffy, and superior. They also hate the Royal Canadian Navy whom they consider quite rightly to be an imitation of the Royal Navy. The Royal Canadian Navy for their part pride themselves on the accuracy of their naval tradition, admire, albeit slightly resent, the Royal Navy, and look down on the Royal Canadian Naval Volunteer Reserve. These and other naval mysteries have been revealed to me in the course of this visit.

That evening B. and I returned in a small landing craft to Portsmouth for me to obtain a landing pass. A tall florid officer with a calm naval manner received me with relaxed politeness but no actual enthusiasm. He remarked casually that he was not a Cook's Tourist Agency. It was not a promising beginning, and although he became exceedingly amiable when he had seen my papers he would not give me a pass. He said it would get him into trouble with the army authorities. I asked what would happen if I succeeded in landing without one. He painted a depressing picture of my being taken up by the Military Police and shot on sight as a spy. I must say that I was wearing just the sort of raincoat that a spy always seems to wear. It was a dirty old Burberry, but in each pocket I had placed a bottle of bourbon whisky for use as bribes. They clanked about a good deal in the course of the interminable jumping from one small craft to another during my travels. Depressed by the refusal of the pass, I repaired to the bar, where I ran into John R., a large young man, dark, with a look of Indian blood, in the RCN, and this was fortunate as his acquaintance was very useful to me. Later on that night I returned to spend the night on board the *Prince William*. The navy atmosphere was novel and cheerful – more fun than the army, suffering less from strain than the air force – in fact, not suffering from strain at all. That night they had a party on board – a formal dinner, then schoolboy jokes and horseplay. At the end the party got rough and the younger ones debagged B. It was then that I realized with satisfaction the dislike of B. was not restricted to myself but was shared by all his "children" of the combined operations.

The next day, Friday the 16th, I got word to transfer at once to the *Prince Henry* our sister ship as she was sailing forthwith for France. We took on troops that night – infantrymen – four hundred and sixty of them – one after another coming up the ship's ladder until watching them coming made you dizzy. Stolid, cheerful, English faces – about half of them looked like boys in their teens. All were top-heavy with the weight of their equipment, staggering as they slid down the incline from the gangplank leading on to the ship's deck, blundering about helplessly like cows caught in a too narrow lane. Their tin helmets covered with camouflage to look like leaves were like some stylized headgear of the kind worn by peasants participating in a fertility festival. The troops were very quiet as we steamed out of Southampton Water. They lined the deck looking back at the pattern made by the masts and derricks against a luminous evening sky. It was one of those moments, common in the war, when everyone shares the same thought. As the sun set we were passing to starboard the white romantic castle on the Isle of Wight where it stands among its woods. No one seemed to know what it was called or who lived there, and indeed it looked like a mirage across the calm waters of the Solent.

Saturday, 17 June, I woke, looked out of the porthole and was disappointed not to see the coast of France. I walked about rather miserably on deck feeling out of place and in people's way. The Captain asked me up to his cabin and talked to me about ways of cooking Peruvian fish. I listened politely. The only thing I was interested in was whether I was going to be able to land without my pass. About eleven a.m. we sighted the coast of Normandy and anchored about five miles off the coast opposite the port of Arromanches. The landing craft came alongside to take off the troops. The Captain sent me a message from the bridge that if I liked to take a chance I could go aboard the landing craft but that if there was any delay in landing the troops the ship could not wait for me – I would have to find my own way back to England. What I needed in order to land was a uniformed escort. I asked B. whether he would go with me. The miserable little man hedged. I asked a moustached Guards officer in charge of troop landing. At that moment my acquaintance John R. whom I had met that drunken evening in Southampton appeared on board the landing craft. I thought he might prove a friend in need and clambered down the ladder among the lines of descending troops, the bottles swaying in my mackintosh pockets.

It was my first experience of the machine-like precision of the landing arrangements about which we read in the newspapers.

The troops in the end were landed but there was nothing very machine-like in the process. By hollering from the bridge at every passing small craft asking for aid and by an exchange of insults with those who refused it, some craft which should no doubt have been taking troops off another landing craft was pressed into our service. Eventually, however, in the midst of shouts, orders, and counter orders, we reached a pontoon bridge and remained stuck there until night-time when we got free and tied up to the bridge.

There is no natural harbour at Arromanches. The artificial harbour which has been constructed is known as the Mulberry and was full of small shipping – the bigger ships ride at anchor outside. It was crowded with troopships, a variety of landing craft, tankers, munition and supply ships, and small tugs in which are seated majors with megaphones who are supposed to have some control over the movements of the shipping. They dash about like sheepdogs. The majors shout down their megaphones in gloomy authoritative tones at the small craft which crowd the Mulberry telling them they must move out of this berth or tie up to that ship and above all keep a safe distance from their precious pontoon bridge which is their chief concern. The captains and crews of the hounded small craft curse and protest but in the end do as they are told.

John R. very kindly asked me to stay on board a Canadian-manned landing craft. Life on board is an intimate business. It has to be in a ship of two hundred and fifty tons – the three officers eat, sleep, and live in a cabin about forty feet by twenty feet in size. The galley opens on to one end of the cabin and the conversation of the crew is clearly audible when the communication trap is open. Life at such close quarters could be hell, but, in fact, it was carefree and cheerful. It was an efficiently run ship, but not run on any orthodox Royal Navy lines but in a peculiarly Canadian way – the lack of fuss and feathers, the humour, and the horse-sense with which the whole business is handled. This atmosphere was due in part to the officers. The Captain was a cool, reserved young man of perhaps twenty-three with serious tastes – Plato, *War and Peace*, Mill on *Liberty* were in the small book-case beside technical books on navigation. He was an ideal Captain, with a simple, rather dry sense of humour, conscientious to a fault, but with an easy, direct way with the crew. The First Officer was a nonchalant youth, imperturbable in difficulties and dangers, easily amused and amusing. My friend, John, was the most unusual and most complex character of the three – a rich man's son, quick-witted, enterprising, exuberant, and uncertain in temper. Between the three they knew how to run the ship and keep happy a crew of boys of nineteen, including a French-Canadian, a Dukhobor, a lumberjack, an ex-rumrunner, a Newfoundlander. They were a tough, good-natured lot who would have been impossible to manage by spit and polish. They enjoyed every incident and welcomed everything but monotony. It was an atmosphere of youth.

Details of Life on a Landing Craft

For breakfast pancakes the size of a large soup-plate with golden syrup. Drinking gin and eating chocolates in a high gale. Listening to German radio propaganda quoting Kipling's "Tommy Atkins" to weaken our morale while German planes are overhead.

The perpetual booming of guns and falling of bombs from the mainland, the knowledge that the Germans are only sixteen miles away behind that cliff and yet here we might be in Canada.

The crew, "Keep your fucking shirt-tails out of the spuds."

The pictures of pin-up girls and John saying, "if only they moved – it is having them suspended like that in one position that gets on one's nerves."

Sunday, 18 June 1944.

It began to blow hard and gale warnings were out. A fine drizzle blew against the portholes. We decided to go ashore and have a look at Arromanches, and walked the length of the rain-swept pontoon which was swaying and creaking in the high wind. No one stopped us at the shore end. No one asked me for a pass. I strolled ashore on to the beach-head in an oilskin coat – and was doubtless taken for a member of the crew. Arromanches looked like a stage-set that had been left out in the rain – a little cardboard backdrop of a French seaside resort, but badly battered about. Port authorities, town majors, naval officers in charge, have set up their quarters in the Hôtel de Ville and in the bigger houses of the town. We walked about among the closed and desolate little villas coloured grey and sand, or biscuit colour – coquettish little affairs – "Mon Repos," "Doux Séjour." The gardens were overgrown with rain-sodden roses, red and white.

The few remaining inhabitants were occupied in salvaging bits and pieces of their possessions or walking about among the débris of the invasion to see if they could find anything which would serve some useful purpose. We went into the church – a big, grey, empty church with a shell hole in the roof above the altar – otherwise intact and the windows unbroken. Before the statue of the Virgin – the usual choco-late-box figure wearing a bright blue mantle – were piles of white roses. There was a Roll of Honour "Mort Pour La France 1914–1918" – too long a roll for a village like Arromanches. No flowers before the statue of Joan of Arc, but St. Thérèse de Lisieux was popular.

Monday, 19 June 1944.

John and I departed by Jeep for the headquarters of the Third Canadian Division. This represented a considerable achievement on his part. He had bluffed the local brigadier into appreciating the importance of my mission, and I found that wherever we went he had built me up to almost embarrassing heights and I was greeted like a visiting cabinet minister.

It was another day of wind and rain with low cloud. We drove along excellent, hard-surfaced roads from village to village looking for the headquarters. Along the roads went an unceasing stream of traffic, trucks, DUKWs, Jeeps, tanks, and interfering with this traffic was the occasional peasant's cart. A red-faced old farm woman riding a bicycle appeared from behind a row of oncoming tanks. She had the same air of going – with a sort of desperate stubbornness – about her own business, which marked most of the local inhabi-tants. In this area the peasants did not seem to have been evacuated. The military say they are helpful and co-operative but not demon-strative. They did not seem much in favour of de Gaulle. In Bayeux two French officers have established themselves as representatives of the French Provisional Government. We saw their proclamations posted on the walls there side by side with those of General Eisenhower.

We went by car over a good portion of the bridgehead – a wind-swept country of high bare ridges and big fields studded with rough wooden poles, as protection against gliders. The German warning signs still left beside the roads, the skull and crossbones and the word *Minen*. There was hardly a field in which there were not either tents or supply dumps – soldiers naked to the waist washing in a wet field, hospitals marked with red crosses, petrol dumps and stores stacked in rows – one of "our" airstrips thick with planes grounded by bad weather. Until the day before, the country had been a dust bowl, now it was being transformed overnight into mud. Our road led through Bayeux and a dozen small Norman villages. I went into some of the shops in Bayeux. It was pleasant to be among French people again – so willing to make every small negotiation into a conversation. They seemed to have lots of food in the shops and luxury goods. The people were full of smiles, glad to see us but not emotional.

The main street was decorated with tricolours, but the demonstrative period, if there ever was one here, was over.

General Keller's headquarters were only a couple of miles from the German lines and at one point we nearly took a wrong turning in our Jeep which would have brought us out behind the German lines. There was little sign of enemy activity except for the almost casual booming of guns. The Headquarters are in the grounds of a château, not in the house itself – a small formal eighteenth-century stucco house – but in the park and gardens. The General, who was living in a camouflaged truck concealed in a mound in the park, emerged on my arrival looking ruddy and confident, just as a General should look, and clad in a khaki pullover and breeches. He talked like a General saying that his men were "in good heart." He summoned a circle of officers and some men standing in the damp park. I read them the Prime Minister's message of goodwill as drafted by me. The General expressed gratification and sent a message to our people at home. I thought his enthusiasm rather muted, and I do not think that the name Mackenzie King makes the military heart beat faster.

I asked one of the officers whether I could go along the line to see my cousins, Peter Smellie and John Rowley, who were with their regiment a mile or two away. He said that a moving vehicle on that road might attract enemy fire to their position and wondered sarcastically whether they would want to see me in these conditions. I said probably not.

A day or two later after my return to the beachhead at Arromanches I ran into Bill Wickwire who was in Roley's regiment and he told me that Roley had been very badly wounded. He had last seen him swathed in bandages from head to foot on a stretcher. He had been returned to a hospital in England as an emergency case. I was now desperately anxious to get back to England to see him, but for the remaining four days we were storm-bound tossing in a landing craft against the pontoon bridge or tied up to a larger ship in a storm-tossed mass of small shipping where a furious north-west gale blew incessantly. We could not cross the Channel by day because of the danger of enemy planes. To manoeuvre at night was difficult and dangerous. Next to us a destroyer out of control was beached. Two tank landing craft were broken up by the storm. All the time until the last day, apart from my worry about Roley, I thoroughly enjoyed myself. Outside – hostile coast, a sweeping gale, clouding skies; inside in the small wardroom we drank gins, told stories, and listened to the wireless until four days later the weather became calm and we were able to return by night to England.

10 July 1944.

It is as if this had been not one war but half a dozen short wars with intervals of truce in between. The last truce ended about one month before D-Day. Since then we have been steadily on the stretch and one begins to add up the reckoning as the end of the war approaches. Roley, wounded, perhaps not beyond cure – Gavin Rainnie, so physically alive, so solid, so racy of health and vigour, blown up in his landing craft before he even reached the beaches – Enid Grant sitting in her farm at Oddington waiting with lessening hope to hear news of Jack who is missing. Jock Colley and Victor Gordon-Ives killed.

The buzz-bombs go on – that poor little Grosvenor girl has her face full of hundreds of fragments of glass from the shattered window in her flat.

Elizabeth and Margery have both had their houses blasted and are trying to think it worthwhile to start again.

13 July 1944.

Morale much improved – we are getting used to the buzz-bombs and also fewer are coming over. People are beginning to come to life again – to ring up their friends and to go out to restaurants. I heard my first fresh piece of scandal today – a healthy sign. Anne-Marie has returned to the Ritz with a new hat and a new admirer. Life marches on.

There goes an air-raid warning. I have been completely unmoved by these buzz-bombs – I was more scared by the early raids at the beginning of the war.

20 July 1944.

Elizabeth's house in Clarence Terrace has been hit by a blast for the third time. She has at last decided to move out now. All the ceilings are down and all the windows broken. She and Alan only escaped being killed by a chance. I hate the disappearance of Clarence Terrace – so will her other friends. It was the last house in London which still felt like a pre-war house. There was always good food, good talk and wine (as long as wine lasted), and a certain style. Then I liked the house itself with its tall, airy rooms and good, rather sparse furniture. I suppose they will re-open it after the war if it is not hit again. Elizabeth's nerves have been under a terrible strain, but she is resilient and if she can get away and get some rest she will be all right. In the midst of it all she is still trying frantically to write her novel.[1]

12 August 1944.

Fine weather, victories, the falling off of buzz-bombs (bugger bombs as Mrs. Corrigan innocently calls them) have improved everyone's spirits. There are bets that we shall be in Paris by the end of September. Meanwhile the casualty lists get longer, and we who need good men in Canada are losing some of our best.

Lunched today with Anne-Marie at the Ritz. She had on a little hat with a crêpe veil – a mockery of a widow's peak. I think she is

---

[1] *The Heat of the Day.*

mourning her lost love, although she hides her scars and her scars never seem more than skin deep.

Elizabeth has moved to Clarissa Churchill's[1] flat, as her house has been blasted once too often. It is high up in a monstrous new block of flats overlooking Regent's Park. She likes the flat which is full of Clarissa's empire furniture, gilt, and maroon velvet – too palatial for the size of the flat. Elizabeth is writing a short story, "The Happy Autumn Fields," and told me about it in an excited way while I lay on a sofa looking out at the sea of green tree tops with here and there an isolated high building.

18 August 1944.

Dined with Michal Vyvyan. He says that to go on fighting the Germans is a waste of men and that people who continue a war after it has ceased to be necessary are as criminal as those who started it. We now dispose of superior power, therefore it is no longer necessary to deploy it militarily. We are like people who hold all the good cards in a bridge hand and insist on playing it out card by card instead of just throwing in the hand and writing down the results. He says we could have had a cessation of hostilities any time in the last six months.

19 August 1944.

The hatred of the more intelligent English upper classes for the age they live in is profoundly discouraging, though less irritating than the shallow optimism, perfectionism, and venom of the Left.

I never seem to put a foot wrong with Jews. I feel at my ease with them. They are more human and more mentally honest than most Gentiles and their minds are alive. Beyond this in my own case there may be a blood connection. I wonder?

I was brought up in the tradition of gentlemanly English culture but it is not deep in my blood. I have not got the English love of things done in due order. Sometimes I think that the English do not care a pin about justice. What they like is seemliness.

---

[1] A niece of Winston Churchill, she later married Anthony Eden.

2 October 1944. Ottawa.[1]

Drove out to the Fishing Club up the Gatineau Valley to which a small group of civil servants belong – younger men – some of them temporary wartime appointments – a very pleasant group – intelligent, unaffected, kind-hearted, and hard-headed. At the Fishing Club the day was overcast with a gun-metal sky, the trees just beginning to turn. I think of this country not as young but as old as nature – ante-dating Athens and Rome – always these hidden lakes and waiting woods.

13 October 1944. Wolfville, Nova Scotia.[2]

The one street of Wolfville is lined with autumn trees – golden filters for sunlight, but there has not been much sun. It is overcast, cool and windless. The old-fashioned, white clapboard houses are so pretty that the village just escapes being a tourist picture postcard. Sandwiched between these charming, early Victorian, *Cranford* houses are the tall, fretted wooden villas of the eighties painted in liver and mustard and the comfortable, shingled, styleless, modern houses with big windows and roomy verandahs. Wolfville is built on a slope – from the woods the orchards spread down to the backs of houses on one side of the street. Behind the houses on the other side the slope ends abruptly in a steep bluff – below are marshes and mud flats stretching into the basin of Minas, an expanse of shifting tides and colours – a mirror for sunsets. Beyond this sea-inlet Cape Blomidon stands up nobly.

The old ladies whom Mother sees in Wolfville are forever spinning their web of daily living, of small worries and jokes, incidents and purchases, sympathies and antipathies, nerves and rests.

I have been re-reading my own early diaries written in my teens and at Oxford and I am so stifled by the fumes of my own personality that I have to overcome nausea to write at all. Yet I am glad to have the diaries. They bring before me a youth who appals me by his silliness and by the banality of his mind. Only the eager appetite for

---

[1] I was on a visit to Canada on leave and for "purposes of consultation."

[2] I was staying with my mother at an hotel in this small town in the Annapolis Valley.

experience is attractive – the astringent notes on people are sometimes amusing, and there is a recurrent sense of the writer's own ridiculousness. The diary describes a life which I had only remembered in a blurred way. The endless succession of people coming and going at home, the dances, picnics, and flirtations. A "social animal," one can see that. Personal relationships and aesthetic or literary impressions (rendered in an appalling pastiche style) dominate. There is nothing worthy to be called an idea from cover to cover, and not one single mention of politics or world events. There is a note of gush mixed with a cynicism about my own motives – altogether an impressionable animal.

20 October 1944. Ottawa.

The feeling in the Department of External Affairs is very pro-Russian and anti-Pole – they do not see this as being inconsistent with our emphasis on the rights of small nations and find it inconvenient to be reminded that it is so. Someone in the Department said to me today that he would be more fearful of a strong Poland than a strong Russia. I suppose it is a remark that he must have read somewhere. It seems extraordinarily silly. The truth is that the old left-wing prejudices still stick. Poland is "reactionary" – Russia is "progressive."

1 November 1944. London.

I reflected coming over on the plane on how obsessed I have been all my life by my determination to forgo nothing. How gently but ruthlessly I have insisted on my pattern at the expense of other people's feelings and my own. Has it all been downright silly? Am I like the man in Henry James's story "The Beast in the Jungle" who found in the end that it was his singular fate to be the man to whom nothing happened?

London seems to me quite meaningless. The illusion it provided has vanished. As Elizabeth says, "It is no doubt an old and interesting city but for me it has come unstuck."

1944 will stand in our memories as the year of fatigue and sorrow when "the silver cord was loosed," etc.

15 November 1944.

Dreamt that I was in the throes of an air raid and woke up to find that it was true. There had been a raid last night but these buzz-bombs and V2s have never made much impression on me, though God knows I was scared enough in the early raids.

I sat about all morning in my dressing-gown in a demoralized state talking about life with the Life Force (my name for the woman who cleans my flat because of her whirlwind energy). We agreed that soft, imaginative people go rotten and bitter much more certainly than those who start dull or hard.

3 December 1944.

The squirrel-faced lift-woman was talking away volubly last night about the English – "The greatest race on earth," she said. "Never has been anythink like us – never will be. Look the way we borne the brunt of the war yet we never talk about ourselves – no swank – we just get on with the job."

The Americans in London are a well-behaved, tolerant army of occupation. They are so polite that one almost hears their thoughts and they are thinking, "These poor, quaint people. They have guts but – backward, reactionary." And the English with their kindly street directions thinking behind shut faces, "These people have not got what it takes – no breeding – an inferior race but, damn them, they have the money and the power. We can only dominate them by character, our national asset from which we can always cut and come again."

The two races and the two armies mingle in street and pub without ever touching except for the collaborating little factory girls who chew gum, wear their hair *à la* Lana Turner, and queue up for movies hand-in-hand with their protectors. The American men are so different with the women. They fondle them in the street, always a hand splaying over breast or buttock. Loose-limbed they amble at the girl-friend's side whispering in her ear, pinching her behind, their two mouths rhythmically moving in unison – so different from the wooden Englishman walking side by side with his girl not seeming to see her except for covert glances and the occasional clumsy touch of his hand on hers.

20 December 1944.

Dined at the Masseys with Rab Butler.[1] I like him better each time I see him. He enjoys his own success so much. He is so malicious and under the don-like manner he is a born politician. He puts out so many tentacles into the conversation and never muffs or muddles what he is saying. He has a trick of praising in general terms before getting on to particular denigration. "I admire X enormously – he is very nearly a great man, but what I think, don't you, has so far held him up has been quite simply lack of intelligence."

All the same he and his fellow Tories understand nothing about Canada. It is discouraging to find this ignorance in the intelligent ones like Rab. A small instance – Rab was trying to show that he appreciated Canada's position in the Commonwealth and said to Mr. Massey, "To show you what I mean I have several times in speaking of Canada to you referred to it as 'your country.' Quite separate from us." This was said in good faith. Any Canadian's reaction would be, "Why the Hell wouldn't you – it *is* our country." Isn't it or is it?

He was talking of the need for Canada becoming the second line of defence, the refuge of the British race, perhaps the future centre of the Empire. "If," he said, "this was presented to the Canadian people on racial grounds they would understand it. Race after all, as Disraeli said, is fundamental." But there are – I reminded him – two races in Canada. "Oh, your French-Canadians," he said, "that would be all right if we had a much closer relationship with France." The Foreign Office cannot get it out of their heads that the French-Canadians are politically devoted to France. Pure ignorance – I only hope to God that they know more about other foreign countries than they do about Canada.

I asked Rab if the country was restive at the delays in implementing social reforms. "Everything in politics can be solved by not making up your mind in a hurry and not getting rattled – procrastination – or I should say – patience."

---

[1] R. A. Butler was Minister (or President of the Board) of Education from 1941 until the end of the war. He had previously been at the Foreign Office, and was to hold many high ministerial posts (other than that of Prime Minister) later.

26 December 1944.

Christmas at Loelia, Duchess of Westminster's. The house is so like a stage set that it engenders a stagey brilliance in people. It looked more unreal than ever in Christmas-card weather, with silver hoar-frost in the park – an interior of crystals and silks seen from the fog-bound avenue. The party were Loelia (who had fits of impatience when she turned on us all and rated the nearest victim, but she is a wonderful creature; coming in from a walk in the cold showed her sudden dark flashing beauty) then the Sitwells and their son, Reresby, Angie Biddle Duke, very smooth – I thought too easy to the edge of insolence, Peter Quennell, emitting a phosphorescent charm.

We went over to the Christmas Ball at Sutton.[1] The whey-faced Duke speaks and moves like a zombie. The ball was an odd mixture – fresh little country-girl neighbours, boy midshipmen, red-faced middle-aged hangers-on of the Duke, and our own group. Then there were American Colonels slapping Duchesses on their bottoms and feeding free lifts, free champagne, free cigars, free silk stockings to the aristocracy, seeing how much dirt they can make the English eat. One said to Loelia, "Since I have come here I find that the Royal Navy stinks, the RAF. stinks and I always knew the British Army stank." Loelia said she very *nearly* threw the bottle of Noilly Prat he brought her out of the door after him, but she had second thoughts. But when he said to young Reresby, "Why do you Etonians go around with your hands in your pockets all the time," he answered like a true Sitwell; "If we had three hands we would keep them all in our pockets if we were inclined to."

An exotic element was added to the ball by the arrival of the Spanish Embassy party, the Duke of Alba's daughter, the Duchess of Montero, cleverly dressed by some dressmaker to look like a Velasquez Infanta.

The house, Renaissance Italianate, is beautiful outside – lovely in its shape against the frost-silvered gardens. Inside it is 1912 Tudor – inescapable panelling everywhere, vast hotel-like rooms, buffets of heat from the grates in the floors, the library full of photographs of women in flower-pot hats and motoring veils.

---

[1] The home of the Duke of Sutherland.

31 December 1944.

After this war the most we can aim at is a breathing-space which, if we are lucky, might last a generation. It is a delusion to talk of permanent peace and there is no "solution" of a "political problem." The latter is the language of mathematics not of politics. The only new element in the permanent human situation is the technical one. As weapons become so much more destructive there is the possibility that the human race may outlaw the more deadly ones and carry on its struggle by common agreement with the less destructive. This would seem unduly optimistic but for one fact, that in this war gas has not so far been used, even by a Hitler.

1945

3 January 1945. Paris.[1]

New Year's Day was magnificent – sun and frost. From the roof of
Saul's flat which faces on the Esplanade des Invalides you have a
panorama of Paris through the sunny mist; the familiar silhouettes
sharpened as the day went on and directly below us ran the Seine, the
colour of chartreuse between the white bleached stone quais. The sun
burnished the melodramatic gold statues on the Pont Alexandre III.
Paris was preserved, untouched physically by the war.

At last I got an opportunity to get out alone into the streets and to
look for Paris. It was like a dream in which you see the woman you
love but cannot speak to her and cannot touch her. The untouched
beauty of the city lying about me in burnished splendour under the
winter sun made the emptiness more sinister. Paris is dead – there is
no movement, no life, no crowds of talking, gesticulating people, no
hum of assurance, no noisy erratic traffic of people and vehicles.
Nothing but a spacious emptiness of the streets and the shabby, silent
passers-by with drawn faces and hunched shoulders, grim, cold,
hungry people. You look at their faces, and pity and nostalgia for the
past seem out of place. The irony of the heroic arches and spectacular
perspectives – the backdrop for their humiliation and their bitter
unresigned endurance. This was how Paris seemed to me, and it
would have been idle to think twice of my past youth there and
memories of old loves when faced with this iron logic of defeat.

---

[1] I was staying with Saul Rae, of the Department of External Affairs, then stationed
in Paris, and his wife.

Everywhere in Paris you are haunted by the Germans. In the flat where I am staying two German diplomats had been living throughout the occupation. They had left in a hurry, their hair ointments and medicines were still in the cupboard, their calendar on the wall, and they had their own telephone switchboard in the salon with a direct line to Wilhelmstrasse. The maid who brought me my morning coffee had brought them every morning for four years their morning coffee. She was a Luxembourg peasant woman with a German accent. I asked her what she thought about the Germans and she said, like one who has sought the advice of a good lawyer and been told what she says might be taken in evidence against her, "There were some who were bad and then naturally there were others who were less bad." Saul says that you often hear people in the shops saying, "Well, after all, the Germans provided coal, they kept the transport running, and when they were here one could buy things."

There is resentment against the Americans and some practical cause for irritation. The American military authorities have demanded all the accommodation which the Germans had had. They are in all the best hotels with the only central heating working in Paris in this icy winter. They have money and, above all – and this is to the Parisians the unforgivable thing – they have food. The United States army rations are incredibly, almost scandalously abundant. They have the only cars in Paris, while Paris freezes and nearly starves. The Allies and a small fringe of rich French have everything they want and live from one party to the next.

In the shops it is not the contrast between French and American but between rich French and poor French which comes into play. No foreigner can afford the prices in these luxury shops, whose goods are, in fact, investments against inflation, but the rich French will buy anything by any means to get rid of currency in which they have no confidence. The astonishing thing is the beauty and variety of the luxury articles displayed. Coming to the shops fresh from wartime London I feel like a simple Russian soldier who has his first view of the western world and its amenities. It is so long since we have seen any object that tempts that we have almost forgotten the lures of vanity. This puritanism melts away at the sight of the Paris shop-windows. Here are jewels and clothes which would make you love your mistress more – simply because you had given them to her. We in England have missed a chapter in the history of taste. Everything is new to our eyes – the fantastic, sumptuous hats, pyramids and turbans of satin and velvet, of fur and of feathers, the new settings for jewels, the new colours of materials, the dramatic brilliance of the presentation in the shop windows.

In the empty boulevards the only traffic is United States army vehicles and a few ancient horse-drawn cabs, or bicycle-propelled hooded affairs which have been invented to try to fill the need for taxis – otherwise the Parisians have no transportation except the Métro.

The Raes' flat belongs to a rich Canadian woman. It is a typical modern luxury flat – great expanse of window, beige carpets, white china horses on the mantelpiece, imitation leopard skin on the bed, and every modern device of comfort, only none of them working owing to the complete absence of fuel. The bathroom was an elaborate mockery with its showers and appliances – no one in the house had had a bath for two months. There was a large salon full of Empire furniture covered in striped satin, but it was too cold to contemplate as a sitting-room. As for my bedroom there could be no thought of sleeping in it. I slept on the sofa in front of the wood fire with a hot-water bottle, a sweater, and all the windows closed. The family spent the day sitting on the floor to be as close as possible to the one minute wood stove in the sitting-room. We ate well on United States army rations.

12 January 1945. London.

Lionel Massey's farewell party for me. If you take twenty or thirty fairly adult and intelligent people and pump them full of alcohol from 6:30 until two in the morning you hear some pretty astonishing things. I do not think the English and Americans quite understand this kind of party. I sometimes think that Canadians, who are at heart a sensitive, pugnacious, voluble, and amorous race, are only released by whisky.

3 February 1945. Ottawa.[1]

I suppose I could have gone on year after year representing my country abroad without knowing much about what was going

---

[1] I had been posted back from London to the Department of External Affairs.

on at home. I am in for an intensive bout of re-education. In the Department I feel like a new boy at school. They all seem to know so much more than I do. I asked myself what I can have been doing in these years when they were informing themselves so fully. Living through the war must be the answer.

18 February 1945.

Pavlov, an officer of the Soviet Embassy, came to a dinner for people from our Department and some foreign diplomats. He was out to *épater le bourgeois* and succeeded. Very cocky and on the offensive – looks like Harpo Marx but with fanatical eyes and a false mouth, nimble-witted and entertaining – the only one from the Embassy who talks freely, but then he is NKVD, and so can say what he likes. He began by attacking, saying that Canada was owned by the Americans and why didn't we have a bigger population? Why didn't the Head of the European Division speak Russian? Why hadn't we provided houses for diplomats posted here as they did in the Soviet Union? Why did we allow the incubus of the church to stifle us? In fact, he thoroughly enjoyed himself at our expense. Norman Robertson[1] was good with him – ironic, sceptical – but he brushed aside argument. It was disconcerting to see how well our people took it. If an Englishman had dared half as much criticism there would have been a free fight, but the bourgeois fall for this proletarian line with inverted snobbery.

24 February 1945. Ottawa.

Staying with dear Aunt Elsie. I had breakfast alone in the dining-room among Elsie's glass tigers and cats and under the eyes of that portrait of the Admiral, her grandfather. The flat is full of tapestries, silver, nice "bits" of furniture, and in the hall a series of watercolours of the old Rowley family manor house in England. You have only to put your nose in the flat to be conscious of "background."

Elsie and I shout at each other at the tops of our voices (she is getting deafer and deafer). We carry on inconsequential conversations

---

[1] Norman Robertson was then Under-Secretary of State for External Affairs. He had been part of the original Department of External Affairs formed by Dr. O. D. Skelton.

from room to room. We meet half-dressed in the hall – she in a silk slip, I in my shirt-tail. We inveigh against the Government, discuss love and the upbringing of children, rehash old scandals. She is incapable of getting into low gear, never wants to go to bed, never sleeps when she gets there, but lies all night listening to the wireless and worrying about her sons at the war.

3 March 1945.

Dinner last night for the Soviet Ambassador, Zarubin. Sat next to the Soviet Ambassadress and asked her how she liked Ottawa after Moscow. She replied with animation, "Moscow wonderful, concerts wonderful, ballet wonderful, opera wonderful, Moscow big city – Ottawa nothing (*nichevo*) – cinema, cinema, cinema."

21 April 1945.

On the train *en route* to San Francisco.[1] Luncheon with Mackenzie King and was charmed by the fat little conjurer with his flickering, shifty eyes and appliqué smile. He has eyes that can look like grey stones or can shine with amusement or film with sentiment. He chats away incessantly – he seems very pleased with himself, delightfully so, pleased with his own cleverness and with his own survival. He talked of the "fun" of parliamentary tactics which cannot, he added regretfully, be so freely indulged in time of war. He talked of the conscription crisis and said that when it was viewed from the historical point of view its most significant feature would seem to be that the French-Canadian Ministers remained in the Government. That is what saved Canada's unity. I irritated him by remarking that our troops must be thoroughly tired by now. He replied, "They have had two months' rest," (*when?* I should like to know) and said, "I knew during the recruitment crisis that they were due for that rest but this I could not reveal."

He described Roosevelt's funeral at Hyde Park naturally and effectively, the silence in the garden and the rightness of the ceremony. He

---

[1] We were on our way to the San Francisco Conference, which was to open in the Opera House there on 25 April and set up the machinery of the United Nations. I was an adviser to the Canadian delegation.

spoke affectionately but not over-sentimentally of Roosevelt himself, adding, "When I last saw him I felt the end might come at any moment. When any subject came up about which he had a complex of worry he collapsed completely. When they called me from the White House to tell me of his death I did not even go to the telephone. I knew what had happened without being told."

Talking of Mussolini he said, "A remarkably finely-shaped head – the head of a Caesar – deep-set eyes full of intelligence. He did a lot of good – cleaned up a lot of corruption, but he had too much power for too long. They worship false gods in Europe – that is the trouble – Europe is too full of pictures of Napoleon and statues of the Caesars."

26 April 1945. San Francisco.

The San Francisco Conference. San Francisco is as lively as a circus – the setting and the audience are much more amusing than the Conference performance. No one can resist the attraction of the town and the cheerfulness of its inhabitants. Nowhere could have been found in the world which is more of a contrast to the battered cities and tired people of Europe. The shock which I felt on arriving in the normality of Ottawa after England is nothing compared with what one would have felt coming from blacked-out London, Paris, or Moscow to this holiday city. The Bay is a beautiful background, the sun shines perpetually, the streets are thronged, there are American sailors everywhere with their girls and this somehow adds to the musical-comedy atmosphere. You expect them at any moment to break into song and dance, and the illusion is heightened because every shop and café wafts light music from thousands of radios. Colours too are of circus brightness, the flamboyant advertisements, the flags of all the Conference nations, the brilliant yellow taxis. This seems a Technicolor world, glossy with cheerful self-assurance. The people are full of curiosity about the Conference delegates. They crowd around them like the friendly, innocent Indians who crowded around the Spanish adventurers when they came to America and gaped at their armour and took their strings of coloured beads for real. The delegates are less picturesque than they should be to justify so much curiosity. There are the inevitable Arabs and some Indians in turbans who are worth the price of admission, and the Saudi

Arabian prince who gleams like Valentino, but in general the delegates are just so many men in business suits with circular Conference
pins in their buttonholes making them look as if they were here for
the Elks' Convention. The exceptions are the Russians – they have
stolen the show. People are impressed, excited, mystified, and nervous
about the Russians. Groups of wooden-looking peasant Soviet
officers sit isolated (by their own choice) at restaurant tables and
are stared at as if they were wild animals. They are painfully self-
conscious, quiet, dignified – determined not to take a step which
might make people laugh at the beautiful Soviet Union. The crowds
throng outside the hotel to see Molotov, that square-head is much
more of a sight than Eden. He is power. When he came into the initial
plenary session he was followed by half-a-dozen husky gorillas from
NKVD. The town is full of stories about the Russians – that they have
a warship laden with caviare in the harbour, etc., etc.

Meanwhile the local Hearst press conducts an unceasing campaign of anti-Russian mischief-making – doing their damnedest to
start a new world war before this one is finished.

The Conference arrangements have so far been conducted with
characteristic American inefficiency. The Opera House in the Veterans'
Memorial Building where the sessions are to be held is like something
out of a Marx Brothers' film. A mob of delegates, advisers, and secretaries mill about in the halls asking questions and getting no answers.
Where are they to register their credentials? Why have no offices been
allotted to them? Where are the typewriters they were promised? To
answer them are half-a-dozen State Department officials white with
strain and exhaustion who have themselves not yet got office space,
typewriters, or the remotest idea of how the organization is to work.
Meanwhile, American sailors are shifting office desks through too-
narrow doors. The San Francisco Boy Scouts are shouldering and
ferreting their way among the crowd (what they are doing no one
knows). Junior League young socialite matrons of San Francisco
dressed up in various fancy uniforms lean beguilingly from innumerable booths marked "Information," but as they charmingly con-
fess they are just "rehearsing" at present and can no more be expected
to answer your questions than figures in a shop-window. All the
babble of questions goes on to the accompaniment of hammering

conducted in all keys by an army of workmen who are putting up partitions, painting walls, eating out of dinner-pails, whistling, sitting smoking with their legs outstretched in the overcrowded corridors. The only thing that is missing in this scene of pandemonium is Harpo Marx tearing through the mob in pursuit of a pair of disappearing female legs.

28 April 1945.

Second meeting of the plenary session again in the Opera House with powerful klieg lights shining down from the balcony into the eyes of the delegates, dazzling and irritating them. The session is declared open by Stettinius[1] who comes on to the dais chewing (whether gum or the remains of his lunch is a subject of speculation). His manner is one of misplaced assurance – unintentionally offensive. (Although the newspapers have described him as handsome, he looks like something out of the bird house at the zoo – I do not know just what – some bird that is trying to look like an eagle.) He makes the worst impression on the delegates. He reads his speech in a lay-preacher's voice husky with corny emotion. The Chilean Foreign Minister reads a tribute to Roosevelt which being translated consists of an elaborate metaphor (which gets completely out of control as he goes along) comparing Roosevelt to a tree whose foliage spreads over the world which is struck by what appears to be the lightning of death but is actually the lightning stroke of victory so that its blossoms, while they may seem to wither, are brighter than ever.

Then comes along Wellington Koo of China, a natty, cool, little man in a "faultless" business suit who reads a short speech about China's sufferings, written in careful English. After him Molotov mounts the tribune in an atmosphere of intense curiosity and some nervousness. He looks like an employee in any *hôtel de ville* – one of those individuals who sit behind a wire grille entering figures in a ledger, and when you ask them anything always say "no." You forgive their rudeness because you know they are underpaid and that someone bullies them, and they must, in accordance with Nature's

---

[1] Edward R. Stettinius was then American Secretary of State and later United States Representative at the United Nations.

unsavoury laws, "take it out on" someone else. He makes a very long speech in Russian, which is translated first into English, then into French, and turns out to be a pretty routine affair. The delegates are by now bored and dispirited. Then Eden gets up and at once the atmosphere changes – you can feel the ripple of life run through the audience as he speaks. It is not that he says anything really very remarkable, but he sounds as if he meant it – as if he believed in the importance of the Conference and the urgency of the work to be done. He is quite beyond his usual form, moved outside himself, perhaps, by exasperation at the flatness and unreality of the proceedings.

I have developed a sort of rash on my chest and rather all over. I am not disturbed by this, as I have always been a great itcher, but the dolt of a hotel doctor has diagnosed it as measles, which must be a medical impossibility as I have had ordinary measles once and German measles twice. However, the doctor is insistent that it is measles. He said he hoped I knew that it was contagious and might spread rapidly in the delegation. I propose to disregard this.

30 April 1945.

Miss Smithson, my secretary, says that agencies – the hotel authorities? or FBI? – have put up a small photograph of me in the women's washroom with printed underneath, "Avoid contact with the above person who is suffering from a contagious disease." This will cramp my style in personal and diplomatic contacts.

22 May 1945.

The backdrop of San Francisco is gloriously irrelevant to the work of the Conference. The people of the town regard the whole proceedings with mixed benevolence and suspicion. Here is an opportunity to make the rest of the world as free, rich, and righteous as the United States but it is hindered by the machinations of evil men. Of the uncertainties, worries, and fears of the delegates they have no idea. They can swallow any amount of this sort of thing – "The Conference is the greatest human gathering since the Last Supper." In the end their appetite for ballyhoo is rather frightening.

But no one could resist the town itself or the luxuriantly beautiful countryside around it, or the spontaneity and chattiness of the inhabitants, or the beauty of the girls – who seem to unaccustomed eyes a race of Goddesses. The town is indeed remarkable for this tall radiant race of amazons; for thousands of sailors who all seem to be on leave with their pockets full and a roving eye for the girls – and for oceans of alcohol in which the happy population float. I suppose there are poor, sick, and worried people here as everywhere else, but the impression is of people without a trouble in the world.

In the hotel dining-room a crooner with a voice like cream sings by request a number dedicated to Mr. and Mrs. Frank Lord because they are just married and on their honeymoon – cameras click – the happy couple bask – no self-consciousness – no sneers – it's "a very lovely thought." At the end of a drunken evening at the Bohemian Club's annual frolic the compère suggests that we should stand and sing two verses of "Onward Christian Soldiers" "honouring our boys in the Pacific" – the audience responds without a blush.

The day is spent in a series of committee meetings which are teaching me several things – the necessity for patience. It is wonderful to see quick-minded men sitting quite still hour after hour listening to people saying at almost infinite length things which could be said in a sentence or two. One becomes, I suppose, inured to boredom. And in combination with this patience the old hands have great quickness. They have been playing this game so long that they know instinctively by now when and how to play the rules of committee procedure or to catch the point of some quite discreet amendment to a motion. They are always on the alert for such things even when they seem to be half-asleep. All this is rather fascinating to a tyro. These are the tricks of the trade. Most men of my age and length of service know them well already.

I mentioned my alleged measles (now vanished) to a newspaper-man as a joke. Tonight there is a headline in one of the evening papers, "Measles at Conference Hotel. Will it spread to the Russian Delegation?" It is true that the Russians are installed on the floor above us in this hotel, but I have no contact with them of any kind.

23 May 1945.

The Conference atmosphere is thick with alarm and despondency about Russia. Wherever two or three are gathered together in the hotel bedrooms and sitting-rooms, where more unbuttoned conversation is permissible there you can bet that the subject is the U.S.S.R. – speculation about their intention, argument as to the best way of dealing with them – whether to be tough and, if so, when – gloomy realization that by unscrupulous conference tactics they may be courting and perhaps winning the favour of the "working masses." This fear of Russia casts its long shadow over the Conference. Meanwhile some of the Latin American and Middle Eastern States, by their verbose silliness and irresponsible sniping, almost induce one to believe that there is a good deal to be said for a Great Power dictatorship. But the Great Power representatives have no eloquent, authoritative or persuasive spokesman in the more important committees. They repeat, parrot fashion, "Trust the Security Council. Do nothing to injure unanimity." There are no outstanding speakers – Evatt of Australia has ability – Berendsen of New Zealand has eloquence of a homespun sort – Rollin, the Belgian, has a clever, satirical mind (I take names at random) – but there is no one of whom you say – a great man – and few indeed of whom you say – a fine speaker.

The British Delegation seems pretty thin and undistinguished now that Eden and the other senior Cabinet ministers have gone. Cranborne[1] is skilful and authoritative in committee – Halifax does not attend – Cadogan seems a tired, mediocre *fonctionnaire*. Webster is always at his elbow with an impressive memory (he can quote the documents of the Congress of Vienna, of the Paris Conference, of the Dumbarton Oaks meeting). His heroes are Castlereagh and Wellington. He takes a donnish pleasure in argumentation and in snubbing people. An excellent adviser – but he should not be allowed his head in policy matters – I do not know if he is – one sometimes sees his hand. The delegation is weak on the economic and social side. There is a grave lack of authority – of men of solid experience, wisdom and moderation, who inform a committee – not so much by what they say as by what they are. Then there is the lack of any

---

[1] Viscount Cranborne (later 5th Marquess of Salisbury) was Secretary of State for Dominion Affairs; Sir Alexander Cadogan, Permanent Under-Secretary at the Foreign Office; Sir Charles Webster, a professor of history, was adviser to the delegation.

representation of the English internationalists or those who have devoted themselves to oppressed peoples and to social causes – that whole humanitarian and social side of English activity goes unrepresented. There were representatives of it, but they have gone home – the brunt of the British representation is borne by a little group thinking in terms of political and military power and with not much feeling for public opinion. As they get more tired they may pull a serious gaffe. They produce no ideas which can attract other nations and are not much fitted to deal with Commonwealth countries.

American policy, or perhaps I should say more narrowly, American tactics in this Conference are similar to British – like the British they hew closely to the party line of support for the Great Power veto while allowing the impression to be disseminated among the smaller countries that they do so reluctantly, that their hearts are in the right place but that they dare not say so for fear of the Russians bolting the organization. One incidental result of this line which the British and Americans may not contemplate is to increase the prestige of Russia. The United States delegation as a whole is no more impressive than the British. There does not seem to be much attempt to understand the viewpoint of the smaller nations or to produce reasoned arguments to meet their objections. On the other hand, the Americans are extremely susceptible to pressure from the Latin Americans who are not doing at all badly out of this Conference. The only American advisers I know are the State Department Team – shifty-eyed little Alger Hiss who has a professionally informal and friendly manner – which fails to conceal a resentful and suspicious nature said to be very anti-British – Ted Achilles – slow, solid, strong physically as an ox, a careful, good-tempered negotiator and a very good fellow – I should not think much influence on policy.

The U.S.S.R. have achieved a most unfavourable reputation in the Committees. This does not result from dislike for the methods or personalities of individual Russians – so far as the Conference is concerned there are no individual Russians – they all say exactly the same thing (and needless to say this goes for the Ukrainian and Bielo-Russkis). All make the same brief colourless statements – every comma approved by Moscow – from which every trace of the personality of the speaker has been rigorously excluded. Their reputation is one of solid stone-walling and refusal to compromise. On the other hand, they are continually blackmailing other governments by posing as the protectors of the masses against reactionary influence. This they have done so effectively that it is quite possible for them to produce a record at the Conference which would show them battling for the oppressed all over the world. The insincerity of these tactics is patent to those who see them at close quarters, but will not be so to the public for whom they are designed. They have great political flair – envisage every question not on its merits but entirely from the political point of view. This causes acute distress to *(a)* the legalistically-minded Latin Americans, *(b)* all social crusaders and liberal internationalists who see "power politics" invading every aspect of the new organization, the social, humanitarian, and even purely administrative.

The intellectual defence of the Dumbarton Oaks[1] proposals has been left to Wellington Koo, which is rather hard on him, as he had nothing to do with drafting them. I sat opposite him and he fascinated me – he looks like a little lizard, darting lizard eyes and nose down close to his papers. When he speaks he displays a remarkable collection of *tics nerveux* – he blinks rapidly and convulsively, sniffs spasmodically, clasps and unclasps his immaculately manicured little hands, pulls at the lapels of his coat and continually removes and then readjusts his two pairs of spectacles. This pantomime does not in the least mean that he is nervous of the work in hand – he is a very experienced professional diplomat, quick-minded, ingenious, and conciliatory. But, of course, he has not – any more than any of the other Great Powers' delegates – the moral authority, eloquence, and vigour which would be needed to carry the Conference – it would take a Roosevelt or Churchill to do that – or perhaps Smuts. The Chinese are an endearing delegation, polite and humorous – but then are they really a Great Power?

The French are among the disappointments of this Conference. The Big Power representatives, however undistinguished individually, *do* represent Power and so carry weight. The French are in the

---

[1] At the Dumbarton Oaks Conference in August 1944, the four Great Powers – Great Britain, China, the U.S.A. , and the U.S.S.R. – agreed on a draft text for the creation of the United Nations.

position of having to depend on their tradition, their professionalism and that assurance of tough and violent precision of language which have always been at their command in international gatherings. But it is just this assurance that they lack. The French delegation here reinforce the painful impression that I formed in Paris – they seem to be *détraqués*. You do not feel that they have France, *La grande nation*, behind them. They are full of *petits soins* and handshakes to other delegates. They are full of schemes and combinations and suspicions. But there is no steadiness or clarity in their policy. They have no one who is a connecting link with the past and who still retains faith and vitality. The national continuity has been broken. They seem just a collection of clever, amiable, young Frenchmen – and old Paul-Boncour is too old and too tired – so is André Siegfried. In fact, you can see the effects of fatigue in the drained faces of almost all the European delegates. Europe (I do not count Russia) is not making much of a showing at this Conference.

In our own delegation Norman Robertson and Hume Wrong are the two most influential senior officials. There could hardly be a greater contrast than that between them. Hume (under whom I worked when he was Counsellor at our Legation in Washington), pale and fine featured, stroking the back of his head with a rapid gesture which suggests mounting impatience. He inspires alarm on first encounter – an alarm which could be justified as he is totally intolerant of muddle, inanity, or sheer brute stupidity. He has style in everything from the way he wears his coat to the prose of his memoranda. He is a realist who understands political forces better, unfortunately, than he does politicians themselves.

Norman understands them very well and has influence with the Prime Minister, but what does not Norman understand? His mind is as capacious as his great sloping frame. He has displacement, as they say of ocean liners, displacement physical and intellectual and he is wonderful company with his ironic asides, his shafts of wisdom, and his sighs of resignation.

5 June 1945.

We are still tormented by the feeling in our dealings with the Russians there *may* be an element of genuine misunderstanding on their side and that some of their suspicions of some of our motives may not be so very wide of the mark. They on their side seem untroubled by any such scruples. They keep us permanently on the defensive and we wallow about clumsily like some marine monster being plagued by a faster enemy (a whale with several harpoons already in its side). Yet they do not want or mean war.

The struggle for power plays itself out in the Conference committees. Every question before the committees becomes a test of strength between the Russians and their satellites and the rest of the world. The other Great Powers vote glumly with the Russians and send junior members of their delegations to convey to us their discomfiture and apologies. This situation reproduces itself over matters which in themselves do not seem to have much political content. But to the Russians everything is political, whether it is something to do with the secretariat of the new organization or the changing of a comma in the Declaration of the General Principles.

Committee 1 of the Commission, on which I sit as adviser, deals with the preamble to the Charter of the United Nations (composed of pious aspirations) and the chapters concerned with the Purposes and Principles of the Organization. It is presided over by a Ukrainian chairman, Manuilsky, said to be the brains of the Communist Party in the Ukraine. My first impression of him was of a humorous and polite old gentleman – an *ancien régime* landowner perhaps. He speaks good French. But I was wrong in everything except the humour – he is quite ruthlessly rude, exceedingly intelligent, and moves so fast in committee tactics that he leaves a room full of experienced parliamentarians breathless. It cannot be said that he breaks the rules of procedure – rather he interprets them with great cleverness to suit his ends. And his principal end is to hurry these chapters through the committee without further debate.

6 *June 1945.*

We had nearly seven hours on end in our Committee on Purposes and Principles. The Chairman, Manuilsky, gave us a touch of the knout when the Latin Americans were just spreading their wings for flights of oratory. He rapped on the table with his chairman's gavel and said, "Gentlemen, we must speed up the work of the Committee.

I propose that no one shall leave this hall until the preamble and the first chapter of the Charter are voted." The delegates gazed ruefully at their blotters – this meant cutting all dinner dates. Yet no one dared to falter in the "sacred task." Paul Gore-Booth, the British delegate, sprang to his feet and said in tones of emotion, "Mr. Chairman I cannot promise that I shall be physically able to remain so long in this hall without leaving it." Manuilsky looked at him sternly, "I say to the British representative that there are in this hall men older than you are, and if they can stay here you must also." So we settled down to hour after hour of debate.

We were after all discussing the principles of the New World Order. The room was full of professional orators who were ravening to speak and speak again. Latin American Foreign Ministers hoped to slide in an oblique reference to some of their local vendettas disguised in terms of the Rights of Nations. The Egyptian representative was hoping to see his way clear to take a crack at the Anglo-Egyptian Treaty under some phrase about the necessity for "flexibility in the interpretation of international obligations." The Syrian delegate saw an opportunity to embarrass the French. The representatives of the Colonial Powers were junior delegates (their chiefs were dining) who were frightened that any reference to "justice" or "human rights" might conceal a veiled attack on the colonial system. All afternoon and all evening until twelve o'clock at night we argued about the principles that must guide the conduct of men and nations. By eleven o'clock there were many haggard faces around the table. The room had got very hot and smelly – dozens of stout politicians sweating profusely in a confined space – outside the streetcars (and San Francisco is a great place for streetcars) rattled noisily and still the speeches went on. The Egyptian delegate was indefatigable in inter-polations. He seemed to bounce to his feet on india-rubber buttocks, "A point of order, Mr. Chairman" and he would fix his monocle and survey his helpless victims. The Peruvian was another inexhaustible plague; he was a professional lecturer who kept remarking, "The Peruvian delegation regard this aspect of the question as very grave indeed, in fact fundamental." Then he would remove his reading spectacles, put on his talking spectacles, brush the forelock back from his forehead, and get into his stride. But it was the Norwegian who moved me to homicide by making lengthy interventions in an obstinate, bleating voice. However, thanks to the knout, thanks to the ruthless, surgical operations of the Chairman, we finished our task in time. The committee was littered with punctured egos, and snubbed statesmen glowered at each other across the tables. The eminent political figures and distinguished jurists of half the world had been rated by the Chairman like schoolboys; but we had finished on time.

12 June 1945.

Lunch in the country with rich, friendly easy-going Californians – a cool, roomy house – none of the stiff, interior-decorated look of so many expensive houses in the East. Californians do not seem to treat their houses very seriously. They are places to sleep and refuges from the heat of the sun. These people seem to swim through life, carried along effortlessly by their good nature and good health. One can hardly believe that they have ever been scared or snubbed or "put in their place" or that anyone has ever exposed them to irony. There were three children bathing in the pool – perfect little physical specimens with nice, rich, easy-going, good-looking, sensible parents – what a way to grow up!

15 June 1945.

Last week I saw an advertisement in one of the San Francisco newspapers which described the attractions of "a historic old ranch home now transformed into a luxury hotel situated in a beautiful valley in easy reach of San Francisco." What a delightful escape, I thought, from the pressures of the Conference! Why not spend the weekend there? I succeeded in talking my colleagues, Norman and Hume and Jean Désy, the Canadian Adviser on Latin American Affairs, into this project, and our party was joined by a friend of Jean Désy, a French Ambassador, a senior and distinguished diplomat attached to the French Delegation. Last Saturday we all set forth by car in a holiday spirit to savour the delights of old-style ranch life in California as advertised to include "gourmet meals, horseback riding, and music in an exclusive atmosphere." It seemed an eminently suitable setting for this little group of overworked and fastidious *conferenciers*. As we approached in the late afternoon up the long avenue, we saw the ranch house set amidst a bower of trees, but when we debouched at the entrance instead of the subdued welcome of a luxury hotel we were brusquely but cheerily propelled by a stout and thug-like individual towards a swaying tollgate which opened to admit us one by one on payment in advance for the period of our stay. Once in the entrance hall we found ourselves in the midst of an animated crowd, but what was unexpected was that all the men were sailors, and young sailors at that, while the women were equally young and some strikingly luscious. This throng, exchanging jokes, playful slaps on bottoms, and swigs out of beer cans, filtered off from time to time in pairs to mount the noble staircase leading to the rooms above. Our diplomatic quintet stood together waiting for guidance among the jostling throng and were soon the objects of remarks. "Who the hell are those old guys?" Finally, seeing that no one was coming to our rescue we set off up the stairs, luggage in hand, to inspect our rooms. Mounting floor by floor we found all the bedrooms in a state of active and noisy occupation, until we reached the top floor where we encountered a large female of the squaw variety. As she appeared to be in charge of operations, we enquired for our rooms to find that only three rooms were available for the five of us.

It was decided among us that the French Ambassador should have a room to himself, while Jean Désy and Hume shared one and Norman and I the other. In our room we found an exhausted maid slapping at some dirty-looking pillows as she replaced them in position. "This is the fifth time I have made up this bed today," she observed. "Are you two *men* sharing this room?" With a look beyond surprise she withdrew. Norman seemingly not in the least disconcerted sank with a sigh into the only available chair and addressed himself to the evening paper. The other members of our party were less philosophical. Hume and Jean appearing in the doorway rounded sharply on me. "Why had I lured them into this brothel? Was this my idea of a joke?" I suggested that we should all be better for food and drink and we descended to the dining-room, a vast, panelled interior already packed with couples dancing to a blaring radio. After a lengthy wait we were squeezed into a corner table where we were attended by a motherly-looking waitress. "Who are all these girls?" I asked her. "And why all these sailors?" "Well, I guess you might call it a kind of meeting place for the boys off the ships and the girls who work near here in an aircraft factory." Meanwhile the French Ambassador was beginning to show signs of controlled irritation as he studied the menu that had been handed to him. Adjusting his spectacles he read out, "Tomato soup, hamburger delights, cheeseburgers, Hawaiian-style ham with pineapple." "For me," he announced, "I shall have a plain omelette." At this Jean Désy, in an attempt to lighten the gloom which was settling over our little party, clapped his hands together and in an almost boisterous tone called out to the waitress, "The wine list at once – we shall have champagne." "Wine list," she said, "I do not know about any list but we have some lovely pink wine – it is sparkling, too." "Bring it," said Jean, "and lots of it." It was not bad – both sweet and tinny, but it helped. For a few moments our spirits improved and we began to laugh at our predicament. Then came the omelette. The Ambassador just touched it with the prong of his fork and leaned back in his chair with an air of incredulity. "This an omelette!" He raised his shoulders with a shrug to end all shrugs.

At this Jean Désy, perhaps stimulated by the wine or pricked by embarrassment at having exposed his French colleague to such an experience, seized the plate with the omelette upon it and said, "I shall complain to the chef myself about this outrage." With this he hurled himself into the mob of dancers and made for a swinging door leading to the kitchen. Some uneasy moments passed at our table, then the swinging door swung open. Jean, still holding the plate with the omelette upon it, was backing away before an enormous Negro who was bellowing above the music, "Get out of my kitchen. Who the hell do you think you are? Bugger off! Bugger off! Bugger off!" Jean returned to our table. "I shall report him," he said – but it was difficult to know to whom. Soon afterwards we repaired to our rooms. As I left the dining-room I heard a girl say to her sailor companion, "Those are a bunch of old fairies sleeping together – the maid told me." The sailor spat, not actually at us, but on the floor, quite audibly.

The night was an uneasy one for me. I was kept restlessly awake by the beery hoots of laughter and the moans and murmurs of passion from the next room. Norman settled into his bed and slept peaceably with his deaf ear uppermost.

When I looked out of the window in the early morning the sun was shining, and a troop of sailors and their girls mounted on miscellaneous horses were riding by towards the adjoining fields, thus proving that horseback riding was as advertised one of the facilities of the ranch. Two small figures, Jean Désy and the French Ambassador, the latter sealed into a tight-looking overcoat, were proceeding side by side down the avenue. I later learned that they were on their way to Mass at a neighbouring church.

By mutual agreement for which no words were needed our party left the ranch before luncheon and returned to San Francisco.

On the way back in the car the French Ambassador raised the possibility that one of the assiduous gossip writers of the San Francisco press might learn where we had spent the weekend and he asked what effect this would be likely to have on the prestige of our respective delegations and indeed on our own reputations. My own colleagues reassured him by saying that in the event of publicity the episode could be attributed to my misleading them owing to my innate folly and vicious proclivities. This seemed to satisfy him.

18 June 1945.

The Conference is on its last lap. The delegates – many of them – are quite punch-drunk with fatigue. Meetings start every day at 9 a.m. and go on until midnight. In addition, we are having a heat wave. The committee rooms are uncomfortably hot and the commission meetings in the Opera House are an inferno. The heat generated by the enormous klieg lights adds to this and the glare drives your eyes back into your head.

We are in a feverish scramble to get through the work – an unhealthy atmosphere in which we are liable to push things through for the sake of getting them finished. The Russians are taking advantage of this state of affairs to reopen all sorts of questions in the hope that out of mere weakness we shall give in to them. Their tone and manner seem daily to become more openly truculent and antagonistic.

Once the labours of the committees are finished, the Articles they have drafted and the reports they have approved are put before the Co-ordinating Committee, who plunge into an orgy of revision. There is no pleasanter sport for a group of highly intelligent and critical men than to have delivered into their hands a collection of botched-up, badly-drafted documents and be asked to pull them to pieces and to point out the faults of substance and form. This could go on forever.

However hot, tired and bad-tempered the other delegates may become, Halifax remains cool and Olympian and makes benevolent, cloudy speeches which soothe but do not satisfy. Senator Connally of the U.S. delegation roars at his opponent, waving his arms and sweating. It is somehow reassuring to come out from the committee meetings into the streets and see the people in whose name we are arguing so fiercely and who do not give a damn how the Charter reads. Sailors hand in hand with their girls – (this is a great town for walking hand in hand) on their way to a movie or a dance hall.

If the people were let into the committee meetings they would have broken up this Conference long ago.

Alice was sitting across the table from me today at the committee meeting, in glowing looks from her weekend in the country and wearing an exceptionally low-cut flowered dress. I was not the only one to be distracted from the dissertation of our pedantic El Salvadorean rapporteur.

Every day going to and from the Conference we pass a Picasso picture in an art shop window – two elongated and distorted forms are in silent communion. They gaze at each other in trance-like still-ness. I find that by looking for a few minutes at this picture I can get into a sort of dope dream.

19 June 1945.

The Soviet delegates have got very little good-will out of this Conference. They use aggressive tactics about every question large or small. They remind people of Nazi diplomatic methods and create, sometimes needlessly, suspicions and resentment. They enjoy equally making fools of their opponents and their supporters. Slyness, bullying, and bad manners are the other features of their Conference behaviour.

Their system has some unfortunate results from their point of view. They have no elbow-room in committee tactics – they cannot vary their method to allow for a change in mood and tempo of the Conference. They are paralyzed by the unexpected. They always have to stall and cable home for instructions. It is unfortunate from our point of view as well as theirs that they should have made such a bad showing, for I think they are proposing to make a serious effort to use the organization and are not out to wreck it.

28 June 1945.

Back in Ottawa the Conference is over. It is going to be a little disconcerting at first living alone again after our group existence in San Francisco. The hotel sitting-room which Norman Robertson and Hume Wrong shared was a meeting place for members of our delegation and there was a perpetual flow of drinks on tap. There we foregathered to talk Conference gossip. The pace of the Conference got more and more hectic towards the end. Meetings would end at 4 or 5 a.m., when we would fall into bed and drag ourselves up three or four hours later. It also became increasingly difficult to relate the Conference to other events going on in the world and form an estimate of the real importance in the scheme of things of what we were doing at San Francisco. While we were there the war against Germany was won, the occupation of Germany took place, the Russians installed themselves in Prague and in Vienna and made their first bid for a port on the Adriatic and bases in the Straits. We were preoccupied with the Battle of the Veto and with the tussles over the powers of the General Assembly and the provisions for amending the Charter. How much were these mere paper battles? How much was the San Francisco Conference a smokescreen behind which the Great Powers took up their positions? These doubts were floating about in the backs of our minds but we had not much time for doubts – the daily timetable was too gruelling.

At any rate, if the Conference was a gigantic bluff, it bluffed the participants – at least some of them.

The final public sessions were decidedly too good to be true. The Opera House was packed with pleased, excited, well-fed people. There was a feeling of a gala performance. On the floodlit stage ranged in front of the flags of the United Nations were standing handpicked specimens of each branch of the United States Armed Forces – very pretty girls from the Women's Forces made up for the floodlighting and wore very becoming uniforms – soldiers and sailors preserving even on this occasion an air of loose-limbed sloppiness.

One after another the speakers mounted the rostrum and addressed us – most of them in their native languages. The text of the speeches in English had been circulated to the audience, but this was hardly necessary as we knew what they would say, and they all said it – in Chinese, Arabic, French, and Russian we were told that mankind was embarking on another effort to organize the world so that peace should reign. We were told that the success of the Conference showed that this ideal could be attained if unity was preserved – that we owed it to the living and to the dead to devote all our efforts to this end. Almost all the speeches worked in a reference to the inspiring example of Franklin D. Roosevelt and a flowery tribute to Stettinius (rather wasted as he resigned next day).

It all went off very well – there was really nothing to complain of – no outrageous bit of vulgarity or juke-box sentimentality. Even that great ape, Stettinius, was rather subdued and contented himself with grinning and signalling to his acquaintances in the audience during the playing of the United States National Anthem. The speakers were dignified and sincere – Halifax, Wellington Koo, Smuts, Paul-Boncour – all spoke out of long experience and were impressive. True, they said nothing, but this seemed an occasion when nothing was better than too much. President Truman made a sensible, undistinguished speech – just too long. (He looks like a sparrowy, little, old, small-town, American housewife who could shut the door very firmly in the face of the travelling salesmen and tramps.) He got the biggest hand from the audience and after him Halifax. They fell completely for Halifax's gilt-edged "niceness." What with tributes to the Great Deceased and bouquets to each other and commendatory remarks on the good work accomplished, the whole thing reminded one of speech day at school. In front of me the Argentine Ambassador and his pretty daughter applauded with polite enthusiasm. There were only two cracks in the surface – one was when Masaryk, the Czech Foreign Minister, said at the close of his speech, "Let us for God's sake hear less talk of the next world war." And the other (for me at least) was when Stettinius asked us to stand "in silent memory of the dead in this war whose sacrifice had made this Conference possible." I suppose it had to be said – it sounded as if we were thanking Lady Bountiful for lending her garden "without which this bazaar would not have been possible." As a matter of fact I did think of some of the dead – of Victor Gordon-Ives, who wanted to go on living and to enjoy country-house culture, collect beautiful things, and make jokes with his friends – of John Rowley and Gavin Rainnie and the other Canadians whose prompt reaction would have been "Balls to you, brother!" Still, I suppose it had to be said, but not by Stettinius in the San Francisco Opera House on a gala evening to the polite applause of the Argentine Ambassador.

5 July 1945. Halifax, Nova Scotia.

Back in my own country among my own people – how different from the easy-going superficial Californians. The surface layer here as everywhere is Americanization – the climate that extends over the whole of this continent – the whole Anglo-Saxon world – babbitry – but here it is a peculiar brand of babbitry without optimism, and it is not deep. Underneath is a queer compound of philosophical pessimism, of rooted old prejudice, of practical kindliness to the neighbour and the unfortunate, of unkindness towards the prosperous, something which has been ironed out in the prosperous fat lands of Upper Canada but which still grows on this rocky soil.

For me, Halifax is full of what Elizabeth calls "mined areas." As I am walking in its streets I am suddenly assailed by memories coming out of a past which is so far away as to be almost meaningless – a street smell, the sharp angle of a tall roof, the cracked, dark red paint on the shingle of a wall – they send me signals that I cannot read. I walk the sunny streets under the trees – everything registers, reminds, torments with hidden hints, sly remembrances, elusive little airs of memories. I am easily bewildered and tired here – it is too much to fit together, and while I observe the changes, the disappearance of shops and houses, there surges a tide laden with old scraps – empty fruit husks, an uneasy wave that goes to and fro, the sensation of change, of time of change – comes so close that it is stifling.

7 July 1945.

Went to lunch at the Halifax Club. An old man sitting in his arm-chair said, "When I get the fish smell coming up from the wharves and the oil smell blown across the harbour from Dartmouth and the smell of the nearby brothels, I ask myself whether I live in a very savoury neighbourhood." The brothels are usually ancient houses in Hollis and Water Streets solidly built in the late eighteenth century, once the homes of merchants, now encrusted with filth, infested with bed-bugs and snotty-nosed brats. Little girls of twelve and thirteen are already in the business, with painted faces and gyrating bottoms – they walk the streets in twos and threes giving a giggle for a leer. This part of Halifax is the old port-town shortly to be swept away. It is not far from Hogarth's Gin Alley. In the midst of these smells of fish, wharf, and brothel lives my maiden cousin, Susie, in the last of the old houses to keep its character. On its outer wall is a mildewed brass plate with "A" engraved in flowery longhand upon it. The glass panel in the door is protected by a fortification of twisted wire-work to prevent drunken lascars from breaking in. This is a last outpost of gentility. It has an obdurate defender. Susie's face is the colour of a yel-lowing letter left in a desk. Her manner is gentle, her obstinacy does not appear on the surface. She would be a happy martyr for her obses-sions – she loves resistance – she is the woman every underground movement is looking for. Thumbscrews would avail her enemies nothing – and she sees her enemies everywhere – the Catholic Church, the American Nation, Modern Commercialism – she tilts at all of them. As for the squalor around her, it shall be kept at bay. It is provided in her will that this old house is to be destroyed at her death. Meanwhile she writes in her childish hand long rigmaroles of family gossip to cousins in England or in Bermuda. She sits under the Copley portrait of the loyalist great-great-great-great-grandfather Byles. (Although practically penniless she refused to sell it to the Boston Art Gallery for $20,000 lest it should fall into the hands of the Americans.) She looks out between the yellow lace curtains at the life of Gin Alley and knows herself as strong as the drunken bullies or the hardened tarts.

8 July 1945. Wolfville, Nova Scotia.

This time it is different being in Wolfville. Perhaps I have been too keyed up and cannot relax, or else I am too well, and this place is only ideal for invalids and the old. The weather has been close and airless with low, suffocating, grey skies. There is to be an eclipse of the sun tomorrow and people say this queer weather has something to do with it.

I miss Elizabeth more and more. When I am working I banish her from my conscious mind by thinking of something that has to be thought of first because it must be tackled at once, so I manage to keep her image at arm's length, but now that I am idle thoughts of her besiege me.

The main street of Wolfville which before seemed so idyllic has lost its charm – in fact it is stifling to me. So many old women spying at the passer-by from behind their muslin curtains – the tight, taut atmosphere of a small town waiting for an event, a scandal, a false step, anything around which to circle and scream like hungry sea-gulls. It makes me feel absurdly sulky, restless and adolescent, yet the people are very kind. It is just that the place gives me a mild attack of the disease of my youth – claustrophobia.

I wonder if the returned soldiers suffer from this disease. I saw two of them today sitting somewhat disconsolately in their hot uniforms on a park bench. What do they make of the home town after months of waiting and fear and exhilaration, after the wild welcoming crowds in the Brussels streets, after the years of their youth in Sussex towns and villages?

9 July 1945.

This is the season for the smells of cut hay and the sweetness of clover – the wild roses are out everywhere. I rush out of this house on a sudden walk streaking along Main Street past the neat white houses with their little lawns and pergolas and right up the hill among the orchards. From there you look down over the dike lands to Minas Basin.

Mother and I spend a good deal of our time with the Sherwoods who are as much a local product as the apples they grow in their own orchards. Gertie is earthy Nova Scotian – she can hardly open her mouth without some localism popping out. "Some person told me" is the beginning of half her gossip, and "Small town – small talk" she says of her own conversation. She notices that the clergyman is wearing a silk surplice instead of a linen one and does not believe that it is because of any wartime shortage of linen – no – it is because his wife thinks silk looks grander. She says of the bank manager's wife, "She calls on everyone, she is the sort of woman who never gets offended." (This is a devastating comment, as in her view people with proper pride are always in a state of "being offended" with some of their neighbours.)

11 July 1945.

Main Street of Wolfville. The brownstone of the Post Office, the greens and reds of the municipal geranium beds. The street itself is still and dusty in the sun – awnings are down over the closed shops. It is Wednesday afternoon – early-closing day – an occasional car passes driven at a sleepy tempo or carts and horses moving at a walking pace. Twos and threes of small boys in overalls with bare feet scour the sidewalks in desultory search for sensation. Men in shirtsleeves sit on the doorsteps – a woman in a white and mauve polka-dot dress passes with a basket of strawberries under her arm. The pulse of the small town beats slowly, rhythmically, steadily – a sense of summer contentment fills the streets.

15 July 1945.

The summer perfection of Wolfville is too much for me – there are too many smells – the rich smell of clover and the juicy, verdant, almost sexy smell of the new-cut grass in the fields behind the house, the wild roses and arbutus, the poppies and the peonies. There are breezes all day long – nothing seems to stand still for a moment – the grass, trees, and flowers shiver and skimmer in the wind and sun. I get hay fever from the smells. My eyes ache from the brilliance of summer colours – the breezes make me lascivious – the beauty makes me restless – there is nothing peaceful about this summer countryside. This indecent display of charms is a standing invitation to lust and venery.

4 September 1945.

Back to Ottawa on a train crowded with returning soldiers. Train after train travels across Canada from east to west laden with them, dropping them off by threes and fours at small towns and in their hundreds at the big cities. The train windows are crowded with their sunburned, excited faces. They lean out in their shirtsleeves, whistling at the girls on the station platforms, making unflattering jokes about Mackenzie King. We passed through one little station where there were a few mugwumps standing about on the platform staring bemusedly at the train and a group of soldiers on the train began themselves to cheer, "Hurray! Give the boys a welcome." The stations are crowded with them striding about self-consciously – men of the world – having proved something about themselves that is plainly to be seen in their sun-paled divisional patches and the ribbons on their chests – the 1939–43 Star, the Africa Star, the France and Germany award, the Voluntary Service Ribbon.

The women look at them fondly, the men respectfully and perhaps enviously. Everyone says, "It is a big moment for them." These are our heroes – the "Flowers of the Nation's Manhood," etc. This is the role – every man his own Hotspur – and they play it to advantage; good-humoured, cynical, knowing their way around – they make the other men look tame and "stay-at-home."

The streets are fuller every day of demobilized soldiers. They wear pinned to their civilian coats emblems of overseas service and rows of ribbons, but you could not fail to recognize them anyway – the straight up and down army back which they will never entirely lose – the sunburned necks and the new clothes. They go in for sporting jackets fresh off the hook – perhaps a souvenir of English fashions.

7 September 1945. Ottawa.

An office day – I get up with a slight hangover but feeling pretty healthy and not gloomy – not anything – just like a bloody clock wound up to run for another twelve hours and off I go to my office in the Department of External Affairs. I read the papers obediently, skipping the story about the gangsters to concentrate on Keynes's statement on economic policy. I cast a wary eye at the social notes. I get down to work. All morning a stream of interesting and informative telegrams and dispatches from missions abroad comes pouring across my desk. I am tempted to read them all and to try to understand what is really happening, but if I do that I have not time to draft answers to the most immediate telegrams and dispatches crying out for instructions. I must skim through everything with my mind concentrated on immediate practical implications. If I try to be objective and to comprehend all the issues I am lost. I draft telegrams and speeches under pressure, short-term considerations uppermost – "Will the Prime Minister sign this?" – "Are we not too short of personnel to be represented at this or that international meeting?" This is the way policy is made on a hand-to-mouth basis out of an overworked official by a tired politician with only half his mind on the subject.

12 September 1945.

Sally Gordon-Ives is here on a visit. She has never recovered from Victor's death in the war. She said, "I suppose he was lucky to be killed young when he was at the height of his enjoyment. Anything is better than being dead in life."

I wish the dead could use our bodies, feel our sensations, see with our eyes. If Victor's spirit lingers in some limbo I should like to lend him this apparatus for living and when I have been dead a little while I should like someone to do the same for me.

22 September 1945.

How devastating it would be to find celibacy bearable – to get fairly comfortably into the habits of chastity and then to find it too much trouble to get out of it again.

I have just been reading a dispatch about the difficulties of life in Moscow. I must say it sounds very much like Ottawa – "For instance, the difficulty of finding a mistress and making arrangements for cherishing her." But the pressure of work keeps me riveted to this spot under an uneasy spell. Just as I get to the point of saying to myself that I cannot stand this life a moment longer a crisis blows up – I am brought in – something has to be done in a hurry – a formula has to be found – a way of getting around things devised – a situation met. I am on a stretch – my will and brain and judgement are called upon. I live on this stimulus.

23 September 1945. Ottawa.

I have come up against a blank wall. There is nothing to do but turn around and face things. I feel myself hardening. I will not be one of life's casualties, nor just a sympathetic character. Middle-age is the time when one is supposed to concentrate on the world's game, care about making a grand slam and watch other people's play. The game has always interested me but never enough to overcome my love of talking and of sensuous perceptions but now I am bloody well going to have my fling at it. The trouble is that it is only for two or three days at a time that I can deceive myself that I do care about this success game. Then I long to throw my cards in and clear out.

EPILOGUE[1]

The diarist did not "throw in his cards and clear out." On the contrary he played them for all he was worth. His diplomatic career is written in the sands of *Who's Who*. He was to become Canada's Representative to the United Nations which he had seen founded at San Francisco, to go as Ambassador to Washington where he had served his apprenticeship, and finally as High Commissioner to the United Kingdom to find himself back again in the grand room at Canada House, where standing under the chandelier Vincent Massey had announced to his staff the outbreak of World War II.

He had one undeserved piece of good fortune in a happy marriage. His wife, Sylvia, during more than twenty-five years has encouraged and supported him with her wit and wisdom in everything he has undertaken, including the publication of this book.

The diaries continue – compulsion dies hard.

---

[1] As written for the first edition of *The Siren Years* in 1974.

DIPLOMATIC PASSPORT

More Undiplomatic Diaries
1946–1962

To
my friends in the Department of External Affairs,
past and present

PREFACE

These journals, covering the years 1946 to 1962, take up where my wartime diaries, published as *The Siren Years*, ended. I ask myself the question, What is the compulsion that makes one put down on paper day after day such a personal record as this? Is it simply an exercise in egotism, or a confessional? Perhaps a little of both, but it may also be an obsession with the passing of time, a sense that life is slipping like sand through one's fingers and that before it vanishes completely one must shore up these remains.

It is said that every fat man has a thin man inside him, struggling to get out. Has every diarist a novelist inside him, struggling to get out? If so, the struggle is likely to be unavailing. The diarist, with his passion for the record – historical, social, or political – too often lacks the power of construction and the storyteller's skill. On the other hand, many writers are marvellous diarists but they tend to regard their diaries as the waste product of their art, material which is not yet fused by the imagination into finished work. Some diaries are written with an eye to publication as a conscious contribution to history. My own were of the private kind. It is true that in my old age I went public, or partly public, but when I wrote them they were for my eyes only. Nor are they at all like the informative memoirs of many of my contemporaries in diplomacy. Yet forty years in a career are bound to be conditioning, perhaps more than one realizes oneself, especially in a career spent for the most part away from one's own country, living the rootless existence of those to whom a place is not a home but a posting, shifting from one foreign capital to another. In this career the representational role tends to take over. The man sometimes merges into the ambassador. The result is not so much pomposity as a smoothness from which all angles and irregularities of temperament and opinion have been ironed out. From this fate diary-writing may have been an escape hatch for me. Diplomacy is a profession in which protracted patience, discretion, and a glaze of agreeability prevail, and it was a relief to break out, if only on paper.

This is the record of years spent in the foreign service of Canada, yet no official business was included in it. Here are to be found no breaches of the sacrosanct Official Secrets Act. From the Department of External Affairs in which I served I took no papers on departure. Buried in their archives is the evidence of my working life. This deliberate omission conveys a curiously lopsided picture, as though the writer, instead of being an industrious and reasonably competent official, had been a detached observer drifting idly about the world. An observer, yes – but what did he observe? Changing scenes and people, politicians, fellow diplomats and journalists, people of fashion or who sought to be so, authors and would-be authors, old aunts and young beauties, people labelled "interesting," and, often more interesting, those without a label. As to the scenes, they shift from Ottawa to Paris, from Delhi to Bonn, from London to New York, and always back to his native Nova Scotia. Thus the journal is an odd mixture of anecdote, reflection, politics, and personalities. It may be thought that this record is too personal for publication during my lifetime. The alternative of posthumous publication seemed to me a bleak prospect, so I let the record stand, with a word of advice to any fellow diplomatic diarist – keep diplomatic discretion out of your diaries and keep the diarist's indiscretion out of your diplomacy. A double life is doubly enjoyable.

1945–1947

In the years 1945 to 1947 the war was just over and the Cold War was just beginning. This was a time marked by one international conference and confrontation after another, at which East–West conflicts were accentuated towards the dreaded danger point of a third world war. Canada was represented at most of these gatherings, either as a participant or as an observer. While based in Ottawa I served as adviser to a series of Canadian delegations to such conferences, so that I was as much abroad as I was at home.

Despite the cloud of gloomy foreboding hanging over the future, these were, for a Canadian foreign service officer, exhilarating years. There was change in the air. Although the Prime Minister, Mackenzie King, was still governed by a caution verging on isolationism, another mood was beginning to prevail in the country. Our pre-war policy of no prior commitments had not saved us involvement in the struggle, and it was increasingly obvious that it was in our interest as Canadians to play our full part in the attempt to build a more sane and stable international order. I do not think that we in the Department of External Affairs approached the task with dewy-eyed illusions, but with a realization that whatever the frustrations, it had to be attempted. A further spur to a positive Canadian foreign policy was provided by the new pride and confidence in our nationhood, born of our achievements in the war and Canada's growing wealth and importance. No doubt, too, the temporary eclipse of so many great nations in Europe and Asia, laid low by the war, thrust Canada closer to a front seat in the world community. These challenges and opportunities met with a ready and eager response in the Department of

External Affairs, which was expanding in size and influence under the leadership of a gifted band of officials including Norman Robertson, Hume Wrong, and Mike Pearson. With the departure in 1948 of Mackenzie King from power, with Pearson as Foreign Minister and Louis St. Laurent as Prime Minister, both convinced internationalists, the political leadership came into being which could use the energy and talents to be found in the department to the full, so that our foreign service gained widespread international respect.

As a relatively junior officer I was only on the margin of decision-making. But there was a continuous interchange of ideas and opinions – rather rare, I think, in Foreign Offices – between the different ranks of our foreign service. We were encouraged to put our views on paper, not only concerning the routine work in hand but on broader questions, so that one had a lively sense of participating in policy formulation. Also, after so many years abroad, I was being inducted into the mysteries, the frustrations, and the techniques of life in a government department. "Power," as Mr. Churchill remarked, "is at the centre," and it was in those years that there was impressed upon me a lesson which I never afterwards forgot. No matter what your relations are with the foreign government to which you may be accredited, or whoever may be your political masters at home at any time, be sure that you are firmly entrenched in your own department and that your relations there are in good repair. Government departments have long memories; they sometimes forgive but they never forget.

Ottawa is a pleasant city. I had good friends and good times there. My work was interesting, yet I was restive. What more did I want? I suppose I shrank from the prospect of existence, year after year, as a completely adapted civil servant. I wanted to have one more fling at life outside the Victorian Gothic precincts of the Department. So that, in January 1947, I welcomed the news of my appointment as Counsellor to the Canadian Embassy in Paris. There was to be a fore-taste of Paris, as I had been named one of the advisers to the Canadian Delegation to the Peace Conference to take place there in August 1946.

The year that I had spent in Ottawa was one of those blissful inter-missions from the servitude of the diary. Either I was too busy to keep it up or the diarist addiction had temporarily relaxed its grip, only to return in full force later, like other incurable addictions. Thus these diaries resume at the Paris Peace Conference.

The Conference was convened for the formulation of the peace treaties between the wartime Allies and Italy and the Balkan states. Its main focus was the controversy over the future of Trieste and the claims and counter-claims of Italy and Yugoslavia for possession of that city. Like all post-war international meetings, this quickly developed into yet another episode of the Cold War. The Canadian Delegation was presided over in a very unconvincing fashion by our declining Prime Minister, Mackenzie King. My own job, in addition to attendance at the plenary sessions of the Conference dealing with the Italian treaty, was to assist in the co-ordination of Canadian policies as prepared by our representatives on the separate committees dealing with the other ex-enemy countries. Our delegation stayed at the Hotel Crillon, in conditions of mingled splendour and inconvenience. It was the Prime Minister's favourite hotel and he had expressed a determination to sleep in the bed in which Woodrow Wilson had slept during the Peace Conference at the end of the First War. This involved delicate negotiations in inducing the hotel management to arrange the temporary expulsion of the lady who had for years resided in this suite. Even the apartments allotted to humbler members of the delegation, like myself, were those which before the war had been reserved for visiting sovereigns or peripatetic millionaires and, during the war, for German generals. (The salon of my own suite still smelled strongly of their cigars.) The hotel service was as urbane as it had been under the German occupation. The food was delicious; the telephone service, despite the presence of priceless antique telephones in every suite, was highly erratic. At times throughout the Conference we were isolated from other national delegations and totally cut off from telephone communication with Canada. Once, in a fit of exasperation, I determined to see for myself who the human agents were in the hotel who could be responsible for this confusion. I expected to encounter an array of overworked telephone operators; instead, I found one plump blonde lady placidly reading a magazine, with a box of chocolates at her side, facing a board on which light signals were frantically flashing from the different floors of the hotel. To these she seemed sublimely indifferent.

"Where," I asked, "are your colleagues?" "I am alone," she replied, giving me a glance of pathos, as though she languished for company, even my own. The frustration of the Crillon telephone system seemed a fitting accompaniment to the frustration of the Conference itself. Met to consolidate peace in Europe, the former Allies were preparing the ground for further conflict.

21 August 1946. Paris.

The *Manchester Guardian* compares the Peace Conference to the situation described in Sartre's play *Huis-Clos*. Like the characters in Sartre's Hell, the nations are trapped by their own past actions and cannot escape. The situation is frozen. The delegates can only repeat endlessly the same arguments and the same gestures. Profound disillusionment and weary cynicism characterize all the delegations except the irresponsible and ebullient Australians.

Even the setting reminds one of Sartre's scene, which was a salon furnished in gilt and plush, of which all the windows had been bricked up. We play out our Hell in the airless Second Empire salons of the Luxembourg Palace. How long is this interminable struggle of wills to go on? The Russians appear to be able to keep it up indefinitely. They have nerves, stomachs, and constitutions of iron. They give the impression of men who have no private lives. We western amateurs have not streamlined our lives enough; we are still in the horse-and-buggy age.

I shall think of this time as dominated by the game of trying to fathom Soviet intentions, of the tactics and strategy of power. International affairs have become a battlefield where the rules of war are relevant, and the strains on the combatants are as gruelling as on the battlefield. You need physical, mental, and nervous strength. But, hardest of all, you cannot afford too many distractions. That is not so bad for the old men who live only for ambition. It is hard on the young; they tire more easily and are more vulnerable to their own mistakes. The Old Boys have made so many that one more or less does not matter to them. Then the young ones have the other battles of love to contend with. They are fighting on two fronts. They must have time to sleep with their wives or someone else will do it for them.

23 August 1946.

In the evenings, when I come back after the day's Conference session is over, General Pope often joins me for a chat in the faded elegance of my hotel sitting-room, with its raspberry-coloured satin curtains. He is a delightful companion, witty and quirky. As Canadian representative on the Commission for the Peace Treaty with Romania, he is always stepping out of the line of his instructions. As we have few direct Canadian interests in the Romanian Treaty, he has been told that we should follow the British lead. He makes a point of doing the opposite. I remonstrate with him, as I have responsibility for co-ordination. "If you imagine that I am going to agree with that soft-centred young prig from the Foreign Office, you are much mistaken," he says. Then we differ about the Nürnberg Trials. I say that such German generals as ordered the massacres of civilians and other excesses deserve to be shot. "And what about the German diplomats," he asks, "who signed documents resulting in atrocities?" "It is different," I say, "for a diplomat to sign a paper. Half the time he does not know what it may lead to. That is not like giving an order to kill." "You and your trade union," he says. "The fact is that the Nürnberg Trials are scandalously unjust and should never have taken place." He may be right.

The only fun I have at the Conference sessions arises from the fact that I have been selected to maintain contact with the Australians. Their Foreign Minister, Evatt, whom we saw in action at the San Francisco Conference,[1] has become insufferably megalomaniacal and irresponsible. He much enjoys undercutting any position taken by the Canadian delegation. Like many Australians, he seems to regard Canadians as mealy-mouthed fence-sitters. He is also very jealous of any Canadian initiative or achievement. Despite all this I much relish my contacts with the Australians. They are such pungently lively company and don't give a damn for the proprieties. The New Zealanders may be nicer but they are tamer.

The other day during the Conference session Evatt made such an outrageous statement about Canadian policy that on the spur of

---

[1] The San Francisco Conference opened in April 1945 and proceeded to the creation of the United Nations. I was an adviser to the Canadian delegation.

the moment I got up from my seat, walked round the table to the Australian delegation, and, bearding him in his lair, said that we must have an immediate apology. He glared at me and I thought he was going to knock me down. But he said nothing. A few moments later he came over to us and apologized profusely.

I have been reading *Darkness at Noon*, Koestler's novel about the Moscow Trials. The theme of the book is the tragedy of those who use unscrupulous means to attain great ends. It is a terrifying picture of the evil courses into which the Soviet bureaucracy has turned. Before the war one might have read it with the feeling that our humanitarian tradition was too deeply engraved for such dangers to threaten us. But can we be sure now? To defeat our enemies we used the atomic bomb, bombing the innocent, flame-throwing, commando tactics, and we imprisoned men without trial. Our newspapers toed the Party line on all these issues. When we were hard-pressed we were willing to use any means to attain our end – victory. Where was the humanitarianism of 1939 (war by leaflets – only the Nazis are guilty, not the German people, etc.) by 1945? So that our humanitarianism is of a fair-weather quality. It is born of stability and prosperity and dies with them. "Let us clear our minds," as Dr. Johnson said, "of Cant." But while we take a holiday from pity and morality in wartime and return to kindness and muddled thinking when the war is over, the Russians are in a perpetual state of war. How can we co-operate with such people? Only for limited and concrete purposes which promise joint advantages, and then watch your partner with a lynx-like eye. No other co-operation is possible. Does this mean that war is inevitable? At any rate it means years of unsleeping struggle for power. It means that all major decisions of foreign policy will have to be taken with an eye to this opponent. Fighting the Germans brutalized our methods of warfare to meet theirs; the struggle for power with the U.S.S.R. will brutalize our methods more and more. They do not believe in our morality for a moment. They think it clever hypocrisy. And after what we have suffered and inflicted in the last few years we are not so sure ourselves of our own moral superiority. Perhaps the Russians are just more logical than we, more brutally consistent. So often we can see, as in a distorting glass but still recognizable, our motives and actions reflected in theirs. We are more scrupulous, more gentlemanly, but how much does that difference matter? Sometimes, as over the scramble for bases, the difference seems to have narrowed down almost to the vanishing point. Yet that difference only divides us from the jungle world they inhabit. And the difference we must stick to – we must think it a strength, otherwise we shall be too much tempted to throw it over. We must demonstrate its effectiveness or we might as well disencumber ourselves of it and plunge nakedly into the struggle. Every act of hypocrisy in which our governments indulge weakens our own faith in that difference. If humane and fair political and social practices only spring from strength and not from fear, then we need to be strong – lest we give way to panic.

24 August 1946.

Fête of the Liberation of Paris.

The Prime Minister's forthcoming departure for Canada will be no loss to the Canadian Delegation and certainly not to the Conference or to the peace-making process. He has produced no ideas and no leadership. He just goes through the motions. He seems principally concerned with petty fiddle-faddle about his personal arrangements. However, if any member of the delegation leaves the hotel for a ten-minute stroll or to keep an official appointment, the Prime Minister senses his absence by some uncanny instinct and, on his return, subjects the absentee to a sad stream of reproach. "At one time it would have been thought a privilege to serve the Prime Minister of Canada. Now it seems that young people think only of their own pleasure." He insists for the record on keeping his personal expenses recorded at a derisory figure. I sat next to him in the Crillon dining-room the other night when he was consuming with avidity a lobster thermidor which must have cost twice as much as his whole daily expense account. He does not grow in stature in one's eyes. Brooke Claxton, the Minister of National Defence, will now take over as Head of the Delegation, which he has been in practice all the time. He has plenty of drive and ability, is most frank and friendly with me, and I like him very much.

The other day, during an interval in the Conference session, I was standing at one of the windows looking out at the sparkling fountains and patterned parterres of the Luxembourg gardens when I became conscious of a person standing beside me. It was Molotov, the Soviet Foreign Minister. He had removed his pince-nez and was wiping them clean with a handkerchief while gazing unseeingly at the scene outside the window. His eyes were red-rimmed, his face naked with fatigue. He looked like a weather-beaten Easter Island monument – but for a moment I had mistaken the old monster for a human being.

13 October 1946.

Bevin's[1] dinner at the British Embassy for Dominion delegations. After dinner Alexander, the First Lord of the Admiralty, played music-hall numbers of 1914 vintage and sea shanties. The party gathered around the piano and sang in a ship's-concert atmosphere of jollity. Mr. Bevin danced with Mrs. Beasley[2] of Australia, and they cavorted about like two good-humoured elephants. Here we all were – "the British family of nations." What a funny collection! The prevailing social tone of the evening was British lower middle class. Since Labour came in in England they are the rulers – the politicians. Their servants of the upper class – the professional diplomats and officials – joined benevolently in the fun, taking the attitude "they are really rather dears and it is nice to see them enjoy themselves in their simple fashion and we must not seem patronizing," except for one who remarked to me, "This is where experience at Servants' Balls and Sergeants' Messes comes in so useful."

The Embassy staff of elegant young and not-so-young Etonians, and the sophisticatedly pretty young secretary of Lady Diana[3] (who had retired to bed with a toothache), had obviously fortified themselves for the evening with every drop of alcohol they could lay their hands on. I could picture the shudders in the Chancery at the idea of an evening with the Dominions, but it was Alexander and Bevin who

---

[1] Ernest Bevin, British Labour politician, was at this time Secretary of State for Foreign Affairs.

[2] Wife of the Australian Ambassador.

[3] Lady Diana Cooper, wife of Duff Cooper, British politician and member of Churchill's wartime government, who was at this time British Ambassador to Paris. Lady Diana was herself a famous beauty and social figure.

made the party a success. They and the Australians are birds of a feather – all old trade-unionists together – members of the New School Tie – same standards, same jokes. You felt at once how English the Australians and New Zealanders are and how un-English the rest of us are: the South African, General Théron; the Indian, a fish completely out of water with his constrained, uneasy smile, being "coped" with by the wives; the Canadians – the Vaniers and myself – so different again.

15 October 1946.

Elizabeth Bowen[1] is here. She has got herself accredited to the Conference as a journalist. We meet every day in the fenced-off area of the gravelled terrace outside the Palais du Luxembourg, where the press are permitted to mingle with the diplomats. We sit talking and drinking coffee at one of the small tables set up there and sometimes afterwards have time for a stroll along the tree-lined walks on the shady side of the gardens, past the statues of dead poets. She is staying around the corner at the Hôtel Condé, still unchanged as I remember it in the twenties, with its narrow stone stairways leading up to the garret bedrooms. We often dine together in one of the small restaurants on the Left Bank. Her being here is the reality which shows up for me the unreality of this sad charade of a conference.

---

[1] Novelist. She was a close friend from the war years (see my book *The Siren Years*).

PARIS

1947–1949

The Diary for 1947 opens on my return to Paris as Counsellor of Embassy.

Our Ambassador to France was General Georges P. Vanier, later Governor General of Canada. He occupied a unique position in the diplomatic community in Paris. He had been a steadfast supporter of de Gaulle and of the French Resistance Movement from the outset. He enjoyed the trust and affectionate respect of French political leaders of varying parties and persuasions. They came to him as to no other foreign ambassador for advice. They confided in his judgement, integrity, and discretion. The Ambassadress, Pauline Vanier, a woman of distinguished beauty and warm charity of heart, carried all before her by her spontaneity. They were fervent Catholics, who lived their faith. French by ancestry, they loved France and believed in her future in the worst of times. As a new arrival at the Embassy I was treated by the Vaniers, whom I had known during the war, as a friend, almost as a member of the family. I much enjoyed working with the Ambassador; despite his distinguished military career he never seemed to me a typical soldier. He was sagacious and subtle, and I appreciated his particular brand of irony and deprecatory understatement, which often concealed a sharp point.

The work of the Embassy was interesting in itself but unrewarding in terms of results. We reported to Ottawa at length on the twists and turns of French politics and the recurrent ministerial crises of those uneasy years when France was still suffering the traumatic effects of defeat and humiliation. No one was better informed than the Ambassador about the French political scene, and he trusted me with drafting many of our dispatches home. Answer came there none. The Canadian government had at that time no discernible interest in France, or if they had, it was not revealed to us. I pictured the fruits of our labours mildewing in the files of some junior officer in the Department of External Affairs. Most of the staff of the Embassy were French Canadians. It was my first experience of working with them as a group, as in those days our department at home was almost entirely Anglo-Saxon in language and mentality. I was stimulated and attracted by my French-Canadian colleagues and made many friends among them, particularly the quick-witted and responsive Jean Chapdelaine and his delightful wife, Rita.

The Embassy was housed in a mansion in the Avenue Foch, erected in the 1920s for one, or both, of those fabled enchantresses of the period, the Dolly Sisters, by a wealthy admirer. During the German occupation it had been in the hands of the Gestapo – a centre to which victims were taken for interrogation. The décor, in pseudo-rococo style with inset bands of pink marble, must have been a sinister setting for the dreadful scenes enacted there. As an Embassy the house was superbly impractical. Typists were packed into passages and boudoirs. The vast marble bath with its solid gold taps was piled high with files and documents, which even overflowed onto the bidet. My own office was in the bedroom in which once the Dolly sisters had romped. My desk, an enormous affair in an unrestrained version of the Louis XV style, was rich in gilt and ormolu, with drawers that stuck when you tried to open them. It was placed between tall French windows looking out on the Avenue Foch.

My first task on arrival in Paris was to find myself somewhere to live which I could afford. Finally I installed myself in an apartment on the Boulevard St. Germain. The house was built round a paved courtyard. My own flat was up one flight of stairs. It belonged to the scion of a family who had owned a Paris department store. There he had lived with his mistress, a well-known actress. This happy state of affairs was brought to an end by the bankruptcy of the department store and by the intervention of his wife, who under some obscure provision of French law now claimed the flat belonged to her. He was determined that it should on no account fall into her hands, and to prevent this he must find a tenant, preferably a diplomat who could not easily be expelled. Our bargain was struck over a bottle of rye whisky, which he had never before tasted and to which he took an instant liking. Two conditions went with the lease: first, that his wife should never on any excuse penetrate into the apartment; second, that I should supply him each month with a case of rye whisky.

My apartment was on the dark side, which suited me, as I dislike brightness in rooms – or people. In fact there was so little light in the dressing-room that I often emerged wearing socks of different colours, sometimes even trousers that belonged to other suits than the coats. As one entered there was a stone-flagged hall with, on the left, a tiny dining-room suitable for dwarves only; on the right, a large and largely unused salon in which spindly chairs and precarious little tables were grouped in uneasy circles. The parquet floor was islanded with dangerously slippery rugs. The salon led directly into the bedroom, the setting for a bed of generous proportions – evidently the scene of action of the whole apartment. Opening out of the bedroom was a small chamber containing a writing-table and an indispensable stove. The winters of 1947 and 1948 were cold ones and much of one's time was spent huddled for heat in front of the stove. I loved this apartment with the passion that some interiors have the power to induce. It had, it seemed to me, been a scene of happiness and I was happy there.

A further part of my bargain with the owner was the continued employment of a manservant who "went with" the place. Yves was of an unguessable age – probably not so old as I then thought. He had started life on an estate in Brittany and had been brought to Paris as a gardener by the old countess who had once owned the whole house in the days when it had been an *hôtel particulier* and who still lingered on in the apartment below us. Yves himself lodged in company with a so-called nephew, a sloe-eyed adolescent, in an attic hovel above. He attached himself to me with bossy devotion, like an old nanny. With his full share of wooden Breton obstinacy he combined great tact – was never in the way at the wrong moment. He had at times a sly smile, conspiratorial without ever becoming indiscreet. He was an excellent plain cook in the provincial style – very good with soup and with a passion for the artichoke which I came to share. In the kitchen he mercilessly bullied a musty old crone who was never permitted to approach me directly but who could be glimpsed bent double over the sink.

My domestic life thus satisfactorily settled, and by no means over-burdened with work, I set about determinedly to extract as much as Paris had on offer and to suppress my persistent traces of guilt at leaving behind me Ottawa civil-servanthood. I approached the Paris scene in the spirit of the Renaissance Pope who said, "God has given us the Papacy, now let us enjoy it."

Elizabeth Bowen came on frequent visits to Paris and her friend-ship which meant so much in my life continued, as indeed it did until her death in 1973.

Socially I moved in different circles which seldom overlapped, a condition which has always appealed to me. Through the friendship of the Vaniers I encountered most of the leading French political figures, also intellectuals like Jacques Maritain and André Malraux. Then there were my colleagues in the Embassy and my fellow diplo-mats. I had friends among the journalists – the closest, Darcy Gillie of the *Manchester Guardian*. Another world was that of the English and American friends who flocked to Paris after the long deprivation of the war, eager for a renewal of the pre-war pleasures of which they had been so long deprived. There was a continuing cavalcade of such visitors with whom the more cosmopolitan French mingled. Some of the actors and actresses in this revived social performance were getting older, but there were spirited recruits from a younger gener-ation. The Parisian arts and fashions – it was sometimes difficult to draw a line between the two (a "New Look" by Dior, a new stage design by Bébé Bérard) – enlivened the scene. Party succeeded party – fancy-dress parties, picnic parties, dinner parties, theatre parties, and house parties. Pre-war social rivalries revived, wits were sharp-ened, scandal took wings, and love affairs came and went as brief as summer lightning. At the British Embassy, Duff and Diana Cooper reigned – there politicians, writers, and artists mingled with the fash-ionables. Under Diana's magic touch, platitude and pomposity shriv-elled – all was warmth and sparkle.

20 January 1947.

Well, here I am back in Paris and installed as Counsellor of Embassy, but why the hell am I here? What possessed me to leave an interesting job, in which I could exercise some influence on events, to walk up and down the Champs-Elysées on a sunny day or to admire the beauties of Paris. Life is not a coloured picture-postcard. As for my work at the Embassy, what do they care in Ottawa for a painstaking analysis of the shifting play of French politics and politicians? Anyway, French politics, although absorbing on the spot, do not export well and are incomprehensible outside France. D. W. Brogan once spoke of "the provinciality of the *Ile de France*." It is quite true. Then, returning to the Paris of my student days as a middle-aged official is like paying a social call on a former mistress. I think of the desolating scene in which Colette's Chéri revisits Léa, when the nostalgic disturbance of his love for her and the shock of his war experience are met with her sensible health recommendations. Yes, Paris has only a bitter little smile for the past. Sufferings and scarcities have contracted her spirit. She has become a *femme de ménage*.

1 February 1947.

Elizabeth Bowen is here. The weather is so penetratingly cold that we spend most of the time sitting close by the stove in my flat, often in company with a bottle of whisky. It is like life on board ship. We sally out on to the windswept decks of the boulevards for a blow and are glad to be back again in the warmth and shelter. I want to see no one else and wish that this good time could last, yet feel that it is transitory. She re-awakens my sympathy for people, my curiosity about situations and ideas; she rehumanizes me.

7 February 1947.

The smell of dusty ivy on a misty winter's afternoon as I go past the enclosed gardens of the big, shuttered houses in the Avenue Foch.

There is nothing in the least mysterious about the French. It is just that they are plainly different from us and for that very reason attractive and somehow formidable. They are gay, but not funny; they make one smile but not laugh; they are so conventional in the grooves of custom, however revolutionary their ideas may be. They have no use for eccentricity – you must be effective in the life here or you are mercilessly brushed to one side. They never tell a story against themselves. After all, why reduce your bargaining power by giving the world a handle against you?

4 March 1947.

During the war we had a simple poster-picture of what was going on on the European continent. It seemed to us an armed camp of enemies – German bullies and satellite zanies – lording it over a vast concentration camp of subject peoples and defied by numerous and heroic resistants. We had to believe that things were black and white; in a war it is a dangerous waste of energy and sapping to the will to admit that one's enemies have mixed motives and sympathies, but it is interesting to take off the wartime blinkers and to indulge in what still seems an unpatriotic luxury of seeing people not just as friends or foes but as people. It leads one to all sorts of reluctant and awkward admissions.

Today, for instance, I spent at Versailles at Beaudoin's trial. He was the Vichy Foreign Minister. It is gospel that the men of Vichy were odious, but there simply did not appear to be any evidence against him at all. I said to myself that I disliked the man, that he had played both sides, that he was anti-Semitic, anti-British, anti-Resistance, a careerist and probably a crook, one of those who had stifled the soul of France. But I could not say, on the evidence produced in court, that he was guilty of any of the precise things with which he was charged.

Evidence came from so many sides, from honest men who had worked with him and whose own reputations were clear, from British Intelligence, from a Free French Jewish fighter pilot. All coincide with remarkable accuracy – he was a patriotic Frenchman who had done his duty as he saw it and, given his own aims, quite effectively. Obviously if he is condemned on that evidence it will be a miscarriage of justice.

27 March 1947.

Mathieu, the Corsican chauffeur at the Embassy, has become almost a friend. He is a man of thirty-five to forty, fat from good eating, and he likes to hear the sound of his own voice, loves a joke, and has immense confidence in his own opinion on all subjects. He can put on a tough, taxi-driver manner and a coarse, rough voice whenever the need arises in the traffic. He takes me out to Versailles to the Beaudoin trial. He misses no points in the trial – in fact, he catches several that I missed. But what first endeared him to me was our common passion for *The Three Musketeers*. He said he had read it at an age when he still believed in love and friendship. I like the way he said that, without bitterness, with a grown-up acceptance of life. Of "Milady" he said, "She is just the woman to excite a boy's imagination – a woman of the world, seductive and so beautiful." (Milady's beauty is indeed one of the unquestionable facts of literature.)

The feeling of liberation that I get in France is because anything can be discussed here and quite naturally too. I can talk about women with Mathieu (the chauffeur) or I can talk about doctrinal differences between the Church of Rome and Protestantism. When he talks about women he does not give me commercial travellers' stories; he talks like an individual, and if he talks about religion it is not to air a few prejudices but to *discuss*. Marcel, the other chauffeur, tells me of how he was put in a German concentration camp and how the older men in the camp went to pieces and wept with despair. "Indeed, I admit that I wept – it was not that I was frightened, but to find myself in prison with armed sentinels, knowing oneself to be an honest man, was enough to make one despair. All the old men were like that but the young ones joked and did not give a damn." What Englishman would tell anyone that he cried when he found himself in a prison camp? He would think no one else had ever done such a thing. The French are not ashamed because they have not set themselves an inhuman standard of behaviour. They are natural men – not public-school boys, or American tough guys, or Nazis, or communist supermen, but natural men.

3 April 1947.

Anne-Marie Callimachi[1] is here on a visit from London. She talks of Romania, from which she was clever enough to escape in time,

---

[1] Princess Anne-Marie Callimachi was a refugee from Communist Romania. Formerly she had been a wealthy political and social hostess in Bucharest.

saying that a communist takeover is richly deserved by her own class, that they have been corrupt and rapacious. However, she still manages to get substantial slices of her fortune out of that country. She is bored with my interest in French politics and says that Paris is the worst place to find out what is happening in Europe, as the French are so self-engrossed. She claims to be in a state of suicidal depression but appears in high spirits, buying new hats and a Modigliani painting, and up to her ears in mysterious financial deals through her banker in Switzerland. We talked of the erotic effects of train travel, due, we think, partly to the motion of the train itself, and always seeming most insistent on the night train from Paris to the Côte d'Azur.

5 May 1947.

The green arches of the park of Chantilly in the April sunshine, the blowing of the paper tablecloths into the grounds of the Lion d'Or, the taste of pâté and red wine warm from the sun, and the sight of M. standing beside the car, her plaid rug over her arm. She scowled into the sun. She is like a statue carved in ivory, her beauty severe and classical. What a fool I am at forty – adolescent dreams that have been dreamed too long.

6 May 1947.

Lunched with Darcy Gillie of the *Manchester Guardian*. He lives with and for books, as a cat-lover might live surrounded by cats. You stumble over insecurely piled pyramids of books when you go to his room. He has a noble cast of countenance and a nature devoid of smallness. I admire and envy him. I wish I knew as much about anything as he knows about North Africa – and never to be boring about it. Yet today he was suffering from a hangover and was less intelligently articulate. I find people more attractive when they are not in "good form," and I felt positive affection for him when, scrabbling among his papers, he cast over his shoulder at me "What year is this? I find it hard to keep up with the revolving years." M. was here in the evening. It was not a success. We had dinner on a small card-table with uneven legs which Yves attempted unsuccessfully to level. I could see that she disconcerted him by bleak glances at the arrangements of the flat. She is beautiful and intelligent, but have we anything in common? I asked her if she felt with me as if she were talking to someone of another generation and had to get me going on a favourite subject, spot my hobbyhorse, and send me off on it. I used myself to do that with older people while cooking up in my mind the unscrupulous schemes of youth. Is she doing the same?

7 May 1947.

Elizabeth de Miribel is an extraordinary personality. I have known her since the war years in Ottawa, when she, an exile from France, with a handful of others upheld the Gaullist cause in Canada with missionary zeal and in the face of all odds. Back in Paris, she now occupies an influential position in the Quai d'Orsay. In everything Elizabeth is larger than life-size – in her range of interests and friends and, above all, in her fanatical enthusiasms. She is out of scale with compromise. The most loyal of friends, she is a despiser of the middle road. She has just come back from Moscow full of the spiritual qualities of the Russian people. "They are so much richer spiritually than the Americans. Their faces are more interesting. There is still a continuity with an old and great civilization which has not been entirely lost to communism." I even fancied that a new way of doing her hair showed Russian influence – it suited the earnest, poetic young woman in a Russian novel and was less Princesse de la Fronde than her usual coiffure.

8 May 1947.

The Poles invite us to the magnificent Hôtel de la Rochefoucauld, which is now their Embassy. Course after course of rather badly prepared food. The Ambassador – squat, voluble, formerly a schoolmaster in Cracow. Reception afterwards – hordes of swarthy Eastern Europeans – thug intelligentsia who look as if they could shoot as fast as they can argue – swarming like termites through the lofty rooms. These cocktail parties and official receptions where dull and tired officials are crowded with tiresome women into brilliant rooms made for leisure, for conversation, for the mannered comedy of intrigue! Clumsy attempts of the state robots to be gay!

9 May 1947.

I had John Grierson, formerly of the Canadian National Film Board, to lunch. He talked about his interest in economic freedom and his belief in a cultural aristocracy – how he was always being asked to lecture on aesthetics when he was really a political scientist. He twisted up his eyes hypnotically behind his spectacles to give me glances of piercing insight. He spoke of the Prime Minister as an "old darling." Grierson is working in UNESCO. What a stew-pot of jealousies UNESCO sounds. God preserve me from having anything to do with it. One look at the people at the UNESCO building was enough. How I loathe international secretariats – they are always so provincial – talking shop all the time and having affairs with unattractive secretaries. They think they are "men of good will" and progressive. They make no allowance to themselves for their egotism and love of power. They have no humility. I am sure the League atmosphere at Geneva would have made a fascist of me.

In the evening at Paul Beaulieu's,[1] a reception for French-Canadian intelligentsia – a world new to me of young French-Canadian students, artists, and actors who are finding Paris for the first time and who have a whole set of new gods unknown to me. Young students came up to me, greeting me with great charm as *Monsieur le Conseiller*, and getting away as quickly as they prudently could to continue passionate discussions among themselves. But they *do* have passionate discussions and they are infatuated with ideas and phrases. And everyone was enjoying just being there and *talking*. After the aridity of diplomatic entertainments and the suspicion which ideas, especially ideas about art or literature, arouse in a group of Anglo-Canadians, it seemed all to be a Good Thing.

Reading Shakespeare's *Romeo and Juliet* – one could get caught in Shakespeare and spend one's whole life (and it would not be long enough) in that world of clues and whispers, glorious vistas, sweet songs and perfumes, breath-taking glooms – in that world so monstrously larger than life.

---

[1] Paul Beaulieu, an officer of the Department of External Affairs and subsequently Canadian Ambassador to France.

Date Most Uncertain.

Weekend in the country with the d'Harcourts – nice French people – in fact, impoverished gentry. A small, shabby château of no particular period (1820-1830?) with bowls of lilac everywhere – in the halls, in my bedroom – so that the whole house smelled of it. They had Germans in the house during the war but it must have been shabby long before that. No signs of a bath anywhere, primitive W.C., but of course a brand-new glistening bidet. They are a very nice family and I liked them all. Comte d'Harcourt takes rather a back seat. His wife is much concerned with local affairs – she sat on some local women's council with a communist woman councillor. She said, "At first the woman was impossible, she must have this and must have that – but she is getting better – already one has got her to use the conditional mood when discussing business and I am lending her some good religious books." This pleasant-looking couple have produced two buxom daughters – short, stocky, peasant types – very nice, simple, and natural (which did not prevent one of them from showing off like mad). Then my friend Emmanuel, their nephew, was there with a sister, a shade less buxom but giving off a slight odour of "good works in healthy country surroundings." On Sunday morning they all went off to Mass and I made a tour of the park, which is encompassed by a high wall. It was a shut-in world of rough grass, trees, and rides in the woods, quite thick undergrowth with violets and other small violet-coloured flowers everywhere. I lay on a cut log in the sun and felt extremely happy.

15 May 1947.

Dined with Maurice Forget (our Military Attaché) to meet General Revers, a famous figure of the French Resistance – his idol. He gives the impression of being deformed due to his immensely broad shoulders and his jutting, underhung jaw. He has charm and quick wit – he is bold, magnetic, vain, and intelligent – in conversation, half-jokingly cynical and extremely outspoken. The company consisted of his wife, another general (retired), who had at one time been in charge of the French Deuxième Bureau and who, in appearance at least, was (to me) a most baffling type, a "simple soldier," and

General Revers's Chef de Cabinet, who has been with him in all the changes of fortune in the Resistance, etc. – a sloppy, clever, intellectual soldier. Most of the conversation turned towards North Africa, as Juin had that day been appointed Resident General in Morocco. General Revers said that the way to preserve the balance there was to set the Berber against the Arab. For thousands of years the Berbers had been in the habit of making raids from time to time on the rich Arab towns. Now was the moment to let them have a go at, say, Fez – the Resident General could shut himself up in the Residence, a little massacring would go on, and after that the French would have no difficulty with the Arabs for some time. As for the Sultan, it was only necessary to back another candidate for the throne to put the fear of God into him. These ideas were advanced with cynical cheerfulness. Maurice Forget says they are quite serious and a Berber rising is just what the French will arrange.

After dinner a young French deputy from North Africa and a French North African newspaper proprietor joined us. The conversation which followed on North African problems was something of an eye-opener to me. Here was a group of men completely sure of themselves, with none of the shaken confidence of the metropolitan Frenchman. To them the Arabs are simply an inferior race. They say that there is no good providing them with improvements – they prefer living in pigsties, and when decent houses were built for them they turned them into pigsties. There is no use paying them more – they have no sense of the value of money; they spend it at once and sit in the sun doing nothing until they are hungry and then work again for a little. The inhabitants of the towns were Semitic in origin and therefore, of course, cowards. All that was needed in North Africa was, as Lyautey[1] used to say, to show strength and then you would not have to employ it. All would be well if (a) the French socialists would leave the situation alone, and (b) the British and Americans would mind their own business and not meddle. For the British there seemed precious little sympathy. The British had intrigued to drive them out of Syria – for that (as the French always say) there is documentary proof. The British had invented the Arab League for their

[1] Maréchal Lyautey, French soldier and administrator in North Africa.

own nefarious purposes and it was a source of some satisfaction that they were now having trouble with it. As for the Americans, they were always prating about democracy but look at the way they treated their Negro population.

10 August 1947.

Paris in mid-August. Weak, plaintive music coming out of a courtyard as one passes by – the houses with all their shutters closed – no one left but concierges and their cats – the Luxembourg gardens under a hot mist blazing with sunset colours of orange and yellow dahlias – a thin jet of fountain. No one to see all this summer luxuriance of foliage and flowers but a few children left behind for some particular reason in Paris – and an old woman in carpet slippers and a scowling gendarme.

11 August 1947.

Picnic organized by Diana to an eighteenth-century folly – La Tour de Retz – now tumbling down and overgrown with ivy, the garden a wilderness of brambles and wild roses. Diana and Cecil Beaton (echoes of how many *fêtes champêtres* of the twenties) suited the place as they draped themselves about a crumbling urn. Duff, who hates picnics, kept wishing that he had a little folding chair to sit on. "How can you!" cried Diana. "To take a chair to a picnic."

Had dinner at the British Embassy. More moments of nostalgia – the Gay Old Times embodied in that antique marionette Lady de Mendel,[1] who still slaps her thigh, kicks up her heels, and smiles with her eyes at eighty-four. "And from that dainty little jewel such a whiff of garlic," said Cecil Beaton. I asked Diana if she remembered my Uncle Harry.[2] "My first love – he lived opposite us in Arlington Street. He paid me my first compliment when I was a little girl – he wrote me a farewell letter before he died. I heard of his *dash* from my father." "What did he look like?" I asked. "My dear, *then* a death's-head."

---

[1] Elsie, Lady de Mendel, fashionable interior decorator and hostess. Her husband, Sir Charles, was an honorary attaché to the British Embassy.

[2] H. K. Stewart, C.M.G., my mother's brother. He was a Gordon Highlander and King's Messenger.

Nancy Mitford to dinner – talking of the horrors of her country childhood – the boredom, the waiting around for something to happen. She said her grandmother used to change the hours of meals in despairing attempts to make – now the afternoons – now the evenings – shorter. "All those women in tweeds taking their cairns for a walk – waiting to die."

As I was driving to the office the other day I saw Nancy walking by herself past the bookstalls on the Quai. She had a floppy old hat on and looked not at all like her smart self, but pale and abstracted, and as she walked her lips were moving. She was talking to herself. She must have been trying out the shape of some scrap of dialogue in her novel. One could hardly believe she was the same person who appeared at dinner last week, her face then brilliant with animation, with that mocking turn-down of the mouth and the eyebrows lifted in incredulous amusement. Then she got into one of her spirals of talk, starting from a mere particle of absurdity that she had spotted in someone and cascading into a fantastic fireworks of invention, in which malice was so mixed with sheer high spirits and comedy that one couldn't call it malice any longer. What a sparkler she can be. How gloriously funny, but I should not relish being the mark of one of her arrows. Then there is, too, in her an undercurrent of bitter, scornful sadness, much less evident now than it used to be in London. Now she is on a crest with literary success, happy love, her charming apartment, and the most stylish clothes in Paris.

14 September 1947.

Lunch with André Malraux, Elizabeth de Miribel, an American journalist, a Swedish journalist, and Catroux. The American journalist crystallized the conversation by asking A.B.C. questions about Gaullism and French politics. Malraux, snorting and snuffling and sweating, replied with a flood of exposition. I am still left, at the end, with the feeling that after the party was over and the juggler had completed his act, when I came to count the teaspoons several of them were missing altogether. Or, to put it a different way, as the Swedish journalist said to me afterwards, "What worries me is that I think that sooner or later these people will get into power and then what kind of a job will they make of it?"

The American was interested (as a "liberal" journalist) to hear a convincing denial of the accusation that de Gaulle is a future dictator. He supposed that Malraux was a liberal too. Reply – "I fought enough to show it." Elizabeth (explanatory): "Monsieur Malraux fought in the Spanish Civil War." The American (incredibly but in good faith): "On which side?" Malraux's answer to the question as to whether he feared power being concentrated in the hands of one man was to say that nothing had ever been achieved in France except through the predominance of one man, and cited Clemenceau, Briand, and Poincaré. (This seemed odd to me as they had functioned under the old Third Republic Constitution and in a régime where there were more parties in France than there are today.)

Malraux thought that there would be no civil war in France unless orders for one came from Moscow; then, with great rapidity and staggering indiscretion, he gave us a map of France in civil war (the Gaullist civil-war map – what a break for the Communist Party and before two foreign journalists and one diplomat!). Here it is: the North, the Northeast, the frontier as far as the Somme – Gaullist; the coast down to and including Bordeaux – Gaullist; Boucles du Rhône – "plutôt Gaulliste"; Paris – Gaullist; Paris suburbs – Communist; Limoges – Communist; the South – Communist; Franche-Comté and Les Landes – a mystery. (In all this he seems to assume that the Socialist Party has ceased to exist and doubtless the MRP too.) It was, he said, a geographical problem, just as the Civil War in Spain had been, and he quoted examples of whole Spanish provinces and regions on one side or the other. He remarked that there was an interesting parallel with the wars of religion in France – the areas of France which had been Protestant then were the areas which were Communist now.

He said that de Gaulle would come to power as a result of financial chaos and collapse. On being asked whether in those circumstances it would be better for the United States to wait to give aid to France until de Gaulle was in power, he first said, "In any case you will give too little," but finally said, "By giving aid in doles now you will only prolong the agony. Ramadier cannot cope with the situation. The United States should choose one party or another. You must disabuse your compatriots' mind of the idea of Right – Left – Centre, with de Gaulle at the Right. That corresponds to nothing real." In fact he was actively discouraging United States aid to France – doing just what we are always accusing the Communist Party of doing – preferring the interests of his party to those of France because he believes that only under his party can France be saved.

Asked about de Gaulle's programme when he comes to power he replied: "We have two plans, one for the *relèvement* of Europe and the other for the *relèvement* of France. France can support herself – the only country in Europe that can." Malraux went on: "France can live off her own resources and is self-contained in a way that Britain is not, is a better bet than Britain for United States support." The barefacedness of this annoyed me.

Malraux impressed me as superficial – a man of letters dabbling in politics. I have no faith in his judgements.

15 September 1947.

Lunch and afternoon at Elsie Mendel's house at Versailles. Décor so familiar to readers of super-glossy fashionable magazines – very pretty it is too. Our hostess was spry – the skin on her antique face stretched like a too-tight ivory-coloured kid glove and the look of death in her eyes, but smart as an old monkey. I got through layers – eighty years – layers upon layers – a millennium of extinct civilizations, through the Roman and Etruscan periods to the Neanderthal woman – when she said that she (or was it her father?) was born in the old de Wolf house in Wolfville, Nova Scotia. It was a really Mendelian party: the little Queen of Yugoslavia; an American half-Cherokee Indian – "You know" (challengingly) "I never say anything behind people's backs that I would not say to their faces. I make a hobby of houses; I have one in Mexico, one in Virginia, one in California, a penthouse in New York, but best of all I like my house in Paris and my little château in the country." When jewels were mentioned – "I have a ceinture of emeralds – so amusing." I sat next to Greta Garbo, but all she said to me was "Pass the salt." But she said it in those husky, mysterious, palpitating tones that have echoed around the globe! She was wearing a Mexican-style straw hat and everyone kept on begging her to take it off. She refused until she went into the swimming-pool and then one saw how clever she had been.

It concealed both her beauty and the ravages in it. She still has that mixture of gaucherie and mystery and that lovely, lovely face. There were half a dozen Hollywood directors or producers, all more or less stout. Also Paulette Goddard, dripping with diamonds – just a gay, pleasant little American housewife, but in the same swimming-pool with Garbo she just did not rate. Old Sir Charles Mendel would not agree. "Wonderful bone structure Garbo has," he said, "but I like flesh – give me Paulette." "Yes," he went on, "I have what Elsa Maxwell would call 'my most intimate friends' here today – intimate acquaintances, that is what *I* would call them. I am a man with a lot of intimate acquaintances." All the people there seemed names out of an old *Vogue* magazine and all *so old*, except the immortal Tony Porson bounding about in the pool like a Neapolitan diving boy.

18 September 1947.

What answers have we to the questioning classes: the poor – the discontented – the young – the clever? One cannot think of the question in terms of "we North Americans" and "they Europeans." It applies to the democratic, anti-communist parties within the European countries. In France are those parties just a front behind which the bourgeois and the racketeers can, in their different ways – respectable or non-respectable – get on with their business? Are they so keen on their short-run interests that they have not even the intelligence and self-restraint to unite to secure their long-run interests? What about the alternative of Gaullism? What are its ideas? Improvement in the machinery of the State to make it stronger, but what is the object of the Gaullist State to be? A revival of patriotism – but is it to be patriotism in the raw or patriotism guided towards the evolution of the State in some advancing direction? A bulwark against communism? But what is on our side of the bulwark? If all our Western democratic civilization can do in Europe is to enable people who are already comfortable to go on being comfortable, *it* won't do. This civilization was sick in Europe long before the war – ever since the First War. Are we seriously bent on curing it or is it a question of enlisting "any allies of whatever origin" against communism?

7 December 1947.

Went yesterday to Nellita's wedding[1] in the Protestant Temple at Poissy – the cold, plain, bare little shrine of a once-persecuted sect. A star pastor had been brought down from Paris for the occasion – a true offspring of Calvin, his mouth a bitter line, eyes of dark fanaticism, twitching hands raised in blessing – a man of spiritual arrogance and probity. The service was very different from the cozy old Church of England or the solid smugness of Presbyterianism. Here the fires of the Protestant conscience still burn – these people might tear the saints from their niches. The church was crowded with Nellita's multitudinous aunts and cousins – dowdy old people full of kindness and rectitude, and inconspicuous young married couples with well-scrubbed children. The bridesmaids were graceful young girl-cousins, unpowdered and unpainted, with fresh skins and dark eyes full of innocence, sweet seriousness, and malice – like girls in a Russian nineteenth-century novel, but doubtless more Frenchly sensible and their moods controlled by Christian cheerfulness. They wore dark-red dresses made by the village dressmakers and had white narcissus fresh from the garden at Poissy in their hair. The pastor indulged in long extempore prayer (that most hateful of vices). He told the *jeunes mariés* that they would "*fonder un foyer – un foyer rayonnant.*" The marriage oath seemed less a solemn abracadabra than a clear promise to break which would be a shame. The thin, clear French language stripped the service of its mystery and beauty and broke the crust of customary acceptance. When the bride and groom answered "Yes," the pastor said: "*Que votre 'oui' soit 'oui,' car il est donné devant Dieu et Son Eglise.*" I felt the enormity of lying to God – no fear entered into this feeling, unless it was the fear that one would never forgive oneself.

So in one way and another I had a very amusing time in that last year of bachelordom in Paris. Yet there was an undercurrent of disarray and loneliness. What all that time I wanted, I finally obtained: a happy marriage. I proposed to Sylvia by long-distance telephone,

---

[1] Nellita McNullty. She married M. Dechaume, a wartime supporter of General de Gaulle.

Paris–Ottawa. When she accepted me I knew that this was the greatest stroke of good fortune of my life, and so it has proved to be. Our marriage took place in Ottawa in January 1948 and we returned to Paris until I was posted back to Ottawa in 1950.

15 May 1948.

This is a toy house, made for a newly married couple to play in. A pretty eighteenth-century villa of cream-coloured stucco. French windows give from the salon onto a small garden – a square of grass, gravel paths – a Paris garden, without a flower, protected by tall chestnuts from the overlooking windows of the banal blocks of Passy flats. These two or three houses on this side of the street are survivals of an earlier Passy, a quiet suburb merging into the Bois at Auteuil. It is the Passy nostalgically described in the opening pages of du Maurier's *Peter Ibbetson* – a place of old-fashioned peace and gentility. The salon with its corner cupboards full of choice "bits" of china and its occasional tables has an almost English look of coziness. Our own few things – the framed silhouettes, the plain, worn Georgian silver, even the mid-Victorian watercolour sketch of my grandmother – look at home here. This is much the sort of house they are used to.

Upstairs we are a little cramped for space. The owner of the house, Mlle de Préval, kept the biggest bedroom for herself. Our bed is really too small. It is an old maid's bed, big enough for Mlle de Préval and her hot-water bottle. The window looks out across the roof which projects over the French windows to the garden. At night we hear the trees moving and smell the garden.

Yves seems very well contented. I think he prefers my being married. It means that there is always someone here to take an interest in what he is doing, someone who can measure his successes and failures. Also, he loves entertaining. Tonight, for instance, we are having a dinner party and all day he has been in a state of happy excitement. He is in and out of the house to buy last-moment things – coloured candles for the table (he has a weakness for coloured candles – I hate them), or more flowers. Only now that Sylvia is here she usually buys the flowers herself. She is in the garden now, arranging them in vases for tonight's dinner. She has always been "good with flowers" – I can remember seeing her doing them at Aunt Elsie's house at Murray Bay one summer years ago. I think even then I knew that in the end I should marry her if she would have me.

Thank Heaven they have brought Sylvia's dress for the party. It is a model, borrowed for the night from one of the big couturiers, and has its name inside it on a tab "*Quand les lilas refleuriront.*" It is made of silvery material with a design of lilac branches and has a long train. She will look cool and graceful and flower-like herself. She seems excited herself too – excited and happy. We were going to row on the Lac Inférieur in the Bois today as it is such a gloriously fine May day. For some time she has been wanting to row over to the island in the lake. It looks so tempting, as though the flowers and trees on the island had some magic more than those on the banks beside us when we stand and look across. But all the boats were taken and there was a queue at the landing-place waiting for them to come back to have their turn. There were boats full of young men and girls – the boys stripped to the waist rowing in the sun – people laughing and calling to each other from boat to boat. There were family parties, too – a stout woman sitting in the stern in a black dress and wearing a black hat – a *chétif* little boy dragging his hand in the water – an old man sitting helplessly in the sun-filled boat. You can smell the boats too – the smell, I suppose, of wood – yet it's more than that. It's a smell of *boats*, and even these tame rowboats in a city park have it.

Tonight after dinner we all go on (except the spare man, who is not asked) to an evening party at the British Embassy for Princess Elizabeth. Royalties have an unfortunate effect on any social gathering. No one listens to anything anyone else, or even they themselves, are saying, because they are so anxious to overhear a Royal word or attract a Royal glance.

19 June 1948.

Reading Malraux's *Human Condition*. In it he makes you share his own passion for conspiracy – a passion which has taken possession of some of the bravest, cleverest men in all the countries of Europe and Asia. For this is a conspiratorial age. Power is running in new channels. This is still only true of half of the world, but will that half corrupt the other? Is this one of the clues to what is going on around us? Where there is power there is also conspiracy? Perhaps this has been true in the most respectable parliamentary democracies, but there are conspiracies and conspiracies. What faces us now is something secret, violent, and fanatical, calling on all the excessive will – the inhuman, single-track obsession – which can apparently be found in the most commonplace men. The professor turned communist – the prostitute turned spy – the public-school boy turned secret agent. Could this not become a new form of excitement as necessary to the nerves as smoking? In France, for instance, everyone has been plotting in the Resistance, or among the collaborationists, or just plotting to save their skins or their fortunes, or to pay off a grudge. They all have been up to something which had to be concealed. It may be that they have taken the habit of it. Is a new pattern developing? Is this a by-product of the omnipotent state? Does it not go on under ministries where the civil servants increasingly control the lives of nations? Is part of our rage against communism the rage of Caliban at seeing his own face in the glass?

21 June 1948.

Not long ago I was sitting next to Diana at a lively luncheon party where the cross-fire of conversation was sizzling away. Twice – three times – I attempted to join the fray without success. Turning to Diana I said: "I cannot understand it. Am I invisible, or inaudible? I have so much to say and no one pays attention to me." She fixed me with her azure eyes. "Something," she said, "must be done about that." Something was – with Nancy Mitford acting as her lieutenant, Diana organized a Ritchie Week, a week of non-stop parties, dinners, even a ball in Ritchie honour. She roped in half Paris – surprised French hostesses found it was the smart thing to join in this charade. Old and new friends showered us with invitations. Whenever we appeared, a special anthem was played to signal our entrance. Verses were addressed to us – on the walls of the houses in our street someone had by night chalked up in giant letters the slogan "Remember Ritchie." Nancy I think it was who had an even more daring inspiration – a clutch of coloured balloons inscribed "Ritchie Week" were let loose over Paris. (The newspapers reported that one of these had floated as far as Boulogne, where it was picked up by the mystified inhabitants, who asked themselves what it might portend.) It was an apotheosis of a kind, and who but Diana could have devised such a fantasy? On the last night of the week, feeling like Cinderella at the end of the ball when she must return to obscurity, I said to Duff, "You don't think, do you, that now we have an *embarras de Ritchies*?" He politely demurred.

25 June 1948. In London on a visit.

Went to the 400 Club. How often have I sat in that precise corner on the right of the band with the eternal bottle of whisky in front of me and with how many different men and women? Only the bottle has always been the same. Listening to the same band for all these years through the war, and before the war – the hours I have spent in that dark little hole with its dirty silk hangings (actually cleaned now, though not changed) while the rhythm of the monotonous, pointless music, of the drink, of the talk, got into my blood. And always with the thought of what was coming afterwards – the postponing of pleasure which heightened the atmosphere and made one talk more outrageous nonsense. Well, it is quite time I stopped going there. I shall go two or three more times until my present bottle of whisky is finished and then give it up, for to find myself at my age surrounded by boy guardees and their little girlfriends – no – it won't do. It is almost as silly as writing this diary.

10 July 1948.

Everyone in Paris is in a disgruntled temper. You can see it in the faces of the passersby in the streets, their lips drawn in a line of bad-tempered stoicism. In the Bois the restaurants are empty, a few dejected waiters gossiping among the deserted tables on the terrace. The trees are turning brown as if it were already autumn. Our house is now as dank and dark as a potting-shed. Rain rattles down on the glass of the gallery roof.

In my office I go to the window and look out at the broad, blank spaces of the Avenue Foch. A sour-faced nurse is lugging a reluctant little boy across the grass under the blue-green dripping chestnut trees. Marcel, my chauffeur, has put on his beret and gone to sleep at the wheel of my stationary car. Inside the Embassy everyone seems water-logged with rain, and we roll up and down the grand staircase with no purpose – or a mechanical one.

7 August 1948.

A restless wind – one feels change in the air – brilliant rain-washed intervals, then sudden grey squalls. The house seemed strange. Yves, the manservant, was away at his son's wedding. The cats, hungry and wild, were snarling at each other and jumping on the tables looking for food. Sylvia, unfamiliar in a blue apron, brought up the breakfast. Later we went for a walk in the Bois – she wore a dress of pale pink linen and her soft-brimmed black hat. People looked at her as if they were saying, "Is she a beauty? No – not really. Oh, wait a minute – perhaps she is."

29 May 1949.

The comedy over the British Embassy Ball for Princess Margaret is worthy of Gogol. First they give out that it is to be for the young people; then it becomes known that they have made a few – a fatal few – exceptions. The fat was immediately in the fire. Men and women are equally frenzied. The men are pretending that they are thinking only of the pleasure their poor, dear wives will miss by not going, or they say, "So far as my wife and I are concerned it is of no consequence. We are too old, I suppose, although no older than the Fordhams" (adding bitterly, "but perhaps we *look* older"). As for the little Princess, she looks a cool little devil with enough in her glance – *maline*, amused, challenging – to turn the boys' heads even if she were not a princess. Neat as a little pin, composed, fresh and dainty in her summer dress with all the Commonwealth and French officials and their wives sweating around her and telling her five hundred times that she has brought the fine weather with her, asking all the right questions with a sweet smile as if butter would not melt in her mouth.

16 October 1949. Geneva.

It is so long since I have been alone as I have been for the past week in the Hôtel de la Paix. I sit here on this Swiss Sunday morning. Outside my window the lake and the mountains are wrapped in a cocoon of fog. Two disconsolate American businessmen in broad-brimmed fedora hats and granny glasses are walking around the Brunswick Memorial, gazing up at it with hung-over distaste. A Geneva Sunday – everyone wonders whether it was worth waking up at all. I am quite alone up here in my double room (will the Department pay for a *double* room?), thinking that I will drink less, that the barber said that in six months I would be bald, that I am forty-three years old, and in a dim way I like this feeling of being alone and taking up again this monologue. I miss my wife – I want her. I am waiting for her, yet this time of recuperation is quietly, sadly pleasant. If ever I am on the edge of nervous desperation – if ever I feel insanity threatening – I shall buy a ticket for Geneva and come and stay at the Hôtel de la Paix. Geneva is the nursing-home of Europe. Who has not come to rest their bodies and nerves after storms, amorous or political? Every dethroned king, exiled intellectual, proscribed politician in Europe for more than one hundred years. Being alone in Paris is despairing, watching the play of love and fashion, being outside it all, walking the merciless boulevards in the brilliant clarity, hemmed in by the stage-sets of architecture, called on at every turn to respond – to enjoy – to live. Here in Geneva one's forces gather – or one has that illusion; the return attack becomes once more thinkable.

OTTAWA

1950–1954

In January 1950 I was posted back to Ottawa from Paris, with the rank of Assistant Under-Secretary of State for External Affairs, and in Ottawa I remained until 1954, becoming Deputy Under-Secretary in 1952 and serving as Acting Under-Secretary for several periods. These years were for me the most satisfying of my professional career. To have reached my rank in the Service gave me a sense of accomplishment. Sharing the management of a government department with all its multifarious problems meant participation in a corporate life and in a corporate loyalty. The Under-Secretary of State for External Affairs, Arnold Heeney, was a great public servant and a warm friend. My colleagues were men and women to whom the job was of exciting importance and to whom hours of work and rates of pay (by no means excessive) meant little compared with the sheer interest of what we were doing. The interest was never lacking, for this was a period in which our country was playing a conspicuous part on the international stage, in NATO, in the United Nations, and in the Commonwealth. In June 1950 the Korean War broke out, and our involvement in it, and the political consequences of the war – in the United Nations, on our relations with the United States, and on our Far Eastern policy – became of dominating importance. During this time I worked closely with our Foreign Minister, Mike Pearson, whom I had known and admired since the war years in London. To be near the operation of power, to live under the tensions of recurrent crises, to participate, in however small a way, in the great game of world politics, all this was immensely stimulating. It also drained away one's other interests, leaving behind it a sediment of dissatisfaction. There was the risk that one's sympathies and amusements with people, one's reaction to the visible world about one, would evaporate, leaving one A Dedicated Civil Servant. The diaries were an escape from this admirable but arid fate. They shut out politics and the office, in an attempt to rediscover an appetite for life.

18 January 1950. Ottawa.

In winter the town seems to shrink in size without foliage and flowers – the smallness of the plots of garden, the nearness of the houses to each other, become plain – so do the drabness and poverty of the architecture. Snow fills up the spaces and seems to bring the buildings closer together. Ottawa has the look of a sub-Arctic settlement huddled together around the Gothic battlements of the Parliament Buildings. The straggling business streets with their Main Street stores and telegraph poles and the untidy mesh of streetcar wires and telegraph lines look like an old photograph of Ottawa in the 1880s. On a day of blizzard when whirling, skirling snow is blown in gusts around the street corners, when cars are embedded in snowdrifts, and people bent forward against the gale stumble and slide across the snow-piled streets, you feel the isolation of this place as if it had reverted to its early days and was no longer pretending to be a modern capital. The cheerful readiness with which people help each other to dig a car out of the snow has in it something of the original spirit of the pioneer community. Ottawa remains in its soul a small town – not quite like the old, small, settled communities of the East, but more a lumbering settlement in the Ottawa Valley. That spirit still pervades the place.

19 February 1950.

The streets are almost clear of snow – that is to say, the middle of the streets and the pavements – for the snow is banked up in brownish-white piles. It is pre-spring, the season of dirty snow, of mild, melancholy weather, of no-coloured skies. Melting snow drips from the window frames with an uneven drip like a leaking bath-tap. On the roofs of the high buildings men with long poles are dislodging great chunks of ice and masses of half-frozen snow. The streets below are barred off so that these snow-slides should not fall on to the heads of the passing citizenry.

There is the dust that must have lain under the snow on the side-walks – pale brownish-yellow dust that blows into swirls where the wind catches it at the street corners. It is not worth tidying up the streets, for it will snow again tomorrow and cover the old dropped cigarette packages, car tickets, newspapers which lie in the dust and are blown with it. In this mild air people yawn and stretch and wish for a good skiing snow. The pressure of winter is relaxed – the icy band of cold around forehead and knees, the knife-cutting wind, the brilliance of sun on ice and dazzling white light on the half-frozen snow. This is neither spring nor winter. It will snow again tomorrow.

26 February 1951.

Buffet supper. The men off in the corner talking shop, the women on the sofa talking servants and babies. No sexy flutters or sentimen-tal approaches between men and women. Flat-footed good sense and practical friendliness tinctured by local hates and irritations. Mrs. Griffin told us of an adulterer run out of town by the adulter-ess's brothers. Four of them went to his hotel bedroom and sat glow-ering at him with horsewhips in their pockets. Mrs. Griffin approved this manner of dealing with the situation, which she said was "good because it was natural." I said nervously that it sounded like the Wild West. "That's what I mean," she repeated, "it's natural."

Blair Fraser[1] says we should tell our newly fledged diplomats "No shirt too young to be stuffed."

Easter 1951.

Today at Easter communion service I felt boredom, irritation, and then hatred secreting itself in my system. I was surprised by the poi-sonous strength of these feelings. Where do they come from? The Devil, people once would have said. The Scoutmaster clergyman in the pulpit, the inoffensive congregation, the midday banality of the middle-of-the-way middle-class Church of England morning service goaded me to near hysteria. I felt that I could not take communion in such a state of mind, but when I had taken my place at the altar rail I felt shaken and dissolved, and went back sadly to my pew in the

---

[1] Blair Fraser, the Canadian journalist, was an old friend.

church, not knowing – or caring to know – whether there was God in the bread and wine.

21 May 1951.

It is not the work in the Department that I dislike; in fact, it absorbs me totally. It is the "surround" that goes with it. There is the underlying assumption that anyone who is not overworked, under-paid, eye-strained, joy-starved – in fact, not a senior civil servant – is frivolous or materialistic, that these are the hallmarks of a higher calling, the stigmata of the faithful. "Poor so-and-so, how tired he looks, how overworked," we murmur in tones in which respect mingles with compassion. Why respect? Why not contempt? That a man should so mismanage his life as to be totally immersed in office work is lamentable, unless he loves it. If he loves it, he is doing what he wants, like another who drinks himself to a standstill, and he has no particular call on our sympathy. A civilized, curious, pleasure- and thought-loving man, reduced to a dreary, weary automaton. What is there to respect in that painful spectacle?

23 May 1951.

The subject I should like to write about is love between brother and sister, growing up together as children in an old house with their grandfather and a couple of aunts, his daughters. They would be orphans, and the boy would be raised on stories of their picturesque or dashing father killed in the war, and their mother who died when the boy was born. As their lives went on they would discover that no man or woman could satisfy them, that the bond between them was so strong that it unfitted them for any other love and made them destructive in love. Entangled with this subject is another, that of the personality of the dead father as interpreted in the old wives' tales of the aunts, acting upon the boy as an influence so much stronger than that of any living person and building his naturally timid nature into rash, would-be-heroic shapes.

Well, back to this diary again. If I must do it, let me make my little messes in private. God knows who will clean them up after I am gone. I hope someone who will not be bored by them. It would be appalling to be a Bore after one was dead – an immortal Bore.

"All the spring goes on without her" – where does that come from? This Ottawa spring is beautiful, but they can have it. I find it quite an effort to remember that this life is real – that it matters whether you do up your fly before going out in the street, or call people by their right names. Only in the office I mean business. Otherwise, there is the habit of not hurting people's feelings, of being on time for dinner, of having three large whiskies between six and eight, and of being a little uneasy about money.

2 July 1951. Wolfville, Nova Scotia, on vacation.

I feel as if I were recuperating after a serious illness. Outside it is perfect June weather – sunlight on a white house – on a slope of neighbouring lawn. The main street is almost deserted at this midday hour. At Frank's Clothing Store the removal sale is slowing down. At Babcock's Restaurant and Soda Fountain Mr. and Mrs. Babcock and the two waitresses are recovering after the rush of the Dominion Day crowds. The Post Office is empty – people collected their mail at the bustling hour of twelve after the Halifax train had come in. In the old-fashioned frame houses behind the roomy porches and the standard rose-bushes, sundry old ladies are resting – resting their rheumatism, their weak hearts, their jangled nerves. The little church on the bluff overlooking Minas Basin is cool, dark, and empty. Light comes through the Sherwood memorial window in crimson-lake puddles. In the churchyard the de Wolfs – the town's founders – lie. From the grassy ledge at the verge of the cliff where the churchyard ends abruptly I can see the whole curve of the land round the water of Minas Basin. The tide is in now, right up to the edge of the dykes and in places seeping through into the dyke land that lies directly below me. Beyond the picture-postcard blue of the water rises Blomidon, swathed in a hyacinth mist, drawing the eye and the imagination – that sombre and dramatic shape dominates the seascapes of mist and water and the receding mauve folds of hills that lie behind it. I am half bored, half enchanted, by this long stretch of June days, by the hot, sweet smells of clover fields, of wild-strawberry patches, the breeze off the water that always keeps the tall elm trees stirring and that blows pollen from flowering bushes in tenderly tended cottage gardens. In and out of the sunny main street too blows the town's gossip – blowing like pollen from house to house, from garden to garden.

11 *November 1951. Ottawa.*

Sunday afternoon again. A grey, dank, damp day – old tin cans lying in dirty slush in the gutters. I walked in from Rockcliffe across the bridge over the grey river which is slowing to freezing-point. The hills, the Laurentians, glow like dark sapphires. Somewhere around the corner a band was playing and soldiers marching back from the Armistice ceremonies. Plump, bright-eyed French-Canadian girls were strolling with their boyfriends through the dirty streets; French-Canadian mothers-of-ten were taking their brood for a Sunday walk, accompanied by their husbands. Rounding the corner by the Château Laurier to go up to my office I thought how very much I should prefer to find myself in a big double bed making love.

27 *November 1951.*

Aunt Beatrice came to dinner tonight – eighty-four – recently (three weeks) widowed, just flown out to Canada after fifty years of county life in Northern Ireland. She sits in her black and pearls, talking about Dundarave, the place which the law of entail has obliged her to quit in favour of an unworthy nephew, and of the follies of the house-maids. She is a plucky old girl with spirit and stoicism. I like it when she talks about her niece being "so good at cartooms – always been artistic." After dinner we looked at old photographs with her – those embalmed moments of lightheartedness at picnics when the men put their straw hats on back to front or enacted facetious courtship scenes with the girls before the camera in the sunlit summer of 1900. How depressing it is to look through these albums now with a survivor of the picnics, skating parties, and weekend gaieties. There is no physi-cal connection, not the slightest, between that laughing girl in the canoe with the towering flowered hat, the tie and starched shirt, and the old woman beside me. "Look," Beatrice says, "at the clothes. How could we have worn them? The hats, my dear, such a suitable outfit to go canoeing in! I was considered very fast for wearing a soft collar to play tennis in. An older married woman told me, 'Of course there is nothing wrong in it, but I should wear a stiff collar in future if you don't want to get the reputation of being a fast girl.'" Those three sisters[1] must have been quite a feature of Ottawa in those days, with quick wits, a great sense of fun, and no money, but determined to be in on everything. Endless flirtations, Beatrice's courtship by Lord Ava – "he wrote me the only real love letter, what you would call a love letter, that I have ever had. The best-looking man I ever knew. Died at Ladysmith in the South African war." And Harold, who proposed to all three sisters, and whose daily letters, lying on the radiator in the hall, were greeted by the other sisters with "Elsie, the daily question is waiting for you on the marble slab." Why do I write about these old sisters? I spend my days with Cabinet Ministers, distinguished (and interesting) civil servants – I am in a good position to report the gossip and politics of society in this little but important place, but

> I have old women's secrets now
> That had those of the young;
> Madge tells me what I dared not think
> When my blood was strong,
> And what had drowned a lover once
> Sounds like an old song.
>
> (*W. B. Yeats*)

When I was young I used to be shocked by the callousness of the old, the casual way they would look at a photograph and say, "She used to be my closest friend. She was so pretty and gay. She married a very ordinary man in Toronto and I don't know what happened to her in the end." I expected, somehow, more feeling, a pause to think of years of friendship, the tragedy of change, the decline of everything – including themselves. Now I think that Proust's ruthless analysis of old

---

[1] The three sisters, daughters of Sir William Ritchie, Chief Justice of Canada, were: Beatrice, Lady Macnaghten; Elsie, Mrs. W. H. Rowley (mother of John and Roger Rowley); and Amy, Mrs. James Smellie (mother of my wife, Sylvia, and her brother, Peter Smellie).

age is not cynical but the simple truth – as the capacity for feeling shrinks, as the freshness of interests narrows, brain and heart contract. I fear it in myself. Or perhaps feeling becomes more canalized – there is less overflow. Two or three human beings out of one's whole world of people seem the only ones truly human.

20 March 1952.

From the world into which I was born, cruelty, violence, and coarseness were altogether excluded. Pain, and even discomfort, were fended off wherever possible. Apprehensions of illness were always in the air, perhaps because illness seemed the only enemy likely to penetrate the defences of my home. Security was – or seemed – complete in those days before 1914 as it has never seemed since. Security in this world and the next, for my parents' generation was the first to retain a belief in Heaven while dispensing with the fear of Hell. It was felt that Hell was a Victorian superstition. Since God was Love and it was unthinkable that he would punish His children with perpetual torment, it would be wrong to darken a child's mind with such horrors. Hell might exist for some unspeakable outsiders, but in any case, like sex, it was not to be mentioned before children.

A sub-fusc day, grey sky dripping on dirty snow. Spring in Ottawa is not a season but one vast mopping-up operation. Civil servants, glum or smug, have now – at 9.30 – been absorbed into the government buildings. The whole population seems mewed up, like the animals in the Ark. The Parliament Buildings, like the Ark, ride high above the surrounding slush and puddle. Silence reigns in the dripping and now almost empty streets. Stenographers are now adjusting in their typewriters the first memorandum (with carbon copy) of this day; their bosses, with or without hangovers, are girding themselves for the day's effort to get nearer the top of their grade. In their homes the wireless whines and housewives prepare lists of purchases for Steinberg's and the A&P. The melting ice discloses an old overshoe, or a French safe, buried throughout the winter under the snow – our Ottawa version of the spring crocus.

This last week has flashed by in days of high-pressure work, absorbed in this absorbing little world where politics and diplomacy merge into personalities. You spend the day working with this group of politicians, officials, and diplomats, then you dine with them and their wives, gossip with them, and drink with them. The dominant theme – the only point in this place – is the pursuit of power. It obsesses the men and infects the women. Other societies may be dominated by money, snobbery, or the search for pleasure. Here the game of political power is the only one that really counts. It creates an atmosphere very uncongenial to love, very unflattering to women – almost any man in official Ottawa would rather talk to a Cabinet Minister than to the most beautiful woman in the room. It is easy to understand this once you are inside the game. You are tuned in to the power waves and you can hardly hear any others, except as "interference." This is the game for middle-aged men – you can even play it into the sixties or seventies with growing expertise, when you would be at a sad disadvantage in the games of love.

17 June 1952. Wolfville, Nova Scotia.

I am here on a visit with my mother. The road into Wolfville runs parallel to the shoreline of Minas Basin. You only see the broad stretch of water and the bold profile of Blomidon at intervals. Most of the time it is blotted out by fields and houses, but even the unseen presence of that magic mountain makes the banality of the main street seem reassuring and cozy. The little town seems like a place met with at the very beginning of a fairy story, before out-of-the-way things start happening – a jumping-off place and a place to which, in the end, one is not sorry to return, to see its lights cheerfully glowing after an excursion into strange terrain.

31 August 1952. Ottawa.

Last night after dinner we went out into the street to watch the Northern Lights. I have never seen them in such magnificence. Anyone who did not choose to call them Northern Lights could not fail to think that this was a revelation of God, his power moving in the firmament; the long, quivering fingers of light seemed alive as they wove their shifting patterns in the sky. At one moment a cone of light at the top of the sky seemed to shed just those rays seen in sacred pictures, and one could expect a Blake-like vision of God the Father. The silent shiftings of these long cones of light and the subtle, swift sliding of one colour into another seemed a performance of intricate music, a manifestation of a vast, benign, and playful intelligence – the music of the spheres. And then suddenly it became for me a most unbearable bore. I went into the house and deliberately picked up a novel and read it, to escape the imposition of sublimity. I felt the same kind of sleepiness, restlessness, and revolt which great music, mountain peaks, and sunsets produce after a brief exaltation in me.

6 December 1952.
    Work.

7 December 1952.
    Work.

8 December 1952.
    Work.

9 December 1952.
    Work.

10 December 1952.
    I am now in charge of the Department of External Affairs.

January 1953.
    Work, work, work.

One day in the autumn of 1953 I told the Minister, Mike Pearson, that I wanted to be posted abroad. He was reproachful and urged me to stay, saying, "I thought you were a *working* diplomat and did not care for a representational job." He was quite right – I was never to enjoy the representative side of an ambassador's role and always to look back upon my days in the Department as the most satisfying of my career. But once my decision was taken I could not wait to go, and I used to fear that I might break a leg on the icy streets of Ottawa and have my departure delayed. With this onset of restlessness came a return to the diaries.

7 October 1953. Ottawa.

This last weekend was warm enough to come up to the Wrongs'[1] cottage in the Gatineau country outside Ottawa. Yet it is hardly warm enough. We had to huddle before a fire last night but today it has turned to this soft, fickle weather, with warm days on sheltered wharves by the lake with the sun on them but, high up here on the verandah, a chilly wind blowing across the lake. Sylvia, at the other end of the verandah, is painting my portrait. She has me writing, clad in a blue dressing-gown, and has made me look like Harold Laski, my least favourite character.

It is very quiet here except for the wind in the pines around the house, the sound of cowbells from the farm nearby where we get water in pails, and the occasional cars passing on the nearby road. The house is full of brown and red butterflies, the colour of the changing leaves. They crawl against the mosquito netting on the verandah, trying to get out. I pick them up very delicately between finger and thumb by their closed wings, open the screen door, and throw them into the air. The verandah floor is strewn with obsolescent wasps, torpid in this autumn air with hardly the spirit left to sting.

The signs are for a peculiar season. Squirrels are making no hoards of nuts; there are no berries on the trees. The bears, driven out of the woods by the forest fires, have come as near as the suburbs. It is too warm for them to hibernate and they go blundering round outlying farms, beating down barn doors in search of food, in an ugly mood, put out of their annual routine.

For my part, like the animals I feel a break in routine. I am once again on the edge of one of those trans-Atlantic migrations which have been the pattern of my life. I am going back to Europe, away from the mindless beauty of these woods and lakes, away from the daily reassurance of making good in a community where there is no attractive way of going to the bad. One fact about Ottawa has from

---

[1] Hume Wrong, Canadian Ambassador to Washington and Under-Secretary of State for External Affairs, and his wife, Joyce.

the first been clear – that for me there is only one temptation here, whisky. How often have I vowed that whatever else this place does to me it is not going to make me into a drunk.

23 October 1953.

There go those Sunday bells from the carillon of the Peace Tower of the Parliament Buildings! I can never forgive Ottawa its Sundays, yet I am conditioned to this place and to the work in the office and am somehow scared of a change and of being turned back on my own resources after the incessant work of the office. It is only a few weeks now before I leave for England and then to accompany the Prime Minister on his tour of the Far East and after that, God knows what. They have suggested my going as Ambassador to Madrid but I cannot face it. There is no work there and one could not live on picturesque views of Spain and visits to the Prado.

This job as Deputy Under-Secretary for External Affairs has been a tough one, requiring toughness in the occupant. It also needs experience. On top of that, it calls for a certain flair for sensing the situation and subjects which are "sensitive," in which a mistake can rapidly become a blunder. I have the experience and something of the flair, but I lack the toughness.

So far as policy is in question, I see policy as a balance, also a calculated risk, as the tortuous approach to an ill-defined objective. All-out decisions, unqualified statements, irreconcilable antagonisms are foreign to my nature and to my training. In these ways I reflect my political masters, the inheritors of Mackenzie King, and I am fitted to work with them. I believe, too, that such temperaments are needed in this dangerous period of history, which is no time for heroics to be paid for in a currency of disaster.

In administration I tend to the concrete and the human and want to break the rules to fit the individual case, the object to get out of people the most effective element that they can contribute. This may lead to injustice but would avoid the worse thing – waste. My ignorance of and contempt for rules and regulations would wreck any system unless counterbalanced by someone who could sustain the necessary framework. But most of the time I am simply rushed off my feet with work, passing by human situations which would be obvious if I had the time to look twice, making decisions by a mixture of know-how and instinct, always in danger of a mistake or a lost opportunity or a damaging delay.

13 December 1953.

It is Jack Pickersgill, always a good friend to me and very close to the Prime Minister, who has suggested my name to Mr. St. Laurent to accompany him on his visit to Europe and the Far East. I am to be his External Affairs adviser, to accompany him on his official calls on prime ministers and heads of state, to keep a record of his conversations with them, and generally to make myself useful. I approach this assignment with trepidation. I do not know Mr. St. Laurent or how I shall get on with him. Also, I do not know the Far East and am nervous lest he pepper me with questions about these countries to which I cannot supply the answers. His daughter Madeleine, his son Jean-Paul, are going with him, plus a small entourage including a doctor, his secretary – the admirable Annette Perron, the clever and charming young Ross Martin from the Privy Council Office, on whom I shall depend a lot for companionship, and an elderly and none-too-efficient valet. We shall fly all the way in an RCAF plane whose captain, John Stevenson, I have just met. He is handsome, humorous, and, I should think, eminently capable.

I intend to try to keep up this diary during the trip but the official and political record will be contained in the telegrams which I shall be drafting for the Prime Minister's approval, so that this will be a matter of personal impressions.

It is to be a tour of goodwill, support, and friendship and no concrete results are expected.

12 February 1954. Bonn.

This is the first moment that I have been able to catch my breath for long enough to return to this diary. We have just arrived here from the Prime Minister's visit to Paris, which, from the political point of view, I found deeply depressing. I have been drafting the telegrams giving the high points of the Prime Minister's interviews with M. Schuman and the other political leaders. Their general outlook on the world was one of profound anxiety and negativism. There was no belief in the European Defence Community in its present form and they had no suggestions for alternatives.

The Prime Minister, his daughter Madeleine, and I stayed at our Embassy, which is a magnificent house in the rue du Faubourg Saint-Honoré. The visit got off on the wrong foot from the start. From the moment that we entered the panelled salon with its chandeliers and elegant eighteenth-century furniture, with a footman bringing glasses of champagne on a silver salver, I could see that the Prime Minister, who was tired anyway, did not at all appreciate this style of "gracious living" (which I know he thinks is "un-Canadian"). The Ambassadress, the beautiful Madame Désy, did not help matters. Encased in satin, she seemed frozen into a formal attitude like an ambassadress in a play. Jean Désy talked with nervous intensity. He is a highly intelligent man but should have sensed that the Prime Minister was not in a responsive mood.

Dinner was even worse. We filed into the beautiful but chilly Louis Seize dining-room and were spaced at wide intervals round a marble table. The food was elaborate, the wines varied, the conversation stilted in the extreme. At times there were pools of silence of several moments' duration. For some reason, and although I was not in any way responsible for the social freeze, I began myself to feel both nervous and embarrassed. I do not know whether it was cause and effect, but, biting on a piece of Melba toast, a loose tooth suddenly came unstuck, falling into my cup of consommé with a plop which was clearly audible in the silence round the table and drew all eyes upon me.

15 February 1954. Bonn.

The contrast in political atmosphere between this place and Paris is extraordinary. There is no mistaking the ability and forcefulness of the German government *équipe*, and owing to the smaller scale of the entertainments offered us we have been able to meet and talk to them on a much more intimate and informal basis than in Paris. Here we encountered a firmness of policy line, energy, and decisiveness. Bonn is a deceptive place, in appearance a sleepy university town, but there is an impression of underlying German dynamism and potential strength. To anyone who, like myself, would prefer to see the French in command of the destinies of Western Europe, this is not altogether reassuring.

The Prime Minister's interview with Chancellor Adenauer went well. I should say, fairly well. Mr. St. Laurent seemed a little disconcerted by Adenauer's cynical outspokenness about international personalities and policies. Our man, no doubt wisely, refused to be drawn and restricted himself to expressions of goodwill and careful platitudes, of which, I must say, he has a steady stock. I was much impressed by Adenauer. There is something very formidable about him. He is like a well-oiled, immensely powerful machine moving in the groove. He emanates authority and an unmistakable *Catholic* touch. His assessments of international forces were realistic. He is adroit, patient, and ironic. His mobility of gait and gesture combine with the mask-like pallor of his face (reconstructed after a motor accident) to leave an impression of agelessness almost uncanny in a man of seventy-six, or is it seventy-eight?

16 February 1954. Rome.

The Italian government is new in office, and insecure. The conversations with Italian politicians have been flimsy indeed; the hospitality on a splendid scale.

Our ambassador here is my old friend Pierre Dupuy, witty, intelligent, one of our best diplomats. There was a funny scene between him and the Prime Minister over the vexed question of exchange of gifts with the Italian government. The Italians have presented the Prime Minister with something handsome in the line of silver and Pierre demurred at the Prime Minister's intention to reciprocate with a signed photograph in a frame which was not even leather but leatherette, and cheap-looking at that. Pierre pleaded for a silver frame, saying "Prime Minister, in Rome do as the Romans do," to which the Prime Minister drily replied, "In Rome *we* do as Canadians do."

The Prime Minister has handled himself throughout these meetings with European political leaders with good sense and dignity, and without pomposity. His charm and warmth and his distinguished appearance are attractive. As a Canadian, one feels proud of him, which is more than I can say for all our travelling Canadian politicians. Madeleine is a great asset. Beautiful to look at, spontaneous and friendly and with a sense of humour. She and her father share a dislike of artificiality and pretence.

The Prime Minister has kept to a line in all his interviews: (1) he has emphasized NATO bonds but refrained from any particular proposal in the NATO framework; (2) he has used the analogy of relations between people of English and French stock in Canada to show how it is possible to cure ancient rivalries and live in productive and friendly relations; (3) he has conveyed throughout that it is enlightened self-interest that has guided Canada in entering into defensive arrangements and in her immigration and trade policies – a frankness which has been appreciated by European statesmen who are a little tired of lofty moral sentiments which conceal interested motives; (4) in his assessment of the risk of war he has expressed his judgement that the U.S.S.R. does not intend war but wants to maintain tension, and this necessitates continued preparedness. On this point there has been striking unanimity among all European statesmen. None believed that aggressive war would be launched by the Russians; none believed in the possibility at this time of a settled peace.

17 February 1954. Bahrein.

Bahrein is flooded. They have had rains here such as never before in their history. But today is a fine day, cool after the rain, a stiff breeze on the sea front. Veiled Arab women pick their way across the flooded streets on stepping-stones. In his hovel shop a bearded and turbaned sage smoking a hookah sells you Gillette blades and Colgate toothpaste. The bar of the BOAC hotel is full of types who seem to be deliberately playing up their parts. The manager, ex-RAF, says, "Franco nearly got me in the civil war. I was one of the bad boys in the International Brigade – born on the Khyber Pass – ask them up there if they remember Cook Sahib. That was my old man." A Danish sea-captain, washed up here because the Japanese took over his ship, describes life in Bahrein: "You wait till the bar opens, drink till lunch, sleep, wait till the bar opens, and drink till dinner, then just drink."

20 February 1954. Peshawar.

Seldom have I come to a place which has had the same instant attraction for me as this. County Cork, the town of Avalon in France, the Isle of Jura, Wolfville in Nova Scotia – all were cases of love at first sight for me. When I awoke this morning it was to hear the Moslem call to prayer floating over an English garden. We are staying at the local Government House. From my window I see an English vista, a village church, hedges, English trees, a cricket ground. The call to prayer and the sound of command and of the bugle are always in the air in Pakistan, yet there is something peculiar to Peshawar, as if we were staying in someone's house when the host was away. The English haunt the place.

21 February 1954.

Up the Khyber Pass. Almost too good to be true, the exhilarating air, the sense of plunging straight into a boy's adventure story – the tough, hard-drinking commander of the Border Scouts whose idea of fun is to stir up a scrap with the Afghans, an atmosphere of virility, adventure, keen air, dramatic heights with the solitary figure of a Khyber Scout perched on a rock guarding the path against the fighting tribesmen with their home-made guns. The sense of adventure, for us at any rate, was spurious. The Pass is perfectly safe now and in another five years will be placarded with Pepsodent advertisements. But cut into the rocks are the emblems of the regiments, British and Indian, who fought in this wild country. The biggest danger I encountered was from the Pakistani colleague who sat in the car next to me sneezing virulently at me as if on purpose till finally I have caught his cold.

On to Lahore. Our knowledge of the subcontinent appears to be restricted to Government Houses. The Government House in Lahore is a cream-coloured, pillared, sprawling mansion, brilliant in sunlight. The bookshelves are filled with out-of-date English novels (many W. J. Lockes) and old sepia-tinted photographs of picnics and polo games. There is tea before breakfast, the bath is drawn. The servants never leave one alone for an instant. An individual bottle of whisky is brought to one's room to prepare one for the interminable Moslem banquets without a drop but water to drink. These drinkless banquets and the endless polite conversation are pretty exhausting. Last evening I went in company with a supercilious maharanee and members of the local smart set to the ball for the end of the Lahore horse show. I might as well have been in the Golf Club in Ottawa – the same kind of talk, the same tunes from the band, but with Moslem ladies sitting in groups, not dancing.

24 February 1954. New Delhi.

From the moment that we arrived at the New Delhi airport we were in a different world from Pakistan – more settled, richer, neater, less of a poor, untidy pioneer country. The contrast between Karachi and New Delhi is overwhelming. Here is a garden city of broad streets and houses set back among green gardens. No refugees, as in Pakistan, no squalor, no stink, modern cars glide over the asphalt. Here the Foreign Office is a fine stone building, solid and gleamingly clean. I thought of the Karachi Foreign Office in the dilapidated Rajah's Palace, open to the sandstorms, untidy, improvised like everything in Karachi. And how different are the people. The Moslems in Karachi seemed straightforward, frank, simple, compared with the alien sophistication of the Hindu, a strangeness lurking just under the surface of the Oxford-educated civil servants with whom we associate. Then there is the mixture of morality and the Machiavellian in their politics, their vanity and subtlety in social relations, the insinuating intelligence, the charm which might just be disconcerting.

We are staying in what used to be the Viceroy's house here, Lutyens' palace, imposing, original, monumental, and monumentally successful, an establishment on the scale of Versailles. Indeed, Versailles in its pompous emphasis is the only palace comparable to this. Hundreds of servants, hundreds of gardeners, hundreds of cooks in the kitchen (I believe there are eight hundred servants in all). Some are turbaned; some, in a curious livery of scarlet and gold, wear flat Chinese hats. A turbaned, bearded father-figure brings in breakfast and stands over you while you eat it. The bathtubs are of marble, built for giants. In the interminable marble halls are yet other attendants who hover and cluster and come bowing forward to put you in one of the lifts which never, to their great chagrin, can they move without a hitch from one floor to another. In the great courtyard standing under every arch, patrolling the Mogul garden, are the soldiers of the Government House bodyguard.

The Prime Minister had been looking forward to this visit and his meeting with Nehru as the high point of his tour. He and Nehru have been conducting a tremendous pen-pal friendship for months. They have been exchanging interminable telegrams of mutual congratulation and esteem, but I am not at all sure how this love affair is going to prosper. It was surprising to Mr. St. Laurent to find that this Wise Man of the East conversed in the style and language of Bloomsbury, a style very far from the Prime Minister's own. However, our High Commissioner here, Escott Reid, seems to think that the talks between them, after a shaky start, are going extremely well. I have not been present at their official meetings, as Escott has taken over. If anyone can make the visit a success Escott can, as in addition to his exceptional ability and charm of manner he is an enthusiastic lover of India.

As for one's impression of Nehru, what can one say? The English painter who has come out here to paint his portrait says that the task is impossible. A thousand expressions flicker across his face. When he met us at the airport he jumped about from one foot to the other, making the gesture of pulling up his long white cotton trousers as if they were slipping down. He kept twisting the red rose in the buttonhole of his long cream-coloured linen coat, and made as if to scratch the top of his white Gandhi hat. He is always in movement, never still, or if he is, his eyes are always moving, or his mouth. He is not the pontifical figure I had expected. Gayer, more mobile, more immediate; impatient, too, between a caress and a barb.

Last night we dined with him – the Prime Minister, Madeleine, and myself. It is, I think, unfortunate from the point of view of a "*prise de contact*" between him and Mr. St. Laurent that Lady Mountbatten should be staying here. She strikes a Mayfair note which the Prime Minister cannot pick up. When we arrived in the hall of Mr. Nehru's house it was she who greeted us, looking charming yet lined and wrinkled from gracious smiling. In the hall was a head of Nehru by Epstein. The Prime Minister remarked, "Well, I suppose that is a very fine likeness." Lady Mountbatten emitted a little cry of horror and said, "Oh, don't tell *him* that. It is too ghastly and must be got rid of." The Prime Minister looked somewhat at a loss.

At dinner there was no real opportunity for any consecutive talk between the two men. After dinner, long pauses in the conversation began to set in. Finally Lady Mountbatten, to break the log-jam, said to Nehru, "Do show the Prime Minister your Tibetan costume and your Kashmiri dressing-gown." At once Nehru jumped to his feet and, slightly stooped, ran from the room. (We do not move as these people do or run in this sudden, lightfooted way.) After a longish interval he returned, clad in a magnificent Kashmiri dressing-gown, then disappeared again, to return in Tibetan dress. He seemed to be much enjoying himself and relieved to escape from conversational effort.

27 February 1954. Viceroy's House, New Delhi.

I have taken to my bed with some kind of throat infection. Outside my window in the darkening dusk the great raised courtyard looks like a stage-set. Any figure appearing there has significance. After a day of silence, at evening there is a monkey chatter of talk from the soldiers below who have come off duty. The flowers in my "sick room" – sweet peas and phlox – have no scent. Perhaps no English flowers smell here.

Last night was Mr. Nehru's dinner in honour of the Prime Minister – white tie and decorations (if any). At the hour of dinner I had a call to go to the Prime Minister's bedroom. I found him standing in the middle of the room, white tie, white waistcoat, tailcoat, long woollen underwear, no trousers. He said, "Here now, I suppose my trousers have been left on the plane." That was precisely what had happened. Everyone else in his entourage had his trousers, but the Prime Minister was trouserless. Like Sir Walter Raleigh throwing down his cloak for Queen Elizabeth to walk upon, I said, "Take mine, Prime Minister," but a second look at his girth and mine showed that this was a physical impossibility. I called one of the innumerable servants to inquire after a pair of spare trousers, but apparently there are none in this vast palace. We sent him running to the nearest bazaar in New Delhi to purchase a pair. The moments ticked by. The Prime Minister was already eleven minutes late for dinner. Finally the servant returned bearing with him an extremely greasy pair of second- or third-hand trousers of such circumference that they had to be fastened round the Prime Minister's waist with safety-pins. During the whole of this agonizing ordeal Mr. St. Laurent remained perfectly unperturbed and patient, with never a word of complaint. My mind boggled at the thought of what Mackenzie King would have said in these circumstances.

Finally we descended to dinner. Turbaned Lancers behind every chair, magnificent flowers on the table, no wine. During the endless dinner party three pigeons flew into the dining-room from the garden through the French windows and perched on the cornice above the fireplace. They behaved very well for quite a long time until boredom with the after-dinner speeches drove them to fly high across the long candle-lit table with protesting cries and out of the windows again.

During the Prime Minister's speech before the Assembly the Indians only applauded the compliments to themselves. I don't believe that, apart from the meetings with political leaders, anything we have said or done on this visit has got across to the minds or hearts of these people. They are easily bored and I think that they have been.

The sentiment heard in government circles is extremely anti-American. The Americans can do no right in Indian eyes. At one moment they are accused of selfish isolationism and neglect of poorer countries, at the next of imperialist ambitions to dominate. There is a great deal of harping on American materialism in contrast to the spiritual values of India. I am beginning to find this very irritating. As a Canadian, I feel quite free to criticize the Americans, but when other people do it I instinctively rally to their defence.

I had a long talk the day before yesterday at one of these endless lemonade-drinking receptions with Indira, Nehru's daughter. She is a handsome woman, but cold. She talked humanitarianism and social reform but in a bloodless fashion, tinged with immense smugness and self-righteousness. I took strongly against her.

A day of sightseeing. Fatehpur Sikri in the morning. Talk of a deserted Mogul capital had put me on the wrong track. I had expected romantic ruins. What I found was a creation of art so totally new to me that it might have been new in time. The completeness, the state of preservation, are due to the accident of its being abandoned by Akbar and thus never plundered or destroyed by armies. Those courtyards, mosques, and pavilions of red sandstone are unhaunted, picked dry of all human context by the heat of the sun. Or is it simply the advantage of my ignorance that I can see these monuments as timeless works of art because I do not know the language of their history which would set them safely in a framework?

The Prime Minister said that he pictured in his imagination the carpets and fountains of the time of the Mogul court. He responds to every impression in India. He seems as interested in ancient monuments as he is in pipelines and the complexities of corporation law. I find it very attractive that a man of his age and in his position should be so open to new impressions. He says that never in his life has he had such a sense of new experience as in this one week in India. Perhaps it is doing the same thing for him as it is doing for me. Yet how profoundly alien India is; nothing responds to my predilections. I do not "love" this country, I am not even "attracted" to it, but I feel it is a multitudinous sea in which one might shed one's personality.

28 February 1954. Colombo.

When we got here last night, Madeleine stretched back in her chair and, kicking off her shoes, said, "Well, I guess I like the small countries." We all knew what she meant. The complexity and sophistication of India, the grandeur of its monuments, the imperial touch, Mogul or British, all imposed their strain. Canadians cannot quite stomach the excessive. Then, too, we are beginning to tire. From Government House to Government House, from dinner party to dinner party, from reception to reception, from interview to interview, from Bombay to Madras. Ceylon seems a holiday after India. The friendliness of the people, the disorganization at the airport. It is a spice island of flowers and fruits and voluptuous foliage.

8 March 1954. Ottawa.

After Ceylon I gave up keeping this diary. Some day I shall try to sort out my impressions of the rest of the trip. At the moment they're a jumble of unrelated details. Jakarta, with Sukarno boasting and posturing; the squalor of war-wrecked Seoul, bad oysters at dinner with horrible old Syngman Rhee, the visit to the Canadian troops at the front in Korea; Tokyo and lunch with the Emperor, where two silences met, the silence of the Prime Minister and the even more extensive silence of Emperor Hirohito, blinking through his thick-lensed glasses; the pointless visit to Manila.

It was at Tokyo that the Prime Minister began to show signs of fatigue. From being tired he began to show signs of melancholy. He seemed austere and more abrupt. I am beginning to fear that this trip has been too much for him.

Honolulu is a boring place, Hawaiian music sick-making. They hung leis of flowers round our necks at the airport, making us – apart from Madeleine – look extremely silly. In my bedroom at the Royal Hawaiian Hotel was a pineapple with a card "Compliments of the Manager." The pineapple was already sliced. I thought it looked delicious and went out for a brief walk, intending to eat some of it on my return. When I got back it had gone. I telephoned the room service and asked, "Where is my pineapple with the Manager's compliments?" "Aloha," a voice replied (they always say "Aloha" in Honolulu instead of "Hallo"). "Aloha, pineapples only left in rooms to welcome guests on arrival." I never saw that pineapple again.

10 March 1954. Ottawa.

Ever since I got back I have been working on the draft of a speech for the Prime Minister to make in the House of Commons about his tour. It was not an easy job but after about eight drafts I felt reasonably satisfied with it. The Prime Minister read it and then said, "Here now, Charles, I suppose you have told me what I *don't* want to say." Rather nettled, I replied, "Prime Minister, I am glad to have been able to clarify your thinking." I went to the gallery of the House of Commons to listen to the Prime Minister deliver *his* version of the speech, which I found absolutely deplorable.

Looking back on my association with Mr. St. Laurent during the trip, I think that though he treated me with so much kindness and consulted me so frequently, I am no closer to him than I was at the outset. As Norman Robertson[1] said of his own relationship with Mr. St. Laurent, "Our natures and our minds do not mesh." Yet I respect him, I admire him, and I could be fond of him if personal relations

---

[1] Norman A. Robertson, twice Under-Secretary of State for External Affairs, Ambassador to Washington, and High Commissioner to London.

meant anything to him, which I think they do not, apart from his devotion to his family. His philosophy of life seems to be a sort of Roman Catholic Rotarianism which does not admit the existence of evil. He lives by Christian rule. I have never heard him say an uncharitable thing. Also, he never praises. His mind is more a lawyer's mind than a politician's, and he is completely free from the vanity and the grudges of political life, hates gossip, does not drink, has great public charm, no small talk, humour *très sec*.

6 April 1954. Amherst, Nova Scotia.

My mother and I are here on a visit for a few days. The wind never stops blowing in from the Tantramar marshes. Only the eye of love could descry beauty in Amherst. It is fascinating to see how different each of these Nova Scotian small towns is from the other. Wolfville is charming, indeed pretty, the houses painted in spotless white, the gardens tended, trees surrounding the colonial houses. Much of Amherst dates from about 1880 when it was "busy Amherst," a boom industrial village-town, now in decline. It is not helped by the unhappy attraction that a kind of maroon sandstone had for Amherst builders and of which many of the buildings, including the post office and the Baptist church in the main street, are built.

The town is at the edge of the marshes, which gives it something of the character of a seaside place. The streets all end abruptly where the marsh begins. Beyond is space and skyscape. An eternal wind blows from those marshes. Yes, it is a peculiar little town.

My mother's family came from here. The only traces left of them are the stained-glass windows (ordered out from England) in the little Anglican church, and the graves on the windy marsh side – "The Honourable Alexander Stewart, C.B., Master of the Rolls" and his children and his grandchildren. In the church there is a brass to the last man in the family, my mother's brother, "Lt.-Colonel Charles James Townshend Stewart, D.S.O., Croix de Guerre, killed in action Bourlon Wood, October 20, 1918." No one in Amherst even remembers the Stewart name now, yet the old man aspired to Found a Family only a hundred years ago and we still live on what is left of his money. We are children or grandchildren of the small town and have never quite got free of its influence. Those dire words, "What will the neighbours say?" still echo in the ears on a hung-over morning.

21 April 1954. Ottawa.

In two weeks' time I leave to take up my appointment as Ambassador to Bonn and Head of the Military Mission in Berlin. Now that I am to leave Ottawa I am beginning to know that I am fond of it and to know how much I shall miss my friends. The truth is that, much as I grumble about life in Ottawa, I have become attached to the place. Today I took my farewell walk along the terrace behind the Houses of Parliament and looked down on that scene that I know so well – the noble wide-flowing river, the Laurentian hills changing colour with every shift of light, and the silvery spires of the Basilica in the middle distance. Then I came back through the quiet tree-lined streets of Centretown, past the sensible red-brick mid-Victorian residences, the ponderous palaces of the lumber barons, and here and there a turreted fantasy, porch and balcony adorned with tortured woodwork. Our own apartment is in the upper floors of this old house, the bedrooms high among the top branches of the trees. In summer the sunlight on the shabby carpets is mottled in a changing leaf pattern; there are sun patches as warm as a summer beach and cooler spots where the leaves keep out the sun. This has become our home, more so than any Embassy could be. Our friends are here – we have become part of this closely knit community. Mike Pearson says that he saw very little sign of my new sentimentality about Ottawa until the day of my appointment abroad.

BONN

1954–1958

When I took up my post as Ambassador to Bonn, the occupation of Germany by the Allied Powers was not yet ended, although official relations with the German government were becoming increasingly close. It was difficult not to think of the Germans with suspicion as the dangerous ex-enemy. The psychological and human breach had not had time to heal – much deeper ran the horror excited by the obscenities of the concentration camps and the brutish nastiness of the Nazi régime which stained the German name. The Germans, for their part, treated the representatives of the victors with the respect which Authority has always commanded in them. There was no resistance and no servility, but the acceptance of a fact – the fact of defeat. While one's social dealings with the Germans were friendly enough, there was too much on both sides that could not be spoken of, or forgotten, to make for real ease. During my years in Bonn this situation was changing. The German people were finding renewed confidence in themselves, the "economic miracle" of recovery was on the way. Germany under Adenauer's guidance was showing itself in advance of France and Britain in understanding the future role of Europe and was becoming the favoured friend of the United States. As the war receded and the Cold War intensified, we increasingly shared fears and interests with the Germans, who were soon to become allies. Then, too, with the ending of the Occupation there came an abrupt change in the attitude of the population. The measured deference due the former Occupying Powers disappeared with almost startling rapidity. At the same time a most definite note of equality – sometimes of superiority – came into German voices. The socially false situation of the Occupation period was over – it was possible to have German friends. I think some of these changes may be found reflected in the small mirror of the diaries.

15 May 1954. Bonn.

It is a glorious May morning. We are just off to Assmannshausen on the Rhine for the weekend. The Cadillac, with friendly and respectful chauffeur (ex-German Army), will draw up in front of the door at precisely 11 a.m. Our luggage will be carried from the door to the car by the amiable Erich, the butler, who will bow us off the premises. The excellent Lena, the lady's-maid, is now engaged in pressing Sylvia's underclothes in the linen room. The parlour-maid has just brought me on a silver salver my Ottawa dentist's bill, which I am afraid to open. The major-domo, Rudolf (ex-Rommel's army), has just presented to me the new gardener, an ex-sergeant-major in the Wehrmacht. So this is the way the War ends! No one could stay sulky on such a fine day with so many people devoting themselves with such cheerfulness to meeting one's every wish. No wonder our heads of mission get an inflated idea of themselves.

17 May 1954.

Just back from our visit to Assmannshausen. A sunny, happy little interlude. Dinner on the terrace looking across the Rhine under arches of wisteria to the accompaniment of sentimental music, drinking lots of red champagne which doesn't make you drunk but gives you the illusion that you can waltz. We did some rough-and-ready waltzing at a small nearby café. Sitting at the table on the terrace by the Rhine I was overcome by a sentimental mood, no doubt inspired by the red champagne but also by the Rhineland atmosphere. The pleasure of intimate talk about feelings, about life, a kind of nostalgia for romantic happiness (for you are looking into the eyes of the other one) – it is the return of the mood of youth, of youth that talks more than it does and dreams more than either, a mood which in New York would seem inconceivably dated, in Paris – beside the point. In Germany I find myself often thinking of the French, their cutting edge of style, the finality of their speech, their contemptuous impatience of blunders. As for Germany, if it is not like England it is not like anything, and of course it is not like England; yet every now and then at the corner of one of those suburban streets, or in the face of a schoolboy, or in the unexpected identity of a word in the language, there is a resemblance, the more disconcerting because the Germans seem so profoundly alien. As for me, I like my foreigners foreign. "*Vive la France!*"

2 June 1954.

This house in the Linden Allee, Cologne, which is the Embassy residence, was built by the owner of a chain of stores in the characterless red-brick suburban style of the 1920s, so different from the ambitious, uninhibited monstrosities of pre-1914 German capitalist mansions. Almost the whole of this bourgeois residential part of Cologne escaped the bombing which wrecked the old medieval city and demolished the factories and the workers' quarters.

There is a garden full of rambler roses on trellises. There is breakfast on the pillared terrace. There are drinks in the evening, when the weather allows, sitting on garden chairs watching the birds poking about in the bowl of the fountain, where a single jet of water gently pisses. There is, of course, a swimming-pool and, next to the pool, a barbecue, the creation of my predecessor as ambassador – a shrewd, kind Western Canadian judge with a folksy vein to which we also owe the tooth-mugs in the bathroom with their alarming inscription "O wad some Power the giftie gie us / To see oursels as ithers see us."

Inside the house the rooms are well-spaced and tall. There is a vista from the marble-paved hall of flowers against the tapestry. There is a colossal fireplace. There is a candelabra hanging from the ceiling composed of bronze cupids which some previous occupant thought fit to clothe with little gilt jock-straps. On the terrace, imprisoned in a wooden packing-case, is a vast male marble nude which used to be in the hall. My predecessors could not live with him. Some day I plan an unveiling ceremony. Supplies and Properties of the Department of External Affairs have repainted formerly dark walls and ceilings of the interior of the house in an effort to induce cheerfulness. All the furniture has been re-covered in bright materials, with a fondness – almost amounting to a mania – for brilliant, strident yellow. Upstairs, *tout le confort moderne* – yet I think the big marble bathrooms stink like badgers' dens. Something wrong with the elaborate German plumbing. The house is pleasant enough to live in, but I hate the German servants' practice of locking the doors and windows from the inside at night. Down come steel shutters over all the ground-floor windows while the butler locks the doors from within and retires with the keys. I have now stopped him from doing this. It gives me the feeling of being incarcerated in a private lunatic asylum.

8 June 1954.

Developing an anonymous public face which expresses only cautious benevolence, controlling the spasms of nervous exasperation or high spirits, getting into the groove, the ambassadorial groove. It is a game, like learning German. Whether it is a game worthy of a grown man I cannot say.

How fortunate it is that the Embassy residence is in Cologne rather than Bonn. For Bonn, like most arbitrarily designated political capitals without a metropolitan tradition, is hard to love. The Germans themselves certainly do not love it. No doubt once as a university town it had its charm, before the politicians and the bureaucracy moved in and the new styleless government office buildings sprouted. In its environs are neat, agreeable residences suitable for residence by civil servants. Its admirers say that "it is a good place to bring up children" – an unenticing recommendation to childless adults like Sylvia and myself. Also in Bonn is the enclave (known locally as the Gold Coast) where the large American community of diplomats and officials is concentrated. There it is possible to purchase at the PX stores all sorts of American goods and to dispense with German shops. There, too, is the American Club, to which we Canadians have kindly been given courtesy membership and where cocktails are properly mixed and Germany seems further away than the Burning Tree Golf Club, Washington, D.C. In Zittelmannstrasse is the Canadian Chancery, to which I am conveyed every weekday in the official car via the Cologne–Bonn autobahn. The Chancery is modestly housed in a medium-sized villa. Its outlook is pleasantly pastoral. At the end of the quiet street is a rough, grassy field where sheep browse – a reminder that until recently this was a village lane on the outskirts of the town. Beyond the field the land slopes down through a municipal park of repellent aspect to the Rhine – an easy stroll to the river's bank when things in the office become too tedious. Bonn seems to me like an acquaintance – agreeable enough unless one does not fancy that particular mix: bureaucracy plus suburbia. Cologne is a very different matter. A flourishing centre of civilization for centuries and now what? The bombardment of Cologne during the war was concentrated on the ancient core of the city. In a series of hammer-blows the medieval walled town and most of its renowned monuments were reduced to rubble. The vast and overpraised cathedral and, oddly enough, the main railway station survived, with the tottering remains of some Romanesque churches and a medieval gateway opening on to the desolation within. Ten years after, on damp days, there hangs in the air of Cologne the stale stink of buried rubble and scorched beams that brings back to me London after a blitz. But here the destruction was more nearly total. When a city has been murdered, does its spirit survive the corruption of the body? The people of Cologne have kept their pride in their tradition of guild and church. Its affinities are with Trier and Aachen; the roots are Roman, the flowering was medieval. The corporate pride is exclusive – one hears its echo in the patronizing tone in which a citizen of Cologne speaks of upstart Düsseldorf, alien Berlin, or Americanized Frankfurt. I have no part in all this – I am an outsider to these memories and to the daily life of the city. Yet I feel an absurd borrowed sense of superiority when I say, "We live in Cologne," as though it were grander to inhabit a noble ruined city than neat, middle-class Bonn.

12 June 1954.

Back from Berlin today, from a visit to the Canadian Military Mission there, which comes under my authority. The Berliners are stout-hearted, with a front-line mentality, like Londoners during the war. They are condescending about Bonn, which they despise as provincial and as being remote from daily contact with the enemy (now the Russians). Visited the reception centre where the refugees from East Germany are given physical examinations and kept overnight before being sent to the refugee camps. The medical side of it is under Frau Doktor Gerhard, a tough sergeant-major of a woman of seventy, full of humour and magnetism. She has seventeen doctors working under her. What struck one was the smoothness of the organization, the incredible cleanness, the neatness of all the buildings in which thousands of refugees are housed. Not a scrap of paper lying on the floors, all clothes neatly folded in the dormitories. This mass of humanity, mostly rather dirty poor people with their miscellaneous belongings, passes through these buildings, living there without squalor or confusion. Imagine what it would be in France! More surprising was the humanity which seemed to accompany this efficiency, especially in the children's quarters, where little blue-eyed, flaxen-haired children of four and five were sitting round tables in pretty, airy nurseries playing with blocks with nurses who seemed kind and devoted. Even the quarters of the criminals and prostitutes who had slipped over the line to the transit camp were spotlessly clean. Did those who made the concentration camps make this?

I went to the interrogation of a woman member of the East German police who said she had deserted to come to the West, but who was suspected of being an East German spy. Narrow face, thin-lipped mouth, blank blue eyes. Something cold-blooded and vapid about her. She recited her story in a high, unfaltering voice, like a learned lesson. As a liar she failed by being too word-perfect. Age about twenty-two, formerly a saleswoman in a small town, then a private, later an officer, in the East German secret police, denounced a woman friend of hers to the police and was herself denounced to the police by her father because she had a boyfriend in West Berlin, hence her flight. She struck me as the type from which the Nazi women jailers came. As a saleswoman no doubt she was efficient, but would have been just as efficient at work in a gas chamber, and would have enjoyed the latter more.

Spent the day walking the streets of Berlin. Among the ruins are the new buildings. Some of the monumental buildings of the past survive like great mastodons of a vanished epoch. In a pile of rubble there would be an ornate doorway decorated with mouldering caryatids and leading to nothing.

14 June 1954.

" 'Damn' braces, 'bless' relaxes." Got up in a bad temper and found this quite useful stiffening during the day. Herr Kleiber, Chef de

Cabinet of the President of the Republic, called and was very critical of the French. It is impossible to defend the French behaviour over the European Defence Community, but none the less it is irritating to have to listen to the Germans sitting in judgement on them, and galling to sense – under their "more in sorrow than in anger" attitude – their contempt for French pretensions, their self-satisfaction with their own record. I am afraid that "rather a Frenchman wrong than a German right" is hardly a possible answer.

Received by Chancellor Adenauer. The more I see of him the more impressed I am by him. He is a very wise and a very wily old man, much subtler than the other German politicians, making them seem raw and provincial.

17 June 1954.

Unity Day celebration at the Bundeshaus[1] of the 17th June risings in Berlin against the Soviet occupants. Looking down from the diplomatic gallery at the rows of middle-aged, middle-class deputies, all listening with restrained boredom to long-winded speeches, I thought, "And these are the chaps who used to listen to Hitler."

The ugliness of the Cologne population is something to be marvelled at. In the crowd outside Cologne Cathedral today listening to the Corpus Christi celebrations, there was not one attractive woman; unglossy, dry hair, pasty or weather-beaten complexions, little boot-button eyes, sack-like clothes, dun-coloured or grey, big bottoms, and a stumping, hausfrau walk. And so many of the men with long, badly modelled noses and high cheekbones, with something goose-like about their movements.

Last night, dinner at the French Ambassador's (François-Poncet's) château on the top of a hill overlooking the Rhine. The choice of the house was designed to impress the Germans and everybody else with the presence of a Great Power – France. It is more successful in general effect than on closer scrutiny. An "eighteenth-century" French château, in fact built by a rich German industrialist in 1912. There were the much-talked-of footmen in scarlet satin knee-breeches and there was the much-heralded cuisine. Not a single

---

[1] German parliament.

German there, all diplomats and their wives, several pretty Latin American women, bored with Bonn and living for their next shopping expedition to Paris. Agreeably frivolous conversation of the kind that the presence of Germans makes difficult. A little diplomatic world under a glass dome.

23 June 1954.

I am trying to learn German. The woman who is teaching me is making me learn the German version of *Little Red Riding Hood* by heart. This is the only German I so far know. Last night we went to a German dinner party. I was seated between two wives of German high officials, stout bodies, little gold crosses on chains round their necks, reddish faces, not a word of English. Finally, unable to stand the silence any longer, I turned from one to the other and launched into *Red Riding Hood*. "Red Riding Hood comes into the wood. She is not frightened of the wolf. When she sees the grandmother she asks, 'Why have you got such big eyes? Why have you got such big ears?'" All this in quite fluent German. The two ladies stared at me in dumb amazement. One of them asked on a questioning note, "Bitte, Exzellenz?" Otherwise, no reaction. However, the German official on the other side of the table, who could not hear what I was saying, came up to me afterwards and complimented me on my fluent German.

18 July 1954.

The servants in this house impose their own restrictions. Sylvia and I must sit solemnly at the long dinner table, taste the wine, be waited upon by butler and maid. When I leave the house for the office I must be bowed to the courtyard gate by the butler, who hands over the red leather dispatch box to the waiting chauffeur. It is impossible to create confusion in this house. Throw your clothes on the floor at night, they are picked up and sorted out by morning. How is one to resist this smoothing-out, flattening-out process which makes an ambassador of you from the collar-button inward?

26 July 1954.

Where are all the former Nazis in Germany? I mean, physically, where are they? They are certainly not to be met in Bonn, or, if they are, they are well disguised. On the evidence of one's eyes and ears one would be led to believe that the entire German population was subjugated by Hitler and a small gang of his criminal associates. Another curious thing is that, of the many ex-officers of the German army I have met, none mention serving on the Western Front. With Rommel in Africa – yes, but mostly they talk of their service on the Eastern Front against the Russians, and the theme of their story is that *they* recognized the communist menace, that *they* were fighting to defend Western civilization against a danger which we were too blind to recognize. As to their casualties in Russia, they are mentioned in a tone which suggests "these died not only for us but for you." If the Nazis have gone to ground, the Jews have vanished into the gas ovens. I have only met one Jew since I have been here. When the word "Jew" is mentioned among the Germans, a self-conscious silence sets in, as if a social gaffe had been made.

The Germans in their dealings with us seem on their best behaviour. Cautious, patient, kindly, friendly people without a trace of arrogance. It is as though they had all received a mysterious order from a hidden leader as to how they should behave.

These new bifocals are tormenting me. I feel like a horse wearing a bit for the first time, or as a boy when I had to wear woolly underwear. And to think that I have to live with these for the rest of my life!

10 October 1954.

A Sunday of getting into the car and motoring somewhere for lunch together and afterwards seeing old churches and castles. The abbey of Maria Laach has stood there by its lake for a thousand years, or as near as makes no difference. It is big, all right, but is it beautiful? At any rate it is startling, like meeting an elephant in a glade. Lunch in a manor-house-turned-motel, the family portraits looking down on fat men and women eating. Then to an ancient church near Bonn. The church made me shiver, and coming back in the car I felt a sudden, shuddering, Sunday-afternoon melancholy. In the mist, youths in belted mackintoshes down to their ankles, and old women in black suits, were stumping along. I wanted to get right into bed and start making love, as a sign of life in the face of those mineral monuments and vegetable people.

25 November 1954.

Dined again with the François-Poncets, guests consisting of rich Rhineland industrialists and their wives. They came from Duisburg and Düsseldorf with their diamonds and minks. The atmosphere was so thick with money that one felt it could be a subject embarrassing in any connection to mention. These people seemed to be a world in itself of big money, very different and quite apart from the local nobility and gentry. The shabby-grand Wittgensteins and their friends live in the lodges of their castles with halls decorated with antlers and no springs in the drawing-room sofa. They are the easiest to get along with. They almost all had English governesses and talk a fluent English interspersed with pre-War slang and Mayfair expressions of the 1930s. They had no opportunity to catch up during the War. All talk of the Nazis with a sort of snobbish disgust. All the men seemed to have served in the army on the Eastern Front.

26 November 1954.

Lunch today with Brentano, who is to be the next Foreign Minister. I had heard that he was a stupid man, but I do not think so. Yet he seemed hardly tiresome enough to make a successful politician. He confirmed what I hear from everywhere, that there is no enthusiasm in this country for rearmament; no one seems keen about it in industry, in labour, or among the intelligentsia. We lunched in icy draughts at the Redoute Club and drank brandy after lunch, which made me sleepy, so that when I left Brentano at the door I absent-mindedly said "Goodnight" to him at two-thirty in the afternoon.

The other night François-Poncet was talking about *Le Grand Meaulnes*. He says it is German and not French in its kind of romantic inspiration. Curious, I have often thought of that book since coming to this country.

The Rhineland has a nervous, boring, neurotic atmosphere but is not commonplace. The obsessive feeling of the place persists, putting everything slightly out of true, distorting, casting strange lights and shadows, always with a persistent, sinister undertone. It is hard to render in words – in music?

Of the social situation and our relations with the Germans, Elizabeth Bowen says, "It is a great, bright, ghastly smile covering an incurably false position." Elizabeth's new book, *A World of Love*, is marvellous, a masterpiece of her own genius. She wrote a lot of it in the sitting-room of this house when she was staying here, and on the verandah of that small hotel in Bonn.

20 December 1954. Hotel Plaza-Athénée, Paris.

I am here for Mike Pearson's[1] visit, spending my time with the Canadian Delegation. Rye whisky in the hotel sitting-room, then a straggle of the delegation, a couple of secretaries, and a tame journalist; we all drift out to some unlikely restaurant or night club for the evening. All day is spent wandering round hotel corridors, waiting for the Minister to come in or to go out, waiting for the typing to be finished, knocking at doors with Draft 3 of the speech in one's hand. Where *is* the Minister? Out buying a present for his wife? A good dose of Canadians. When I went to the plane to see them off I felt I'd like to stay and arrive home for Christmas, coming down in the snow and icy wind at Dorval, flying on down to Halifax. I thought what hell it would be to be an exile, to see a plane leaving for Canada and to know that I could never go back.

24 December 1954. Cologne.

Wild wind blowing. Yesterday it blew the scaffolding off Cologne Cathedral. It came hurtling down from the high tower into a narrow street, scattering the people like a thunderbolt from Heaven and sending them scurrying into side-streets and shop fronts for shelter. The household is disorganized by the new dachshund puppy we have just bought. A long-haired dachshund, an attractive little creature. It peed in the middle of the new dining-room carpet where no table, chair, or rug can conceal the damage.

The Vice-Chancellor, Blücher, came to lunch. He represented Germany at the Queen's coronation in London. His eyes filled with tears when he spoke of the significance and beauty of the coronation ceremony and of the kindness of Princess Alice. He said that here was a lesson for Germany, and expressed deep nostalgia for the monarchy. Blücher struck me as rather commonplace and absurdly vain. When

---

[1] Pearson was then Secretary of State for External Affairs.

we were talking of different German accents and which was the best, he said, "I do not want to boast, but you could not possibly do better than listen to my accent." He is anxious to play a part in foreign affairs and he indicates that his views are wider and less narrowly political than those of Adenauer.

26 December 1954.

Overcast weather, rushing wind, mire in the fields, swollen, dirty little rivers, trees snapped by the gale. We are sitting in the upstairs sitting-room among the presents for today's children's Christmas party – children of the staff, Canadian and German. The presents include Indian headdresses, teddy bears, jigsaw puzzles. The radio is going full blast but I am afraid to touch it for fear of breaking it for the third time. The puppy, now called Popski, is locked in the bathroom and barking incessantly. The German servants are delighted with their presents, delighted with our Christmas party, the cook making endless cakes covered with marzipan flowers.

1 January 1955.

Had an obscene-looking upside-down egg with shreds of ham adhering to it for breakfast. Began rereading *Swann's Way* in my bath and thought of when I first read it in a cold bath in my lodgings in Earls Court Road over the creamery during the heat wave of 1932 when I was earning four pounds a week as a reporter for the *Evening Standard*, and then later in Paris she and I read Proust aloud to each other in the intervals of making love.

2 January 1955.

A New Year's party last night, all English. A lady called Mrs. Tusket said, "Hamlet was only fourteen years of age." How does she know? Did some friend of his tell her? She said that it is a part that is played too old by men too old for it. Sat next to an Englishman after dinner who said, "After nine years in Germany I have been offered a job in Rhodesia, so my wife and I are off. Quite remunerative, the job, with a house thrown in." I asked, "Is Rhodesia a colony on its own or part of a federation?" "No idea," he said, "never been in Africa except in Tangiers for one day and that's no guide."

3 January 1955.

Holiday. Spent the day playing with the dog, reading *Swann's Way*. Tea before the fire, house still hung with Christmas cards, greyness outside. Hamlet was not fourteen as Mrs. Tusket pretends, but over twenty-four, as the Anglican archdeacon has proved to me from the evidence of the Yorick scene.

The evening party last night – danced with a pretty Irish woman. Asked her, "What do women mean by security?" She said, "I could give you a ribald answer to that one. We want to know *it's* there. Anyway," she said, glancing out of the corner of her green eyes, "that's one thing I've never bothered my head about. Security I care nothing for."

9 January 1955.

The servants are calling for Popski up and down the house. They adore him and spoil him incessantly. He will be lucky if he doesn't turn into a self-centred little neurotic.

The German men are good company. They enjoy jokes, although preferring the one about the other man slipping on the banana peel. They have a streak of adolescent cynicism. But they are not hypocrites, they are not platitudinous. Although they may be deceitful about their intentions, they are frank and rather indiscreet about their feelings. They are by nature terrific talkers. Their most striking lack seems to be grace, style, elegance. The so-called festival gaiety of the Rhineland depends on immense quantities of beer or wine, and ends in moon-faced boorishness.

A bold, unstable race. They have the attraction of vitality and the fascination which the adventurous exercise. They are not a middle-aged race as so many of the English and French are (not to mention Canadians).

I was thinking today about the ups and downs through which so many of the diplomats here in Bonn have passed during the course of the war years. So many of the Europeans have been in exile from their own countries, the Dutch Ambassador for one, living in a bed-sitting-room in London, then – with the liberation of the Netherlands – becoming Governor General of Indonesia in a palace with a hundred servants. François-Poncet, *Figaro* hack, French Ambassador, a prisoner of the Gestapo, and now Ambassador again. As for the Asians, many of them have served their term in prisons during the colonial period, whereas the communist diplomats have of course had a training as revolutionaries. Yet all this variety of experience is triumphed over by the extraordinary force of the convention of the diplomatic corps, a caste which envelops everyone, so tenacious of its privileges that it has maintained a sort of eighteenth-century enclave in the modern world, ruled by privilege – manners good, bad, and indifferent – and, above all, rank.

A Bavarian gentleman came to lunch today. Brilliantly blue eyes a little too expressive, a bachelor, takes immense trouble over his fingernails. He had an odd expression for near-Nazis, saying they had "a brownish tinge" (an allusion to the Brown Shirts). He said, "I never had any sympathy for the Nazis, yet after all even I fought in Hitler's army. But then, you people were allied with communism. So there you are. I remember the first time I said 'Heil Hitler.' It was to get into a military hospital to take a present to a sick friend; otherwise they would not have let me in. But I was never a Nazi. Not that I suppose you will want to check up on that, but it is a fact." I felt like saying, "It's not your guilt or lack of guilt that interests me, it's your experiences. Tell me what it was like to live through all that."

There was a domestic crisis today. The butler, Erich, has been having an affair with one of the housemaids. His wife has found out and insists that he should leave and go to Munich to start a restaurant with her. In talking to me he burst into tears, saying he didn't want to leave and that women were terrible – the same all the world over – so unreasonable. In fact I am very anxious to keep Erich as he is an extremely good butler with a sympathetic although weak character. I have suggested to him that I would pay the rent of his wife's house in Munich if she wanted to go there and he could join her at some indefinite period in the future. He seems inclined to accept this, but no doubt when his wife has talked to him he will change his mind.

12 January 1955.

Started the day with a very irritating conversation with François-Poncet on the telephone in which he got the better of me. What a genius the French have for putting one in the wrong. It is a great mistake to discuss business with them in their own language. Even a stupid Frenchman, which François-Poncet certainly is not, can score off one with that weapon in hand.

A professor of chemistry from Bonn University to lunch today. He talked about conditions in his former university of Leipzig. He is in touch with his colleagues there and says that the régime bears hardest on law and the humanities. Scientists have no trouble and are doing very good work, with excellent pay.

13 January 1955.

I cut my throat this morning when shaving and have gone about all day looking like a failed suicide. The sitting-room is full of hyacinths, white, pink, and mauve, and smells delicious. I must go and dress for the fancy-dress ball at the French Embassy. False beard. Erich says it makes me look like a Russian prince. I think it makes me look like a commissar. Sylvia looks lovely in her costume.

15 January 1955.

I am certainly lucky in the staff of the Embassy. John Starnes, the Counsellor, would make a better Ambassador than I. He has an acute, questioning mind and a grasp of German affairs. He is also a companion and friend with whom one never has a dull moment. Helen, his wife, is a delight – lovely to look at, funny, and equal to any occasion. Pam McDougall, the First Secretary, is handsome, humorous, and exceptionally able. The Air Attaché, Doug Edwards, and his wife Lois have become what one could call "boon companions" of ours. We knew them in Paris days when he was at the Embassy there. He is the easiest of company and she is witty and attractive. The younger members of the staff, Peyton Lyon and Frank Stone, are among the most promising of their generation in the public service.

16 January 1955.

Luncheon party here today, including the Wittgensteins and her mother, old Countess Metternich. She was English by birth, the daughter of an admiral, and her mother was a Miss Kenny from Halifax, Nova Scotia. She said to me in earnest tones, "Have you ever seen Thornvale, outside Halifax? It must be a beautiful house. My mother always told me that it was far finer than the Metternich castle." In fact, Thornvale is a Victorian wooden villa. I was much amused by this piece of Nova Scotian loyalty and I backed it up strongly, saying, "Your mother was quite right. Thornvale is indeed magnificent and makes most German castles seem quite insignificant." Countess Metternich gave a sigh of deep satisfaction. The Wittgensteins are becoming friends. She is very pretty and a great charmer – she certainly charms me.

Little Prince Wittgenstein embarked on a series of questions about Canada. "Canada is part of the Commonwealth but not a province of the United Kingdom?" I agreed. "Why then do you have a Governor General?" I tried to sketch out the constitutional position of the Commonwealth and the monarchy. He looked very suspicious, as though I was concealing something, probably our subordination to Britain.

21 January 1955.

Went to an English cocktail party in honour of the new clergyman just out from England. The English colony is riddled with fights over running the English church here.

A member of the German Socialist Party (SPD) to lunch. A clever, cynical little man, but sincere in his immovable suspicion of creating a German army in any form. He kept on saying, "We do not know what it will be like. We can only judge by the record." Indeed, if we encourage the Germans to be rearmed it will be very largely our responsibility. There is no enthusiasm for it, partly due to full employment in this country, partly to the fact that the Germans have felt protected by the Occupation forces and now by NATO troops. The mood of the younger generation seems to be one of indifference to slogans and causes. They had enough of that growing up under the Nazis. They want to settle down, get good jobs. There are many early marriages. I was talking the other day to one of the refugees from the lost territories in Prussia, where he had been a landlord. He said he and his generation would never be reconciled to the loss of these lands, nor would this generation of German refugees from Czechoslovakia ever accept their exile, but he said his own sons were typical of the new generation in being bored with the whole subject and wanting to settle down to a good paying job in Düsseldorf or Frankfurt.

On the other hand, many people with whom I have talked believe that once the new German army is in existence the Germans will toe the line, and that the German tradition of militarism is deeper than any passing mood. One of the NATO military attachés said to me the other day, "Good martial music and a few parades and they will be back where they started." But the question is – do we want them back where they started? We can't have it both ways.

I had a long talk with Beaudissen the other day about all this. He is a German officer with an anti-Nazi record who is consultant to the German government on measures to be taken to ensure that the new German army will be different from the old, without its dangerous aggressive tendencies. He is a nice, well-meaning man but does not carry much conviction, at least to me. He talks of a citizen army, an army which would not feel itself separate from the people – not a state within a state, but an army of individuals who are not military robots but have a sense of belonging to the civilian community. He talked of a tank crew as the ideal size of the group where political discussion could develop individual initiative, and he linked this with the concept of mobility and the tendency away from the mass concentration of troops. He said that it was necessary to curb the caste character of the German army and make it more socially democratic. But he went on to admit that a great deal had been done in this way by Hitler, and that Hitler's army had been much more democratic in spirit and composition than any German army of the past. This social democratization had gone furthest in the air force, yet the air force was the most fanatically Nazi element in the armed forces. I imagine that this talk of democratizing the German army may be beating a dead horse and that the dangers in the future will not be from the remains of an hereditary officer corps but from those trained in the new tradition of German militarism – the ex-officers and NCOs of Hitler's army.

23 January 1955.

How I loathe dances. Why do I always drink too much at them? Why do I build up these killing hangovers? I should like to be living alone, or almost alone, by the sea somewhere, allowed three visitors a week, chosen by me, lots of books (and perfect eyesight to read indefinitely), solitary walks, and short sprees to places of my choice with people of my choice.

The Rhine is in flood up to the tops of the lamp-posts on the Rhine road outside the Bundestag. I was thinking this morning of my old boarding-school in Canada, a red-brick building on a hill, now – thank God – burnt down. There was one boy, a wall-eyed, bandy-legged, log-witted giant who hated me (or did I imagine that?) – at any rate, tormented me. I swore that later in life I should be revenged on this sadistic son-of-a-bitch. To my undying shame, when I met him in London in 1939 as a grown-up Toronto broker I not only did not kill him on sight, I shook hands with him, a betrayal of myself as a boy.

At that school the headmaster and most of the masters were Englishmen. The system of prefects, fagging, etc., was not natural to the Canadian scene any more than the cult of cricket. It was an alien system and I think it set up strains of which the boys were not conscious but which disturbed them. By 1922 or 1923 we had certainly ceased to be colonials but were not yet fully a nation. It was an Awkward Age. The idea of Empire, of which Canada was proud to be a part, was still alive to the older generation who sent their boys to this school, but my contemporaries were young Canadian nationalists without knowing it. Their Toronto conservative fathers imposed things English on them but they remained like a Sunday suit and stiff collar worn for the occasion. Nothing could stop the natural slip into North American habits. Old Silver Balls, as we called the headmaster, said he wanted the school to be "an oasis of monastic seclusion in the desert of commercial modernity." He got a horse-laugh from the boys. He was a Wykehamist and he wanted to make Wykehamists of these future Canadian brokers, bank managers, lawyers, and insurance men. His defeat was total. Although I had just come from an English school, I was a schoolboy and so, as a matter of course, on the other side of the barriers from the masters. Besides, I was not a natural Wykehamist.

The scene from my window this evening: Claus, the cook, is standing at the door in his white chef's cap, which he never removes indoors or out, except I suppose when he goes to bed. The door has been thrown open by the butler to let Popski out for a pee in the garden. The night-watchman is standing by with a torch to light Popski's way and the chauffeur is watching the gate lest he should slip out on to the road.

Lunch today with Charles and Natasha Johnston of the British Embassy. They are the people I like best here. The new Greek Ambassador and his wife were there. She is a big ox of a woman with dyed hair and a loud voice, a wonderful mimic, very funny, just what we need to lighten life in Bonn.

There is an article about me in *Time* magazine which says, among other things, that I have been "pepping up diplomatic dinner parties for twenty years." What a ghastly epitaph for my tombstone!

29 January 1955.

Dinner with Terence Prittie and his wife. He is the *Manchester Guardian* man, an Anglo-Irish Etonian, intelligent and entertaining. When he puts on his granny glasses he looks dreary and respectable; when he takes them off he looks a little pugilistic. He has no faith whatever in the changed character of the Germans and says that Beaudissen will get nowhere in changing the German military and that one day there will be a showdown between the Protestant Church in the eastern zone and the Communists over the future of East German youth. Sat next to an Englishwoman at dinner who said, "My only problem is that my son should be my daughter and my daughter should be my son."

In the afternoon went to a German film, *Canaris*, in Bonn. There was an old news film showing Hitler's entry into Vienna. At his appearance the German audience burst into laughter, mocking and hating laughter. It was an extraordinary performance.

Diplomatic dinner in the evening. A terrible row over the placing of the guests. No fewer than three ambassadresses claimed that they had been wrongly placed at table, and one threatened to leave.

Popski is gnawing one of Sylvia's evening slippers. Every time we try to get it from him he shoves it under the sofa and when our backs are turned hauls it out again.

1 March 1955.

Alone in the house. Sylvia has flown to Canada to see her mother before she dies, if there is time. I felt so sorry for her as alone she stepped on to the plane to leave.

11 March 1955.

My official visit to Hamburg. This visit is going better than I expected and I may even do some good for German–Canadian relations. Dinner last night at the Anglo-German Club. Businessmen and consuls, Englishmen who had spent twenty, thirty, forty years in Hamburg and spoke German with old familiarity. Germans who had been born in Liverpool or educated in Scotland and spoke English with homely local accents acquired in their boyhood. It gave me an idea of the character of Hamburg as a twin sister of Liverpool or Glasgow, tied with England in peace or war for decades or centuries. I like this community of shipowners and merchants. I have been on a tour of the newly built areas of Hamburg, which cover the square miles of the densely built city totally destroyed in the three-day air-raids.

They are constructing a new city of space, light, greater privacy, and less density of population per acre – a planner's dream.

12 March 1955.

After dinner drank brandy with the British Consul and he took me for a tour of the Reeperbahn. A most unvicious place with the atmosphere of a Hammersmith *palais de danse*. A nude woman emerges from a bubble bath and an attendant showers the soap off her bottom, all to slow music, then up go the lights, dance music, a collection of women in snuff-coloured dresses or sweaters and skirts waiting to be danced with, waitresses or tarts tittering and drinking beer. At every corner nude displays and then a solo dance by a lady in a lace gown who represented refinement. It all seemed clean fun suitable for children and grandmothers. Indeed, there seemed to be a lot of grandmothers around, stout elderly bodies in groups or with their husbands. There seems nothing between these shows and brothels.

13 March 1955.

I had lunch yesterday at Friedrichsrühe with the Bismarcks. The house is situated in a great forest of firs and was destroyed by a bomb during the War, which also killed the Swiss Consul and his wife, who were staying at the time with the Bismarcks. The new house is built on the foundation of the old. Their house party was standing about in the drawing-room, talking. Then the door burst open and Prince and Princess Bismarck bounced in as if released from a circus cannon, he with a pink face and a pink carnation in his buttonhole, she a Swede with the "international society" manner, opening her ever-so-blue eyes very wide at one as she talked. Age around fifty, quick in conversation, mischievous and mocking. She has her social twin sisters in London, Paris, and New York. Her husband is a member of the Bundestag but he is not, I think, taken very seriously.

17 March 1955.

The day began badly. Popski escaped from his room and came into mine at five in the morning and woke me up. I lost my temper with the poor little bugger and began yelling at him like a banshee, and threw boots at him. All day I felt sad, sensual, and sloppy. Sylvia arrives today from Canada with her aunts, Elsie and Beatrice, who are coming to stay. I have been getting the servants to put flowers in their bedrooms; Claus is cooking up a steak-and-kidney pie for their lunch.

The possibility of nuclear warfare looms over all hopes. It looks as though this unhappy generation will have to pay an enormous overdue bill for all the follies and sins of the human race, and by comparison every previous generation, whatever its fate, may have been lucky not to be born in the twentieth century.

20 March 1955.

It is lovely having Sylvia back again. I am enjoying this visit of the old girls. Aunt Elsie (now seventy-five) is, of course, my old friend and ally. How many nights at her apartment at the Roxborough in Ottawa we have sat up together talking about life, love, and politics, and drinking whisky. I love her for her warm, generous heart and for being so funny, but she has got terribly deaf, and there is something touching about her impatience with her own deafness. She has still kept her wish for happiness and still suffers from childish disappointments. She says she hates old people, that they are empty of everything, like old paper bags blowing about. Perhaps I shall hate the old too when I am old. Being sorry for them gives me a feeling of being younger than I am. Talking of age, Aunt Beatrice is now eighty-seven. She is, as usual, full of stories of Dundarave, the Irish estate where she passed her married life – also long anecdotes beginning "On one occasion when we were staying at Brown's Hotel . . .," which is a signal that she will go on for twenty minutes. All the same, I admire her spirit and her toughness. She is perfect with the German servants, who appreciate her "grand manner" and respond to her bossiness. In some ways she is a natural German herself.

I can't think why I am haunted by that bloody boarding-school. Looking back it seems to me that a miasma of sexual prurience, excitement, and fear hung over those boring days and dream-filled nights. Of course, I was an insufferable boy – but who isn't, at fourteen?

Tomorrow is supposed to be the first day of spring, but still snow on the ground. Sylvia and Aunt Elsie have just left for church (Aunt Beatrice disapproves of religion). Popski is barking despairingly in the garden where he has been left to amuse himself for an hour. An unmistakably Sunday feeling in the house today. Can even the nuclear bomb change Sunday?

The Wittgensteins and old Countess Metternich to dinner last night. Countess Metternich and Aunt Beatrice are made for each other. Monica Wittgenstein was mocking the social aspirations of the Cologne bourgeoisie in tones familiar all the world over wherever the hard-up gentry talk of the newly cash-conscious.

At dinner at the Starneses' was a German ex-officer, a handsome bob-sleigh champion, who figure-skates near here. He had been on the Eastern Front and said that when the Germans came into the Ukraine he went with them right into the villages on his motor-bike and that the Ukrainians threw so many flowers and so much food and butter to the German troops that he was lucky to have his tin hat on or he would have been brained. He said all the Ukrainians wanted was independence, or at least a show of it, and if the Germans had pulled a Grand Duke out of Paris and set up a Ukrainian state they could have settled any quantity of Germans there and have secured the agricultural produce of the Ukraine. He went on, "None of you on your side would have cared and we could have got away with it, but that little Austrian pup Hitler had to go and blow up the holy places at Kiev and turn the people against the Germans. Then he imported narrow-minded German schoolmasters and made them Gauleiters who oppressed the people and lived on champagne. When the War began I thought it was a crusade against communism, but after serving on the Eastern Front I soon discovered that it was not a crusade. I had two old White Russian aunts living in Berlin as émigrées, naturally violently anti-communist, but as the campaigns on the Eastern Front went on and the destruction of Russian cities began, they began to say that this was a wicked war against Holy Russia and to listen to Stalin's speeches on the radio."

2 April 1955.

The two old girls are having a social success here. We have taken them round to a lot of parties and they seem to be very much enjoying themselves. Aunt Beatrice got into a misunderstanding yesterday at a diplomatic party with the South African Ambassador. She said, "I do not approve of your government's policies in South Africa." The Ambassador, thinking he was up against a gentle, liberal-minded old lady, began a long-winded explanation of how devoted his government was to the best interests of the black population when Beatrice interrupted him to say, "I don't mean that at all. I think you should take a much stronger line with them. Shoot them down if they give you any trouble."

Went into Cologne with the aunts. I had to stagger round the jewellery shops with them, carrying a bag of asparagus, vermouth, and cheese, while they had every diamond in Cologne out to compare unfavourably with their own rings. I cannot think that Aunt Beatrice needs any more rings. Her old hands are already laden with four outsize cat's-eyes, one large diamond, and one mammoth dark opal, known in the family as "the frog."

15 May 1955.

Chip Bohlen has suggested my flying to Moscow with him for a visit, as he is American Ambassador there now. I think I might do this. I am in the mood for a fresh start. From now on not a single day is to be thrown away as you chuck in an unsatisfactory hand at poker. Today is windy, sunny, lilacs blowing in the wind, everything in bloom, a feeling of exhilaration like a morning in one's youth, a restless mood, up one minute, down the next. Yet one must be wary of the dreams and projects which swarm in one's mind as the sun plays on lilacs and chestnuts as you walk quickly past the neat white houses of the English suburb of Cologne to buy the Sunday papers.

12 June 1955.

Sitting alone on a bench in Sud-Park with my eyes closed, thinking that I used to imagine what it would be like to be an old man sitting alone on a bench in a park. Perhaps when my heart grows as small as a peanut I shall be a cheerful and sociable old man like my grandfather and like I was in my heartless youth. There is rain on the rhododendrons and the roses. A brooding resentment settles in this climate like a low cloud that hangs never far away over the Rhine Valley. Then brief passages of sunlit elation. Yesterday – or was it the day before? – the clergyman came to lunch. "Blessed be the poor in spirit," he quoted. What does that mean? I understood better today when Mrs. Chichester came to lunch, so smug in good works, so qualified for salvation. She was indeed "rich in spirit," quite overpoweringly so.

Now what could be fairer than this rose garden with the roses just out, a swimming-pool waiting for me around the corner, caviare for lunch with a little white wine, a valet tenderly brushing my morning coat. My hopes and unsung struggles would make the average man laugh himself sick and say, "Affectation and nonsense."

Reading André Maurois's account of George Sand's love life and her ghastly, claggy letters to her lovers. How did they put up with her? How much nicer to have had as a mistress an obedient, co-operative, brown-skinned maiden who could not speak a word of any known language but was graceful and usually half-nude, and to live with her in a clean, sunny house in a valley in Ceylon.

1 July 1955.

Our National Day. A reception here this afternoon – five hundred guests and it will certainly rain. It started out fine this morning but is already clouding over and the birds by their twitterings are obviously expecting rain. Diana Cooper and Frank and Kitty Giles[1] staying here. Frank is so intelligent, so open to new ideas and impressions. As for Kitty, she makes everything and everyone around her alive – who could not love her? Everything went swimmingly. We sat out a lot on the terrace among the roses while the atomic air exercise "Carte Blanche" went roaring over the garden. Diana was adorable but has the bad effect on me of making everyone else seem dull.

Sat next to the Ethiopian Minister's wife at dinner last night and fell a little in love with her – an exquisite, intelligent, dark statuette dressed by Dior.

There is not enough to do in the office and I hate an office that is going at a slow pace where every little snippet of business is magnified to fill in time. I have a goose of a German student as a language teacher. He stinks so much in this hot weather that I can hardly bear having him sitting next to me on the sofa.

23 July 1955.

Haus-Assen. Staying with the Von Galens for the week in their schloss in Westphalia. A family of five daughters, a refugee aunt from the Sudetenland, an English school-friend of the daughters, the only son of the house, an Oxford friend of his, an Austrian archduke, and two little local barons are all staying in this moated sixteenth-century house. (The moat is solid with a beautifully coloured green scum with a dead fish on the surface and some very live ducks swimming about in it.) The Von Galens very welcoming, extremely nice. Their girls with English-schoolgirl voices calling "Mummy" and "Daddy" from the garden. Racing Demon after dinner. My host explained to me the difference between the barbarous Prussians and the West Germans, whose civilization goes back to Charlemagne. There were so many at dinner that the young ones sat at what they called "the cat's table," the

---

[1] Frank Giles, British journalist, since Editor of the *Sunday Times*, and his wife, Lady Katherine Giles.

one for the children. I wished I had five daughters. We have a circular room in Biedermeier style with a balcony over the moat.

We all walked over to the vegetable garden and ate currants and raspberries, talked in a desultory way, drifted down lanes and around farm buildings. Their son is on vacation from Oxford – Christ Church – a breath of undergraduate goings-on.

25 July 1955.

A long argument last night after dinner with Mike Handler of the *New York Times*, who attributes all the evil in the world to Adenauer and Dulles and says that as Adenauer is now in fact United States Secretary of State, why not name him so? An American woman was there, rather drunk. She says that all her friends in New York came from the three per cent of successful people in *all* fields.

Sylvia says that this is the end of summer. The heat is over. The roses in the garden are dead or dying. The pink ramblers look rather disgusting in their vegetable decay. There is a feeling of break-up in the house. We had last night one of our last and least successful dinner parties of the season. The butler, Erich, is leaving. The other servants are anxious to go on their holidays and so am I. We can hardly be bothered to train the dog any more. We shan't be seeing him again for a month and then perhaps we shall all be different, including Popski. Our first year in Germany is over. I want to get away now from this queasy climate, the quilt of low cloud, hazy in heat, dark in dank weather.

7 August 1955.

A newly appointed special consultant in the German Foreign Office came to dinner last night. He has spent the greater part of his life in Russia, as has his wife. Their parents were members of the German colony in St. Petersburg. They have the accent and the charm and the naturalness of manner of White Russians but are very German. They were complaining that the Russians in their own view know everything better than everyone else, but I felt inclined to reply, "So do the Germans, so do the French, all three are know-it-all nations. The English do not know it all and don't wish to. They just know that they are better."

26 January 1956.

I am getting quite fond of the new butler, Karl, but my God he is obstinate! This morning I asked him to pack my dark-blue suit to go to Soest. He said, "The suit is dark but it is not blue," to which I replied, "Please pack my *dark-blue* suit." We stared at each other without yielding.

Motored to Soest in wind and snow. Great double trucks interlocked in collision along the autobahn. Volkswagens crushed like tin cans. The Germans are the most frantic drivers in the world and their roads are strewn battlegrounds. Got to Soest five minutes before dinner, changed in a rush with my drink in my hand. Roger Rowley is in command of the Canadian Brigade. This was the occasion of the visit of General Gale, the Commander-in-Chief of the British Army on the Rhine, and Lady Gale, who had come over for the night in their private diesel train from their schloss, which Lady Gale tells me has four drawing-rooms and takes twenty-one servants to run. General "Windy" Gale is like a bloodshot old bulldog barking amiably. His hackles rose a bit at the sight of an Ambassador, and a Canadian Ambassador at that. I dare say he thinks it quite superfluous for us to have any diplomatic representation at all, but we circled around each other in fine fettle. Lady Gale was the success of the party – red hair, plump, fiftyish, shrewd, and good fun. Played games until three in the morning. The Army are tough. Roger came into my room at dawn while I was asleep – in uniform, off to manoeuvres.

27 January 1956.

I lunched today with Von Welk, who looks after Canadian affairs in the German Foreign Office. We meet for lunch twice a month at the Adler, a restaurant that specializes in the food the Germans best understand – venison. Von Welk and I discuss our problems in Canadian–German relations. He snorts and crinkles up his brown eyes, looking at me with a dachshund expression. For some reason I am much drawn to this unattractive man with whom I seem to have nothing in common. He is stiff and rude at times, but never pompous. He can be malicious, but he is not boring. There is something dowdy about him which inspires a sort of confidence. He might do a double-cross, but he himself is not a lie.

4 February 1956.

Have been staying with Norman and Jetty Robertson in London, where he is now High Commissioner. Norman was at his most delightful, with his wonderful, wide-ranging curiosity and interest in everything and everybody, his pleasure in his own cleverness, his mixture of boldness in thought and of caution. Isn't he in the long run profoundly on the side of constituted authority although he enjoys dissecting it? He is a non-believer of Presbyterian origin. How different in mentality is a Presbyterian from an Anglican agnostic, not to mention a Roman Catholic one. You can renounce your own faith but its particular imprint remains. I measure myself against Norman and I know that he is a wiser and better man than I am. I came away even fonder of him than I was before and I tremble to think what he would make of this diary. "Burn it," he would say, and I have little doubt that he is right. I love Jetty too. Her receptiveness, responsiveness, and funniness charm me. I enjoyed London – the stucco streets in the mist, with a great red sun in the fog. I liked meeting chaps for lunch in clubs and taking women out to restaurants and all the comings and goings, encounters, and gossips of London life.

17 March 1956.

One of the drearier diplomatic days. Went to the St. Patrick's Day reception at the Irish Embassy, a cheerless and squalid party unworthy of Ireland. A pile of dried old shamrocks for the guests, looking like a garbage heap, stout and watered Irish whisky to drink, and no warmth in the welcome. Dined at the Belgian Embassy. The new Ambassador and his wife have made it magnificent, the only Embassy with any style in Bonn. The dinner party had no spark. Afterwards we sat islanded in little groups in the enormous rooms. First I bored the Greek Ambassadress, then I told two long and boring stories to some people on a sofa. Then we talked about why dentists become dentists. The Portuguese Ambassador talked about Goa, and we came home.

Every middle-class German in every city is this morning starting out with his briefcase clasped firmly in his hand, wearing his long mackintosh or belted leather coat, off for his week's work, and through the half-ruined, half-rebuilt streets of the German cities goes an army of workers of all classes. The whole of Germany is like a vast school with no idle boys in it. Here everyone obeys the rules, no one protests. They cut down the only charm of Bonn – the noble trees lining the streets. There is no protest. People try to make the best of it and say, "It is *brighter* now." Brighter indeed!

22 April 1956.

Spent the whole day working on my telegram to Ottawa about the German situation and afterwards read it to Sylvia, something I never do with political dispatches. She seemed far from enthusiastic. I know it is not clear and interesting enough to hold her attention, but I despair of making it more so without over-simplifying. I sympathize with political journalists who try to make things reportable and interesting and keep them true. I think that most get to a point when they don't want to know any more about the subject. They have decided on the line they are going to take in their articles and it is confusing and encumbering to learn something new which does not fit into the picture. My trouble is a little different. I find it hard to recommend a policy except under pressure. I cannot construct in a void, and our relations with Germany are almost a void. I left off writing and went for a solitary walk when I met my friend Admiral Campbell-Walter, RN, who has some ill-defined naval job here. He was very red in the face from celebrating the christening of one of his ratings' children. I like him very much. He is a kind of male ex-beauty, very handsome and with many conquests to his credit. He began early to learn the arts of love from Queen Marie of Romania when he was a young naval lieutenant.

Blair Fraser, the Canadian journalist, was here the other day. He is courageous, honest, and intelligent. He thinks that the Liberals are in trouble in Canada and that they will lose the election. They have depended for much of their influence on the support of a small group of publicists, professors, civil servants, and men of influence, and it is this group whose support they have lately lost.

5 June 1956.

The aunts are again staying with us – Elsie much older but still wonderful, Beatrice ageless and clear in the head but with some strange words. For instance, she says she was "dumb struck" and that someone was "criss-crossed" instead of "double-crossed." On June 2 we went over to Groesbeek Cemetery in Holland for the dedication by the Duke of Gloucester of the Canadian part of the cemetery where John Rowley is buried. It was a sunny day. The cemetery looked almost cheerful on one of the few hills in Holland. The Duke of Gloucester, very pink in the face, with popping azure eyes and wearing across his uniform the azure ribbon of the Garter, read a speech from a piece of paper held in very shaky white-gloved hands. Afterwards when I was presented to him he mumbled, "I didn't know there were so many [inaudible] around here." I couldn't think what the missing word could have been – graves? Canadians? – so I judged it safer to make no reply.

8 June 1956.

Today there was a very large and very mixed-up lunch party at our house, assembled together for the old Pells. Old Pell is an American diplomat, retired. He looks like an American senator and comes from a "grand American family." His wife is a full-busted seventy, with a lace shawl and a cupid's-bow mouth incongruously painted on a Republican lady's face. She is fond of old English music-hall songs, believes in yoga, eats no meat, and considers that all American husbands are unfaithful with women younger than their wives. All American divorces are, according to her, caused by American husbands playing on their wives' strong maternal instincts to release them from the bonds of matrimony so that they can remarry younger wives. "The American success woman is a myth. If you could only see into their hearts," she said, "you would know that they are hiding the scars inflicted on them by mainly immature and worthless American men." The new Australian Ambassadress attempted several times to interrupt by quoting U.N. statistics on divorce which proved something – just what, I never could make out. Later in the day little Del Dongo came to dinner, a nice Hungarian refugee whom I befriended in Canada, a sort of grown-up Catholic choirboy. He brought with him Father Heim from the Papal Nunciature, a shy Swiss priest who is writing a book on ecclesiastic heraldry and whose brandy glass broke in his hands after dinner. God and the Catholic

Church know whether they enjoyed themselves, but they ate and drank willingly.

16 June 1956.

My usual business lunch with Von Welk. What is developing between us is as near to friendship as I have had with any German man and a sort of mutual trust, but with a misunderstood word it could crack up. Today he was very critical of Adenauer, much more openly so than he would have dared to be a short time ago. Altogether the Germans are getting more and more articulate and bold in what they say, as the Occupation recedes.

Dined with the Jakopps, German business people who live around the corner from us here in Cologne. She is plump and might be sentimental, wore a sort of handcuff of diamonds and emeralds. The German women began talking among themselves about the privations and adventures of the years just after the war, 1946–47, telling anecdotes about the shortages, how if they were asked to a reception by foreigners they would try to eat everything in sight because they were so hungry; how they would share one cigarette among a group of them, passing it around the circle; how if they had to make a journey they got lifts in coal trucks. All this was not said in a self-pitying vein or with bitterness – at times as if it seemed funny in retrospect. It shows how much safer, more prosperous, more sure of themselves the Germans are, that they can talk in this way. I must stop writing this diary now as Karl has come in to say, "Tea is served." Anyway, it is only a sort of acknowledgment for a day of life to write the diary at all, a "bread-and-butter" to God but one that must more often bore than please Him. How often the human race must bore God. I picture a cosmic yawn and His self-question, "Was it worth while creating them?"

18 June 1956.

Yesterday was wrecked for me by the discovery that the dentist had put a gold tooth in my mouth. Of all things in this world I abominate it is the gleam of a gold-toothed smile, so today I went back to the dentist again and demanded that he begin all over and make it silver. He was crimson with irritation and mortification at this reflection on his skilful work on the ambassadorial teeth, but in the end he promised to change it. God, to think that I should end up bald, with gold teeth and hairs coming out of my nose!

23 June 1956.

Still the same sunless summer. We have passed through midsummer's day without a sunny day. The visit of the Minister of Economic Affairs of Ontario has been a diversion, although an unlikely one. This "little Napoleon" has enlivened us for the last two days by his absurdities. Mistrusting me by instinct as representing the federal authorities, he has treated me throughout with unctuous politeness while bullying and insulting the junior members of the Embassy staff. Yesterday I had a reception for him of German bankers and businessmen. The Minister arrived an hour late, when the Germans were just on the point of departure. The old aunts have left to go home to Canada and we shall miss them. They bring a breath of spontaneity and fun into the stuffiest gathering, and Elsie, even deaf and ill at seventy-eight, has more heart and vitality than most of the people I know and I really love her.

29 June 1956. London.

Spent the day with Mike Pearson and the Prime Minister and discussed European policy questions and Canada's relationship to them with Mike. The Prime Minister seems sunk in melancholia. He certainly appears to find no fun or interest in politics and perhaps he had better get out of it.

12 July 1956. Cologne.

My cousin Wilfred Ponsonby is staying here from England. He and Lance Pope were talking as we lunched on a sunny terrace on the Rhine about their exploits when they were prisoners of war in Germany – of getting over the wire, of the brilliant but abortive escape when Lance got out dressed as a German general in a uniform made in camp, only to be caught a few hours later while changing in a nearby wood into civilian clothes. But mostly they talked about tunnels – the incredible feats of engineering, concealment, and patience which went into the digging of these tunnels by underfed prisoners suffering from the lassitude of malnutrition, and how, after months of digging, on the day before the big break-out they were given away to the Germans by a spy in the camp. All day I have been thinking about this kind of staying power, this continuous bending of all energies and ingenuity to the idea of escape and the techniques of achieving it, the turning of everything to one purpose. In the afternoon to an odious reception, mostly Baltic barons and their county wives. Talked to one woman who, when I asked her if she liked Bonn, said, "Wherever *mein Mann* is, there I am happy." I nearly laughed in her face.

At this point the developing crisis over the Suez Canal began to overshadow the international scene. As there are so many references in the following diaries to Suez, it may be helpful briefly to recall the history of those events which not only altered the balance of power in the world but affected relations between individuals and led to such bitter and divided personal feelings.

The seizure of the Suez Canal by President Nasser of Egypt in July 1956 led to the intervention by the British and French to retake the Canal. The plan worked out at secret meetings with the Israelis was for Israel to attack Egypt, and then the British and French would go in, ostensibly to separate the combatants. On October 29, Israeli forces crossed the frontier and captured Egyptian border posts, and by November 5 British and French paratroopers landed in Port Said, to be followed by the arrival of ships carrying the main assault forces.

These developments caused consternation in the United Nations, in Washington, and in Ottawa. L. B. Pearson, then Minister of External Affairs, went to the United Nations in New York. He was shocked at the action of the British Prime Minister, Anthony Eden, in sanctioning an enterprise which would antagonize the Arab world, split the Commonwealth, and put such a strain on Anglo-American relations. The idea of a United Nations Emergency Force was not a new one but it was his initiative and his diplomatic skill that brought it into being. Throughout, he worked in close co-operation with the Secretary-General, Dag Hammarskjöld. The United Nations Force was intended to proceed to the Suez Canal area on the withdrawal of the Anglo-French expedition. On November 4 the Canadian resolution setting up the Force was introduced in the United Nations General Assembly by L. B. Pearson and approved by the Assembly.

Meanwhile, the U.S.S.R. was occupied in crushing the two-weeks-old Hungarian people's rebellion. Now they proposed that the United Nations give military assistance to Egypt. When the Security Council refused to discuss this proposal, the Russians addressed threatening notes to the United Kingdom, France, and Israel. On November 6 the Franco-British invasion of the Suez Canal Zone was halted when Prime Minister Eden agreed to a cease-fire in view of the formation of the United Nations Emergency Force, of the United States' opposition to the operation, and of a heavy run on the pound sterling. So this ill-conceived venture ended in humiliating failure and the subsequent resignation of Prime Minister Eden on grounds of ill health. In England the role played by Canada in this whole affair aroused mixed feelings. On the surface there was appreciation of the fact that Pearson had helped the British out of an increasingly impossible situation. Yet there was also resentment at the lack of Canadian approval and support for the United Kingdom government. The Prime Minister, Mr. St. Laurent, had indeed made a public statement extremely critical of the United Kingdom and of France. Canadian opinion was divided; the Conservative Opposition launched a bitter attack on the government, claiming that they had sided with Nasser and the United States against Britain and France. The government's handling of the Suez crisis may have had some effect on the 1957 election, which brought the Conservatives to power for the first time in twenty-two years. Thus Pearson was out of office when he received the Nobel Peace Prize for his contribution to peace-keeping. With the change of government in 1957 and the arrival in office of the Diefenbaker administration, Pearson was succeeded as Secretary of State for External Affairs by Sidney Smith, who in turn was succeeded in 1959 by Howard Green.

14 September 1956.

The shadow of the Suez crisis is over everything, so perhaps this little Bonn world does not look so bad when war might threaten its disappearance. Could we really be headed for another war, or only the humiliation of all that is left of Britain's greatness? Is it to be a bang or a whimper? The weakness of the British position is that people do not believe in their shopworn phrases such as "free men everywhere" and "world opinion." The point is that "free men everywhere" are far from convinced that the principle of freedom is endangered by Nasser as they knew it was by Hitler.

15 September 1956. Battle of Britain Sunday.

I do wish the English would stop saying that the choice is between war and their having to pay one and sixpence more for a gallon of petrol because it would have to come around the Cape, because this argument cannot make them many converts.

We went to the Battle of Britain Sunday service in the little RAF church here and had gin and tonic afterwards on the lawn of the RAF Mess with the Air Vice-Marshal, who thinks there will be a war and blames it on the Foreign Office. Spent the afternoon reading the Sunday papers about Suez until I could read no more and turned to the *Towers of Trebizond* by Rose Macaulay.

16 September 1956.

A break from the crisis in the form of a visit to Bonn by the King and Queen of Greece. There was a reception for them last night at Schloss Brühl.[1] Quite a spectacle. The royal procession leaving between a bowing row of guests looked like an early movie of court life in old Vienna. Schloss Brühl was lighted with candelabra wreathed in roses. The rococo décor had all been renewed and looked theatrical. There were striped marquees in the candle-lit gardens and music "off." There was a touch of Balkan royalty about the uniforms of the Greek court officials. I shook hands with the manager of the hotel responsible for the catering and said, "Good evening, Your Excellency," mistaking him for one of my obscurer colleagues. He looked profoundly gratified. The Soviet Chargé d'Affaires came to me (why me?) and said, "Can I go home now?" like a little boy. I said severely, "No, the King and Queen are still here and you cannot leave until they go." He looked quite desperate.

---

[1] The eighteenth-century palace outside Cologne used by the German government for official entertainment.

7 October 1956.

Just back from spending the night in Wiesbaden with Sylvia. Down the Rhine road in a mixture of rain and shafts of sunlight, weather which suits the poetic and dramatic style. Lunched in a restaurant under an old castle on a crag above a village, the village decked with flags for the Weinfest. Drank thin, sour, ice-cold wine and went on a tour of the castle, now a museum. The horrid life lived in that castle by those medieval troglodytes in armour; the small, dank, dark, slit-eyed rooms into which they crowded! The Ritterhall was full of armoured figures and one imagined the echo of the brutish laughter of these sinister iron robots who, once unarmoured, must have thronged around the fireplace roasting an ox or a disobedient serf. It was a giant's lair from a frightening fairy tale, a place for tortures, with dungeons deep in the rock. In the museum hangs a bearded mask with openings for eyes. This was made red-hot and pressed over the victim's face; also the first chastity belt I have seen – a thin opening in the iron which nothing substantial could penetrate and a hoop around the body, the key given to the butler and only to be opened if the husband did not return from the Crusades after three years. Down we came from this dismal place and when I saw in the Wiesbaden Gallery the portrait of a young knight in ornamented Renaissance armour with a fair killer's face, there in the background was just such a Rhine castle on a crag. I thought of those proud whelps being engendered in the dark curtained bed in that top turret chamber behind the thick stone walls with the slit-eyed view down the precipitous tower wall to the broad Rhine flowing between swelling hills. Wiesbaden after this was a welcome return to civilization. I like these German watering-places as well as anything in Germany. They have an agreeable touch of cosmopolitanism. The hotels are good, even luxurious. They can make a decent martini at the bar. The water is boiling hot in the baths. It is pleasant to stroll through the arcades of the casino or to walk along the allées in the garden. We mildly gambled and ate partridge cooked in the German style with sauerkraut and grapes, which made Sylvia feel sick.

8 October 1956.

A visit from a German diplomat concerned with Canada, a large, florid gentleman who emanated scent and appeared to me to be suffering from a hangover, not taking it quietly but trying to override it, thus giving the impression of too much manner. He had uneasy hazel eyes, a faint trace of a duelling scar across his pink cheek, and heavy white hands emerging from cream-coloured silk cuffs worn rather long in the English manner. He was certainly in no condition to discuss the Air Training Programme or any other Canadian–German question. Later Aga Fürstenburg came in for one of our absurd German lessons. We are reading a Simenon detective story in German but she interrupts the whole time to gossip in English. She is very good company but my German is not progressing. I had been told how after the assassination plot against Hitler she had hidden two of the plotters in her apartment in Berlin. I asked her how she got away with it and why she was not suspected. She said, "The Nazis never did take me seriously." Perhaps that was the best protective colouring in that jungle.

I am becoming attached to Aga. She now gives me lessons three times a week. We had met at the house of mutual friends who heard my complaints about the German teachers I have hired up till now and, knowing that she could do with the extra money, suggested her name to me. From the moment that she strolled into my office for the first lesson, I might have known that all serious hope of my mastering the German language had vanished. Aga must be about my own age – in the late forties; tall, leggy, she resembles a giraffe, with a giraffe's expression of absent-minded *hauteur*. This is her first experience of teaching and she has a novel approach to the subject. "What has prevented you from learning German better," she says, "is boredom. You will never learn if you are bored. So don't bother with the grammar. What do you read to relax?" "Simenon," I replied. "Good. I like him very much myself – we'll start with him." "But he writes in French." "That doesn't matter. His books are translated into German. You shall have your copy and I mine. We shall read together – you will translate the German into English as we go along, with my corrections, of course." This system, if it can be called a system, is not working very effectively, as Aga is always breaking into my laborious translating with some startling and scandalous story of life in Berlin under the Nazis when she was employed in some ill-defined capacity in the Foreign Office, or the private lives of our Bonn acquaintance. Her stories, told in a mixture of French, German, and English, often leave the solid ground of fact and leap into the upper air of fantastic fun and cruel wit. When inspiration fails she sinks back on the sofa, opens her handbag, and, extracting a small brown bottle of Unterberg, takes a sip of it and with a sigh turns back to Simenon. (I have myself experimented with Unterberg, the German health drink or pick-me-up – a noxious concoction with quite a kick to it.)

Aga comes of an aristocratic Westphalian family. A brother with whom she is on quarrelling terms now lives in the family schloss, but her grown-up life was spent in Berlin and one can see traces in her of the hectic, sophisticated, despairing Berlin of the twenties when she was young. When the Russians entered Berlin she came as a refugee to Bonn. She has one deep attachment from the Berlin years – Baron Zetsé Pfuel. Like her, he has a record of anti-Nazi courage. He and Aga give the impression of having seen both better and worse times together, and of having been cast up on these shores after the storms of their lives had subsided, leaving them empty of any future. I find Zetsé an attractive figure, with his striking looks and his high spirits which can change quickly to gloom. Like Aga, he has a reckless tongue. Through them I have met some of the refugees from East Prussia and Berlin – they bring with them a whiff of cynical wit and debunking frankness quite different from the Rhinelanders. They form a little world of their own in Bonn, crowded into small, shabby apartments, having escaped with nothing; taking odd jobs where they can find them and free meals from their Rhineland friends and relations. They remind me of the White Russian refugees I knew in my youth.

Aga surprised me the other day with a sudden outburst – "Why do you people pretend to sympathize with us Germans in wanting reunification of Germany? What a farce! We all know that that is the last thing you want. Why should you want a bigger Germany? Of course you don't trust us. Why should you? Why pretend?" I was on the point of protesting, but to do so would be an insult to her intelligence. I said nothing. The silence marks our mutual understanding and its limits.

31 October 1956. Halifax, Nova Scotia.

I am here on a visit home to see my mother and today I have been walking the streets of the town. Halifax has lost its peculiar flavour of a nineteenth-century garrison town and its look of faded gentility. For a long time people used to say that the citizens of Halifax never painted their houses but let them look shabbier and shabbier to avoid high tax assessments. That reproach can never be uttered again. People have gone hog-wild with the paintbrush and the houses have blossomed out in pinks and greens and pastel shades. Rather touching to see these old-fashioned houses having another fling at life, but so many places that used to be gardens are now Esso stations.

The day of my "coronation,"[1] as my mother calls it. Why did I ever get involved in giving this address, particularly in the Cathedral, where I am to make a speech to – among others – the King's College students? The speech itself is a respectable collection of second-hand ideas expressed in the usual clichés. As I walked across the old golf links, following a path I used to take on my way to King's College when I was a student there, I thought of what I should be saying to these young men. "Don't be taken in by vain old buffers like me. Escape if you can from the terrifying conventionality of this atmosphere. Don't be trapped by fear or affection into conforming over anything that matters." I looked among the students I saw on their way to the Cathedral for a bespectacled, self-conscious, angular youth – for myself when young – but they all looked very free and easy and neither self-conscious nor angular.

6 November 1956.

The international situation is taking on a nightmare aspect. Mr. St. Laurent says that the Soviet ultimatum to the United Kingdom does not make him tremble in his boots. That is as may be, but I must get back to Bonn at once. I cannot be caught in Halifax at a time like this, not that my presence in Bonn will make the slightest difference to anything.

13 November 1956. London.

I hate being in London when so much is at stake for the English and when I do not feel at one with them. I am haunted by memories of 1940 when I felt such a complete identity with the Londoners. It

---

[1] I had been awarded an honorary D.C.L. by my old University of King's College.

seems like a desertion on my part and no doubt many of my friends here think that it is a desertion of them on the part of Canada. Elizabeth Bowen says, "What if we *are* wrong? If one of my friends made a mistake or committed a crime I would back them up. It is as simple as that." She has a raging contempt for the U.N. and its moral palaver. I said to Michael the other night, "It is not that I am troubled by the so-called immorality of the Suez action, it is just a question of what the international traffic will bear or will not bear and our assessment is different from yours." But feeling runs high and one has to be careful even with one's friends. Anne said to me, "Don't desert England – how can you?"

18 November 1956. Cologne.

Three o'clock on Sunday afternoon, the hour of my birth and always the lowest point in the week for me; the inexpressibly melancholy sound of voices drifting up to the window from the foggy suburban street. I am trying to go over and over in my mind this beastly Suez affair so that I can decide on the line to take in talking to my diplomatic colleagues and to the Germans. It is one thing to criticize the English to their faces or to my fellow Canadians. It is quite another thing to criticize them before foreigners and before those who hate them. My friend the Admiral came in this morning for a drink. We were both very careful in discussing Suez to keep unemotional for fear of another row between us over politics, and he kept on calling me "Charles" affectionately to show that there was "no offence" after our last argument. I would have reciprocated if I could have remembered his first name. Derek Hoyer-Miller (the British Ambassador) very nice, very friendly and understanding of our position.

21 November 1956.

Today is Repentance Day in Germany and a holiday. I don't know what they are repenting – they have plenty to choose from. Sylvia and I went for a walk this afternoon in the grounds of Schloss Brühl. It was a fine, clear early winter's day, the last roses frozen and the walks in the park carpeted with bronze leaves. I came back to read the English papers and felt sick at heart at the pass to which British prestige has been brought, and divided between my certainty that their government's policy has been a colossal, disastrous blunder and my emotional sympathy for the English, particularly when isolated and when so many are turning against them. Today the servants found a revolver behind the wall in an upstairs room in this house. It has been lying there since street fighting when the Allied troops fought their way into Cologne. Perhaps a German soldier had thrown it there to get rid of it.

Called on Couve[1] and found him very objective over Suez. (By that I really mean that he agreed with me.) But he did say that the situation in France is different from that in England because in France "we are all involved; the whole population except the Communist Party and a few isolated individuals are in favour of our action over Suez." I again reflected how little like a Frenchman Couve is, with his reserved, cool manner and his English clothes, but perhaps the difference is only skin deep or perhaps it is because he is a Protestant.

25 November 1956.

Another Sunday. Went to the RAF Chapel across the street, which is really just the upper room of a house very much like this one. The Welsh clergyman read with beautiful, unaffected appreciation the lesson from Ecclesiastes, "Remember now thy Creator," etc. The mournful majesty of it echoed disturbingly around the room. It makes most of the Old Testament prophets sound like angry old men shouting their terrible denunciations and shrieks for vengeance. The clergyman preached against sloth. The congregation of young men sang vigorously. This is called "stirring-up" Sunday.

I hope that in Ottawa they realize that the time has come to help to save the face of the British over Suez. The British will be there long after Eden has gone and will remain the best bet in a bad world. They should not be humiliated, and Canada should be the first to see that. I hope that we are not too much influenced by unreal majorities of the United Nations. As for the Russian ultimatum, shall we yet see Russian tanks rumbling through the suburban streets of Cologne on

---

[1] Couve de Murville, the French Ambassador. He succeeded François-Poncet and was later Foreign Minister of France.

some such dark Sunday afternoon as this, and where then will be our complaints about being bored?

27 November 1956.

Lunched with the diplomatic colleagues. And endless discussion over protocol. If you are giving a dinner "in honour" of someone, is it possible to put the wife of the guest of honour on the right-hand side of the host – in other words, higher up than invited Ambassadresses? The answer of most of the colleagues is "No, it would be grossly improper." The Italian Ambassador has sent members of the Diplomatic Corps an invitation to dinner for the President of Italy, who is visiting Bonn, but he has sent it in the name of the President instead of in his own name. The question arises whether a Head of State can issue invitations when he is on foreign soil or whether it must be his Ambassador who does this.

By tacit agreement, Suez and events in Hungary are not discussed in a diplomatic group of this kind, but only between pairs of individual ambassadors, to avoid emotional rows.

The Yugoslav Ambassador called, an intelligent man more interested in politics than in protocol. He is bitterly disappointed by the turn of events in Hungary but he is more anxious to blame the West than the Russians.

30 November 1956.

In the evening, dinner at the Campbell-Walters'. My host, the Admiral, was in a melancholy and silent mood but Mrs. Campbell-Walter more than made up for it. Their daughter, the beautiful Fiona, was there with her new husband, the millionaire Heinie Thyssen. She was wearing the famous great pearl which he has given her and which has had so much publicity in the press. Fiona is that rare article, a real beauty – not just pretty or handsome or attractive, but a Beauty. She combines this with very quick wits. She is very unselfconscious about her looks. I thought of how the greatest beauty of them all, Diana Cooper, talks of "the face" as if it were not part of her but a valuable possession which had to be taken care of. Heinie Thyssen's attitude towards Fiona always seems to me to be that of a connoisseur who has added to his collection rather than that of a lover. He has indeed collected at least one earlier decorative wife in addition to so many superb works of art. Fiona's younger sister Sheila was there. She is a pert, funny girl and greeted me by saying, "How are you, you old whisky-slinger?"

Reading Beckford's diaries. They are very fascinating reading but *any* diary has a certain fascination for me, even the most trivial ones. We are buying another dog, this time a Schnauzer. We thought a little brother might be good for Popski, whose ego is getting completely out of hand. The only trouble is that I suspect that this new puppy is a "disturbed personality." He has a very mad look in his eye.

Tonight we are giving a dance in honour of Roger Rowley's daughter Andrea, who is eighteen. Everything has been left to the last moment. At this very moment workmen are pulling up half the loose tiles in the dance floor and hammering in some new ones. They say they will cover them with some quick-drying cement that will dry in an hour, but I picture it sticking to the shoes of the dancers and rooting them to the floor – a motionless ball. Then "they" sent only half-bottles of champagne, so that there is only half enough, so that we are involved in an illicit deal with the French Club – but will the champagne be here in time for the dance? We have asked far too many people for the size of the house. It is a physical impossibility for 110 people to dance in that hall, and still acceptances are coming in, including people who are not on any of the lists. Who the hell, for example, is Lord Chelsea? I think it must be a spoof name.

1 December 1956.

The dance seems to have been a great success. It certainly went on long enough. I got so exhausted at one point that I retired to the w.c. and sat there reading Beckford's diaries with a whisky in my hand. The door unexpectedly opened and two of the girl guests came in. They gazed at me in horror and amazement and fled.

There is a ridiculous flurry in the German socialist press today against the Canadian Army, saying that a Canadian soldier bit the ear off a German in Dortmund during a row over parking a car. The press have been after me on the telephone about it, one journalist asking me if I could make "an educated guess" as to what had really happened.

19 January 1957.

Back from Ireland after staying with Elizabeth at Bowen's Court. Got into a conversation on the plane with a young Irishman who was returning from London to live in his native County Cork. He said, "You get tired of the city, but in the country there is nothing to get tired of." I pondered this elliptical remark.

How can one convey the fascinating flow of Elizabeth's talk, the pictures of places and people, the continual surprise and pleasure of her choice of a word, the funniness, poetry, and near-brutality of her view of a situation? One day we went off to the wedding of the daughter of the farmer who lives by the gate of Bowen's Court and who was marrying a young man who has a shop and runs the post office in Kilmallock. The very young bridegroom was as pale as ashes. After the wedding the bride and groom were photographed standing in the church porch and off we drove to the wedding breakfast in a country hotel twenty miles away. There were clans of Hodginses and Harrises, all "strong farmers," all Protestant. Their Catholic friends who could not go to the church stood at their doors in Kildorrery village and waved the bridal party a send-off. At the wedding breakfast I sat next to old Aunt Hodgins, toothless but talkative. We spoke of Life and she said, with a sidelong glance at me out of her bright blue eyes, "And what are we all hoping for?" There was Irish whisky and champagne and a speech from the eighteen-year-old best man, a country boy, in which he compared the bridesmaid to the Queen of Sheba.

On another day we drove over to Muckross. Elizabeth said of that wild, steamy, strange County Kerry country that it suggested temperament, with an unexplained, unreasoning flash of joy followed by darkling, curdling weather when the lakes turned from sunny blue to black. She showed me some of the Bowen topography, the scenes where some of her short stories are placed.

Elizabeth says that her next book is to be called *A Race with Time*. She says that she knows its title but not yet exactly what it is to be about. There will be a "star-shaped" plot with characters and events converging on a point in time. She is working very hard at her present book, writing all morning on most days and in the early afternoon. She says that when a woman becomes a widow she goes back to the arts and crafts of her youth in attaching friends and combining people and, in order not to be lonely, returns to her earlier gregariousness.

Talking of writing she said, "I could give a very good vivid description of the road past Headington where I used to walk every day, but who would want to read it unless something happened there?" She says that she does not want to write a subjective autobiography. She wants to invent, or rather that it comes more naturally to her to invent.

19 February 1957.

I have excluded from these diaries almost any reference to office work or mention of members of the Embassy staff or descriptions of any official business or negotiations with the German government. I have absolutely no wish to write about such things, which anyway are covered by memoranda and dispatches in the office. Then there is another consideration – security. I have always been almost excessively "security-minded." In addition, this house is full of German servants of varied backgrounds. Then Bonn is, I think, riddled with spies of different persuasions. The result of all this is that the diaries have a very unbalanced look as though I were a man of leisure who did nothing but go to parties and never did a day's work. The truth is that I very much like office work and very much enjoy the transaction of business. Indeed, my main complaint about this post is that there is not enough business to transact. As a result of leaving out any political or diplomatic record the diaries would be of less interest to readers, but this does not matter as I do not intend that there should be any readers. I have provided in my will that all my papers should be destroyed at my death. Why then do I write the diaries? It is a compulsion, like smoking.

21 February 1957.

I went over today to Dortmund to open an exhibition of Eskimo art. I have already opened three exhibitions of Eskimo art and am becoming sick of the sight of it. This exhibition was in the museum at Dortmund and the museum officials had told me that they had very few funds to provide refreshments, so I sent over several cases of rye whisky. The people at the museum had never seen rye before and the Director asked me if it was "a kind of liqueur or a sort of wine." After the speeches were over, tall glasses filled with undiluted rye whisky were handed round on trays and drunk recklessly, so that before the reception was over everyone was more or less drunk. It was by far the most successful exhibition of Eskimo art I have ever attended, although towards the end of the evening things got somewhat out of control. A German art critic came to me and said that he knew that the Eskimo objects were not genuine but were copies made in Germany of objects sculptured by a German sculptor called Arndt. However, he promised that he would not reveal this in the article he wrote in tomorrow's paper about the exhibition. I could not convince him that he was mistaken. He went on repeating in a drunken fashion, "I promise not to tell, Your Excellency, I promise not to tell," until two tears began to run down his cheeks. One of the senior officials in the museum was a large, masculine lady with a broad, noble forehead, wearing on her finger an outsize signet ring. She seemed strongly attracted by a chinless young woman from the Cultural Division of the Foreign Office and they ended in a warm embrace and the promise that they would spend the evening together. The reception ended with group photographs which I shall certainly treasure.

I had a letter today from Anne in which she wrote to me of the time when we were young in the twenties. Few of my contemporaries, male or female, married young. She was an exception. In those days we would have thought it a premature descent into the dreary world of middle-aged domesticity. As politics did not interest us, nor religion nor money unless it fell into our laps, we must now wonder what did interest that generation. I can only speak for myself. I was after Experience. I lived in the private conviction that intense, strongly poetic, dramatic Experience lay in wait for me. I longed for a condition in which reality lived up to literature. Meanwhile I did little to bring this state about. I was a "mirror dawdling down a lane," but I was a talking mirror. I only loved solitude when I knew that company was round the corner.

As I was thinking of those days a scene swam into my mind. It is Paris, some time in the twenties. Here is a random group of friends and acquaintances picked up in night-clubs, joy-rides in borrowed cars, and casual couplings. We had all been together for days and nights, spinning about the town in a nonsensical saraband, intoxicated with our own youth and with the cocktails of the time – Alexanders, Sidecars, White Ladies. Now we stood drinking, talking, and laughing together in some bar, making a noise, showing off, under the eyes of a disapproving couple of men who are quietly shooting dice in a corner of the bar. (That is what we wanted, disapproval and attention – insufferable and enjoyable behaviour.) There was Basil, the enfranchised son of a rural dean, a rubber-faced joker and lecher; Jo from Missouri, a bright-eyed, solemn girl who knew better but wanted to savour dissipation in Paris; a silent, wooden Scottish textile millionaire in a checked jacket; a pale, plump White Russian who could do card tricks and was employed in the perfume business; and of course Lavinia, skinny, flat-chested, lovely long legs, hyperthyroid eyes, skirts to her knees, the Lady Lavinia, a lost lady in the Michael Arlen fashion, a Bright Young Thing now a trifle tarnished, heroine of endless escapades, figuring in a fashionable novel. Her gaiety now gone a trifle shrill, her wit blurred with drink, yet eager for enjoyment, she could still spark a party. There was a gramophone in this American bar and we kept pestering the bartender for our favourite tunes, moaning jazz laments, "Sweet Chee-ild, You're Driving Me Crazy" – the tunes of futility and longing.

22 February 1957.

I have been seeing a great deal of Brentano, the German Foreign Minister, in the last weeks. We seem to get on rather well and this may prove useful. I am beginning to speak German quite fluently but only social German. I never speak it when I go to the Foreign Office. It is very risky to do business in a foreign language and my German is certainly not up to it. Even in "social" German I mistrust myself for fear of giving just the wrong emphasis, greater intimacy than I feel, a cruder judgement than I intend, or just a joke that does not come off.

17 March 1957.

Went to the airport to meet Sylvia on her return from Canada. What my life would be without her I cannot imagine. She was so sweet and looking beautiful. She rises to all occasions, never fusses or nags. I am a lucky man and I know it.

5 April 1957.

I have a spring cold in the head and the spring goes on without me. This morning began badly by my throwing a ball for Popski which scored a direct hit on one of the china urns which we bought in Marseilles. It came crashing onto the black and white stone tiles of the hall, making a splendid row.

In the afternoon a German in jackboots came to see me. He has been pestering me for an interview for days. He says that he has been wrongly arrested by the Canadian police as a former Nazi, whereas he claims that he was only a driver in a transport division. He stood very straight and it was a question whether in his emotional state he would hit me on the head with a blunt instrument or burst into sobs. I felt sad and weary for his desperation and I gave him ten marks. His battered pride moved me. He probably should have been shot long ago and would get scant sympathy from his fellow Germans. Karl, the butler, said, "Yes, he was lucky before in the Nazi days. Now things are not good for him. What does he expect?"

I wonder whether the Air Attaché should have given my secretary a book called *The Strangler in the House of Lust*, with illustrations.

23 June 1957.

Zetsé Pfuel, Aga's friend, told me last night that he and his wife had escaped from Berlin on the last train which left for the West when the Russians had already entered the city. He said that on the morning of their departure his wife informed him that she was going out to have her hair done. He protested and said that it was very likely that she would never get back through Berlin to the station in time for departure and that the Russian troops were moving into the centre of the city. She said, "If you think that I am going to stay with your rich cousins in the Rhineland and arrive at their house as a poor refugee with my hair straggling down my back you are very much mistaken." Zetsé then went back to his Ministry, burned various files, and went to the station where his wife was to join him. He said he never put in such an agonizing hour as the hour he spent waiting for her. She arrived exactly two minutes before the departure of the last train, with her hair done.

Then the talk turned to life in Germany during the war. One couple who had a country house in Westphalia said that, while they were not Nazis, they went along with the régime. There was nothing else that they could do. The garage proprietor in the neighbouring village was a Nazi official. All the villagers were under his control. If they had not kept on good terms with him it would have been impossible for them to buy anything in the village. As it was, their lack of enthusiasm was already suspected and they were treated with great coolness by the local people. If they had openly opposed the régime they would have been at once deported to a concentration camp. This had already happened to their cousins in the neighbourhood. They said that most people knew something of the horrors of the concentration camps but by no means everything. It was very dangerous to try to find out any more, as the only result would be to land up in one of the camps oneself. I often wonder whether we Canadians would have been much more willing than the Germans to defy Hitler once the country was in his power.

5 January 1958.

A few months ago when we were coming back from the weekend in Paris and the train was coming in to Cologne station, I looked out at the bulk of the Cathedral looming against the grey evening sky and found myself saying, "We are home again." How inconceivable it would have seemed to me, nearly four years ago when we came here, ever to have this feeling of familiarity verging on affection for this place and these people. One senses in the Germans a controlled neurosis, admires the control and mistrusts the neurosis. They have such immense potentialities for achievement and such a contribution to make to Europe. They are like a friend of whom one could say, "He will go far if he does not go too far."

NEW YORK

1958–1962

In January 1958 I took up my new appointment as Permanent Representative of Canada to the United Nations. During that year Canada was a member of the Security Council and I served a term as President of the Security Council. I remained at the United Nations from 1958 to 1962.

When I arrived in New York in 1958 it was as the representative of a country well-known as a strong supporter of the United Nations. Mike Pearson, the former Minister of External Affairs, had been the embodiment of this policy. With the coming to power of the Conservative government in 1957 there was no falling off in Canadian support for the United Nations, which was backed up by widespread favourable opinion in the country. The Conservative ministers of External Affairs, first Sidney Smith and then, in 1959, Howard Green, were active in United Nations affairs. Howard Green devoted much of his time and energy to the United Nations and, in particular, to the cause of disarmament. The position of Canadian Permanent Representative to the United Nations was thus considered by the government to be an important one. I had had a fairly extensive experience of the United Nations since 1945, when I had been an Advisor to the Canadian Delegation to the San Francisco Conference, which founded the Organization. Since then I had served as Advisor, Observer, or Alternate Delegate at a series of sessions of the General Assembly and the Security Council and I had taken an active part in United Nations disarmament negotiations. I looked forward to the pressures and excitement of my new job and to the change of scene from Bonn to New York, and I was not disappointed. The years I spent at the United Nations were the most stimulating, if sometimes the most frustrating, of my diplomatic career.

For me the attraction of the United Nations was as a centre for international negotiation – a unique meeting-place of diverse group-ings and interests and a framework for the resolution of problems or at least the papering-over of cracks and the averting of explosions. I was less impressed by the global ideology, the "one world" language of some of its more Messianic supporters, and I had few illusions about its ultimate effectiveness in peace-keeping or disarmament. I enjoyed the combination of public and private diplomacy, the open sessions of the General Assembly and the Security Council, and the long-drawn-out bargaining behind the scenes which preceded every public declaration. All of this was of absorbing professional interest to any diplomat, particularly one who like myself preferred negoti-ation to representation. It is true that the eons of boredom endured during speeches in the General Assembly took a heavy toll, but at least one did not have to speechify oneself. That was best left to one's political masters. Indeed, to seek – worse still to obtain – personal publicity at the United Nations is, for the career diplomat, the kiss of death. It is resented by the politicians and deplored by one's fellow members of the Service.

I had many friends among journalists accredited to the Organ-ization. I had, in my youth, aspired to journalism and had served a turn on Beaverbrook's London *Evening Standard*. I never could under-stand the mistrust and alarm with which some diplomats viewed the press, for in the two-way relationship between diplomat and journal-ist the diplomat often has quite as much to gain as the journalist. I was to find this even more true later, when I was Ambassador in Washington. Certainly I learned more, not only in information but in wisdom, from that great man Walter Lippmann than I could ever repay, and James Reston knew more of American political life and politicians than any Ambassador could absorb in a lifetime.

Although I found the United Nations job a fascinating one, it was not good for the diaries. The attempt to combine the pace of work with the pleasures of New York meant that I had less time to write the diary regularly. I notice too, in these diaries, an increasingly caustic note. The close association with my colleagues in the hothouse atmosphere of the United Nations building, while it led to close friendships, could breed irritability. If I sometimes wrote disparagingly about my profession and its practitioners, allowances should be made for temporary exasperation. I would never myself have exchanged the diplomatic career for any other. Diplomats have never, as a group, been much loved. They are accused of many things – starchy manners and over-supple consciences, secretiveness and deviousness. In fact they are a hard-headed, knowledgeable, tolerant lot, often more long-sighted than their political masters. Of course, there are joke figures among them, petty-minded and pretentious, but that is true of every occupation. As for our own Foreign Service, it stands comparison with any I have ever encountered. Certainly the men and women who worked with me at our Mission in New York were among the ablest and most respected at the United Nations. Naturally a diplomat's effectiveness is ultimately determined by the confidence he inspires in his own government. It is sometimes supposed that there is an inbred mistrust between the permanent civil servant and the politician. Having served under five prime ministers I cannot subscribe to this notion. The worst case is the combination of a suspicious or insecure Minister and an unimaginative or smug official. Those who are safely ensconced in the permanent civil service may sometimes forget that politicians, however temporarily powerful, and at times arrogant, are always walking a tightrope of risk from which the fall is oblivion. My own sympathy tended to be with the risk-takers.

Whether or not it has proved to be a wise decision to locate the United Nations in New York, for me personally it was a happy choice. Sometimes New York tired me, but I never tired of New York. Many of our friends there neither knew nor cared anything about the United Nations; they lived in other worlds of interest and amusement. Elizabeth Bowen came on frequent visits to the United States, lecturing or as writer-in-residence at American universities, and was often in New York where she had so many friends and which she so much enjoyed, although during this time she was in the throes of a financial crisis which resulted in the sale of Bowen's Court, her beloved family home in Ireland.

Looking back upon the New York chapter of my life I still feel, as I wrote at the time, that I should make a libation of gratitude to the Goddess of Liberty at her gates. These diaries terminate with my appointment in 1962 as Ambassador to Washington, a new challenge for the diplomat and a change of scene for the diarist.

20 January 1958. New York.

Today I presented my Letters of Credence to Dag Hammarskjöld. He twinkled at me and turned on the charm. What is he like? Modest conceit, subtlety, vanity, intimacy switched on and off, an intriguing little creature. Is he to be the "Saviour of the World"? He would probably make as good a shot at it as anyone else. He talked of Mike Pearson, of their working so closely together at the time of the Suez crisis and the setting up of the U.N. peace-keeping force. He seems to look on Canada as a member of an inner circle – the "Scandi-Canadians" is his word – who, together with Ireland, are particularity dedicated to the United Nations and share his objectives and his point of view. He wants to get Geoff Murray, the number two in our Mission, on his own staff. I do not welcome this, as Geoff is one of the ablest operators on the U.N. scene and his experience and ability will be invaluable to me, but I suspect that Hammarskjöld will prove persistent about this. He has the reputation of taking up new people who attract his attention – and sometimes dropping them again.

In the long bar at the U.N. I met John Hood, the Australian Representative. We had three or four jumbo-sized Manhattans each. I don't know if this is the order of the day at the U.N. In the afternoon walked in Central Park – icy wind, cloudless blue sky, the wild animals shrunken in their cages, bored jaguars, comatose pumas, a wild-animal smell that hung about one for an hour afterwards. To a cocktail party in the evening. I had forgotten how much the Americans love talking on social occasions about international affairs and how earnestly distressed they are about the conduct of everyone everywhere – the French in North Africa, the Germans in Germany, the Russians, and of course the Americans themselves. "Aren't you depressed about the international situation?" as an opening gambit in conversation at a cocktail party always makes me feel like persiflage.

23 January 1958.

Entering the U.N. building is like going aboard a vast, gleaming ship moored off 42nd Street. You might have turned at the entrance to wave goodbye to the passing New Yorkers left behind in the street, before joining the motley crowd of your fellow passengers on the voyage outward-bound – the compass pointing to far horizons – the weather uncertain, with gale warnings out – and the final destination unknowable. One after another the gleaming black Cadillacs, pennants fluttering, sweep onto the curving driveway before the great glass doors, and out step the diplomats, dapper in their dark business suits, heading for the entrance with the air of preoccupation of men who have grave matters on their minds. Following come their juniors, swinging briefcases purposefully. The uniformed guards at the front door have the business of knowing them all by sight and nation, and giving each a respectful yet friendly greeting. They do it well. The U.N. guards do everything well, from managing the mass exodus at the end of a public session to controlling the unruly in the public gallery. They are picked for strength as well as intelligence. The bartenders at the long bar know the drinking preferences of half the world. The telephone operators and the lounge receptionists can track down an Ambassador for an urgent long-distance call from his capital at any hour of the day or night. The interpreters are sophisticated, tactful, tireless artists of language. These are the indispensable crew without whom the ship would founder. They could teach a lesson in good temper and good manners to some of the delegates. An escalator leads up from the entrance to the upper level of the Assembly Hall and the Council Chambers. As one ascends one mingles with the incoming colleagues – "There is a point I should like to raise with you before the vote this afternoon. Could we meet in the usual corner in the Delegates' Lounge in half an hour?" or "Have you had a reply yet from your government about sponsoring our resolution?" You step off the moving staircase together, and separate. The day has begun.

25 January 1958.

I am spending a day and night with the Robertsons at our Embassy in Washington. Norman[1] seems stimulated here and is stimulating. This morning I had a ranging run over the possibilities of negotiations with the Russians with him and Ed Ritchie,[2] Norman seeing all sides but steering his purpose through his own subtleties. He said he has a few friends here – Dean Acheson, Walter Lippmann, and Frankfurter. He describes them as a sort of mandarin group *"not set* in their ideas but now become conservative or contemptuous, what proper mandarins should be," and then he adds, "Perhaps I am becoming 'set' myself." I can see no signs of it. Went to the National Gallery with Sylvia, and there among the Aztec death masks was Sammy Hood[3] – lounging, affectionate, welcoming – an El Greco in an old Etonian tie.

17 February 1958.

I loathe this official apartment in Sutton Place. There is no privacy, not a single door anywhere in the apartment, every room opens out onto another room, the furniture comes from Grand Rapids, the paintings are bad oil paintings by bad Canadian painters almost all in oranges and yellows of autumn colouring in the woods – a subject which should be put out of bounds for all Canadian artists. We have one maid, and by a curious stroke of fortune she is a German. Her salary is as much as that of the entire staff in Cologne, her name Matilda, her cooking inferior. Popski of course peed on the carpet on the day of his arrival. I can't say I care what he does to the carpet. It is a repulsive colour and covered with a sort of scurf that scuffs off on your shoes and gets all over your clothes. Every single time the elevator goes up or down Popski barks.

5 March 1958.

I started the morning as I have most of the preceding mornings – studying the Constitution and the Rules of Procedure of the United

---

[1] At this point Canadian Ambassador to Washington.

[2] A. E. Ritchie was to succeed me as Canadian Ambassador to the United States and was subsequently Under-Secretary of State for External Affairs.

[3] Viscount Hood, then British Minister in Washington.

Nations and, in particular, of the Security Council, on which I am now the Canadian Representative. We have before us the crisis over Tunisia, and French actions there.

Lunched today with Bob Dixon, the British Representative. He seems very nice and intelligent with gentle manners, almost a bedside manner. What do the British make of one – "a sort of foreigner" who wears English clothes and has an English accent, but is he *sound*?

The British Delegation are still recovering from the wounds inflicted on them by the Suez crisis, when they were virtually ostracized by friends and allies, not to mention the enemies. Their line about Canada, and Mike Pearson in particular, is one of appreciation and admiration for our role at that time, but I think these sentiments come from the head and not the heart. In their hearts they feel that their true friends were those like the Australians, who backed them up to the hilt. It is from Moore Crosthwaite of their Delegation that I get a less guarded version of their reactions. He is becoming a friend.

13 March 1958.

What an extraordinary coincidence it is that not only is Matilda the cook German, but my secretary at the Mission is of German origin, highly efficient and very German in temperament. Went to one of the regular meetings of the Commonwealth Representatives today. Why is the British Representative always in the chair at Commonwealth meetings? Would it not be much better to rotate the chairmanship among the Commonwealth Representatives? Today Bob Dixon said to Arthur Lall, the Indian Representative, "I *think*, Arthur, that you will find mine is really quite an innocent little suggestion." "Too little and too innocent," said Lall, and I felt for him. Aly Khan is the news here. He has come as Representative of Pakistan. From elevator girls to sober-sided U.N. officials – they are all after him. Even when the men pretend to despise him as an amateur in international affairs, they want to get close to him so that they can tell their wives that this glamour boy is really only a balding little sallow-faced man. Bob Dixon's line is, "We should, I think, all do our very best to make him at home in the U.N. He is trying very hard." Exactly like a headmaster talking of a rich but erring boy who has come to his school with all registered intentions of "going straight." Arthur Lall is

taking a line of extreme agreeableness, almost amounting to flirta-
tiousness, with the newcomer. Lall with all his pleasant manners gives
off such a shine of malice from his highly polished surface and combines it with intellectual ability and an air of moral irreproachability.
The fact that he has quite a good opinion of himself is the first, but
perhaps not the last, impression left by him. Aly Khan's modesty and
sense of humour are an attractive contrast.

16 March 1958.

As I write in the so-called den, Matilda moves maddeningly about
in the sitting-room saying "Pfui" to Popski when he barks. Now she
has begun Hoovering the carpet. She will end by driving me out into
the street in a rage. There goes that infernal little beast barking again.
Shall we ever escape from this flat-trap with its scurfy beige carpets,
its dentist's-waiting-room furniture, its unopenable and unshuttable
steel-framed windows? I am starting to look for a new apartment but
the people in Ottawa are obstructing me at every turn.

17 March 1958.

St. Patrick's Day – a glorious day without a cloud. Went to meet
Jules Léger[1] last night at the airport. The plane was two hours late
and I sat happily alternating my reading between Descartes in a
paper-bound edition and *Eloise in the Plaza*. In the afternoon to the
Metropolitan Museum – the look of pride in the portraits of adventurers and dukes of Renaissance Italy, not vulgar assurances but the
native vitality and splendour of men clothed in brilliant colours
wearing strange hats, like birds of show and birds of prey with foreign
markings, natives of another world. Where has that pride and splendour gone?

How much I like Jules. How wise and witty he is.

2 April 1958.

I had lunch with the Soviet Representative. He seems a homely
old body, tough but not dehumanized. "We consider," he said, "that all

---

[1] Then Under-Secretary of State for External Affairs; subsequently Canadian
Ambassador to France and Governor General of Canada.

religious wars have always been based entirely on economic motives. The name of religion merely masks the real motive, for example the Crusades." I said, "I cannot remember the economic motives for the Thirty Years War or the French religious wars, can you?" Apparently he could not. Brushing the question aside, he reverted to the Crusades.

In the afternoon we went to Mabel Ingalls's[1] farm in the country. She seemed in a nervous frenzy, jumping up from her chair to half open the window and then immediately shutting it again, smoking incessantly, quoting great names and then dashing them away again. Dorothy Osborne[2] sat with her long legs stretched out in dark-green woollen stockings and made her jerky, witty comments in her take-it-or-leave-it voice. Among the other guests was a young couple who touched hands for a moment in physical recollection and could not help smiling at each other. Also a German count who could not – would not – believe that I was a Bad Shot. After lunch we threw things for the dogs to play with in front of the sitting-room fire. Rain streamed down in slanting slats across the flank of the mountain that Mabel has just bought to save it from the common herd and their motels, across her lake, her fields, her woods, her farms. We went home at 4 p.m. precisely. "What's your hurry?" growled Mabel.

18 April 1958.

Lunch with Engen, the Swedish Representative, and walked the sunny streets with him to his office. Banners hung from the tall buildings in the heat haze, vistas stretched, glass gleamed. Oh I love, absolutely love, New York, at any rate on a fine day in spring I do. Engen has a soft charm, a subtle intelligence, and a "progressive" outlook.

2 May 1958.

A feeling of respite today after my first day as President of the Security Council. Afterwards a journalist asked me what it was like being "up there in front of all the klieg lights with all the people watching. Can you give us the human angle or are you too hardened a diplomat?" The truth is that I very much enjoy the Security Council.

---

[1] Daughter of J. P. Morgan, the banker.

[2] Officer of the Department of External Affairs.

It is rather like a court of law. When one is acting as the head of one's own delegation one is pleading a case, interjecting, cross-examining like a barrister. When one is in the chair one is interpreting the rules, keeping order, presiding like a judge. It is much less tiring than a diplomatic dinner party. The issue before the Security Council was the Soviet veto of the Northern Defence Zone. The Americans have prepared an International Arctic Inspection System and we have worked closely with them over this. Dag Hammarskjöld has supported it, much to the rage of the Russians. The "non-committed" countries were at first undecided as to the line they should take. What was decisive was the Soviet attitude, the blank lack of compromise, the Gromyko "nyet." We were back in the Cold War. Even if our tactics had been subtler, this would have changed nothing. During the disarmament negotiations this summer and even up to the last few weeks it has been possible to see some merit in the Russian case. This had its own consistency, but in this last week a new – or rather a return to an old – attitude has come about. Now they don't even bother to make a case. What does this change mean? A new access of strength from an unexpected quarter? Or the cover-up for a reappraisal? In the evening I had a television interview with Stan Burke. When the question-and-answer part of the interview was over they took what is called a reaction shot, during which he and I had to sit looking at each other for two interminable minutes before the camera. The more we gazed at each other eyeball to eyeball the more I felt a sensation of embarrassment which he perhaps shared.

9 *May 1958.*

Jetty[1] has been staying with us, looking young and pretty. When old Frederic Hudd[2] was boring her with the price of shad roe and his desire to acquire a brass-and-bronze platter with the head of Bacchus carved in relief upon it, she curled up on the sofa and went to sleep, looking like a young girl. As for old Frederic, he too looks younger now that the menopause is over. His face is thinner, his aquiline nose juts out like the nose on a death-mask although he is far from dead

---

[1] Jetty Robertson, wife of Norman A. Robertson.

[2] Formally senior official at Canada House, London.

but pink and perky, and in his relations with his host and hostess, Sir William[1] and Lady Stephenson, he makes me think of an undergraduate staying with two old people who "wait up for him" of an evening. After dinner he caused the lights to be turned out and recited the *Morte d'Arthur*, looking like a noble old Merlin himself. An actor he is – a ham actor. He is a Dickensian figure to me, one of those eccentrics whom the hero David Copperfield, or Pip, meets as a boy on his way upwards in life. I hope I am on Frederic's "prayer list," for although he says he is a phoney I should like his prayers. They might be potent all the same.

19 May 1958.

Oh this doorless flat, everyone's perpetual awareness of everyone else. It is like having no eyelids. At this moment Matilda is vacuuming the sitting-room (why at this hour?). If rays of hatred could strike her body through the archway that opens out from this parody of a library into the sitting-room, then dead at this instant would she fall. But who the hell do I think I am – Proust? – needing a cork-lined room to write a masterpiece when I am only scribbling this diary. Are my susceptibilities so exquisite? What would I do if my "dream children" were crying and shouting all around me? A crotchety old bore I am becoming. I have been reading *Justine* by Durrell. It depends on the mood – if you are irritated it will irritate you and you will say it is all shreds and patches of mysticism, aestheticism, and mandarinism. But wait – let the ingredients settle and the brew is seductive, disturbing, with strong, rancid flavours. Now as Popski barks I hear Matilda say in her plaintive, high voice, "When he and I are alone together he is never like this, never barks. It is funny, very funny," and she gives a wild pipe of mirthless laughter. She is developing a mania for Popski and a sort of jealousy of us in competition for his love.

19 May 1958.

Mike Pearson and Maryon are here. He is taking part in a seminar on the TV – "In Search of an American Foreign Policy." He is in

---

[1] Sir William Stephenson was Director of British Security Co-ordination in the Western Hemisphere, 1940-46, and subject of *The Quiet Canadian*.

splendid form, entertaining and so intelligent, quite undismayed by political misfortunes. Maryon looking very handsome and being very funny and very much on the mark in her comments. I thought that the TV show itself was a dispiriting performance, conveying an impression of ineffectual uneasiness on the part of the Americans participating, with a note of sophomoric cynicism struck by the British Representative, Nutting.

24 May 1958.

These last days have been spent dabbling in this murky Lebanese crisis in the Security Council, where the Lebanese charge of interference in their internal affairs by Egypt is before the Council. Aksoul, the Lebanese Representative, comes to see me in the apartment at all hours for consultation, sometimes accompanied by his very decorative wife, who is herself no slouch in diplomatic negotiations. Last night when Aksoul was outlining the dangers facing the Lebanon, Popski came barking into the room and Aksoul said to me, "It is very nice to have a pet dog but is it so nice in such a small apartment?" – a question God knows I have often asked myself.

This Lebanese business is very tricky and one that could be dangerous, and as President of the Council I have to tread warily. Here my ignorance of the Middle East makes it difficult for me to gauge Arab reactions. I hate dealing with an area which I cannot see in my mind's eye and with people whose motives I cannot assess. Part of the difficulty is my ignorance of the history of that part of the world, which leaves me without terms of reference.

3 June 1958.

Our new Minister of External Affairs, Sidney Smith, has been here for a visit. He has been extremely kind and understanding in his dealings with me and I like him. He is shrewd enough too, but all the same I ask myself what can be the secret of his success. It is certainly not force of intelligence or grasp of issues. And he does talk such nonsense. Last night he began comparing Canada to his thirteen-year-old daughter, "both adolescents at the difficult age." He says, "We must not let ourselves be treated like Tunisians." What can he mean?

15 June 1958.

This Tunisian crisis, caused by the French bombing of a Tunisian border village, has exercised my mind and my feelings too without respite for days. I live in the U.N. like a termite in cheese and my personal life has disappeared. I stay on and on in the evening in the office until I suppose the staff say, "He works because he has nothing else in his life."

What is disturbing is the resentment which has grown up between us and the British over the Middle East – echoes of Suez involved. I should like to be in agreement with them, even – if necessary – against the United States. That used to be the state of affairs. For example, over Korea we worked well together. I wish I could talk to some Englishman freely and have it all out – perhaps Harold Beeley or Humphrey Trevelyan,[1] not Bob Dixon. He would just pretend to agree with me. What worries me is what worried me at the time of Suez and was not a moral question but a sharp divergence as to the possibilities. They seem to me to be suffering from an aberration and in pursuit of it to be oblivious of their loss of reputation. They proceed by indirection, pretend to scruples, perhaps even feel them, but they do not count the full cost in the Middle East or clearly see the end in view.

21 June 1958.

Last night I went, at his invitation, to call on President Heuss (President of the German Federal Republic) whom I had known when I was posted in Bonn. The moment I got into the hotel sitting-room I was transported back to the peculiar atmosphere of all such German gatherings. There was a real wish on their part to make a graceful gesture to a former Canadian Ambassador to their country. There was even genuine friendliness, and the old man himself was as charming and natural as ever, yet still the occasion had a sort of stuffiness and clumsiness like so many German official

---

[1] Sir Harold Beeley, then Deputy U.K. Representative to the U.N., later Ambassador to Egypt; Sir Humphrey Trevelyan, formerly British Ambassador to Egypt, then Under-Secretary at the U.N., later Lord Trevelyan.

gatherings. This was mainly produced by the gang of officials surrounding the President. What do I feel when I look back on the Germans and my relations with them? I feel a sort of twisted liking for them and admiration too, but their lack of ease is painful, as is their incessant struggle to impose themselves and an undercurrent of doubt as to whether they are succeeding, the incessant grinding of their *will* to stamp a rigid form on their self-consciousness, to button up their nature.

26 June 1958. Ottawa, on a visit for consultation.

I am off for a walk around the poop-deck of Parliament Hill which overlooks the river where I have so often walked in the past trying to regain balance after some crisis in my Ottawa life. When I see the tired, aging men who are my friends and who work in the Department I think it is as well that I don't have to face that ordeal. There is something wrong here but it is the same thing that it has always been – overwork, the panic desire to escape before they get too old, and the fascination of being in the centre of things, these pulling in opposite directions. I know that dilemma and I have no desire to go through it all over again.

2 July 1958. New York in a heat wave.

I am alone in the flat. Sylvia has stayed on in Ottawa. Matilda and Popski are away on a holiday. I sleep in one bed and then in another and I never make up the one I slept in last. I leave my dirty clothes in piles on the floor. If the light doesn't work, I'm too lazy to change the bulb, so just move to another room. Elizabeth writes that Bowen's Court is becoming for her a barrack of anxiety and that she has to face the fact that she cannot keep it up any longer and must sell it. She writes, "I am getting bored here and that is a fact. I suppose it is the effect of hardening my heart. When one can no longer afford to support an illusion one rather welcomes seeing it break down, or perhaps, in this case, run down," but does she really know how much leaving Bowen's Court will hurt when the time comes?

Had dinner last night with an old friend from Nova Scotia, now a very successful New York career woman. It was interesting to see how the acquired layers of New York "graciousness and culture" came peeling off after the third drink. Thank God they did.

16 October 1958

I spent the morning trying to work on the Minister's (Sidney Smith) speech on disarmament to be delivered to the General Assembly. The truth of the matter is that I am discouraged as I have been working on disarmament now off and on for months and I can see no prospect of achieving anything substantial. The same unreality hangs over so many of the activities of this year's General Assembly – the abolition of apartheid, the bill on international human rights, peace in the Middle East, peace in the Far East, disarmament. Who thinks we can achieve any of these things? It is likely to be easier to get to the moon. Anyway, diplomats are only small craftsmen and there are no statesmen.

John Holmes came to lunch today. He is here with the Delegation as special adviser. John is probably one of the most liked diplomats in the United Nations, a real asset to Canada. He should be in this job instead of me. He gets on easy terms with all, the more exotic the better. Indo-Chinese princes, Polish communists, Indian intellectuals – all eat out of his hand.

Well, I must get on with that speech. I can't leave all the work to John just because I am suffering from "cosmic disillusionment." He has been through all that himself and come out a patient, modest Christian (although not Christian by faith he certainly is by temperament).

For my part, I lost my temper in a most un-Christian way with Krishna Menon, who is heading the Indian Delegation to the General Assembly, yesterday. It does not seem by his attitude today to have done any harm at all to our relations, rather the reverse. The odd part is that I have a grudging, suspicious admiration for the creature. I can't help seeing that he has political imagination and a kind of wild, malicious high spirits. When he comes into the Commonwealth delegation meetings he flutters the dovecotes just for the fun of it. Poor old Alan Noble, the head of the British Delegation, who is chairman of the committee, is like an ineffectual schoolmaster trying to keep a brilliant bad boy under control. Just how bad is Krishna Menon? Perhaps worse than we think.

20 October 1958.

I spent all last evening with Sidney Smith and John going over the speech until I got quite bleary-eyed and was also suffering from indigestion caused by bad curry. Sid has a dual personality. First there is the over-confident, wordy, artful one – and then, over his shoulder, there is a perceptive, sensitive Sid who appears to judge his companion harshly although he always gives way to him. This is an unkind way to write of him. He has been exceptionally friendly and nice to me. He wasn't too bad working on the speech, either. When he gets hold of a point of policy he sticks to it, and he changed the tone for the better and some of the individual phrases. The text we were working on for this speech was John's and I dare say he must have felt a bit bruised as his text was being mauled and battered about, but he is so patient and objective that he gave no sign of irritation, as I certainly would have done.

It is still before breakfast and the red sun has just risen over the river. I have been standing on the balcony looking down to where it broadens towards Brooklyn Bridge and beyond to the sea. I love that widening of the river. I don't know how I shall live without it when we change apartments.

5 November 1958.

As I was walking along 34th Street near Pennsylvania Station while waiting for my train to the country (it was a brilliantly fine morning), a certain gentleman caught up with me and, walking a few blocks together, we joined in conversation. "New York," he said, "is a murderous city. You have to know what you can do here and what you can't or you get yourself a bad ulcer. That is why I walk every morning for an hour before I go to my business." He was the manager of Coward's Shoe Store, a wise man sent from God, for as he talked, glancing at me from under his battered hat with sharp, dark eyes, I felt my own tension relax and I walked happily among the skyscrapers, the slum door stoops, the cheap restaurants, and the building sites down by the river under a blue heaven.

7 November 1958.

I wrote off in answer to that nice little German Gräfin's letter about Aga Fürstenburg's death. Mine was an empty, careful letter. She must have known that Aga and I were friends. Poor Aga, "warm-hearted, courageous, witty" I wrote of her. But that is not the point. Unhappy, near-desperate, turning herself and everything else into a joke, with her "grande dame" manner and her wild gossip. She remained hopelessly attached to her Prussian baron but I think she was not lucky in love or money. She had no reason to live and did not like it much, but she was much more alive than those who have reasons for living and do like it.

16 November 1958.

Weekend with the Angels at their farm in Connecticut. A Sunday-morning walk under the grey sky through a country of small fields enclosed in grey stone walls, and back to drink bourbon out of Victorian moustache cups (Mr. Angel collects them), in company with a group of pleasant late-middle-aged couples. This is a converted farmhouse, full of charm. The Angels and their friends have lots and lots of money, but never too much in evidence. They're people who have travelled, collected good furniture, shot big game, farmed the land, run businesses or law firms, "kept up" with art, literature, and politics. Most have been married several times. (The interests they have, these Americans! The information they have modestly and unemphatically accumulated while also accumulating so much else.)

15 December 1958.

At last the General Assembly is over and yesterday the Canadian Delegation got off by plane for Ottawa. The weeks of pressure all day and late into the night are over, and the effort of keeping so many balls in the air. I have tried to run a private social life on the margin of the great circus of the General Assembly. I have even succeeded in doing so, at the moderate cost of a ruined digestion.

20 December 1958.

On the Ocean Limited between Moncton and Amherst on my way to Halifax for Christmas leave, during an interminable wait. Why is the train waiting? Frozen up, I suppose, in the midst of this waste of snow and scrubby fir trees. It is darkening quickly outside the train windows and is getting cold inside this compartment. Probably the heating goes off when the train is not in motion. There! she gave a jolt. Does that mean that we are going to move? No, not an inch, and we'll be four hours late arriving.

Yesterday, sitting alone in the long gallery of the Windsor Hotel in Montreal, I opened my eyes on the dark panelling and the windows inset with armorial glass and the large, obscure paintings in their immense frames. The gallery was half-lit and silent, with snow coming down the well shaft beyond the sightless glazed windows. The housekeeper came along and switched on a table lamp. "A little light might help," she said, "such a beautiful room, and it's all to be demolished next year. They will never replace a ceiling like that."

I determined to take a taxi and go out to Sainte-Anne-de-Bellevue to see my cousin Gerald. There he was in a corner of the ward among all the other ex-servicemen of the First War. He has been moved now from the mental ward. He looked tiny, shrivelled and shrunk, plucked-looking, with huge blue eyes in his ageless face. He sat up straight in his wheelchair with his destroyed hands in his lap. Round his shoulders was a scarlet shawl. We forced conversation with each other across his bed-table about the Queen, Russia, his pills. "Things," he said, "are not too bad with me, and not too good." I talked to his nurse by the door. She praised his courage in standing pain; never a groan or a movement of impatience. Is there something uncanny about him, I thought, as he watched us talking with an ironic expression; a sort of saint has he become? I thought of him writing a card to my mother in the depths of his melancholy madness, "*Nil desperandum*," and I thought if he could say that, shall I always be able to?

5 *February 1959. New York.*

It *is* the most uncanny thing that whenever I try to write or read, Matilda the German maid appears and begins to tidy, to water the plants right under my nose, to turn down the bedspreads, to empty the ashtrays. The moment the woman sees one settling down to work she comes in to fuss like a bluebottle. We are back in our high-up twenty-first-floor apartment, with the wind beating off the East River. High up as it is, it did not prevent our being robbed the night before last. Yes, a burglar came into this very bedroom between three and four in the morning and stole from the drawer by my bed what money there was, which unluckily was too much. It is strange to know that he, or she, was probing about in the dark while we stupidly, blindly, slept, and the burglar coolly got away with the money from the sleeping suckers. Being robbed makes one feel such a damn fool.

21 February 1959.

I am doing an assessment of the personality of Cabot Lodge, who is spoken of as a possible Secretary of State to succeed Foster Dulles. I have struck up a real friendship with Cabot, unlikely as it seems, as no two people could be more different. He is full of courage and energy, extremely impatient, and permanently at odds with Dulles. I think any American Representative at the U.N. will always end up on bad terms with the State Department. Living and operating in the atmosphere of the United Nations inevitably changes one's point of view. There are tactical advantages to be gained here. There is the temptation of publicity and popularity, not appreciated by Foreign Offices at home, and this is particularly true of the New York–Washington axis. Cabot's weakness is his emotionalism, which would indeed be a fatal weakness in a Secretary of State who had to negotiate with the Russians. I am never sure whether this emotionalism is genuine or whether it is a stunt for public consumption.

I find him very good company. When Mrs. Roosevelt was here with the American Delegation and I was sitting beside her at dinner, I said to her, "I am very fond of Cabot," and she drew back her lips over her teeth and said, "How very interesting. You are the first person I have ever met who was *fond* of Cabot Lodge."

22 February 1959.

Old John Stevenson, who was for so many years the London *Times* correspondent in Ottawa, came in for a drink. I like him, but he is full of scurrilous and inaccurate stories. Strangely enough, as he has got older he has almost stopped being a bore and seems to have returned to an earlier self – more considerate, more affectionate, less apt to hog the conversation. I have noticed that onset of mildness and moderation in aging old egotists before now. It is perhaps a sign that their end is not far off.

Talking of bores, I made a speech to the Bullock Forum about the United Nations yesterday which bored me almost as much as it must have bored the audience. In return they gave me a silver replica of Nelson's dress sword in the form of a paper-opener.

In the afternoon to a cocktail party at Mary McCarthy's. Elizabeth Bowen says Mary would say anything about a friend, but do anything to help him, or her.

8 March 1959.

I sit here trying to write. Matilda, her hair in curl-papers, comes tidying things under my nose. Then she begins to shake two bath-room mats out of the window on to the terrace. Then she changes the cigarette in my ashtray beside my notebook so that all the smoke goes into my eyes. She has a passion for Popski. She takes him away for weekends with her to stay with her German sister – puts him in a box with an air-hole in it. He seems to accept this with resignation, although he has bitten her three times.

I am reading a book about the American Revolution. As I was brought up in a nest of United Empire Loyalists, I always instinctively sympathize with them, but I am swinging to the side of the Revolution. How insufferable it must have been for the Americans to be patronized by petty British officials and third-rate line officers.

What am I to do about these damn diaries? I know what I *should* do – destroy them. Perhaps the bank will be bombed with them in it, perhaps I shall lose them. I don't want to leave them as a mess behind me, which might cause pain or hurt people's feelings. It is very odd how little mention there is in them of my working life.

Talking about work, I have done about five drafts of a long paper on Germany, German rearmament, the possibilities of reunification, Canadian policy towards Germany, and I was pleased to hear that my piece is to be used by the Prime Minister as the basic paper on the subject for his talks with Harold Macmillan.

23 March 1959.

Dag Hammarskjöld lunched here the other day to meet Elizabeth Bowen, who is here on a visit. They both set out to please each other and succeeded. He does not relax easily in the company of women and most women do not take kindly to him. The sexual element is missing and he cannot be bothered replacing it by cozy persiflage. Women sense a certain chill. Elizabeth, I thought, would not be drawn to him – a neuter Swede could not be attractive to her. As it turned out, she was at first surprised, then charmed and amused. With his customary quickness he caught on at once to the fact that this was no sentimental lady novelist but a mind as capable as his own of dealing in general ideas. From this understanding there was only a jump to pleasure in each other's company. He left behind him the mountaineer idealist and sparked with witty, clever sketches of people and places, absurd situations, and indiscreet imitations of public personalities – a side of him that he too seldom shows and perhaps deliberately keeps under surveillance. This was for him a day out of school. When Elizabeth exercises her charm it can attract anyone from the charwoman to the Duke of Windsor, with whom she got on so well that evening in Paris. She is desperately worried about money and says she is more and more irritated by what she calls the Fortnum and Mason troubles of the rich, such as the cost of double-silk linings for drawing-room curtains.

1 June 1959.

Alastair Buchan[1] is here today and we have been sitting drinking gins and tonics on the terrace. He has just come back from Ottawa and says that the atmosphere there is very claustrophobic. This is partly due to the Diefenbaker régime and the bad relations between the government and the civil service resulting from the suspicion of Ministers, and particularly the Prime Minister, that the higher civil servants may be disloyal to the government, or even plotting with the Liberals against them. In a way this suspicion is comprehensible. In the long years in Opposition the Conservative Members of Parliament, particularly the Western Members of Parliament, have been living a somewhat isolated life in their rented houses and apartments in Ottawa. They have seen the cozy, intimate relationship between Liberal Ministers and civil servants, mostly living cheek-by-jowl in

---

[1] Hon. Alastair Buchan, journalist and author, and the son of John Buchan, Lord Tweedsmuir. He was Director of the Institute of Strategic Studies.

Rockcliffe, their children attending the same schools, their wives in and out of each other's houses, intimate old friendships between senior civil servants and Ministers, and so they have come to believe in a sort of conspiracy against the government. It is true, I imagine, that most of the influential civil servants in Ottawa have Liberal sympathies, certainly very few are Conservatives, but I think they are much too loyal to the tradition of an impartial civil service to work against the government. Unfortunately, this intense suspicion of their motives and behaviour may create the very animosity that it fears.

8 June to 13 June 1959. Ottawa.

I arrived on a hot, thunderous evening and drove straight to the Country Club for dinner to meet the new Minister of External Affairs, Howard Green. The taxi-driver said that in this weather he had to change his shirt twice a day because it stuck with sweat to the back of the car seat. At the Country Club the senior members of the Department were standing about in a rather stilted, uneasy way waiting to meet the "new boss." I could hear Norman Robertson's[1] host laugh coming through the windows into the Club, where I was hastily pouring myself a preliminary drink. As it turned out, the dinner went surprisingly well and the Minister made a very good start with us. He was skilful and tactful, with an ironic sense of humour. What kind of impression the members of the Department made on him it is harder to say.

In the afternoon I went to see my brother Roley's swearing-in as a judge of the Supreme Court. Nothing has ever given me more deep satisfaction than his now being what his nature, ability, and heredity meant him to be.

28 June 1959.

Marshal Berland came to lunch with me today. He talked of Elizabeth. He loves and reveres her for her goodness, intelligence, and generosity of heart. So, twenty years later, she is still able to mould, to inspire, and to amuse another young nature. I told him that even

---

[1] Norman A. Robertson had returned from Washington and was now Under-Secretary of State for External Affairs.

when she was gone, and however long he lived, her quickening influence would still work on his imagination. He seemed today to me to be like myself when young – a mixture of romanticism, quick sympathy, and quick cynicism.

We dined with the Japanese Ambassador, my new friend Matsudiara. He is quite unlike any other Japanese I have met. He is worldly and witty, and is extremely indiscreet. He plays the Japanese hand cleverly at the U.N. but is not, I think, quite at ease with the Afro-Asian group of nations, of which Japan is of course a member. Indeed, there does not seem to be much natural sympathy between the Japanese and the Africans. The Afro-Asians as a group are proving increasingly difficult to deal with. Either in bilateral negotiations or with the Commonwealth members in a Commonwealth framework, relations are easier, but as a group the Afro-Asians are showing an increasing tendency to take up extreme positions and to produce resolutions full of sound and fury and quite inoperable. This, of course, is not only true of Afro-Asians.

Another new friend – or one who could become a friend – of a very different kind is the poet Howard Moss, whom I met through Elizabeth. How funny and perceptive he is, charming, and with a fibre of integrity.

We are beginning to make the move from this apartment in Sutton Place to the new one in Park Avenue. Matilda does not go with us. Meanwhile, she has bought a new *toupet* which makes her look like a housekeeper in a detective play.

15 August 1959. Stonington, Connecticut.

I have the precarious feeling that I shall be interrupted at any moment as I am sitting up here in the cool top room of this pretty little house, or simply that I shall get too sleepy because it is so hot and still outside in the garden and so silent in the house, except for the faint clinking of dishes being washed in the distant kitchen. The noise of insects strumming tunelessly, or according to their own tunes, fills the air. There are three or four other people staying in the house. "What it must be in this heat in New York!" everyone says. This is a woman's house – wallpapers "enchantingly gay," the house painted pink outside, a former farmhouse but it has left the manure pile far, far behind. There is a garden, or rather an enclosed lawn, shaded by immense maples (or are they ash? I must look) and walled with a stone wall about the height of a man. I know I bored my hostess, Mary, last night. She looked quite effaced with boredom, her face like one in a murky mirror. She is a delightful creature, with mind, feeling, and wit.

16 August 1959. Stonington.

Hotter still today, although a faint breeze is moving in the branches of the tree outside the window. Prideaux, the drama critic of *Time* magazine, has joined the house party. He is a cozy character but could bite if he chose.

Stonington is a charming little town, eighteenth-century white clapboard houses with fanlights over the doors. In one Mrs. Carlton Sprague-Smith practises chamber music and collects white Wedgwood stone china. In another Miss Bull perfects fine book-binding in a pre-Revolutionary hide-out in her herb garden. We dine on terraces here and there with these acquaintances and they in turn come for drinks in the garden, but tonight it is too thundery for the garden. Perhaps if I went downstairs I might get a drink, although it is really too early for one and it would not do for me to help myself from our hostess's whisky when she is not about.

22 August 1959. New York.

We are in the final stages of moving from the flat. We camp in the sitting-room with garden furniture. Nothing is left in this place but beds, TV, and toothbrushes, and the incessant wind blowing from the air-conditioner. Sylvia has been working packing things all day for the last two days, while I have been sitting reading. Last night she asked me would I move the window-box from the ledge on the terrace. I went out, picked it up, but it was heavier than I thought and I dropped it on the front of my foot, breaking two small bones. Serves me right for being so lazy. The chauffeur took me to Saint Luke's Hospital to have a cast put on which will be with me for a month. Sylvia says it is the last time she will ask me to help with moving anything.

22 September 1959.

We are installed in the new flat. It is much larger and rented principally for entertainment during the General Assembly. The Supplies and Properties Division of the Department of External Affairs has spent a good deal on doing it up but for some mysterious reason they refuse to renew the wooden seat on the w.c. of the spare room. I pointed out to them that prongs of wood had come loose from the seat and were sticking out, to the danger of anyone sitting on it. Still they refused. Finally, today, I telephoned them and said that as the Minister was coming to stay it would be their responsibility if any of these wooden prongs stuck into the ministerial bottom. They gave way at once and I have now authority for a new w.c. seat. Truly, the Department of External Affairs works in mysterious ways.

27 September 1959.

Howard Green, the new Minister of External Affairs, has arrived for the General Assembly and we have started, he and I, by having a falling-out. I am upset about this as I feel a rapidly increasing admiration and affection for him, but at the Delegation meeting this morning he publicly rejected my advice. It has to do with the French action in Tunisia, and my pro-French predilection got the upper hand of me. I must say that my support for French positions seems a one-sided effort, as the French never make the slightest attempt to accommodate us. Does he think that as an official of the suspect Department of External Affairs I am working against him in some way? On the policy question he may be quite right and I quite wrong. In fact, he probably is right.

1 October 1959.

All is well again between me and the Minister. He is very impressive in dealing with other delegations but I am sometimes rather alarmed by his technique and the way in which he sweeps aside arguments and opposition. However, he does not seem in the least alarmed. He certainly gave Bob Dixon the surprise of his life yesterday. I couldn't help laughing in my bath this morning when I thought about it. Bob, as chairman of the Commonwealth meeting, made a statement on policy at the Assembly which he hoped would be acceptable to us. He produced these views with quiet, persuasive confidence and was about to pass on to another item on the agenda when the Minister said, "In our best judgement, that simply doesn't make sense." I think there will be quite a lot of broken crockery left about when the Minister returns to Ottawa and I can see that I am going to have to pick up a lot of the pieces. Those who think that they have got a nice tame Canadian in the new Minister are very much mistaken. He is a very shrewd politician. He is also admirable in his pursuit of objectives in which he tenaciously believes, particularly in the field of disarmament.

2 October 1959.

Strauss, the German Defence Minister, came today for talks with the Minister, accompanied by the German Ambassador to Ottawa, Dankwort, and a group of German officials. While Strauss was talking to the Minister, Dankwort kept whispering to me about nothing in a low voice, thus reminding me of that irritating trick of German officials. When their superiors are present they always talk in a low, reverent murmur as if they were in church. Strauss put on a performance of jovial, shrewd frankness which was very nearly convincing. Despite his grossness he can be attractive. The Minister, who has not seen a German since he killed some of them in the First World War, was fascinated by the interestingness of Strauss's talk, his disregard for platitude, his realism and no-nonsense approach.

15 January 1960.

Outside the door the official Cadillac awaits and I begin to think of what is to be done today. In the office my secretary (except when she suffers from a delaying migraine) waits, gently and satirically. She reminds me of my oversights with a tiny pinprick. The incoming telegrams are piled before me, the news of the world extrapolated for my benefit. These chalk-blue messages and white replies contain a scenario of the World's Game. They inform and they disguise. A riot or a revolution comes to one without the movement of fear or rage, couched in the cool telegraphese of our Chargés d'Affaires. Policy is indicated in faint loop-like shapes. It is to be flexibly firm and firmly flexible. Aims fade into a Technicolor sunset of world peace, the Declaration on Human Rights excludes the nightmare and sounds like an invitation to a plate lunch at the Waldorf. Disarmament is to be complete, but hate they cannot regulate. This paper world breeds paper conflicts in the mind, starchy debates between the one hand and the other, and peering to descry the barricades on which we ought to die. It is no go, all that; it is none of our business anyway, for we are diplomats, not meant to think or feel but to manipulate and remember and to shift the papers from the "In" box to the "Out."

Then there is the little matter of personal relations with other governments and, most important, with one's own. How to put things – in a way – you know – in a certain fashion which does not offend and yet disturbs. How to hide the needle in the bundle of hay.

Of course, Canadians are different. There is no malice in us. We are the family doctor whom no one has called in for consultation. We are the children of the midday who see all in the clear, shallow light.

16 January 1960.

Certainly one does not at any particular time of life from day to day feel the same age. On one day one may feel a premonition of what it will be like to be really old, and on another one awakes again an adolescent. Quivers of restlessness, flushes of vanity, tail-ends of impossible dreams disturb. One even craves the moral anarchy – like a lost innocence – of adolescence. Oh for the breakdown of Values, those weights upon the lids of life!

The Argentine Ambassador says that the access of sensuality in middle-aged men is called in his country "*le démon de midi*," after a forgotten novel on this subject by Paul Bourget. He says that the title refers to a phrase in the Psalms, which I must look up.

I telephoned my mother today in Halifax. I don't know how to deal with her old age. Perhaps when I am with her, by refusing to admit it I seem to make light of an unbearable affliction. My pretence that she is as she always was may be superficially flattering but may seem like silly patronage (who does he think he is taking in?), and am I not forcing her to play up to my pretence? Is that love? In love all barriers are down, and she has always tried to pull them down to show me the truth. She is indeed preoccupied with the business of dying and sends courageous and despairing signals as she is drawn away on an irresistible tide, and yet they say to me, "How amusing your mother was yesterday! Isn't she wonderful!"

24 January 1960.

I wonder if I can write at all without echoing the truly terrible style in which this book *Advise and Consent* is written. Norman Robertson says that it is "a good political novel." For him and for me it comes pat on the occasion. This is what we are up against in Ottawa – the jungle of politics. Of course, we have always been up against it, but for some illusory years we seemed cushioned against its savageries; in the jungle of politics when the powerful beast strikes one can hide or run, melt into protective colouring if any can be found – but don't wander unarmed in the deceptive sunshine of the glades or you may get badly bruised, finally mauled. I have just been talking to such a victim of power politics. He will live, but will he ever fully recover?

I had lunch today with David Walker.[1] He has just finished a new book. He said that as he was getting towards the end of it he developed a fear that he might die before he had time to finish it and hardly liked to go near the tractor on his farm in case he met with a fatal accident. When David told me this I had a flash of the deepest, most hopeless envy. What would I not give to feel myself the carrier of a book in which I believed!

28 January 1960.

I am a little worried by my speech yesterday. Huntingdon Gilchrist said I had given people something to think about. I felt that this was just what I had not done.

With luck – I mean, if nothing goes wrong, illness, scandal, disfavour of the great, or conspicuous failure – I may expect to stay on at the United Nations for two or even three years. Then there is a possibility of the Under-Secretaryship in Ottawa. But it may be that they would prefer to offer it to someone younger, and perhaps they would do better to do so. Then there is the possibility that Washington

---

[1] Canadian novelist.

may become vacant and they may want a useful, non-controversial successor and I might be the one. Or there is Delhi soon to be vacant – and to be resisted at all costs. Two or three more postings and it is all over. Then retirement and we call it a day.

Harold Beeley of the British Delegation, whom I think of as an educated man, told me that he could never read philosophy and could not understand a word of it. This made me feel better about my struggles with Stuart Hampshire's book.[1] But it does all the same seem idiotic that two grown men like him and me, who are reputedly intelligent at their jobs and who have had expensive educations, are apparently incapable of following a discussion on questions of mind conducted in what looks – deceptively – like plain English.

9 February 1960.

I think and hope that Canada is respected in the United Nations. Or is it just that we are regarded as "respectable"? We seem to have assumed the role in many of the world's troubles as an objective bystander, willing to help if it does not cost too much, given to tut-tutting over the passionate unreasonableness of other people, and quite given to political moralizing. It seems to me that we Canadians have been lucky enough so far to ourselves be spared any "moment of truth." I think there is altogether too much glossing over of the real issues in our statements on defence and foreign policy, both by the Government and by the Opposition. There is also a dated "progressive" political vocabulary which is supposed to give a mildly advanced look to our policies but which is often very superficial and could be misleading.

21 February 1960.

I spent the morning with Hammarskjöld, who was in marvellous form, giving me vignettes of the political leaders with whom he has been dealing – Salazar, de Gaulle, and Franco. He is certainly the most charming, witty, intelligent companion and a delight to be with, glinting with malice and playing with political schemes, ideas, devices, and stratagems.

---

[1] Stuart Hampshire, the British philosopher, had published *Thought in Action* in 1959.

9 March 1960.

March is perhaps the most unpleasant month in the year. Dirty snow in the streets and the cracking and raking of a snow shovel on the pavement, raw sunlight, hard blue sky, and a back-breaking wind.

For some reason I woke up today thinking of Anne. I seemed to see her at the front door of Lapford as her brother Tony and I drove up the avenue in his battered second-hand car, coming from Oxford, where we had begun to be friends. There she stands, her dark head consciously averted, flanked by her mother and her two Chekov aunts. Lapford Grange was enclosed in a green Devon combe. The house was comfortable, rather shabby – not that one noticed – and full of people. I see a young girl, a Romantic Young Girl, with a strongly developed feeling of herself as a Romantic Young Girl, yet with a streak of realism, no silliness, she delights precipitately in her cleverness, she is avid for life, grasping for it. She is sensuous, sentimental, easily in tears or laughter, deliciously eager.

Yes, I remember her, looking like a Russian girl in one of the novels she loved, with her untidy dark hair, her mesmeric dark eyes, her fine-wristed hands. How she talked, with what urgency!

Then I began thinking of Oxford and, inevitably, of Billy Coster, that meteor of my skies till he blunted his wits with drink and became an embarrassing bore. He belonged to the Scott Fitzgerald age and was like Diver in *Tender Is the Night*; like him in his social fascination and his underlying truculence. He was a sexual nihilist, not to be confused with a neuter. He spoke and seemed like an Englishman and I thought of him as the only American who was not like an American. I think now that his was a very American tragedy. In his last phase during the War he lived almost entirely with dart-playing London pals whom he had picked up at his fire-watching station, and sought solace in a semi-platonic friendship with a good-natured barmaid. He thought the English lower classes better friends than his own class and he romanticized them. He would drink beer, port, and whisky all in one hour. He tried to escape from America, from money, and from sex, and died in his mother's arms in an alcoholic clinic in California. I loved Billy and laughed with him and drank with him and talked with him for hours on end. Later, we were both at Harvard as post-graduates and hated Cambridge together. If he appeared today as he first was, how life would come to life. How truly awful it would be if he appeared again as he ended. Dear Billy, how he would have hated the United Nations. He loathed cant. He also thought he loathed snobbery, but he was a New York gentleman and in his heart believed it hard to beat the Costers and the Schermerhorns. No one seems to remember him now – not even his relations. Perhaps he was an embarrassment from which they are delivered. His mother is dead, too – fascinating, funny, with her handsome face and wild stylishness. I see her in trailing tea-gowns, in the sitting-room of some hotel suite in London, Paris, or New York, upbraiding, mocking, and moaning over her children and applying her own disastrous touch to their general débâcle. And where has all the money gone? To "little Matilda," I suppose, the child of the Paris Ritz, married to a duke – must be nearly forty by now. I might sit next to her at dinner without recognizing her. But Billy is Down Among the Dead Men. If he is in Paradise, it is the Oxford of his youth, where he shone briefly in the warmth of friendship and the sparkle of high spirits.

We were all "children of the twenties." But is that phrase just an escape-hatch to excuse messy, self-indulgent, frivolous lives? Is it like blaming alcoholism on heredity, or crime on "something that hap-pened in one's childhood"? In fact, is there anything in this twenties business? Not much perhaps, but something. The famous frivolity marked us, as did the fashionable despair. We also were "rebels without a cause."

13 April 1960.

On this fine spring morning with the sun and the cool breeze and New York traffic sounds coming up from the street I feel hungry and cheerful. Elizabeth is up the Hudson at Poughkeepsie, having taken on a seminar at Vassar. She says the whole place is threaded with stories, a frieze of young creatures drifting across the campus, the girls going to collect their letters like going to collect eggs on the farm, and the girl coming back reading a letter as she walks and smiling to herself. Elizabeth says hang on to the diaries – they could be pruned and published as "The Diaries of Mr. X."

14 May 1960.

A large, cheerful lunch party today at the Piping Rock Club in Locust Valley. More and more rich Americans, and how endlessly many there seem to be and how endlessly much money they seem to have – and when you think of all the other rich Americans who don't happen to be meeting one at lunch or dinner in the month of May 1960, the thought becomes quite oppressive. Then there is this talk of private planes and swimming-pools and "We have taken a floor at the Plaza for six months," "Her mother has inherited the most divine villa at Como," "He has the largest collection of Fabergé in the world," "They own two miles of private beach on the Sound," "Our plantation near Charleston" – and what is nice is that they are all rich together. Ambassadors, too, are collected for social occasions – the house-trained ones.

15 August 1960.

Just back from my holiday in Nova Scotia. The Minister has arrived by plane from Ottawa. Went back to the hotel with him from the airport. Of course, in spite of my instructions, no one from the Delegation had inspected their rooms. The heat was appalling and there was no air-conditioner in their sitting-room. Naturally, my flowers for Mrs. Green had not been delivered. Then there was a meeting over his disarmament speech. Tommy Stone, Wally Nesbitt, Ross Campbell, Geoff Murray, and myself – what a lot of high-priced help! The speech was immensely long but I think very well reasoned.

20 August 1960.

The first morning that I can breathe again after five days of the Minister's presence in New York, during which he brought off a very neat little ploy on disarmament, sent up his prestige, and got what he wanted by a mixture of toughness and shrewdness that surprised and impressed his fellow professional politician, Cabot Lodge, while at the same time stealing the show from him. I think Cabot may have thought that he was dealing with a nice old boy from the sticks who was a little slow in the uptake and could be patronized with his usual effortless effrontery – but it did not work out like that. This exercise demonstrated the advantage of taking an inflexible and clear-cut position at

the start, in our case a middle position towards which the "uncommit-
ted" countries in the U.N. gyrated. During this time I was somewhat
irritated by Mark, who came down with the Canadian Delegation. He
has all the virtues but occasionally relies too much on possessing
them. He "cannot tell a lie," when no one actually is asking him to do
so, so why the protuberant stare of aggressive integrity? Someone said
of him, "He is a stallion." Yes, but a stallion with a conscience.

22 August 1960.

"When will this weather change?" the doorman asked as I stepped
out from under the apartment-house awning into the heat of 62nd
Street. These hot, sticky days seem to have been with us for so long that
we have lost track of dates and can hardly remember when they began
or what went before them. The cool sparkle of early autumn seems a
distant mirage. Central Park is not really any cooler than the streets
but I go there every morning to walk over the burnt grass and under
the dusty trees before we have breakfast in the apartment. I get my
first cup of coffee in the Zoo cafeteria and take it out onto the
terrace. The coffee tastes of dishwater, the terrace tables have not yet
been cleaned, and when I put my elbow on the green-painted table
surface, grains of sugar stick to the sleeve of my coat. At a nearby
table Zoo attendants in open-necked khaki shirts are gossiping
about the animals. Sometimes I overhear something that interests
me – the cause of the squabble between the gorilla and his mate, the
reason why the lioness lies moaning on her back with her paws in
the air. The animals are still half asleep at this hour, but they have
already come or been pushed out into their outdoor cages. They seem
cross or reluctant to begin their day. Only the seals are enjoying themselves, the sole cool creatures in New York, gliding and snorting in the
dirty water of their pool.

Inside the apartment, breakfast is waiting on the small table
between the windows in Sylvia's bedroom, the *New York Times* beside
one chair, the *Herald Tribune* beside the other. Popski is lying on the
unmade bed, his head burrowing under the sheets, his rump immo-
bile. Anne, the new maid, brings in more coffee. Her morning face is
like her evening one – round, porcelain pink and white. She must
have been a pretty girl, plump probably even then.

Outside the windows is the racket of the electric drill as they burrow away at the destruction of the apartment-house next door. You can see down into rooms like our own, minus their ceilings. Sylvia is a thorough newspaper reader. She questions what the Medical Association say in their statement. I read the foreign political news and about animals and architecture. After the egg comes a cigarette. Shaving, thank God, is over, the face in the bathroom mirror packed away till another day.

Static are the morning rooms as I go round them – an unfinished glass of rye, a vase of bronze chrysanthemums, the television doors are open but the drawing-room shows nothing, eternally cool and grave it is like a place in another house. The rooms are linked up by a dark corridor running along the apartment, hung with dubious portraits of unwanted ancestors. At the end is my bedroom, darkest of all and darkened further by the hanging woods of the tapestry facing my bed. I cannot see the colour of my socks in this green gloom.

On the silver tray in the hall (crest of the fighting cock of the Prevosts) are the bills and the invitations. "His Excellency," "the honour," "overdue," and notes of thanks for "a delicious evening." The car is waiting to take me to the office.

Every day and every night this week has been occupied by the Security Council meetings on the Congo. Ever since the Belgians granted independence to the Congo in June that country has been in turmoil. The Belgian officials and technicians cleared out at once, and there are less than a score of Congolese university graduates in the country and no trained officials. The result is chaos. Then Katanga, the province where the copper belt is, seceded from the central government. The Belgians have sent in troops to ensure the evacuation of their remaining nationals and the Russians are accusing them of "imperialist aggression." Now the Secretary-General has been authorized by the Security Council to send a United Nations military force to restore peace there and we are contributing a Canadian signals detachment. My head is woozy with sitting up half the night at these Security Council meetings. My mouth's stale from smoking endless cigarettes, my stomach irritated by nipping out to the bar with my fellow delegates during the translations of speeches. My great friends and allies on these occasions are Freddy Boland, the Irish representative – wise and imperturbable; Nielsen, the Norwegian – a steady friend in all U.N. crises (the Norwegians seem the nearest to the Canadians of any of the Scandinavian delegates, much nearer than the Swedes or the Danes); Jim Plimsoll, the Australian, and I should say my closest friend at the United Nations – so quick, intelligent, and sensitive. It has been gratifying during the last few days to see how other delegations have rallied round to Canada's defence in the face of persistent attacks on us by the Russians. Yet of course people do inevitably play up to the Russians. That bloody Kuznetsov attacked me personally in the most insolent terms tonight for the support that Canada is giving to Ireland for the presidency of the Assembly. He said this was a Cold War move on our part. I said that he knew perfectly well that our Minister was, as he had so often proved, totally opposed to the Cold War. He replied that in any case Canada had no independence of its own and this was proved by the fact that we were members of NATO. I lost my temper at this, but my temper has got very frail anyway from sitting it out in this vast hot-box of New York, and I also lost my temper with the waiter at the Côte Basque restaurant. Went to a stifling cocktail party at my colleague's, the Indian Representative. God, how tired we are all going to be by the time the coming General Assembly is over! And *what* an Assembly it promises to be, with Khrushchev, Lumumba, Krishna Menon, Nkrumah, and Castro!

11 September 1960.

Things are going from bad to worse in the Congo. The Congolese Premier, Lumumba, has declared that he has lost confidence in the Secretary-General and has demanded the withdrawal of white troops from the U.N. forces. Meanwhile, a mob of Congolese soldiers has attacked and severely beat up fourteen Canadian members in the force at Leopoldville. I have been living much more in the Congo than in New York and it now seems quite possible that I shall be asked to go there. I very much want to do this but I doubt whether it will come off as I think the Russians would object because they disapprove of Canada, as a member of NATO, having anything to do with the Congo. They are, of course, attacking Hammarskjöld violently. The Scandinavians intend to stick to him through thick and thin.

It is raining. There go the church bells in the rain-soaked air. I have been reading short stories – O. Henry's, Chekov's, and Edgar Allan Poe's – with pleasure, except for Edgar Allan Poe, a writer I have never been able to endure.

26 September 1960.

I have just come in from my morning walk in Central Park and have paid a visit to the macaws and heard the lion giving its waking roar. The Prime Minister[1] is in New York for the United Nations and has made no effort whatever to contact or consult me. So I sit in my room waiting for a telephone call. I am determined not to approach him. Of course, I should have known what Prime Ministers think of resident ambassadors (when they think of them at all). They simply think that they are "officials" and as such a mixture of flunkey and clerk.

3 October 1960.

When will Butterball (as I now call the maid, Anne) have my breakfast ready? I have to listen to Khrushchev and Menon today at the General Assembly. The Americans have refused the Eisenhower–Khrushchev meeting, and who would have expected them to accept after the wholesale insults fired at them by Khrushchev, whose behaviour is becoming more and more Hitlerian? The spectacle of all these dictators coming here to New York and strutting and orating and bullying reminds one of the Bad Old Days when Hitler and Mussolini were in bloom and busy breaking up the League of Nations. I feel an increasing disgust for what is going on at the United Nations. The incessant work carries me through time with the speed of light.

Elizabeth has written to me again encouraging me to keep my old diaries rather than burn them and to consider later publication. If I ever do publish them I shall call the book *Flies Around My Head*. I remember as a small boy being horrified by the sight of a horse in a field with its entire face covered with flies and the way it charged up and down the field trying to shake them off.

The United States Delegation are not at all satisfied with the Canadian record at this General Assembly. In fact, I now learn that

---

[1] Mr. Diefenbaker.

they have reported that their relations with our Mission here in New York have been so bad for the last two years and that we (I?) have been so unco-operative that they have given up approaching us. In view of my close personal friendship with Cabot Lodge and the many appreciative things he has said about me, I must say this surprises me. The truth of the matter is that the Americans dislike and mistrust the present Canadian government and all its works. Wadsworth, whom I have known for years and who is now heading the American Delegation, has never attempted to make the slightest human contact with me from the first day he arrived here. The United Nations is full of misunderstandings, worse this year than ever, and this poisons personal relationships. People associate their colleagues with the policies of their respective governments and mistrust the man because they dislike the policy. This is inevitable but often mistaken. Half the time the man you think incarnates a hostile attitude is fighting his own government to get that attitude changed.

27 November 1960.

Mike Pearson is here today from Ottawa. He and I had a talk today about the United Nations Secretariat. Last night he said to someone at dinner, "Charles has done all right. He comes of an old Conservative family and has succeeded in ingratiating himself with the Liberals."

1 January 1961.

Shall we or shall we not go to Haiti for our holiday – that is the question. Matsudiara, the Japanese Ambassador, says, "Don't go near it, it is frightening and sinister," but Loelia Westminster[1] says, "Yes, go and get me some voodoo charms to braid in my hair the way the Haitian women do." Loelia is here on a visit. How much I like her, her looks and her friendship! I am just going up to drink vodka with her in the blood-red *garçonnière* which she has been renting.

Matsudiara came into the French Embassy last night, sat down before the fire with a glass of champagne in his hand, looked round the New Year's gathering, and said, "There will be a world war within

---

[1] Loelia, Duchess of Westminster, later the Hon. Lady Lindsay of Dowhill.

two years. I have just been telling that to the Japanese press corre-spondents and I foretold to the month the coming of communism in China. Also," he went on, "there will be communist revolutions in all the Caribbean states." In the wake of these announcements the company paused for station identification. If Matsudiara happened to be right, how would one get the most out of these two years left to us? Madame Schébéko, a White Russian refugee, told me once that if only she had been sure of the date of the coming Soviet revolution she would at once have bought two fur coats and a Rolls-Royce, to get as much satisfaction out of these as possible before all her money was taken away from her.

It is raining! – the darkest, dismallest New York day imaginable, but I continue to love New York in all seasons, and in spite of any-thing I may say about the United Nations I enjoy being there and would not exchange it for any post in the foreign service.

22 January 1960.

I have been reading Horace Walpole's letters all morning instead of working on our next disarmament resolution. He charms me still as he did when I was a boy of fourteen and read his letters for the first time, when I absurdly wrote that his style was "natural." I think I must have meant "high-spirited." Horace Walpole was troubled by nerve storms but, lucky man, was untroubled so far as we know by the flesh.

Sylvia says that when she is listening to me talking with the Minister on the telephone I come back and say that I have stood up to him and put my views extremely firmly, whereas she had the impression that I agreed with every word he said. A very wifely observation.

Drinks with Charles and Marie Noetbeart. What good friends they are. Marie, unchanged since Ottawa days, as pretty and amusing as ever.

The General Assembly is meeting and yet it is not functioning. Shall we ever extricate ourselves from the morass of the Congo? I still hope so much to go there and have a look at it. The Congo to me has become a country of the mind. I am obsessed by it and more inter-ested in travellers' tales from there than in those from the moon.

Last night I dined at Pat Dean's[1] with members of the British Delegation. I urged them to use all their influence to get the Belgians, or as many as possible of them, out of the Congo, but I recognized resistance, tenacious, unargumentative. Then the question of barring arms shipments to the Congo came up. Their new Minister came out with, "When one thinks of all the arms being smuggled all over the world, one wonders why the fuss about arms for the Congo." I thought, "There go we diplomats! If an issue does not suit you, break it up into parts and make it relative. If it comes to that, when one thinks of all the adulteries being committed in the world, what does one adultery matter?"

12 March 1961.

To put myself to sleep I tell myself stories. How flat, trivial, lacking in imagination, and repetitive they are, so that I go to sleep through boredom. By comparison my dreams are works of surrealistic art, brilliant films in the newest continental mode, rich in endless invention, in scenes of hallucinatory brilliance. Even the small "bit parts" in these dreams are rendered with uncanny intensity. As to emotions – fear, love and desolation, danger and narrow escape, lust and nostalgia – the themes are endless and images crowd to express them. If I could tap the sources of dreams, no writer of this age could touch me. There is no doubt I dream like a genius.

At the close of my speech last night Dean Acheson said, "You were superb." "So were you," I replied. "I always am," said Dean.

Walked through the Park to the Plaza Oak Room bar for morning vodka martinis with Sylvia on my arm. She looked lovely, eyes very blue. She has been so patient and sweet during all the storms of the last few months and the strains of the General Assembly. Then we went to the French seventeenth-century exhibition at the Metropolitan, which was badly chosen and arranged. It left an impression of showy, mediocre pictures. Even the Poussins were the poorest I have ever seen; only two Claude Lorrains saved all.

I have been reading Pope's *Rape of the Lock* and now *The Essay on Man* – "In Folly's cup still laughs the bubble Joy."

---

[1] Sir Patrick Dean, then Permanent Representative of the U.K. to the United Nations; later British Ambassador to the United States.

25 March 1961. Washington, D.C.

No, I do not want to come here as Ambassador. Yet if they offered it to me I should probably not refuse it. Why not? Why not tell Norman Robertson that, as a friend, I ask him to save me from it?

As for the brilliant company of the New Frontiersmen and -women, if last night's dinner party is an example I'm afraid it is just a group of clever bureaucrats and their clever or artistic wives meeting after a hard day's work in the office. And must I leave my beloved New York? I feel inclined to make a libation to the Goddess of Liberty at her gates.

Isaiah Berlin, speaking of Adlai Stevenson, told Elizabeth that he hated "a liberal mob." That phrase keeps echoing in my mind irrespective of party labels.

Pope's philosophy is thin and he skates over the depths. It is a day-lit jingle but consider how he slides into poetry and out again. Yet he does not seem to me a religious man like Doctor Johnson. He is a monster of accomplishment rising to genius.

18 September 1961.

A shocking tragedy. Dag Hammarskjöld has been killed in an air accident in the Congo on his way to arrange a cease-fire in the fighting there. Was it an accident? Who will ever know for sure. So many people for so many reasons may have wanted him out of the way. I think his vision of the future of the United Nations will die with him. I also feel his death as a painful personal loss. While he was too detached to be called a friend, I shall so much miss the stimulus of working with him and the pleasure of his companionship.

22 November 1961. New York.

Lunched today with the Libyans. I sat next to a bearded Oman prince and idiotically asked him how he liked New York. He said, "It is just like home," and sniggered slyly.

Coming through the swinging doors of the U.N. Building I encountered the Romanian Permanent Representative. I have struck up a kind of odd relationship – almost friendship – with him. He has to return to Bucharest and says he longs for it. In fact, I am sure he dreads it. He went on insisting so much about this that it became embarrassing. Then suddenly that great white slug seized my arm and said, "I am a human being, you know." Of course the poor bastard is a human being – that's his trouble.

The Finnish Ambassador says if you stay long enough at the United Nations you will find that "all the heels are wounded." One's skin gets rubbed thin from the close commerce with one's colleagues in this claustrophobic place, and as a session of the United Nations goes on, personal relationships become more and more strained. Even with my great friend Jim Plimsoll, the Australian, it was a shock last night, when I voted against the Australian resolution, seeing his amused, pale, ironic face turn crimson with irritation as he came over to my chair and, standing over my shoulder, kept repeating, "It's not personal. I know it isn't you, but how *could* you vote the way you did?"

Before the curtain goes up on the official performance of the General Assembly and the Councils and Committees of the United Nations, the scenery has to be put in place, the parts of the players rehearsed, scripts compared. And this is done when little groups of actors huddle together in low-voiced confabulation or drift towards each other casually – but by arrangement – in the corridors of the Assembly Hall or in the wings of the Security Council. Often each carries with him a sheet of paper, the text of his country's forthcoming Resolution, for which he seeks support from other delegations. Or there are points of procedure to be picked over – under which provision would it be best to proceed, or which amendment of the text (often pencilled on the typewritten page) will be most likely to attract support or at least avert defeat by inducing benign abstentions when the Resolution comes to the vote? It is as well to keep these exchanges as inconspicuous as possible, certainly out of earshot of the enemy, for there – on the other side of the lounge – the enemy are gathered in similar preparation for the fray. They are planning the defeat of one's government's cherished project or, more damaging still, an amendment of their own which will, by an extension or rearrangement of language, enlarge the scope of the Resolution and water down its intention so that no credit will redound to your country and there will be no headlines in the press at home to the greater lustre of the government in power.

And now, talking of governments, here comes with soft feet across the carpet towards us an elegant lady, her hair beautifully braided – the multilingual telephonist. "Mr. Ambassador, there is an urgent call for you from the Minister of External Affairs in Ottawa. Would you care to take it now? He is waiting on the line." "Waiting on the line" – that will never do. With hurried apology to my colleagues, with controlled speed – one does not run but moves quietly to the voice of the master – "Hello, Charles. How are things down there? Got everything lined up for our Resolution? Who's supporting – how many co-sponsors?" "What? only nine countries? We'll have to do better than that. What about Australia? No, darn it, we didn't vote for *their* Resolution. India?" "So they want to make it more like an Indian Resolution, do they? Charles, you'll have to get more co-sponsors quickly. I want to make an announcement in the House of Commons tomorrow. Twist a few arms – I know you can do it. Good luck, and let me have the additional names later in the day." It is all very well, but where is one to find these "additional names"? I have already canvassed all those delegations which are in sympathy with our Resolution. I have even incorporated some of their amendments into our text as bait for their support. I wish the Minister was here to twist a few arms himself. No doubt he could do it; he is a practised politician and vote-getter. All day I go from pillar to post seeking out even the most unlikely allies and by late afternoon I am still one short of a total of twelve co-sponsors. But I have reached the end of the line. No one else is interested in the Canadian resolution. I go into the lavatory and, standing at the urinal next to me, buttoning up his trousers, is the Ambassador of Haiti. I barely know the man – our relations with Haiti are minimal. The Duvalier régime is not popular at the United Nations. "Excellency," I say to him in my most polished French, "may I have a word with you?" He looks surprised, almost affronted, at this approach to him in this place. I draw him into the washroom. I do not attempt to explain the merits of our resolution; I simply say, "I am offering Your Excellency a unique opportunity to associate your country with a great initiative in the cause of peace." I venture the suggestion that President Duvalier could not fail to approve. I point out that as the list of co-sponsors appears alphabetically, Haiti would rank high on the printed list, above other important nations. The Ambassador, a small, stout, elephant-coloured man, pauses and stares at me through thick horn-rimmed glasses, and then, "Excellency, I shall have to consult my government." "I fear," I reply, "that the list closes this evening. Would it be possible to have an answer before midnight tonight?" The Ambassador bows and emerges from the washroom. At 11:30 he telephones me – Haiti accepts. I have achieved twelve co-sponsors.

9 December 1961.

I am having difficulties with the Indian Delegation and in particular with the Indian Representative. What prevents him from being what at first sight he seems – a silver-haired, wise Indian civil servant, devoted, highly intelligent, and industrious? What is wrong with him? Why does the oil of malice in him rise so easily to the surface? I should like to know his whole story. Has he been so much snubbed in the past to develop this india-rubbery self-assurance, these ingratiating, pawing gestures? Perhaps that may explain his insistence on his position as an ambassador and his wife's detestable arrogance towards her so-called inferiors. The other night when they dined at this house I put her on my right, on the other side a very intelligent, entertaining member of the Department of External Affairs who is down here on a visit. During the whole of dinner she never spoke one word to him, in fact, turned her back on him. He was not of sufficient rank for her to talk to.

Descartes says that one proof of the existence of God is man's sense of his own imperfection; that this sense of imperfection would not exist unless there were a perfect being. I think of a picture, Piranesi ruins, with some figures of men and women in the foreground. The scale and grandeur of the ruins give the measure of the people, the men and women posed against them illustrate the scale of the walls and pillars. Without God there is no scale of measurement. Man swells into a nervous monster. And yet there are plenty of modest and noble men and women who live without God and plenty of monsters who believe in Him.

15 January 1962.

The die is cast. I am to go as Ambassador to Washington. I suppose I could have flatly said "No," but who would turn down the biggest job in the profession? My hesitation has been partly due to my own blank ignorance of so many of the issues involved between Canada and the United States, particularly the trade and economic ones. (When I said this to my mother she replied, "Well, you'll just have to learn about them, won't you.") I also shrink from the prospect of returning to normal diplomatic life with all its tedious formalities and conventionalities. The United Nations spared one a lot of this. There is little time for such things in this hothouse of international intrigue, where one stumbles from crisis to crisis. I prefer this speeded-up process to a more leisurely pace. However, perhaps I need not worry about tedium in this new post; on the contrary, all the storm signals are out for foul weather between Washington and Ottawa. Relations between the two governments are bad and show signs of getting worse. This was brought home to me when I went to Ottawa for my interview with the Prime Minister on my appointment and also during my visit to Arnold Heeney, our present Ambassador in Washington. Not only are there substantive differences of policy involved, but the atmosphere is poisoned by the mutual aversion of the Prime Minister for the President and the President for the Prime Minister. President Kennedy seems to regard Mr. Diefenbaker as a mischief-making old man who cannot be trusted, whereas Mr. Diefenbaker sees the President as an arrogant young man and a political enemy. In such a situation the role of Canadian Ambassador to Washington promises to be a tricky one. This does not dismay me, but I ask myself why I have been selected for it. Arnold Heeney, a warm friend, has urged that I should be his successor. The Minister, Howard Green, has adopted me as his candidate for the job and has been working on the Prime Minister in my favour. I am grateful for his support; I have always had respect and affection for him. As for the Prime Minister, I think he finally made up his mind that I was the safest available bet for the post, and I wonder whether my Conservative family connection helped him in my case to overcome his endemic suspicion of members of the Department of External Affairs. During our interview I had the impression that he was preoccupied, self-isolated, and, far from enjoying the exercise of power, was overpowered by it.

I hear on all sides that the present government is extremely unpopular in Washington and that the Americans say that every communication they receive from us is a protest or a complaint against them. Also, they are beginning to give us the cold shoulder and their reaction to any Canadian official visitor is a snub. I do not think that this perpetual nattering at the Americans will get us anywhere. I am all for standing up to them on a real question of principle or policy but snapping at their heels all the time is undignified and unproductive. I suppose, however, that they must be getting hardened to this treatment. It is what they get from most of their allies, in intervals of their asking for favours. The British, with their usual realism, ever since the humiliation of Suez, never stop making up to them. At one time we had pretensions to consider ourselves a "bridge" between the United Kingdom and the United States. What a bad joke that looks now! I doubt all the same that the British have much influence on United States policy. The Americans in their present mood do not welcome advice from anyone, least of all from the present Canadian government. I think that one difficulty I shall experience in Washington is finding a basis for communication with the American official world. In the past we have had speedy access to United States government departments on an informal footing which has sometimes been envied by other foreign governments. This has been advantageous to us in some ways but it has its drawbacks. It has meant that our agreement with the general direction of United States policy has been taken for granted, so much so that we hardly seem to be regarded as a "foreign" government at all. When we differ from them on anything important they seem much more surprised and irritated than when dealing with "foreign" countries from whom they can expect trouble. It becomes a sort of family quarrel; always the worst kind. And then, too, the disparity between us has been immensely increased since the War. Now the United States is the greatest military and economic power in the non-communist world, with no British Empire to offset it. The old neighbourly relationship between our two countries was never, of course, based on equality between us, but the inequality was less glaring than it now is.

This enormous access of United States power is reflected inevitably in the men who wield it. A diplomatic colleague who was with me in Washington before the War said the other day, "You will find that the American official has become much 'grander' than he used to be," I have encountered this attitude myself during my visits to Washington but "grand" is not quite the right word for it. The personal friendliness and informality are still there. It is rather that they have developed a complete impermeability to advice, criticism, or comment of any kind, combined with the patient courtesy that one extends to the well-meaning irrelevance. I think that this is an element in the irritation that our Prime Minister feels and that other Canadians may share. No doubt we do not make sufficient allowance for the world-wide responsibilities which the Americans carry on their shoulders. However, any assumption of superiority, conscious or unconscious, has always been peculiarly difficult for Canadians to swallow, prompting the very Canadian question, "Who the hell do they think they are?"

My own problem may be that American friends, knowing of my long association with Mike Pearson, may show a certain sympathy for me in serving under Mr. Diefenbaker. This must be discouraged from the start. I like and admire the Americans, I am devoted to Mike, I shall do anything I can to keep relations on an even keel between Canada and the United States, but if it comes to a showdown of any kind there must be no question as to where my loyalties lie.

24 January 1962.

Farewell party given for us by the San Miniatos.[1] The Windsors were the feature of the evening. I sat next to her. She has developed a curious, disconcerting tic. When she stops talking, her lips meet and part tremblingly like a nibbling rabbit, or as though she were talking to herself. Indeed, she seems ravaged but unsated, her green eyes brilliant with anticipation of a party at Mrs. Cafritz's[2] in Washington next week. But then, she is easy, conversable, engagingly full of curiosity, and with a nose tilted for scandal. The Duke, royally red in the face with a white carnation in his buttonhole, expatiated to Sylvia on the impossibility of his having black men to dinner and wondered how we bore this portion of our lot at the United Nations. The room was full of jewels which mattered more than the names and numbers of the players. The Duchess's Schlumberger bracelet of coal-dark

---

[1] The Duke and Duchess of San Miniato. The Duchess is Canadian by birth.

[2] Well-known Washington hostess of the period.

sapphires and small diamonds, our hostess's cabochon rubies, my neighbour's enormous black pearl, like a slug crawling over her finger from the foliage of diamonds, and, out-soaring all, the diamond necklace of a Russian lady of endless antecedents, whose still-lovely face is permanently framed in an envelope of gauze. "Does she take it off," they asked her husband, "when she goes to bed?" "No, never," he replied, "but it isn't that that I mind. It is that her diamonds scratch." Café society is not a cinch. These people bought or charmed or clawed their way into this enclosure. There is less room for nonentities here than in ordinary society. The room is full of adventurers and adventuresses, from born ladies who got sick of being ladies to slightly shop-worn countesses from Brooklyn or the Bronx, and one white-skinned young beauty with a pile of red hair and sardonic eyes. This is a slippery arena and I was glad to see my dear friend, our hostess, dauntless Gladys, steering her way with a certain rough, tough, shy, bold authority.

2 April 1962.

As my departure from New York becomes imminent, I have been reflecting on the United Nations and its claim to be a world community – and on the tragic fate of Dag Hammarskjöld. The world community was to be incarnated in the United Nations, but the incarnation has never really taken place. Its prophet – and, since his death in the Congo, its martyr – was Dag Hammarskjöld. Its religious ceremony, so it seems to me, is the concert of classical music (chosen by Dag) which is the prelude to the meeting of the General Assembly. There are the delegates from more than half the world gathered together – for once in silence – with reverent expressions on their faces, listening to the strains of Beethoven and Bach, their souls presumably lifted above mundane differences into an ethereal world of music in which their common humanity is made manifest. The concert lasts about an hour – the unity of mood among the listeners lasts no longer. There is also the chapel or room of meditation – undenominational, of course – to which it must have been hoped that delegates would repair to cool their tempers exacerbated in the heat of debate and to contemplate the latter end of things. I have looked in there once or twice myself. On those occasions it was empty, except for a member of the U.N. security guard pacing up and down at the entrance, to guard it against defilement.

There used to be a common saying – I forget who originated it – that "the United Nations is no better than its members." That indeed was a truism abundantly proved, but the very fact that it had to be stated shows that there is a widespread expectation – or at least hope – that the whole will turn out to be more than its parts. There is support for the cause of the United Nations (nowhere more than in Canada), and this cause is felt to be something superior to the sum total of the different nations represented there. It is to be an emanation of the good intentions, the better selves, of these nations, working together for peace and the dignity of man. A spirit brooding upon the waters of a troubled world. Of course, many of those who devote themselves to the cause are hard-headed, able men and women, not easily deluded by optimism but sustained by a purpose. There is, however, an element of mysticism and also of muddle in the minds of many of its supporters. They expect miracles and are disillusioned. For this, Hammarskjöld himself – the symbol of the United Nations – bore some of the responsibility. He himself was a mystic but he was far from muddled. Like Mahatma Gandhi, who in some ways he resembled, he combined a fervent faith in the unseen with a very keen eye for the scene before him. He knew – none better – the task he had set himself and he approached it with spiritual humility and intellectual arrogance. The task was to speed the evolution of the United Nations from a meeting-place of nations into an effective instrument in international politics – to make of it what some mistakenly believe it already is, a cohesive force. He knew that the odds were against him, but he had been a mountaineer. Over the fireplace in his own room was suspended a mountaineer's pick – it was not there for nothing. He would set out to scale the mountain and if he failed to reach the top the fall would be precipitous. This was the risk that added zest to the enterprise. Meanwhile, like any experienced climber, he would assess the chances, study the terrain, and hire the most trustworthy guides – his own secretariat. The mountain that he set himself to conquer was that of exclusive, aggressive nationalism, deeply rooted in history and engendering conflict. For all his skills, it proved too much for him. His failure can be attributed too simply to

Soviet resistance. This was the precipitant, but it was also a convenient screen for the reluctance of others, especially the Western Great Powers, to accord him the support he would have needed. How then did he go wrong? It was partly a failure of patience, partly an overplaying of his hand. These were the political errors. Beyond them was a deeper failure – the failure of the doctrine he sought to embody – the doctrine of supernational solidarity. It was too insubstantial – too fleshless; it might take hold of men's minds but could not appeal to their passions. The air at the top of the mountain was too thin for common humans.

27 April 1962.

It is half an hour before train time, the suitcases are packed. There is no necessity for me to lug them all into the hall – that is precisely what we gave five dollars to the doorman to do – but I know I shall be pressured into doing it myself. Before breakfast this morning I went for a farewell walk in the Park and, standing on the bridge, quickly and sadly said goodbye to my beloved New York. It has served me well and would have done even better for me if I had had more initiative to plunder its gifts. I shall never in any foreseeable or unforeseeable future live in this place again. It is painful to leave, but this must be concealed from Washingtonians, as they no more appreciate hearing good things of New York than New Yorkers do of Washington.

STORM SIGNALS

More Undiplomatic Diaries
1962–1971

To my niece Elizabeth Ritchie
and to the memory of
Elizabeth Bowen

PREFACE

This will be the fourth volume of these undiplomatic diaries. It covers the years 1962 to 1971, beginning with my appointment as Ambassador to Washington and ending when I quit the post of High Commissioner to London and said goodbye to the Foreign Service.

I should from the start warn the reader what not to expect. This is not an historical memoir or a study of the role of Canada in international affairs. Recently a spate of memoirs and studies of this period have appeared. Some are valuable contributions to history – some less so. All were written with the wisdom of hindsight which is denied the diarist.

As a boy I wrote, "I prefer diaries to memoirs. They are less made up afterwards." They are also less flattering to the ego of the author. It is a temptation to revise the record when one comes across opinions about people and events which have since proved to be wrong. That temptation has to be resisted. Also, one does not want to hurt the feelings of the living or cause distress to the friends and relatives of the dead. Yet if one irons out all pungency of comment the sanitized text becomes so bland as to be unreadable. The only real answer to the problem would be for the diarist to die before publication or for those mentioned in the diary to die before him – either seems an extreme solution.

This record is only a footnote to History. Yet History, if not at the centre of the stage, is always in the wings, for the diarist played a small part on the fringes of the drama. Politics dominated the Washington years, and politicians – good, bad, and indifferent – come and go throughout the story. So too do my diplomatic colleagues. Diplomats are not a particularly popular breed and my old profession, like all professions, has its trivial, sometimes ludicrous, side, but most of its practitioners are hard-headed, humane, and tolerant people who devote much of their energies to the peaceful solution of intractable international problems and the prevention of violent international collisions. As to our own Foreign Service, it contains some of the best brains and most devoted public servants in our country.

Though the framework of this journal is that of the diplomatic career, the diaries themselves are highly personal. The scenes and people appearing in them are an oddly assorted company, not chosen in order of importance or according to the rules of protocol. Why else does the diabolical dachshund Popski usurp space which should be reserved for his betters? Why does the snapshot of an eccentric encountered by accident replace the portrait of a friend whom I saw every day?

In this book statesmen, or would-be statesmen, rub shoulders with authors, society hostesses; old friends reappear and a younger generation begins to enter on the stage; the scenes shift from Embassy life in London, Washington, and Paris to the streets of Ottawa and the south shore of Nova Scotia. It is a peculiar book because it reflects the changing moods of the writer, ranging from gloom and nostalgia to exhilaration and amusement, written from day to day, sometimes from hour to hour. We diarists are peculiar people; we may appear harmless, yet we can be dangerous. We write things down, awkward things sometimes, indiscreet things, things better forgotten. We should be banned. No doubt we soon will be, for we have no union or lobby to defend us. Diarists are by definition non-joiners; theirs is not a group activity. Our only plea in defence might be that we find Life so interesting that we are not willing to see it slip between our fingers without leaving a trace behind.

WASHINGTON

1962–1966

After four years as Permanent Representative to the United Nations I left New York on April 27, 1962, to go as Canadian Ambassador to Washington. My appointment there took place at a time of strained and worsening relationship between the Kennedy administration and the government of Prime Minister Diefenbaker. I had been chosen as Ambassador at the urging of the Secretary of State for External Affairs, Howard Green, and after a prolonged period of indecision on the part of the Prime Minister as to the best candidate for the job. I hardly knew Mr. Diefenbaker personally, and my interview with him prior to my appointment was of the most cursory kind. Howard Green, on the other hand, I knew well. I had worked very closely with him in my capacity as Permanent Representative to the United Nations and I had developed a respect for his ability and integrity, and a personal affection for him. I had serious misgivings myself about my suitability for the Washington post, principally on the grounds that I had not enough knowledge of the trade and economic issues between our two countries. However, the outgoing Ambassador, Arnold Heeney, sought to encourage me in every way possible, and this, combined with Howard Green's confidence, overcame any hesitations I might have had.

To be an ambassador in a capital when relations between your own government and the government to which you are accredited are bad, and getting worse, is always a tricky situation and is a difficult hand to play. I had spent happy years in my youth as Third Secretary in the (then) Canadian Legation in Washington. I had many friends there. So my wife Sylvia and I were warmly welcomed, and there was not the faintest reflection, in the hospitality with which we were greeted, of the clouds on the political horizon. However, pleasant as this was, it had little to do with the realities of politics. I had only been in Washington a very short time before this was brought home to me. The occasion was a private party at which the Secretary of State, Dean Rusk, was present. To my surprise, he took the occasion to launch an attack on the policies and attitude of the Canadian government in such forthright language that Walter Lippmann, who was among the guests, said to me afterwards that in all his experience he had never heard such terms used to an ambassador about his government. There could be no doubt in my mind, or in anyone else's, of the personal quality of the President's dislike of Mr. Diefenbaker, whom he regarded with supercilious aversion and whose policies seemed to him to have an anti-American bias. Nor could there be any doubt that the Prime Minister reciprocated these sentiments. In Mr. Diefenbaker's case there was anger and irritation, particularly with the President's somewhat arrogant and offhand style. More profound was Mr. Diefenbaker's suspicion, which deepened into conviction, that the President was in close sympathy with the Canadian Leader of the Opposition, Lester B. Pearson, and would not hesitate to interfere in our domestic affairs to bring about a change of government.

For an embassy to be in disfavour with the White House at a time when the office of President was at the height of its power and influence was a disconcerting experience. The word had swiftly percolated down into every department of the United States Administration. As an example, I recall that when, while discussing a minor tariff item, I expressed a differing view from that of the American official involved, he replied that he had the authority of the President for his interpretation and asked me whether I "intended to call the President of the United States a liar."

Despite these strains and stresses, my personal relationship with the State Department and White House officials remained cordial, even friendly. They seemed to regard me more in sorrow than in anger, and their attitude implied – and sometimes more than implied – that I could not, as a reasonable man, be at heart in sympathy with the policies of the Diefenbaker government. While this eased personal relations, it was sometimes more difficult to deal with than outright hostility.

With the Secretary of State, despite his initial outburst, I was on good terms. I respected him as a devoted public servant who had his own difficulties with the White House, and I admired the clarity and precision with which he could outline a case. I enjoyed the earthy sense of humour which underlay his Buddha-like exterior. He struck me as a first-rate executant, rather than an originator, of policy. As he was to demonstrate later during the Vietnam war, he, like many Washington officials, was totally impervious to any idea or suggestion which did not originate in Washington. The United States version of consultation with their allies meant listening patiently to their views and then informing them of American decisions.

McGeorge Bundy[1] at the White House was always available to me, and at times of crisis I would see him two or three times a week. It was a delight to encounter that steely intelligence, that far-ranging competence, and that sharp wit. He was also invaluable as a mirror of the President's moods and methods.

28 April 1962. Washington.

The first day in Washington. Outside the window in the garden the cherry blossoms, pear blossoms, and magnolias are in the perfection of early bloom. A sturdy Italian gardener mops his brow in the heat. The overgrown box hedges scent the air. Inside, a cheerful, polite little Spanish maid trots in and out with breakfast trays. The house exudes the confident, quiet charm of a much-loved and admired Beauty. In all this paradise only Popski is vile. He barks edgily among the bird song and an eye has to be kept on him lest he pee on the acres of pale-coloured carpet.

29 April 1962.

Harold Macmillan is here on a visit to President Kennedy. He met with the Commonwealth Representatives this afternoon. He is certainly my favourite Prime Minister. Talking of Russia he said, "I pin

---

[1] At the time Special Assistant to the President for National Security Affairs, he left government in 1966 to become President of the Ford Foundation.

my faith on them gradually getting more like other people, more and more wanting the same things, so that over generations the differences between us and them will narrow. Meanwhile, do not yield to them but avoid picking quarrels." I hope that this pragmatic point of view is the right one but I am far from confident. Of the Common Market he said, "If we do not join the Common Market, do you imagine that in twenty years' time there will be any question of the President of the United States going to the trouble, as today, of consulting the Prime Minister of Great Britain about anything? Why should he do so? We should have dwindled into a small, unimportant island. Europe with its tens of millions would go on without us."

Mike and Maryon Pearson at dinner last night. Mike looks in fighting trim. He does not expect to win the coming election but he hopes to reduce the government's majority or to prevent them from getting an absolute majority.

7 May 1962.

This prolonged period of waiting to present my Letters of Credence to the President is beginning to get on my nerves and I am wondering whether this delay is deliberate on the part of the White House. Max Freedman, the Winnipeg journalist,[1] says that we are in danger of a state of affairs in which American officials groan when they see a Canadian coming. They think from experience that we are going to grouse over one of our grudges. (As they have a grudge a minute from one ally or another, they must be getting hardened to it.) Max looks back to a time when the Americans turned to us for advice, when we discussed common problems, when Dean Acheson[2] dropped in to this Embassy to compare notes with our Ambassador, Hume Wrong. Now we drop in to protest, and always in the name of Canadian interests, not on the assumption of shared responsibilities. We are reluctant to admit that we are involved with the United States and have adopted an attitude of some detachment, which we associate both with independence and with moral rectitude. Of course no one wants us to agree with every American policy, but there should

---

[1] Max Freedman was with the *Winnipeg Free Press*.

[2] Former United States Secretary of State – statesman and author.

be a dialogue based on common inescapable commitment. By all means let us stand up to them, but let us talk to them rather than protest to them. Look at the British. Ever since Suez they have been diligently cultivating at every level their contacts with the United States. What an absurdity it would be now to claim that Canada is a bridge between the United Kingdom and the United States. We are the odd man out and it is we who have put ourselves in this position, not only by the content of our policy but by the manner of it. Meanwhile this southern spring weather goes on and I wait day after day in this silent and beautiful house with its cool vistas, mirrored reflections, and blond carpets which muffle sound. From the garden rises the scent of box – strong, sweet, and sexy. It blooms in abandon in what was once a formal rose garden with paved paths and disciplined box hedges; at some time the box got out of control and now luxuriates like a jungle of the Amazon. There are flowers everywhere and all in bloom at once – cherry blossoms, magnolia, azalea, wisteria – and in the Judas tree scarlet cardinals flashing from branch to branch. All this is too much after the stone-and-steel landscape of New York. My brain feels drugged and drowned in all this languid sweetness, this trilling of birds and splashing of water in the goldfish pool.

Popski may feel the same. He has just been sick on the upstairs carpet from an indigestible meal of magnolia blossoms.

26 May 1962.

I presented my Letters of Credence to President Kennedy. His reception of me, while perfectly civil, was, I thought, distinctly cool, and I came away with the impression that this reflected his attitude towards the Canadian government and particularly towards Mr. Diefenbaker. He seemed deliberately to be creating "a distance." The conversation was routine and with longish pauses. During one of these the President half rose from the rocking chair in which he was sitting, stretched out his arms, and said, "Shoo, shoo." For a moment I was frozen in my place. The thought passed through my mind that I might be the first ambassador in history to be shooed out of the White House. I didn't see that behind the sofa on which I was sitting, coming through the French windows out of the garden, was his young daughter, the little girl Caroline, leading her pet pony. They hastily backed out of the window into the garden but my reaction will give some idea of the uncomfortable coolness of the atmosphere created. What impression did I have of the President? I had not quite expected the waxy pallor of his skin. I felt that the man and the image coincided with uncanny precision, as though he was indeed a TV image rather than a human being. Even during our strained conversation his calculating, live intelligence was clear, as was the cutting edge of his will and the jauntiness of his manner.

28 May 1962.

My grandmother, Eliza Almon, was a girl of eighteen in the year 1838 when she wrote her diary, which I have just been reading. Her life was outwardly narrow and funless. She was not an adventurous or pleasure-loving girl and, as she had no eye for character, landscape, or anecdote, her diary is damn dull except in one particular. As to her daily existence, she lived at Rosebank, then a country house on the outskirts of Halifax. The property is now engulfed in streets, though the old stone gates with their rose emblem remain. It was a life of reading, studying French and Italian, sewing, helping with the "housekeeping," going to church twice on Sunday, and walking over to a neighbouring house, Oatlands, on the North-West Arm, to see a female friend. Her reading list is wide for a miss in Nova Scotia in those days. It includes Chateaubriand, Byron, Scott, Ford (*The Witch of Edmonton*), Fanny Burney, Disraeli, volumes of French memoirs, and of course Shakespeare, but the real drama of her diary is her spiritual life. Church attendance and good works did not interest her. It was the inner life that absorbed her, and she wrote that she would "more than any temporal evil that could befall me fear being left to the Form of godliness without its life and support." This theme grows in strength and intensity as the journal goes on. It was to be the theme of her life, and she shared this passionately personal religion with her cousin James. When they wrote to each other it was to discuss the sermons they had heard. When she married him she persuaded him to give up the world in the form of a promising career at the Bar and become an unhappy and ill-suited evangelical country clergyman. She died of diphtheria at the age of forty-two, leaving my father and his brother and sisters motherless children. After her death she was always spoken of by the family as a Christian, selfless saint, but my poor grandfather went on fulfilling his duties as a clergyman without heart, enthusiasm, or interest – perhaps without faith?

30 May 1962.

Went to the Cathedral and heard a full and eloquent sermon, but I can't abide sermons, even the best of them. Arnold Heeney, my predecessor here, was a pillar of the Cathedral, which is more, I fear, than I shall ever be. He is a thoroughgoing Christian of the Anglican persuasion, and his religion, I am sure, guides him steadily in life. During the sermon I kept thinking of the gospel for the day, which included "Knock and it shall be opened unto you." Will it be opened for me? Or don't I knock hard enough? The other day I met a young red-haired Canon of the Cathedral (at any rate, young for a canon) and asked him what was the essential quality for a clergyman, and he won my heart by at once replying "compassion." Then he added, "That is what *I* think; others would tell you 'leadership.'"

This is a somnolent Sunday afternoon. Sylvia is asleep in the garden room, Popski asleep in the library, the servants have disappeared to their quarters for a long siesta. Even the birds have gone off the air. It should be a day for reading poetry rather than the prose of T. H. White, author of *The Making of the President, 1960*, a useful, informative book about the workings of American politics. I am filled up to the throat with its gassy, fluent style. It is the story of an American hero by an American hero-worshipper; "There is no ceremony more splendid than the inauguration of an American President," etc. etc. It's all a bit too much to swallow on a hot summer afternoon.

2 June 1962.

Encounter with a leading name-dropper. He began in top form, firing two governors general, the Leader of the Opposition, a French duchess, and John D. Rockefeller across my bows and all but sinking me. Then he began to talk of the Art of Living. I told him that the words meant nothing to me. He admitted modestly that his own understanding of the Art went back to his aristocratic Viennese origins, but he thought I had mastered it, up to a point. "But no," I insisted, "I shall never understand the Art of Living." After three cocktails he rather relaxed and I found myself remembering that I had liked him when we were younger, perhaps before he had so completely mastered the Art of Living.

I walked this morning in Dumbarton Oaks Park by the brown, quick-running stream, then into the close, dark woods of the bird sanctuary and on to the grassy path by the big meadow. Talked at the entrance gate with the gardener, a gnarled, ageless troll. "Been working here for twenty-two years," he told me. "Twenty-seven acres to keep up and not a man or boy to help me." I remember walking in this park in 1939 on the day before I left Washington for my posting to London, and how I came back that morning to the garden of the house in Georgetown and, biting into a peach at breakfast, fancied that I was biting into the fruit of my future in London ... how I would write a masterpiece, meet the famous, have a flat of my own and a mistress to go with it. A bright dream – it all came true, except, of course, the masterpiece.

5 June 1962.

Lunched today with Scotty Reston, the Washington correspondent of the *New York Times*. He has been a good friend to me since I came here and is wonderful company. He and Walter Lippmann, and in a different way Henry Brandon,[1] are a refreshment and a stimulus after diplomatic society. They are also far more important in the political world of Washington than any ambassador. I spoke to Scotty about my unsatisfactory conversation with the President, and by way of consolation he said that in any case the President had not much use for professional diplomats and thinks them a lesser breed of men who are useful if they produce facts or memoranda but do not take the risks or face the decisions of politics. He says that this attitude dates back to the days when the President's father was Ambassador in London, and to the contemptuous view that old Kennedy took of his diplomatic staff.

9 June 1962.

Went to New York to hear Prince Philip make a speech to the Wildlife Fund, which was really an excuse for me to revisit New York.

---

[1] Henry Brandon, correspondent for the London *Sunday Times*.

The city was tricked out in all its best and sending electric impulses of energy into its victims. The women on the streets were as fresh as paint. Girls hipped along the avenue, disdaining the look in the men's eyes. Old painted shrews from Vienna days and matrons from Wisconsin peered into the windows of Bergdorf Goodman. Husky, helmeted workmen, stripped to the waist, lounged over lunch beneath the girders. Inside the monster buildings, middle-aged time-addicts watched for the elevators with hop-eyed intensity and shifted from foot to foot. In Central Park schoolmarms were lining up squads of kids to look at the elephants and watch the seals dive.

13 June 1962.

Dinner the other night with Susan Mary and Jo Alsop.[1] Seeing Susan Mary brings back memories of all the gaieties of the time in Paris when we first met. I delight in her company and feel that among so many acquaintances she is a friend. Jo is an original, a brilliant journalist and talker, but cantankerous. There is a great cult for him in his circle in Washington. The other day someone said to me, "You must come on Thursday. Jo is coming and is in a very good mood." I felt inclined to answer, "I'd love to come if *I* am in a good mood."

I had a note today from Freddy Boland, the Irish Representative at the U.N. and an enlivening friend. How much of the friendships made at that time depended on the shared talk of the U.N.? In that U.N. shop there were friendships formed closer than between most diplomats. Those who served together at the U.N. are like soldiers who served together in the trenches – no matter which side we fought on, we know something of the rough-and-tumble of international politics that other gilt-edged ambassadors do not know. When I left, one of my colleagues said, "Don't worry about the workload in Washington. Your problem there will be boredom."

And I am ashamed to say that I *am* bored, and this despite the office responsibilities and the incessant social life. It is something to do with this place, this beautiful, bland city, after the high-pressure

---

[1] Joseph Alsop, author of column "Matter of Fact," syndicated through the *Washington Post* and later the *Los Angeles Times* syndicates, and his wife, Susan Mary, authoress.

excitement of New York. This mood has been intensified by reading Durrell's *Mountolive*, which treats of the fate of an ambassador, of the attrition of human ties to which this profession can lead, and of the airless state in which diplomats learn to breathe. Oddly enough, the ambassador in this book has as a companion a pet dachshund who, like Popski, pees on the Embassy carpet.

I suppose if one yawns one's way through a summer day it finally finishes. I can hear the swish of the Spanish maid's broom on the terrace as she sweeps up the dead blossoms fallen from the overspreading acacia tree. The potent smell of box comes in waves from the garden through the still air up to my bedroom window. I have taken off my shirt in this heat and I smell of boxwood as if I were oiled in a bath essence. Damn it, should I take up golf, as the nice New Zealand Ambassador advises? Or hand round the collection plate in the Cathedral with a carnation in my buttonhole? Or shall I end up as that joke figure, a dirty old man?

16 June 1962.

One of the features that emerges from my talks with American officials is their negative attitude towards the Commonwealth. Any reference to its importance in the world falls on deaf ears or elicits an occasional conventionally polite agreement. There are, I think, several reasons for this. The Americans do not like the fact that it includes so many neutralist nations and that it cannot be counted on to support them in an East-West confrontation. There still remains a residual jealousy of it as a hangover of British world leadership. They are now thinking in terms of continental blocs on a global scale, and the Commonwealth cuts across this concept. Or perhaps they simply estimate that it has no future, that its bonds are loosening and will loosen further, that it is a dead duck – or at any rate a dying duck. In terms of Canadian–U.S. relations there may be another consideration at the back of their minds. If the Commonwealth declines or disappears, there will finally be an end to the Canadian balancing act between London and Washington, and we shall inevitably drift further into the American bloc. Certainly London would not raise a finger to prevent this, indeed would view such a development with complete indifference. However, the continued existence of the Commonwealth is important for Canada in other terms – not only because of the advantages of Commonwealth preferences for us but because in its present multiracial form it is partly of our making. We were instrumental in the evolution of Empire into old white Commonwealth, and white Commonwealth into new multiracial Commonwealth. The preference system is perhaps not essential to its continuance but it is an important part of it and a part that is important for Canada. Why should the Americans approve the European Common Market and disapprove of Commonwealth preferences?

19 June 1962.

Henry Brandon of the *Sunday Times* says that the Canadian government has succeeded in alienating both London and Washington by a mixture of self-righteousness and self-centredness. I think we have got to start looking at developments in the Western world and to try to assess our relationships to them anew. There is no sign of this in the parochial character of our elections. But the United States cannot really be indifferent to the fate of their biggest trading partner and their continental defence partner, so what are their calculations? Are they waiting for us to fall into their laps? Do they discount as mere bluff the anti-Americanism now rampant in Canada and make the calculation that we have got to give in to them in the end, probably hat in hand, and that the rest is posturing?

29 June 1962.

Lunched today with Jim Barco, of the U.S. Mission to the U.N., and the Soviet Ambassador and Madame Dobrynin. Dobrynin skates with skill and ease over the thinnest ice and allows himself a latitude in conversation unlike that of any Soviet ambassador I have ever known. To think that one would live to see the day when Russian and American diplomats gaily joked together about the U-2 incident. Dobrynin is certainly one of the most skilful operators I have encountered in the career. He and I got to know each other when he was in the U.N. Secretariat in New York and are by way of being very friendly. Madame Dobrynin has much smartened up since those days – very cheerful and chatty when she used to be severely silent, and with her hair curled instead of being austerely drawn back from her forehead, her original Soviet-Communist-wife image considerably modified by life in the United States.

30 June 1962. Evening.

Voices and music from a next-door party sounding from behind the screen of heavy-leafed trees bordering the garden. The music plucks at some lost feeling. The women's voices sound languorous and enticing. It is true, no doubt, that the encounters between people at that party are as forced as at the party I have just left, that most are looking beyond each other's left ear to sight someone more important to talk to. The laughter in most cases does not contain in its volume one hundredth part of real laughter and is as tasteless as frozen ham, but perhaps it is worth coming to a garden setting under the glassy, unreal light of late evening if two people on the outskirts of the party remember it as the moment when they first met, and carry the memory that it was *there* that it all started.

4 July 1962.

A cool, overcast national holiday on which we are going out to the country. Tennis for others, and a barbecue. I do not much enjoy these American days in the country. There is so much hanging about, and there are so many children and young-to-middle-aged mothers watching with half an eye that they don't get into the deep end of the swimming pool. Besides, no one ever goes for a walk.

Mitchell Sharp has come to see me. He has gone into politics and just failed by a small minority to beat the Minister of Finance. He appeared flushed with political excitement. To see a quiet civil servant so transformed is astounding – his discovery of himself as a "national figure" and the inaugurator of new election techniques, etc., is remarkable. But most of all, at the wave of a wand he has become a revelation to himself of his own possibilities. Perhaps I should go into politics!

9 July 1962.

A mixed day. In the morning I went to see George Ball[1]. He is one of the most intelligent and attractive figures in the State Department,

---

[1] U.S. Undersecretary of State.

but in negotiation, without being unfriendly, he has shown very little understanding of our position and no disposition to concede anything. In the afternoon, Dick Howland of the Smithsonian Institution came to see me. I was trying to induce him to lend the Hope Diamond from their collection for a Canadian exhibition. We had a very pleasant talk about pictures and people. But he won't part with the Hope Diamond.

15 July 1962.

A neurotic weekend with the servants: the Spanish-speaking maids, with tears filling their large, dark eyes as they tried to explain their devotion to us and their desire to have more time off; Sylvia and the cook, without a common language, stare at each other in dismay and irritation; Colin, the butler, ex-Royal Navy, is a young Scottish martinet, very bossy with the maids, disliked by Sylvia, most meticulous in looking after my clothes, extremely conscious of his status as a butler, which he seems to think gives him dictatorial power over the rest of the staff. Meanwhile, the chauffeur was drunk again last night. I have seen this coming on. If I had spoken to him day before yesterday, when the first signs were visible, I might have stopped him. But as it was disagreeable, I put it off, as I always do put off disagreeable things. And now, I must get rid of him. I suppose if he had not got drunk tonight he would have done it a month or so later. Tonight he drove us right past our house, up the drive into a restricted area at an American military establishment, and stopped the car outside the front door, having apparently mistaken it for our house. I think he has tried to stop drinking but can't. Yet Arnold Heeney kept him on for seven years and never allowed it to come to this. Perhaps it is my fault, in the effect I have on him. I drove the chauffeur in New York nearly out of his mind, and now this chap has taken to the bottle. If he is dismissed at his age, what will happen to him? How can I give him a recommendation, a drunken chauffeur? He's through. Yet he fought in the Dutch Resistance, he's a real man, he's responsible, a professional, never had an accident and probably never will. He has sacrificed his life and career. I might do the same tomorrow, though not for the same reason. How can I judge him? I'll have to discuss it with Harry Stewart at the Embassy and see if something could not be found for him. Damn, damn, damn!

A horde of people are coming to a reception here tomorrow and I am not looking forward to it. It is not that I get bored with other people – it is that I get bored with hearing myself talk to other people.

27 July 1962.

Do the Americans realize that our differences of outlook from them in international affairs make us more valuable to them than if we were mere satellites? I sometimes doubt it. For example, in nuclear matters we are dead against continued tests, so they foolishly accuse us of letting down NATO. Yet now in the anti-test Geneva negotiations we have been able, because of our anti-test attitude, to develop a relationship with the neutral nations which we could never have achieved otherwise, and which has been helpful to NATO. If we had, at U.S. urging, pushed anti-communist protests in the Indo-China Commissions too far and broken out of the Commissions, the whole machinery would have collapsed, and that presumably is not what the United States want. They sometimes give the impression that they do not trust us, but in the long run they do. Why otherwise would they want us in the Organization of American States (which I hope we shall not join)? Now there is a new test case in our policy towards Cuba. Our position is perfectly justifiable, but we have not thought through its implications and simply take the line that as the Cubans have not seized our banks, etc., why should we pull American chestnuts out of the fire? This begs the question as to whether there is a dangerous Communist threat in South America. Sometimes we grudgingly admit this as a possibility. Do we consider what has happened in Cuba as a popular social revolution and not a Russian-inspired Communist takeover? Is our attitude affected by the fact that, like Cuba, we are a neighbour of the United States? It is unthinkable that anything similar to developments in Cuba should occur in Canada, but if it did, should we not regard this as our own business and resent intervention? In general in our dealings with Communist countries we have tended to be against the policies of economic strangulation (even more against military intervention). While we have never spelled out our views, they seemed to amount to the proposition that economic pressure, sanctions, etc., applied to

Communist countries, so far from making them more amenable, make them dig their heels in more deeply. Presumably this is the philosophy behind our trade with China. Of course, our economic interests are the concrete reasons for our policy, but in the background is a philosophical difference as to how best to deal with Communist countries, and our position, though obscurely defined, is basically different from that of the United States.

The more I am involved in diplomatic and political affairs, the more I set store on private feelings. I prefer my loved ones to any political allegiance, and hope I always shall. Henry Brandon talks of his friendship with President Kennedy, with whom he is on easy, almost intimate, terms. I listened with interest and a growing sense of my own lack of contact with the President. Apart from the political strain between him and Diefenbaker, perhaps I am myself out of date – Old Hat in the New Frontier. Washington has always been like this. The "In" people make the "Outs" feel even "Out"-er. It is the same in Ottawa.

12 August 1962. Halifax, N.S.

We have escaped from Washington for a couple of weeks to come down here with Roley[1] and Bunny and to see my mother. Today is overcast and claggy, the same weather they have had here all summer. Never a day without the sound of the foghorn. It is Sunday, after lunch. It is impossible to believe that one will ever come to life again, impossible to picture life except as a yawn. I cannot walk again in the dank park among the firs and hemlocks. I can't go on reading *Vanity Fair* as I am bogged down among Amelia's tender tears and rhapsodies and I will not skip to get back to Becky Sharp. Popski is bored too. We should never have brought him here. He is driving me mad this afternoon. I mean that not in the casual conventional sense – there really are moments when I tremble for my sanity and fear that if he does not stop barking something will crack in my skull and I shall start barking myself. Poor little brute, he is terrified of the steep, slippery staircase in this house. It takes all his courage and resolution

---

[1] My brother, Roland Ritchie, Justice of the Supreme Court of Canada, and his wife, Bunny.

to launch himself from the top step, as if it was a precipitous ski slope, and then he slithers and crashes to the bottom.

Roley is lying asleep in a deck-chair on the damp lawn, looking like Sylvia's sketch of himself. Sylvia and Bunny are making cucumber sandwiches because the Misses Odell are coming to tea. They are Cranfordian, genteel spinsters, unpopularly invited by me. My mother has taken to her bed, totally exhausted by her family. My niece Eliza[1] has simply gone off the air. A dull Sunday afternoon, but not repulsive. As a family we are happy together, glad to be together, enjoying each other's company more than that of other people, though tomorrow we give our first – and last – cocktail party. The matter of the list of guests has given rise to reproach from my mother because we have not invited a certain couple whom the other guests do not know and may consider socially inferior. The argument for not inviting them is that they would not enjoy coming as they would only be uncomfortable and incompatible. My mother treats this with scorn, as being nothing but snobbery. I am alone on her side.

26 August 1962. Washington.

I have just returned from Ottawa, where I was summoned to attend Dean Rusk's visit. I flew back here with him in his private jet and had a long talk with him on the plane about all outstanding Canadian-American problems. As on previous occasions, when we are alone and he is out of the office, he talked to me very frankly and told me what was worrying him about our relations, dropping the cautious politeness which he used in his presentation to our Ministers. He talked to me as if we were two officials who shared common assumptions, rather than a Foreign Minister and an Ambassador. If I encourage him in this I cannot complain of the bluntness of his language, but I must not give him the impression that I am detaching myself from the position of our government. It is sometimes a fine line to walk.

Is there something sly about Rusk, a demure slyness like an unfrocked Abbé? Yet I respect his ability and enjoy his company.

---

[1] My niece, Elizabeth Ritchie, daughter of Roley and Bunny, is called Eliza in these diaries to avoid confusion with Elizabeth Bowen.

28 August 1962.

The Department of External Affairs is becoming more and more a branch office of a huge expanding bureaucracy. Our Foreign Service is becoming more and more like other Foreign Services. This is inevitable, but it does not suit me. I loved the old, small, ramshackle Department where eccentricity was tolerated and where everyone was a generalist who flew by the seat of his pants.

The Victorian Gothic of the East Block was the perfect setting for the Department as it was in those days. The building makes no concessions to efficiency and is a standing rebuke to progress. How many of the waking hours of my life I have spent there; how well I know the dark attics with windows at floor level, one of which I shared as a junior with Temp Feaver and Alfred Rive, and later, on my progress upward in the Service, the spacious rooms with their monumental fireplaces, which were reserved for senior officials. How often have I trod those echoing stone-floored corridors and caught the dusty, musty smell that lingers there from the 1870s. How often have I paused, leaning on that ironwork balustrade that looks down on the pit of the entrance hall, trying to pull together my thoughts before an interview with the Minister or the Prime Minister of the day in his office in the corridor beyond. And how often, too, have I paused there again on my way back after the interview, to curse myself for being talked out of the point of policy that I was trying to make.

I thought I knew every inch of the old place, yet the last time I was in Ottawa I made an unfortunate mistake. Hurrying on my way to see Mr. Diefenbaker about the current crisis, I darted into what I mistook for the men's WC. What was my horror when I heard outside the toilet closet the sound of women's voices! Fortunately, my presence was concealed by the swinging door that screened the closet – screened, but only to knee level. I determined to stay there until the coast was clear, and tucked my trousered legs around the toilet bowl on which I was seated, to avoid identification. The wait seemed interminable. I had had no notion of how much hair-patting, nose-powdering, and lipstick touching-up goes on among females in these places. No sooner would one leave than another arrived; there was no empty interlude. As to the chat among them, it became positively embarrassing when I heard one of the secretaries giving a living imitation of one of my more tiresome colleagues dictating one of his long-winded memoranda. At last I could stand it no longer. I was cramped from the position in which I was seated, and I was apprehensive as to what more I might overhear – perhaps an imitation of myself. So I swung open the partition and walked through them, without looking from left to right lest I should have the awkwardness of recognizing someone whom I might afterwards encounter in a corridor or office. An astounded hush descended on the ladies at my appearance. What they said afterwards I shall thank God I never knew.

31 August 1962.

I rang up Vincent Massey yesterday and said that I wanted to call on his "experience and imagination" in developing our academic and cultural relations with the United States, as I am very conscious that this side of things is being neglected and that being Ambassador to the United States should mean more than just negotiating in the old civil-servant way with government departments. But I have no capacity for launching a project of my own in this domain. Vincent, I thought, sounded a little cool and dry and said, reasonably enough, that he had no ideas "out of the blue" but invited me to stay with him later in the autumn so that we could talk the matter over.

I saw in the National Gallery today a Crucifixion by (I think) Matthias Grünewald. Christ's body on the cross is in a state almost of dissolution; the face and position of the head show a collapse beyond the pale of sustained suffering. This is the mortal body that dies in corruption. It brought me with a shock to understand that Christ's becoming Man meant that he too came to this subhuman stage of collapse, so different is this picture from the noble, consciously suffering figures on the cross in most renderings of the Crucifixion. Also there is in the Gallery a curiosity of a picture – Christ in limbo among the lost souls. One somehow forgets about that period when Christ "descended into Hell."

29 September 1962.

I have just come back from New York. Yesterday I was walking along Fifth Avenue in the air and light of early-October New York, with the women passing in their newly fashionable bowler hats, and

I was on my way to vodka martinis at the Côte Basque with my pocket full of money. The sun shafts lit on a pansy designer's window full of flowers in baroque vases and it looked as gay and artificial as the designer's dream of it. Men whistled in the street, middle-aged women smiled ineffably, construction workers in scarlet- and wasp-coloured helmets squatted together munching midday sandwiches. In the Central Park pool the seals drifted lazily, half under water. No one for the moment was being robbed or raped or thinking of jumping from fourteenth-floor windows. It was benign October in the well-loved, over-praised city.

Oh, how have my contemporaries attained their self-esteem, how have they added, brick on brick, to the stable structure of a personality that can be turned inside out, public and private, and look the same? Oh, to have principles, to have faith, to have grandchildren, to grow up before you grow old.

30 September 1962.

The Canadian government has certainly made it abundantly plain that we are against nuclear arms as one is against sin, and this moral attitude is shared by the most sophisticated (Norman Robertson) and the least so among Canadians. It is exemplified in the figure of Howard Green. It is not only a moral attitude, but also hygienic; the two often go together in Canada. Fallout is filthy in every sense of the word. This reaction, strong in many parts of the world, is particularly strong at home. It is from this soil that our disarmament policy grows. That policy may not be rational, but it is very Canadian. Don't forget that for most of our history we were protected by the British navy and now we are protected by the United States' nuclear bomb. All this may be peculiar, it may be unjustifiable, it may be irrational, it may be irresponsible – but no political leader of any stamp is prepared to go to the Canadian people and tell them that they must have nuclear arms or store nuclear arms. This may change with a change of government; if so, gradually. This is a deep policy difference between us and the United States. At any rate, so long as the present government lasts, (a) we will not fill the Bomarc gap; (b) we don't want nuclear arms for the RCAF overseas; (c) we will not store nuclear weapons; (d) we are against the resumption by the United States of nuclear tests. The

United States wants all four of these from us. They are exasperated by our attitude, but so far they are holding their hand. It remains to be seen how long they will resist the temptation to bring pressure upon us of a kind that might bring about a change of government.

As it turned out, the diarist did not have long to wait to witness both American exasperation and American pressure. The precipitant was the Cuban missile crisis in October 1962. The Canadian government resented the United States' delay in informing them that the Russians were installing offensive weapons with nuclear warheads in Cuba, all the more so as Canadian forces were an integral part of NORAD, the defence organization of North America. The Prime Minister considered that, at this moment of crisis when the issue of peace and war was at stake, Canadian support had been taken for granted without adequate consultation. The President was involved from day to day, indeed from hour to hour, in the most testing crisis of his career. The handling of the crisis involved speed, accuracy of timing, and secrecy. In view of the reluctance of the Canadian government to be involved in any action likely to be provocative to the U.S.S.R., it is hardly to be wondered at that the Americans did not wish to become embroiled in discussion with us of the daring moves that they were contemplating to meet the Russian threat. Their reluctance to consult no doubt seemed to them justified when Ottawa hesitated to put Canada on a state of alert, only finally doing so on October 24. Even then, further friction arose when the Prime Minister asserted that the President had asked him to declare a state of emergency in Canada when no such state had been proclaimed in the United States itself. The atmosphere of mutual recrimination that followed between Washington and Ottawa made this a difficult time for the Canadian Ambassador. I regarded the subject matter of the dispute and the high degree of security involved as excluding it from my private diaries. At the time, it was my task, and by no means an easy one, to expound our position over nuclear arms and to explain that we could not go along with any decisions of theirs which might risk a nuclear war without the opportunity to make an informed and independent judgement. Our government had its own responsibilities to the people of Canada. This point of view was represented in Cabinet most tenaciously by our Minister of External Affairs, Howard Green, who in addition had staked his international reputation on his opposition in the United Nations to nuclear testing and at home to nuclear arms on our soil. As to the Prime Minister, I doubted whether he had deep conviction on the nuclear issue, and thought him more influenced by his resentment at Canada's being taken for granted by the United States. The split in the Cabinet over the issue resulted in the resignation of the Minister of National Defence, Douglas Harkness, who favoured the acquisition of nuclear weapons by the Canadian armed forces.

In January 1963 General Norstad, the American retiring NATO Commander, visited Ottawa and at a news conference stated that Canada would not be fulfilling its NATO commitments if we did not acquire nuclear warheads. I found it impossible to take seriously the American official explanation that he was speaking not as a U.S. representative but in his former NATO capacity. This was another American turn of the screw to bring down the Conservative government. In that same month Mike Pearson reversed his previous stand and in a public speech advocated the acceptance of nuclear weapons by Canada.

16 December 1962.

Dined last night with Bill and Mary Bundy. Bill is now in the Defense Department[1] and Mary is the daughter of Dean Acheson, and very much his daughter too. They are New Frontier and so a welcome change from the collection of ex-ambassadors, Republican businessmen with jewelled wives, and outdated hostesses whom I have been seeing lately. Mary says that her parents are "the gazelle and the lion" – Alice beautiful, gentle, retiring; Dean proud, active, and lord of the jungle – but that now in old age their roles are changing. Her mother sits on Democratic committees while her father more and more loves writing, reflection, and pottering in his potting shed.

At the Bundys' were the Winklers of the French Embassy and the Geylins, he a journalist and his wife, Sherry, an auburn-haired

---

[1] At this time, William Bundy was Deputy Assistant Secretary of Defense for International Security Affairs.

romantic beauty. The Winklers are the only diplomats in Washington who seem universally acceptable. They glide unemphatically from coterie to coterie, welcomed and cherished by all, and are leaving shortly, without any excessive regrets, to return to Paris.

Elizabeth [Bowen] is here. I said to her today that the chilly exhilaration of her new book, *The Little Girls*, must spring from revenge. "Oh yes," she said, implying "you don't know the half of it."

Looking about at the people in the room she remarked, "God has not made enough faces to go round."

19 December 1962.

Lunched with Scotty Reston. I like him very much as a friend and an enjoyable companion. Underneath his Americanism is a Scottish subsoil very down-to-earth. I also find him invaluable as a barometer of the political temperature in this city. It is not only that he is extraordinarily well informed, but he has a flair not only for news but for the changing moods, psychological as well as political, of this volatile country. He can sniff a shift in the wind quicker than anyone I know. At the moment he talks in terms of the New Frontier pragmatism. Its practitioners like to think of themselves as tough, young, and hard-headed. McNamara is their hero. I admire them, within limits, but mistrust the application of the business computer to international affairs, particularly when it is allied to power and the love of power.

22 December 1962.

When I woke this morning and saw sun on the melting snow I closed my eyes, pulled the eiderdown over my head, and wished that I lived by myself in an isolated autumnal château in France with high walls round it, with books, a fire in the library, the smell of leaf mould in the garden outside. It was last night's dance that did me in. The guests were all old friends, my Washington pals – twenty-five years later – bringing out into society some their daughters and some their granddaughters. Conversation was a ghostly echo of old jokes and flirtations. Some have been friends or lovers of others; now their children dance together into another generation. Standing in the doorway of the ballroom, beside two ex-young men of my former dancing generation, I was overwhelmed with such a sense of strangeness to think that this grey-haired old guy was I, that youthful eyes travelled over me with that total unseeing indifference which one reserves for lampposts. I did not feel sad, only almost dizzy with the impact of time, hit in the solar plexus by it.

But time stood still when I saw the eternal Tony Balásy waltzing, waltzing in the style he learned in Budapest before the First World War. Gentle, sociable, herbivorous Tony, a gentlemanly giraffe, now nearly seventy. He was the friend of my early days in Washington when he was in the Hungarian Legation, then during the war in London. When Hungary entered the war on the Nazi side he had the courage to resign from his country's diplomatic service, and now has some minor job in Washington and lives in bachelor solitude in a hotel here. Is there something spectral about Tony? A phantom is he? with his elongated, fleshless figure and those bony hands that grip one at the elbow as his mild voice murmurs, "'Allo, Charlie old man."

27 December 1962.

If only one could discard the wardrobe of stale thoughts, concepts, habits, desires, fancies – bundle them off to the old-clothes man. Perhaps that is what Heaven is, to be rid of this accumulation.

A completely still, completely colourless day, of a desolating dullness. It reminds me of some day in my childhood, when I stood alone in the melting snow in a mouldering backyard, wondering what on earth to play.

Only the greedy, ill-tempered little birds are alive in the still garden, engaged in competitive pecking at the food which Sylvia has hung in a bird's hors-d'oeuvre tray from a tree. I am like the old man in Byron's *Don Juan*, trying to get through a long day – "at sixty I wait for six." Damn it, I had forgotten that 350 people are coming to this house this very afternoon to swizzle and guzzle, and the cook is preparing prodigies in the kitchen while Colin, the butler, sets up trestle tables and bars and clears the room of obstructive furniture.

I must stop scribbling and work on my notes for tomorrow's meeting with the State Department on the Nassau Agreement.

28 December 1962.

Had lunch with an old State Department friend in the gloom of the Cosmos Club, surrounded by dreadful portraits of dreadful old men. He is mourning the death of his ninety-nine-year-old mother. (He himself must be nearing seventy.) Apart from intervals of diplomatic travel he has always lived with his mother and her death has shattered him. His friends find it hard not to find something comic in his stricken state of bereavement. His sister has sensibly – or cruelly – insisted on selling the family home, dispersing the old servants. Now he finds himself exiled to a world of clubs and dependent on luncheon invitations from dowagers. He talked to me today of his lucky escapes all his life from emotional entanglements. He has indeed escaped everything – except Mother. But who is to say that in his love for her he hasn't had as full a life as his contemporaries who married, begat, and took chances?

Reading Genet at disturbing intervals. Am I an existentialist without knowing it? He writes that to utter the words "we doctors" (or "we diplomats"!) shows that a man is in bondage, that that "we" is a parasitical creature who sucks his blood. Perhaps this is what one senses in one's friends who have "improved" with age – that in improving they have diminished from fear of freedom.

29 December 1962.

Went to St. John's Church (the old small church opposite the White House) – poinsettias, carols, and comfortable pews. That old tart Mrs. X was sitting in front of us with a black velvet bow affixed to her doubtfully-auburn hair. Episcopalianism is a long way from existentialism. Then Sylvia and I, accompanied by Popski, went for a married walk. How I do love Sylvia. I can see her now through the window, trundling about the garden in her beige coat with the fur collar. I can hear her scraping earth out of a flower pot and the knocking of the trowel against the pot's surface. It is a mild winter day with a spring sky and some failing snow still on the ground. The birds in the garden are bustling. I feel an after-church drowsiness coming over me and could fall, like Alice in Wonderland, down a deep, deep well.

Yes, I did fall asleep and now it is three o'clock on Sunday afternoon, the day and hour of my birth and always the low ebb of the week for me. But I must bestir myself – Susan Mary Alsop and Dick Howland are coming to tea.

Later: It was very pleasant, tea and cinnamon toast before the library fire, and with Dick and Susan Mary a rich and varied diet of Washington gossip – political, social, with the arts thrown in.

21 January 1963. Corpus Christi, Texas.

This non-stop tour through Texas has addled my wits. I have given the same spiel in every town – "how happy I am to set foot on Texan soil for the first time," "the links between Canada and Texas," how "Canada is big and so is Texas." Well, there is the famous hospitality, the good nature and friendliness of the people which no one but a crustaceous old boor could despise. Then one is always appreciating, going "ooh, aah, how big it is, how beautiful." No one here ever says anything critical about their own town, each rejoices in living in the best community in Texas (or the world!). This perpetual self-praise rises hourly to Heaven, like incense. Texas is another dimension; it is a cult, too, from which no dissent can be tolerated. It has its converts, not all born Texans. The tall clean-cut young man with the cowboy hat and the Texan accent who has been showing us around Dallas is one of these. When I asked him what part of Texas he came from, his accent seemed to change as he replied, with some embarrassment, "As a matter of fact, I come from Prince Edward Island." The most frightening city in Texas is Dallas, which consists of tall office buildings and hotels entirely surrounded by mile upon mile of carparks. In one direction are the segregated homes of the rich, in another the segregated homes of the poor. The heart of the city has been eliminated. There are no side streets, no small shops, and nothing familiar to attach to. All the inhabitants I have encountered have the same absolutely smooth surface of relentless good humour and optimism. Yet I suppose someone in Dallas must have time to read, to idle, to mope, to be critical and bad-tempered.

This is the Bible belt, grown rich yet clinging to its values. The oil world is of course an international fraternity. These people are as much at home in Saudi Arabia and Iran as they are in Calgary or Dallas. They fly round the world at the drop of a hat, yet they remain closed to all alien ideas, tone deaf to outside influences. They carry the assurance of their own superiority with them wherever they go. And it is a many-sided sense of superiority. They feel superior in health, techniques, hygiene, and morals, and certainly superior in friendliness.

The Texans I have met distrust and despise the following: the President of the United States, Washington and all its works, New York City and all its inhabitants, the eastern United States in general, foreigners, Catholics, Irish, Mexicans, and blacks, and, as a combination of all that they distrust most, the United Nations. I keep trying to steer the conversation away from the fact that I have served in the United Nations, as any discussion of that organization leads straight onto the shoals, and I am not here on a conversion mission.

Yet everywhere we go – kindness, courtesy, warmth of welcome. This courtesy of theirs is not only on the surface; they will take trouble, do things which are tiresome for them and which put out their lives, and then say, with real warmth, "It is *our* pleasure."

25 January 1963.

How strange it is always to be seeing one's country from abroad as I do. One becomes very conscious, perhaps over-conscious, of the showing that Canada makes in the eyes of others. Perhaps one begins to care too much about what others think. Also, one builds up a sort of ideal Canada in one's own mind which may have increasingly little to do with reality. What depresses me is the thick coating of self-congratulation which covers every Canadian official statement. This eternal boasting to Canadians about their own achievements when heard abroad sounds painfully embarrassing, especially when combined with a sort of Rotarian optimism about the future in which all Canadian politicians of every party indulge. As for the material with which the Department of External Affairs supplies us for dissemination to the press, it is headed straight for the editorial wastepaper basket. Much of it consists of the texts of speeches (frequently out of date) by Canadian Ministers, aimed at their own constituents and with no relation whatever to American interests and concerns.

I am lucky to have Basil Robinson as No. 2 in this Mission. He has a good tough mind and great sensitivity to the currents of politics, which he has learned in a hard school during his service in the Prime

Minister's Office. And he has a passion for integrity and fairness. In addition, I feel him to be a friend and an enjoyable companion. But I think he has his own dry, ruthless yardstick of judgement in which sentiment, I believe, plays little part. At any rate, he avoids making me feel that I am a schoolmaster who has neglected to do his homework and is lagging badly behind the cleverer boys in the class, besides being morally somewhat questionable. This is an attitude conveyed by some of the smugger members of our Department. I find it tiresome. Politicians are infuriated by it in their dealings with the Department. Basil and Ross Campbell are the boys to watch. Ross plays things with more dash – tough little bird. I wonder how he'll end up. He is extremely fertile in policy expedients. Basil is used to the winds of politics but, as a good civil servant, he holds onto his hat in a political gale. Ross might throw his hat over the windmill.

In order to make the following entries comprehensible I should recall that on January 25, 1963, the Prime Minister made a statement in the House of Commons in which he made it clear that he did not regard the storage of nuclear weapons on Canadian soil as part of our NATO commitment. At the same time he indicated that his understanding of the Nassau Agreement, reached a month earlier by President Kennedy and Prime Minister Harold Macmillan of Britain, was a justification for a few months' more delay in arming the Canadian weapons system. On January 30 the Department of State in Washington issued a press release challenging the Prime Minister's interpretation of the nuclear negotiations which had been taking place in secret between the Canadian and United States governments. The Prime Minister was infuriated by what he saw, to use his own words, as "an unwarranted intrusion in Canadian affairs." I had been finding the delays, ambiguities, and indecision of the Diefenbaker government on the subject of nuclear weapons on Canadian soil not easy to explain and defend in Washington. But the heavy-handed and overbearing action of the State Department in lecturing the Canadian government in a public press release seemed to me intolerable. While the State Department protested, with some reason, that they had been obliged to put the record straight over the Nassau

Agreement, there could be no doubt in my mind that they welcomed this opportunity to injure the government of Mr. Diefenbaker. The State Department press release had been approved by McGeorge Bundy at the White House. Later it was said that the President regarded this as a blunder on Bundy's part and that he had never himself seen the text of the press release. However, knowing Bundy's political sensitivity and closeness to the President, I considered that he never would have approved the press release unless he knew that it echoed his master's voice.

On February 5, 1963, the Diefenbaker government was defeated in the House of Commons on a non-confidence motion opposing the government's nuclear policy.

Meanwhile, I had been recalled to Ottawa as an indication of the government's displeasure and as a rebuke to the United States. The Prime Minister and Howard Green were anxious to prolong my absence from Washington, perhaps for a period of weeks, as a further indication of their displeasure with the United States government. I took the line in conversation with them that my absence from Washington would not be particularly shattering to the United States government, and I was allowed to return to Washington.

6 February 1963.

Just back from Ottawa. The government was defeated last night. I have been living politics for the last week and feel drained and left without a private thought or feeling after the continuous excitement of this crisis. What a substitute politics are for private life, and what an appalling inner emptiness and surrounding stillness must descend on the politician who is finally and irrevocably OUT. The road ahead in Canadian-American relations is sure to be full of slippery paths and perhaps some precipitous drops. It may also mean the end of my tenure of the Washington Embassy as a small by-product of the general confusion and débâcle.

Oh, those hours in the Prime Minister's Office with Mr. Diefenbaker and Howard Green, two old men, old cronies, old scarred soldiers of political battles. It was indeed an education for me. I had arrived in Ottawa in the hope of repairing the damage caused to the relations between our two countries, but I soon realized that the government was not interested in patching things up and hoped to win an election on the issue of United States interference in our affairs.

In Ottawa during this crisis it was twenty-eight degrees below zero, with winds blowing the icy snow round the corners and buttresses of the Gothic buildings on the Hill. Hurrying figures, their coat collars turned up, grasping briefcases, their heads down against the wind, pushed forward to Cabinet conclaves and parliamentary sessions. The whole scene was shrouded in the falling snow, and further mists hung over the river and the airport, completing the effect of isolation from the outer world which I felt so strongly in Ottawa, the peculiar capital of a peculiar people. Then to come back to this bland and sunny scene, this classical architecture, the wide-spanning bridges and broad perspectives, this illusion of rationalism. Apart from my opinions as to the issues at stake, my feelings are very tangled. While I disapprove entirely of the manufactured anti-Americanism of the government, yet deep down I feel satisfaction at hearing the Canadian government finally lash out at the omniscience and unconscious arrogance of Washington, and I am not immune to that fever of irritation with the United States government which at home could become a national rage – could, but I do not think it will.

10 February 1963.

Dear Oatsie Leiter, that generous-natured beauty who brings a breeze of high spirits into this town, wanted me to meet her friend, a political lady. We met, but it did not work. She engaged me on the subject of the Common Market, on which I have just written a long dispatch. The conversation was for me like a lesson out of school hours. I stopped listening and looked. Her pink face was eroded by many suns in Swiss skiing resorts or the winds that blow on yachts in Southampton Harbour.

11 February 1963.

The government seems to be falling to pieces, leaving the Prime Minister more and more isolated in his suspicions, narrow stratagems, and sterile prejudices. How will it all turn out? Where shall we find ourselves after the election on April 8? And, incidentally, where shall I find myself?

Diana Cooper[1] is here on a visit and as usual I find myself talking more frankly to her about my dilemma than to anyone, excepting, of course, Sylvia. It gives me a sense of stimulus to feel that that irreverent, irrepressible Beauty is next door. She is withstanding the siege of old age with all flags flying. I said to her that I thought I had got to the stage in life of throwing in my hand, ceasing to seek for adventure, and "settling down." "Don't," she cried immediately, "don't *do* that," fixing me with her fabulous eyes. "I thought you might advise it," I said. "What, me? Never!" said with immense energy. She has been lunching with the President at the White House. He asked her whether she thought that the loss during the First World War of so many gifted young men who had been the circle of her friends had altered and weakened British political life. She said no.

Today we lunched with Mr. and Mrs. Phillips of the Phillips Gallery, my favourite art gallery. As it is small, one can sit down, and, as in no other art gallery in the world, one is allowed to smoke. I am very much drawn to the Phillipses. He is a bald, rather tired millionaire, with a wedge-shaped head. Mrs. Phillips is a painter and a gallery politician. Her face is worn, not by wind and weather but by exposure to masterpieces. The Lippmanns were there. Walter Lippmann, ever since I have been here, has been a wonderful friend to me. In wisdom, experience, and knowledge of the world he is head and shoulders above most journalists and politicians and, of course, ambassadors! Just before lunch there was a startling crack and the bottom fell out of the glass which Sylvia was holding in her hand. Bourbon and assorted fruits gushed onto the exquisite Aubusson carpet.

12 February 1963.

I am feeling the strain of these last weeks and completely lost my temper with a political lady next to whom I was sitting at lunch. She had been described to me as "a perfect darling," but I found her a perfect pest and was irritated by some remark she made reflecting on the Canadian government which normally I would have passed over without notice. Also, I keep asking myself whether I could have

---

[1] Lady Diana Cooper – widow of Duff Cooper, British politician; famous beauty and social figure.

avoided this crisis if I had foreseen the State Department press release in my encounters with Mac Bundy. But I do not think this would have made any difference.

The feeling of happiness that I experience in dreaming seems a kind of moral or social weightlessness and, with it, a gaiety, sometimes hilarity, which is, as they say, "out of this world." This weightlessness is like that shown in ideal pictures of blessed beings floating in clouds, but it does not seem, in the case of my dreams, to be a reward for good works. Dreaming sorrows are morally awakening and enlarge the sympathies. Last night I dreamed of her, with both joy and sorrow.

16 February 1963.

I want to arrange a date for lunch with Dobrynin, the Soviet Ambassador, next week. He and I have lunch every now and then. He is very pleasant company, a genial six-footer, a gleam of humour in the glance behind his rimless spectacles. He is tenacious in argument, shifting his ground but always returning to the point. Our talk has usually turned on the German role in NATO. He speaks of the dangers of renascent German militarism encouraged and supported by the Alliance. I argue that from the Russian point of view Germany in the NATO framework, contained and supported by nations who have themselves had experience of the German aggression, is safer than a revived Germany free of restraints. But I make no headway. It is the American-German linkage that he fears. Perhaps he thinks that Canada might be a softening influence on American policy. If so, he is mistaken. Even if we had such an intention, we would not have the influence.

I had at one time thought of leaving my diaries on my death to my niece Eliza, but why burden the girl with these stale leftovers of a life? Better burn the lot. Eliza is the last of us – no more male Ritchies. The good Lord has decided to discontinue the experiment! She is beautiful and intelligent, subject to gloom, to precipitous moods; has not yet found herself, but with a streak of daring; great charm. I love her and she means more and more to me each year. I am also fascinated by the idea of her future, of what the story of her life will be. I know one thing she will never be – a BORE.

17 February 1963.

I had lunch with my new pal, the Greek Ambassador, Matsas. He is an old aesthete, very astute and also a tremendous old gossip. He has written several enormously long plays, one of which he has lent to me to read. He says that in Europe people say frightful things about their dearest friends – and to them – but go on in friendship, while the Americans never say an unkind word and one can only judge their feuds and hatreds by their significant silences when a name is mentioned.

18 February 1963.

Henry Brandon and Nin Ryan here for lunch. Between them they know all the private scandals, inside stories, of Washington politics and society.

I am in the midst of an argument with the Department at home. What a jealous old hippopotamus the Department is, whose service is perfect submission and who never forgets even if she sometimes has to forgive.

Can the Diefenbaker government live on? I can hardly believe so. How much does it count against the government that the press, many – if not most – businessmen, all civil servants and academics are against them? Not perhaps as much as one thinks. Meanwhile, so far as my own reputation is concerned, I have presided over this Embassy during a time of collapse in Canadian-American relations. Some must surely say that I might have done something to prevent the deterioration. My grandfather put an inscription on his second wife's tombstone: "She did what she could." Hardly flattering to the lady. I suppose that might be the verdict on my efforts. If there is to be a change, won't the new government say to themselves, "Let us start with a new man in Washington"? Then what becomes of old Ritchie? Banishment to our mission in Berne? A kind friend said to me the other day, "In this Canadian-American row it's *you* I am sorry for." Well-meant, no doubt, but misplaced. I do not relish being an object of pity.

20 February 1963.

The Breeses here today with their son. They are my oldest friends in this town. Billy I have known since the days when he was in the U.S.

Legation (as it then was) in Ottawa. His mother was kind to me when I was a newly arrived Third Secretary in Washington – had me to stay in her house for weeks. Nora is so lovable, warm-hearted, with a quick spontaneous wit all her own. It is a relief from official life to go to their country house, Longview, outside Washington, like a return to a happier, less responsible time in my life. Thank Heaven for the earlier friends made in this city in my youth and who have remained friends – the Ourousoffs, Anne Perin, Cynthia Martin, and a few others. When I am with them, all the competitiveness and one-upmanship that infect Washington seem to fall away.

Lunch with Diana Cooper. She says that it is necessary for a happy marriage that husband and wife should sally forth separately into the world so that each can bring home something fresh "to put into the vase."

21 February 1963.

Another old friend who is staying with us is Alastair Buchan. I first met him when he was a schoolboy at Eton and spending the holidays with his parents at Government House in Ottawa. I was his best man when he married Hope at Oxford during the war. Then he was a young officer in the Canadian Army; now, after a successful career in journalism, he is becoming known as an expert in international studies. I saw a lot of him during the war in London. We used to have those long, uninhibited conversations, the kind of endless, engrossing talk, well-laced with whisky, which one had with friends in those days when one was unguardedly experimenting with ideas and indiscreetly revealing one's own affairs. Now we are both married, sobered (he more than I, as he drinks nothing), and our friendship is in another key. He has both shrewdness and wisdom and is widely informed on what is going on here and in London, and also in Ottawa. He knows Canada and Canadians from the inside as few Englishmen do and he has an instinct for the country, as his father John Buchan[1] had before him.

The cook has given notice. She could not stand Colin any longer, with his bossy, butlerian ways. Indeed, Sylvia can hardly stand him

---

[1] John Buchan, Baron Tweedsmuir, the novelist, was Governor General of Canada, 1935-1940.

herself. He despises all womankind. His only devotion is not to me, but to my clothes, of which he is a stern but loving critic, proudly attached to certain of my suits and shirts, contemptuous of others. Himself·a natty dresser, he is insistent that however I may feel inwardly I must make a good outward appearance. A cocky, curly-haired Scottish introvert, he makes few visible friends, but may have his own resources. It is sad about the cook. She was a good cook, too. Who was it – Saki? – who said "She was a good cook as good cooks go, and as good cooks go she went."

22 February 1963.

Dined at Bill and Mary Bundy's, with her parents Dean and Alice Acheson, and Bruce Hutchison. Bruce is a voice of integrity in Canadian journalism. If this sounds pompous, he isn't. If I had to point to a man who represents what I think of as embodying Canadian qualities, it would be Bruce. He makes friends with those in power but never gives an inch in his estimates of them. And he has a salty, quirky side to him. Dean has a bee in his bonnet about the British – that they are a useless lot who have lost their way in the con-temporary world. When I first knew him before the war he was a familiar of the British Embassy; in style, in appearance, even in his London-looking clothes, he is the nearest of all Americans to an upper-class Englishman or Anglo-Canadian. Perhaps that is why he feels free to castigate the British as though he were a member of the family, sitting in a London club among his peers. But his attacks will not be seen like that in London. The mixed feelings that the English arouse among those who have too much admired them are of little interest to the English. They want practical results and do not care whether they get them from someone who does not know one school tie from another. I have seen this operating in Canadian terms. Canadian Tories have, or used to have, a devotion to the "British con-nection." When they went to London, as Diefenbaker did, they were more at odds with the British Establishment than Liberal politicians who have no devotion to "Crown and Altar."

After dinner Dean Acheson attacked the concept of a multilateral force and said it was all nonsense. He said what was needed was sixty divisions of Europeans. As to the commander, he could not be either

American or French and might well be a Canadian. Dean says he would put all possible pressure on the Germans to provide military forces. The English would be reluctant to join, he thinks, but might do so if they saw the Germans getting in there first. The Europeans should leave no ground role to the United States. Their sixty divisions could exert pressure on the East bloc and would change the whole picture and lead to, if not reunification, at any rate the withdrawal of twenty Communist divisions from East Germany. He puts all his money on the German contribution and says that NATO is at present a machine without a purpose because we have no intelligible German policy. At any rate he says that if the Europeans will not defend themselves, the United States will not continue to do so.

24 February 1963.

Day before yesterday there was a silly flap in the press about my interview with Rusk. Harold Morrison printed a story that Rusk had "refused to pose with me" for a photograph, and this was spread all over the Canadian newspapers. People will say I have an unlucky touch, but I feel an almost lighthearted fatalism about these misadventures.

1 March 1963.

John Watkins is here, retired from the Service and setting off to Europe to live a little in Paris and follow the sun to Marrakesh. He is an ageless creature, with his crinkled face, small almost-black teeth, and the gleam of intelligence and amusement in his sharp glance. I am fond of him, but there is something impersonal and detached about him that would prevent my claiming to be his friend. I stayed with him when he was Ambassador in Moscow. He said to me, "If you want to understand the Russians, come with me to the railway station tonight." We drove down to the station and there on the platform were dozens of recumbent bodies, wrapped, some of them, in what appeared to be old sacking to keep out the cold, while others stomped up and down, hands in pockets, collars turned up, whistling and talking. Whole families with small children were encamped in corners. "All these people," John said, "have been waiting for their train for twenty-four hours, and they may be waiting for another day and night. They take all this cold and discomfort quite philosophically.

They are without impatience, and the passage of time does not affect them. They have a different time sense from us. Russians are always waiting." When he was in Moscow, John knew more Russian artists, musicians, and members of the intelligentsia than anyone else in the diplomatic corps. He is himself by taste and temperament more a member of the intelligentsia than an ambassador, and eschews formality. He is a curious by-product of the Ontario farm where his old aunts still live (or did till recently). Himself an incorrigible bachelor, they seem his only family attachments.

2 March 1963.

I have been reading Blake's poetry all morning and now am off to lunch with George Ball of the State Department. I want to get on a steady even keel with him, but my own government rocks the boat every time. Only a little more than one month before the election. Today I decided not to go to the Gridiron Club dinner in case someone made an unflattering reference to Diefenbaker and created a further incident. This is indicative of the artificially poisoned state of our relations with the United States. Read *The Loved and the Lost* by Morley Callaghan. At last, a novel not "about Canada" but which takes place in Canada and which shows men and women as walking, talking Canadians, and not written by a visiting Englishman or an expatriate Romanian, but by a real live Canadian. It is not the greatest novel in the world but it does bring us into the territory of literature and so adds a dimension to living in Canada. One thing that makes for thinness in the air at home is just the lack of this dimension. A cityscape remains a private world until it has been put into words. But winter Montreal, thanks to Callaghan, and Halifax, thanks to Hugh MacLennan, are now on the literary map.

5 March 1963.

The world of Carpaccio . . . What is the meaning of that figure who appears so often in his pictures, of a young man with long blond hair, sometimes as a bowman, sometimes a courtier, sometimes one of a crowd? His back is always turned to us. What is his face? The face of violence? So it must be in the bowman when he looses his arrows at some suffering saint. And why do those whom he faces in these pictures always avert their gaze from him? Or perhaps he is just a stock figure from a drawing book, chosen to illustrate the tensions of back leg muscles and the turn of the neck. It is sad to see Carpaccio, with his curiosity, his joy in faces, forms, animals, and colours, turn into an old bore in his later pictures. His Christs are repulsive from the start – barber's blocks with somewhat wig-like hair parted in the middle and epicene lips showing in a chestnut beard. Yet his figure of Christ dead is quite different – an elongated corpse with a dark, unshaven face of a young man killed in an accident.

8 March 1963.

One more month before the Canadian elections. For the first time since I joined the Service I am toying with the idea of getting out of it. No, I never shall – I am too inured to it, and perhaps softened by the luxuries that go with it. Yet I seem powerless to prevent the multiplying incidents which are worsening relations between Washington and Ottawa.

10 March 1963.

Sylvia is away and I am in the house alone. This is a house of reflections, green in summer and now, in spring, reflections of cloud moving and light changing. It is a house of many windows. These upstairs rooms are very quiet, just the swish of traffic on Massachusetts Avenue and of branches moving in the slight spring wind. But early in the morning there is the nerve-tapping noise of the woodpecker in the garden, and later Popski begins barking and goes on and on. I wonder if the spring is driving him mad.

To look around and not always see the same things – it's impossible but it would be heavenly to shift the angle of vision.

17 March 1963. Snee Farm, South Carolina.

We are staying here with Tommy Stone and Alix.[1] Tommy is in tremendous form. He gets and gives so much fun in life. He is more

---

[1] Thomas Stone, Canadian diplomat, Ambassador to Sweden and subsequently to the Netherlands, and his wife, Alix.

than the Life of the Party (that would be a desolating description of a friend). Like all performers he is moody and can be pugnacious in a cause, as he was during the war when he espoused the Gaullist cause and pressed it on a reluctant Canadian government. This is the plantation house which he lent to Sylvia and me for our honeymoon. It is a very beautiful place and we were very happy here, except that Sylvia took against the Spanish moss which hangs from the live oak trees round the house – but that did not spoil the honeymoon.

Today there was a luncheon party here. A Southern gentleman with a very loud laugh told stories which he himself found uproariously funny. Jack Wheeler-Bennett was at lunch. He is on a visit to this country. He and I talked about Germany. (His book on the Nazi war machine is by far the best thing ever written on the subject.) Today he was describing his visits to Kaiser Wilhelm at Doorn Castle in Holland and his interviews with Goering before the war. He is a fascinating talker, but his slight stammer gave the opportunity for the anecdotalist to interrupt with another story.

Much as I am enjoying this visit, I do not think that I should have relished plantation life in the Old South. Some of my Johnston forebears had a place called Annandale outside Savannah and were driven out as Loyalists in the American Revolution. They put in claims for compensation to the British Treasury, enumerating their slaves and acres, I suspect much inflated. The Treasury gave them derisory compensation. The British have never been generous with Loyalists when they were liquidating imperial possessions, as the Anglo-Irish know. Too much loyalty can become an expensive bore. Now the name Annandale has survived as a trade name for a paper company in Savannah and the Southern plantation owners who supplanted the Loyalists are ousted by Northerners. *Moral*: Don't be on the losing side. Incidentally, one of the Johnston ladies of Annandale set a record for carrying propriety to the point of imbecility. Her flounced dress caught fire from a lighted candle. She needed help to get out of the dress but alas there was at that moment only a man-servant in the house. Modesty forbade her to call him in lest he see her disrobed. The flounces flared and she died from the effects of the burns.

3 April 1963.

I took Michael and Andrew Ignatieff,[1] ages fifteen and eleven, to lunch at the Jockey Club. There was no difficulty about conversation, as when any gap threatened we talked about food, in which both of them are passionately and discriminatingly interested. Andrew is an ageless original and a comic. Michael is a young Russian gentleman of the liberal school, with perhaps a touch of the youthful prig. But that will wear off, and he is intelligent, interested in everything, articulate – his father's son. But the observant young are on our heels and can't help noticing our vanities and absurdities.

8 April 1963.

Election day. Everyone seems to feel that this is no ordinary election. For some of my fellow civil servants the Liberals seem a sort of normalcy which is called stable government and seems to mean a return to the old middle-class, middle-of-the-way, reasonable, responsible, familiar Canada. But in the process of the election campaign, what is happening to the good name of Canada and the unity of the country? Have we begun to destroy this, and how long is the destruction to continue?

Princess Hohenlohe explained to me at lunch that there was one word of which she did not know the meaning, and that one word was "fear." So fond was she of animals and so confident in their understanding of her love for them that she believed that she could easily walk into a lion's cage, if necessary. I explained that I thoroughly understood the meaning of the word "fear" unless temporarily distracted by interest or desire. The Admiral and a senior State Department official listened to this exchange in silence.

13 April 1963.

In the morning in this house there is a concert of smokers' coughs, Sylvia and I and Colin the butler. Colin was attacked in the street the other day by a man who was attempting to steal his money. He says

---

[1] Sons of George Ignatieff, Canadian diplomat, subsequently Provost of Trinity College, University of Toronto, and later Chancellor of the University of Toronto.

he threw himself on his back on the pavement and kicked out at the man's stomach. His technique was successful, and the man fled. A woman we know slightly was raped in Rock Creek Park just outside our house at 9:30 in the morning. Instead of concealing the fact, with great pluck she went straight to the police, gave her name and all the details, and said they were welcome to publish them if it led to the apprehension of the rapist.

14 April 1963.

The government is out. Diefenbaker is gone and Mike is in. The wreckage is strewn all around – Ministers with whom I have been dealing in these past years now are relegated to powerlessness. I must at once write to Howard Green to express my respect for him and my gratitude for his steady support. I shall not be writing to Diefenbaker. I consider his disappearance a deliverance; there should be prayers of thanksgiving in the churches. And these sentiments do not come from a Liberal.

23 April 1963.

The new government has been in office less than a week but already one can register a change of atmosphere. So far as I am concerned, I am dealing with someone familiar. Mike Pearson has already telephoned me three or four times. This change does not mean that everything is going to be simple and straightforward in Canadian–American relations, but at least I understand and share Mike's objectives in international affairs. Of course we are still in the honeymoon period. The danger lies in the political weakness of the government and its need for quick political returns.

28 April 1963.

Just one year today since we came to Washington, so Colin tells me. He seems to have a phenomenal memory for past dates and events. Perhaps, like myself, he keeps a diary.

Behind Massachusetts Avenue, if you take a turning up to the left, are the houses of the well-to-do, pink brick in the shade of their trees. Up and down, the well-heeled streets wander into Crescents and Places, peaceful in the sunny morning. On the sidewalk four delivery men stand gazing at a new desk to be moved through a too-narrow gate. A red-headed boy is now jumping from foot to foot, to land on alternate squares in the pavement. Alternations of tree shade and sunlight as you approach the escarpment of flats, and then, downhill, into the rawer sunlight of Connecticut Avenue. Staring through a peephole into a waste of shit-coloured mud where the bulldozers nozzle, I see a workman poised on the edge of a crater in the stance of Donatello's *David*. Unexpectedly, I have already arrived at the church. Inside, the dark brownness of crossbeams and high-backed pews, the muffled air at first seeming cool, then stuffy. The eye is drawn to the coloured windows, small and low-set, blue and saffron and the red of throat pastilles. Not a mote is moving in the stillness. Behind closed eyelids the hangover operates – plunging into the subsoil, jetting up into an implausible stratosphere. When the eyes are open they rest on the silent glow of the coloured windows, the rows of dark pews, and the paler vista of the aisle.

4 May 1963.

I am going to Hyannisport with Mike for the meeting between him and the President, and tomorrow I leave for Ottawa for a week's consultations with the government.

10 May 1963.

Back from Hyannisport. The meeting between the President and Mike was tinged with euphoria. The atmosphere was that of clearing skies after a storm – the clouds of suspicion covering Canada–U.S. relations had parted, the sunshine of friendship shone. There was also an undercurrent of complicity between them, as though they had both escaped – like schoolboys on a holiday – from under the shadow of an insupportably tiresome and irrational Third Party and were now free, within limits, to crack jokes at the expense of the Absent One. Indeed, it was mutual relief at the departure of Mr. Diefenbaker from power which gave added savour to the encounter between them. The President and the Prime Minister have much in common – at any rate on the surface, for their natures are different; Kennedy is more ruthless. As companions they are congenial – perhaps the Irish touch in both. They enjoy the same style of humour. More important, they talk the same political language. Their views on international affairs are not widely different, allowing for the permanent difference between the world view of a Great Power and that of a Middle Power. On Canadian-American issues both share the will to achieve solutions to problems in a cool climate without the inflamed rhetoric of the last years. The working sessions at Hyannisport were brisk and businesslike. The log-jam of pending issues was broken. It became possible to make progress on a whole range of questions from balance of trade and the Columbia River to air-route agreements for trans-border flights. We have made a new start; it remains to be seen whether the sweetness and light last.

For my own part I made no substantial contribution to this meeting of minds. Mike was more than capable of dealing with the President without advice from me. We had only one long talk the first evening of our visit, when we had a walk by the seashore and he outlined some of his preoccupations about the coming talks. He had come accompanied by a squad of officials from Ottawa to whom he could turn for factual information. Otherwise he played it by himself and, as usual, played it skilfully.

At dinner the talk was lively and far-ranging, settling in the end in a discussion of the future of Germany. Of the distinguished company assembled at Hyannisport I most enjoyed that of Annette Perron, the Prime Minister's indomitable secretary. We had travelled the world together with an earlier Canadian Prime Minister, Mr. St. Laurent, and we had a cheerful reminiscent reunion over several post-dinner drinks.

I was installed in Bobby Kennedy's house in the Kennedy compound and retired to bed in an atmosphere of outdoor sport and Roman Catholic piety, surrounded by pictures of sailboats and by crucifixes.

1 July 1963. Washington.

Our National Day prompts the question: can our country survive as an independent, united sovereign state – a reality, not a fiction? Or must we fall into the embrace of the U.S.A.? We struggle in the net, make fumbling attempts to find our way out, but all the time are getting deeper in, in terms both of our defence and of the control of our economy. Diefenbaker tried, in relations with the U.S., to be a sort of pocket de Gaulle. It didn't work. We have not the will or the means to be sufficiently exorbitant.

When I asked an old pal of mine how he kept so cheerful he said, "I see life through rose-coloured testicles."

The woman next to me at lunch yesterday said of her son, "He isn't as bright as his father, but he is *so* beautifully oriented."

"Poetry strips the veil of familiarity from the world and lays bare the naked and sleeping beauty, which is the spirit of its forms." Shelley, *A Defence of Poetry*. "The veil of familiarity" . . . sometimes it lifts for a timeless moment as it did for me this early morning when I came back from my walk in the park to find the house still sleeping. I entered it like a stranger and saw all things afresh – walking through the silent rooms wondering, fingering like a child in a house of mystery. I look about me to take solitary possession. The only motion in the shrouded stillness is the light breeze sifting in from the empty gardens. A cardinal flashes past the window on its way to the drinking bowl.

Talking of poetry and poets, this book of Doris Moore's about Byron leaves a trail of questions behind it. She defends the poet fanatically, but doesn't her record work against him? How was it that he left behind him such envy, hatred, and malice among those who knew and survived him, so that for decades the rows among them raged on? Was he unlucky in his loves and friendships or did he carry some poison with him? Men and women were carriers of the Byron infection. Thirty years after his death his wife, his sister, Caroline Lamb, could not get him out of their systems and re-fought his battles.

The influence of the dead on the living – what an endlessly fascinating subject. I believe that my two uncles, Harry and Charlie, one dead the year I was born, the other hardly known by me and dead when I was a child, have by their legends influenced me more than any living man. There must be a medium to carry the current from the dead to the living, sometimes a living survivor, sometimes the written word. My mother was such a medium. The dead lived through her talk. Even their voices and gestures were in the room with you. These were private ghosts, known only to a few. Byron, by the genius of his personality, greater even than his poetry, has changed countless lives . . . usually for the worse? But he gave them a role to play and a sense of freedom in playing it, even if most were pinchbeck performers. The Byronic virus lasted more than a hundred years – is it now finally extinct?

2 July 1963.

Blazing heat. Woke up early to the whirring sound of the air conditioner and the conviction of the airlessness in the street outside where no leaf stirred. Heat kept at bay by air conditioners is like pain frozen out by a local anaesthetic – in both cases, you know it's there.

Yesterday the Canadian Club had a reception of three hundred people in this house. There are quite a lot of lonely, homesick Canadians living in this town, many of them government employees who come from small places in Canada and are not having so very much fun in this gracious city and missing their friends and relations at home. We sang "O Canada," standing about on the terrace with the written songsheets in hand. Very few people knew all the verses. Sylvia said it moved her and made her want to cry. It was moving when sung like that by a group of Canadians abroad and in the open air and without music. It sounded less like a national anthem than a Highland lament or a nostalgic French-Canadian song full of pride and yearning, not at all martial. It was a good party. How hot the servants were, and how hard they worked. Colin was in his element, ordering everybody about, and old Isobel, the cook, was cheerful, her wild hair hanging about her in elfin locks.

6 July 1963.

The Americans are intensely irritated by our new Budget,[1] which is being attacked in violent tones by the press. I lunched today with Bill Armstrong at the Jockey Club. He is a good friend to Canada in the State Department and not at all averse to making it known that in this role he has much uphill work to do. At one point he said that when he was arguing with the other American officials for an understanding of Canada's position over the Budget, they said to him,

---

[1] The Budget introduced by the Minister of Finance, Walter Gordon, was considered in Washington to be anti-American.

"What Canadians need in financial questions is a psychoanalyst's couch." But then, to the Americans, the irrationality of their allies and their own rationality is an absolute assumption. To do Armstrong justice, he glimpses this. As for our position on this and on nuclear weapons, I am not far from sharing American bewilderment over our tergiversations. These must be called typically Canadian, the reflection of a divided mind. How else was our country held together in the first place? How else will it be held together in the future? Only some do it more expertly than others. If Canada cannot logically work as an independent, unified nation, we are all the same determined to make it work.

Went down in the afternoon to the State Department to see Bill Tyler, who told us nothing about Kennedy's visit to Europe except that the President had lost his suitcase en route with his father's tortoise-shell shoehorn in it, and had found it again on return to New York.

Perhaps, after nearly five years in the United States, I have quite unconsciously begun to accept American assumptions more than I realize. At any rate, I see their difficulties through their eyes, for to the Americans almost everything, and certainly any development in international affairs, constitutes a "problem" to which there must be a "solution." And what spurs them on is the feeling that there is a Russian boy in the class, perhaps more hard-working, who may come up with that "solution" first. Hence they are incapable of leaving anything alone. Also, any "solution" offered is better than none at all. I cannot see that the United States policies which protected and enriched the Western world are wrong. I think they have a more grown-up understanding of the danger of nuclear war than any other government except the Russians'. I share some of their irritation with the ceaseless needling and ungenerous pettiness of many of their allies who depend upon them and vent on them their own resentment of the fact. I think the Americans are right to be continually alert to the Communist danger from which they saved Europe by the Marshall Plan and by the presence of their forces there. Nor do I think they have been guilty in their relations with Canada. I think they have been patient, considering their power. And yet, *yet*, the more I concede them to be right, the more I am subject to fits of what I think claustrophobia. They are *everywhere*, into *everything* – a wedding in Nepal, a strike in British Guiana, the remotest Greek island, the farthest outpost of Donegal, the banks of the Limpopo. All countries' private and domestic affairs are of interest to the Americans; in all do they, in a measure, interfere. Everywhere they carry with them their own sense of their own superiority, their desire to improve, to preserve, to encourage what is deserving, to obliterate what is "feudal," "reactionary," "Communistic"; to advance, with banners flying, The American Way of Life, which of course we all must know is the way of progress and enlightenment for all mankind.

8 July 1963.

Had a letter today from Joe McCulley, who was Headmaster of Pickering College, Newmarket, Ontario, when I was there teaching French in 1931. It made me think of that time which I so much enjoyed, although I was a damn bad teacher, sometimes going to sleep in the middle of one of my own classes. One difficulty was my own very uncertain grasp of the subject I was supposed to be teaching. I could speak and read French but my knowledge of the finer points of French grammar, especially the irregular verbs, was so shaky that I had to mug them up the night before I went to class. There was a boy, Llyn Stephens, who knew them better than I did. He would sometimes interrupt as I was teaching, to correct me. Much later in life he became Counsellor at our Embassy in Bonn when I was there as Ambassador. It was a repeat performance. His knowledge of German was far superior to my own, but he no longer corrected me – at any rate in public.

Pickering was an experimental boarding school, founded originally by Quakers. There were no punishments, no compulsory games, and the minimum of discipline. Surprisingly, the system worked remarkably well. This was largely due to the personality of the Headmaster. Joe was then a blond, handsome six-foot crusader, overflowing with enthusiasm. At the same time he had a glance which missed nothing that went on in the school and from which no adolescent subterfuge was concealed. He ruled by magnetism combined with a domineering instinct for command. It seemed unlikely that I should become a friend of this hearty extrovert, yet friends we were.

After the school day was over I would often repair to his study, and over a bottle of rye whisky we would talk together for hours. The dramas, personalities, and intrigues of school life gave us plenty of food for conversation. After the second or third whisky we would launch out into wider fields. He would expound his Rousseau-esque vision of the perfectibility of human, and particularly boys', nature. All that stood between the most recalcitrant or idle boy and his happy and fruitful development was the narrow prejudice or brutal mishandling of his upbringing. In vain I pleaded the influence of heredity, as against environment. In vain I argued that while vice might be curable, stupidity was incorrigible. He swept all such objections before him and sometimes, in the final stages of the evening, would recite to me in sonorous tones Tennyson's "Ulysses." We parted, warmed not only by whisky but by the glow of friendship. Not all the masters shared my enthusiasm for Joe. Some questioned his scholarly qualifications, others resented his technique in discussion, particularly an irritating phrase of his in argument – "Let me clarify your thinking."

My happiness in those early days at Pickering was in part a happiness of contrast. My own experience in the conventional Canadian boys' schools I had attended was deplorable. I had been a miserable schoolboy, untidy (glasses mended with bits of string), uncoordinated in athletics (the English sergeant-major used to say, "Come and watch Ritchie on the parallel bars. It's as good as Charlie Chaplin any day"). I was a natural bully-ee (if that is the word for the bully's butt). I was always late for classes, so spent hours doing detentions – i.e., writing moral maxims in copperplate – a social misfit cursed with an English accent from my prep school in England; a garrison-town colonial Nova Scotian among the alien herd of smug Upper Canadians. At Pickering I felt that I was getting my own back on a system which had bruised me. So I had a lot in common with those of the boys at Pickering who had themselves either been expelled from or left under a cloud the schools they had previously attended, to come to the freedom and ease of Pickering. Also, having been unpopular as a boy, I found myself popular as a master. Somewhat adolescent myself for my age – I was twenty-four – I shared the rapid transitions of adolescents from hilarious spirits to inspissated gloom. Mentally grown-up, I was temperamentally adolescent. The boys had a sort of cult for me, treating me as something between a mascot and their own freak, in some cases almost their friend. They sensed that I was not interested in improving or influencing them and that I had none of the schoolmaster's way of measuring them. I sought amusement, incident, personality among them as I would have done among my own contemporaries. In the classroom I rarely had trouble in keeping discipline because I viewed classes as they did, as tiresome routine that had to be got through. I was not an inspiring teacher, but the boys did just about as well in exams in my subject as in any others. With younger boys from the Junior School, whom fortunately I rarely had to teach, I could establish no relationship. They found me incomprehensible and uninteresting. Their jerky restlessness, always clattering, banging, and shouting, made me tired, and I never seemed to have the answers to their incessant questions.

Miss Ancient, or Anan as she was always called, was the school matron. It was through her that I had first heard of Pickering College. She had been first my father's secretary and later my brother's governess. At Pickering her sitting-room was a refuge from schoolrooms and school corridors, and from the permanent company of schoolboys and masters – an undilutedly male world. After my early-morning class I used to join her there for coffee and gossip. She was then, I suppose, in her forties or fifties, tallish, flat-chested, and her sympathetic dark eyes gazed somewhat reproachfully at the world through gleaming pince-nez. She was the soul of sincerity, upright and conscientious in all she attempted; an intelligent woman with something touchingly clumsy about her gestures. "My fingers are all thumbs thith morning," she would say in her thick lisp. She and I became friends in those sessions in her sitting-room. I think of her with affection and with sympathy, for her life as the plain daughter of a penniless clergyman had not been an easy one. She had finally found a haven at Pickering where her devotion to the Headmaster was so total that a word of praise or recognition from him made her day, as his occasional impatience with her fussing ruined it. She took a darkly suspicious view of the masters' wives, particularly any one of them who attracted Joe's favourable attention or failed to give full recognition to her status as school matron. In particular she resented one, a beautiful woman with an opulent figure whom the older boys much lusted after. "I suppose," said Anan, "that she has what they call thex appeal." She spoke as though it were an unpleasant, perhaps contagious, disease. Anan's own duties included charge of the school sick-room. Herself stoical, she had no time for malingerers; one half-Aspirin was her maximum cure for all forms of pain, and she had an awkward, impatient touch on the sufferer's pillow.

Almost all the other masters except Joe and myself were married men. I often spent my evenings dining and drinking in their hospitable houses. I made friends among them and in the course of doing so learned to understand the rewards and frustrations of the school-teaching career, and to admire the devotion they brought to it. I got rid of my mistaken preconceived notion that schoolmastering was a secondary kind of occupation – "Those who can, do, those who can't, teach" – and came to see it as being important and engrossing. Yet as I moved into my second year at Pickering I was increasingly restless. The atmosphere of youthfulness, at first stimulating, began to be oppressive. Boys were perpetually barging into my sitting-room and lounging about talking and sprawling. No sooner had I got rid of one lot than there was another knock on my door. I began to get bored with their company. They sensed this and seemed to become more boring. Boredom breeds bores. Then, too, it was more and more apparent to me that the teaching profession, admirable as it might be, was not for me. I lacked the wish to mould or to instruct. I saw myself an old crustacean washed over by successive tides of youth. My practical dilemma was that despite years of expensive education I had no qualifications for any alternative job, and 1931 was a notoriously bad year for the unemployed. My only resort was to return from attempting to educate others to being myself further educated. I applied for a fellowship at Harvard, where I had already spent one year as Commonwealth Fellow on leaving Oxford. There were two fellowships on offer: one to proceed to France to explore the significance of the word "*sensibilité*" in eighteenth-century French literature, the other to advanced studies in the origins of the First World War. I coveted the first and obtained the second. It was to prove a turning-point, for had I been delving into "*sensibilité*" in the cafés of Montpellier I should not have been in Boston to take the examination for the Department of External Affairs and ergo I should not now, as an aging Ambassador, be sitting at my desk in Washington wasting the government's time with this excursion into the past when I should be studying the statistics of Canadian lumber exports.

5 August 1963. Halifax, N.S.

I am here on another brief visit to see my mother, who has been increasingly ill lately. She varies much from day to day. Suddenly today the clouds of melancholia and weakness parted, and she was restored to me as she used to be. It was like something happening in a dream. She had returned to take possession with her full nature of that decrepit old body which an hour before had seemed to belong to an equally decrepit old spirit. I was in the presence of a really fascinating woman. It is sad to know that by tomorrow this former Lilian will have disappeared again into the shadows, but it was worth coming here to be with her for these few hours. Does her brain suddenly clear? What part does boredom play in her afflictions? These questions may be important for oneself some day, if one lives long enough to be in the same case. The doctor says she "talks between the lines," which is a good description. She talked today of religion. She is of two minds about it. She prays without really believing, a process which I share with her. She said to the Dean, fixing him with those extraordinary eyes which even now have not lost all their power, "Do you *really* believe that Jesus Christ is here in this room with us when you are giving me Communion?" She said the Dean answered that she mustn't worry her mind with such questions. "He couldn't really answer me and I shouldn't have asked him. He has his living to make, like everybody else. Being a clergyman is his occupation. How else, at his age, could he earn his living? Anyway, I dropped the subject and offered him a glass of sherry. He accepted, which showed he was a human being."

She dreams, she says, of the next world, "a cold, immense emptiness in which I wander." "But then," she added brusquely, "I pay no attention to such thoughts. It's all nonsense."

A few hours later when I left her she seemed to have recovered from her gloom, because when I asked her how she felt she said, "Fine. I could knock *you* down."

27 August 1963.

Return to Washington. The private world of the family in Halifax is already beginning to recede. The pain over my mother's tragic state will become calloused over. That last evening in Halifax I spent wandering about the streets in the centre of town, past old houses once the homes of family friends, now run-down, decayed, some divided or replaced by parking lots or office buildings. I paused at street corners, seeking for landmarks and seeing the new city which is springing up on all sides and which will be identical with every other city in North America. I was composing in my mind a requiem for shabby, memory-laden old Halifax.

Back here I am switched abruptly into the present by the Prime Minister's voice on the telephone. Mike is in one of his querulous moods. He asks my advice, brushes it off as irrelevant, then circles back to it, picks up a point I have made, turns it inside out, and makes something of it. What emerges more clearly every day is that the Hyannisport honeymoon is already over. Things have never been the same between us and the Americans since Walter Gordon's Budget.

28 August 1963.

Sylvia has not yet returned. This big house is empty, apart from the servants, and very empty it feels. It was like a Victorian sentimental engraving today when Popski found his way to my lonely side and licked my nose. It is a long time since I have lived alone and I agree with what other solitaries have told me – that the loneliest moment is the early evening, about six o'clock. Also, there is being in bed alone. On the other hand, I rather like having the morning to myself.

Today I went into the town to watch the civil-rights parade, which is, of course, mainly concerned with civil rights for blacks. Washington seemed a ghost town. The population, thoroughly scared of some outbursts of violence, had almost shuttered themselves in their houses. The only other ambassador who had ventured forth was my Greek colleague, Matsas. He says that the other one hundred and three ambassadors have barricaded themselves in their embassies. He himself seemed as debonair and carefree as usual, and takes a very frivolous view of the colour problem.

29 August 1963.

Farewell frivolity. Abandon dreams of visits to New York. A non-stop stream of official visitors from Ottawa is impending – Cabinet ministers and their acolytes, senior and less-senior civil servants – and I must plunge into a crash course in interest rates and the levels of North American rivers. What is going on in my own Department? None of my friends there write me about the real state of play. They won't put an indiscreet word to paper, but over the second post-dinner drink it all comes out. What do the young men in the Department think of the Old Boys like myself? What do they think of Norman Robertson? Who will succeed him as Under-Secretary? At one time there was a movement on foot "in certain quarters" to drag me back into the job. It seems to have died away. Mike sometimes implies in his half-joking way that I am not "close enough" to the President – what ambassador is? But on the whole, he seems to like having me here. He appreciates that I am not trying to carve myself a place in the limelight – also he knows that I know what he wants done without his having to spell it out.

Dinner with the Inter-American Bank Board. Best food in town, but when I retire, no bank will invite me to be on its Board and I can't blame them.

In the evening the first diplomatic party of the new season. Do these functions at which the diplomatic corps take in each other's diplomatic washing serve any purpose? Certainly not that of pleasure-giving. Perhaps they reinforce the feeling that "Here we are, all in the same boat" – as though diplomats were embarked together on a cruise ship in foreign waters, unable to get away from each other, jealously comparing each other's accommodation, the places allotted to them in the dining saloon, and their relative precedence at the captain's table, and united in their insistence on their rights as passengers – on such voyages friendships are formed, usually transient but sometimes long-lasting, confidences are exchanged, alliances are consolidated and dissolve or reform before the voyage is over.

Here in Washington there is a latent sense of grievance in the diplomatic corps. They complain that they rarely have access to the President – even in some cases to the Secretary of State – that U.S.

authorities do not attach enough importance to ambassadorial rank, that the important U.S. Senators rarely accept their invitations to dinner, and when they do, often excuse themselves at the last moment.

Today it was a National Day reception. If the number of sovereign nations increases at the current rate and if all are represented in Washington, there will soon be one of these every day of the year. Now some countries are cheating and in addition to celebrating the day they acquired independence or the birthday of their monarch or the glorious revolution when they got rid of their monarch, they give receptions to memorialize any episode in their histories that takes their fancy – a military victory or a transient coup d'état. Other people's National Days are regarded by the corps as a public nuisance and a public duty. They are taken with deadly seriousness by the newcomers on the international scene, particularly the Africans. Maturer nations view them with fatalism, like a woman's attitude to the monthly curse. We have ourselves been delivered by a stroke of diplomatic skill on the part of my predecessor, Hume Wrong, who convinced Ottawa that, as there is no "Canadian colony" of any number in Washington, it was a waste of money for the Embassy to have a National Day reception. It was clever of Hume, because the other embassies in Washington are in the same position as Canada in having few of their nationals here. Apart from bored State Department officials and a handful of senators and fellow diplomats, most of the other guests at these functions are the members of Washington society who do not rate an invitation to a meal. As someone said to me today, "Perhaps we could fit Mrs. X into our National Day. We must have her inside the embassy." A few ancient dames of this breed still survive from the days when I was first in Washington in the 1930s and they have been eating their way like termites through the free embassy refreshments ever since.

A new form of torture is the National Day reception prolonged into a National Film Showing. Unless one is very nippy at getting through the exit, one is herded into a hall in the embassy, parked on a little gilt chair, and subjected to a film portraying some sanitized version of life in the Host Country. These films feature everything from folk-dancing to dam-building, with a lot of boring scenery thrown in – majestic mountains, broad rivers, and vast plains, the latter populated by herds of wild animals stampeding Hell-for-leather for the nearest water-hole – and making one long to stampede oneself.

31 August 1963.

I lunched today with John Sharpe of our Embassy. I have come to have a great liking for him. He was just developing flu, so had an extra drink or two and talked more freely than usual. He tells me that many of the wives in the Department of External Affairs are complaining about diplomatic life abroad because it "unsettles" the children. Why is everybody so frightened of being unsettled? I think it's the best thing that can happen to a growing boy or girl or, indeed, to their parents. It seems that the young-middle-aged lot want to get back to Canada. They have seen through the illusion of exotic adventure abroad and adopted another illusion, that life in Canada has become "tremendously exciting" and that the country is "on the move." Well, it may be so, but I did not notice it in Halifax.

Bob Farquharson, our Press Attaché, since his stroke is always searching for words. The meaning is in his head but the right speech symbol is mislaid. How distracting that must be, always to be looking for words that one cannot find. It's bad enough looking for things about the house – lost spectacles and lost money.

1 September 1963.

I am putting on a belly. That's what comes of trying to develop a "philosophy of life." Meanwhile, there is the question of my future. I think they may leave me here for eighteen months or so. They won't want to appear to change me so soon after the change of government, as it might look as though they were replacing me because I was a Conservative appointee and this would not look good from the point of view of our Foreign Service. Jules Léger, I hear, may be going to Paris. Heaven help him if he has to have dealings with intractable de Gaulle.

2 September 1963.

I am going to switch from drinking rye whisky to drinking Scotch, as I like the latter less and hope I may drink it more slowly. This res-olution has been brought on by a long evening, indeed almost a night, since it lasted until 4 a.m., drinking and talking with Scruff O'Brien, the No. 2 Canadian naval man here and a good friend of mine. A restless, intelligent, adventurous man, very Irish and very Canadian, and I like him.

3 September 1963.

I dined with the Australian Ambassador and Lady Beale. They are about the best company in town. Howard Beale says that someone said to him, "President Kennedy is a bore." This revolutionary statement gave us all food for thought, especially Lady Beale, to whom it was particularly welcome, as the President has certainly "un-charmed" her. On the other hand, Alice Longworth, the oldest of all old White House hands, said to me the other day, "Jack Kennedy is a broth of a boy and I love him." I am amused by Alice Longworth, the doyenne of all Washington hostesses and the daughter of Teddy Roosevelt, but I do not love her. I sat next her the other day at lunch. She looked like a witch, in her big black shovel hat. She is amusing in a gossipy, bitchy way, but not, I find, very funny or congenial.

The Kennedys are given to inviting groups of philosophers, musicians, actors, and writers to the White House. This is a welcome change but I don't know how deep this Camelot culture goes . . . not very far, I fancy.

8 September 1963.

Our new Minister of External Affairs, Paul Martin, arrived on Sunday evening to stay in the house for two nights. I much enjoyed his visit and his company. He is French enough and Irish enough to like a warm, pleasant social surface, and is good company. He is very serious in his approach to his new job, and is widely read and informed about international affairs. He is very much the inheritor of the Liberal tradition in which he was raised – "progressive" but basically cautious and realistic. The first evening we sat and talked. The next morning we had a breakfast party. Colin was in his full glory, deeply gratified to have a Foreign Minister staying in the house. He produced an enormous breakfast in the English-country-house tradition, with numerous side-dishes over flames. The guests included

U.S. Senator Morse, who talked absolutely non-stop throughout breakfast, entirely and exclusively about himself.

15 September 1963.

A new officer, Michael Shenstone, has arrived at the Embassy and came to see me today – quick-witted, quick-moving, highly intelligent, ruffled hair, dark eyes gleaming behind spectacles. What must it be like to be a junior officer with me as an Ambassador? My eyes used to be sharp for the absurdities and pretensions of those under whom I served. No doubt theirs are equally so. I don't mind being thought absurd by my juniors, but I should not relish being thought pretentious. What do I, for my part, expect of the people on my staff? Obvious things – intelligence and hard work. What do I chiefly deplore? Long-winded wordiness in speech or on paper. Also, I am embarrassed by incurable stupidity, especially if combined with a conscientious devotion to duty. It is difficult to know how to report on such cases when they come up for promotion; one cannot name any remediable faults, but one cannot conscientiously recommend advancement. Then I don't like fluffiness of mind which cannot get to the naked point. That is not so much stupidity as superficiality, often accompanied by self-esteem. Or, as Anne-Marie Callimachi used to put it: "He is thinking too much for the amount of brains he has."

I fear that it is not a liberal education, or any education at all, to serve under me. In my own young days I was indeed educated by senior men in the Service. Despite all those years passed as a student at universities, that was the only effective education I received – education as fitting one for action as distinct from acquiring knowledge. Hume Wrong was Counsellor in Washington when I was first posted here in 1937. I can still see him going through my draft dispatches with his red pencil, looking up across his desk at me with something between amusement and despair or leaning back in his chair stroking the back of his head with a rapid gesture of controlled exasperation at some muddled sentence or sloppy thought. (A morsel of praise from him would make my day, for he was no easy praiser.) Style and content he would scrutinize with impatient patience. He would annotate my text in his precise, elegant script, and put a stroke or an exclamation mark of horror beside some solecism. To accompany him on a visit of official business to the State Department was another kind of education. He would arrive for an interview with his arguments and the facts marshalled in his mind in impeccable array, and on his return to the Embassy he would dictate his account of the meeting – a model of clarity and verbatim recall – accompanied by his succinct comments and recommendations. Looking back, I now realize that in those days Hume was an unhappy, frustrated man. For although he had such a realistic grasp of policy questions, he was not able or willing to accommodate himself to politicians. He had fallen into disfavour with his peculiar Prime Minister, William Lyon Mackenzie King. In addition, he could hardly curb his contempt for the intellectual shortcomings of his own Head of Mission. Perhaps he was always better in dealing with those under him than those above him. I not only admired Hume, I came to love him as a friend. His cool perfectionism was only the surface – he was warm in his affection. I still often wish that I could turn to talk to him, to hear his acute and biting comments on personalities and events, and to know that here was one man who had never known the meaning of subterfuge or subservience.

22 September 1963.

When I was a young bachelor in Washington my mantelpiece was piled high with invitations to dinners, luncheon parties, and dances. I attributed this to my social and conversational charms. Now I realize that anyone in trousers serves the purpose in the desperate hunt for a spare man for dinner in this widow-populated city. When an apparently case-hardened bachelor takes it into his head to get married, there is lamentation among the hostesses as they cross his name off their lists: "How could he be so inconsiderate?" Death among the elderly single men is unavoidable, but marriage is unforgivable. Among the remaining bachelors my old friend Sammy Hood[1] is undoubtedly the pearl of price. Not only is he charming, with looks of infinite distinction, but he loves dining out and gives delightful parties in return. And on top of all this, a diplomat and a Lord. Sammy is made for Washington. He blossoms here, surrounded by affectionate friends, amused and interested by everything and

---

[1] Viscount Hood, British diplomat and Minister in British Embassy, Washington.

everyone. He makes one suspect that there is a lot to be said for bachelordom, provided one puts friendship before passion. For in a gossipy small town as Washington is, there is no place for lovers. In this and in many other ways it resembles Ottawa. Indeed, Ottawa might be described (in oyster terms) as Washington on the half-shell.

2 October 1963.

To a concert of chamber music at Dumbarton Oaks. Mrs. Bliss greeted us with regal affability. It's a miracle! She hasn't changed in the twenty-five years since first I crossed her threshold – the same tall, svelte figure and erect carriage, the same eager interest in all things cultural, from modern Brazilian poetry to pre-Columbian art. Heaven knows what her age must now be. Washington hostesses are notoriously ageless – they remain embalmed in their own image till one day they crumble into dust, untouched by decrepitude. Artistic hostesses, intellectual hostesses, social hostesses, political hostesses – reigning deities of the Washington stage! There are still a few survivors of those I knew in my youth – Alice Longworth, terrifyingly sprightly, and dear Virginia Bacon, the best-hearted, most downright of the lot, whose dark old house with its family portraits and long gallery still echoes the politics and gossip of half a century. But where is Mrs. Truxton Beale, whose soirées were so famous? And where Miss Boardman, of simple, unassailable dignity? And musical Mrs. Townsend? And where bustling, worldly Mrs. Leiter? And handsome, clever old Mrs. Winthrop Chanler, who had stepped from the pages of Henry James? Washington still abounds in hospitality and there are plenty of cultivated, decorative ladies who in a variety of styles keep the tradition going. I could name a dozen at this moment. But they lack one attribute of their predecessors – they are not formidable. Those old girls could dish out a magisterial snub and crush a social or political offender with the raising of an eyebrow. Manners have become milder.

Of course now, as then, there are hostesses and would-be hostesses. To an old Washington hand it is both funny and pathetic to see the struggles of some newly arrived political wife or aspiring ambassadress attempting to surprise with novel entertainment or calculated unconventionality. Old Washington, which has seen so many such ambitions blossom and fade, looks on with a basilisk stare.

18 October 1963.

Lunched today with Allan Dulles.[1] I have been seeing something of him lately. He is not as impressive intellectually, or in force of personality, as his brother Foster or his redoubtable sister. His mind seems to jump about. When seen in the domestic setting it is difficult to think of him as the ruthless spy-master. This afternoon he was shambling around in his carpet slippers, fussing with his notes for a joint TV show, on the subject of American burial practices, with Jessica Mitford and Adlai Stevenson, a bizarre trio. I very much like Mrs. Dulles – she has such individuality and a touch of the unexpected. The other day when I was paying a visit to my beloved Phillips Gallery I saw Clover Dulles standing in front of that great Renoir of the dancing couples in summer sunshine. Her lips were compressed in a line of disapproval and her brow furrowed in puzzlement. When I came up to join her and made some conventional remark about the exhilarating beauty of the picture, she said, "I can't agree. What is all this fuss about? Why do they look as though they were enjoying themselves so much? I can't see why a lot of sweaty red-faced Frenchmen in straw hats prancing about with stout females is so wonderful. I'm certainly glad I wasn't there myself."

Incidentally, one of the Klees at the Gallery has been stolen. These pictures are so small that they could almost have been slipped into the thief's overcoat pocket. How I wish it had been my pocket.

28 November 1963.

"Less than a week ago," we all keep repeating to each other in bewilderment and horror. Yes, it is "less than a week ago" since I was in Boston making a routine speech at some civic affair organized by the Mayor. When I sat down at the end of my speech the Mayor rose to his feet and, instead of the conventional thanks, he said, "I fear that I have some extremely bad news to announce. The President of the United States has been assassinated." Sylvia and I walked out into the sunny Boston streets in a state of shock. People were standing at street corners or walking along the pavements weeping openly, a sight I have never seen before. Now the original shock seems buried under

---

[1] The former head of the C.I.A.

these shoals of tributes and eulogies pouring in from all over the world and the hundreds of shifting TV images of the assassination and its aftermath. What can one find to say? The adventure is over, "brightness falls from the air," that probing mind, that restlessness of spirit, are snapped off as if by a camera shutter. We shall no more see that style of his, varying from gay to grim and then to eloquent, but always with a cutting edge.

Now for the anticlimax – to L. B. Johnson. We have come from the hills to the plains.

Bobby Kennedy remains untamed among the flood of public grief. His silence is significant of a deeper and different kind of grief.

29 December 1963.

Now at the year's end I look back on this last year in Washington and try to sum up my impressions. In the first place, there is the life of the office, the management of the Embassy itself. Once a week I sit at the end of the long table in the Chancery library, with its panelled walls and Grinling-Gibbon-style carvings, where Sir Herbert Marler used to sit with such ponderous dignity when he was in my place and I was a young man. Down the length of the table are representatives of the various government departments stationed here in Washington, also of the armed forces and the Bank of Canada. The Ambassador is supposed to have overall authority for the multifarious activities of Canadian representatives here. It is an almost impossible task to keep track of so many and such varied specialized activities and to know and assess so many varied personalities. Our own people from the Department of External Affairs I of course know well. I have an extremely able No. 2 in Basil Robinson. The younger men from External Affairs on the staff I see very often and they are a very good lot. I manage to keep up with most of the current work conducted here by other government departments. All the same, a great deal escapes me. There are a multitude of direct department-to-department contacts between Ottawa and Washington between officials who have known each other, very often, for many years, while ambassadors have come and gone. Their contacts are close and informal, by telephone Ottawa–Washington, Washington–Ottawa, or by their frequent visits. The armed forces, of whom there are hundreds stationed here in Washington, have their own close relationship with their American counterparts. The Bank of Canada and the Federal Reserve are in touch daily. Many of their conversations, which affect the whole economy of Canada and thus bear heavily on Canadian–American relations, take place on the telephone. Such conversations are not reported, except in the most general terms and not always then, to the Ambassador. All these direct relationships form a valuable ingredient in Canadian foreign policy. The Ambassador, however, is often hard put to it to obtain full knowledge and understanding of all the activities for which he bears a wide measure of official responsibility.

Then there are the frequent visits by Cabinet Ministers and officials for bilateral meetings with the Americans, and each of these Ministers arrives with his own team of experts fresh from the Ottawa scene and highly conscious of the political power-struggles and intrigues going on at home. Sometimes the Ambassador finds himself occupying a figurehead position in such negotiations. This, for example, was particularly true during this year's negotiation with the Americans over the Interest Equalization Tax, when I watched with silent admiration the superb and sustained diplomatic performance of Louis Rasminsky, the Governor of the Bank of Canada, in convincing the Americans, much against their previous stand, that the interests of the United States would best be served by granting us an exemption from the tax.

What, I wonder, was a diplomat's life like before the invention of the telephone? Ministers and officials, particularly of course officials of my own Department, are on the telephone to me almost daily, and so, quite frequently, is the Prime Minister. None of them seem to pay the slightest attention to the regulations supposed to govern the use of the telephone in the interests of security. Cabinet Ministers are particularly irresponsible in what they say, but then I should think, one way or another, the Americans know virtually everything that goes on in the activities of the Embassy if they are sufficiently interested to find out. Mike has never been particularly careful on this score. The fact that I have known him for so many years, however, makes it easy for me to pick up his meaning and intention from a half-phrase, sometimes even from the tone of his voice. In these recent years since he has been in politics I have been more and more struck by the tenacity with which he pursues his objectives. He does not proceed in a straight line, but crab-wise. If he meets an obstacle, he turns aside, even appearing to forget his intention, but he always comes back to what he was originally seeking. In his conversations with his American counterparts or in the days when, as Foreign Minister, he played such a part in the United Nations, he showed extraordinary facility in devising compromise, in finding a formula, often scribbled on the back of an envelope in the heat of debate. Indeed, his diplomatic footwork is amazingly nimble. One aspect of his character of which one has to beware, and which often leads the unwary into misunderstanding, is his acute dislike of any personal unpleasantness. Thus he often leaves the impression of agreeing to more than he intends to fulfil. People leave him with the impression that he has adopted their views when in fact he is simply trying to save their faces. Indeed, I have found that ready agreement on his part to any proposition is a negative sign. When I worked with him in the Department of External Affairs, I found that if he praised any proposition I put to him, it was speedily put aside. If, on the other hand, he poured forth a stream of objections and appeared to brush the proposal away, it was a sign that he was taking a serious interest in it. From the personal point of view it is, of course, a relief and a stimulus to me to be dealing with a Prime Minister who is also a friend.

My relations with the State Department are also, of course, easier since the change of government, although they never were difficult on a personal basis. Apart from Rusk himself, I see a good deal of Bill Bundy, a very nice and very able man. He and his wife Mary are personal friends. In general, the State Department strike me as highly competent but extremely cautious in the expression of their views. I wonder whether this is a hangover from the McCarthy years and the attacks on the State Department for supposedly left-wing inclinations. American officials are less willing to discuss alternatives, less speculative and less forthcoming, than the Foreign Office in London. They also seem somewhat less individual in their views than our own people at home. They tend to run to a pattern. There are outstanding exceptions. One is George Ball, a forceful, original mind, very tough in negotiation but very civilized in conversation. (He shares my love and admiration for the novels of Anthony Powell.) Another outstanding exception is Averell Harriman.[1] That old man is younger in mind and in spirit than many of his juniors, and has more political imagination; multi-millionaire, a former politician, he is totally without pomposity. Of the older men, Dean Acheson, now on the fringe of affairs, is my closest friend. I have known him and his beautiful and perceptive wife, Alice, since my early days in Washington. It stimulates one's mind just to be in the room with him. He has such immense style, intellectual and social. His vanity is endearing. We often go during the weekend for lunch with the Achesons at their country house. He always runs up the Canadian flag when I arrive. He is a kind of Canadian himself by ancestry and in temperament. This makes for difficulties with him, as he feels perfectly free, as if he were himself a Canadian citizen, to launch into the most violent attacks on Canadian policy, and in particular on Mike Pearson, for whom he has conceived strong mistrust. Once at his house after lunch he attacked Mike's reputation in such terms that I thought that as we were talking of my Prime Minister I should perhaps leave the house, after having in vain attempted to contradict him. However, as he then turned to an equally lively attack on most American political figures, I felt that it would be idle and absurd to make a scene and that my admiration and friendship for him were more important than anything he said.

Then as to my dealings with the White House this year, there has been the pleasure and stimulus of working with Mac Bundy. His company gives me the same kind of pleasure as that of Dag Hammarskjöld or Isaiah Berlin – the quickness of his mind, that network of live intelligence. To some, Mac's intellectual cocksureness might be putting-off, but then they are all cocksure here, all the leading officials – Ball, Acheson, Rusk, McNamara, and so on, right down the line. And at the top, in the Presidency, there is no humility, no self-doubt. The cast of thought in Washington is absolutist. It is true that there are a number of incompatible Absolutists, often in embattled struggle with each other, but all are Absolute for America, this super-nation of theirs which charges through inner and outer

---

[1] At this time Harriman had just left the post of Assistant Secretary of State for Far Eastern Affairs to become Undersecretary of State for Political Affairs. From 1965 to 1968 he was to serve as Ambassador-at-Large.

space engined by inexhaustible energy, confident in its right direction, the one and only inheritor of all the empires and the one which most fears and condemns the name of Empire, the United States of America, exhorting, protecting, preaching to and profiting by – half the world.

I don't know what I should have done since I came to Washington without my journalist friends. Some of my colleagues mistrust journalists, some are simply scared of them. I have always enjoyed their company. After all, I once tried to be a journalist myself – and failed. In Washington the top journalists wield more influence and have more access to the seats of the mighty than any diplomats. For example, Walter Lippmann. Walter is one of the most interesting minds I have encountered, also one of the most congenial companions. I have lunched with him at regular intervals this year and we go to the gatherings at the Lippmanns' house where one meets some of the inner circle of Washington influence. Then Scotty Reston has proved to be as good a friend to me as he has to other Canadian representatives and to our country.

As to the diplomatic colleagues, I have seen less of them than I used to do at the United Nations, yet we are often in and out of their Embassies and they are often here. David Ormsby-Gore, the British Ambassador, was the closest to President Kennedy of all the diplomats, although I don't know how much British influence affected the major policy decisions taken in the White House. The same question arises about my opposite number, Walt Butterworth, the American Ambassador in Ottawa. Walt is an able and aggressive operator. He has known Mike Pearson since years ago when he was a junior in the American Embassy and Mike was in the Department of External Affairs, and he sees him very often on an intimate social basis. Again, I rather doubt that he influences Mike's political decisions.

Thank God we have many friends in this city who have nothing to do with politics (except that everyone in Washington, directly or indirectly, has something to do with politics). Sylvia likes it here very much. She has a lot of women friends and it is a great place for women's group activities. She knows more Senators' wives than I know Senators. I think she is thoroughly enjoying herself. As for me, what a fortunate day it was when she said she would marry me.

I am lucky in having a lot of old friends here who date back to before the war. Some of these are actual born-and-bred Washingtonians, "the cave-dwellers," who have seen the ups and downs of so many political reputations, the coming and going of so many confidential advisers to successive presidents. Since I came back to Washington this time we have made a lot of new friends. Yet someone remarked to me the other day, "In this town no one is missed when they go away and no one is forgotten when they come back." Yes, Washington is a movable feast. Personally I am not in favour of capitals created purely for political purposes – Washington, Ottawa, Bonn. I think the capital of a nation should be in one of the great cities where the political process is not isolated. There is a claustrophobia about federal capitals.

Well, goodbye 1963. It closes on the note on which it opened – politics, the fascinating, dangerous world on whose fringe I live and whose muddied waters I try to keep my head above.

Here the diaries abruptly end, not to be resumed for nearly four years. What has become of the missing years? The volumes were perhaps lost in subsequent migrations from one diplomatic post to another? Left in the drawer of a hotel bedroom in Paris, London, or New York? Or did they ever exist at all – was I visited by one of those merciful intermissions when I abandoned the diary habit?

Of my remaining years in Washington, till my departure early in 1966, only a few of my notes remain and these have mostly to do with the disastrous Vietnam War which was so soon to darken the Washington scene, to twist and distort political – and sometimes per- sonal – relationships. As anyone who has lived through the last World War knows, a nation at war requires total support from its friends, not qualified approval, still less wise advice from the sidelines. Our Canadian support for the Americans over Vietnam was more explicit than we always recall in retrospect, but it did not meet the demand. As Ambassador in Washington I found myself once again represent- ing a Canadian government that had not come up to American expectations. There was not the acrimony which had marked the Diefenbaker–Kennedy exchanges; the mood now in the White House and the State Department was one of disappointment, a "more in sorrow than in anger" mood, though the anger was to come later. My own official record of this period is embalmed in the archives of the Department of External Affairs. What follows is no comprehensive account of relations between Canada and the United States on the Vietnam War or on any other of the many subjects of negotiation between the two countries during that time. It was compiled from notes taken at the time.

Lyndon Baines Johnson in his solemn hour lumbers to the podium to face his fellow Americans. The portentous utterances are lowered slowly into the waiting world. An impressively firm yet benevolent statesman enunciates the purposes and aspirations of the nation. The undertaker's tailoring encases a hulking, powerful body, something formidable by nature but dressed up and sleeked down. The President is not to be mocked. His displacement – as they say of ocean liners – is very great. He is a man of Faith, a man of ideals and of sagacity, and above all a man of power. No greater power has been in history than in this incarnation. He is our nuclear shield, leader of the West, dispenser of aid, sender of satellites, spender of billions, arbiter of differences, hurler of thunderbolts. The President of the United States of America! Foreign ministers and potentates gather at his gates. "How did you get on with the President?" That is the question, and woe betide the one who fails to pass the test. If the Jovian countenance fell into sullen furrows, then no more loans – no more arms. The chill spreads rapidly through the furthest confines of the administration. Lips tighten all down the line to the humblest desk officer in the State Department. What it is to be in the Presidential Doghouse! I have been there once or twice – or my country has. They are still civil in the government offices – civil and chilly – but give them a drink or two after dinner and it all comes out with rough frankness. Your government has erred and strayed from the way and the sheep-dogs are at your heels barking you back into line. Disagreeable it is at times – even offensive. Your Prime Minister may be harshly censured, but a word of criticism of the President of the United States of America and the heavens would fall with a weight appalling to contemplate.

Even when the sun of favour is shining, there are outer limits for a foreigner to exchanges of thought with the Washington higher management. For one thing, the President never listens – or at any rate never listens to foreigners. He talks them down inexhaustibly. The phrase "consultations with allies" is apt to mean, in United States terms, briefing allies, lecturing allies, sometimes pressuring allies or sounding out allies to see if they are sound. The idea of learning anything from allies seems strange to official Washington thinking. The word comes from Washington and is home-made.

When LBJ first came to power – in those few months when he counted none but well-wishers in Washington – that good friend of Canada, Scotty Reston expounded to me the pleasing notion that, as the new President was inexperienced in international affairs and as Mike Pearson was an international figure, there could be a fruitful and friendly working relationship between them. The President would turn to Mike for advice as a neighbour, one he could trust in a homely dialogue across the fence. It did not work out like that perhaps it could never have been expected to do so. When Mike Pearson came on his first official visit to Washington there was little stirring of interest in the White House. The President had much to occupy him; the visit seemed treated as of marginal importance. The Prime Minister's opening speech under the portico of the White House consisted largely in a heartfelt tribute to J. F. Kennedy – natural, inevitable so soon after the assassination, but not particularly heartwarming to the President. The President responded by a reference to our "undefended border." At dinner at the Canadian Embassy the President seemed bored. The Canadian government's gift of an RCMP English-type saddle brought a mumble that it "had no pommel." One saw it relegated to the White House attic. Yet the Prime Minister was not easily discouraged. He was determined to break through the ice and melt it with his charm and humour. He succeeded – or appeared to succeed. Before the visit to Washington was over he had had a long, private talk with the President which put the two of them on a footing of frankness. The President was genial and gossipy.

There followed an invitation to the Pearsons to go to the presidential ranch for the weekend. What effect – if any – this further intimacy had on the President is unknown. The ranch life seemed to the Pearsons a sort of burlesque circus. The hookers of bourbon at all hours, the helicoptering to visit neighbours, the incessant telephoning, the showing off, the incoherence and inconsequence of the arrangements – all disconcerted Mike. What disconcerted him even more was the impossibility of having any continuous discussion with the President, any exploration of political questions. The President was free with some fairly scabrous gossip about his fellow Senators. He would unexpectedly throw across to the Prime Minister a secret telegram or report which he was reading – thus making a demonstration of the easy, trustful way he felt about him, but there was none of that exchange of views on international or bilateral matters which had characterized the Prime Minister's meeting with Kennedy at Hyannisport in 1963.

All the same, the visit had been a success in political and personal terms. LBJ appeared to take to Mike and that, in terms of Canada–United States relations, was much gained. Every time the President saw me at an official reception he would send the warmest greetings to the Prime Minister, whom he described to me on one occasion as the head of government he "felt closest to."

Then came the thunderclap. The Prime Minister's speech at Temple University in Philadelphia on April 2, 1965, advocating a pause in the bombing in Vietnam – and the President's reaction to it – are part of political history, and this is not an historical record. The President's reception of the speech was sulphurous, and the relationship between the two men never fully recovered. No doubt LBJ believed that an attempt had been made by one he thought to be a friend "to dictate United States policy in his own backyard." When the Prime Minister arrived in Philadelphia he found a telegram from the President inviting him to lunch at Camp David. The telegram had been dispatched before the President had read the text of the speech. I accompanied the Prime Minister to Camp David – an occasion unfortunately unforgettable. Presidential aides Mac Bundy and Jack Valenti met us at the little airfield – no President. They were like schoolboys escorting the victim to the headmaster's study for a sharp wigging or possibly "six of the best." With strange innocence the Prime Minister and I were not fully prepared for what was to come. We anticipated that the speech would not be popular. Indeed, the Prime Minister's expressed reason for not consulting the President in advance of making it had been that LBJ might put pressure on him to excise the reference to a pause in the bombing.

Camp David could be a cozy mountain retreat – with a large, rough stone fireplace and the kind of pictures that go with it – but it was not cozy that day. LBJ received us with a civility that only gradually began to seem a trifle cool. I noticed with mild surprise that, contrary to his custom, he drank only one Bloody Mary before lunch. I made so bold as to have two. At luncheon the general conversation was made impossible because the President talked almost continuously on the table telephone. Part of the time he was receiving reports on bombing operations in Vietnam, at other times he seemed to be tidying up any telephone calls remaining at the bottom of his list – some fairly trivial ones that could have waited. Mike was left to make conversation with Lady Bird, Mac Bundy, and myself. He talked of the day's flight over the battlefield of Gettysburg, of his long interest in the battle and in the Civil War in general. Lady Bird was receptive – he made a joke and she distinctly smiled. Mac and I at intervals made a remark.

Lunch was over and there had been no mention of the speech. Over coffee the Prime Minister took the leap. "What," he inquired, "did you think of my speech?" The President paused before replying. It was the pause when darkest clouds lower, pregnant with the coming storm. "Awful," he said, and taking Mike by the arm, he led him onto the terrace.

What followed I witnessed mainly in pantomime, although from time to time the President's voice reached us in expletive adjuration. He strode the terrace, he sawed the air with his arms, with upraised fist he drove home the verbal hammer blows. He talked and talked – phrases reached Mac and me as we stood fascinated, watching from the dining room which gave onto the terrace through the open French windows – expostulating, upbraiding, reasoning, persuading. From time to time Mike attempted a sentence – only to have it swept away on the tide. Finally Mac suggested that he and I should take a walk through the wooded hills and leave our two masters together.

Our conversation was a reproduction in minor key of what we had just been witnessing. Mac, with the gentleness of a deft surgeon, went for the crucial spots. Perhaps, he suggested, he had not got his message across to me in our last conversation when he had reminded me of the undesirability of public prodding of the President. (I had in fact conveyed this message to Ottawa.) Why had the Prime

Minister chosen the United States as the place for such a speech? Why had there been no prior consultation with the President? Did I realize that the Prime Minister's plea for a pause in the bombing coming at this time might inhibit the very aim he had in mind? The tone was friendly but the scalpel was sharp. I countered by saying that the substance of the speech was a Canadian policy statement and in our view a wise one. The Prime Minister was speaking as a Nobel Prize lecturer at an academic occasion; he must deal with issues affecting the peace of the world. The thought of interfering in United States policy was far from his mind. Finally, losing patience with unanswerable questions about the choice of place and occasion, I added that I could assure him that the United States would never have a better or more understanding friend than the present Prime Minister.

By this time we had wound our way back again to the house. In the dining room we found Jack Valenti. The three of us looked out again at the terrace – the two figures were still there and the drama seemed to be approaching a climax of physical violence. Mike, only half seated, half leaning on the terrace balustrade, was now completely silent. The President strode up to him and seized him by the lapel of his coat, at the same time raising his other arm to the heavens.[1] I looked at Mac in consternation, but he was smiling. "It will be all right now," he said, "once the President has got *it* off his chest." Shortly thereafter LBJ and the Prime Minister re-entered the house and we took our departure. The President this time accompanied the Prime Minister to the airport and patted with him with geniality.

That night when I got back to Washington I rang up the Prime Minister, who had returned to Ottawa. I was emotional. I said to him that I had never been prouder of him than now. Indeed, he was both right and courageous in what he said, and the President would have done well to listen.

Some weeks later I was lunching with the indomitable Dean Acheson, who attacked Mike and referred critically to his speech. Once again I explained the background and defended the substance.

---

[1] It has been stated that the President grabbed the Prime Minister by the back of the shirt collar and held him off the ground. I saw nothing of the kind and do not believe that this ever happened. It would indeed have been an intolerable insult.

"Oh," said Dean, "you will see that bouncy man come back here and do it again."

The next year when the Prime Minister received the Atlantic Pioneer Award of Federal Union Incorporated at Springfield, Illinois, he made a speech dealing with issues involving the relationship between the United States and its NATO allies. The speech was thought in Washington to imply some measure of criticism of U.S. attitudes. Again rumbles reached us from the White House. Ambassador-at-Large Averell Harriman was sent to Ottawa to seek clarification. At the White House, Walt Rostow, who had succeeded Bundy, spoke of the Prime Minister's "egregious" speech and of the President's displeasure and "Why," he asked, "did he come into the President's own backyard to make such a speech?"

I heard myself replying much as I had to Mac Bundy on the earlier occasion a year before. But I thought I might guess the answer. Perhaps the Prime Minister had neither forgiven nor forgotten his encounter with the President on the terrace at Camp David. As Dean Acheson remarked, he was "a bouncy man" and he had bounced right back.

LONDON

1967–1971

When in 1966 I left Washington it was to go as Canadian Ambassador and Permanent Representative to the North Atlantic Council in Paris. It seemed that this would be an appropriate and enjoyable assignment. I had had a long experience in matters affecting NATO, dating back to the early days of the Alliance. I had been a student in Paris, and later served in our Embassy there, and I looked forward to returning to a city I loved. As it turned out, I was not a very effective member of the Council and could not recapture the Paris of my younger days. I saw it as a beautiful and historic city that had, in some mysterious way, "come unstuck" in my imagination, an old love revisited when we had little left to say to each other.

In my working life, I succeeded an old friend, George Ignatieff, who had brought enthusiasm and energy to the task. I had neither. Perhaps the strenuous years at the United Nations and in Washington had temporarily drained them out of me. Also, I found the North Atlantic Council itself a curiously unsatisfactory body, despite the able men who composed it. The work itself, covering as it does all aspects of the Alliance, could not fail to be interesting and important, but one had a sense of remoteness from the real centres of power in the NATO capitals where the decisions were reached. A complicating factor for a Canadian Representative was the policy which our government had adopted in relation to France. De Gaulle had pulled the French military forces out of NATO while France still, of course, remained a member of the Alliance. The French action was resented by other NATO governments. The Canadian government, however, partly for understandable domestic reasons, was anxious that the links with France should be maintained and that the French should be made to feel that, while we regretted their decision, nothing should be done to widen the breach between France and her NATO allies. This attitude was not popular with the other members of the Council, who tended to see it as a form of appeasement which the French had done nothing to merit. I do not think that the French government much appreciated our efforts. Indeed, Hervé Alphand, then at the head of the Quai d'Orsay (and an old acquaintance of mine from the days when we had both served in Washington), seemed to regard our efforts to placate General de Gaulle with a certain amount of cynical amusement.

Meanwhile, the decision to move the Council from Paris to Brussels had been taken. The Canadian government and its Representative were not favourable to the change – the government on grounds of policy, its Representative on grounds of preference. Although Paris might no longer cast the same spell of illusion, it was still highly agreeable. We had a charming flat, a genius cook, interesting colleagues, and varied friends. The ministerial sessions of the Council gave one an opportunity to see the Foreign Ministers of NATO in action; the discussions in the Council touched on issues affecting the political balance of the Western world and of East–West relations. My daily walks in the Bois de Boulogne were a pleasure. But I had my eye on London. The tenure of Lionel Chevrier as High Commissioner was nearing its close. There was a possibility of a political appointment; on the other hand, a professional diplomat might be chosen. In the event, when Mike Pearson appointed me I felt it to be a recognition that the hand I had played in Washington had not, after all, been so badly played. More than that, I felt it a gesture of friendship from one who was reticent in expressing friendship. I was grateful not only for the appointment but for the friendship.

I had very much wanted the London posting. Who would not? It is, to use a detestable adjective, a "prestigious" appointment. The attractions are obvious: to reside in London in a fine house, to be given the entry to varied English social and political worlds. I had reason to be delighted with my good fortune. It was to be my last post before retirement and I looked forward to it in a spirit best expressed by my friend Douglas LePan, who wrote, in congratulation, that my motto should be that of the Renaissance Pope – "God has given us the Papacy, now let us enjoy it."

London meant something more for me than my official position. As a child in Nova Scotia it was the London of Dickens which merged with my mother's stories of her own London experiences to create in my imagination a multitudinous city, the only scene for the full spectacle of life. When I was a schoolboy in England, London was the promised land at the end of term, the cornucopia of theatres and treats. When I was an undergraduate at Oxford, London meant the Big World where one's friends sank or swam when thrust out into the business of earning a living. Later still, I myself was to be one of these, a fledgling journalist on the *Evening Standard*, living in a bed-sitting room above a grocer's shop in the Earls Court Road. London had by then become a workplace, seen without illusion, as familiar as an old shoe. Coming back to it in war was a different matter. Under the bombs, one had a fellow feeling for every passerby in the streets. War and shared danger gave birth to a sense of community which peace had never achieved. We pitied those who were not with us in London in those days.

So, with memories tugging at my elbow, here I was back once again; back, but with a difference. Before I had, as a Canadian, slipped in and out of the interstices of English life. Recognized in no social category, I had the freedom of the city; I was familiar without belonging, an insider-outsider. Now I came as the official representative of Canada, tagged and classified, also handsomely housed. The residence of the Canadian High Commissioner – 12 Upper Brook Street – was originally a typical upper-class town house. It had been bombed out during the war and was largely reconstructed. The result was satisfactory, but somehow lacked conviction, like a woman with a facelift.

There was ample space for entertainment; the rooms were shapely and spacious. The long drawing-room had originally been decorated in glowing colours with rich fabrics imported from Paris. Later the Anglo-Saxon taste of some of the incumbents had been unable to stomach these splendours and had opted for middle-brow beige and genteel lime green in curtains and coverings. The pictures were a mixed bag – Canadian artists rubbing shoulders, not always happily, with their English neighbours, a Group of Seven iceberg staring blankly at a Mortlake tapestry of cupids disporting themselves in a pillared pleasance.

It required five servants to run the house. Of these, the butler was paid by the government, the cook and the maids out of my allowances. As to the fare provided there, the food – as always, under my wife's direction – was excellent. An inspired cook herself, she knew the difference. The wines were passable. The dinner table accommodated thirty, the drawing-rooms comfortably up to three hundred. The chauffeur, John Rowan, and his wife and son had an agreeable apartment in the basement. John was, and is, a remarkable man. He accommodated himself with tact, while preserving his own complete independence, to a succession of High Commissioners, each one very different from his predecessor. The official car was the largest, most indecently ostentatious vehicle to be seen in London. (It has since been sold to an undertaking firm and must add class to any funeral, rivalling the hearse in length and gloomy grandeur.)

My office in Canada House was on a scale to match the car. It had been the dining room of the old Union Club from whom the Canadian government had originally purchased the building. I knew the room well from the years when Vincent Massey had been High Commissioner and I, as his private secretary, inhabited the adjacent cubbyhole. How often had I trod the acres of carpet that separated the entrance from the outsize desk behind which the small figure of the High Commissioner was seated. How often had I stood looking over his shoulder while he peered dubiously at the drafts of speeches I had written for him. It was under the great chandelier that hung from the middle of the ceiling that he had stood when, in 1939, he had announced to the staff Canada's declaration of war. Vincent Massey had been a distinguished representative of Canada. He was a well-known and respected figure in political, social, and artistic circles in London. He had dignity without pomposity, intelligence and charm. Here I now was in his place; it remained to be seen what I could make of it.

The times had changed, and so had the relationship between Britain and Canada. In the days of Vincent Massey the Canadian government, under the leadership of Mackenzie King, was obsessed by the suspicion that Whitehall was plotting designs against our nationhood and trying to draw us back into the imperial framework. Our attitude, however, was ambiguous, as Mackenzie King himself demonstrated when he chose as the title for his own book on Canada's war effort, *Canada at Britain's Side*.

Now, in 1967, the ambiguity had been resolved, but what had taken its place? We no longer harboured fears of British dominance. We had finally emerged from the motherhood of the British Empire, only to struggle for breath in the brotherly embrace of Uncle Sam. There were still enduring ties, rooted in history and common institutions, which gave Britain a special place in the affection of Canadians – at any rate of Anglo-Canadians. We were allies in NATO, fellow members of the Commonwealth, owing allegiance to the same Queen. There was extensive trade between us; there were innumerable special links between groups – professional, business, and cultural. Every spring, London was inundated by our fellow countrymen. They came for the historic sights, for the theatre, for the charms of London and the English countryside, sometimes to visit scenes where they had served in the war or for reunions with friends and relatives. The affection for England was there, but British influence was gone. No future Prime Minister was ever likely to call his book *Canada at Britain's Side*. We and the British were excellent friends who had known each other for a long time, but we were no longer members of the same family. If our attitudes had changed, so had those of the British. With their loss of influence had come some loss of interest. Canadians were well liked in England; Canada was esteemed. There remained the bonds of the past, but our future was no longer any concern of theirs. If our preoccupations were with the United States, theirs were increasingly with Europe.

The relations between the Canadian and the British governments in the years when I was in London were, for the most part, untroubled, or, as they say in official communiqués, "cordial and friendly." They offered no challenges or ordeals to a Canadian High Commissioner. After Washington, this was a rest cure. The drama was not in London, it was in Paris. It was French policy, with its impact on the future of Quebec, that was of absorbing interest to the Canadian government.

The advent of Pierre Trudeau as Prime Minister in April 1968 did not affect our relationship with the United Kingdom. There was a very different style and a shift of emphasis, not of policy. Mike Pearson was well known and liked in London. He was also a strong supporter of the Commonwealth and of NATO. Trudeau at first showed no great enthusiasm for either. While his somewhat flamboyant behaviour on his first visit to England in January 1969 got plenty of press notice, his official contacts with the United Kingdom government went smoothly and satisfactorily. He and the Prime Minister, Harold Wilson, got on well together. It gradually became apparent that, despite the talk then prevalent in government circles in Ottawa of our military withdrawal from NATO, nothing of the sort was seriously contemplated; also, the Canadian government would continue to play a positive role in Commonwealth affairs. Nor did the coming to power of the Conservative government in Britain in 1971 make any real difference to Canadian–United Kingdom affairs. The new Conservative Foreign Secretary was Alec Home. I had never experienced anything but friendliness from George Brown when he held that office in the Labour government, but Alec Home was quite exceptional in his wisdom, tolerance, and charm. Our day-to-day relations with the Foreign and Commonwealth Office were conducted with Dennis Greenhill, an effective and sensible realist. At Buckingham Palace the Queen's secretary, Michael Adeane, I had known since Ottawa days when he had been an A.D.C. at Government House. One of the most astute of men, he is also the best of friends.

In Marlborough House, the seat of the Commonwealth Secretariat, the Canadian Secretary-General, Arnold Smith, a former colleague in the Department of External Affairs, deployed his enthusiasm, skill, and patience in dealing with problems more difficult and demanding than those which faced the High Commissioner.

There was a large and competent staff at Canada House, among whom I counted some very good friends. It often occurred to me that the place could function quite satisfactorily without any High Commissioner at all. The atmosphere of the office was congenial. I had with me, in Geoff Murray, Jerry Hardy, and Louis Rogers, very able Deputy High Commissioners. We had entered a new age of administration. The monstrous growth of regulations, the avalanche of forms and bureaucratic paraphernalia, created a jungle in which I was lost. I had been trained in a simpler era when External Affairs was smaller. The change was inevitable, but I could not get away from the conviction that self-regulating bureaucracy took up too much time which should have been devoted to the formulation and execution of policy. There was too much harness and no bloody horse! Louis Rogers, who had come to Canada House after being our Ambassador to Israel, understood both policy and administration. He controlled his impatience with my administrative ineptitude and enlivened the working hours by his sardonic wit. His wife, June, was stimulating in talk, lovely to look at, the daughter of my old chief, Hume Wrong. I had known her since she was a child.

As there were few policy questions at issue between our two governments, the functions of the High Commissioner were largely those of a representative and a reporter. There were speeches to be made and ceremonial occasions to attend. There was also the multifarious daily business involved in our close trade, cultural, immigration, and tourist relations with the United Kingdom. There were frequent – all too frequent – visits of Canadian Cabinet Ministers and delegations of officials; there were press conferences and briefings. There were close contacts to be maintained with the Agents General of the provinces in London, and with the Canadian colony there.

There was reporting on the British political and economic situation for the inattentive ears of Ottawa. There are few echoes of these reports in the London diaries, which reflect a varied and lively social life and scarcely dwell at all on the public events which formed the substance of dispatches to Ottawa now lying dormant in the files of the Department of External Affairs.

The years I spent as High Commissioner in London, although enjoyable personally, were not an inspiriting period in British history. The country was wracked by strikes and industrial disputes. Under uninspired political leadership the nation seemed increasingly fragmented, with every group pursuing its own particular interests. Yet the notion that England was a "sick society" was a superficial judgement. The country was indeed suffering from social and economic ailments which took forms peculiar to England. But the disease was to spread to other industrialized nations, including our own. Throughout the stresses and strains of these years the underlying strength of

British character and British institutions remained intact. The English themselves were – as they had always been – kindly, ironic, and stoical. Britain remained one of the most civilized countries in the world, if civilization is to be judged by standards of tolerance and humanity.

2 October 1967.

London is a fever of hope deferred. Some day (?) I shall get on top of this job, lead my own life, make my mark. What mark? A first-class reporter who knows all and everyone; a counsellor whose counsel is sought; host at a present-day Holland House; loved but not inconveniently, sought after but not pressed, liked and respected by my own government but at a distance; no more ministerial visits; good cook, interesting books, no chocolate-covered chairs in the "guest suite"; reputation of a brilliant speaker but never having to justify it by making any more speeches; taken as natural by the young.

6 October 1967.

Yesterday was quite different. I walked in Hyde Park under a cloudy sky. Damp oozed from the grass beneath my feet. I carried an old borrowed umbrella, tied together with a rubber band. I had just been reading Virginia Woolf's *Mrs. Dalloway*. It had reopened a way of feeling and seeing that belonged to its time – an anarchic mixture of exhilaration and sadness. As the seagulls scattered and swooped over the park expanses, restlessness and dead wishes stirred. I thought, too, of Life (and we know how Virginia Woolf loved talking of Life).

I went into the Griffin in Villiers Street, near Charing Cross Station, to meet Elizabeth [Bowen]. It is perhaps to become our London equivalent of the Plaza Bar in New York. We sat drinking, talking, and eating cold beef sandwiches. She looked – and was – extraordinarily young (there must have been some quality in the day that made it a pocket in time, a day out of the steady progression). She began to talk about the figures of Bloomsbury she had known in her youth – Virginia Woolf, the Stracheys. It was a sudden outbreak of her old brilliant, individual, visual talk, which has been muted lately. She made me see the ingrowingness of that little Bloomsbury world, their habit of writing endless letters to each other, of analysing, betraying, mocking, envying each other. She spoke of the kind of pains of jealousy and treachery which they inflicted on each other. She thinks that that kind of intellectual, professional, upper middle-class, like the Stracheys, tends more to corruption than any other class and that, in that sense, they are "clogs to clogs." Elizabeth is approaching the last chapter of *Eva Trout*. God knows how it will be received. Her delight in it is catching. The people she can't now bear are those who say nostalgically to her, "I did so love *The Death of the Heart*."[1]

In the afternoon a Brigadier and his wife came for drinks, she a tiresome woman with that air of tucking away what you say to her with disapproval, as if she would take it out of her bag when she got home and, if necessary, report it to the Proper Authorities.

27 October 1967.

Went to Colchester for the Colchester oyster feast. Rather fun, these little excursions and getting glimpses of the endless groupings of English life. This week the Distillers in the city, and the Warrant Holders' Banquet, and now this little world of Colchester. All the local worthies and bigwigs – Ted Heath,[2] who made a speech and spoke of the typically Essex faces in the audience. I looked down from the high table at the long, pale faces with very pale blue eyes and colourless hair and total lack of expression – Essex types? It rained. I don't care for Colchester oysters and I noticed that neither the Mayor nor the Aldermen touched them. I sat next Lady Allport, wife of the man who heads the Mission to Rhodesia, and did not charm her, which was a pity as she did rather charm me. Next to her, on her other side, was the head of the Boilermakers' Union, whom she described as a "very cozy character."

1 November 1967.

Popski's attitude towards us has changed since his long incarceration in kennels during the quarantine period on his arrival in England. I think we made a mistake in visiting him when he was

---

[1] First published in 1938.

[2] Edward Heath – then Leader of the Opposition, subsequently Conservative Prime Minister.

caged up in the kennels. He greeted us with frantic excitement, but when we walked away from him he was in despair. I believe that he came to think that we had deserted him and never forgave us.

Since he has been released and come to this house, he lives by preference most of the time in the kitchen. When we call him he comes, allows himself to be patted for a moment, is perfectly polite to us as though we were distant acquaintances. I am sure he bears us a deep grudge for – as he thinks – abandoning him in prison.

5 November 1967.

It is at this precise time – 11 a.m. – that Sylvia is going into the operating room. She fell day before yesterday and broke her hip. The doctors said that she could either remain in bed for six weeks without moving, so that the bones might heal naturally, or have a pin put in to hold them together. She chose the latter, as she couldn't bear the prospect of the total inaction. I am unreasonably nervous and depressed about this operation, which I am told is quite a routine one. How much she means to me, and how lonely I should be without her, how much married I have become. The thought of the actual operation sickens me. The weather is depressingly black, the house deadly silent (this house, like the house where Lytton Strachey spent his youth, has developed elephantiasis, disproportionate swollen growth).

6 November 1967.

I went to the banquet in the Guildhall given for the President of Turkey and sat next Mrs. Mulley, who is the wife of the Minister of State at the Foreign Office. Her husband was a Cambridge don, but it bored him, so now he is a politician. How does one make that transition? Politicians always seem to me a race apart, like actors, and I am surprised to find that they nearly all once plied ordinary trades. The laundry had sent someone else's shirt back and I wore a collar sizes too big for me, but no one knew or cared.

Sylvia has come out of the operation. It has gone very well. She was already sitting up a few hours after regaining consciousness and asking for *newspapers*.

21 November 1967.

Mike Pearson has arrived, and Maryon. I felt such affection, attraction, for them when I saw them arriving at the airport. He seems happy at being here, and young – much younger than I am. Lunch with Blair Fraser[1] at the Travellers. This was my day for liking people, although I have always liked him and find him admirable. With us elderlies much depends on the day, state of fatigue, health, etc. We have our recoveries, and can be almost human.

Mike's press conference very dreary; it dragged and he knew it. The British press uninterested – no angle for them.

3 January 1968. Doodles to replace a diary.

I can pray for myself but it seems a presumption to pray for others.

"'Damn' braces, 'bless' relaxes" Blake.

I cling to rationalization like a man hanging on to his pants to prevent them falling down.

The burrows of the nightmare, the stuff that dreams are made of; endless riches piled in those caves of sleep, mixed with rubbish and wildly comical juxtapositions. This is what Buñuel is after in his films, and catches, and the lewd delights!

The Turner Venetian scene over the fireplace "floods the room with colour" – and it does.

Wheeler-Bennett would be the best to do Vincent Massey's biography, but he cries out for Proust, a Canadian Proust.

Is there any point in balancing one's prejudices with "fair-mindedness"? Why not turn purple with prejudice and passion, make no allowance? Why not give way to envy, and to blind loyalty too? Come on, join the human race.

20 January 1968.

Garwood, the butler, has his endearing side, also an infuriating side. Last evening I said to him, "General Anderson would like a dry martini *on the rocks.*" He made a martini with ice *in the shaker* and

---

[1] Canadian journalist.

poured it. I said, "That is not a martini on the rocks." He said, "Yes, sir, it's just the same, *not to worry*. I have a reputation for my martinis." "I was restrained from pursuing the argument by the presence of a guest" (as Mr. Pooter[1] would have said), but the guest, Bill Anderson, said when Garwood had left the room, "He certainly won the battle of the rocks." I laughed, pretty grudgingly. As a General, Bill has a sharp eye for victories and defeats.

Garwood and Popski make a pair. I don't know how two such egotists get on together. Garwood recognizes Popski's tactical skills, sometimes calling him "the General" or "Your Royal Highness," at others addressing him good-humouredly as "you silly old fool." Popski has been given the stone out of an avocado pear and will not let anyone go near him in case they try to take it away from him. He bangs it on the parquet floor, making a considerable racket for a small dog with a small object.

21 January 1968.

Beryl Saul and her two sons are staying here. Her husband, Bill, who was my Military Adviser in Paris and of whom I was fond, died suddenly two weeks ago at forty-eight years old of a cerebral haemorrhage. She is in a state of shock. Her eldest son is a parachutist in the British Army, just back from Aden. His batman was shot in the back by an Arab terrorist. "He was the most innocent boy I ever saw, wouldn't have hurt a fly. What were we fighting for in Aden anyway? Was it worth his life?" The second Saul boy wants to join the Department of External Affairs. Both had been brought up in the Canadian military tradition, as of course was Bill Anderson, who dined with us last night. So we have been seeing quite a lot of the Canadian military. They are the descendants of the old Canadian Permanent Force, the class and kind of people I was accustomed to in Halifax in my youth – Canadians modelled on a British tradition.

22 January 1968.

Called on Polish Ambassador in the morning. He is pessimistic about British recovery. He says that the United Kingdom has for years

---

[1] Mr. Pooter is a character in *Diary of a Nobody*, by George Grossmith.

had the lowest rate of investment in Europe, so there is no base for a recovery founded on the export drive. England, he says, is hampered by her class system and is not drawing upon all the human material available in the country. I questioned this latter bit but I don't know if I am right. This seems to me a democratic society, but what does one mean by that? British society seems pulverized, its different segments living unto themselves, innumerable private pockets and groups and individual interests. The only solidarity seems to be that of the young against the old, and vice versa.

I got Hardy[1] to qualify the gloom of his telegram about Wilson's future as Prime Minister. It is too easy to be carried away by these gusts of opinion. Wilson is not through yet, though many I meet wish he were.

Lunched alone on sausages and mash at the Griffin – "There is a table free, love, in the corner."

Went to the National Gallery and saw a celestially blue Bellini Madonna, "such a forgiving blue" as Stephen Tennant would have said. John Maher says the National Gallery is too near to go to and I am going to prove the opposite.

10 March 1968.

Reflections on a spring Sunday afternoon . . . The picture of the world from the TV and the Sunday papers is an apocalyptic one – race war, war between the generations, collapse of the financial system, Vietnam, collapse of moral values, erosion of parliamentary government, etc., etc. America in trauma, England full of self-disgust, and everywhere swarms of protesting students – in Warsaw, Cambridge, Tokyo, Rome, in America, Canada, in China, in Europe – hordes of angry milling masses of placard-bearing youth. Student riots – a preliminary to revolution? What kind of revolution? Against what, and for what? The casualties or near-casualties of this day in time include internationalism (the decline of the United Nations and the Commonwealth), the multiracial society (racial struggle in America, in England, and now in Kenya), the concept of "one world" (nationalism is everywhere rampant). Is some vast shudder going through

---

[1] J. E. G. Hardy – Deputy High Commissioner.

the frame of man-made society or is it all inflated and inflamed by the news media?

Today Sylvia and I went in this mild grey weather for a mild and happy little expedition to Richmond. We walked along the tow-path, past dilapidated hotels, to the Star and Garter, where we had lunch for only £1.10 and looked out on the famous view of the bend of the river. Then we took a mini-taxi to Ham House.[1] How strange it is, unlike any other house in the world. To think of that coarse, sinister, scheming couple – the Lauderdales – plotting in these little over-decorated rooms among the japanned cabinets in the baroque décor under the floridly painted ceilings. Ghosts that Horace Walpole said, when he visited the house in 1770, he would not give sixpence to see. One would give more than sixpence *not* to see them.

11 March 1968.

I wonder, sometimes, about my various predecessors in this house. I suppose they had the same marital conversations about servants and allowances, plus talk, in their case, of their children, and they made love in the same bed and looked out at the same chimney-pots and ended by "loving London."

I was so touched and pleased that Peter[2] came with a present of six pairs of silk stockings for Sylvia. I recognized him in this gesture more than anything he has done since I met him again. He told Sylvia that he had come to see me because I sounded so low on the telephone.

12 March 1968.

Frederic Hudd[3] died last night. At the end, he said that he wished he had married, and that he had had a lonely life. General and Mme. Ailleret were killed in a plane accident yesterday. Two ways of dying – a stroke following old age and years of senility, or a plane crash. Which would you choose?

---

[1] Ham House, Richmond, Surrey – originally the home of Lord Lauderdale, Scottish politician in the reign of Charles II.

[2] Peter Elliston, an old friend from boyhood in Halifax.

[3] Former Deputy High Commissioner, Canada House.

Garwood, the butler, is back, "on the wheel" as he puts it. He looks years younger for his illness.

For some reason, when I woke up this morning I was thinking about butlers. I could write a book about "Butlers I Have Known." In their lofty idea of their own position and their devotion to protocol, in the gravity of their public façade, they much resemble certain ambassadors. Indeed, they often look like them physically. On one unlucky occasion at a cocktail party, I called out, rather impatiently, to the passing servitor, "Bring me another whisky, please," only to realize a moment later that he was a newly arrived Ambassador of notorious prickliness and self-importance. However, butlers can get their own back as effectively as diplomats. Once, at a reception in Ottawa, I encountered an ex-butler from one of our embassies, now – with his wife – catering for parties there. An old Cockney he was. He greeted me with the remark, "I just said to my wife when I saw you: 'My God, how Mr. Ritchie's aged; *my God*, how he has aged!'" I tried to indicate my lack of interest in this train of thought, but he went on repeating it with intense conviction.

12 April 1968. Weston Hall.

Staying with Sachie and Georgia Sitwell for Easter. We had a day at the races with Kisty Hesketh[1] and her party from Easton Neston. High spirits in a cutting wind at the races. Lunch in a drafty tent – shivered with cold and thoroughly enjoyed myself. Back to Weston for tea (cinnamon toast and chocolate cake).

Now I sit writing in this little bedroom overlooking the garden where first I came twenty-eight years ago, and I remember the intoxication of the first visit when the name Sitwell was a key to a fabulous landscape with figures. Sachie is now recovering from an operation but refuses to be daunted by illness. They have both been so affectionate and welcoming – I love them.

20 April 1968.

We have a new Prime Minister – Trudeau – and I try, from reading articles about him, from talking to his friends, to penetrate to the

---

[1] Christian, Lady Hesketh.

man. Nothing so far said or printed reveals him to me, nor did my own meeting with him. I recall something enigmatic about him which struck me even at that time, long before his present celebrity, something inhuman (the word is too strong) beneath the courteous, charming manner; too much all-of-a-piece, perhaps, the cultivated, intelligent, cool observer?

21 April 1968.

It is time that Elizabeth returned. What if she never did? Some day she won't.

In St. James's Park, sensually happy in the morning, sensually sad in the evening.

Read Malraux's *Anti-Memoirs*. I started it as a duty and was discouraged and surprised to find how many French words I do not understand. Then I read on and something else irritated me – there was too much talk of Destiny. I began to suspect inflation, and a peculiarly French form of inflation, but I persisted and was rewarded, engaged, swept along by the marvellous rhythms of language and brought up short by the telescoping of thought and image.

22 April 1968.

Just back from a weekend staying with Huntley Sinclair for the Badminton Horse Show. Huntley, an old friend from early Ottawa days, came over here in the RCAF during the war and has stayed on and married a very nice and very wealthy woman. They live in a big house of Cotswold grey stone, with a Lutyens wing and a view of the Stroud valley.

The Queen is staying nearby with the Duke and Duchess of Beaufort, and was at the morning service in Badminton church. She had a word with me on the way out of church about Trudeau's succession as Prime Minister. (I had told her some days ago that I felt certain that he would win over his competitors.)

The Queen has treated me with the greatest kindness and informality since I have been here. And she has no more devoted admirer than I. It is not only loyalty to the Throne (and I have always been a royalist) but fascination with the personality of the woman who occupies it.

2 May 1968.

What would we do without Jean Halton? She is the widow of Matthew Halton, the brilliant Canadian journalist, and we are lucky enough to have her as social secretary at Canada House. It's a tricky job, as, in addition to our own official entertaining, she has to cope with the stream of applications by Canadian visitors for invitations to the Royal Garden Parties and the Trooping of the Colour. The applicants do not always realize that these invitations have to be shared out among all members of the Commonwealth. Those who do not get invitations sometimes become disgruntled, and Jean copes with these and all other social problems with her mixture of charm, good humour, and friendly firmness.

6 May 1968.

A blowing day of wide skyscapes. Sylvia wore her purple suit with a new flowered blouse and we walked together in Hyde Park, watched a sailing boat capsize in the Serpentine, and came home to lunch on trout and asparagus.

The new Canadian government is apparently contemplating some measure of military withdrawal from Europe and perhaps from NATO itself and putting increased emphasis on the continental defence of North America. I am planning to write a dispatch on this subject and have been thinking it over. One argument for the change would be that it would make us slightly more independent of the United States' continental defence umbrella. At first sight this argument is not impressive. Our additional contribution to continental defence would be a flea-bite. Then there is the fashionable argument that money saved from NATO should go into aid and peace-keeping. There is disillusionment, too, with the failure of the Atlantic Community idea and our concept of Article 2 of the Treaty. Also there is the influence of de Gaulle and the French military pull-out from NATO. Some may even believe that by retreat from NATO we might improve Canadian–French relations and take the French heat off Quebec. After de Gaulle's behaviour in Canada this would be kissing the boot that kicked us. Such appeasement would not affect de Gaulle but only encourage him.

There is also the widespread feeling (how widespread I doubt) that NATO is becoming regarded in Canada as an "old-fashioned" military alliance. The very word "alliance" savours to such critics of power groupings and does not fit with our image of ourselves as "progressive." The further dangerous implication is that it is dated to believe in the political or military aggressiveness of the U.S.S.R., especially in Europe. How far does Trudeau share these notions?

At any rate it seems to me quite unthinkable that we should contemplate leaving NATO in the foreseeable future. A unilateral precipitate announcement of troop withdrawals would be messy but not quite so bad. It would gravely embarrass our NATO allies. A phased redeployment of Canadian forces after consultation with our allies could be justified in terms of an increase in our North American responsibilities. It would be disintegrating in its effects on the Alliance, perhaps pointless in terms of positive results, but not fatal.

8 May 1968.

Went down on the morning train to Hythe to spend the day with Elizabeth.[1] I was an hour early at Folkestone, so Elizabeth was not there to meet me. I walked in the sun round some playing fields and tulip beds and had a happy drink alone in a pub where skippers off the Folkestone-Boulogne boats were reminiscing. Then Elizabeth called for me in the car and we lunched in the hot sun at the Hotel White Cliffs, at Dover, where the glass-ended lounge looks across to the esplanade, to the equable blue channel and the boats coming in and out. It has always been warm and sunny when we have gone together to Dover and we are always happy there and always have Dover sole and Pouligny-Montrachet for lunch and walk afterwards under the cliffs which look as though they would topple over the line of late-Georgian houses, in one of which my aunt, Lale Darwall, ended her days. Then we walked out on the long pier and the weather changed to grey and the landscape looked "like a photograph," as Elizabeth put it. She said that she remembered in her youth coming back from adventures in France on such a day, to find, with sinking heart, England looking just like that.

In the afternoon I read Lady Cynthia Asquith's diaries about the brothers and lovers and sweethearts who went out to die in the 1914-18

---

[1] Elizabeth Bowen had bought a house in Hythe, Kent.

war, while the house parties and flirtations and gossip went on at home, and Ego and Ivo and Basil were on the casualty lists or reported "missing, presumed dead." The sadness and waste of it all and the triviality of the gossip combined to depress me. We have come such a long way since then that for all their worldliness they seem innocent – and brave.

Coming home I stood in the light rain alone at Sandling Station waiting for the train – a little station, probably shortly to be suppressed.

5 June 1968.

A dark, rainy morning. The Pearsons, who have been staying here, will be off to the airport for Canada in a few minutes. The shooting of Bobby Kennedy, with its play-back to the assassination of JFK, has given a nightmarish flavour to the last twenty-four hours. Mike says that people in Canada will be smug about it and will say "it couldn't happen here." It only accentuates one's feeling that Canada must not, shall not, be absorbed into that runaway American society which is like a giant plane out of control.

A quiet last evening of the Pearsons' visit – Sylvia and Maryon playing Russian bank, Mike and I watching soccer on the TV, a brisk argument on the future of NATO after dinner, Mike saying that we *will* withdraw our forces from Europe, that NATO is an "old-fashioned military alliance," that our future lies more in the North American continental sphere. It's this last bit that I find difficult to absorb.

19 June 1968.

London seasonitis. Morning of breathless exhaustion, like a swimmer weakening a long way from land, land being in this case our holiday at Chester. Deterioration of human relations because of always having to break off conversation just as it might come to a point, in order to rush to change for another party. Undue dependence on alcohol to buoy one up for another encounter, smoking frantically in the car in traffic queues, always twenty minutes late for a luncheon or a dinner party; always a day behind in little thank-you notes for a day-before-yesterday's dinner party, or condolence notes to widows whose mates have finally fallen out of the race due to strokes or heart attacks from just one day or night too much; decline of sexual energy from too much social stress – and all this is self-inflicted (All of Us on All of Us), and still there is the whole of July ahead of us.

22 June 1968.

A muggy, claggy day, a day to sit on a park bench wrapped up in a raincoat like an old tramp, with some crumbs to feed the ducks while waiting for the mild drizzle to come down. But in fact I am away, top-hatted, to the commissioning of a Canadian submarine at Chatham, and to pass in review the crew, and to orate from a dais. And Sylvia, very nervous, is to present the Captain of the submarine with a large crest-engraved silver cigarette box. *There*, that is Commander Swiggum at the door, to A.D.C. us, sitting in the car all the way to Chatham, thus impos-ing a certain measure of chat. Better have a pee now and not have to arrest our great black hearse at some Esso station on the rain-wet road.

8 July 1968.

Back from Stansted after a most enjoyable weekend with Eric and Mary Bessborough.[1] Eric says that from his bed he sees nothing but tulips. His bedroom is hung with Dutch paintings of tulips and with beautifully articulated watercolour drawings of tulips; in all the vases are more tulips. Tulips and macaws – not only paintings of macaws, but real live ones. When not infuriated in a cage, biting the hand that feeds them, they fly free in glorious Technicolor from tree to tree, making a wickedly unfriendly noise, but undeniably ornamental. During lunch on the terrace, as I was putting a piece of pâté to my lips, a macaw swooped down and flew away with it.

Peter Ustinov came for lunch. Is he the clown country gentleman in a nineteenth-century novel? Broad, pale, heavy hands; broad Russian nose; mimicry and wit with the very edge that Russians can find for pretensions and affectations. A lumbering, friendly, comical creature who could change mood with the speed of a bear.

27 July 1968.

In the parks, under the sulky sky and on the used-up grass, the couples lie, length to length. They follow an undeviating protocol in

---

[1] The Earl and Countess of Bessborough. Stansted is their country house in Sussex.

their embraces – kiss, kiss, hug, hug, no copulation; hour after hour they entangle thus without culmination but with convulsive twitching of blue-jeaned buttocks. Dotted about in conveniently sited deck chairs, elderly men watch them, uncross their legs and gaze absently at the clouds above. Children throw balls over the recumbent writhers. Tired ladies in ones, or sometimes twos, close their eyes in unsimulated indifference, and adolescents seated in groups discuss over the recumbent bodies whatever it is that adolescents do discuss.

30 July 1968.

Dinner at the Apéritif with Elizabeth. The bartender remembered me from the days more than twenty years ago when I used to go there and sit on a high bar-stool drinking martinis and waiting for Margot, cursing her for always being three-quarters of an hour late and in an accumulating rage which changed in a jiffy to pleasure and relief when her tall figure finally came through the door with a rush of modish, Mayfair-ish excuses, interlarded with "darlings." Then there was always the promise of the night ahead – a promise often unfulfilled, and put off with the most blatant lies about her visiting sister-in-law, etc., lies which had to be swallowed because I was only a substitute, a filler-in, a role which, apart from the frustration it sometimes involved, really suited me better than being No. 1, with all its claims.

1 August 1968.

I have been thinking about the forthcoming Commonwealth meeting in London and the role of Canada and of Trudeau in it. He is a new figure whose advent will be greeted by British public opinion and by his Commonwealth peers with curiosity and interest. He may be the star of the Conference; the others are mediocrities. The popular press will be after him, his speeches will get a good play. He is in a position to be heard, if he has anything to say. What is his thinking about the Commonwealth? Is he interested? I doubt it.

Will there be a tendency to expect Canada to take on Britain's role? I don't think so – it's plainly impossible. Arnold Smith, as Secretary-General, will want us to take a more positive part, possibly over Rhodesia. So will Nyerere and Kaunda, who flatter and actually believe in us. All this is very tempting – its multiracial quality is popular in Canada; also it corresponds to a real but not deep-rooted trust in Canada by the Africans. But the terrain is dangerous. Expectations can easily be built up and disillusionment can result. The British might be prepared to push us into a more ambitious role. It will cost us more in aid – perhaps we can afford that? We should, in talking to the Africans, not "hot them up" but try to cool them off. There is realism among them underneath. We should not get mixed up in their politics or in the protection of British interests, which a Commonwealth Peace Force would have meant. We should stay right away from African freedom fighters. We mustn't be used by Harold Wilson and must remember the possibility that the Conservatives may be in power in England before long.

Unless we do propose to be the champions of the Africans and assume a new Commonwealth leadership there is nothing much in the way of a role for us. Our posture should be a sensible middle-of-the-way realism, using the Commonwealth as an opportunity for numerous bilateral contacts, showing a general disposition that it should continue and being willing to contribute to this end. The Commonwealth has links in a world where there are not too many, and can help in finding compromises provided these are not so illusory as to rebound against their originators. As to the Monarchy – in the Commonwealth context – it is a useful limited device.

20 August 1968. On holiday in Chester, N.S.

This south shore of Nova Scotia with its mixture of small fishing villages and sea inlets sparkling in sun and wind, squat white farmhouses sheltered by trees and set in rough meadows, has a flavour all its own, never pinned on paper by painter or writer. And the small towns, some with almost as many wooden churches as there are wooden houses, look a standing invitation to peace and suggest the alternative of a life in which retired hours could pass swaying in a hammock in the shelter of a verandah. Gulls float and settle, a colony of them on a hillside; solid big-bellied fishermen rear chunky big-bellied sons who already as children have the promise of their fathers' strength.

King Street runs down to the sea, quite a steep hill at the top which descends gradually at the end. On the right-hand side of the street stands this small shingle house in which we four people live – Roley and Bunny and ourselves. I love the house as if it were my own, especially my bedroom, which I would change for no other. It is absolutely as plain as an anchorite's cell, with white painted table and dresser, a chair of unpainted wood, a square mirror hanging on the wall which faintly distorts the features, a hard square bed, and that is all. And I am happier here than anywhere. Outside, the tree-lined street; above, the blue of a sea sky and a glimpse of the blue of the sea itself. Sailing boats in the harbour, and the islands beyond – Quaker, Saddle, and, farther away, Tancook, to which the ferry goes twice a day and once on Sunday. In the gardens of Chester grow nasturtiums, in colours that defy their poor-genteel neighbours, the petunias – colours that pierce the eye and make the heart beat faster – gay, brilliant common nasturtiums in borders and bowls, planted round rocks or even telephone poles. By the roadside and at the foot of meadows near the sea are wild roses, smelling of rose, while the tame ones in gardens are scentless.

21 August 1968.

What a curse is the tiresome gambit of "being offended" which infects some people. At any one time you may rely upon it that someone you know is in a state of "being offended" with someone else. The injured party conveys this state by degrees of coolness, huffiness, and standing on dignity. "Being offended" leads to the second stage – Hurt Feelings. It can be most easily softened by a stroke of misfortune suffered by the offender. In that case, the offended one can, magnanimously, forgive all, but the offender must not hope to escape unscathed if he attempts to continue serenely on his way with a casual apology for the offence.

I should know. I have just "offended" an old acquaintance here. I have also burned the bottom of the electric kettle.

22 August 1968.

Suffering from crisis agitation and the sense of being cut off here. I know that I can contribute nothing, but I feel so restless that I take no more real pleasure in this holiday. The Czech crisis has been the focus of my restlessness. The thought of those brutes of Russians moving into Prague, stamping out individuals and liberties, reimposing that suffocating regime, makes me almost physically sick. I should think some kind of protest must be registered by the helpless U.N. If we have resolutions about "war-mongering Rhodesia" and don't mention the invasion of Czechoslovakia, except under our breath, the U.N. should shut up shop.

23 August 1968.

The holiday is over. From one day to another Chester has lost its charm for me. I know every board in the board wharf – which is rotting and which is firm; I know every knot-hole in the wood; I know each of the six wild roses in the sloping field. If this euphoric peace, rest, and happiness lasted with me for little more than two weeks, what *will* my retirement be like?

27 August 1968. Ottawa.

Back in Ottawa for three days of consultations. Woke early in my small room at the Château Laurier hotel. How is it that the Department of External Affairs always manage, in the friendliest way, to get the worst accommodation in any hotel or on any airline? But my window, which will not open, looks out on the canal locks and, on the other side of the canal, above the screen of trees, the Gothic towers, conical green copper roofs, and iron fretwork pinnacles of the East Block point upwards to an overcast sky. I took my morning walk round the poop-deck of Parliament Hill overlooking the river and towards Eddy's pulp factory and the Gatineau Hills beyond, the same walk I have paced at intervals for thirty-five years, in every weather and at every turning of my career, in decision and indecision, in panic and exhilaration. Parliament Hill has not changed. The only addition to its population of frock-coated Victorian statues is a monstrously comic – or comically monstrous – version of Mackenzie King, sculpted apparently in shit in the style favoured in Communist countries at the height of the Stalin epoch. It could be a work of revenge by an inspired enemy.

28 August 1968. Ottawa.

A brilliant early autumn Canadian day. I bolted into the French-Canadian Roman Catholic cathedral for a few minutes to seek sustenance, only to find myself involved in a funeral service, and escaped just before the corpse. One day in Ottawa has gone a long way towards destroying the health and spirits built up in three weeks in Nova Scotia, and I have yet to have my interview with the Prime Minister.

In the Ottawa "Establishment" there is uneasiness; they don't quite know what to expect from Trudeau. They feel a distinctly cool breeze blowing. Many of them now realize that they are getting older and suspect that they soon may be considered out of date. They cluck nervously.

29 August 1968. Ottawa.

I saw Trudeau yesterday. I was talking in his outer office to his secretary, a young French Canadian, when, by a change in his expression, I realized that someone had glided silently into the room and was standing behind me. I turned, and it was Trudeau, looking like a modern version of the Scholar Gypsy in sandals and open-necked shirt, as if he had just blown in from Haunts of Coot and Hern. He is physically altogether slighter, lighter, smaller than his photographs suggest. His air of youth – or is it agelessness? – is preternatural in a man of forty-eight. It is really impossible to connect him with the Office of Prime Minister. The manner is unaffected and instantly attractive; the light blue eyes ironical and amused, but they can change expression, and almost colour, to a chillier, cooler tone. What is behind all this? After this talk with him I am not perceptibly nearer the mind or motive. I rely on others. Some speak of his great intelligence, his power of organizing Cabinet; others speak of his pragmatism; yet others of his Thomist cast of thought. The truth is that all are baffled by an enigma, and so also am I.

30 August 1968. Ottawa.

The Prime Minister began our interview by asking me whether I thought that the Department of External Affairs was really necessary and, if so, why? I said that I viewed the Department as an instrument for the protection and advancement of Canadian interests abroad and not as a seminar to discuss abstract policy considerations. I think that Trudeau has got it into his head that the Department is divorced from the real interests of Canada and is embarking on international projects which have no firm basis in Canadian needs, and that this has been characteristic of the Pearson era.

I find the climate in Ottawa very anti-NATO. There is a great deal of talk of neutrality for Canada based on the Swedish model. Marcel Cadieux[1] is not in favour of these trends and told our new Minister of External Affairs, Mitchell Sharp, that we had "no expert on neutrality" in the Department. The British connection is far from popular. I am told that a visit by the Prime Minister to the United Kingdom might "cover his Anglo-Saxon flank," as he must do some things which will annoy the British.

1 September 1968. London.

Back in London, in a dazed condition after a sleepless night on the plane. This house has an uninhabited look and one sees how quickly, when we are gone permanently, it will take on the featureless face of an official residence. It's partly the way the servants "place" furniture – always in straight lines – so that a woman's first gesture on coming home is to give sofa and chairs a pull and a push, to bring them into a nest-like form. But there is no wife here to "build a nest," as Sylvia remains in Canada for a few more days. Also, no flowers in the house. I look at London with indifference, and the blank August residential streets show no response. It is hard to believe that only a month ago the place abounded in friends and acquaintances, the telephone rang incessantly, and every post contained notes and invitations.

2 September 1968. Hythe.

A girl got into the railway carriage where I was seated alone waiting for the train to start from Charing Cross. I knew from the instant that she appeared that she felt herself embarking on an adventure, perhaps going to meet a lover. She was pale, dark eyes enlarged with excitement, anticipation, nervousness. (It turned out in later talk that she was on her way to Deal to stay for the first time with her young man and to meet his family.) She was so charged with feeling that at random she shot some arrows in my direction. I closed

---

[1] Under-Secretary of State for External Affairs.

my eyes in pretended sleep and opened them to find her dark glance looking directly into mine. Then two women got into the carriage and planted themselves for the remainder of the journey, one with elephantine knees.

Elizabeth was waiting for me at the station exit at Folkestone. I heaved my suitcase, heavy with whisky and shoes, into the back of her car and off we drove to Hythe. I find her subdued in mood and wonder if she is ill, exhausted perhaps by her permanent cough. I seem to do all the talking. Do I ever give her a chance? The weather is sunless and cool, with a wind that bangs all the doors in this house.

5 September 1968. London.

Dined with the Hardys and found myself face to face with their son, a boy of eighteen — me at the age when I wrote my early diaries.[1] I imagined myself skinned alive by his electric eye. What would he write in *his* diary? Myself – a gabbling, infinitely old parrot, quite outside the range of human sympathies. At the same time, his physical shyness was such that he could not bring himself to draw his chair into the group of the conversation and was no doubt cursing himself for his own gaucherie.

6 September 1968.

People talk of a second childhood, but am I having a second adolescence? Sylvia returns tonight, and a good thing too. This bedroom is beginning to stink of self. Walking round Grosvenor Square the other evening I contemplated, as a task for my retirement, the editing of my own diaries. They seem to me at the moment so trivial as to be completely unpublishable, even if they were not full of indiscreet or unpleasant references to "living persons" which would cause hurt feelings.

7 September 1968.

This morning I have been having an early walk in the park. It is blazingly fine and already hot. A couple of youths waking up in their

---

[1] Later published under the title *An Appetite for Life*.

sleeping bags and putting their heads out of their cocoons. I might like to sleep like that in the park all night, coiled up in a sleeping bag. I read some of Harold Nicolson's diaries. Diaries are unlovable things and in the long run put one off the writer.

My young cousin Mary Carscallen has been staying the night and has just left, bubbling with her adventures on the Continent, where she and her girl friend have been roaming. Another pair of adventurers – this time male – hove in view in the persons of another cousin, young Roger Rowley, and his friend Larry O'Brien. These two sports have shaken the dust of Rockcliffe from their feet and are questing.

I have been looking, for the first time in years, at my old diaries. They summon up for me impressions, memories, colours, rooms, faces, which are not visible on the written page. It is like reading a play which *I* have seen acted with the original cast and others have never seen.

Dinner at the Painted Hall, Greenwich, for Finance Ministers. Reception at the Banquet Hall, Whitehall, for Athlone scholars. Lunch at the Beefsteak.

25 September 1968.

The Burmese Ambassador called and kept on saying, "Difficult world; very, very difficult," and sighing. Burma probably has plenty to sigh about.

Went to Gatwick Airport to meet our Minister of Finance, Benson. Reception for them here in the afternoon. I made a presentation of Canadian books to the University of Birmingham's representatives and had them to tea. Nice librarians – another world, full of intrigue too. Read Powell's *Afternoon Men* and was back in my own twenties. Did Time ever string ahead indefinitely like that – time to be endlessly wasted, time for interminable hesitations and endless conversations?

1 October 1968. Plymouth.

Sylvia and I are here on an official visit to Plymouth. We are staying in this house which used to be Lady Astor's and has been left to Plymouth on condition that nothing in it should be changed. Every snapshot remains in place, and her copies of the works of Mary Baker Eddy, with salient passages underlined in red by her. An old housekeeper, Florrie, who dates from the Astor regime, goes with the house, which is in a terrace facing on Plymouth Hoe and the sea beyond. The house, although not a bit ghostly, gives one a soothing sensation which could also be stifling – a sensation of silence and immobility. Everything, once and for all, sealed into its place. This seems all the stranger when one looks at the faded photographs of civic occasions which line the walls and in which the figure of Nancy Astor, like an electric marionette, seems always to be springing about in gesticulation or protest. It is odd to think of that disturbance which must perpetually have swept through this house being displaced by this dead calm of ticking clocks and great cow-like objects of mahogany furniture. I find that to leave the house is like pulling oneself with effort out of a quicksand which could engulf one.

Well, we shall be gone in five minutes, and the Plymouth episode over. Mayor and Mayoress, store managers and newspaper editors, the librarian and the city clerk, will all vanish down a hole in my memory and only the feeling of this silent house facing the level grey sea will remain, and a sense of old-fashioned comfort and permanence which could change to one of being walled up, breathless, in the past.

16 October 1968.

St. James's Park on a fine autumn morning. The pelicans flapping their great wings in the sun and yawning at each other (at least it looks like a yawn – it may be part of a courtship ritual for all I know). I have been rereading those diaries written when I was eighteen. They have stripped away layers of accumulated experience and exposed nerves which I thought dead but which are all too much alive. I started reading them with detachment, but I soon wanted to change them, to leave out this or that which just would not fit in with my later edition of my own youth. Then I began to realize that I was not reading the diaries of a stranger to see if they had any literary interest, but was involved in a more dangerous enterprise. Now I cannot get away from that adolescent that was – and is – myself. How silly he is, and how sharp; how early the twig was bent into the worldly posture; how powerfully, when I thought myself alone, was I the subject of influences and policies on the part of others; how little have I later achieved, except the damning diary. What has it all amounted to, these forty-five years since I wrote in my bedroom at The Bower as now I write in my bedroom here in London? My "career" – the work and interest – yes; the achievement I count for little. Only love in one form or another, social exhilaration, solitary walks, and a few books, have left traces. Everything else has slipped between my fingers. As for God, I lived without Him all my youth, and was I better or worse for that?

18 October 1968.

I don't know what has got into me this morning. I am itching with old grudges and angry retorts which I didn't make at the time. They got under my skin like splinters and have stayed there, only coming out later. Perhaps this mood has been brought on by reading Tolstoy's life, that cantankerous old monster. I am beginning to be bored and overpowered by Tolstoy – there is so much of him.

Walked in Regent's Park with Sylvia. Ducks and dahlias, roses not yet bitten by the frost, and in the upper canal discovered the hideout of the black swans. Lunched with Arnold Smith. Our professional interests differ: he wants to keep the Africans in the Commonwealth; I am interested in relations between Canada and Britain. But I like him personally very much.

20 October 1968.

Donald Mallett to lunch – a friend, perhaps the last of them for me. Went afterwards to the Balthus pictures at the Tate – the claustrophobia of adolescent afternoons, young girls enclosed in curtained rooms singly and in pairs, all slouched in chairs day-dreaming mindlessly, erotically; a Paris street scene that I would buy if I could.

Splendid reviews in the American papers of *Eva Trout*. I am so delighted from every point of view. Also, having been, in these "unfashionable" years for [Elizabeth] as a novelist, always a continuing believer in her genius, I feel such satisfaction at this chorus of praise.

Young Roger Rowley staying in the house. He, Eliza, and Peter

Elliston for dinner last night. A bizarre evening for me, as I had just been soaked in the early diaries in which Peter played the central part. "What," I said to him, "have we two to show for our lives, not in terms of 'success' or 'failure,' but in living?" "Nothing, nothing at all," Peter said in his new dry voice of realism. Yet the next moment he was off on a fantastic saga of embroidered invention just as rococo as his youthful extravaganzas.

27 October 1968.

The day of protest marches through London. Demonstration against the U.S. Embassy next door expected. I can hear somewhere in the near distance the sounds of horses' hooves – that must be the mounted police. U.S. Marines are installed in the Embassy and closed-circuit TV is on the roof. What is this protest march protesting against? Everything. And what does everything mean? I am as out of touch with this protest as if I lived on another planet. And the young whom I happen to know seem to understand it as little as I do. Sexual freedom, social freedom, outrageous clothes, long hair – if they want these I am all in favour. I also sympathize with the fun of protesting, but the social and political meaning of the "permanent revolution" is gibberish to me. A protest against this permissive society – isn't it punching a pillow?

Roger leaves today. I shall be sorry to see him go, which is more than I can say for some of my guests. He makes me laugh and he is attractive. Moreover, he has a lot of sense.

Do I envy these young men? Not really. Those decisions and indecisions affecting one's whole future loom so large, and what the family expects of one, what one's contemporaries think of one, how to get hold of a girl, or how to find a job. It's agony shot through with high spirits.

12 November 1968.

I saw Eliza riding in the park yesterday morning, trotting along on a grey nag with her red hair flying in the wind. She wants to buy a stallion from Zsa Zsa Gabor to save it from being gelded.

In the Communications Centre the cypher clerks are on to me about tax-free cigarettes and drink. It is outrageous that they can't have them. Why shouldn't they get some droppings from the diplomat's table? Why the bloody hell can't they? They work as hard as, or harder than, anyone, and everything depends on them and no one pays the least attention to them.

The Lord Mayor's dinner at the Guildhall. Technicolor brilliance of robes and uniforms under the klieg lights, especially the Archbishop's violently purple robes. What an old stage-stealer he is. The Prime Minister [Harold Wilson] standing no nonsense from the City in his speech, which was coldly received. How they hate him! Then a series of drippingly mellifluous exchanges from the Lord Mayor, the Archbishop, the ex-Lord Mayor – reciprocal compliments, jokes, tributes, resounding affirmations of Faith in Youth, sound as ever to the core but with a few rotten spots; the Commonwealth (these tributes sound hollower each year); Britain (hopefully); and the City of London and all that it stands for.

15 November 1968.

In the afternoon dedicated a plaque at the veterans' Star and Garter Home at Richmond, in the company of the United States Ambassador. Made a short and "stirring" speech.

In the evening chaired a big dinner at the Canadian Club. Wore a bloody silly chain and medallion round my neck like a Mayor. Made a fulsome speech introducing Earl McLaughlin – quite disgusted myself.

That woman whom I met at the reception the other day – did I say too much to her? I thought I saw the small-town tightening of the lips, that remorseless glint of satisfaction at having heard scandal and intending to retain and retail it. A walk in Regent's Park, seagulls in sunlight, last roses, copper beeches, swinging my umbrella, exhilaration.

Stout men in Homburgs and double-breasted overcoats walking in pairs and discussing how to beat the new government financial regulations.

A lady came for a drink and began, "It means so much that there is still graciousness to be found in the world." We asked where. "At Claridge's, where I am staying. The flowers in my room, the exquisite manners of the waiters."

1 December 1968.

I like making love as much, if not more, than anything. What else do I like as much, or nearly as much? In some earlier diary I write that what I liked most was the kind of conversation in which characters and motives were dissected. That now seems to me trivial. I do like walking alone in public parks – St. James's Park; Bois de Boulogne; Central Park, New York; Point Pleasant Park, Halifax, Nova Scotia; Christ Church Meadow; Magdalen Park, Oxford; Sud-Park, Köln; the Luxembourg Gardens, Paris; Dumbarton Oaks park, Washington, D.C.; along the canal in Ottawa; round the poop-deck overlooking the Ottawa River; along the Rhine-side walk at Bonn. I like sinking into a movie after a good lunch. Reading would once have come first on my list – I still can't imagine life without it; looking at pictures – yes, in a responsive mood. The transient glow of hospitality given. Some seaports I like, and a town hotel or country house which is unfamiliar. Smoked salmon and hot baths. I don't know if I *like* drinking but I have to, and I like the effects – sometimes. Smoking is another *must* and only rarely a pleasure. Are addictions different from pleasures?

Things I hate most – flying, or preparing a speech, or reflecting on my own unworthiness.

Lunched at the Travellers with my old friend Tony Payne, now Rector of Lichfield. He arrived in a period shovel hat which would sell well in the King's Road. We had a very good lunch – whisky, then chops and Club claret and Stilton. Tony is in a Retreat in Great College Street for a week. I asked him, "Can you smoke there?" He said, "Yes, on the roof." "Would I like it?" "I don't know how much of a man of God you are." Hard question to answer. Tony and I parted in a glow of friendship.

13 December 1968.

All-day sessions of the Anglo-Canadian Continuing Committee on Trade and Economic Relations. I was in the Chair and listened, understanding a little here and there. Lunch for thirty men here at the house. Cocktails given by the RCMP for the Intelligence Wallahs. One of the English Intelligence people had had dealings with

Norman Robertson over cases of people being blackmailed, etc., by the other side. He said that Norman's wisdom and compassion were those of a saint.

3 January 1969.

Waiting for Trudeau. Message telephoned anonymously – "He will not leave the airport alive." So, we start the drama with melodrama; so, I am off to the airport.

5 January 1969.

First meeting between Trudeau and Harold Wilson. The conversation started on NATO. There was a good and full discussion which I do not record as I make it a rule not to include accounts of confidential political and diplomatic negotiations in this diary.

Trudeau said that he was impressed by Wilson's apparently relaxed mood, by his taking time for random conversation. He added that Wilson was a fully political animal as he, Trudeau, was not. He said he would never spend a whole weekend, as Wilson does, talking politics and getting officials around him and going over with them all the speeches he would later make at the Commonwealth Conference. Trudeau was impressed by Wilson's intelligence and dialectical skills. I think that Wilson and Trudeau enjoyed each other and got on perhaps better than Mike and Wilson.

23 January 1969.

Scattered impressions of Trudeau's visit. The press have concentrated quite largely on his "love life." He attacked them for this at his press conference, but he is himself largely responsible. He trails his coat, he goes to conspicuous places with conspicuous women. If he really wants an affair, he could easily manage it discreetly. This is a kind of double bluff.

I lunched on gammon at the Travellers' club and afterwards read a pornographic book in the library. It is the most beautiful room in London. We used not to have any sex in the club library but now it is everywhere, like petrol fumes in the air.

I believe that this notion of the younger generation – embattled and different from any other – may turn out to be a huge hoax. It is certainly a huge bore.

24 January 1969.

Went down in the train from Charing Cross to Hythe for the day. There was Elizabeth waiting at the Central Station, Folkestone. God! how will it be if I must outlive her. We walked on the lees at Folkestone in the mild spring weather under the groin of the cliffs and went back to her house, Carbery, for dinner. She showed me the outline of her new book, *Pictures and Conversation*. Yesterday was the London birth day of *Eva Trout* and the reviews are just beginning to come out, and already she is at work on the new book. In it she asks the question "Is writing allied to witchcraft?" We drank a lot of 1949 Burgundy and I waited in the dark night, Burgundy-filled, at the little Sandling Station for the London train to come in.

25 January 1969.

A fully spring day of early sunshine in which Sylvia and I walked cheerfully together. I came back and read an old memoir of the fate of my great-great-aunt Catherine, a beautiful, high-spirited girl given to too much novel-reading, who was driven mad by her family and by an overdose of laudanum and thought she was being dragged over broken bottles. She died young and insane.

Matthew Smith says that at my reception at Canada House, to which Trudeau came so reluctantly, Trudeau attacked him for wearing a dinner jacket and told him that he ought to be out in the street joining with the other demonstrators instead of swanning around at a social occasion.

27 January 1969.

I heard Sylvia saying to Bruna, our "wonderful maid," "Mr. Ritchie does not like bacon or fried egg for breakfast." Poor Bruna – she goes into the hospital tomorrow to have a cyst or cancer removed from her breast. Think of her on these black London mornings, getting my Goddamned fried egg ready, toting it up in the lift, toting it – untouched – down again, taking the dog round the block in the dank morning air, and all the time worrying, worrying, "Will they remove my breast?"

Lunch and dinner for Cardinal, the President of the Quebec Council; elaborate food and lousy speeches, but none so bad as that of Whitlock, the Under-Secretary of State for Foreign Affairs, who quoted Rupert Brooke – "Some corner of a foreign field that is for ever England" – and spoke of World War graves to this group of Quebeckers who regard those wars as British imperialists' ventures in which their countrymen were used as cannon fodder.

5 February 1969.

Recovering from flu and from the jungle of high fever, restless turning in the "burrows of the nightmare." In that fetid region all the paper mottoes of faith and conduct are swept out of touch and sight.

I spent the afternoon recovering in bed. Read *Antony and Cleopatra* and became so moved and inflamed by it that I could not get to sleep at night.

10 February 1969.

Back from Stansted. The two days there were extraordinarily happy and healthy. I was exhilarated to wake up to the famous parkscape from my bedroom, the "rides" through the forest, the black trees with a snowy foreground and the sky cold and cloudless with visibility to infinity, infinity all enclosed in the woods and avenues of Stansted. The familiar enchantment of the place operated once again. Everything pleased. Driving round the estate with Eric in his new Land Rover, watching the pigeons rise from a field of kale, watching Mary paint flower pictures in her attic studio, and standing in the library before a fire of great logs, turning over photograph albums.

1 March 1969.

Eliza has come to stay. She and I walk round the Square in a mild thaw from a small snowfall, two tall figures nodding heads, a rustle of talk, plans, contrivances, phrases for dealing with dilemmas, rattles round as we mimic communication together.

Young Marshall from Ottawa came to see me about the visit of the Canadian Parliamentary Committee, with the suggestion that all their briefings here should be tape-recorded and attended by the press. Of course this means that no one will speak frankly. All this is in the name of "participation," to build up parliamentary committees so that they feel they are participating in the formulation of policy, that all options, including neutrality, have been considered and all voices heard. I am divided about all this; I see what Trudeau is driving at. He is impressed by the alienation of people from their government and their feeling that foreign and defence policies are formulated mysteriously and imposed on them. He is indeed undertaking to change the system of Cabinet solidarity and the organization of Executive and Legislature; "broaden the base," and also secure a new kind of "General Will," incarnate in himself. He may be right in his diagnosis of the gravity of the social disease. As to the cure, he is looking for it by an apparently endless process of review, of digging institutions up by the roots to examine them, of shaking up Establishment figures. And then what? He is not really a revolutionary. Is this process aimed at the reversal of alliances or at real economic and social programs of change? No. Is it just a grandiose and perhaps necessary manoeuvre to establish communication? How much of it is done with mirrors? Well, I am with him so far, but is he with me? I think he believes that diplomats as a class are an organized lobby against change. Perhaps he is right – especially elderly diplomats.

Met horrible literary female, and felt a shuddering repugnance for this malicious, round-heeled, blowsy *bore*.

16 March 1969.

Two and a half more years, with luck, of living on a millionaire's income in a London mansion of the kind that disappeared from ordinary life thirty years ago, with five servants, a chauffeur and the biggest car in London, with whisky and cigarettes virtually free – and presto! down we go to a heavily taxed middle-class income; from invitations to Buckingham Palace and Chatsworth to the company of a few old friends, if any left after an absence of years; from being surrounded by the young, who find it convenient to lodge here, to seeing only contemporaries; from a diversity of company to relative isolation; from influence and inside information to neither of either. On top of all this – old age, impotence, loss of hair and memory!

23 March 1969.

I am having my portrait painted. An artist – even a bad artist – can create mayhem around him. I have a craving to destroy the portrait – and perhaps to destroy the painter.

Eliza plays her scales over in the long drawing-room in the half-light of this grey Sunday afternoon. She props her music against the Barbara Hepworth bronze. Facing her is the ill-fated portrait, still on its easel. The floor is strewn with the matting on which he stood while painting. When the artist departs, the room will revert to its parlour-like sterility. Yesterday Eliza and I went to Chiswick. The sun came out and went in again. There were colonies of purple and yellow crocuses on the lawns. We went into the house and stood in a window embrasure of an empty, unfurnished little panelled room, looking out together at the cypresses and urns and obelisks and *allées*. Then we went to Chiswick Mall by the river and watched blue-sailed boats scudding before the March wind, and chose a house in which to live called Strawberry House – Georgian, with a vine-clad balcony overlooking the river.

15 April 1969.

Walking through St. James's Park I encountered that Gypsy woman whom I have seen telling people's fortunes. I decided to try mine. She took my hand, looked at it, and instantly said, "They will never make a gentleman out of you." I can remember nothing else in the fortune.

I had a long talk with Jerry Hardy about politics. The truth is that he and I know that there is no interest in Canada in tightening relations with the United Kingdom or in reporting home on British policies. Dispatches from Paris are read because French politics affect our future as a nation, whereas Britain has virtually no influence at all. The "British connection" seems to be receding out of view. Only the Crown remains.

In the evening went to a crowded cocktail party and accidentally stepped on my hostess's toe. She gave a real squeak of anguish.

17 April 1969.

They are going to make me a Companion of Canada, so now I am a registered member, in good standing, of the Canadian Establishment.

I was going to write that my mother would have been pleased, if she had been alive, but I don't think she would have understood what it was all about. The only awards she respected were "real" British awards.

McMillan, the president of the CNR, came to lunch. He is a Winnipeg Westerner and spoke of the revolt of the West against the Trudeau regime, saying that in the Party caucuses in the West there is a strong underground movement of Western separatism.

More Westerners in the afternoon, including an oil-business couple. I took very much to her but not so much to him. There was an air of over-used charm about him and he smelt of hair essence or after-shave cream or something, and kept referring to Canadians as "Canucks." Perhaps he is an American.

20 April 1969.

Woke feeling levitated, put on my blue pullover, taxied to Regent's Park, walked happily with my head full of projects in the spring sunshine by the rock garden, to and fro over the bridges; looked at some nesting coots; saw three nuns quacking away together on a bench; knew that I had not too long to live; remembered that day Elizabeth and I walked down the road by the Park lined with flowering cherry trees. It was during the war, and I was recovering from flu and it was my first day out. It must have been the same time in April as today, because the fruit trees lining the road were just in bloom.

Went down to lunch at Knebworth with the Cobbolds, charming elderly couple (about my age). They garden together, clear out the undergrowth in the "wilderness," making do with one gardener where once there were sixteen. (The gardens of England's Stately Homes before the Fall must have been the most over-staffed organizations in history.) The Cobbolds have three upstanding, nice-mannered, intelligent sons, and the appropriate quota of grandchildren. Lord Cobbold is a former Director of the Bank of England, now Lord Chamberlain. Has a grace-and-favour house in St. James's Palace overlooking the courtyard. Knebworth, built by Bulwer Lytton – or rebuilt by him – is a German romantic fantasy of the 1840s, unfortunately tidied up by Lady Cobbold's uncle, Lutyens, who was appalled by the gimcrackery, which is the only point of the house, and wanted to uncover and restore the original uninteresting fourteenth-century house.

Now the remaining nineteenth-century heraldic figures, gargoyles, and Victorian armorial bits and pieces are quite literally falling off the exterior. Warnings out everywhere – "Beware of falling stone-work." We had excellent roast beef for lunch.

12 May 1969.

In the morning went to a NATO commemorative service in the new Guards Chapel built to replace the one destroyed in the blitz. I was revolted by the sermon from a sanctimonious old Dogan plastering over this necessary military alliance with pseudo-Christian pi-jaw.

In the afternoon, as an escape from an east-windy grey day in Oxford Street I popped into a German film entitled *Sex and Love*. It was the kind of thing to give pornography a bad name. I came away fearing that I might have been put off sex for life.

The French Embassy party in the evening ostensibly given for the Finnish Ambassador and his wife, but nobody spoke to them and they looked like Finns out of water.

18 May 1969.

Went down on the train to Devon with Derick Amory, former Chancellor of the Exchequer, former High Commissioner to Ottawa, and could, I believe – if he had wanted to – have been Prime Minister. I am becoming very fond of him. He is ironical, invalidish (terrible wounds from the First War, served again in the Second), now a Director of the Hudson's Bay Company. He lives by faith or stoicism, covering permanent pain. In dealing with people he pushes away all directness with kind inquiries and malicious asides. He spends his weekends with his old aunt (eighty-eight) in her bungalow in the grounds of her Tudor former house. We stayed there for the night. Derick's aunt is a redoubtable old Anglo-Irish woman, lost a husband and a brother in the First War and all her three sons in the Second War, now shrivelled, shrunken, wearing an old felt hat and gardening boots as she stumped into the yard to greet us. But in three minutes her recalcitrance, quick-wittedness, and engagingness were apparent. Round the garden we went with her. She was fond of this flower, disparaging about that flower, asking no questions, giving no answers, occasionally a crooked smile – and she had us!

20 May 1969.

To the Mounties' Musical Ride at the Devon Agricultural Show. Many bulls, cows, goats, sheep, in procession before the Mounties got a look-in. Presented prizes, took the salute (slight uncertainty on my part as to when to take off my hat and when to put it back on again), toured the tents, tasted local cheese, drank local small cider. Most tricky was my visit to the "Lines" of the Mounties. I patted horses' necks, started talking to each member of the Mounties' team, began to run down on matey chat, knew they knew it, felt a fool. Suppose they only saw a silly old man – what does it matter?

22 May 1969.

Macdonald, President of the Privy Council, and Mrs. Macdonald are here on a visit from Ottawa. We gave a luncheon for them today. He has the reputation of being one of the most "with it" Ministers, close to the Prime Minister and opposed to the old establishment. One of his staff warned me that Mrs. Macdonald is strongly anti-English. But in spite of my "Englishness" I got on very well with her. She is an extremely attractive woman, tall, fair, fresh-skinned, and her talk has freshness too. She is, however, imbued with the anti-External Affairs virus.

5 June 1969.

Yet another Cabinet Minister – Pepin, the Minister of Trade and Commerce. Went to the airport to meet him. I had never seen him before but guessed as he came off the plane that he would be carrying a spare suit on a hook under a cellophane cover, and I was right. He is big and jovial, and looks a cross between an Assyrian emperor and Groucho Marx. Very easy and open in manner. A group of us went back to the Dorchester to work on his speech. It is a long time since I have put in such a session, yet how many hundreds of times I have done it and with so many different Ministers – battles of wits, will, prestige, over the inclusion of one civil servant's draft or the substitution for it of another; attempts by civil servants, gently, firmly, persistently, to eliminate the Minister's wilder, bolder – or just more vote-getting – passages in the text. Block that metaphor! Drop that joke! A final exhausted tug-of-war over the elimination of the word "despite" in paragraph 4.

Home, and a quick change, and to Anne Fleming's party. Literary figures, a don or two, and Andrew Devonshire. Our hostess, Anne, looks sadder and more human since her husband Ian Fleming's death. Diana Cooper, in a pyjama suit, greeted me in joke tones of thrilling sincerity. In the next room Elizabeth and Stuart Hampshire stood murmuring by the bar. The writer Leslie Hartley sat on a sofa like a giant panda, being patted and petted, making mumbling and inconclusive sounds. He is loved by all. Our hostess, in grey and diamonds, was alternately pert and pensive. Of herself she said, "In my youth I did what I wanted and never knew guilt. Women's frustrations are different and simpler than those of men, and come from not getting what they want, usually something quite uncomplicated – a husband, a lover, a home, children – but men suffer from not knowing what or whom they want."

14 June 1969.

Went to a stupid reception at the Dorchester given by the Sheik of Abu Dhabi. It was full of hawk-nosed sons of the desert with lustrous eyes, and oil men, and Foreign Office Middle East experts who would like to be oil men. When I was presented to the Sheik he said, condescendingly, "We have heard of your country and its good reputation."

Dinner with Elizabeth. She thinks that one is born with "innate ideas," reflections of the social and mental climate of one's parents. If this is so, in my own case the idea of loyalty (and its obverse, disloyalty) was a dominant. Loyalty, but not necessarily fidelity. She thinks that instead of being awarded the Order of Canada I should have been knighted. I explained that this was impossible for a Canadian, and that in any case I did not want a knighthood. I should feel a damn fool among my friends at home, being addressed as "Sir Charles." In fact I am very pleased to have this award. After all, I have acted for my client, Canada, for thirty-five years and defended its interests like a son of the law and swallowed my own prejudices in the process.

27 September 1969.

A muggy, murky, misanthropic day. Went to the doctor about my itching legs. He has always been such a sensible, reassuring practitioner, but I believe that he has now gone mad. He had a speck of froth on his lips and his kind horse face looked blurred. Without ado upon my entry he asked, "Shall I read you some of my poems?" Then one poem followed another, sunsets, leaves turning . . . "You see, I paint in words." And then, odder and more personal ones, one called "The Midnight Doctor of Hythe." "Why Hythe?" he asked on a puzzled note. He is in fact Elizabeth's doctor also. In his dream he is driving around the sleeping town in his Mini thinking of those lying awake in their beds tortured by anxiety, on whose heads he might lay a calming hand. Later in the day he telephoned me to ask my advice about a letter he is writing to *The Times* which he believes "will bring the Government down."

On my way back from the doctor's I sat in a deck-chair in the park and must have dropped my wallet, which unfortunately had £40 in it.

4 October 1969.

I went to Oxford to my old college for the annual dinner of the Pembroke Society. After dinner, when the very old and the young had gone to bed, my sixty-odd-year-old surviving contemporaries got together at one of the tables in Hall and the serious drinking began, a new bottle of whisky being ordered every five minutes. I would not have recognized any of them if I had fallen over them in a London street, but in that Hall, where we had all sat together drinking when young, their faces gradually got attached to earlier faces once belonging to them, and we peered and stared at each other through the mists of time and whisky.

On the morning after, I pensively promenaded the meadows and lanes and quads of grey, autumnal, out-of-term Oxford, encountering by the way several of last night's convivial contemporaries. We passed each other with averted eyes, nursing our separate hangovers.

5 October 1969.

Earlier in the day I had lunch with an old painter. He tells me that some young women are "gerontophiles," meaning that they prefer old men. He says he has a list and offered to lend it to me. At lunch there was a woman who said, "I know my husband is an old lecher but there are so many pansies about that I prefer him like that."

The afternoon was depressing. I had to read to the "Canada-based staff" the Minister's telegram about the withdrawals of personnel and the new economies. I thought it best not to try the Pollyanna note but to give them the treatment direct. I was upset by the whole proceeding because of the botched and clumsy way it is being done under this absurdly poised time gun and for the wrong reasons – almost non-existent economies – when it could and should have been done over a period of time as a process of reorganization and a re-targeting of the functions of the Department. The present exercise is being conducted in a cloud of public and political criticism of the Department. It seems almost punitive and gives our people to think that their work has all been a waste of time and that the Department would like to shuffle them off anywhere to get them off the payroll. Louis Rogers says that my morale is bad.

Ted Heath said to me the other day, "You Canadians have a good Foreign Service; why are you buggering it about?"

24 November 1969.

Lunched with a group of super-rich oil men at the Dorchester, organized by Roy Thomson,[1] who said it did him good to hear talk which seldom got below the level of a billion dollars. I found the conversation fascinating, though sometimes incomprehensible. Plainly I had been invited as a social or symbolic gesture – I came with the flowers, the smoked salmon, and the wine, to show that the old pirate knew the amenities.

I am not at my ease with tycoons, except, for some reason, Jewish ones.

In the office we spend two-thirds of our time administering ourselves and coping with the swarm of regulations that our new "management approach" has resulted in. Questionnaires, union contracts, program budgeting, task forces, goals targets, ratings, policy analysis, computerized forecasts. There is no policy work in the office, and Louis Rogers and I are both bored.

---

[1] Lord Thomson of Fleet; Canadian newspaper owner.

4 December 1969.

I was thinking back today to my October visit to Ottawa, Trudeau's capital and court, ruled by an icy enigma. He seems to have cowed Parliament, the Civil Service, and his Cabinet colleagues. He does not bully – his method is more oblique, a mixture of chilly scorn and scorching impatience, and all overlaid with the quick, disarming smile.

How well does he govern Canada? He has been quick to see the need to hold and weld into political society the young and the outsiders. He has attacked and is demolishing the obsolete assumptions behind the criminal code. His rule is only at its outset. He has joined battles but not yet won them. Will his method work in Canada, a country traditionally governed by compromise, by subterfuge, all wrapped up in the opaque jargon of politicians who learned their style from Mackenzie King? Will Canadians long endure Trudeau's explicitness of will and his caustic language? Could these begin to goad and irritate? Behind this question lies the limit of his power and his quest to extend it. Some say that this quest for power will lead him to an American or Gaullist conception of the Executive; that he plans by stages to bring not only the Civil Service but Parliament itself to heel. Yet he is a cautious man – he shows more than he moves. First there is a resounding defiance of established policy and patterns; then prudent pragmatic withdrawal, with still some ground gained; then a sally in another direction. So in the end he is compelled, like every Canadian Prime Minister before him, to a balancing act – to enrage one section of the population one day, to appease them the next, to play one region or interest or prejudice or race against another. This he does with virtuoso effect.

Is Trudeau a surgical analyst come in to cut off the layers of inefficiency and out-of-date ideas? Can he construct something solid in the place of what he wants to change? Again a question. Every statement about Trudeau crumbles into its contradiction. An intellectual, yes, but *is* he? If so, his conversation does not reveal one. A social swinger, yes, yet not at ease socially. A power-loving French-Canadian politician, but how different in tone and temper from any of that breed. What then has one got to go on? He is a dandy, an actor, a loner, a secret – even a shy – man.

He dominates the Canadian scene without a rival. The Opposition, at any rate the Conservative Opposition, is feeble and sterile. This is how things look in December 1969 – how will they look two years from now? The going will get tough for Trudeau. He could end up as an exploded myth. His problem will be not only to establish "mastery" but to produce radical solutions to match his radical criticisms. Or he could turn out to be a sphinx without a secret.

As to the international scene, they say that Trudeau would like it to get up and walk away. Also, he is reacting against what he thinks to be the over-responsiveness, busy-body-ism, do-good-ism, of his predecessors, and hence to their instrument, the Department of External Affairs. There is animus in his reaction. He would like not so much to destroy the Department as to serve it a very sharp lesson. What is that lesson? Part of it is simply to come to heel. But there is more to it than that. He has genuinely concluded that our operation is over-extended, wrongly targeted, and out of date. Just as he has set up a task force on the role of the soldier, so he wants a categorical answer to the question no one has ever satisfactorily answered – What is the role of the diplomat? The answer he would like would be a cybernetic answer, a computer answer, something that could be shown on a graph, an extrapolation, something fished out of a "think tank," for he has a weakness for this language and these concepts. What he does not want is an answer from the Department which implies a mystique, a trade secret, something elect, inherited from Trudeau's predecessors and shared between them. He has a right to put the questions, but not to the animus with which he puts them. It is true that there has crept into the Foreign Service a note of both self-congratulation and self-pity which irritates others besides the Prime Minister. It is true that a portion of the work done by the Service is not focused on concrete Canadian interests, that telegrams assiduously and conscientiously prepared sink into the Department without a trace, without response or influence. This unreality is partly a function of size. At the insistence of the politicians we have opened many missions which are far from essential, and at our own instigation we have over-padded many of our missions abroad. It is time that we and all the other Departments functioning abroad took a look at our operations and expenditures.

11 December 1969.

To see Burke Trend[1] at the Cabinet Office. He says, and I think so too, that the great task that faces our political leaders is to humanize the computer age, to give back to people a sense of connection with the growing scale and impersonality of modern technology. He wants Wilson and Trudeau to talk about this when next they meet. Certainly Trudeau is one of the few politicians to be impressed with this question of the dehumanization of our life and environment, which is really behind so many of the protest movements of our times.

Went to the Beefsteak Club and was richly rewarded as Harold Macmillan[2] was there in wonderful form; witty, wise, wide-ranging talk.

Margaret Meagher is staying with us. She is very good value, down-to-earth in a Nova Scotian way.

Bobby Rae,[3] now a Rhodes Scholar at Balliol, came to lunch. Intelligent, left-wing views, student power at the University of Toronto. Dislikes Trudeau as being much too conservative.

12 December 1969. Manchester.

Having got drunkish the night before, I had to rise at 6:30 on a pitch-black morning, pile into my clothes, and set off with Sylvia by train for my visit to Manchester. On the train they gave us a huge breakfast – sausages, bacon and eggs, God knows what – I couldn't touch it. I wondered how I would get through the day, though in fact got through it very well. There is nothing like being treated as Royalty, and being gracious back, to bolster morale, and one sees how those in the public eye go on and on forever and never lose the taste for it. Manchester lived up to its reputation for murk. On arrival we were escorted down the platform by the station-master and Rolls-Royced to the Manchester Liners' new building which I was to open. I was met at the door by Stoker, the Chairman of the Company. Then I swung a bottle of champagne (which to my surprise broke, as it

---

[1] Sir Burke Trend, Secretary of the Cabinet.

[2] Rt. Hon. Harold Macmillan, British Prime Minister 1957–1963.

[3] Bob Rae later became leader of the Ontario New Democratic Party, and premier 1990–1995.

should have done, on the first shot) to launch the new building. Then unveiled a totem-pole, then shook hands with two hundred people, then, after a very long lunch in a very hot room, speeches by Stoker and myself, both attempting to be facetious. He is a "whirlwind of energy," with a nice Scotch wife and a son who wants to be an artist. He presides over a container shipping line, and all the talk was of the container trade from Manchester to Montreal. I found this interesting and instructive. The container business is progressively eliminating dockers – another example of making people unnecessary. No more dockers, no more porters. Why not no more diplomats? How our Prime Minister would love to computerize the whole Foreign Service and eliminate the human element. After lunch we all bundled into buses and drove, in the driving rain, along the ship canal to see the containers being lowered into the ships. Later Sylvia and I went to stay with the Lord Mayor and Lady Mayoress for the night in the Town Hall in which the Mayor resides. It must be one of the most stupendous buildings of the Victorian age, built at the peak of Manchester's greatness. The State Apartments were vast, gloomy, decorated, painted, tiled, panelled, frescoed; there were outsize stone and marble staircases and ironwork everywhere. The Mayor and Mayoress gave a dinner party of the local magnates for us. The Manchester people are very forthcoming and not at all gentlemanly – what a relief!

The next day we set out after breakfast in the Mayoral Rolls for a tour of the city. It was raining, with drifting fog patches which mercifully obscured some of the new housing units, great grey blocks of prefabricated flats, sited in a sea of mud. By contrast the little old (Industrial Revolution) bleak hutments with outdoor plumbing looked almost cozy. They are hauling Manchester out of the nineteenth century at a great rate and building, building, everywhere, as they are in the vast industrial sprawl through which we passed in the train on our way home to London, giving one a notion of the huge industrial wealth and strength of this country. And everywhere new housing, high-rises, and terraces in former fields.

16 December 1969.

Kenneth Clark in *Civilisation*, discussing Turner's use of colour, writes: "Colour was considered immoral, perhaps rightly because there is an immediate sensation which makes its effect independently of those ordered memories which are the basis of morality."

Since I was eleven years old, perhaps before, I have at intervals played a kind of game in which I opened my eyes, looked about me, and willed myself to blot out all except what I at that moment saw before me, pretending that all was completely new, seen for the first time. So, too, with people. I have looked at my loved ones with an eye, and listened to them with an ear, from the outside. I have had at such times a sense of moral irresponsibility, a sort of self-induced drugged state, intensification of vision, dissociation from the human element. This game is dangerous. It has sometimes led to words and actions which would never have been in the linear order of my behaviour. These "fresh beginnings" have in fact not been beginnings, but escapes from habitual behaviour. They are a form of aesthetic immoralism, often bringing later remorse, but highly delightful at the time.

Diana erupted into Wilton's today to join me for lunch wearing trousers and a yachting cap with "HMS *Indomitable*" on it. She was in a gale of spirits from having parked her car with all four wheels on the pavement after banging into a van. She is not only accident-prone, I believe she revels in accidents and risks. She is, now nearing eighty, a woman for all ages, equally enchanting to that ninety-year-old billionaire Paul Getty, to up-and-coming politicians, to writers and artists, waiters and policemen, to philandering skirt-chasers, homosexuals and lesbians. Yet this Pied Piper plays no soothing or well-worn airs; she is unexpected, fresh as a clever child, has kept her immaculate beauty, and wears the lost glamour of pre-1914 with a touch of slapstick. She enjoys the company of the rich, but hasn't forgotten what it is to be hard up. She tried to save me money on the luncheon by insisting on one lobster cutlet only between us, but Mr. Marx, the proprietor, circumvented her and managed to charge me £10.

15 February 1970.

Weekend at Hythe. Cold, sunny weather, but quite warm when you had been walking briskly up and down the sea-front past the Victorian seaside lodgings, past the 1920 bungalows (one of which is the seaside house in *The Death of the Heart*). Sun on calm blue water, a few stoutly coated figures fishing at the water's edge, passing dog-walkers all muffled up. The curve of the bay, Dungeness in the distance, and behind me the romantic view of Hythe topped by its church tower. Then walking back past the now leafless trees of Lady's Walk (which are in dripping leaf when Karen and her lover walk there in *The House in Paris*[1]), and so on up the hill to Carbery. Elizabeth does not join me in my walks. She says that neither of us ever stops talking and that when she talks as she walks the cold air catches in her throat and makes her cough. Her mind is now fixed on Ireland, going to live there. She says she will prowl around a little Regency terrace at Clontarf and choose a house there, or somewhere like it, not too far from Dublin. She will stay at Hythe only as long as I stay in London.

10 March 1970.

Lunched today at the Carlton Club with a Conservative peeress. She and I are not made for each other. She kept asking me questions like "Is it compulsory in Canada for every individual to *destroy* any waste paper in his possession?" I said, "No, I don't think so. Probably most people just chuck it out." "But I am assured, on very good authority, that it *is* compulsory in Canada." (Well, if she knows, why the hell ask me?)

As I was lapping up my machine-made turtle soup my nose began to spout blood, drops falling on the virgin snow of the tablecloth. I bolted off past the tables of Conservative MPs to the Gents', and tried to ice my nose. When I returned to the table, the peeress said, in a brisk voice, "That shows you have been overdoing things."

22 April 1970.

Particles of the past disturb my vision of today. I cannot throw away the scratched gramophone record of my particular experience. The needle is stuck in the groove and plays the same old tunes. Never more so than during this visit to Mary in the beamed and raftered cottage that she has left me in her will. She is one who "lives in the past." That sounds to be a dreary occupation. I am not so sure that it

---

[1] Published in 1935.

is. In these last years when she has lived alone a loveless life of small friendships and village squabbles, she has gone over and over the past with such absorption that it has become far more real and vivid than the daily jogtrot. However, her version of the years which we shared is wildly different from my own. Which of us is lying? Perhaps neither. So much for history. Certainly I do not come well out of her story. (Elizabeth once said, "There is no woman who can't knock a man off his perch if she tries hard enough.") Yet as she and I sat side by side on a slatted wooden bench in her sunny garden, it seemed we were two old people turning over pages in a book we had written together. Who else but we two knew of this or that? "Is the smell of melting tar on a road still your favourite scent, Mary, as you said that day when we walked back from the beach house? And what about Mrs. Pulsifer in the seaside lodging, calling upstairs, 'Breakfast is ready, bar frying the bacon.'" Now Mary says she loves her dog more than any man or woman.

8 May 1970.

For more than a week this hot, fine, flawless weather has gone on. I spend hours of each day in the parks, among the strollers and the lovers (two are making love in a group of daffodils!). The sun is drawing out the scent of the wallflowers. The burnished cavalry of the Household pass slowly down the Mall. Buckingham Palace has been refaced smart for the Queen's return from Australia. The Season is getting under way.

More echoes of the past at Laurence's cocktail party. Laurence himself, whom I remember as a musical stripling, is a puce-faced and portly ex-opera singer. His cousin Marcie (an old flirt of mine) is now a broad-faced peasant with crinkled apple cheeks. There was a florid gentleman in a spotted tie there. I did not identify him, until the moment of departure, with an elegant and dissipated figure who was at Oxford with me and whose circle of "Golden Youths" I envied. We spoke of Billy Coster.[1] I said, "Billy haunts me." "Me too." But as we talked of him he seemed to recede into a mocking laugh.

---

[1] William Bay Coster, an Oxford friend.

19 October 1970.

How much I miss Norman Robertson – how often I wish that I could talk to him. Nobody replaces him for me, or ever will.

Back again to the diary after an immense interval and in a very different climate, for now we live in a climate created by others, those few in Quebec who have, in one of the most extraordinary exploits in our history, held up a nation to ransom.[1] They have sought out the vulnerable parts in our society and are twisting and twisting the knife in them. Here in London they want to put Canada House under police protection, and also our house. I cannot believe that if I were kidnapped the present government would pay one cent for my ransom. At home it sounds like war but it is not – it is blackmail. Our immense Anglo-Canadian reserves of security – never a revolution, never a civil war, never a defeat, never an enemy occupation, never a humiliation – are at last being drawn upon. Our unbroken national luck has turned, and anger and fear combined may break down our national basis of compromise. Mike Pearson on TV was wise to remind us of this danger. Today a newly arrived French Canadian on the staff said to me, "I am ashamed to be a French Canadian. I feel I should skulk through the streets." I said, "That is complete nonsense. We are all in this together. All Canadians feel the same." But do *all* Canadians? I feel and think insistently about this sombre tragedy.

20 October 1970.

The funeral of M. Laporte. Every time the telephone twitches I expect more bad news from Ottawa. I have spent most of this last week on the long-distance telephone talking to Ed Ritchie[2] at External Affairs and then relaying messages to and fro between him and Dennis Greenhill at the Foreign Office about the kidnappings. Fortunately one could not have two more sensible and unwordy men to deal with.

---

[1] On October 5, Jasper Cross, the British Trade Commissioner in Montreal, was kidnapped by the terrorist Front de Libération du Québec. This was followed by the kidnapping and subsequent murder of Pierre Laporte, Deputy Premier of Quebec.

[2] Under-Secretary of State for External Affairs.

1 November 1970.

Elizabeth is just back from Ireland where she had revisited Bowen's Court[1] in a busload of Catholic nuns, priests, and acolytes. The house, she says, is gone without a trace; the ground where it stood so smooth that she could only identify the place where the library was by the *prunus* tree that once used to obscure the light in one of the windows. She says it is better gone than degraded. She is happier, she says, in a different way, now than ever before – the happiness of old age, the day-to-day kind, sensuous pleasure in the visible world. She wants to go on *living*, and so do I.

I suppose Jasper Cross must be dead by now. A small, scruffy collection of Communists were presenting a petition today at the door of the United States Embassy as Elizabeth and I came back from lunch. The other day we had to evacuate MacDonald House because of a bomb scare.

31 January 1971.

Lunched with Ted Heath, now Prime Minister, at Chequers. He was very brisk with his no-nonsense manner and his determined joviality. I like the man because he treats me as a friend, or a friendly acquaintance. Of course I knew him quite well when he was Leader of the Opposition. I feel at ease with him, which I rarely do with Prime Ministers while they are in office. They are usually all right before and after. I certainly never felt at ease with his predecessor, Wilson.

1 February 1971.

I have been re-reading Thackeray's *Pendennis* and recovering from the itch. Pendennis is a young barrister in the 1830s, a man-about-town. After all, *has* London life changed so much since then? Or rather, is the life-style of such young men so very different? *Pendennis* is a sort of English version of Flaubert's *Sentimental Education*. Very acute it is, too.

In the evening went to meet the Quebec Police delegation, who are here for consultation with the British. The head man is a Norman

---

[1] Elizabeth Bowen's family home in County Cork.

French Canadian, blue-eyed, strawberry colour. Every so often you see that pure Norman type in Canada. He spoke of the FLQ and said that to them separatism was only a jumping-off place. What they really wanted was a revolution against the "Establishment." He spoke as an intelligent policeman, saying that if you read nothing for three months but Che Guevara, Marx, Mao, etc., it would not be at all difficult to think as they do.

After he left, a dreary little party here of middle-aged people talking about Youth. Always the repetition of the same boring senti-ments...."I didn't know whether it was a boy or a girl"..."Mind you, I can tolerate long hair provided it is clean"..."They are brought up too soft".... "They despise money but they are always looking for a handout." My trouble is that I can understand the misbehaviour of the younger generation, but not their aspirations.

14 February 1971.

St. Valentine's Day. Went to see Nancy Mitford in hospital where she lies – dying? She says that people always tell her that she would not really have enjoyed living in the reign of Louis XIV because of the horrors of the medical treatments, but that, judging by her medical experience in the last few years, she might just as well have lived in the age of Louis XIV. She tried some jokes and so did I. We drank a little of her champagne. I brought her a bunch of freesias that I got off a barrow at the Marble Arch. I was touched – and surprised – at her being so glad to see me, but felt, as I often do visiting the sick, that I talked too much and nervously, hoping to amuse. Later I walked in the windy park feeling very sad about Nancy and about life.

28 March 1971.

Yesterday was a day of inexplicable exhilaration, of total happi-ness. Sylvia and I went down to Woodstock for the night. We arrived in the late afternoon and walked in Blenheim Park. The landscaped lake, the theatrical bridges, the woods behind, were all misted over as though seen through gauze in the ballet *Swan Lake*. It was like walking by the lake in the Bois together when we were first married, and the bedroom up the twisting staircase at the Bear Inn was a kind of bird-cage, like our bedroom in the rue Singer in Paris.

29 March 1971.

I can no more imagine life after retirement than life after death. When I wrote to Ed Ritchie and told him that I did not wish to "cling to this job," I meant precisely the opposite. I *do* wish to cling to this job, and of course he knows that I do.

Elizabeth is in the Hythe Nursing Home. There is a sky above which makes you disbelieve in God – an opaque, inexorable sulk, unchanging, like a mood that is going to last forever.

Douglas LePan comes to see me. He has begun to write poetry again after twenty years of silence. He and I drink together. We are friends.

24 April 1971.

The Duchess of Kent here for a tea party for Dr. Best of insulin fame. The thing about Royalty (which she must have learned after, or just before, entering that enclosed order) is the slow-motion bit – never hurry, just cool it and keep every step, every gesture, every word, limpidly leisurely. It is a game of control. If any of the other actors in the scene get out of phase by word or gesture, control them with the slightest jerk of the reins. It's dressage. No wonder Princess Anne is good at it – she was trained that way. And against this background, conversation of dedicated platitudes; any throwaway line from the Royalty sounds, to the uninitiated, like an indiscretion.

In the afternoon to St. Paul's Cathedral. The Duchess of Kent says that it would be impossible to be inside that Cathedral without believing in God. I feel exactly the opposite, as if I were in a magnificent, poorly filled opera house.

26 April 1971.

Weekend with the Sitwells. We drove over to Easton Neston. As always there was a wonderful and enjoyable mix of people there coming and going, up and down the grandiose staircase past the statues in their niches and the painted grisailles, in and out of the superb drawing-room with its elaborate plaster-work. In all the rooms, seated or semi-recumbent figures lounging, talking, reading, making their entrances and their exits. A house of echoes and reflections – echoes on the stone staircase, on the long parquet-floored gallery, on the paving stones of the hall, reflections from the long windows which frame the formal gardens and the ornamental water. Our hostess, dear Kisty, is a charmer, so clever and so funny and a Scottish naturalness about her.

19 May 1971.

A letter from the Department – "I regretfully must confirm that you should plan your retirement at the normal date, that is, September 23, 1971." So that's that. It will take some sharp hustling to get out of this house by that date, with two months of the London Season and continual entertaining coming in between, and then the dead month of August. It is the end of thirty-seven years in the Foreign Service.

They, particularly Louis Rogers, are trying to get me out of my spacious office in Canada House and into a utilitarian third-floor box in MacDonald House. No – I and my office go together.

6 June 1971.

Walked in Kensington Gardens. I had got up very early – 5:30 a.m. – pulled on my pants, old sweater, collected key and three cigarettes. The park was completely empty. The morning was fine, foreboding heat, the sun just risen. I walked and walked till I came to the statue of Queen Victoria sculpted by her daughter which stands in front of Kensington Palace. Turning round the statue I came under the vine trellis into the garden. After so much green of trees and grass, its yellows and browns and pinks, the red of the tulips and the brown of the wallflowers, burst on my eyes with a delightful shock. I was alone and happy. For some reason I thought of my mother and remembered how she used to challenge us boys to look straight into her eyes and how we tried and always flinched before that potent, mocking, mysterious gaze, something leonine about it, not feline.

14 June 1971.

Itching like hell – I wonder whether this is the change of life.

I am emptied and flattened by the hours of Wagner with Loelia.[1]

---

[1] Loelia, Duchess of Westminster, now Hon. Lady Lindsay of Dowhill.

The second Act of *Tristan* vented its full power. Never that I can remember have I been so totally transported into a realm of passion and tragedy which was yet quite credible. I feel as if Loelia and I had been consumed and exhausted in the same revelation. I thought of ringing her up and asking her how her Wagner is settling down, but she is at Ascot with her husband. The loss of credibility and the lessening of interest comes in the third Act, with the endless dying of Tristan. Never underestimate Wagner's capacity for stretching a duet. We were in the theatre for six hours.

Earlier in the day I lunched at Aspinall's, the new club in Berkeley Square. All the people who used to go to the West End restaurants have now migrated, either to the new gaming clubs or to Chelsea and Knightsbridge. At the table next to us were a quartet of young bucks – quite a change from the arty Chelsea world. Perhaps with the revival of Edwardian women's hats this year will come revival of the Edwardian gamblers and womanizers, the earliest progenitors of Mayfair.

12 July 1971.

Returned to London from a Disraelian weekend in the country at the d'Avigdor-Goldsmids. Gloriously hot weekend; roses, roses all the way. House running on the velvet wheels of the rich. The diversified and diverting company staying in the house included my now-favourite writer, Anthony Powell. What more could one ask? Powell himself is unalarming to an almost alarming degree, young in manner, extremely nice, natural and charming.

16 July 1971.

End of the Season – and what a Season! Lunched with the Queen Mother. On the dining-room table great silver bowls of outsize sweet peas breathing over us, and the Queen Mother, herself breathing charm. This life of semi-friendship with Prime Ministers and members of the Royal Family will finish in six weeks' time and I shall have vanished from the scene as if I were dead, only if I were dead there would be a memorial service for me and *they* all would come.

Dinner at Claridge's with Elizabeth. She had spent two days with Rosamond Lehmann at Cumberland Lodge, Windsor Park (nicknamed Spook Hall), where there was a psychic convention. Elizabeth said there was much talk of reincarnation and that it gives one a pretty poor idea of God's resources to think that He could run out of inventing new people and be reduced to using the same old material over and over again. Elizabeth was in splendid form, but she is not cured. I fear for this winter when I am away in Canada.

John and Anne Maher are staying with us. We are a very companionable quartet. Anne seems to me as young in spirit as when I first knew her forty years ago, and I love her dearly.

27 September 1971.

We have left the house and are staying for a brief interlude at the Dorchester. Back last night on the night train from Scotland from staying with the Adeanes at Balmoral. Everything we do is now a last time – most certainly the last time I dine with the Queen at Balmoral.

25 October 1971. Ottawa.

The menacing wail of the vacuum cleaner wielded in the inept hands of our new cleaning woman comes nearer and nearer up the passage to my closed bedroom door, seeking what it can devour. The rain has peed itself out and on the still-wet streets the last leaves are falling. It is an autumn morning, still mild before the snow flies.

I am baffled by all this talk of the cultural opportunities of Ottawa, the Renaissance life one can lead at the Centre for the Performing Arts. I would rather walk the quiet back streets, beyond the cluster of high-rise apartments, down to the poorer quarters where a sort of sing-song, ding-dong life crawls along. The old sit on porches and stare. A little girl kicks up leaves in the gutter and chases a grey cat. China ornaments of no cultural significance encumber small windows choked with potted plants. Swarthy, big-bellied Italians park their dirty, dented old cars up wide alleys. Chinese children are playing football on an asphalt yard. On corner lots stand up the grey rock churches of the French-Canadian faith, flanked by priests' houses and seminaries, cheerless formal repositories, but preferred by me to the hulking red sandstone of the United Church, embodiment of gloomy, dowdy dullness.

At the cocktail party yesterday someone asked me point-blank across a roomful of people, "To what do you attribute your success as a diplomat?" I was somewhat taken aback by the question and was incapable, or unwilling, to make an answer, like ladies asked to account for the flavour of their curry soup. . . . "Oh, one just adds a snatch of pepper, a dash of salt and a few condiments."

All the same, the question has set me thinking, not so much of success or failure in the diplomatic career as of the profession of diplomacy, and specifically of the Canadian Foreign Service in which I have spent nearly forty years of my life and to which I am now saying goodbye.

. . .

Yet it was to be some time before I set down on paper the following reflections on diplomacy and diplomats – particularly the Canadian variety.

DIPLOMATIC ATTITUDES

Diplomacy is a matter of communication. The first diplomats were no doubt the messengers sent from one cave to another to establish friendship or to issue defiance. Like ambassadors today, if the messages they bore were not agreeable to the recipients, they were apt to be unpopular (no doubt on the McLuhan principle that the medium is the message). Sometimes they were decapitated and their heads returned to the senders. Now they are declared *persona non grata* and are recalled by their own governments in a huff or as a prelude to hostilities. Yet sooner or later, after the war is over, the business of diplomacy is resumed and diplomatic channels are reopened. The process will continue indefinitely unless humanity succeeds in blowing itself off the earth's surface.

It is argued that the traditional methods of diplomacy and the system of representation abroad are out of date. Also, that the diplomats themselves are, in training and outlook, out of touch with the realities of today's world.

It is certainly true that the role of the diplomat has changed and is changing, and that diplomacy is being conducted in new spheres and by new methods. It would indeed be very extraordinary if, when every social and political institution is changing so rapidly, the diplomatic career remained as a sort of fossil of the past; if it did so, what young man of ability and ambition would wish to enter such a profession?

Much of this material appeared in *Spectrum* (Volume 3, Number 2, 1983), a quarterly publication of the Canadian Imperial Bank of Commerce, under the title "As Others See Us – Canada's Image Abroad."

Difficult, sometimes painful, problems of adjustment, together with new challenges, face the diplomat of today. His position is a vulnerable one. He is a generalist surrounded by experts. In a period when quantifiable coefficients are the instruments for assessing job performance, how does one measure such qualities as skill in negotiation, coolness in crisis, and experience in international affairs? And how does the diplomat fare in the company of specialists in a technological age? International negotiations cover so many fields undreamed of in the past, whether it be the environment, tariffs, energy, the law of the sea, the protection of human rights, monetary policy, or sport, that one can hardly think of an area of human activity which is not on the agenda of an international gathering.

Linked with this proliferation of new areas of negotiation has been the development of multilateral diplomacy, where negotiations are not just between two nations but among many. The United Nations is of course the most obvious case, but there are now more than 150 international organizations. Multilateral diplomacy, with its lobbying for support, its dealings with international secretariats, the variety of its subject matter, is a new phenomenon requiring both political skills and expert knowledge.

It is a strange paradox that while traditional diplomacy is under fire from so many quarters, diplomacy is one of the growth industries of this century. When I returned to Canada House in London in 1967, the number of foreign diplomats and their wives there entitled to varying degrees of diplomatic privileges and immunity totalled more than 3,300 – more than double the number when I had last been stationed in London in 1945. All foreign service offices, like all other branches of bureaucracy, have increased vastly in size. New nations, between sixty and seventy of them since the last war, have come into being and have sent their new diplomats all around the world. In return, older nations have posted their diplomats to the new states.

Serving Canada abroad is an enlightening experience. The Canadian identity emerges very clearly when seen from the outside and when Canada appears as an actor on the international stage. Any foreign diplomat who has had the experience of negotiating with Canadians would recognize on sight our particular Canadian mix of goodwill and hard-headedness, of friendliness and touchiness. He would also, I think, respect the Canadian instinct for conciliation and realistic acceptance of the limits of the possible, mingled though it is with a strong dose of self-righteousness. These qualities do not seem to be more Anglo-Canadian than French-Canadian. Indeed, seen from abroad, all Canadians, whatever their differences of origin, seem much more like each other than like any other race or nation, including the races from which they spring.

In the longer perspective there also emerges a continuity in Canadian attitudes in international affairs. Despite changes of governments and varying emphasis in our foreign policies, it would be almost possible to foretell a Canadian national reaction to an international problem or crisis. The very vocabulary in which Canadian views are expressed has not much altered. It has a moralistic preaching tone which strives, sometimes inadequately, to express a real strain of idealism. Yet this idealism is inevitably strongly diluted by the realism of a great trading nation with the material interests of its people to safeguard. Any policy which drifted away too far from our national interests into an atmosphere of ideal international aspirations would have no roots at home.

When I entered it in 1934, the Department of External Affairs was as small as Canada's place then was on the map of international politics. Since then, of course, it has increased enormously in size and in complexity of organization. At the start we were anxious to differentiate ourselves from traditional Foreign Offices, to eschew diplomatic trappings and to display an almost-ostentatious lack of ostentation. The profession of diplomacy is, however, an international trade union which, whatever the national or individual styles and origins of its members, stamps them all with its hallmark. The Canadian diplomat, like all other diplomats, lives a peculiar amphibious existence at home and abroad. Abroad, one enjoys privileges, allowances, and a special status. At home, one is a civil servant among tens of thousands of others, and the quicker one adjusts to the change the better.

For the foreign service officer who is interested in policy and the mechanics of power, service at home is more important than service abroad. If he hopes to exert any influence on affairs he must make good his position in the department. The longer he remains abroad, remote from the political and departmental infighting in Ottawa, the more his influence tends to decline. He must first have established a base of trust and friendship at home in order to count on continued support, and this relationship must be steadily maintained. He who forgets this does so at his peril.

Power is at the centre, as Winston Churchill once remarked. It is in Ottawa that all the decisions are made that affect our policy abroad. Much has been written lately in Canada, as well as elsewhere, about the decision-making process in foreign policy, and much of it has been written by political scientists whose journals explore the subject, sometimes with the aid of graphs or models of behaviour. These methods have produced studies of value, although often couched in language so specialized that those actually involved in the decision-making – the politicians and officials – might find it hard to follow them without taking a language course. Such studies are conducted in a cool climate of reasoned analysis which is remote indeed from the pressure-cooker of politics.

In reality, decisions are often taken in reaction to unexpected developments in the international field – a sudden revolution, a change in interest rates abroad. At home there are pressures from other government departments with their special interests and responsibilities, and there are waves of public concern and agitation about particular causes. Sometimes policy swerves from its course from the urgent necessity of the government's winning a by-election, or because of a rash reply given by a Minister to an awkward question in the House of Commons. Then there are the time and human elements. As to the time element, in an age of instantaneous communications it is speeded up to a matter of moments in which a decision may have to be reached or a previous decision reversed. A telephone call from one national leader to another may do the trick. The human element involves not only the personalities of our politicians and their advisers but the effects of strain, fatigue, or ill-health.

Diplomats, when serving abroad, live in a different world, a world of official immunity. They are outside the law of the country where they are stationed. Diplomatic immunity is far from being an artificial anachronism. Without it, diplomats stationed in hostile countries could easily become the victims of trumped-up charges. Diplomatic immunity is often misunderstood and causes irritation to the local inhabitants. The aspect which causes most irritation is the diplomat's ability to park his car wherever he likes. In recent years the number of parking tickets issued to diplomats in one capital – London – and left unpaid numbered, over a ten-month period, more than twenty-six thousand. I am glad to say that, although not in law bound to do so, the personnel of Canadian missions abroad are under instruction to pay such fines.

There is no aspect of diplomatic life which appears to the outsider more artificial, and indeed sometimes more absurd, than that of protocol. There is a type of diplomat to whom matters of protocol come to assume absorbing fascination; there are others who regard them as a necessary evil. Protocol is best understood as a reflection of the extraordinary sensitivity and touchiness of the nation state. Nations, in their relations with each other, of which diplomats are simply the agents, behave very much like temperamental prima donnas. They fear "losing face" or being upstaged. They use the nuances of a snub or the extra cordiality of a gesture as a means of registering the temperature of their relations with other states. At what level of representation is a visiting Canadian Foreign Minister welcomed at the airport on arrival in a foreign country? How many guns are fired in salute for the arrival of a visiting Head of State? What is the degree of warmth or coolness expressed in an after-dinner toast? These apparently trivial things form a sort of code, carefully weighed and noted in the diplomatic community. They may be the first indications, the red or green light, in relations between states indicating degrees of friendship or hostility.

One of the features that separate diplomats in the higher ranks from others in the communities in which they live is their housing. This has always been a sensitive question for Canadians. Some critics would like the style of life of Canadian representatives abroad to reflect that of the average Canadian middle-class home. In practice, in most countries, ambassadors are housed in conditions quite different from anything that could be afforded by the local inhabitants. This dates back to the days when there were plenty of large private houses staffed by many servants, and the ambassador's residence was one of many, instead of standing out as an exception. One justification for maintaining these mansions is the necessity for entertaining. How much is diplomatic entertaining justified? Sometimes its value is greatly exaggerated, yet it still goes on all over the world. The Embassy provides a setting for hospitality to visitors from home and the local colony of Canadian residents, for entertaining politicians and officials in the country to which one is accredited and visiting Canadian Ministers. All this requires a certain scale of physical "plant."

Perhaps finally this whole way of life will disappear for one very simple reason – there will no longer be servants available – and ambassadors will have to retreat to modest flats and mount their dinners and receptions at the local hotels. They will then be faced by the great and growing problem of physical security. When I was in Washington, the Prime Minister, Mike Pearson, came on a visit and we gave a dinner for him and the President, L. B. Johnson, and their wives. This involved the presence in the Embassy residence and grounds of some twenty United States security men. The cook threatened to leave. "They kept tracking through my kitchen," she complained, "while I am trying to cook the dinner." She also resented having to prepare a light repast for the security officers simultaneously with the dinner upstairs.

Women diplomats in the higher ranks are still something of a rarity in all Foreign Services. In our own Foreign Service we have had a handful of distinguished women diplomats – too few and too far between. The unsung heroines of the Foreign Service are the women in its administrative and secretarial ranks; without whom the whole operation would speedily collapse. The attractions for Canadians of representing their country abroad are less than they once were. With the opening up of missions in so many new countries, the ratio of unhealthy, remote, and boring posts has increased. Then, too, some wives of foreign service officers – and this is increasingly the case – have interesting, remunerative jobs at home and do not look forward to the prospect of giving them up in order to accompany their husbands to a foreign post. Yet the wife of a foreign service officer can make all the difference to the success or failure of her husband's posting abroad. If she enjoys the stimulus of meeting a variety of people, if she finds an interest in getting to know other countries and cultures, the husband and wife make a doubly effective team. I do not know how effective Sylvia and I have been as a team – I do know that without her I could not have carried on. She has risen to every occasion with zest and without fuss.

By its very nature this is a career of adjustments not only to changes of place but to changes of policy and changes of political masters. This involves conformity, but when does the conformity stop? What happens in the process to the personal convictions of the individual?

It is sometimes suggested that diplomats have suspiciously supple consciences, and accommodate themselves all too easily to changing régimes and switches in policy; that they serve not only their country "right or wrong" but any government in power "right or wrong." There is a lot of truth in the saying that "there are old diplomats and bold diplomats, but there are no old bold diplomats." It is not a profession for men of fiery political opinions. They should go into politics and fire them off there – but that does not necessarily mean that all diplomats are a race of spineless time-servers without views of their own. Certainly there has been no lack of debate and dissension over policy in the ranks of our own foreign service. Most of the important – and some of the unimportant – decisions in our foreign policy have been the subject of discussion in which professional diplomats played an active part, sometimes seeing their views prevail, sometimes being overruled by the Foreign Minister or the Prime Minister. If overruled, these same officials proceeded to defend abroad the policies which at home they had tried to alter. This for some was a painful duty, but they had no doubt that it was their duty. If that is what is meant by conformist, a good diplomat is a good conformist. Once a line of policy is adopted, and it is a matter of explaining it and defending it abroad, there is no longer any place for personal differences. It is the diplomat's role to convey as accurately and as cogently as possible the policy of his government. If he aired his own views to a foreign government or to the press, he would be misleading them. However much he protested that his view was personal, it would be believed that it reflected in some measure the views of his government. An ambassador or a senior official in a Foreign Office is only worth while listening to if his interlocutor believes that he is in close touch with the opinion of his own government and has authority to express it. The ambassador's personal opinions are of no more importance to a foreign government than those of a taxi driver, and often less interesting.

Of course, there are outer limits to loyalty, and if one believes that the policies of one's government are evil or dangerous to the interests of one's country, one has always the recourse of resignation. It must be admitted that on the whole, diplomats do not resign readily. They sometimes console themselves with the reflection that if they left the service, a more dangerous and undesirable person might be appointed in their place.

A diplomat is a civil servant at the orders of his government who happens to be serving part of his life abroad. Under the orders of his government, yes, but under how many and how different governments in the course of a lifetime? As for myself, I have served under six Prime Ministers in the course of my career – a mixed bunch, one might irreverently remark. Some I have known better than others; most I have observed at pretty close quarters at home and abroad.

The only people to whom Prime Ministers can talk on a basis of real equality are other Prime Ministers. I have been present at many such "face-to-face" meetings between Canadian Prime Ministers and their counterparts in foreign countries. In addition to the importance of the official agenda for discussion between them, it was fascinating to watch the manner in which they took each other's measure. There was always a period of small talk between the great men, customarily led off by a few mild jokes. Nothing of significance at this stage was said by either party, but if they were meeting for the first time they seemed to sense, not only on political grounds but on grounds of sympathy or aversion, whether this relationship would bear fruit in future. This matter of personal rapport or distaste between the leaders of nations is one of those elements in international affairs least easy to forecast, escaping all computerized data and baffling the planners, but by no means negligible in its effects. Two examples are the personal antipathy between President Kennedy and Prime Minister Diefenbaker, and the personal friendship between Mr. St. Laurent and Mr. Nehru. It is not always the antagonist in the international arena who arouses personal mistrust – it is sometimes the ally.

In the conduct of Canadian foreign policy the effects of prime-ministerial or ministerial statements on international issues which are aimed at vote-getting at home, without regard for the long-term consequences abroad, are much to be feared. However, what really counts in the daily conduct of foreign policy is that the Secretary of State for External Affairs should have a strong position in Cabinet and be able to make his views prevail. A Foreign Minister may be a charming chap, much liked by his officials, but that is of little use if the policies he is advocating are regularly shot down by his colleagues or overruled by the Prime Minister. Of course, in the worst case one may have a Minister who is both disagreeable and ineffectual.

It is notoriously difficult to get Canadian news into the columns of the foreign press. As I know all too well, it is easier for the camel to enter the eye of the needle than to get a well informed Canadian political story or considered editorial comment into the columns of the press of London, Paris, or New York. Perhaps this is in part simply because our news stories are not very sensational; perhaps if we indulged in more revolutions, or more spectacular scandals or crimes, we would receive more attention. There are far too few Canadian journalists permanently stationed abroad and too many journalists accompanying visiting Canadian ministers. Our actors, singers, and artists contribute enormously to a fuller view of Canada.

Politicians of all stripes are very prone to tell us what a great people we are and what a magnificent future awaits us if we vote the right way, or, alternatively, to chide us for backsliding if we do not fulfil their expectations by conforming to their policies. Fortunately, Canadians have enough common sense not to swallow all these congratulations and admonitions. Canadian governments have always had a tendency to dish out good advice to other nations, calling upon them to behave themselves in conformity with our high moral standards, and to cease and desist from disturbing actions. We are a little too apt to insist by contrast upon the purity of our own intentions. We have the more cause to be careful of the susceptibilities of other peoples because we are extremely susceptible to criticism of ourselves by others. This prickly sensitivity is not an asset to us.

We show to our best advantage in our association with the developing nations. We ourselves have gone through a colonial stage in our history and know something of the birth pangs of emerging nation-hood. Our relationship with such countries also brings to the surface the idealist strain that has always played a part both in our aid pro-grams and in our peace-keeping initiatives. In general, we are happier when we can fulfil a practical and humanitarian or peace-keeping role, and this has brought us many good friends around the world. We resent condescension, real or imagined. "Who the hell do they think they are?" is the common Canadian reaction. Sometimes this attitude comes into play even in our relations with those with whom we have the closest ties of friendship and affinity – the British, the French, and the Americans. We condemn in others what seems to us snobbery, cultural or social, whereas while we have no class structure in the European or even the American sense, we have many social and cul-tural dividing lines of our own, and quite a plentiful crop of snobs.

It is a well-worn platitude that in a democracy foreign policy should be based upon an alert and informed public opinion, but to repeat a truism does not make it come true. The fact is that most people, most of the time, are not much interested in foreign policy except when it touches their pockets or involves some special group organized for a particular cause. This lack of interest is reflected in this country in the paucity of public debate in and out of Parliament and the scrappy coverage (with some honourable exceptions) of international affairs in the press. Thus, informed public opinion is, and is likely to remain, in a minority.

It is, however, a minority essential to the conduct of foreign affairs, for a policy which has no real roots in public opinion is apt to be an artificial construction which may sound plausible on paper, but which collapses at any real test. The universities and the press have, of course, an indispensable part to play, informing and sustaining public interest. In Canada we have been fortunate in having an aca-demic community who are making valuable contributions to our knowledge and understanding of foreign policy issues.

Those who operate in the field of international relations, politi-cians and professional diplomats, depend upon such informed comment. Even criticism is preferable to indifference; otherwise they may come to feel that they are functioning in a void, and no one likes to feel superfluous, not even an ambassador – or, indeed, an old ex-ambassador.

As to the vexed question of our national identity, it appears that, in the long run, despite all our self-doubts and divisions, we have an instinctive sense of what it means to be Canadian and no intention of relinquishing the privilege. Sometimes this seems clearer viewed from a distant perspective than closer at home.

EPILOGUE

As it turned out, my farewell to diplomacy did not lead to a farewell
to the Public Service of Canada. For on December 9, 1971, I was
appointed Special Advisor to the Privy Council in Ottawa. My diary
entry for that day reads as follows: "They have announced my appointment to the Privy Council. The front-page headline of the *Ottawa
Journal* says 'Government Crumbles' and, directly below, 'Ritchie Joins
the Prime Minister's Office.' It sounds as though I had been called in
to prop up the edifice. In reality this job has nothing to do with party
politics. What precisely it *has* to do with remains to be seen. At any
rate it gives me one more hand to play before I throw in the cards and
clear out for good. Then I shall delve once more into the toppling piles
of my diaries to see if anything can be unearthed that will bear the
light of day."

INDEX

Beasley, Mrs., 262
Beaton, Cecil, 279
Beaudissen (German officer), 337, 339
Beaudoin (Vichy Foreign Minister), 272, 273
Beaulieu, Paul, 276
Beck, Józef, 42
Bedford, 12th Duke of, 162
Beeley, Sir Harold, 385, 401
Belgium, 57, 406, 411
Belinski (Polish acquaintance), 123, 127
Bell, Clive, 193
Bell, Vanessa, 112
Bennett, R.B., 65, 72, 123–24
Benson, Edgar, 532
Berendsen, Carl, 225
Berland, Marshal, 394
Berlin, 112, 122, 139, 325, 326, 327, 358, 368
Berlin, Isaiah, 412
Bessborough family, 39–40, 71, 91, 524, 540
Bevin, Ernest, 183, 262–63
Binyon, Laurence, 151
Bismarck, Prince and Princess, 341
Bliss, Mrs. Robert Woods, 18, 488
Blitzkrieg (1940–41), 71, 73, 74, 80–81, 83–84, 95, 107–8, 111–12, 122, 165
Bloomsbury group, 132, 193n, 512–13
Blücher, Vice-Chancellor, 331–32
Blum, Léon, 121
Bohlen, C.E. ("Chip"), 344
Boland, Freddy, 406–7, 439
Bonn, 305, 306, 321, 328, 348–49, 365; American diplomatic community in, 324; Belgian Embassy, 348; diplomatic corps in, 333–34, 362; Zittelmannstrasse (Canadian Chancery), 324–25
Borden, Sir Robert, 5
Boulogne, 62
Bowen, Elizabeth, 132, 136, 146, 150, 151, 161, 162, 164, 168, 173, 179, 180, 182, 184, 190, 191, 192, 240, 270, 271, 360, 364, 375, 392–93, 394–95, 520, 546; *Heat of the Day*, 8, 204; author first

meets, 101, 131; her books, 133; *Death of the Heart*, 143, 513, 553; on friendship, 149; and Virginia Woolf, 149, 158, 174; in Ireland, 153, 386, 557; on writing, 155–56, 174, 365; house bombed, 203, 204, 205; "Happy Autumn Fields," 205; at Paris Peace Conference, 263; on relations with Germany, 330–31; *A World of Love*, 331; *A Race with Time*, 364; at Vassar, 403; on Ritchie diaries, 403, 408; *The Little Girls*, 452; on Bloomsbury group, 512–13; *Eva Trout*, 513, 534, 539; in Hythe, Kent, 522, 531, 539, 553–54; *Pictures and Conversation*, 539; illness, 559, 562
Bowen's Court, 364, 375, 386, 557
Bower, The, 4, 84–85, 136, 179
Bowra, Sir Maurice, 184
Bracken, Brendan, 123
Brandon, Henry, 438, 441, 445, 462
Breakers, 20–22
Breese, William and Nora, 462–63
Brentano, Dr. Heinrich von, 330, 367
Brogan, D.W., 271
Brown, Dudley, 12
Brown, George, 510
Bruce, Stanley, 42, 44–45
Bruna (maid), 539–40
Buchan, Alastair, 55n, 90, 393, 463
Buchan, John, Baron Tweedsmuir, 463
Buchan, William, 55n, 91, 101
Bull, Miss, 396
Bullitt, William C., 108
Bundy, Mary, 451, 464, 492
Bundy, McGeorge, 433, 458, 461, 493, 498, 499–500
Bundy, William, 451, 464, 492
Burke, Stanley, 382
Burma, 532
Butler, R.A., 209
Butterworth, Walter, 494
Byron, Lord, 473, 474
Byron, Robert, 40–41, 50, 145, 146

Cadieux, Marcel, 530
Cadogan, Sir Alexander, 225

Moore, George, 170, 193
Moreau (Belgian refugee), 168
Morgan, Charles, 175
Morocco, 115, 278
Morrell, Lady Ottoline, 193
Morrison, Harold, 465
Morrison, Herbert, 162
Morse, Sen. Wayne, 486
Mortimer, Raymond, 146, 184
Mosley, Sir Oswald, 19n, 41n, 183
Moss, Howard, 395
Mountbatten, Lady, 311–12
Mountolive (Durrell), 440
Mrs. Dalloway (Woolf), 512
Mulley, Mrs., 514
Murray, Geoff, 376, 404, 510
Mussolini, Benito, 38, 114, 220

Nassau Agreement (1963), 453, 457–58
Nasser, Gamel Abdal, 353, 355
NATO, 308, 407, 444, 451, 461, 501, 505, 506, 510, 521–22, 523, 530, 544
Nazis, 321, 326, 328–29, 330, 334, 337, 357, 368, 369
Nehru, Indira, 313
Nehru, Jawaharlal, 311–12
Nelles, P.W., 195
Nesbitt, Wallace, 404
New Delhi, 310, 312
Newport, 20–22, 124
New Writing, 49
New York, 114, 322, 346, 375, 381, 387, 388, 405, 410, 411, 421, 439, 448–49; Central Park, 376, 405, 449; Metropolitan Museum, 380, 411; Park Avenue (Ritchies' apartment), 395, 397, 405–6; Sutton Place (Ritchies' apartment), 378, 380, 383, 388, 390, 395, 396
New Zealand, 66, 115, 259, 263
Nicolson, Harold, 138, 532
Nielsen (Norwegian representative to U.N.), 407
Niven, David, 138
Noble, Alan, 387
Noetbeart, Charles, 410
Noetbeart, Marie, 410

NORAD, 450
Normandy, 195–203
Norstad, Gen. Lauris, 451
North Africa, 64, 109, 278
North Atlantic Council, 505, 506
Northern Lights, 301–2
Norway, 59, 66, 113
Nova Scotia, 20, 297, 301, 316, 389, 436
Nuremberg (Nürnberg), 24; Conference (1938), 40–41; Trials, 259
Nutting, Anthony, 132
Nye, George, 108

O'Brien, Larry, 532
O'Brien, Scruff, 485
"O Canada," 474
Odell, Ella, 23–24
Official Secrets Act, 252
Organization of American States, 444
Ormsby-Gore, David, 494
Osborne, Dorothy, 381
Ottawa, 164, 181, 206, 207, 219, 236, 241–44, 256, 298, 304, 317, 488, 562; Parliament Hill, 386, 528; Rockcliffe, 394; social life, 295, 301; in spring, 300; in winter, 294–95, 459
Ourousoff, Mr. and Mrs., 463
Oxford, 5, 17, 44, 76–78, 101–2, 105, 181, 206, 402, 547

Paget, Lady Victor, 141
Pakistan, 309, 310, 379
Paris, 17, 164, 204, 215–17, 270, 271, 274, 279, 331, 505; Bois de Boulogne, 286, 288; British Embassy, 262, 270, 279, 286, 289; Rue du Faubourg St.-Honoré (Canadian Embassy), 306; Avenue Foch (Canadian Embassy), 268, 271, 288; Hôtel Condé, 263; Hôtel Crillon, 257–58; Hôtel de la Rochefoucauld (Polish Embassy), 275; Louvre, 117; Luxembourg Palace, 258, 262, 263; Passy (Ritchies' house), 285, 288; Boulevard St. Germain (Ritchie's apt.), 268–69
Paris Peace Conference (1946), 256, 257–63

refugees, 65, 66–68, 78, 168; and internees, 68, 72; at Garnons, 69–70; air raids, 69, 71, 73–74, 75, 76, 78, 107–8, 111–12, 118, 139, 140, 204, 208; revisits Oxford, 76–78, 101–2; on sexual happiness, 95–96; attitude to Americans, 107, 108, 114, 122, 144–45, 208; tea with Queen, 110–11; feelings about Canada, 168–69, 172, 190; religion, 171, 180; D-Day, 193, 194, 195–200; in France, 200–203; visits Canada, 206–7; visits Paris, 215–17; posted to Canada (1945), 217; San Francisco Conference (1945), 219–36; postwar career, 242–43, 245; marriage, 245
— 1946–1962: Ritchie Week, viii–ix, 287–88; advisor at Paris Peace Conference (1946), 256, 257–63; Counsellor to Canadian Embassy in Paris (1947), 256, 267–68, 270, 271; on French-Canadians, 268, 276; friendship with Elizabeth Bowen, 270, 271; on the French, 271–72, 273; on aging, 275, 290, 299–300, 342; marries Sylvia, 284–85; posted to External Affairs in Ottawa (1950), 293–94, 296, 300–301; on diaries, 294, 296, 365; religion, 295–96; on official Ottawa, 300–301; Deputy Under-Secretary of State for External Affairs (1952), 302, 304–5; External Affairs adviser to St. Laurent (1954), 305–15; mother's family, 316–17; Ambassador to Bonn (1954), 317, 321–69; on boarding school days, 338, 341; on nuclear warfare, 341; awarded honorary D.C.L. (1956), 359; on youth, 366–67
— 1958–1962: Permanent Representative of Canada to U.N., 373–421; President of Security Council (1958), 373, 381–82, 384; on diaries, 374–75, 392, 408; on diplomats, 375, 399, 411, 413; and cousin Gerald, 390; apartment robbery, 390–91; on youth, 403; on dreams, 411

— 1962–1966: Ambassador to Washington, 431–501; on grandmother, 436–37; religion, 437; friendships formed at U.N., 439; on aging, 452–53, 460; Texas trip (1963), 455–56; viewing Canada from abroad, 456; defeat of Diefenbaker government (1963), 458; on diaries, 461, 495; position in Washington, 462, 467, 484; Loyalist ancestors, 468; as Pickering College teacher, 476–79; as schoolboy, 477; Embassy staff, 486; duties as ambassador, 490–94; friends in Washington, 494–95; Canadian Ambassador and Permanent Representative to North Atlantic Council (1966), 505
— 1967–71: High Commissioner to London, 507–63; Canada House staff, 510–11, 535–36; duties of High Commissioner, 511, 523–24, 548; making his mark, 512, 534; on politicians, 514, 573; on world events of 1968, 517–18; on butlers, 519; meeting with Trudeau, 529–30; on diaries, 531, 532, 533–34, 535; on protest marches, 535; pleasures in life, 537; on aging, 541; portrait, 542; Companion of Canada, 542–43, 546; FLQ crisis (1970), 556, 557; on younger generation, 558; retirement (1971), 559, 560, 561; appointed Special Advisor to Privy Council (1971), 576
Ritchie, Ed, 556, 559
Ritchie, Elizabeth (niece), 446, 461, 534, 535, 540, 542
Ritchie, Lilian (mother), 4–5, 20, 36, 38, 206, 240–41, 399–400, 416, 446, 473, 480, 481, 543, 560
Ritchie, Roland (brother), 4, 60, 155, 181, 189, 193, 194, 203, 394, 445, 446, 527
Ritchie, Sylvia (wife), 289, 290, 328, 335, 340, 341, 346, 349, 356, 367, 396, 406, 410, 411, 432, 443, 454, 468, 524, 558;